Musical Communication

Musical Communication

Edited by

Dorothy Miell
The Open University

Raymond MacDonald
Glasgow Caledonian University

David J. Hargreaves
Roehampton University

OXFORD
UNIVERSITY PRESS

*This book has been printed digitally and produced in a standard specification
in order to ensure its continuing availability*

OXFORD
UNIVERSITY PRESS

Great Clarendon Street, Oxford OX2 6DP

Oxford University Press is a department of the University of Oxford.
It furthers the University's objective of excellence in research, scholarship,
and education by publishing worldwide in

Oxford New York

Auckland Cape Town Dar es Salaam Hong Kong Karachi
Kuala Lumpur Madrid Melbourne Mexico City Nairobi
New Delhi Shanghai Taipei Toronto
With offices in
Argentina Austria Brazil Chile Czech Republic France Greece
Guatemala Hungary Italy Japan South Korea Poland Portugal
Singapore Switzerland Thailand Turkey Ukraine Vietnam

Oxford is a registered trade mark of Oxford University Press
in the UK and in certain other countries

Published in the United States
by Oxford University Press Inc., New York

© Oxford University Press, 2005

The moral rights of the author have been asserted

Database right Oxford University Press (maker)

Reprinted 2007

ISBN 978-0-19-852936-1

Foreword

To draw upon the belief of the highly influential American musical figure Harry Partch, that the individual's path 'cannot be retraced, because each of us is an original being', brings forth the observation that it seems an extraordinarily challenging task to present an in-depth text on musical communication. Music is as complex, inexplicable, and unknowable as those who participate in it. What does "participation" actually mean when dealing with this fluid art form? Is "sound" music or is "music" sound? The sound of a bird outside may be an annoyance whilst we are still sleeping or it could entice us to get up and enjoy the day ahead. It may allow us to slow our tempo down and focus on other sounds of nature, ignite memories of childhood, or it may be source of wonderment for our children. Suddenly that one little bird has created a myriad of emotions through how we observe, relate, and digest its sound. What "orchestra" is each of us creating with our incessant internal chatter and how does that affect how we relate to the external "orchestra" of everyday living? Each of us has our own personal relationship and lifelong journey with music, which begins in the womb. Therefore, the admirable and in-depth research and observation from all contributors to this book must be seen as an ever growing journey of exploration and curiosity.

Our speech is a form of music which overflows with inflection, phrasing, dynamics, rhythm, punctuation, tempo, expression, and emotion. Sign language is an even more enhanced form of music because the imagination plays a greater role in the process of direct observation, focus, and extreme concentration; one does not allow external distractions to "visit" the experience but instead the whole body vibrates with infectious exaggerated expression, taking the dynamic of "silence" in to the heaviest, the loudest, and certainly the most expressive dynamic of all. "Silent practice" is crucial for me to experience, as a performing musician, because everything is perfectly formed in my mind, with no element of fear coming into play whatsoever; the challenge lies in bringing this perfect internal state out into an external situation such as a concert hall with noisy air conditioning, a cough from the audience, poor acoustics, and so on. Silence is the ultimate music but I imagine it is only its experience in death which can enable it to be seen as the pinnacle of life.

Music is our everyday language - there is no such thing as being "unmusical". To play an instrument is but one small aspect, albeit an important one, of what music really is. Each moment of the day presents for us a kaleidoscope of tempo, rhythm, pitch, texture, and dynamics which connects every living soul. Perhaps this is why I am keen to say that music is our everyday medicine just as food, water, and shelter are – it is completely accessible to each and every one of us but how we choose to relate to it is something that only we ourselves can control.

While some of the aspects of this book are outside the scope of my current experience, I am particularly pleased that it is addressing music as applied to socially excluded groups, particularly the physically and mentally challenged who experience music in ways that often I do not understand. There is no question in my mind that to experience music only through the ears is like eating your food without any indication of what it tastes like. You are satisfied in that it fills you up and keeps you alive, you experience the texture and temperature of the food, but under no circumstances can you say you have truly "experienced" the food and how that relates to your body and mind.

For me personally, I have to open up every fibre of my being to be a giver and receiver of sound. This is reiterated in my observations with children through my myriad of percussion instruments. How can I explain the over-whelming physical change of the little deaf/blind boy with uncontrollable body movements who was placed lying under the bass end of my marimba? For him to go from totally uncontrollable and exaggerated movements to extreme stillness was something that no one around him had ever seen him do. How could I or his dedicated carers follow this up? Was it the sound of the marimba, the piece of music being played; was he enjoying the fact that I was creating similar movements to him with my sticks; was his stillness a display of excitement; or was he frightened? His alert face and eager eyes and my gut reaction was an indication that music is something that does not have a place in the exam room, it has a limited place in the recording studio but it most definitely has a place as a living, breathing art form whereby we all must open ourselves up to share and learn from each other.

This little boy helped me "listen" to the journey of the sound – the preparation of the sound, the process of its execution, the giving of the sound, the life of the sound throughout the space, and the death of the sound - he helped me to understand the difference between interpretation and translation and, most of all, he helped me to understand that I am the sound. He openly expressed himself in receiving the sound which is something that can be a challenge in our Western concert halls. He made me realize that no one has possession of the sounds because they are out there for us all to breathe. Perhaps this is why I enjoy performing in places like India or South America where the audiences openly participate physically whilst I'm playing. They may suddenly shout out in excitement or clap in heightened moments of pieces or stand up anytime during the performance. They are living for the moment, they are part of the music too and they want to celebrate that. It is very infectious because again one can sense a breathing art form that is truly shared and celebrated without any spoken word creating a barrier and where class barriers are completely eliminated.

However, one must also consider the extreme audience reactions to the likes of Igor Stravinsky's Rite of Spring or the music of Bob Dylan or Dmitri Shostakovich. Was it just the political message being portrayed and the unfamiliar combination of sounds in relation to what was experienced in their everyday sound world which provoked the audience in these examples or was it the confidence and fearlessness with which these sounds were projected? In performing groundbreaking works like the Rite of Spring, the musicians were being challenged physically in what they were being asked to do on their instruments so they are likely to have had a completely different view on the sound to that of the audience.

Music Therapy or Sound Therapy (as I prefer to call it) is a recent and exciting field of medicine in development. It comes at a particularly opportune time, in so much as that the mushrooming options for delivery of all music forms via technological advances allows the inexpensive yet high quality delivery of audio to individuals. Technology such as the miniscule MP3 players, music and sound creating software, and suchlike allow for extreme portability for peripatetic and outreach teachers to deliver what might otherwise be financially restricted in these current times of financial cut-backs in curricular music in our schools. However, I am still wary of the fact that reliance on manufactured sound, even if "live" musicians have participated in the recording, causes our listening skills to become one-dimensional. We totally lose the experience of "feeling" the music throughout the body. The reliance is solely on our ears and so we are reverting back to eating without tasting.

This invites the observation that the explosion of audio delivery methods via the Internet and other technological means and the expectations of the audience during performance has led to a change in the general public's listening skills. Until possibly the 1960s when the Rock n' Roll explosion occurred accompanied by the review of stagecraft and the production of those events, audiences were content to attend an event and purely listen. Nowadays, as well as listening they desire all their senses to be stimulated. Though it may be argued that the decline in audience attendance - in particular to Western classical concerts which still cling to the belief that the audience is there only to listen - indicates that for a large percentage of the potential audience the single stimuli of sound only is no longer sufficient. By comparison, the manufactured pop groups prevalent in Western pop culture are enjoying considerable success despite questionable levels of skill. Yet, on the whole they are able to fill huge arenas night after night with high ticket prices. This level of success has also been maintained by the genuinely talented popular rock icons who also perform using enhanced and theatrical production methods.

And so, through this book, observations, debates, and discoveries will reveal themselves. It gives me hope and satisfaction to know that the sharing of these observations can only help to make the world a better place.

Evelyn Glennie

Cambridgeshire, UK

April 2005

Contents

Communication in learning and education

Cultural contexts of communication

List of contributors

Gary Ansdell is currently Head of Research at the Nordoff-Robbins Music Therapy Centre in London, where he is Director of the research degree (MPhil/PhD) programme. He is also Honorary Research Fellow in Community Music Therapy at the University of Sheffield and Visiting Fellow at Trinity College of Music, London. He trained at the Nordoff-Robbins Centre, London in 1987 and later at the Institut für Musiktherapie, Universität Witten-Herdecke, Germany. He has worked with many client groups in the UK and Germany (currently in adult psychiatry). From 1994–7 he was Research Fellow in Music Therapy at City University, London, during which time he completed his doctoral thesis: *Music Therapy as Discourse and Discipline*. His book *Music for Life* was published in 1995, and he has co-authored (with Mercédès Pavlicevic) *Beginning Research in the Arts Therapies: A Practical Guide,* and the recently published *Community Music Therapy.*

Jeanne Bamberger is Professor of Music at the Massachusetts Institute of Technology where she teaches music theory and music cognition. Her interests include musical development and learning, in particular issues of representation among both children and adults. She was a student of Artur Schnabel and Roger Sessions and has performed extensively as piano soloist and in chamber music ensembles. She attended Columbia University and the University of California at Berkeley, receiving degrees in philosophy and music theory. Her most recent books include (1995) *The mind behind the musical ear* (Harvard University Press), and (2000) *Developing musical intuitions: A project based introduction to making and understanding music* (Oxford University Press).

Margaret S. Barrett is Associate Professor in Music Education at the University of Tasmania. Her research interests include the study of: children's musical thinking as composers and notators; creativity in music and the arts; children's communities of musical practice; the meaning and value of the arts in children's and young musicians' lives; the developmental psychology of music; and aesthetic education. Margaret has published in key journals in music and early childhood education and contributed book chapters to a number of edited collections in music education. She was National President of the Australian Society for Music Education (1999–2001) and is editor of *Research Studies in Music Education.*

Charles Byrne is a Senior Lecturer in the Department of Creative and Aesthetic Studies, Faculty of Education, University of Strathclyde. Charles taught music in secondary schools in and around the Glasgow area from 1979 to 1993 and was also Musical Director of Glasgow Schools Youth Theatre. In 1990 he combined his interests in theatre and composition by writing the musical, *Dreams for GSYT*. His research interests include the teaching and learning of composing and improvising in Scottish secondary schools, thinking in music and aspects of flow theory in music education. Publications include articles for the *British Journal of Music Education,* the *International Journal of Music Education, Music Education Research* and *Psychology of Music.* Charles is a member of the editorial boards of two international music education journals.

Martin Clayton studied at the School of Oriental and African Studies in London, being awarded degrees in Music and Hindi (BA, 1988) and Ethnomusicology (PhD, 1993). He is the author of *Time in Indian Music: Rhythm, Metre, and Form in North Indian Rag Performance* (Oxford University Press, 2000) and has also published on topics including the history of comparative musicology, British-Asian music and Western music in India. A former editor of the *British Journal of Ethnomusicology,* he also co-edited the acclaimed collection *The Cultural Study of Music* (Routledge, 2003). He is currently Senior Lecturer in Ethnomusicology at the Open University, where he directs the AHRC-funded project 'Experience and Meaning in Music Performance'.

Annabel Cohen (B.A. McGill; M.A., Ph.D. Queen's) is a Professor of Psychology at the University of Prince Edward Island, Adjunct Professor in the Dalhousie University Faculty of Graduate Studies and Fellow of the Canadian Psychological Association. Having published on tonality and transposition, she directs two primary research programs in music cognition: one on the learnability of music across the lifespan and the other on how music influences the experience of film and multimedia. Her research is supported by NSERC, SSHRC, and the Canada Foundation for Innovation. She is a consulting editor for several journals in the field of music psychology.

Initially a classical guitarist, since 1986 **Ian Cross** has taught and conducted research in music and science at the University of Cambridge where he is now Reader in Music & Science and a Fellow of Wolfson College. He has published widely in the field of music cognition. At present, his principal research focus is on the exploration of music as a biocultural phenomenon, involving collaboration with archaeologists, psychologists and engineers.

Jane W. Davidson, Professor of Music Performance Studies, University of Sheffield, has a background in music psychology, musicology, vocal perform-ance, and contemporary dance. She has written more than ninety academic articles and book chapters on performance, expression, therapy, and the deter-minants of artistic abilities. Her edited volume the *Music Practitioner* explores the uses of research for the practising musician. A former editor of *Psychology of Music*, she is currently Vice-president of the *European Society for the Cognitive Sciences of Music*. Jane also works as a professional stage director in opera and music theatre, having collaborated with Andrew Lawrence-King, *Opera North*, and *Drama per Musica*.

David J. Hargreaves is Professor of Education at Roehampton University, and has previously held posts at the Universities of Leicester, Durham, and the Open University. His books in psychology, education, and the arts, have been trans-lated into 14 languages. He was recently awarded an honorary Doctorate by the University of Gothenburg, Sweden for his work as Visiting Professor in Music Education Research in that University since 1993. He has appeared on BBC TV and radio as a jazz pianist, and is organist at his local village church.

Patrik N. Juslin is associate professor of psychology at the Department of psychology, Uppsala University, Sweden, where he teaches courses on emotion, perception, and music psychology. He is the director of the inter-disciplinary research project *Feedback-learning of musical expressivity (Feel-ME)*. He is a member of the *International Society for Research on Emotions*, and received *ESCOM's* Young Researcher Award in 1996. He has published numerous arti-cles in journals that include *Psychological Bulletin, Emotion, Journal of Experimental Psychology, Music Perception,* and *Psychology of Music*. He also edited the book *Music and Emotion: Theory and Research* for Oxford University Press together with John Sloboda.

Scott D. Lipscomb is an Associate Professor in the Music Education and Music Technology programs in the Northwestern University School of Music. His primary area of research is the cognition of music in the context of motion pictures and animation. He has presented the results of his research at regional, national, and international conferences and has published articles in *Psychomusicology, Selected Reports in Ethnomusicology,* and has contributed chapters to numerous edited volumes on music communication, film music, and the application of technology in the music classroom.

Raymond MacDonald is Reader in Psychology at Glasgow Caledonian University. He is an associate editor of *Psychology of Music* and the *International Journal of Music Education* and is conference secretary for the Society for Education Music and Psychology Research (SEMPRE). He has also been Artistic Director for a music production company, *Sounds of Progress*, working with ind-ividuals who have special needs. He is an experienced saxophonist/composer, who performs internationally and has recorded many CDs. He is currently director of the Glasgow Improvisers Orchestra.

Janis McNair is the Development Officer for the Centre for Political Song at Glasgow Caledonian University. Established in January 2001, the Centre exists to promote and foster an awareness of all forms of political song. Janis gradu-ated from Strathclyde University with a BA (Hons) in Politics and Sociology in 1998 and has been combining her passion for politics and music ever since.

Dorothy Miell is Professor of Psychology in the Social Science Faculty at The Open University, UK, and member of the University's Centre for Research in Education and Educational Technology. Her research interests lie in studying communication in close relationships, particularly the effects of such relationships on identity development and on the nature of collaborative working in creative tasks such as music making. She has recently co-edited *Collaborative Creativity* (2004, Free Association Books, with Karen Littleton) and *Learning to Collaborate, Collaborating to Learn* (2004, Nova Science, with Karen Littleton and Dorothy Faulkner). She is associate editor on the journals *Psychology of Music, International Journal of Thinking and Creativity* and *Journal of Social and Personal Relationships*.

Adrian North obtained his PhD on responses to music in everyday life in 1996. He has published numerous journal articles within music psychology and has also co-edited two books with David Hargreaves (namely *The social psychology of music*, Oxford University Press; and *Musical development and learning: the international perspective*, Continuum). He is currently a senior lecturer in psychology at the University of Leicester.

Mercédès Pavlicevic is Director of the Music Therapy Master's programme, and Associate Professor at the Music Department, University of Pretoria, and Visiting Researcher at the Nordoff Robbins Music Therapy Centre in London. She has published *Music Therapy in Context* (1997); *Music Therapy – Intimate Notes* (1999), *Groups in Music: Strategies from Music Therapy* (2003), and with Gary Ansdell, *Beginning Research in the Arts Therapies* (2001) and *Community Music Therapy* (2004).

John Powles is Research Collections Manager at Glasgow Caledonian University, managing Archives, the Centre for Political Song (since its launch in January 2001), Heatherbank Museum of Social Work, and Special Collections. John has worked at GCU for the past 21 years, before which he spent several years working for the Forestry Commission and for North Sea oil companies. He is particularly interested in the music, politics, and lifestyles of the 1960s 'countercultures', and, above all, in the work and influence from 1960 to today of Bob Dylan.

R. Keith Sawyer is Associate Professor of Education at Washington University in St. Louis. He studies collaboration, conversation, and creativity, and his work has been published in journals in psychology, sociology, philosophy, and education. His most recent books include 'Explaining creativity: The science of human innovation' (Oxford, 2005) and 'Group creativity: Music, theater, collaboration' (Erlbaum, 2003).

Michael H. Thaut, a native of Hamburg, Germany, is currently Director of the School of the Arts and Professor of Music and Professor of Neuroscience at Colorado State University. He received his PhD from Michigan State University. His major research focus is on the neurological basis of rhythm and time perception in the brain and biomedical applications of music. He has over 130 scientific publications and has (co)authored several books. He has also established the field of Neurologic Music Therapy, the first historical paradigm of music therapy based on neuroscience research. His European musical training included the Mozarteum Academy of Performing Arts in Salzburg, Austria. As a former professional violinist (and folk fiddler) he has several recordings in the classical and folk music genre and an extensive performing career. One of the leading German Anthologies of European and North-American Fiddle Music was edited by him. He continues to enjoy tremendously his dual career as artist and scientist.

David E. Tolchinsky is a commissioned screenwriter (MGM, Touchstone, USA Networks, Montecito Pictures), whose feature film, Girl (screenwriter/associate producer), is in regular rotation on cable and available from Sony. He also composes sound/music for film, new media and installation projects which exhibit internationally. He was originally trained as a composer at Yale (BA), went on to get Certificates in Digital Audio Processing and Composing with Computers from M.I.T.'s Media Lab, and an MFA in Film/Video Production from USC School of CN-TV. He is currently an Associate Professor of Radio-TV-Film at Northwestern University, Director of Northwestern's Creative Writing for the Media Program, and Co-Director of the Program in Sound Design.

Graham Welch holds the Institute of Education, University of London Established Chair of Music Education and is Head of the Institute's School of Arts and Humanities. He is Chair of the Society for Education, Music and Psychology Research (SEMPRE), recent past Co-Chair of the Research Commission of the International Society for Music Education (ISME) and holds Visiting Professorships at the Sibelius Academy and the Universities of Sydney, Limerick and Roehampton. Research and publications embrace a variety of aspects of musical development and music education, teacher education, psychology of music, singing and voice science, special education and disability.

Graeme Wilson is currently a Research Fellow in the Psychology Department of Glasgow Caledonian University. His PhD in Psychology, from the University of Glasgow, investigated separated fathers and their co-parental role; previous research work includes investigating children's collaboration on musical composition, and the musical identities of musicians with special needs. He has worked in Scotland and abroad for many years as a saxophonist, arranger and composer including performances with the Scottish National Jazz Orchestra, a wide range of recordings, and facilitating music workshops for musicians with special needs. Currently, he is collaborating with video artists on a number of projects to produce live, free improvised soundtracks.

Susan Young is lecturer in early childhood studies and music education at the School of Education and Lifelong Learning, Exeter University, UK and Senior Research Fellow with the Centre for International Research in Music Education at the University of Roehampton. She trained as a classical pianist at the Royal College of Music and in Dalcroze Eurhythmics at the Institut, Geneva and has taught music to children of all ages in a range of formal and informal settings. She has written and presented widely on the topic of music education, particularly in the early years.

Chapter 1

How do people communicate using music?

David J. Hargreaves, Raymond MacDonald, and Dorothy Miell

Introduction

Music is a fundamental channel of communication: it provides a means by which people can share emotions, intentions, and meanings. Music can exert powerful physical and behavioural effects, can produce deep and profound emotions within us, and can be used to generate infinitely subtle variations of expressiveness by skilled composers and performers, such that highly complex informational structures and contents can be communicated extremely rapidly between people. Music is something we do with and for other people, and which through its communicative properties can provide a vital lifeline of human interaction for those whose special needs make other means of communication difficult.

The rapid technological changes that have taken place over the last two decades or so have led to equally rapid changes in the diversity and availability of music, and in the ways in which people engage with and 'consume' it. The digital revolution, and the corresponding developments in miniaturization and portability of music recording and playback equipment, mean that virtually any music can now be heard at any time by many listeners around the world, some of whom can carry their entire music libraries around wherever they go. These changes also mean that many more people have the means of composing, recording, and performing their own music than at any time in the past.

The ubiquity of music in everyday life, and the corresponding diversification of musical behaviour, probably explain why there has been an explosive increase of interest in music psychology over the last two decades or so. We have described elsewhere how the discipline has expanded and diversified into several sub-disciplines (Hargreaves *et al.* 2002): the contemporary cognitive, developmental, and social psychologies of music each have their own theoretical priorities, empirical research foci, and practical applications. Our present focus on musical communication in this volume cuts across these traditional divisions: our central interest, as the title indicates, is on how people use music to communicate with each other. The search for answers to this *how* question, and to the related question of *why* people communicate using music, form the subject matter of the rest of this book. The authors of the forthcoming chapters use a variety of theoretical approaches, covering many areas of empirical research, carried out in many different contexts, in trying to provide some answers.

These primary 'how' and 'why' questions immediately raise three others, however, which we need to tackle at the outset in drawing up our agenda in more detail: these are the 'what', 'who', and 'where' questions of musical communication. In establishing *what* is communicated, we need to be clear about the parameters of what we mean by 'music'. Most people have a common and consensual view about the different genres, styles, and idioms which constitute music, and we shall return to this issue in more detail later in the chapter. Having said this, it is also worth considering John Cage's argument that chance and random events, or even silence, could be construed as 'musical' if they occur within an artistic context. It is the artist and the listener who ultimately decide what is and what is not musical, even though their views might not necessarily coincide. Different sounds (or the absence of them) become musical when people collectively imbue them with musical meaning, and an important aspect of this is the social and cultural context within which those sounds exist.

In this book we adopt a very broad view of our subject matter: we conceive of musical communications as ranging from an infant's response to its mother's song, or the beginning attempts of an elective mute to move in time to a rhythmic stimulus, to audience reaction to recorded and broadcast music, or to a complex group improvization involving interactions between performers and audience, as well as to talk about music. This view also implies that the contents and functions of different musical communications can vary widely: Cross (this volume) points out that music is inherently ambiguous, and 'has a sort of "floating intentionality"'….it can be thought of as gathering meaning from the contexts within which it happens and in turn contributing meaning to those contexts' (p. 30). Musical meanings could therefore include political messages, social conventions and ceremonies, nationalistic pride, altered states of consciousness, interpersonal signals, commercial messages, as well as aesthetic pleasure, deep emotional states, and complex ideas. Specific considerations of the broader social context should enable us to develop our understanding of the referential complexity of musical meanings.

This broad view of what constitutes music leads to the fourth question, namely *who* are the communicators and recipients of musical meaning?

Here again, our view is very broad: as we have suggested earlier, it goes well beyond professional musicians, working in artistic contexts, to include situations in which the composer and the performer, who may indeed be one and the same person, are not formally trained or skilled musicians – they might be children, therapeutic clients, or indeed chanting football crowds. Each of these groups uses music to communicate specific physical, cognitive, social, and/or emotional messages to its audience. Animals also communicate using musical sounds, of course, and Olivier Messaien's use of bird song in his work illustrates their immense subtlety and complexity: but as Merker (2000) and Cross (this volume) point out, music appears to play a unique role in the individual and social development of human beings, and the predisposition to engage in musical activities seems to be a biological adaptation, acquired through evolution.

Our approach to the fifth question, namely *where* does musical communication take place, should by now be apparent: we move well beyond most traditional models of musical communication, which typically deal with 'art music', presented in artistic contexts, by encompassing the numerous forms of music that we encounter, often involuntarily, in everyday life. Musical meanings can be context-specific, as we have seen here, and we follow Hargreaves and North (1997) in our focus on the specific places, times, and other people present in situations involving music, as well as on the broader historical and cultural contexts of musical behaviour.

The attempt to deal with the contexts of musical communication, as well as with all the participants involved in the process, sets a very broad and ambitious agenda. To summarize, we might define the aim of the book as being 'to explain the musical, social, and cultural processes that underlie the eventual realization of the acoustic performance event (by the composer, performer, arranger, and all others involved), the means by which they lead to the listener's response, and thence to short and long-term effects upon arousal level, cognition, emotion, and subsequent behaviour'. We see the specific link between the performance event and the response as the defining property of communication: there are different theoretical views of this link, as we shall see in the next section.

Contextualizing musical communication

Most models of musical communication have been influenced by the information transmission model of communication, which was initially formulated by Shannon and Weaver (1949). This model, which is illustrated and described in more detail by Cohen (Chapter 4, this volume) is based on the view of a communicator who uses a channel to send information to a receiver; the sender, the channel, and the receiver can take many forms, but the central characteristic of the model is that the information moves in one direction – from sender to receiver, and not vice versa. Cross, Cohen, and Juslin, in their chapters in this volume, discuss some of the issues involved in applying this model to music, most of which revolve around the idea that a good deal of musical communication is much more interactive and re-creative than is suggested by the idea of information being passed from one person (e.g. the performer) to another (the listener). This view implies a kind of power relationship in which the performer takes the active role, and the listener is purely a passive recipient: this is not the case in many forms of musical communication, since the 'listener' may well play an active role in shaping the content and meaning of the message.

The development of psychology within the 1960s was largely dominated by the 'cognitive revolution', with an emphasis on information processing models of memory, attention, and thinking. These analysed the flow of information through the human cognitive system, attempting to specify what goes on between the input to the system (usually a stimulus) and the output from it (such as a behavioural response). The mechanisms proposed were directly analogous to those employed by the computer in coding, storing, and processing data, and in making some kind of output. This cognitive influence was clearly apparent in music psychology in the 1980s, which was dominated by laboratory-based studies of the effects of stimuli such as isolated tones, intervals, and harmonies. This history may partly explain the continuing influence of transmission models on the study of musical communication, though more recent developments in music psychology have moved well beyond the laboratory in trying to deal with complex musical behaviour in real life contexts. The time seems right for a reconceptualization of musical communication which adopts this broader theoretical approach, which views traditional transmission models in a new, broader context. Let us briefly consider some of these models before we deal with the broader perspective.

Johnson-Laird (1992) focused on the ways in which communicators use symbolic codes to transmit messages to their receivers. They 'code', or construct some kind of representation of the message they wish to communicate, and then transmit the representation in such a way that the receiver can decode the message, so that the transmission of the message is dependent on their mutual understanding of the symbolic coding system. Kendall and Carterette (1990) have formalized and developed this idea by proposing a three-stage model of music communication (shown in Chapter 18 of this volume, see p. 385) which attempts to show how those musical meanings which are encoded by the *composer* are transmitted via the *performer* to the *listener*. This model suggests that the performer decodes these meanings, recodes them within the performance and thereby transmits them to the listener, who needs to undertake another decoding. Each of these processes is dependent on the shared implicit and explicit knowledge of all three participants in the chain, and is influenced by the context and environment within which the process takes place – although the model does not specify the latter in any detail.

Juslin (Chapter 5, this volume) has proposed a clear and explicit summary of this view in his illustration of the process by which emotion is communicated in music (see p. 87). He follows Kendall and Carterette (1990) in showing a 'communication chain' in which the composer has a causal influence on the listener, and in which communication occurs when the expressive intentions and meanings encoded by the composer are eventually decoded by the listener (as an affective response). The chain moves from the composer's intention (usually encoded in the score), to the performer's intention, which gives rise to the acoustic features of the performance; this results in the listener's perception of those features, including the detection and recognition of relevant patterns in them, which may or may not ultimately result in an affective or emotional response, i.e. the induction of a new mental state. Juslin is also keen to emphasize that the communication which occurs in this hypothetical chain goes further than musical expression, in that the composer exhibits the *intention* to express a specific concept or state, and that the listener is able to *recognize* this intention.

Our proposed move beyond transmission models, and towards locating the study of musical communication within complex real life situations, means that we need to look more closely at the ways in which individuals interact with other people, objects, and situations in their immediate environments – and especially those relevant to a particular domain of activity such as music. This leads us to a consideration of social cognitive theory, and Bandura's (1986) approach provides an excellent starting point. Central to Bandura's approach is his view of the nature of human agency – 'how people exercise influence over what they do' – which leads to the principle of *triadic reciprocal causation*. This transactional view of the relationship between self and society is based on three major classes of determinants – behaviour; internal personal factors (cognitive, affective, and biological events); and the external environment. In Bandura's view, each of these three determinants exerts a mutual influence on each of the others, such that the whole system is 'reciprocally deterministic', and in a constant state of dynamic change. People themselves create social systems – but are themselves influenced by those systems in turn, so that human behaviour is a product of both social influences and internal psychological factors.

Social cognitive theory led Bandura (1997) to develop his views of self-referent thought, and with a particular emphasis on *self-efficacy:* 'Knowledge structures representing the rules and strategies of effective action serve as cognitive guides for the construction of complex modes of behavior' (p. 34). These self-efficacy beliefs remain grounded in social and contextual factors, however: some situations demand individual effort and skill more than others, and individuals' perceived self-efficacy varies accordingly. Business executives may place a high value on their entrepreneurial or money-making skills and place little importance on cultural values and learning, for example, whereas university professors may prize the latter whilst devaluing their abilities in everyday practical matters, or indeed in money-making! This highlights the important implication that self-efficacy is not a general or non-specific personal belief, but is grounded in particular contexts and domains.

The related ideas that human agency and knowledge exist within the social world, that they are domain specific, and that they are mediated by internal constructs such as self-efficacy, forms the basis of our own attempt in this chapter to develop a new contextual explanation of musical communication. We propose that there are three major determinants of the musical communication process, as we defined it earlier, namely the characteristics of the music itself; those of the people involved (i.e. the composer, performer, and/or listener); and those of the situation in which it occurs. Grounding our model in the specific domain of music limits the wider psychological applicability of our predictions and insights, of course, but we are nevertheless able to incorporate Bandura's principle of reciprocal determinism, suggesting that each of these three major determinants exerts a mutual influence on each of the others. The idea that musical experience depends on the interrelationships between the person, the music, and the situation is not new in music psychology, of course, but it has not previously been applied systematically to the analysis of communication.

The incorporation of reciprocal determinism, which we have operationalized as 'reciprocal feedback' in our model, is the first main feature of our attempt to contextualize the explanation of musical communication. The second is our adoption of broader definitions of the three determinants – of the people involved, of 'music' itself, and of the social contexts within which it occurs – than has hitherto been the case.

Most previous models of musical communication have been conceived with reference to a live art music performance in which a skilled performer plays pre-composed music to an audience – i.e. in effect, to musical performance in the Western European art tradition. As we suggested earlier, our definition of the performer goes well beyond this: we consider that musical communication can be said to take place when the 'composer' and 'performer' may not be trained, skilled, or professional musicians, and we consider that musical communication takes place outside of the artistic contexts of the concert hall or recording studio, which could include recorded performances, such as those in broadcasting, the media, and cinema, or even listeners' reactions in everyday situations such as shops, leisure environments, or the workplace.

We shall return to examine these issues in more detail when we consider which characteristics of the person, the music, and the situation influence musical communication, and how they do so. More generally, however, we concur with Juslin (this volume) when he concludes that 'most previous research on expression, perception, and induction of emotions has neglected *the social context* of musical emotion, including everything from the situation in which the musical activity takes place to the wider socio-cultural context' (p. 106), and contend that contextual models of musical communication will need to extend the notion of transmission in adopting this broader perspective.

A reciprocal feedback model of musical communication

Our 'reciprocal feedback' model is created by combining two parallel component models: one attempts to specify the main personal, musical, and situational variables which give rise to a musical *performance*, and the other attempts the same task to explain the *response* to music in a specific situation. The two components are combined such that musical communication is conceived of as occurring at their interface, so that the critical link, or 'spark' of musical communication, exists when a specific performance event gives rise to a listener's response. The resulting model is intended to represent a view of musical communication which goes beyond previous transmission models (a) by taking into account the many relevant personal, musical, and contextual variables, and (b) by virtue of its incorporation of the reciprocal causal influences of all its components. This first attempt will inevitably neglect some of the relevant variables: but it nevertheless represents a preliminary mapping of some of the main developments in current research within the psychology of music.

Musical response

Figure 1.1 shows a more elaborate and detailed version of the musical response model outlined by Hargreaves *et al.* (2005): it describes the various different determinants of a specific response to a given musical stimulus at a particular point in time. The *music* itself can be analysed, and for experimental purposes be seen to vary, in many different ways. A full exposition of this is the subject of music theory, of course, an account of which is way beyond our scope here, but we can nevertheless indicate some of the main factors which are of interest from the point of view of the study of communication.

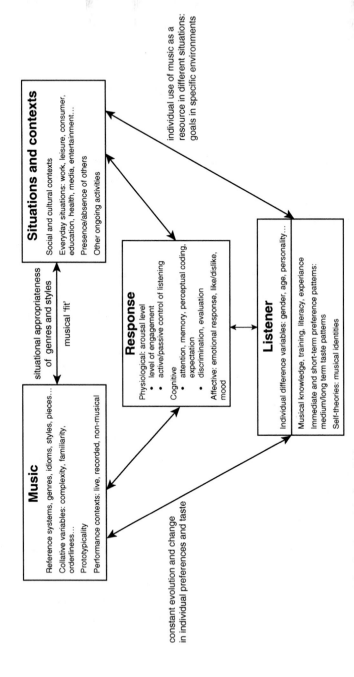

Fig. 1.1 Reciprocal feedback model of musical response.

First, we can conceive of the concept of musical style or genre in terms of several different levels of generality, and music theorists have suggested various ways of conceptualizing and classifying stylistic phenomena. Nattiez (1990), for example, proposes six different levels of musical style which range from the very culture specific – a specific work by a particular composer – through to the completely non-culture specific – the universals of music (e.g. pitch, rhythm) – via a series of intermediate levels (a style during one phase in the life of a composer, intermediate genres and idioms, and systems of reference within which styles are defined (e.g. tonality). This is a useful conceptual framework, though empirical research on the perception of musical styles and people's preferences for them (see e.g. Hargreaves and North 1999) is fraught with methodological problems, not the least of which is that the extra-musical influences on many popular genres and styles, notably those from the media and the fashion industry, mean that they are subject to constant and increasingly rapid redefinition.

Second, an extensive body of psychological research has been conducted within the approach of experimental aesthetics, a good deal of it deriving from the theoretical background established by Daniel Berlyne (see e.g. Berlyne 1971). Berlyne suggested that the listener 'collates' the different properties of a given musical stimulus, such as its complexity, familiarity, or orderliness, and that these 'collative variables' combine to produce predictable effects on the level of activity, or arousal, of the listener's autonomic nervous system. The level of arousal is related to liking via an inverted-U function according to which liking is highest at intermediate levels of arousal, and correspondingly lower at both low and high levels. Berlyne's arousal-based approach was challenged in the 1980s by another group of researchers (e.g. Martindale and Moore 1988) who argued instead that preference is determined by the *prototypicality* of different stimuli, i.e. by the extent to which a particular musical piece is typical of its class. Their explanation, in terms of neural network models, was that more prototypical stimuli give rise to stronger activation of the salient cognitive categories in people's mental representations of music, and that this is the main determinant of aesthetic preference. North and Hargreaves (2000a) have proposed a reconciliation between these two views: whilst the detailed issues are beyond us here, there can nevertheless be no doubt that the properties of the music itself exert important influences on musical response.

The performance contexts in which music can be heard are far more varied now than at any time in the past: whereas live performances were the only way in which music could be heard in the nineteenth century, the development of the mass media and more recently of global digital communication mean that music – live, broadcast, or recorded – can be heard in an almost infinitely wide range of settings, in the developed world at least. The development of the Walkman, of the internet, and of high capacity MP3 portable players mean that listeners can carry their entire music collections with them wherever they go, so that music has indeed become a 'sound track to life': two recent studies have suggested that well over one-third of the everyday lives of many people in the UK involve music in some way (Sloboda *et al.* 2001; North *et al.* 2004). Furthermore, both of these studies found that very few music-listening experiences take place in the absence of any other activity: the vast majority of music listening takes place while we are involved in other activities. This makes understanding the sensitive interplay between the musical and extramusical phenomena that occur during musical communication all the more important (Carlton and MacDonald 2004).

This means that people's experiences of and uses of music are much more varied than in the past, and that its evaluation in terms of traditional artistic or aesthetic criteria may not be appropriate in many cases: music is heard and used in 'non-musical' contexts, and listeners' responses to style, genre, and quality are inevitably affected. This leads on to the reciprocal feedback relationship between the music and the listening context: as illustrated in Fig. 1.1, different styles and genres are seen as appropriate to varying degrees in particular, listening situations. Research on music and consumer behaviour (see Chapter 19 of the present volume) shows this very clearly: a shop selling fashion wear to young people will typically play loud pop music, whereas an up-market furniture store may discreetly play Vivaldi or Mozart.

The creation of appropriate 'in-store ambiance' by retailers, which is designed to increase sales by priming the appropriate cognitive networks in customers, leads to the idea of the musical 'fit' with specific products and environments: sales are maximized when this 'fit' is high.

Situations and contexts can vary in many respects, of course, and some of the key variables are shown in Fig. 1.1. Broader cultural influences might derive from specific regional or national institutions, such as the particular music which is associated with sports clubs, political movements, or national figures. McNair and Powles' analysis (present volume) of the role of music in sustaining particular subcultures is a good example of this, and Folkestad (2002) has undertaken an intriguing analysis of the role of music in national identity.

An increasing body of research in the social psychology of music is beginning to show how specific social or institutional contexts can exert a powerful influence on the responses to music within them (see North and Hargreaves 1997*a,b*). Adrian North and David Hargreaves have carried out a series of experimental studies in everyday settings including restaurants, bars, banks, shops, computer assembly plants, exercise and relaxation clubs, and on-hold telephones.

This work shows that music fulfils many different cognitive, social, and emotional functions by demonstrating that it has the power to influence behaviour as diverse as consumer product choice and shopping behaviour; work efficiency; time perception and the preparedness to wait in queues; speed of eating and drinking; efficiency on cognitive tasks; people's moods and emotional states; their attitudes to different surroundings, and the likelihood of their staying in them. These behavioural effects are also influenced by other associated features of the listener's immediate situation, including the presence or absence of others and/or simultaneous engagement in other ongoing activities: we shall return to this issue when considering the performance model in Fig. 1.2.

Our proposal is that people in contemporary society use music as a resource, such as in managing situation-specific emotional states or moods: we use music in order to achieve certain psychological states in different everyday situations. This illustrates the reciprocal feedback relationship between 'situations and contexts' and 'the listener' shown in Fig. 1.1. North and Hargreaves (2000b), for example, have shown that people have specific arousal-state goals in specific environments, and that they consciously use music to achieve these goals. This can have very obvious practical implications: Mitchell (2004), for example, has shown that the tolerance for and experience of experimentally-induced pain can be significantly varied by listening to preferred music as compared with other auditory stimulation.

Another unusual feedback relationship between 'situations and contexts' and 'the listener' is shown in O'Hara et al.'s (2004) field tests of the Jukola, an interactive MP3 jukebox which allows a group of people in a public space to democratically choose the music being played by means of networked handheld wireless devices. O'Hara's team found that the process of voting and choice involved gave rise to 'discussions around music, playful competition, identity management and sense of community' (p. 145), which represents an intriguing way in which music can be used as a group as well as an individual resource.

Listeners vary with respect to the 'individual difference' factors on which all people vary, such as age, gender, and personality, and these can have a greater or lesser influence on their response to music (see Hargreaves 1986): these are shown above the horizontal line in Fig. 1.1. Shown below this line are those other factors which are more specifically music-related, such as musical training, knowledge, and experience, and these are likely to be particularly salient in determining responses to music. We shall say more shortly about the different components of responses to music: for the purposes of the model, we have focused on those relating to musical preference and taste. Most people have strong and distinctive patterns of preference: immediate, short-term reactions to given stimuli or pieces at given times gradually accumulate to give rise to medium- and longer-term taste patterns, which tend to be more stable: and we have used the term 'musical identities' to refer to the ways in which these patterns can become an important part of individuals' personal identities (Hargreaves *et al.* 2002).

Although these medium- and long-term patterns are relatively stable, they are nevertheless subject to continual change as each listener encounters new stimuli: Fig. 1.1 illustrates this as a reciprocal feedback relationship between the music and the listener. Individuals' immediate responses to new stimuli are shaped by their longer term taste patterns: but significant new experiences can correspondingly feed back into the system and change those longer term patterns, as the preference or identity system is in a constant state of evolution, change, and re-negotiation.

The response to music itself, shown at the centre of Fig. 1.1, has many components, and can be conceptualized in many different ways. The figure briefly summarizes just three of the main foci of psychological investigation (for a more detailed review see Abeles and Chung 1996). At the physiological level, as we saw earlier, Berlyne's proposal was that music can determine the level of arousal of the autonomic nervous system, and that this is probably implicated in some way in musical likes and dislikes: there is also a growing literature on the emotional effects of music, which can be observed at the physiological level (Juslin and Sloboda (2001), and Juslin, present volume). We have summarized two of the subjective concomitants of arousal level as individuals' level of engagement with the music, and the extent to which they are in active control of their listening, or being passive respondents. When people use music as a resource, as just discussed, they exert active control over factors such as genre and volume, and are likely to be highly engaged: when simply exposed to the piped music in a supermarket or restaurant, on the other hand, their level of engagement may be so low that they are not even aware of its existence. High levels of engagement can also produce physical and other behavioural responses, which could include dancing, foot tapping, and so on.

There is an extensive literature within the cognitive psychology of music which deals with the internalized rules, strategies, and operations which people employ in musical behaviour, and Fig. 1.1 mentions just a few of these: a good deal of research effort has been devoted to investigating the phenomena of attention, memory, perceptual coding, and expectation in listeners' responses to tones, intervals, scales, melody, harmony, and other aspects of musical structure (see e.g. Deutsch 1999). Musical preferences and tastes are dependent on the discriminations and evaluations that people make by employing these cognitive mechanisms: but they also involve affective components, which include aspects of emotion and mood. Responses to music in real-life situations incorporate affective as well as cognitive components: the relationship between these is a central problem in social psychology, which is beyond our scope here.

Musical performance

The corresponding reciprocal feedback model of musical performance, shown in Fig. 1.2, is based on the same principles as the musical response model shown in Fig. 1.1. Our conceptualization of the *music* is broadly similar: variations occur with respect to basic stylistic and genre distinctions, to collative variables and prototypicality, and there are many other distinctions which remain unexplored. One feature which we have added to the performance model's description of music is the extent to which it is necessarily rooted in artistic contexts: as we indicated earlier, previous models of musical communication have restricted themselves to the performance of art music, usually within the Western tradition. The extent to which silence, chance events, and so on can be considered as art works when presented in certain contexts was mentioned earlier, but we have included them in the model to reinforce our earlier point that we are adopting as wide a definition of music, and of who might be a performer, as possible.

Our account of 'situations and contexts', and of the reciprocal feedback relationship between the factors involved and those within the music, need little further comment as they duplicate those in the response model. One factor which does require further elaboration with respect to performance, however, is the presence or absence of others. Our definition of 'a performance' within the model includes recordings and broadcasts as well as live performances: and the presence of other performers and an audience in the live situation clearly opens up many more channels of potential communication than for sound produced by a loudspeaker. The physical setting of a live performance gives rise to normative expectations about the appropriate audience response, and this varies according to genre and style: Western 'classical' audiences usually listen in silence (although this has not always been the case), and rock audiences frequently dance, sing, or interact with the performers in other ways (cf. also Clayton, Chapter 17 of this volume).

Juslin (this volume) uses the phrase 'acoustic performance parameters' as part of his illustration of the musical communication of emotion, and this refers simply to the physical characteristics of the sounds which form the performance. As we have just suggested, the performance medium is likely to have a profound influence on the communication process: recorded performances could include piped music in commercial environments, for example, and broadcasts could include live as well as recorded performances on television as well as radio or the internet: all of these dimensions will influence the ways in which listeners are likely to respond. Alongside different performance media, we can also distinguish between different performance contexts: three prominent contexts are composed music, improvised music, and music in which the audience forms an integral part of the performance, such as in the ways in which contemporary club DJs can be seen to use audience reaction to shape their performances (see Brewster and Broughton 1999).

Different performance media, contexts, and conventions are dependent on the cultural traditions of different societies: the formalized conventions of Western European art music have radically different expectations of the 'performer' and the 'listener' from the more informal traditions of musics in Africa or South America, for example. The wide variations between these different traditions also imply varying definitions of the 'performer' and the 'composer' as well as of the 'audience': the performer *is* the composer in many forms of improvised jazz, for example.

For clarity of exposition, we have made a clear separation between the 'performer' and the 'composer' in the model. In Fig. 1.2, the factors that are listed above the horizontal lines in the lower two boxes show our working definition of who constitutes the performer and the composer, and those listed below the horizontal lines refer to the factors or dimensions along which they can vary. Performers within Western art music are largely either instrumentalists or vocalists, and take part in solo, small group, or larger group (e.g. orchestral) performances. We have already made clear, however, that our definition of performers as well as of composers includes those involved in informal music-making, such as children singing, clients in therapeutic contexts who produce musical improvizations, and other 'performances' which take place outside conventional 'artistic' contexts.

Looking in more detail, we can see that performers also vary with respect to 'individual difference' factors such as age, gender, and personality. Performers differ on specifically musical factors such as their level of instrumental, interpretative, and expressive skill: and the nature of specific performances are determined by performers' expressive intentions (as shown in Juslin's 'communication chain' illustration, see Chapter 5), as well as by psychological factors which determine performers' internal states. These might include arousal level, performance anxiety, and other motivational states which are receiving increasing attention within psychological research (see Williamon 2004). As well as the intrinsic desire to produce an excellent musical performance, motivations might include other perceived outcomes, such as receiving applause and critical acclaim; increasing record sales and earning large appearance fees; setting fashion trends; or passing examinations.

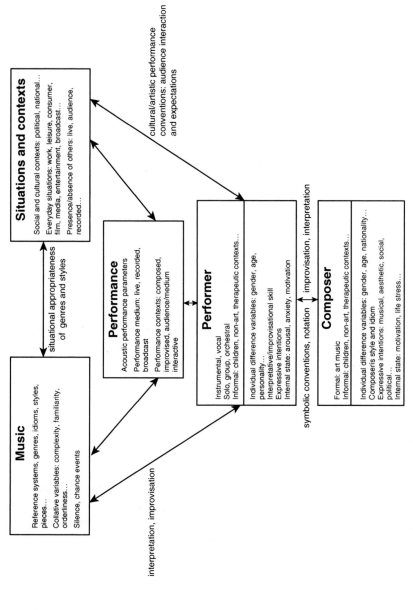

Fig. 1.2 Reciprocal feedback model of musical performance.

These latter examples illustrate the reciprocal feedback relationship that holds between the performer and the factors within 'situations and contexts'. The cultural and artistic performance expectations of different musical genres and different societies give rise to certain expectations about the behaviour expected of performers and of audiences: some Western rock stars are expected to behave in a way that others would see as outrageous, for example, and audiences can consciously or unconsciously encourage them to do so.

There is a corresponding reciprocal feedback relationship between the performer and the music itself, and this is most clearly seen in improvised music. Many jazz musicians report that their most successful improvised performances occur when they experience rapport with the audience, and with other members of the performing group: the new musical ideas that they create and develop become interdependent with their internal states and feelings (MacDonald and Wilson 2005). This is clearly apparent in the work of the pianist Keith Jarrett, whose solo improvizations, recorded in the 1970s, have received widespread critical acclaim. Jarrett brought his own distinctive approach to total improvization to a huge worldwide audience. He developed harmonic sequences, rhythms, melodies, and structures from scratch, having made no advance plans and deliberately trying to clear his mind of any preconceived ideas before the performances, which could often last an hour or more. The direction, mood, and structure of each marathon improvization were dependent on his own mental state and concerns at the time, on the particular concert situation, and on the audience reaction and feedback. In the liner notes to the concert recordings, Jarrett writes of: 'One artist creating spontaneously something which is governed by the atmosphere, the audience, the place (both the room and the geographical location), the instrument; all these being channelled consciously through the artist so that everyone's efforts are equally rewarded, although the success or failure belongs completely to the artist himself' (Carr 1991).

Jarrett's approach undoubtedly marks him out as a pioneer of musical communication within the world of free improvization. However, other communities of musicians, notably, but not exclusively, in Amsterdam, Berlin, Chicago, and London, also explored the notion of the performer as instantaneous composer during the 1960s and beyond (Lewis 2004). Critically acclaimed ensembles such as The Association for the Advancement of Creative Musicians (AACM), The Spontaneous Music Ensemble, and AMM all had an explicit focus on developing strategies of musical communication that celebrated the instantaneous realization of musical composition in performance (Bailey 1992). An important feature of their approach, crucially relevant to this chapter, is that these musicians, while not working within an academic context, were fundamentally interested in the wider theoretical, psychological, cultural, social, and political implications of musical communication (Durrant 1989). This approach was and still is viewed as part of a move towards the democratization of musical communication, which is in opposition to the elitist and status-driven conceptualizations of musical performance in the Western art tradition (Reason 2004).

These are clear examples of the composer and the performer being one and the same person, which leads us on to consider the additional factors which come into operation when they are not. In most Western art music, the composer is formally seen as the generator of the 'core product', and occupies the apex of a status hierarchy lower down which is the performer, whose role is to pass on the product to the listener, who is still lower down the hierarchy (see Cook 1998): this is the position implicitly adopted by most existing theories of musical communication. In this situation, the composer communicates with the performer by means of the written score, which involves shared understanding of some form of symbolic convention, such as staff notation. The use of graphic and other forms of notation, and their potential effects on musical communication, are explored elsewhere in this book (notably Chapters 6 and 7).

As in the case of the performer, composers also vary with respect to 'individual difference' factors such as age, gender, and personality: their particular musical languages, and the styles and idioms within which they work, may well be more distinctive and idiosyncratic than in the musical world of professional performers, who may be called upon to work in many different genres. (There are some notable exceptions to this, of course: Igor Stravinsky and Miles Davis, though working in completely different fields, both created and/or worked within several different idioms and styles over the course of a single lifetime). Composers' expressive intentions in a sense form the essence of the 'core product' referred to earlier, and these are determined by various musical, aesthetic, social, political, and other motivational factors. As in the case of performers, the working lives of many composers are notoriously bound up with particular psychological and other motivational states, including life stresses, the difficulty of earning a living from composing, the struggle for public recognition, and so on.

Musical communication

By combining the response and performance models, we are now able to propose a model of musical communication which takes into account all of the factors reviewed in this chapter: it is shown in Fig. 1.3. Figures 1.1 and 1.2, for clarity of illustration, appear in two dimensions: in order to combine them we need to move into three dimensions. We can conceive of the performance model in three dimensions as a pyramid (tetrahedron) with the *music, situations and*

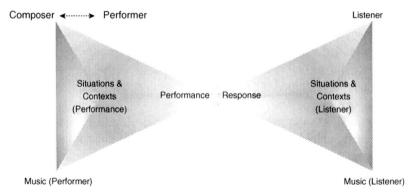

Fig. 1.3 Reciprocal feedback model of musical communication.

contexts, and *composer/performer* variables interactively giving rise to the *performance;* and of the response model, correspondingly, as a pyramid with the *music, situations and contexts*, and *listener* variables interactively giving rise to the *response*. The two pyramids can then be rotated as shown in Fig. 1.3 to produce a model in which musical communication is defined as the 'spark' which occurs when the performance event gives rise to a response.

The model also illustrates the distinction between the music as seen from the points of view of the performer and the listener, as well as that between the situations and contexts as seen from the points of view of the performer and the listener. This allows us to represent the possibility that the representations of the music by the composer and the listener – the former's expressive intentions and the listener's affective response, in terms of Juslin's 'communication chain' illustration – may be quite different from one another, although that need not necessarily be the case.

To reiterate what we pointed out earlier, this double tetrahedral model represents a view of musical communication which takes into account important social and contextual variables, which goes beyond 'art music' contexts, and whose principle of reciprocal feedback indicates that the causal relationships between each of the three major determinants operate in both directions. In each of these respects, it goes beyond the transmission models which have hitherto been proposed: but we need to be clear about its status in this respect. The double tetrahedral model is based on the communication of information between the performance event and the listener, and so remains, in essence, a transmission model: it does not specify any alternative theoretical explanation for the way in which communication occurs. Its two components, the perform-ance and the response models, are not based on information transmission, however: the proposed reciprocal feedback mechanisms which link the boxes in Figs 1.1 and 1.2 are intended to represent the causal relationships between the three determinants of the performance/response in each case rather than any flow of information as such.

It would therefore be inaccurate to describe Figs 1.1 and 1.2 as 'transmission models', even though we could do so for Fig. 1.3: and this obligates us to specify what exactly is the purpose of the performance and feedback models. The answer is that by specifying as many of the personal, situational, and musical factors involved as is possible at this stage, and by advancing proposals about some of the causal interrelationships between them, we can generate new theoretical predictions that might not otherwise be possible. It would be unrealistic to claim that all of the factors influencing musical communication are included within these three models: but they do nevertheless attempt to cover the main issues that have been investigated by psychological research to date, and might thereby stimulate more precise and comprehensive formulations. Detailed consideration of the five questions which we posed at the outset – the 'how', 'why', 'what', 'who', and 'where' of musical communication – should enable future researchers to address this new agenda.

Plan of the book

In deciding on the structure of the book, and in inviting contributors, we consciously adopted a multidisciplinary approach: as a result, there are chapters by, for example, psychologists, music therapists, music educationalists, and ethnomusicologists. Although these disciplines represent different ways of understanding musical communication, our text makes no claim to be exhaustive. It is most strongly influenced by our own roots within psychology, and contains chapters written from different theoretical perspectives within psychology, including cognitive, social constructionist, physiological, and evolutionary approaches. Although some of these perspectives may be viewed as mutually exclusive, we make no attempt to offer any value judgements or comparative evaluations, preferring to leave these to the reader.

We devoted a great deal of thought to the best way of dividing the book's varied chapters into coherent and conceptually meaningful themes, and eventually settled on four sections, namely *Cognition, Representation and Communication; Embodied Communication; Communication in Learning and Education;* and *Cultural Contexts of Communication*. The first three chapters of the book (including the present one) are not included within these subheadings as they offer wide-ranging views of the topic of musical communication, and discuss broad issues that cut across all of the other sections.

In Chapter 2, Ian Cross develops his evolutionary view of the functions of music. He presents clear evidence, on the one hand, that humans are predisposed to engage in music-like activities, such that music can be considered to be part of our biological heritage: but paradoxically, that music is also inherently ambiguous, taking a multiplicity of forms and fulfilling many different functions according to specific social and cultural conditions. In Chapter 3, Keith Sawyer starts from the same point of view, suggesting that 'there is evidence that musical ability is a genetic, biological competence': but he then goes on to develop the argument that 'the evolutionary origins of music and language lie in sociality' (p. 51). He describes some of his own attempts to identify and characterize some specific interactional mechanisms which are held in common by both musical and verbal interaction, and expresses his belief 'that we enjoy music because it represents, in crystallized form, the basic processes of human social life.... As we listen to a performance, we are exposed to the distilled essence of human sociality' (pp. 46–7).

The first section of the book, *Cognition, Representation and Communication,* offers four chapters that share a focus upon cognitive psychological issues: we see their detailed consideration as a fundamental part of any comprehensive explanation of musical communication, and as complementing the wider social and cultural issues involved. Annabel Cohen presents a comprehensive and historically grounded overview of the relationship between musical cognition and musical communication in Chapter 4, highlighting that the brain imposes limits on what can be communicated. Patrik Juslin undertakes a similarly comprehensive review of the literature on emotional communication in music in Chapter 5. The topic of music and emotion enjoys widespread public as well as academic interest (see Juslin and Sloboda 2001), and encompasses a significant number of fundamental issues concerning musical communication.

In Chapters 6 and 7 respectively, Margaret Barrett and Jeanne Bamberger focus on musical notation, considering how the use of different notational conventions can shape musical perception and performance. Barrett looks in detail at children's invented notations, and Bamberger draws on three very different case studies – of a musically untutored nine-year-old, of two gifted young violinists, and of a professional string quartet – in demonstrating how the rules and syntax of notation crucially influence the process of musical communication.

The second section, *Embodied Communication,* draws together four chapters that focus on emotional, physical, and biological aspects of communication. In Chapter 8, Michael Thaut examines some of the neurological bases of musical communication, using behavioural evidence from psychophysical studies and from studies using brain imaging and brain wave recordings.

This work not only illuminates our understanding of the neurophysiological processes mediating rhythm perception and rhythm production, but also has implications for the use of music in therapy and medicine. Gary Ansdell and Mercédès Pavlicevic pursue the importance of the notion of 'music as communication' in the therapeutic field in Chapter 9, reviewing interdisciplinary research on the relationships between health and social interaction in relation to contemporary music therapy, and asking some fundamental conceptual questions about its future. They argue that placing the idea of 'music as communication' at the centre of music therapy 'can embody and foster a humanistic value system of musical dialogue as companionship and community – as ways of being musically with people in need' (p. 195).

In Chapter 10, Jane Davidson deals with three central aspects of musical communication in investigating the role of the human body in producing a musical performance, namely how biomechanical constraints operate; how expressive intentions and social codes influence the production of a perform-ance; and how that production is subsequently interpreted by co-performers and audiences. She uses three case studies from her own research to illustrate these issues – a classical pianist, a jazz singer and accompanist, and a pop band. Graham Welch specifically considers the role of human vocalization and singing in musical communication in Chapter 11, reviewing its neurological and physiological origins and its role in early infant–parent relationships, especially in the communication of emotion. From this perspective, Welch suggests that musical communication is integral to human vocalization and emotional expression.

The three chapters in the section on *Communication in Learning and Education* all look at young peoples' musical communication in learning contexts, both formal and informal. In Chapter 12, Margaret Barrett explores the notion of a 'community of practice' in relation to children's music-making in informal settings, illustrating her analysis with examples drawn from her own research on children's play in such activities as handclapping, chants, and musical games. Susan Young highlights some key features of musical commu-nication of young children aged 2–4 in Chapter 13, proposing that this can provide a template for musical communication in later years. She emphasizes the importance that music has in sustaining and developing relationships and in doing so, demonstrates a link between her own work and that of music therapists. In Chapter 14, Charles Byrne investigates the classroom environment, exploring those verbal and musical features of music teaching which seem to promote musical communication and learning. He considers the ways in which teachers think and talk about music, and proposes a theoretical model of interaction in the music classroom.

The final section of the book, *Cultural contexts of communication,* looks at a range of different contexts in which musical communication takes place and attempts to delineate a number of key processes involved in each of these situations. In Chapter 15, Raymond MacDonald, Dorothy Miell, and Graeme Wilson present an account of how talk *about* music in informal settings can play a crucial role within the musical communication process. Rather than examining how music itself communicates, this chapter focuses on the ways in which talk about music serves a number of personal, social, and musical functions for both young people and professional musicians, and which can therefore be viewed as an important aspect of musical communication itself.

In Chapter 16, Janis McNair and John Powles examine the role of music in creating, communicating, and sustaining identities based in particular sub-cultures. They point out that music and song can cause, facilitate and reflect social, cultural, and political change, such that music can be seen as a powerful medium for communicating intellectual and emotional messages: and they draw specifically on 1960s protest music, notably the music of Bob Dylan, and on hip-hop culture to illustrate these issues. Martin Clayton takes an ethnomusicological approach to communication within Indian raga music in Chapter 17, showing how this can operate through non-auditory as well as auditory channels. He suggests that non-verbal and auditory features of a performance can combine to create a cultural Gestalt whose intrinsically musical features are part of a social milieu that must be considered in its entirety for a full appreciation of the communicative potential of the music.

Scott Lipscomb and David Tolchinsky return to cognitive models in Chapter 18 to explore musical communication within a cinematic context. They present several empirical and theoretical models of film music perception and the role of music in film, and illustrate some of the many ways in which a film's soundtrack can not only contribute towards but also expand upon the meaning of a film's narrative, and on what it communicates to the audience. In the final chapter of the book, Adrian North and David Hargreaves review the research literature on the effects of music within consumer contexts, grounding this in the debate between those within the music industry who argue for the commercial benefits of piped music, and those campaigners who object that the background music which is 'piped' into shops and stores represents an invasion of personal freedom. They present clear evidence which shows that background music can influence the speed of customer activity, perceptions of the ambiance or atmosphere within a retail outlet, the experience of time spent waiting in queues, and output in the workplace.

The power of music is immense, and the contents of this book represent just a first step towards our understanding of the 'how', 'why', 'what', 'who', and 'where' of musical communication. We have attempted to set out a new agenda, and look forward to the challenge being taken up by future research.

Acknowledgements

Like its predecessor *Musical Identities* (MacDonald, Hargreaves and Miell 2002), this book has its origins in a series of seminars which we co-ordinated in 1998 which were funded by the British Psychological Society and entitled *Social Psychology of Music: Theoretical Advances and Practical Applications.* We would like to thank the BPS for this support, as well as Leslie Bunt, Tony Wigram, and Colwyn Trevarthen who, whilst not contributing chapters to the present text, presented articles at the seminar on musical communication which helped to shape our ideas about what to include. We would also like to acknowledge the help and support of Linda Hargreaves, who first suggested the idea of the 'double pyramid' model developed in this chapter; Jon Hargreaves, for doing the indexing; Tracy Ibbotson; Karen Littleton for being a most supportive and stimulating colleague as the ideas for this book developed; Patrik Juslin and Adrian North, for their critical comments on the present chapter, and Graeme Wilson.

References

Abeles, H.F. and Chung, J.W. (1996) Responses to music. In *Handbook of music psychology,* (ed. D.A. Hodges). San Antonio, TX: IMR Press.

Bailey, D. (1992) *Improvization: Its nature and practice in music.* New York: Da Capo.

Bandura, A. (1986) *Social foundations of thought and action: A social cognitive theory.* Englewood Cliffs, N.J.: Prentice-Hall.

Bandura, A. (1997) *Self-efficacy: The exercise of control.* New York: W.H. Freeman.

Berlyne, D.E. (1971) *Aesthetics and psychobiology.* New York: Appleton-Century-Crofts.

Brewster, B. and Broughton, F. (1999) *Last night a DJ saved my life.* London: Headline.

Carlton, L. and MacDonald, R.A.R. (2004) An investigation of the effects of music on thematic apperception test (TAT) interpretations. *Musicae Scientae,* 7 (special issue), 9–31.

Carr, I. (1991) *Keith Jarrett: The man and his music.* London: Grafton.

Cook, N. (1998) *Music: A very short introduction.* Oxford: Oxford University Press.

Deutsch, D. (ed.) (1999) *The psychology of music* (2nd ed.). San Diego, CA: Academic Press.

Durrant, A. (1989) Improvization in the political economy of music. In *Music and the politics of culture,* (ed. C. Norris), pp. 252–82. New York: St. Martin's Press.

Folkestad, G. (2002) National identity and music. In *Musical identities* (eds R.A.R. MacDonald, D.J. Hargreaves, and D.E. Miell). Oxford: Oxford University Press.

Hargreaves, D.J. (1986) *The developmental psychology of music.* Cambridge: Cambridge University Press.

Hargreaves, D.J., Miell, D.E., and MacDonald, R.A.R. (2002) What are musical identities, and why are they important? In *Musical identities,* (eds R.A.R. MacDonald, D.J. Hargreaves, and D.E. Miell). Oxford: Oxford University Press.

Hargreaves, D.J. and North, A.C. (eds) (1997) *The social psychology of music.* Oxford: Oxford University Press.

Hargreaves, D.J. and North, A.C. (1999) Developing concepts of musical style. *Musicae Scientiae,* **2**, 193–213.

Hargreaves, D.J., North, A.C., and Tarrant, M. (2005) Musical preference and taste. In *The child as musician: Musical development from conception to adolescence,* (ed. G.E. McPherson). Oxford: Oxford University Press.

Johnson-Laird, P.N. (1992) Introduction: What is communication? In *Ways of communicating,* (ed. D.H. Mellor). Cambridge: Cambridge University Press.

Juslin, P.N. and Sloboda, J.A. (eds) (2001) *Music and emotion: Theory and research.* New York: Oxford University Press.

Kendall, R.A. and Carterette, E.C. (1990) The communication of musical expression. *Music Perception,* **8**, 129–64.

Lewis, G. (2004) Improvised music after 1950: Afrological and Eurological perspectives. In *The other side of nowhere: Jazz, improvization and communities in dialogue,* (eds D. Fischlin and A. Heble), pp. 131–63. Connecticut: Wesleyan University Press.

MacDonald, R.A.R. and Wilson, G.B. (2005) The musical identities of professional jazz musicians: A focus group investigation. *Psychology of Music.*

MacDonald, R.A.R., Hargreaves, D.J., and Miell, D.E. (eds) (2002) *Musical identities.* Oxford: Oxford University Press.

Martindale, C. and Moore, K (1988) Priming, prototypicality, and preference. *Journal of Experimental Psychology: Human Perception and Performance,* **14**, 661–70.

Merker, B. (2000) Synchronous chorusing and human origins. In *The origins of music,* (eds N. Wallin, B. Merker, and S. Brown). Cambridge, MA: MIT Press.

Mitchell, L. (2004) *An experimental investigation of the effects of music listening on pain.* Unpublished PhD thesis, Glasgow Caledonian University.

Nattiez, J.-J. (Trans. C. Abbate) (1990) *Music and discourse: Toward a semiology of music.* Princeton, New Jersey: Princeton University Press.

North, A.C. and Hargreaves, D.J. (1997*a*) Experimental aesthetics and everyday music listening. In *The social psychology of music* (eds D.J. Hargreaves and A.C. North). Oxford: Oxford University Press.

North, A.C. and Hargreaves, D.J. (1997*b*) The musical milieu: studies of listening in everyday life. *The Psychologist,* **10**, 309–12.

North, A. C. and Hargreaves, D.J. (2000*a*) Collative variables versus prototypicality. *Empirical Studies of the Arts,* **18**, 13–17.

North, A.C. and Hargreaves, D.J. (2000*b*) Musical preferences during and after relaxing and exercising. *American Journal of Psychology,* **113**, 43–67.

North, A.C., Hargreaves, D.J., and Hargreaves, J.J. (2004) Uses of music in everyday life. *Music Perception,* **22**(1), 41–77.

O'Hara, K., Lipson, M., Jansen, M., Unger, A., Jeffries, H., and Macer, P. (2004) Jukola: Democratic music choice in a public space. *Proceedings of the 2004 conference on designing interactive systems: Processes, practices, methods and techniques.* Cambridge, MA. Symposium on Designing Interactive Systems Archive.

Reason, D. (2004) Navigable structures and transforming mirrors: Improvization and interactivity. In *The other side of nowhere: Jazz, improvization and communities in dialogue*, (eds D. Fischlin and A. Heble), pp. 71–87. Connecticut: Wesleyan University Press.

Shannon, C.E. and Weaver, W. (1949) *The mathematical theory of communication.* Urbana: University of Illinois.

Sloboda, J.A., O'Neill, S.A., and Ivaldi, A. (2001) Functions of music in everyday life: an exploratory study using the Experience Sampling Method. *Musicae Scientiae,* **5**, 9–32.

Williamon, A. (ed.) (2004) *Musical excellence: Strategies and techniques to enhance performance.* Oxford: Oxford University Press.

Chapter 2

Music and meaning, ambiguity and evolution

Ian Cross

Humans as animals

From a biological perspective, humans are unusual animals. Not only are we the single truly bipedal mammal, we have brains that are much larger than would be warranted by our body size. It seems reasonable to assume that this large brain comes together with the immense cognitive flexibility that humans possess, a flexibility that enables us to manipulate our environments in extraordinarily complex ways. This cognitive flexibility is not the only attribute that appears to mark us out from all other species. Humans are also capable of an immense social flexibility; the ways in which we can interact with others are extremely diverse and can be immensely sophisticated. Some of this capacity for diversity of social interaction we share with our nearest evolutionary neighbours, the apes; indeed a close correlation between degree of social flexibility and the size of the neocortex in the brain has been found across the primate and hominid lineages (see Dunbar 1992).

But perhaps the most salient and unique feature of humans that seems to underlie our cognitive and social flexibility is the capacity to communicate in language, whether spoken, signed, or written. While other species are self-evidently able to communicate with other members of the same species by sound, sight, touch, or smell, only humans have the capacity to communicate to each other information about complex states of affairs in the material and social worlds. Despite the best efforts of researchers over the last thirty-odd years, neither chimpanzees nor bonobos, our closest evolutionary relatives, seem capable of employing communicative media to express their perceptions, desires, intentions, or attitudes with the level of syntactic and semantic sophistication that seems to be naturally acquired by an average five-year old human child (see Conway and Christiansen 2001).

The human capacity to communicate through language is perhaps the one unique marker that differentiates us from all other species, and it is natural to think of this capacity as intrinsic to our cognitive and social flexibilities. Communication through language, enabling complex and useful information to be represented and exchanged, seems to be the principal guarantor of our intellectual powers and of our cultural complexities, features that are likely to have had considerable potency in enabling humans to have emerged as a highly successful species over the 200 000 years or so in which modern humans have been in existence. In other words, it is highly probable that language, in enabling and sustaining our cognitive and social proficiency, was an adaptive factor in human evolution (see Pinker 1994); it enabled humans, individually and in groups, to communicate useful and accurate information to each other and hence to survive and reproduce in situations where other species could not.

Like language, music can also be conceived of as a communicative medium; indeed, both seem to fit equally well within a widely used theoretical model of communication, the 'information theory' model of Shannon and Weaver (1949). In this model a sender makes use of a channel to send information to a receiver; the sender and receiver can be any type of entity, the channel can be constituted of any medium, and the information that is sent may take any form. In a musical context, one can think of the sender as the performer, the receiver as the listener, the channel as the air, and the information transmitted is the sonic patterns that constitute the music. Analogously, in language, the sender is the speaker, the receiver is the listener, the channel is the air, and the information sent is the patterned fluctuations of air pressure that constitute the sound of speech. The model seems to provide a basis for considering music and language to be analogous systems of communication, setting aside for the moment the nature of the information that is communicated.

But while this model seems to fit most instances of language use quite well (and perhaps fits all instances of animal communication, see Seyfarth and Cheney 2003), it is not clear that it is so generally applicable to music. Although in perhaps most musical situations in contemporary western global culture, it is easy to categorize participants as sender or receiver, performer or listener, there are many musical situations which may not yield such clear distinctions. The members, say, of a recreational choir, or of an amateur rock band, may rarely if ever fulfil the role of performer; for them, music may be more a medium for participatory interaction where all are equally and simultaneously performers and listeners than a medium for display, for communication of musical information to 'passive' listeners. Moreover, the interaction is likely to take the form of synchronous and synchronized sound patterns and behaviours rather than the asynchronous and alternating sonic sequences that are typical of speech. Similarly, if we look to non-western musical practices, many seem to have as their raison d'être not the transmission of musical information from active performer to passive listener but collective engagement in the synchronous production and perception of complex patterns of sounds and movement (see Arom 1991; Blacking 1976). Music in these guises does not seem as easily assimilable as is language into the model of communication provided by information theory.

Music

So where does this leave music? Is it, to quote Steven Pinker (Pinker 1997), simply 'auditory cheesecake', a human faculty that pretends to communicate but that is more or less parasitic on many of the abilities that underlie language and that has no real function other than to tickle the senses? Is music merely an opportunistic and non-adaptive exploitation for solely pleasurable purposes of capacities to communicate that have arisen in humans through evolutionary processes for the serious business of survival? It has been argued by Miller (2000) that music was in fact an adaptive factor in human evolution, playing a role in processes of sexual selection through the opportunities it afforded for the communicative display by performers of the 'protean' or unpredictable intellectual and social attributes that rendered them and their offspring more likely to survive in an uncertain world. However, this view, and that of Pinker, both rely on the 'conventional' idea of music as requiring participants to fulfil roles of performer and listener, and as we have seen this does not appear to be generally applicable to all manifestations of music. If we are to understand music as a communicative medium it seems that we must look beyond the notion that music exists as sonic information communicated from performer to listener, and it may be that we must also look beyond the model of communication provided by information theory.

For most musicologists and for almost all ethnomusicologists, music is not just sonic pattern. Music involves action and interaction. Indeed the structure of its sonic patterns may be as much determined by the actions that produce them as by any abstract considerations of sonic design, as both Baily (1985) and Nelson (2002) have shown is the case for, respectively, the music of the Afghan dutar and the improvization of blues guitar solos. In music, sound and action may be intrinsically interlinked, and action in music is, more often than not, a form of interaction that is typically expressed in terms of entrainment to some common temporal framework or pulse. In the western concert hall this fact is only overtly evident in the actions and interactions of the performers, but it is very likely that many audience members will covertly engage in surreptitious finger or foot tapping, conducting, or regular and expressive head and upper body movement that is entrained with the musical sound. It should be noted that even were a member of the audience at a western concert to show no overt signs of movement, the *acquisition* of the capacity to listen and respond appropriately to concert music is likely to have involved movement, as we shall see. Moreover, Petr Janata and others (see Janata and Grafton 2003) have shown that even 'passive' listening to music can involve activation of brain regions concerned with movement.

Outside the confines of the concert hall, the 'action' and 'interaction' dimensions of musical participation can be less covert and may be extremely ostentatious. Indeed, in many non-western contexts active and collective entrainment with the sonic structure of the musical sound seems to be as much a part of the music as is the sonic structure of the sound itself, perhaps evidenced in the lack of distinction made in certain societies between what in the west might be separately categorized as music and as dance (Gourlay 1984). The intelligibility of the sonic structure of music may even depend on its contextualization in collective movement, as is evident in, for example, many of the musical practices of the *campesino* culture of Northern Potosí in Bolivia (see Stobart and Cross 2000).

And finally, the issue of what – if anything – music is communicating must be addressed. Whereas in language it is usually possible to specify the subject of an utterance with some precision, this is almost never the case for music. Music appears to be a strangely malleable and flexible phenomenon. The meaning or significance of a musical behaviour or of a piece of music can rarely be pinned down unambiguously; music appears to be inherently ambiguous (see Kramer 2003). As Langer (1942, p. 195) puts it '...music at its highest, though clearly a symbolic form, is an unconsummated symbol. Articulation is its life, but not assertion; expressiveness, not expression. The actual function of meaning, which calls for permanent contents, is not fulfilled; for the *assignment* of one rather than another possible meaning to each form is never explicitly made'. This ambiguity has been conceived of as valuable within social and political contexts. Lydia Goehr (1993, p. 187) suggests that 'music has no meaning to speak of, and hence can be used to envision an alternative culture and political order while escaping the scrutiny of the censor'; Devereux and LaBarre (1961, p. 369) propose that 'In addition to viewing art as a harmless safety valve, society and the artist alike consider the artistic utterance as *unrepudiable* in form but *repudiable* as to content...'. In effect, one and the same piece of music can bear quite different meanings for performer and listener, or for two different listeners; it might even bear multiple disparate meanings for a single listener or participant at a particular time. Music has a sort of 'floating intentionality' (the word 'intentionality' here simply means 'aboutness'); it can be thought of as gathering meaning from the contexts within which it happens and in turn contributing meaning to those contexts.

Music seems to be inherently ambiguous, yet it is intuitively plausible that music is a communicative medium. How, and what, then, is it communicating? In order to explore this it is necessary to consider whether or not the model of communication provided by information theory is in fact adequate to account for all aspects of human communication. This model postulates that information is sent to a receiver who decodes the information encoded in the message received. When applied to human linguistic communication, this requires a very close match between the capacities of the sender and of the receiver. The capacities of the sender and receiver must be similar enough for the receiver to be capable of all the processes that are necessary to decode the message accurately. In effect, this model presupposes that sender and receiver both possess a body of shared knowledge that will render the information that is communicated unambiguously intelligible. This seems to be a reasonable proposition in respect of language; one might expect that a speaker and a hearer belonging to the same language community might be bound by the same set of rules and conventions that they can both bring to bear so that the speaker's message is intelligibly decoded by the hearer.

Music and meaning

However, this model can be questioned, at the very least on the grounds that while a pool of mutual knowledge seems plausible, it can never be guaranteed, hence neither can the intelligibility of a linguistic message. Without the certainty of mutual knowledge there will always be a degree of ambiguity in linguistic communication. The exchange of a verbal message requires that inferences are made by the hearer as to the speaker's intended referent, and that inferences are made by the speaker in respect of the hearer's capacity to identify the speaker's intended referent. So, for example, the sentence 'This land belongs to the Duke of Sutherland' would have quite different import when spoken by the Duke's bailiff to a tenant farmer during the Highland Clearances in the nineteenth century and when spoken by a guide to a group of tourists visiting the north of Scotland in the present day. Sperber and Wilson (1986) have analysed the implications of this requirement for inference at length in developing a theory of *ostensive-inferential communication* in which a speaker is characterized as not simply broadcasting a message to a listener but as producing a stimulus that is intended to change the cognitive environment of a listener by seeking to achieve some degree of resemblance between a speaker's and hearer's thoughts (Sperber 1996). This theory claims that human cognition is geared to the maximization of *relevance*, defined by Sperber (ibid.) as a human 'tendency to optimize the effect–effort ratio' in any particular situation and hence minimize the cognitive load involved in processing the information that an individual encounters. For Sperber and Wilson, a presumption of relevance by both speaker and hearer is what frames and guides processes of inference in human linguistic communication and reduces the ambiguity inherent in a communicative act.

Accepting that a degree of ambiguity seems to be inherent in all (even linguistic) acts of human communication, music's apparent ambiguity does not debar it from being considered to be a communicative medium. However, language has referents – it is *about* something – and hence language can be said to communicate information about states of affairs. Indeed, aboutness or *intentionality* can be considered intrinsic to any act of communication. But what is it, if anything, that music can be said to be *about*? What information is music communicating? A view that was put forward by Hanslick in the late nineteenth century and that still has considerable currency is that music is about nothing other than itself. As music unfolds in time, it articulates complex structures that relate to, and perhaps refer to, each other. And it is certainly the case that music embodies what Leonard Meyer has called 'evident' meaning. For Meyer (1956, p. 37), music's evident meanings are 'those that are attributed to the antecedent gesture when the consequent becomes a physico-psychic fact and when the relationship between the antecedent and the consequent is perceived'; this relationship will depend on the expectations that the antecedent aroused and on whether or not the consequent fulfils or abrogates those expectations. The ongoing abstraction of evident meaning in a piece of music by a listener or performer will depend on the continual making of inferences – 'generation of expectations' in Meyer's terms – which may or may not be fulfilled as the music unfolds.

The types of information that underlie and that may constitute music's evident meaning have been the focus of a great deal of cognitive-psychological research over the last half century. This has explored in depth the nature of the human capacity to abstract a range of types of musical information, such as which notes or musical events are more important, stable or 'closural' (final) than which other notes or events, which sets of events belong together and which belong to separate groups, which groups of events appear to be dependent for their identity on other sets of events, etc. (see Deutsch 1999). Here it is important to note that, just as with language, the making of appropriate inferences appears to depend on the degree to which a listener or performer is embedded in a given musical culture, although some types of inferences might be more universally and cross-culturally available than others. For example, Castellano *et al.* (1984) showed that the frequency distribution or total sounding duration of different pitches in passages of North Indian music were powerful determinants of listeners' attributions of different degrees of stability to different pitches: the more frequent or the longer total sounding duration, the more stable the pitch was perceived to be. This applied equally to western listeners with little previous experience of North Indian music and to Indian listeners with considerable experience. However, Indian listeners were also capable of finer degrees of distinction between the perceived stability of pitches, a capacity that appeared to be related to their previous experience of or exposure to music of that particular kind. The seeming universality of the strategies that could be employed by both sets of listeners probably reflects generic learning processes that are common to all humans, irrespective of cultural background, whereas the different discriminatory skills of the Indian and western listeners can be thought of as arising from particularizations of those learning processes operating over the long term in specific and different cultural contexts. The inferences that are made in the abstraction of evident meaning from music appear to be dependent on individual and cultural histories, and on both generic and specific attributes of the cognitive systems that make them.

However, the idea that music is solely about itself was under attack from the outset. As already noted, many if not most cultures' musics appear to be embedded in broader suites of cultural practices. The ethnomusicologist Philip Bohlman (2000) claims that 'all human beings produce music and that expressive practices do not divide into those that produce music and those that produce something else, say ritual or dance. Music accumulates its identities… from the ways in which it participates in other activities…'. And music's self-reflexive aboutness can scarcely account for what John Booth Davies (1978) has called its 'darling-they're-playing-our-tune' dimension. For most members of contemporary western culture, music bears meanings that extend beyond the 'music itself'. One obvious candidate for what music might be about – for what it might *intend* – is emotion.

Emotions can be defined as complex, dynamic, and integrated states of brain, body, and mind which arise in response to environmental stimuli (and here the environment might be thought of as being as much cognitive as physical), and both prepare the body for appropriate action and impact on the functioning of perceptual and cognitive processes (see LeDoux 1998; Damasio 1995). It seems entirely uncontentious to characterize music as portraying or eliciting emotions. How, and indeed, whether, music does this has been the focus of a great deal of recent research (see Juslin and Sloboda 2001), much of which appears to confirm Meyer's (1956) proposal that the unfolding of music's evident structure modulates the affective states of both listeners and performers, probably in part by mirroring the temporal forms of emotional brain–mind–body states (ibid, p. 79) and those of correlates of these such as gesture or linguistic utterance (see Lavy 2001). In addition, as Lavy points out, music may be involved in the elicitation of emotion as much by virtue of its 'raw' sonic attributes as by its structure, and, as Scherer and Zentner (2001) note, by its capacity to embody and to connote specific cultural referents.

Music seems to have the capacity to communicate, hinting, alluding, connoting, and referring not only beyond itself but to itself. It does appear to be 'about' itself in the evident meanings which are bound to its structure and become apparent as the music unfolds, allowing for the elicitation of emotion in the listener and performer. And music also means by virtue of the connotations that it embodies, perhaps best expressed, to quote Meyer (1956), as 'connotative complexes'. As Meyer (ibid, p. 265) states, 'Music does not [for example] present the concept or image of death itself. Rather it connotes that rich realm of experience in which death and darkness, night and cold, winter and sleep and silence are all combined and consolidated into a single connotative complex'. ... 'What music presents is not any one of these metaphorical events but rather that which is common to all of them, that which enables them to become metaphors for one another. Music presents a generic event, a 'connotative complex', which then becomes particularized in the experience of the individual listener.'

Moreover, music's meanings can be less or more explicit according to the contexts in which it is encountered and according to the degree to which the constituents of the musical 'sign' may bear specific significances. For instance, it is likely that the experience of western art-music would allow for a greater latitude in apparent meaning than would that of a piece of music employed in the context of a Hollywood film. Two different solitary listeners to a CD of Beethoven's *Grosse fuge* might well abstract quite different highly personal and intricate emotional significances from the music's complex evident structure. If the listener has considerable previous experience of Beethoven's oeuvre, the ongoing flow of the piece might be registered as a continual struggle between the apparent implications of the fugue's subjects and their constant metamorphoses in their traversal of harmonic space. For a listener with little experience of Beethoven's late style, the abruptly pitching subjects might evoke images of a sea-storm, or it might impel a sense of emotional disequilibrium; their diffuse harmonic treatment could be experienced as destabilizing and threatening, or it could be felt as somehow grave, objective, and detached. The situation might be quite different and much less obscure in respect of music experienced in the context of film; the very low-pitched semitonal ostinato overlaid by a non-tonally related horn call at the outset of the film *Jaws*, overlaid on an otherwise fairly innocuous underwater scene, signifies to the listener/viewer that something big and unseen is out there in the water (only big things can produce low-frequency sounds) and that it may well be hunting (horn calls, in western culture, are conventionally interpreted in terms of hunting topics – see Agawu 1991) – hence fear and perhaps terror may be wholly appropriate, and fairly universal, responses.

In many respects the ways in which music means, and the information that it may convey, are similar to those of language. Language also hints and alludes, it may even refer to itself and connote through its sounds as well as its structure, as in poetry (see, e.g. Vendler 1997). It can certainly be employed to elicit emotion! Even a very recent attempt to delineate the human faculty for language (Hauser *et al.* 2002) puts forward a narrow and exclusive definition of language that could equally well define music; Hauser *et al.* suggest that language is a unique human faculty because of its recursive capacities (roughly speaking, recursion is the capacity of a system such as a linguistic grammar to embed entities in themselves (such as clauses within clauses) so as to enable the generation of an infinite (in theory) range of expressions from a finite set of elements). However, the property of recursion seems to be as much a feature of music and of the experience of music as of language (see Lerdahl and Jackendoff 1983; Horton 2002). These similarities appear to validate the notion that music may be just an offshoot of language. Viewed in evolutionary terms, it seems that Pinker may have been right; the human faculty for music may indeed be parasitic on the human faculty for language, simply exploiting capacities that have arisen for evolutionarily adaptive ends.

However, music does appear to have an efficacy that is different from that of language by virtue of the specific features that differentiate it from language. Whereas perhaps the most prominent feature of language is its capacity to be deployed so as to narrow down the range of its possible referents (see Sperber and Wilson 1986; Deacon 1996), music *by itself* does not appear to be capable of doing so. In the limit, language can express semantically decomposable propositions; it can refer unambiguously to complex states of affairs in the world. Music, however, seems to embody an essential ambiguity, and in this respect it can be suggested that language and music are at the opposite poles of a communicative continuum, almost meeting in the middle somewhere near poetry (Cross 2003c). This inherent ambiguity, together with the quality of the actions and interactions that were noted earlier as being integral to music, suffice to differentiate music from language. Music's attributes of *embodying*, *entraining*, and *transposably intentionalizing* time in sound and action (see Cross 2003a) enable it to be efficacious in contexts where language may be unproductive or impotent precisely because of its capacity to be interpreted unambiguously, and it can be suggested that the emergence of musicality is likely to have been crucially adaptive in processes of human evolution.

Music can be efficacious for groups, for individuals within groups and for individuals. If one imagines a group of people involved in a collective musical behaviour, their individual behaviours are likely to be co-ordinated within a temporal framework and thus stand in more-or-less predictable relationships in respect of each other. This endows the collective activity with a high degree of coherence which is more than likely to help establish a strong sense of group identity in this directed and synchronized modulation of action, attention, and affect (see McNeill 1995). It is even feasible to propose that such collective musical behaviour engenders sufficiently similar affective and cognitive dynamics in the participants that one could conceive of the music as eliciting or instantiating forms of intersubjective experience (see Benzon 2001). The reinforcement of group identity or the instantiation of a form of intersubjectivity can function in collective musical behaviours not only because of the music's capacity to entrain but also because music allows each participant to interpret its significances individually and independently without the integrity of the collective musical behaviour being undermined. Music's inexplicitness, its ambiguity, or floating intentionality may thus be regarded as a highly advantageous characteristic of its function for groups; music, then, might serve as a medium for the maintenance of human social flexibility.

In addition to this efficacy at the level of the group, music may be efficacious for individuals within groups which are engaged in collective musical behaviours. This is perhaps most evident if we consider a group of children interacting musically. Here it may be that social flexibility is not just being maintained but formed. Music's powers of entrainment, together with its ambiguity, may allow each participating child to explore forms of interaction with others while minimizing the risk that such exploration might give rise to conflict, effectively underlying the gestation of a social flexibility (see Cross 2003a). One only has to envisage a group of children interacting verbally and unambiguously rather than musically to see (and hear) how quickly conflict is likely to emerge in linguistic rather than musical interaction!

For individuals, any efficacy for music beyond the purely hedonic seems harder to articulate, but a clue might be found in Meyer's notion of 'connotative complexes', where he implies that music does not so much embody metaphors as constitute a metaphorizing medium, one through which seemingly disparate concepts may be experienced as interlinked. While it is more than feasible that music fulfils this role for mature members of a culture, it seems more viable to suggest that music's efficacy at the level of the individual may be greatest in infancy and in childhood.

Over the last twenty years it has become evident that infants and children, though hugely flexible in that their neural systems are immensely plastic, are not general-purpose learning machines (see, e.g. Spelke 1999). Rather they seem to be predisposed to pick up certain types of information and to deal with it in particular and distinct ways. So, for example, even a very young infant will show that it has expectations about the likely behaviours of animate objects that are quite different from those which it exhibits in respect of inanimate objects. Similarly, even extremely young infants can respond appropriately to facial expressions. These capacities emerge too rapidly to be explained on the basis of the operation of a general-purpose learning mechanism. Moreover, they seem to be specific to the particular domains within which they are displayed. An ability to deal with information in one domain, for example, the physical world, is unlikely to be transferable to another domain, say, the social. Infants seem to be predisposed to pick up and deal with information in these distinct domains rapidly and effectively.

Yet the hallmark of the human species is a generalized ability to deal with information that is not specific to any particular domain. It is in the emergence of this domain-general intellectual flexibility that music is likely to play a role. Music's floating intentionality, its potential for its meaning or aboutness to be transposed from one situation to another, allows that one and the same musical act might be co-opted by an infant or child in dealing with information in two quite different domains. This could help in the emergence of the capacity to relate or to integrate information across domains, and assist in the emergence of a domain-general competence. In effect, early musical, or rather, proto-musical, behaviours may be functional in individual development in giving rise to a *metaphorizing* capacity. The attributes of music that may facilitate this transposition of its significances and hence allow the *redescription* of information across domains (see Karmiloff-Smith 1992) may lie in its capacity to mirror forms of emotional and cognitive dynamics (see Cross 1999). Alternatively, it may be that positive emotions evoked in an infant's or child's engagement with music are directly beneficial in cognitive processing, particularly in affording the conditions for rich integration of representations and enhanced exploratory behaviour (see Damasio 1995).

Indeed, individual musical behaviours in childhood have been characterized as fundamentally exploratory and children seem to be predisposed to engage in music-like activities from birth. Over the last ten years a considerable amount of research has demonstrated that caregiver–infant interactions in many cultures have musical or proto-musical attributes, incorporating exaggerated pitch contours and periodic rhythmic timings in their structure, involving turn-taking and a close linkage between sound and movement, with similar or the same 'musical' interactions occurring in a wide variety of contexts. Even very young infants can engage in music-like or *proto-musical* behaviours– which involve not only sound perception and production but also movement (see Papousek 1996) – and they are highly motivated to do so.

It is notable that in the earliest years proto-musical and proto-linguistic behaviours appear to be indissociable; the infant's early manifestations of linguistic capacity and of musicality are more likely to co-occur than to be displayed separately. In the course of the infant's development, linguistic and proto-musical behaviours can be thought of as gradually differentiating out from this common suite of complex and communicative behaviours; linguistic behaviours become increasingly bound by considerations of relevance (after Sperber and Wilson 1986) so as to constrain the extent to which they can substitute one for another in the linguistic contexts in which they are deployed. However, proto-musical and musical behaviours are likely to retain a degree of 'floating intentionality'; for the child, they are likely to continue to be appropriate in a wide range of dissimilar situations and types of information, their individual and social functionality being closely tied to their effective ambiguity.

Music in evolution

Overall, it appears that music plays crucial roles for humans in individual and social development, and that a predisposition to engage in music-like activities seems to be part of our biological heritage. That biological heritage is, by and large, a consequence of the operation of evolutionary processes, and it can be suggested that music may have played a significant role in human evolution.

The intellectual and social flexibilities that mark out modern humans seem to have emerged in the hominid lineage sometime within the last seven million years, the likely date of the last common ancestor of humans and of our nearest relatives, the chimpanzees and bonobos (see Foley 1995). For about the first five million years of that separation, the main feature distinguishing our ancestors from the contemporaneous chimps was likely to have been posture; our early ancestors, the australopithecines, were bipedal. In terms of cognitive capacities, it's likely that the australopithecines were much closer to chimps than to ourselves. Around two and a half million years ago, *Homo habilis* emerges, with a brain capacity about 66 per cent greater than the australopithecines and the first evidence of the consistent manufacture and use of (albeit primitive) stone tools. Around two million years ago *Homo ergaster* appears, with at least double the brain capacity of the australopithecines and a considerably more robust physique, marked particularly by a barrel-shaped – as opposed to pyramidal, or ape-like – rib-cage; with *Homo ergaster* there is a leap in the sophistication of the stone tools produced and employed. While the australopithecines, *habilis*, and *ergaster* all originated in Africa, *ergaster* was the first to disperse beyond Africa into Eurasia. Between seven and five hundred thousand years ago, *Homo heidelbergensis* appears in the archaeological record, the predecessor of both the *Neanderthals*, who arise some three hundred and fifty to two hundred and fifty thousand years ago, and ourselves, modern *Homo sapiens*, who seem to have emerged as an African species some two hundred thousand years ago (see White *et al.* 2003).

Successive hominid species had ever larger brains, and left traces of progressively increased sophistication in dealing with tool manufacture and use, and exploitation of habitat. However, within each species, from *habilis* to *heidelbergensis*, the archaeological record suggests a kind of cognitive conservatism. As Mithen (1996) and others have suggested, whilst each successive species developed increasingly complex skills in dealing with the problems of survival, within the behaviour of each species these skills appear to have been restricted to relatively narrow domains. This suggests that while the cognitive capacities of each of our predecessor species were increasingly highly developed, in certain respects they were also somewhat inflexible. Only with the advent of *Homo sapiens sapiens*, modern humans, do we find unambiguous evidence for a capacity to transfer skills flexibly from one domain to another – a generalized cross-domain intellectual capacity – together with the ability to make use of symbols, the earliest evidence for symbolic behaviour consisting of engraved pieces of ochre found in South Africa and dated to 77 000 BP (Henshilwood *et al.* 2002).

It would appear that none of our predecessor species possessed anything like the degree of flexibility of modern humans in producing complex technologies, exploiting natural resources, and perhaps in managing social relations with each other; it is this intellectual and social flexibility (or, as Henshilwood and Marean (2003) put it, a capacity for 'fully symbolic *sapiens* behaviour') that marks us off from our hominid predecessors. As this chapter has suggested, music (and I include dance in this) appears to play a significant role in the achievement or enhancement of cognitive flexibility as well as being efficacious in the rehearsal (and hence the acquisition) of competences in managing social relationships. It is only with modern humans that we find evidence for musicality, in the flexibility of our cognitive and social capacities, and it seems feasible to propose that music emerged with modern humans and helped to stabilize our cognitive and socio-cultural capacities; it may even have been critical in the emergence of these crucial capacities (see Cross 1999). And of course it is only with modern humans that we find unambiguous evidence for musical behaviours in the form of musical instruments in the ancient archaeological record.

The earliest musical instrument yet found is a bone pipe from Geissenklösterle in southern Germany, dated to about 36 000 BP, and a large assemblage of musical bone pipes has been found in Isturitz in southern France covering a time-span of some 15 to 20 thousand years and first appearing at around 30 000 BP (see D'Errico *et al.* 2003). These are, for the time, extraordinarily sophisticated objects, and it's notable that the dates to which the earliest is attributed is around the time of the earliest appearance of modern humans in Europe. In other words, almost as soon as modern humans reach Europe they are leaving traces of sophisticated musical behaviours, which strongly suggests that humans brought music with them out of Africa and to me, and to many others, strongly suggests that musicality constitutes a specific and unique attribute of modern humans. It should be noted here that there is no sound evidence for Neanderthal musical instruments; claims that a 'Neanderthal flute' was found in Divje Babe in Slovenia (see Kunej and Turk 2000) have been countered on what appear to be incontestable archaeological grounds (see D'Errico and Villa 1997).

This is not to suggest that music arose *ab initio*, full-blown, with the emergence of modern humans. It is more likely that components of musicality were possessed to some degree by our predecessor species, but that only with modern humans did an integrated capacity for music appear. It is likely that human musicality is built from a number of disparate capacities that arose in response to a variety of evolutionarily selective pressures at different times and over different time-scales in the hominid lineage, some of which may be tentatively identified. The evolutionarily adaptive value of social flexibility might have underpinned the probable use by *Homo ergaster* of complex vocal signals (control of which would have been enabled by the barrel-shaped chest) to communicate affect or emotional state in order to regulate social interactions; the same factor may well have led, with *Homo heidelbergensis* to the modern human vocal tract, which would allow the articulation of the full range of vocal sounds (including musical sounds) of which modern humans are capable (see Morley 2002). The selection pressures of sociality may also have impacted on the rate of individual maturation within the hominids; each successive species appears to be progressively more *altricial* than its predecessors (consecutive species spending a progressively longer proportion of their total life span in a juvenile state). The need to accommodate to population structures with an increasing proportion of members with access to juvenile modes of cognition and behaviour may have favoured the emergence of something like musicality as a means of assimilating the exploratory value of such modes of cognition and (inter)action into the adult behavioural repertoire (see Cross 2003*b*).

To return to the point made at the outset of this chapter: humans are unusual animals. We are intellectually and socially flexible to a degree that seems to differentiate us from all other animal species. Yet our capacities have arisen largely in the same way in which the capacities of other species have arisen, through processes of evolution; we are different from them, but the mechanisms through which *we* became *us* are of the same kind as those through which *they* became *them*. If we got rhythm and we got music (and it does appear that we are unique amongst primates in both of these capacities, see Merker 2000), then we probably got them the way we got everything else – through evolution. But it is very likely that without the emergence of musicality our species would have seemed far less different from our evolutionary neighbours; without music, we might not have become fully us.

Finally, the claim that musicality has its roots in processes of human evolution does not mean that musicality is explicable in terms of those processes. The meaning of music is not reducible to its significance in human evolution. Music in present day societies takes a multiplicity of forms and fulfils a wide array of functions, from the underpinning of ritual to the articulation of filmic narrative, from the shaping of interaction in dance to the socialization of infants in song, from the evocation of connotative complexes in the concert hall to the framing of adolescent rites of passage. In all these situations music takes identities and plays roles that cannot be explained solely in terms of the features that may have made it efficacious in evolution. Yet at the same time music's powers in the present are likely to be underwritten by the features that appear to have rendered music functional in evolution: its potential to keep people together in time, and to clear a social and mental space for the unhindered exploration of the capacity to mean.

References

Agawu, K. (1991) *Playing with signs: a semiotic interpretation of classic music.* Princeton, NJ: University Press.

Arom, S. (1991) *African polyphony and polyrhythm.* Cambridge: Cambridge University Press.

Baily, J. (1985) Music structure and human movement. In *Musical structure and cognition,* (eds P. Howell, I. Cross, and R. West), pp. 237–58. London: Academic Press.

Benzon, W. (2001) *Beethoven's anvil; music, mind and culture.* New York: Basic Books.

Blacking, J. (1976) *How musical is man?* London: Faber.

Bohlman, P. (2000) Ethnomusicology and music sociology. *In Musicology and sister disciplines,* (ed. D. Greer), pp. 288–98. Oxford: Oxford University Press.

Castellano, M.A., Bharucha, J.J., and Krumhansl, C.L. (1984) Tonal hierarchies in the music of North India. *Journal of Experimental Psychology: General,* **113**, 394–412.

Conway, C.M. and Christiansen, M.H. (2001) Sequential learning in non-human primates. *Trends in Cognitive Science,* **5**, 539–46.

Cross, I. (1999) Is music the most important thing we ever did ? Music, development and evolution. In *Music, mind and science,* (ed. S.W. Yi), pp. 10–39. Seoul: Seoul National University Press.

Cross, I. (2003*a*) Music and biocultural evolution. In *The cultural study of music: a critical introduction,* (eds M. Clayton, T. Herbert, and R. Middleton), pp. 19–30. London: Routledge.

Cross, I. (2003*b*) Music and evolution: causes and consequences. *Contemporary Music Review,* **22,** 79–89.

Cross, I. (2003*c*) Music, cognition, culture and evolution. In *The cognitive neuroscience of music,* (eds I. Peretz and R. Zatorre), pp. 42–56. Oxford: Oxford University Press.

D'Errico, F. and Villa, P. (1997) Holes and grooves: the contribution of microscopy and taphonomy to the problem of art origins. *Journal of Human Evolution,* **33,** 1–31.

D'Errico, F., Henshilwood, C., Lawson, G., Vanhaeren, M., Tillier, A.-M., Soressi, M., *et al.* (2003) Archaeological evidence for the emergence of language, symbolism, and music-an alternative multidisciplinary perspective. *Journal of World Prehistory,* **17,** 1–70.

Damasio, A. (1995) *Descartes' error: emotion, reason and the human brain.* London: Picador.

Davies, J.B. (1978) *The psychology of music.* London: Hutchinson.

Deacon, T. (1996) *The symbolic species: the co-evolution of language and the human brain.* London: Allen Lane.

Deutsch, D. (ed.) (1999) *The psychology of music.* London: Academic Press.

Devereux, G. and LaBarre, W. (1961) Art and mythology. In *Studying personality cross-culturally,* (ed. B. Kaplan), pp. 361–403. Evanston, IL: Row-Peterson.

Dunbar, R. (1992) Neocortex size as a constraint on group size in primates. *Journal of Human Evolution,* **22,** 469–93.

Foley, R.A. (1995) *Humans before humanity.* Oxford: Blackwell.

Goehr, L. (1993) 'Music has no meaning to speak of': on the politics of musical interpretation. In *The interpretation of music: philosophical essays,* (ed. M. Krausz), pp. 177–90. Oxford: Clarendon Press.

Gourlay, K.A. (1984) The non-universality of music and the universality of non-music. *The world of music,* **26,** 25–36.

Hauser, M.D., Chomsky, N., and Fitch, W.T. (2002) The faculty of language: what is it, who has it and how did it evolve? *Science,* **298,** 1569–79.

Henshilwood, C.S. and Marean, C.W. (2003) The origin of modern human behavior: critique of the models and their test implications. *Current Anthropology,* **44,** 627–51.

Henshilwood, C.S., d'Errico, F., Yates, R., Jacobs, Z., Tribolo, C., Duller, G.A.T., *et al.* (2002) Emergence of modern human behavior: middle Stone Age engravings from South Africa. *Science,* **295,** 1278–80.

Horton, T. (2002) Some data that falsify spreading-activation accounts of global context effects in tonal music. In *Proceedings of the 7th ICMPC, Sydney,* (eds C. Stevens, D. Burnham, G. McPherson, E. Schubert, and J. Renwick), pp. 223. Adelaide: Causal Productions.

Janata, P. and Grafton, S.T. (2003) Swinging in the brain: shared neural substrates for behaviors related to sequencing and music. *Nature Neuroscience,* **6,** 682–7.

Juslin, P. and Sloboda, J.A. (eds) (2001) *Music & emotion: theory and research.* Oxford: Oxford University Press.

Karmiloff-Smith, A. (1992) *Beyond modularity.* London: MIT Press.

Kramer, L. (2003) Musicology and meaning. *Music Times,* **144,** 6–12.

Kunej, D. and Turk, I. (2000) New perspectives on the beginning of music: archeological and musicological analysis of a middle Paleolithic bone 'flute'. In *The origins of music*, (eds N. Wallin, B. Merker, and S. Brown), pp. 234–68. Cambridge, MA: MIT Press.

Langer, S. (1942) Philosophy in a new key. Cambridge, MA: Harvard University Press.

Lavy, M. (2001) Emotion and the experience of listening to music: a framework for empirical research. University of Cambridge, Cambridge (www.scribblin.gs).

LeDoux, J. (1998) *The emotional brain: the mysterious underpinnings of emotional life*. London: Weidenfeld & Nicholson.

Lerdahl, F. and Jackendoff, R. (1983) *A generative theory of tonal music*. Cambridge, MA: MIT Press.

McNeill, W.H. (1995) *Keeping together in time*. London: Harvard University Press.

Merker, B. (2000) Synchronous chorusing and human origins. In *The origins of music*, (eds N. Wallin, B. Merker, and S. Brown), pp. 315–28. Cambridge, MA: MIT Press.

Meyer, L.B. (1956) *Emotion and meaning in music*. London: University of Chicago Press.

Miller, G. (2000) Evolution of human music through sexual selection. In *The origins of music*, (eds N. Wallin, B. Merker, and S. Brown), pp. 329–60. Cambridge, MA: MIT Press.

Mithen, S. (1996) *Prehistory of the mind*. London: Thames and Hudson.

Morley, I. (2002) Evolution of the physiological and neurological capacities for music. *Cambridge Archaeological Journal*, 12, 195–216.

Nelson, S. (2002) *Melodic improvization on a twelve-bar blues model: an investigation of physical and historical aspects, and their contribution to performance*. Ph.D thesis. City University London, Department of Music, London.

Papousek, H. (1996) Musicality in infancy research: biological and cultural origins of early musicality. In *Musical beginnings*, (eds I. Deliège and J.A. Sloboda), pp. 37–55. Oxford: Oxford University Press.

Pinker, S. (1994) *The language instinct*. London: Allen Lane.

Pinker, S. (1997) *How the mind works*. London: Allen Lane.

Scherer, C. and Zentner, M.R. (2001) Emotional effects of music: production rules. In *Music and emotion: theory and research*, (eds P. Juslin and J. A. Sloboda), pp. 361–92. Oxford: Oxford University Press.

Seyfarth, R.M. and Cheney, D.L. (2003) Signalers and receivers in animal communication. *Annual Review of Psychology*, 54, 145–73.

Shannon, C. and Weaver, W. (1949) *The mathematical theory of communication*. Urbana, IL: University of Illinois Press.

Spelke, E. (1999) Infant cognition. In *The MIT encyclopedia of cognitive sciences*, (eds R.A. Wilson and F.C. Keil), pp. 402–4. Cambridge, MA: MIT Press.

Sperber, D. (1996). *Explaining culture*. Oxford: Blackwell.

Sperber, D. and Wilson, D. (1986). Relevance: communication and cognition. Oxford: Blackwell.

Stobart, H.F. and Cross, I. (2000. The Andean Anacrusis? rhythmic structure and perception in Easter songs of Northern Potosí, Bolivia. *British Journal of Ethnomusicology*, 9, 63–94.

Vendler, H. (1997). *The art of Shakespeare's sonnets*. London: Harvard University Press.

White, T.D., Asfaw, B., Degusta, D., Gilbert, H., Richards, G.D., Suwa, G., *et al.* (2003) Pleistocene Homo sapiens from Middle Awash, Ethiopia. *Nature*, 423, 742–7.

Chapter 3

Music and conversation

R. Keith Sawyer

In interviews with Chicago jazz musicians that I conducted in the early 1990s, many musicians compared musical communication to conversation:

> [The ensemble] influences it the same way as if – we're having a conversation now ... when I start talking about it, I start thinking about it, putting bits and pieces together, coming up with ideas on how I feel about things, and that way it helps me ... I can start to know myself better through my conversation and interactions with the world around me, and it's the same thing up on stage, the same exact thing. By talking to people up on stage through your music, you can start working on stuff you've never heard and never done ... you need people to play with ... when I do it, I'd find that there are these things coming out of myself, which I didn't even know were there, I'd never heard them, I didn't know where they came from ... but playing with the others triggers it, so maybe consciously or subconsciously you'll hear that thing, that you're trying to find ... by listening to what other people have to say, and by talking to them about it, it's like talking about – really great music, it's guys getting together and talking about how sad or lonely they feel, or how happy or angry (Sawyer 2003a, pp. 28–29).

But jazz musicians weren't the first to notice a connection between music and speech. In the nineteenth century, both Darwin and Spencer discussed connections between music and speech, coming to opposite conclusions. Darwin wrote: 'the rhythms and cadences of oratory are derived from previously developed musical powers' and that 'musical sounds afforded one of the bases for the development of language' (1871, p. 593), whereas Spencer believed that music derived from speech (1891, pp. 400–51). In the last 10 years or so, scholars of *biomusicology* have extended these observations, arguing that music and speech have similar evolutionary origins (Wallin 1991; Wallin *et al.* 2000).

Beginning in the 1960s, both linguists and musicologists have attempted to identify formal parallels between music and speech. The most famous attempts have been at the functional levels of prosody and syntax; for example, Lerdahl and Jackendoff (1983) drew on generative theories of language to develop their theory of musical phrase structure (see also Brown 2000). Many theorists applied this approach to entire compositions, attempting to explain what one might call the 'syntax' of music by analogy with generative grammar

(Feld 1974; Hatten 1980, 1990; Nattiez 1975, 1977; Powers 1980; Ruwet 1967, 1972). Several scholars have applied the generative grammar approach to jazz improvisation (Johnson-Laird 1988; Perlman and Greenblatt 1981; Steedman 1984); the parallels are perhaps most explicitly laid out in a 1981 article titled 'Miles Davis meets Noam Chomsky' (Perlman and Greenblatt 1981), where the authors drew analogies between the deep structure of a sentence and the harmonic chord structure of a jazz standard, and between the words of a sentence and the melodic fragments, or 'licks', that musicians weave into their solos.

However, by the end of the twentieth century it was largely believed that these attempts to connect music and language had failed. They suffered from two main problems. First, anything but the most superficial parallels between music and language were difficult to discover at the functional levels of syntax and semantics. Second, these approaches had difficulty explaining musical *performance* – particularly improvisational and ensemble performance, and the influence of social and cultural context – in part because they were inspired by the Chomskian division between competence and performance.

In these efforts to compare music and language, the interactional influences among performers characteristic of group creativity have been completely neglected (cf. Benzon 2001; Sawyer 1996). In this chapter I take a different approach. Like these prior scholars, I argue that music and language have similarities as communication media, and that we can gain insights about both by comparing them. However, in contrast to prior approaches that explore the syntax or semantics of music, I examine the *pragmatics* of musical and verbal communication. I explore the common observation that jazz is like conversation by focusing on the nature of musical communication in improvising groups.

My primary research interest is everyday conversation, and I began to study musical improvisation after I observed that everyday conversation is creatively improvised – there is no script that guides a conversation. My empirical research has focused on three types of improvised discourse: improvisational theater, children's fantasy play, and everyday conversation (Sawyer 1997b, 2001, 2003b). In my theoretical writings, I use these improvisational phenomena to address several issues in contemporary psychology and social theory – issues of textuality, discourse, Bakhtin's *heteroglossia* of multiple voices, and the tension between structure and practice. The perspective I present here derives from the empirically grounded attempt to identify and characterize specific interactional mechanisms which are held in common by both musical and verbal interaction (Sawyer 2003a).

I conclude by proposing an explanation for why people enjoy listening to music. I believe that we enjoy music because it represents, in crystallized form, the basic processes of human social life, the same social processes that the child internalizes during development. Musicians in an ensemble communicate with each other, and these interactional patterns replicate the essential interactional processes found in all human communication. As we listen to a performance, we are exposed to the distilled essence of human sociality.

Improvisation and group creativity

Group performance is often referred to as *jamming*. The term 'jamming' was first used by jazz musicians; a 'jam session' is an impromptu gathering of musicians with the purpose of improvising together. The term has a positive connotation; when a performance goes particularly well, the musicians might say 'we were really jamming tonight'. In the last several decades, the term has been widely used outside of jazz to describe any free-flowing creative group interaction (e.g. Coates 1997). The *American Heritage Dictionary* defined the jam session as both a type of jazz performance and also as 'an impromptu or highly informal discussion' (1982).

Jamming refers to the collective activity of a group creating together, and it suggests a high degree of improvisation and informality. Group creativity is found not only in music; it is essential in many problem-solving groups, such as a brainstorming session at a small high-technology company, a group of teachers collaborating to develop a new curriculum, or a family working to resolve a financial crisis. In group performance, the creativity of the performance depends on an intangible chemistry between the members of the group. In jazz, for example, no single musician can determine the flow of the performance: It emerges out of the musical conversation, a give-and-take as performers propose new ideas, respond to other's ideas, and elaborate or modify those ideas as the performance moves forward (Berliner 1994).

Even in scored classical music, interaction and communication are critical. As Weeks (1996*a*) found in his studies of orchestral rehearsals, much of the musical communication among musicians is hidden from the audience during a performance, and the intention of all involved is to give the audience the somewhat misleading impression that the musicians are reading 'the musical text as the composer intended it, under the direction of the conductor *then-and-there*' (p. 248). In Weeks's analyses, ensembles constantly communicate to coordinate the temporal features of the performance: the initial tempo of the piece; the rate to slow down the tempo in a ritardando – a passage in which the composer has indicated that the tempo should slow down; and the relative durations of the fermata, a mark on the score that indicates that a note should be held for an indeterminate length of time (1996*b*).

Orchestral performance becomes particularly improvisational when one of the performers makes a mistake, playing a wrong note or losing the tempo of the piece. Weeks (1990) analysed the interactional processes that occurred during the rehearsal of a chamber group of seven musicians that had no conductor. He documented how a cellist and pianist executed a series of 'collaborative maneuvers' (p. 211) to recover from several mistakes made by the cellist, so that the performance could continue in such a way that the average listener would not notice the variation. The covering-up action involved a retrospective redefinition of the mistake, redefining it by modifying the scored performance that immediately followed so that it retroactively seemed to have been the correct note and tempo to have played (p. 216). The ensemble's modification resulted in dropping almost 2 beats from the scored performance. Weeks (1990) concluded that 'although the score has served as a guide, the determination of the specific place the group is at a given moment is thereby a complex *collaborative accomplishment*' (p. 219).

This kind of close analysis of performance reveals that both improvisational performance and scored performance depend heavily on musical communication. I believe that improvisation is the purer example of musical communication – the Weberian 'ideal type'. Because improvisation is the ideal type, we can more clearly see in it the key characteristics of all musical communication: process, unpredictability, collaboration, and emergence.

Process. The purpose of a jazz improvisation is not to generate a created product that will later be scored or performed. Instead, the performance is its own goal; the communicative process is the product. The audience is of course interested in individual artistry; but they also attend closely to the interactional dynamics among the members of the group. Musical communication is not just an ephemeral element of 'performance practice'; it's central to the art of improvisation.

Unpredictability. In a jazz improvisation, no musician knows exactly what is going to happen next. At each point in the jam session, a musician can choose from an almost infinite number of musical possibilities. Each musician has to listen closely to all of the others, and no one musician can single-handedly determine the future course of the performance.

Collaboration. A musician cannot know how his playing will be interpreted and elaborated by the others. The eventual musical meaning of an improvised phrase is determined by a collaborative, emergent process. Referring to a musical conversation between a trumpet and bass, bassist Richard Davis commented: 'Sometimes you might put a idea [*sic*] in that you think is good and nobody takes to it. ...And then sometimes you might put an idea in that your incentive or motivation is not to influence but it does influence' (Monson 1996, p. 88).

In other words, a musician cannot know the meaning of her own playing until the other musicians have responded. This *retrospective interpretation* is quite common in musical performance; Gioia (1988) noted that the jazz musician cannot 'look ahead at what he is going to play, but he can look behind at what he has just played .... he creates his form *retrospectively*' (p. 61). Because no single musician has complete control over how or even whether a new musical idea will be picked up, the group's performance is fundamentally collaborative.

Emergence. Band members often say that when the group dynamic is flowing, the performance that results is greater than any one individual; the whole is greater than the sum of the parts. Each individual performs at a higher level than he or she would have been capable of alone. Many scholars now use the term *emergence* to refer to complex systems in which the whole is greater than the sum of the parts. In the terminology of these *complexity theorists*, a creative ensemble is a *complex dynamical system*, with a high degree of sensitivity to initial conditions and rapidly expanding combinatorial possibilities from moment to moment (Sawyer 1999, 2003*a*). In complex systems, the global behaviour of the entire system is said to emerge from the interactions among the individual parts of the system. The group performance is thus at a higher *level of analysis* than the performers that collectively generate it.

Musical communication results in the collective creation of a shared creative product. I use the term *collaborative emergence* to refer to emergence in creative groups (Sawyer 1999, 2003*b*). In collaborative emergence, the direction in which the group will go is difficult to predict in advance. The flow of the performance cannot be predicted even if the analyst has unlimited advance knowledge about the skills, motivations, and mental states of the individual performers. We cannot explain musical communication by analysing any one performer; we have to analyse the communicative dynamics among the members of the group.

To explain musical communication, we have to focus on the interactional dynamics of the group, rather than the internal mental states of the performers. I discuss three different intellectual traditions that do this: the aesthetic philosophy of American pragmatism, studies of interactional synchrony, and conversation analysis.

John Dewey: music as experience

In his 1934 book *Art as Experience*, John Dewey detailed his aesthetic philosophy. Dewey placed the core of art in the *experience* of art. 'Experience' was the central concept of Dewey's philosophy; Dewey defined experience as interaction with people or the physical environment: 'experience is the result, the sign, and the reward of that interaction of organism and environment which ... is a transformation of interaction into participation and communication' (1934, p. 22).

Experience refers to the emergent and temporal nature of an organism's interaction with its environment.

Dewey used this general theory to explain the nature of aesthetic experience. He argued that a work of art captured the temporal flow of the artist's experience, and that by viewing the work, the viewer was able to recreate that temporal experience. The most aesthetic works were those that best captured the crystallized essence of human experience. Because Dewey's theory of experience focuses on the temporal and emergent nature of action in the world, the essence of art is in the creative process that generates it, not in the finished work: 'the *product* of art ... is not the *work* of art' (Dewey 1934, p. 214). The product is only valuable because it is indirectly a representation of that original experiential process. The product then invokes the same experience in the viewer: the 'work' of art is not the static product, but is 'active and experienced. It is what the product does, its working' (p. 162).

Dewey's theory of art as experience lends itself naturally to musical communication. Because so much of human experience is social, many artworks are aesthetic because they crystallize the essence of social life. He often compared aesthetic experience to everyday conversation: 'Acts of social intercourse are works of art' (1934, p. 63) because they are both interactional, and both are temporal and emergent. Dewey wrote 'Moliere's character did not know he had been talking prose all his life. So men in general are not aware that they have been exercising an art as long as they have engaged in spoken intercourse with others' (1934, p. 240). Especially in casual small talk, we do not speak from a script; our conversation is collectively created, and emerges from the actions of everyone present. We collaboratively determine where the conversation will go, what kind of conversation we are having, what our social relationship is, and when it will end (Sawyer 2001).

Because his core theory focused on the interactive nature of experience, Dewey believed that communication is the essential property of art: 'Because the objects of art are expressive, they communicate. I do not say that communication to others is the intent of an artist. But it is the consequence of his work' (1934, p. 104). Dewey wrote 'Because objects of art are expressive, they are a language' (1934, p. 106). Dewey's aesthetic theory was a communication theory of art.

Because of its temporal dimension, music is the most essential art in Dewey's aesthetic theory (1934, p. 184). Although Dewey does not mention improvisation explicitly, his metaphoric descriptions of experience, often emphasizing rhythm, would seem quite familiar to jazz musicians: 'all interactions ... in the whirling flux of change are rhythms. There is ebb and flow ... ordered change' (1934, p. 16). Dewey's vision of 'experience' is that of an improvising artist.

Dewey's communication theory of art makes improvisation, collaboration, and emergence central to all creativity. Even when an artist is alone, there is a public and social aspect to his creativity: 'Even the composition conceived in the head and, therefore, physically private, is public in its significant content, since it is conceived with reference to execution in a product that is perceptible and hence belongs to the common world' (1934, p. 51). Dewey drew on a language metaphor to emphasize this point: 'Language exists only when it is listened to as well as spoken .... Even when the artist works in solitude ... the artist has to become vicariously the receiving audience' (1934, p. 106). All art is communication; and music is the purest of the arts, because it is the most like everyday lived human experience.

Interactional synchrony: the biology of music

We evolved to be fundamentally social organisms, and this sociality is accomplished through symbolic communication. Recently, biologists have begun to propose that we are hard-wired to communicate, both verbally (e.g. Dunbar 1996) and musically (Ansdell and Pavlicevic, this volume; Wallin 1991; Wallin *et al.* 2000). There is evidence that musical ability is a genetic, biological competence (Peretz and Morais 1993). Several of these scholars have followed the pragmatist G. H. Mead (1934), an important colleague of John Dewey, in proposing that the evolutionary origins of music and language lie in sociality (Dunbar 1996; Ujhelyi 2000).

Dewey argued that we enjoy music primarily because it is ensemble performance, and the communicative interaction among members of the ensemble replicates the pragmatic and interactional patterns of all human communication. If this is true, then it seems likely that when we listen to music, we draw on the neural circuitry that evolved to manage everyday social life. Our enjoyment of music would then be deeply programmed in the genetic core of our being.

Wallin (1991) first argued that the neural circuitry of the brain was hard-wired to respond to music. There is some recent evidence for this hypothesis: temporal patterns of human cortical activity have been discovered to track the pitch contours of tone sequences, and they track more accurately when the tone sequences are more similar to musical melodies (Patel and Balaban 2000). The brain tracks melodies better than random sound sequences.

But most of this brain imaging work focuses on the internal processes of a single brain, rather than the uniquely social nature of musical communication (cf. Benzon 2001, p. 44). In most musical traditions, music is performed in an ensemble, in front of an audience. Group musical performance can only work when the performers are closely attuned to each other. They have to monitor the other performer's actions at the same time that they continue their own performance, to be able to quickly hear or see what the other performers are doing, and to be able to respond by altering their own unfolding, ongoing activity.

In other words, the performers have to manage what some behavioral scientists have called *interactional synchrony*. The term 'interactional synchrony' was coined by Condon and Ogston, who analysed videotapes of speakers and hearers frame-by-frame and found that 'the speaker and hearer look like puppets moved by the same set of strings' (Condon and Ogston 1971, p. 158). People can synchronize an incredible number of verbal and nonverbal behaviors in as little as 1/20th of a second (Condon and Ogston 1967). The coordination of rhythms between two people has also been theorized using the concept of *entrainment* (Condon and Ogston 1966), a term originally used by physicists to describe the mutual phase locking of two oscillators (Pikovsky *et al.* 2001). In entrainment, one person's rhythms become attuned to another, almost like a tuning fork. Musicologists have analysed similar phenomena using the concept of *groove* (Berliner 1994; Keil and Feld 1994; Monson 1996) and *coupling* (Benzon 2001).

Interactional synchrony is thought to have a biological basis (Burgoon *et al.* 1995). Evolutionary theorists have argued that proto-humans used rhythm to coordinate social activities long before the evolution of language (Benzon 2001; Donald 1991), and that musical communication evolved in parallel with linguistic ability (Brown 2000; Richman 2000; Wallin 1991; Wallin *et al.* 2000). Infants show evidence of interactional synchrony with their parents as early as 20 min after birth, and it appears in chimpanzees and even in interactions between dogs and their human owners. Interactional synchrony has been hypothesized to serve several important biological functions: for example, its early emergence in infancy may provide physical safety and comfort (Condon 1980), and it helps to facilitate social interaction with parents (Cappella 1991). There also seems to be an important cultural component to synchrony; synchrony is much harder to attain if the participants are from different cultures, because different cultures seem to have different interactional styles, and these differences can disrupt interaction timing (Burgoon *et al.* 1995, p. 23; Lomax 1982).

A few researchers have examined the role of interactional synchrony in musical performance. Several researchers have compared musical interaction in jazz to the interactional synchrony between mother and infant, noting the many studies that show that we are born with an ability to engage in rhythmically coordinated interpersonal interaction (Papaeliou and Trevarthen 1994; Schögler 1998, 1999–2000). Studies of *intersubjectivity* by developmental psychologists (Trevarthen 1979; Tronick *et al.* 1980) – who videotape mothers and infants to examine how pre-verbal infants synchronize to their mother's facial expressions – show how the developing child uses this instinctive ability to become adapted to adult social life.

Studies of interactional synchrony show the importance of focusing on the entire group. As Scheflen wrote, 'If we observe only one person or one person at a time, there is no way we will observe synchrony or co-action or interactional rhythm' (1982, p. 15). Focusing on one single brain is insufficient, because synchrony is a socially emergent complex systems phenomenon. By closely focusing on micro-second aural and visual actions, these studies have shown that musical performance cannot be understood by analysing individual performers' actions in isolation. Rather, these studies have demonstrated that ensemble interaction is a complex systems phenomenon, and that musical communication must be the primary focus. However, because these studies focus on such a small micro level, they represent only a first step in the study of interaction in ensembles. In musical performance, interaction occurs at many temporal levels, and includes social, cultural, and semiotic processes in addition to rhythmic ones (cf. Monson 1995).

Studies of interactional synchrony provide a new perspective on the conversational metaphors of jazz musicians; they suggest that jazz improvisation is like conversation because both require interactional synchrony, entrainment, and coupling. These findings provide empirical evidence to support John Dewey's theory of art as experience. Although videotape recorders did not exist in Dewey's time, Dewey nonetheless had the key insight that the detailed temporal dynamics of human social life were critical to lived human experience. The essence of music is musical communication, and musical communication is aesthetic because it has so much in common with everyday social life.

The pragmatics of musical communication

Music is a kind of communication, but we can be led down the wrong path by language metaphors, because so many language theorists have proposed that we use language to conduct a one-way communication of meaning from one brain to another. Reddy (1979) referred to this as the *conduit metaphor*: the idea that conversation is a polite turn-by-turn exchange of ideas, bouncing back and forth like the ball during a tennis match. The traditional way of comparing language and music – by comparing the syntactic structures or generative grammars of sentences and melodies – assumes the conduit metaphor.

Since the 1980s, empirical studies of conversation have discovered that the conduit metaphor is often inaccurate (Duranti and Brenneis 1986; Goodwin 1981). Listeners influence the construction of a sentence, right in the middle, with carefully timed gestures, eye movements, and single-word comments.

Speakers often overlap their utterances, and these overlaps are collaboratively synchronized and regularly structured. Conduit theories do not capture the truly collaborative nature of spoken language. For the same reasons, conduit theories miss the key features of musical communication: its processual, collaborative, emergent aspects (also see Cross, this volume). This is why comparisons of music and language that focus on generative grammar have failed: because music and language are more similar in their communicative, collaborative aspects than in their internal syntactic structures (Sawyer 2003*a*). Musical performance is a collaboratively emergent social process, and its analysis requires a focus on interaction, practice, and pragmatics.

Instead of structural approaches that focus on notes, syllables, and phrase structures, to explain musical communication we need a new approach based on the semiotic concept of *indexicality*. An *index* is a sign which requires an association between the sign and its object. The classic example of an index is the weathervane, which 'indicates' wind direction. In language, *deictics* are indexical; these are words whose referent cannot be known apart from a context of use. For example, we cannot know what a pronoun such as 'I' and 'you' means apart from its context of use. Likewise, with temporal constructions like 'now' or past, present, and future tense, we cannot know what time is meant without knowing when the utterance occurred.

Peirce's notion of indexicality was further elaborated by Jakobson in his analysis of the *poetic function* of language. Silverstein (1984) pointed out that Jakobson's writings on indexicality and poetics (e.g. 1960, 1971) implied that some forms of indexicality are dependent on broader structuring principles of a text; for example, a word placed in line-final position has implicit indexical relations with other words in other line-final positions, which can vary depending on the overall structure of the poem. Much of Jakobson's work was focused on exploring continuities across poetic language and everyday speech. The poetic function is even more central to music than language, because so much of the structure of music is based on parallelism, repetition, and transformation.

Indexicality emphasizes the socially creative nature of musical communication. Musical improvisation requires constant creativity from the performers; creativity rests in introducing novelty in the form of a new musical idea, while remaining consistent with what has come before. To remain musical, the performer is required to play something that retains musical coherence with the emergent performance. Each musician is constrained by what has come before and what has been agreed upon in advance: the key of the piece, the song's harmonic structure, and the past musical ideas proposed by the other players. In the presence of these constraints, jazz requires each performer to offer something new at each point, ideally something which is suggestive to the other musicians. Of course, the degree of constraint of any given moment of performance can vary significantly; but there are constraints on how rapidly it can change, which in turn may be dependent on the genre or the social context of the performance. An evolving performance constrains a performer on several musical planes simultaneously: tone or timbre, mode and scale permitted, rhythmic patterns, specific motifs, stylistic references, and references to other performances or songs. At any given moment these different planes may be differentially constrained. Thus as with conversation – where a participant is required to maintain coherence with the flow of the conversation – a musician's creativity is constrained by the flow of the group's improvisation.

Each member of the ensemble constantly suggests new musical motifs, concepts, styles, and moods, and sometimes implicitly references other songs or other performances of the same song. These new ideas are always indexical – their meaning is heavily dependent on the immediate context. And each musician's new idea is subject to a social process of evaluation; the entire group collectively determines whether it will be accepted into the emergent, ongoing performance. They collectively have the option of accepting the idea (by working with it, building on it, making it 'their own'), rejecting it (by continuing the performance as if it had never occurred), or partially accepting it (by selecting one aspect of it to build on, and ignoring the rest). This evaluative decision is a group effort, and cannot be identified clearly with any specific moment in time, nor with any single individual. The performance may evolve for some time before it becomes clear what has or hasn't been accepted. In many cases the performers do not know what will happen until after it has happened, because no single individual has the authority to make these evaluative judgments. This uncertainty is due to the complex interplay of individual creativity and group evaluation found in musical communication.

Why we like music

In this short chapter, I have summarized John Dewey's aesthetic philosophy, studies of interactional synchrony, and studies of everyday talk. All of these studies converge to give us an integrated perspective on why we like music: We like music because it represents, in crystallized form, the essence of human social life.

John Dewey's aesthetic theory is based on his theory of *experience*, the temporal nature of living and acting in the world. And art represents a peak experience, experience captured and structured so as to communicate itself most effectively to an audience. Dewey's is a social theory of art as shared living in the world, and music is the purest art – not because it is not representational, as Walter Pater famously wrote (1873/1986, pp. 86–88), but because it is the most temporal and interactional.

How can these theories help us understand why we like music? For an answer, I find it helpful to turn to recent *sociocultural* theories of psychology. Sociocultural theories are based on a nineteenth century sociological insight: that each person's mind is formed in development by internalizing social structures and practices.[1] This idea was at the core of the pragmatist theories of Mead and Dewey; in Mead's evolutionary account, pre-verbal gestures became internalized to form the earliest primitive human minds (Mead 1934). And for Dewey, the experience of encountering the world became internalized to form the mind. Because the mind comes from social life, the mind itself is fundamentally social. And if music and rhythm predated language – as Darwin believed – then the deepest roots of the mind might be musical communication rather than verbal (Benzon 2001).

The preverbal child uses his instinctive ability to interactionally synchronize to grow into intersubjectivity with his parents. And after a child acquires language, intersubjectivity becomes more sophisticated yet again, as children learn to engage in the everyday skills of conversation: taking turns, showing attentiveness, indicating confusion, asking clarification. Conversation, like improvised music, is unpredictable, collaborative, and emergent. Recent studies of musical development have likewise shown that children grow in their ability to engage in collaborative, intersubjective musical communication (Miell and MacDonald 2000; Morgan *et al.* 2000).

Sociocultural psychologists are primarily developmental psychologists; if the mind forms by a process of internalizing social interaction, then it would have significant implications for developmental psychology (Rogoff 1990, 1998; Nelson 1996; Cole 1996). If the mind is formed by internalizing social life, and social life is fundamentally communicative and collaborative, then the internal structure of the mind must also be a sort of internal social microcosm. And music is fundamentally social and communicative – after all, all music has its origins in improvisational group performance. Even when we're listening to music at home alone, it still taps into our social brain, evoking the social world that we all have within us, the internalized social world that defines us as human beings.

Conclusion

Psychologists who study creativity have focused on *product creativity*, creative domains in which products are created over time, with unlimited opportunities

---

[1] Socioculturalists often associate this 'internalization' idea with Russian psychologist Lev Vygotsky's writing in the 1920s, but it was then already common in the nineteenth century sociological theories of Marx, Durkheim, and others.

for revision by the creator before the product is displayed (Sawyer 1997*a*, 2005). Product creativity is found in artistic domains such as sculpture, painting, and musical composition. In product creativity, the artist has an unlimited period of time to contemplate, edit, and revise the work. The creative process is usually invisible to the public.

Unlike product creativity – which involves a long period of creative work leading up to the creative product – in musical performance, the process *is* the product. A jazz ensemble collaborates on stage to spontaneously create the performance, and the performance that results emerges from the musical interactions among multiple band members. There is no director that guides the performance, and no score for the musicians to follow. The art is in the process itself; the audience sees the work as it is created.

Our desire to explain music has been stymied by psychology's general focus on product creativity, because to explain music, we have to start by explaining musical communication, and to explain musical communication, we have to start by explaining improvisational group performance. Although rudimentary musical notation has been found even in Ancient Greece, notated music was not common and conventionalized until the thirteenth century Franconian system (Grout and Palisca 1996); before that time, there was no division of labour into composer, conductor, and performer, and all music was oral tradition. To explain how humans evolved a capacity to perform and enjoy music, we have to focus on music as improvisational performance.

Music is the essence of human social life because music is the purest form of communication, 'the distilling of social life to its simplest forms and moves' (Benzon 2001, p. 64). Musical communication is not a conduit-like transfer of a message from one performer to another; that would be too linear, too individualistic, and too reductive. Instead, musical communication is an emergent property of social groups in complex interaction. Musical groups have all of the properties associated with complex systems, including inter-subjectivity, interactional synchrony, entrainment, unpredictability, and sensitivity to initial conditions. To understand musical communication, we need a theory of communication as a fundamentally social and collaborative activity.

References

Benzon, W.L. (2001) *Beethoven's anvil: Music in mind and culture.* New York: Basic Books.

Berliner, P. (1994) *Thinking in jazz: The infinite art of improvisation.* Chicago, IL: University of Chicago Press.

Brown, S. (2000) The 'musilanguage' model of music evolution. In *The origins of music*, (eds N.L. Wallin, B. Merker, and S. Brown), pp. 271–300. Cambridge, MA: MIT Press.

Burgoon, J.K., Stern, L.A., and Dillman, L. (1995) *Interpersonal adaptation: Dyadic interaction patterns.* New York: Cambridge University Press.

Cappella, J.N. (1991) The biological origins of automated patterns of human interaction. *Communication Theory,* **1**(1), 4–35.

Coates, J. (1997) The construction of a collaborative floor in women's friendly talk. In *Conversation: Cognitive, communicative and social perspectives,* (ed. T. Givon), pp. 55–89. Amsterdam: John Benjamins.

Cole, M. (1996) *Cultural psychology: A once and future discipline.* Cambridge, MA: Harvard University Press.

Condon, W.S. (1980) The relation of interactional synchrony to cognitive and emotional processes. In *The relationship of verbal and nonverbal communication,* (ed. M.E. Key), pp. 49–65. New York: Mouton.

Condon, W.S. and Ogston, W.D. (1966) Sound film analysis of normal and pathological behavior patterns. *Journal of Nervous and Mental Diseases,* **143**, 338–47.

Condon, W.S. and Ogston, W.D. (1967) A segmentation of behavior. *Journal of Psychiatric Research,* **5**, 221–35.

Condon, W.S. and Ogston, W.D. (1971) Speech and body motion synchrony of the speaker-hearer. In *Perception of language,* (eds D.L. Horton and J.J. Jenkins), pp. 150–73. Columbus, OH: Charles E. Merrill.

Darwin, C. (1871) *The descent of man, and selection in relation to sex.* London: J. Murray.

Dewey, J. (1934) *Art as experience.* New York: Perigree Books.

Donald, M. (1991) *Origins of the modern mind: Three stages in the evolution of culture and cognition.* Cambridge, MA: Harvard University Press.

Dunbar, R. (1996) *Grooming, gossip, and the evolution of language.* Cambridge, MA: Harvard University Press.

Duranti, A. and Brenneis, D. (eds) (1986) *The audience as co-author. Text special issue, Volume 6 number 3.* Amsterdam: Mouton de Gruyter.

Feld, S. (1974) Linguistics and ethnomusicology. *Ethnomusicology,* **18**(2), 197–217.

Gioia, T. (1988) *The imperfect art: Reflections on jazz and modern culture.* New York: Oxford University Press.

Goodwin, C. (1981) *Conversational organization: Interaction between speakers and hearers.* New York: Academic Press.

Grout, D.J. and Palisca, C.V. (1996) *A history of Western music.* (5th ed.). New York: Norton.

Hatten, R. (1980) Nattiez's semiology of music: Flaws in the new science. *Semiotica,* **31**(1/2), 139–55.

Hatten, R. (1990) The splintered paradigm: A semiotic critique of recent approaches to music cognition. *Semiotica,* **81**(1/2), 145–78.

Jakobson, R. (1960) Closing statement: Linguistics and poetics. In *Style in language,* (ed. T.A. Sebeok), pp. 350–77. Cambridge, MA: MIT Press.

Jakobson, R. (1971) Shifters, verbal categories, and the Russian verb, *Selected writings of Roman Jakobson. Volume 2: Word and language* (pp. 130–47). The Hague: Mouton.

Johnson-Laird, P.N. (1988) Freedom and constraint in creativity. In *The nature of creativity,* (ed. R.J. Sternberg), pp. 202–19. New York: Cambridge University Press.

Keil, C. and Feld, S. (1994) *Music Grooves.* Chicago, IL: University of Chicago Press.

Lerdahl, F. and Jackendoff, R. (1983) *A generative theory of tonal music.* Cambridge, MA: MIT Press.

Lomax, A. (1982) The cross-cultural variation of rhythmic style. In *Interaction rhythms: Periodicity in communicative behavior*, (ed. M. Davis), pp. 149–74. New York: Human Sciences Press.

Mead, G.H. (1934) *Mind, self, and society*. Chicago, IL: University of Chicago Press.

Miell, D. and MacDonald, R.A.R. (2000) Children's creative collaborations: The importance of friendship when working together on a musical composition. *Social Development*, 9(3), 348–69.

Monson, I. (1995) Commentary on Keil. *Ethnomusicology*, 39(1), 87–9.

Monson, I. (1996) *Saying something: Jazz improvisation and interaction*. Chicago, IL: University of Chicago Press.

Morgan, L., Hargreaves, D., and Joiner, R. (2000) Children's collaborative music composition: Communication through music. In *Rethinking collaborative learning*, (eds R. Joiner, K. Littleton, D. Faulkner, and D. Miell), pp. 52–64. London: Free Association Books.

Nattiez, J.J. (1975) *Fondemonts d'une sémiologie de la musique*. Paris: Union Generale d'Editions.

Nattiez, J.J. (1977) The contribution of musical semiotics to the semiotic discussion in general. In *A perfusion of signs*, (ed. T.A. Sebeok), pp. 121–42. Bloomington, IN: Indiana University Press.

Nelson, K. (1996) *Language in cognitive development: Emergence of the mediated mind*. New York: Cambridge University Press.

Papaeliou, C. and Trevarthen, C. (1994) The infancy of music. *Musical praxis*, 1(2), 19–33.

Patel, A.D. and Balaban, E. (2000) Temporal patterns of human cortical activity reflect tone sequence structure. *Nature*, 404(2 March), 80–4.

Pater, W. (1873/1986) *The Renaissance: Studies in art and poetry* (Adam Phillips, ed.). New York: Oxford University Press.

Peretz, I. and Morais, J. (1993) Specificity for music. In *Handbook of neuropsychology*, (eds F. Boller and J. Grafman), Vol. 8, pp. 373–90. New York: Elsevier.

Perlman, A.M. and Greenblatt, D. (1981) Miles Davis meets Noam Chomsky: Some observations on jazz improvisation and language structure. In *The sign in music and literature*, (ed. W. Steiner), pp. 169–83. Austin, TX: University of Texas Press.

Pikovsky, A., Rosenblum, M., and Kurths, J. (2001) *Synchronization: A universal concept in nonlinear sciences*. New York: Cambridge University Press.

Powers, H.S. (1980) Language models and musical analysis. *Ethnomusicology*, 24(1), 1–60.

Reddy, M.J. (1979) The conduit metaphor: A case of frame conflict in our language about language. In *Metaphor and thought*, (ed. A. Ortony), pp. 284–324. New York: Cambridge University Press.

Richman, B. (2000) How music fixed 'nonsense' into significant formulas: On rhythm, repetition, and meaning. In *The origins of music*, (eds N.L. Wallin, B. Merker, and S. Brown), pp. 301–14. Cambridge, MA: MIT Press.

Rogoff, B. (1990) *Apprenticeship in thinking: Cognitive development in social context*. New York: Oxford University Press.

Rogoff, B. (1998) Cognition as a collaborative process. In *Handbook of child psychology*, *5th edition, Volume 2: Cognition, perception, and language*, (eds D. Kuhn and R.S. Siegler), pp. 679–744. New York: Wiley.

Ruwet, N. (1967) Linguistics and musicology. *International Social Science Journal*, 19, 79–87.

Ruwet, N. (1972) *Langage, musique, poésie.* Paris: Editions du Seuil.

Sawyer, R.K. (1996) The semiotics of improvisation: The pragmatics of musical and verbal performance. *Semiotica,* **108**(3/4), 269–306.

Sawyer, R.K. (ed.) (1997*a*) *Creativity in performance.* Greenwich, CT: Ablex.

Sawyer, R.K. (1997*b*) *Pretend play as improvisation: Conversation in the preschool classroom.* Mahwah, NJ: Lawrence Erlbaum Associates.

Sawyer, R.K. (1999) The emergence of creativity. *Philosophical Psychology,* **12**(4), 447–69.

Sawyer, R.K. (2001) *Creating conversations: Improvisation in everyday discourse.* Cresskill, NJ: Hampton Press.

Sawyer, R.K. (2003*a*) *Group creativity: Music, theater, collaboration.* Mahwah, NJ: Erlbaum.

Sawyer, R.K. (2003*b*) *Improvised dialogues: Emergence and creativity in conversation.* Westport, CT: Greenwood.

Sawyer, R.K. (2005) *Explaining creativity: The science of human innovation.* New York: Oxford University Press.

Scheflen, A.E. (1982) Comments on the significance of interaction rhythms. In *Interaction rhythms: Periodicity in communicative behavior,* (ed. M. Davis), pp. 13–22. New York: Human Sciences Press.

Schögler, B. (1998) Music as a tool in communications research. *Nordic Journal of Music Therapy,* **7**(1), 40–9.

Schögler, B. (1999–2000) Studying temporal co-ordination in jazz duets. *Musicae Scientiae,* **3**(suppl.), 75–92.

Silverstein, M. (1984) On the pragmatic "poetry" of prose: Parallelism, repetition, and cohesive structure in the time course of dyadic conversation. In *Meaning, form, and use in context: Linguistic applications,* (ed. D. Schiffrin), pp. 181–98. Washington, DC: Georgetown University Press.

Spencer, H. (1891) *Essays, scientific, political, and speculative.* (Vol. 2). New York: D. Appleton.

Steedman, M.J. (1984) A generative grammar for jazz chord sequences. *Music Perception,* **2**(1), 52–77.

Trevarthen, C. (1979) Communication and cooperation in early infancy: A description of primary intersubjectivity. In *Before speech: The beginning of interpersonal communication,* (ed. M. Bullowa), pp. 321–47. New York: Cambridge University Press.

Tronick, E.C., Als, H., and Brazelton, T.B. (1980) The infant's communicative competencies and the achievement of intersubjectivity. In *The relationship of verbal and nonverbal communication,* (ed. M.R. Key), pp. 261–73. The Hague: Mouton.

Ujhelyi, M. (2000) Social organization as a factor in the origins of language and music. In *The origins of music,* (eds N.L. Wallin, B. Merker, and S. Brown), pp. 125–34. Cambridge, MA: MIT Press.

Wallin, N.L. (1991) *Biomusicology: Neurophysiological, neuropsychological and evolutionary perspectives on the origins and purposes of music.* Stuyvesant, NY: Pendragon Press.

Wallin, N.L., Merker, B., and Brown, S. (eds) (2000) *The origins of music.* Cambridge, MA: MIT Press.

Weeks, P. (1990) Musical time as a practical accomplishment: A change in tempo. *Human Studies,* **13**, 323–59.

Weeks, P. (1996*a*) A rehearsal of a Beethoven passage: An analysis of correction talk. *Research on Language and Social Interaction,* **29**(3), 247–90.

Weeks, P. (1996*b*) Synchrony lost, synchrony regained: The achievement of musical coordination. *Human Studies,* **19**, 199–228.

Chapter 4

Music cognition: defining constraints on musical communication

Annabel J. Cohen

Introduction

The mind enables musical communication but it is also a limiting factor. This chapter examines musical communication from the point of view of these capabilities and limitations. It argues that a cognitive theory of musical communication must define not only what is communicated but also what can not be communicated. The argument is developed in a historical context, touching first on the early years of experimental psychology, then the period of behaviourism, and, finally, the present cognitive era. Several experimental paradigms are reviewed to demonstrate how the capacities and limitations of music communication can be quantified. A brief comparison between language and music literacy is drawn, and a plasticity framework for understanding the role of early music exposure is also presented. It is concluded that a foundation now exists for the creation of a fairly complete though complex quantitative cognitive representation of music communication.

History of experimental approaches to music communication

Early experimental psychology (1850–1920)

To the nineteenth century founders of experimental psychology, music raised important questions. This is exemplified by three of the most influential scientists, each of whom held a prestigious professorship – Gustav Fechner and Wilhelm Wundt at Leipzig, and Hermann von Helmholtz at both Heidelberg and Berlin.

Gustav Theodor Fechner (1801–87) and psychophysics

With the ambitious aim of providing an 'exact theory of the relation of mind and body', Fechner (1860/1966, p. xxvii) developed the field of *psychophysics*, the systematic study of the relation between the physical world and its mental representation. According to the translator of Fechner's book *Elements of Psychophysics*, 'Fechner's early interest in music appears in his chapter on the psychophysics of tones' (1860/1966, p. xxi). Through psychophysics, he attempted to quantify the functional relation between physical and mental events. Part of Fechner's approach was to establish laws that governed changes in sensation that were just detectable. He began with determining the limits or thresholds of sensation, including, of course, tones. Fechner's interest extended beyond elementary lawful relations among tones to broader aesthetic issues, the topic of a later book (Fechner 1876).

Hermann von Helmholtz (1821–94)

Like Fechner, Helmholtz was a polymath for whom music played an even more significant scientific role. His *Sensations of Tone as the Physiological Basis of the Theory of Music* (1887/1954) drew attention to melody, tonality, scales, and the physics of sound including the role of harmonics. In *Physiological Optics* (1896/1962), he proposed the notion of *unconscious inference*, the idea that based on past experience, the mind guesses the physical cause of the subjective impression created by the energies impinging on the sense organs. These empirically based guesses or expectancies determine perception.

Wilhelm Wundt (1832–1920)

Wundt had worked briefly with Helmholtz on studies of perception before establishing the first experimental psychology laboratory in Leipzig in 1869. His *Principles of Physiological Psychology* (Wundt 1874) discusses musical combinations of tones as well as aesthetic issues. In the area of aesthetics, Wundt postulated maximum preference for a moderate level of intensity as opposed to lower or high levels, as depicted in Fig. 4.1 (Berlyne 1960 pp. 200–1).

Other psychologists, such as Theodor Lipps (1905/1995), Wundt's doctoral student and Carl Stumpf (1883, 1890), Wundt's peer in Berlin, directed attention to perception of piano tones, tonal fusion, melody perception, and musical talent. Ernst Mach (1886/1897), the philosopher, physicist, and psychophysicist, also included chapters on tone perception in his book *The Analysis of Sensations*.

Implications

The nineteenth century scientists encouraged the analysis of the mental representation of music and its components. Their insights remain relevant. Fechner's aim of relating objective and subjective worlds predates a goal of

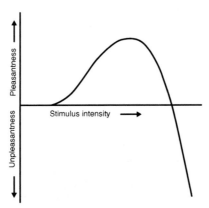

Fig. 4.1 Wundt Curve. The relation between liking for music and its complexity. Based on a diagram in Berlyne (1960, p. 201).

cognitive psychology; in addition, his focus on defining limits sets the stage for the present argument that to understand representation in music communication it is necessary to understand precisely what information can and cannot be represented. Helmholtz' concept of unconscious inference precedes similar contemporary accounts of perceptual and cognitive phenomena including those of music cognition research. For example, the first seven notes of the *doh re me fa so la ti doh* scale, (i.e. up to *ti*), will prime an expectation of an eighth note *doh*. Even fewer notes of the scale will prime the entire scale (Cohen 1991; Krumhansl 1990). Inference, or expectation, also plays an important role in the work of music theorists such as Leonard Meyer (1956) and Eugene Narmour (1990, 1991). The latter proposed a theory of *Implication–Realization* which assumes that listeners unconsciously generate implications or inferences after each tone they hear. Notes that match a preceding implication are *realized*; notes that violate the implication create surprise (e.g. Schellenberg 1996, Schmuckler 1997; Thompson *et al.* 1997). Finally, the aesthetic theory of Wundt, summarized as the Wundt Curve, became a building block in the 'new experimental aesthetics' of Daniel Berlyne (1971, pp. 86–91) a century later.

It is remarkable how much progress in music psychology was made during an era in which recording of sound only became possible towards its end. Experiments might resort to hitting tuning forks, or to inviting the local violinist to play tones to listeners who held Helmholtz resonators to their ears (Fig. 4.2). The period of behaviourism that followed had the advantage of technological innovations like phonographs and tape-recorders, but the climate was no longer receptive to musical problems.

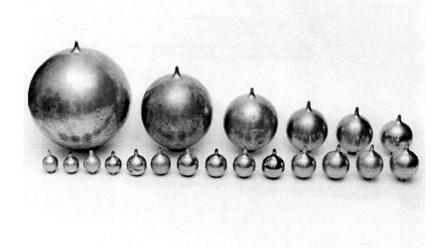

Fig. 4.2 Helmholtz Resonators. A set of Helmholtz resonators (manufactured by Koenig 1870) used to illustrate that listeners could hear out individual components of complex tones. Each resonator vibrated in sympathy with a particular frequency, and this vibration could be heard when the resonator was placed to the ear. (Courtesy of the Clarendon Laboratory Library archive, University of Oxford).

Behaviourism (1920–60)

John Watson and behaviourism

Few, if any, of the insights of the early experimental psychologists reviewed earlier had led to obvious applications. In contrast, by studying animal behaviour, Russian physiologist Ivan Pavlov had discovered the conditioned reflex, a principle of learning. In an influential article, the American psychologist John Watson (1913) recommended the behaviourist approach, urging psychology to focus on 'objectively observable behaviour'. According to the strict behaviourist view, introspection was an empty pursuit as were the topics of mind, thought, creativity, beauty, and imagery. Because music involves all of these topics, its neglect during this period was not surprising.

The stimulus and experimental method

From approximately 1920 to 1960, behaviourist research increasingly characterized psychology laboratories, typically entailing the conditioning of rats or other animals. The behaviourists developed strong methodologies: the use of research design, control of variables in experiments, and statistical analysis. Their concept of *stimulus* referred to the independent variable in an experiment that systematically affects responses of the participant. Conditioning studies sometimes used tones as stimuli (e.g. Pavlov 1928; Razran 1949). Watson himself emphasized sound as a conditioning stimulus (1916). The connection between the function of a tone as a conditioning stimulus and its function in music perception was rarely addressed (for an exception, see Humphrey 1927). One behaviourist study by Blackwell and Schlosberg (1943), however, suggested that the octave functioned similarly in both humans and rats. In this study, rats learned to press a bar when a particular tone frequency sounded, and their response *generalized* to the octave of this tone. Later researchers referred to this as evidence for an inborn or innate response to this musically significant octave relation (e.g. Deutsch 1969). Despite the behaviourist chilly climate for research on anything 'mental', some psychologists nevertheless maintained a strong interest in music (e.g. Seashore 1938/1967).

Gestalt psychology

A small group known as the Gestalt psychologists, most notably Wolfgang Köhler, Kurt Koffka, and Max Wertheimer, focused their attention on mental structure (see Ash 1995 for a review) though it was not in keeping with the behaviourist trend. For the Gestaltist, music was a clear example of organizational phenomena. Melody was the prototype of the Gestalt since *gestalt* means structure or pattern in German (though it is difficult to define precisely). Christian von Ehrenfels (1890), a philosopher of the earlier period who was passionate about music, is considered the originator of Gestalt psychological thought. His article in 1890 (also a shorter version published in English in 1937), entitled 'On Gestalt Theory', argued that one of the best examples of the Gestalt is *melodic transposition*. In melodic transposition, two melodies that begin on different pitches can be recognized as having the same tune if the corresponding pitch relations are the same within each melody. Although the elements, the tones, differ from melody to melody, the whole melodic pattern is still preserved. As a simple example, think of a birthday celebration in which different people begin the *Happy Birthday* song on different notes. Gestalt psychologists also introduced the principle of *Prägnanz* which meant 'the simplest and most impressive structure' (Ash 1995, p. 1 and p. 133) and is associated with 'simplest aesthetics' (Ash 1995, p. 185). To account for perceptual structure or grouping, they introduced laws of organization based on principles such as proximity, similarity, and good continuation (Ash 1995, pp. 224–5). The early description of Gestalt phenomenon challenged psychologists in the next historical period for a more precise explanation. Post-behaviourism developments in communication or information theory provided some tools and answers.

Cognitive zeitgeist and communication theory (1960 – present)

The prominence of behaviourism receded after the Second World War. The need for a measure of communication efficiency and accuracy had become important during wartime and had led to a mathematical theory of communication (Shannon and Weaver 1949) otherwise known as information theory. Unintentionally, its components, as depicted in Fig. 4.3, offered metaphors for mental processes and provided a new way to think about the mind. Consider such terms as *source* of a message, the *message* itself, *receiver* of the message, the *information channel* through which the message passes, and *noise* that prevents perfect transmission. Consider one mind as the source of a musical message. The message is a musical idea that is ultimately expressed as an acoustical energy pattern. This pattern travels along an information channel within a second mind, the receiver. The accuracy of transmission of the message depends on both the degree of noise and the capacity of the information channel. The correlation between the source and receiver (i.e. comparing the message at the beginning and end of the channel) represents the efficiency of transmission, from one mind to the other. A high correlation confirms that transmission is effective. With respect to music communication, consider as one example, the correlation between the mind of the performer and the mind of the listener. See Moles (1958/trans. 1968) for a specific illustration (pp. 10–11) and for an extensive application of a mathematical theory of communication – information theory – to music.

In the 1950s, the developing computer technology (or information processing technology) provided additional metaphors for mental phenomena. Terms such

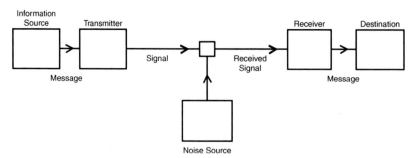

Fig. 4.3 Elements of a Communication System. Image redrawn from Shannon and Weaver (1949, p. 7).

as *data, programs, memory*, and *storage* served as vocabulary for discussing mental phenomena that were taboo during behaviourism. This terminology helped those psychologists who realized that they could no longer avoid the problems of how the brain carried out tasks of recognition, communication, thinking, memory, creativity, and problem solving. Closely aligned with communication theory, the information processing approach assumed that perception was not immediate but occurred in stages, which took a finite amount of time and was associated with capacity limitations which could sometimes be overcome by recoding (Haber and Hershenson 1980, pp. 293–4). These assumptions apply to music in the following way. Although subjectively, it seems that music perception is immediate (turn on the compact disk player and hear the music), many processes occur, each of which takes a finite though short amount of time. From the peripheral hearing mechanisms to the higher cortical mechanisms, musical information is transformed from the real world into mental representations. Each stage limits the to-be-transmitted information. Recoding musical information in particular ways may assist in overcoming these limitations.

There is then a need to identify the different stages of transformation of the real-world music-stimulus information and to examine the accuracy with which the information is preserved from stage to stage. Fortunately, 100 years after the beginning of experimental psychology, a technology had developed for controlling sound precisely. Computer-controlled tone generators and high quality headphones and tape recorders represented the first major advance, and studies to be described took advantage of this new level of control. The later discovery of digital synthesis enabled presentation of almost any musical sound to listeners in experiments. Yet it is important to appreciate that very simple sound stimuli can contribute to understanding how humans acquire and use knowledge, the primary concern of the new spirit of the time, cognitive science (Harnish 2002; Sternberg and Ben-Zeev 2001).

Experiments showing the limitations on music communication

Absolute judgment

Procedure

Consider a set of tones differing only in highness and lowness of pitch. How many tones can an individual identify with absolute accuracy by saying, 'I know, that tone is the lowest I heard, that one is the 4th lowest, that one is the 2nd highest, etc.?' The experimental method for answering this question is absolute judgement. Its simple though rigorous procedures and analytic techniques came out of communication theory. In studies conducted in military communication research laboratories (e.g. Pollack 1952, 1953), a listener was presented with a set of items (or stimuli) each of which had a name or symbol designated by the experimenter. The set of items might be 12 tones of the chromatic scale, for example. The name assigned is typically a number, such as *1* for the stimulus with the smallest value on the dimension, *2* for the stimulus with the 2nd smallest value on the dimension, etc. If there were 12 items in total, than the number *12* would be the name given to the tone with the largest value on the dimension (the highest or loudest tone).

Early studies revealed accurate identification up to only five frequencies or five loudnesses. Confusions arose as the number of items increased beyond that. Given the potentially infinite number of frequencies or loudnesses, memory for only five of them seems like a big limitation. In his celebrated article 'The magic number 7 ± 2: Some limits on our ability to process information', Miller (1956) summarizes the early evidence for the limited capacity on information processing for many sensory dimensions, including auditory dimensions like frequency and intensity. Miller also observes that the memory limitation can be improved by: (1) recoding or structuring groups of items into meaningful chunks, and (2) by increasing the number of dimensions on which the items vary (for example, changing both frequency and intensity of the tones).

In music, the limitation of around seven coincides with seven different notes in the musical scale (*doh re me fah sol la and ti*), and the first seven harmonics of a complex tone. This series of harmonics furnishes a wealth of musical material (major, minor, dominant seventh chords and all 12 musical intervals except the semitone). Because each of the 12 musical intervals (two-note combinations) has an inversion, the set of intervals also reduces to just six basic intervals. Thus, several small sets (diatonic tones, overtones, intervals, relative durations, and metres) furnish building blocks for an infinite variety of music. This small number of items fits well within the 7 ± 2 limit on the ability to remember and transmit information. Still, the question remains, how can the limitation on absolute judgement be overcome? Experiments described as follows review attempts to improve memory for tones through special training, inclusion of musical structure, and altering the probability that any particular tone will occur.

Improving memory for tones

Cuddy (1968) compared two methods of training memory for 10 tones separated by semitones. The first training method, designated *series* training provided feedback about the correctness of response after every trial. The second method, designated *reference* training, provided feedback on only one of the 10 tones in the set. Surprisingly, feedback on the single reference tone improved memory for the entire set of tones and was superior to the series training.

In a further study, performance was superior for a set of 12 tones spaced as the major triad structure as opposed to a set drawn from the chromatic scale or from the frequency continuum covering the same four-octave range (Cuddy 1971). In another study, the role of the probability of presentation of tones was examined for its effect on memory for a set of 9 tones (Cuddy *et al.* 1973). In a *biased-probability* condition, one tone was presented on 1/3 of the trials and each of the other tones was presented on 1/12 of the occasions. In the *equal-probability* condition, all tones were presented with equal probability (1/9). Performance per tone was better in the biased-probability condition even though most tones had been presented less frequently than in the equal-probability case (i.e. less opportunities for learning). The results suggested that listeners were able to exploit the redundancy within a set of tones to facilitate memory through establishment of an anchor or reference. Sensitivity to statistical pitch characteristics of melody was also shown by Oram and Cuddy (1995) and Eerola *et al.* (2001).

In another study exploring the role of the major-triad structure, an absolute judgment study was conducted using a set of nine 5-note melodies – one melody representing a major triad (*doh me sol me doh*) and the others representing a systematic set of distorted approximations to this major triad. Listeners with a great deal of musical experience could take advantage of the major triad structure so as to better identify the various melodies absolutely (Cohen 1994, 2000). This and other studies comparing listeners with various levels of musical training suggest that musicians may more easily bring what they know to new musical situations to facilitate musical communication.

Summary and implications

Studies of absolute judgement of tones define the limitations on memory for tones and the following ways of overcoming the limitations: (1) a learned reference tone facilitates tone memory more than learning every tone in the set, (2) tones from a set of musically (harmonically) related tones are easier to identify than a set of tones chosen randomly from the same range, (3) tones from a set having biased probabilities are easier to remember than from a set having equal probabilities, and (4) musical training facilitates the ability to take advantage of available structure.

Absolute judgement studies are highly controlled in terms of the stimuli, procedure method, and analysis. Sceptics may question the possibility of learning something about musical communication from something so 'unmusical'. In response, consider the implications for understanding one of the most important music-theoretic concepts, tonality. Tonality refers to the establishment of a reference tone, tonic, or sense of key in most Western-European music as well as in music of some other cultures. As I have previously argued (Cohen 2000), if an established reference note in absolute judgement studies can facilitate memory for all the tones sequentially presented, then this benefit should apply whether the tones are in an experiment of absolute judgement or in a musical piece presented for pleasure. The reference tone overcomes memory limitations and permits the listener to keep track of more notes in the piece than would otherwise be possible.

Thus to understand at least some aspects of musical communication, it is useful to consider the information-theoretic concepts of the set of tone-events, the size and structure of the set, and the probability of occurrence of each tone event. From the mathematical theory of communication, the amount of information increases with (a) the increasing number of events or tones in the set and (b) equi-probability of occurrence of each item (Garner 1962). To illustrate the first point, everyday experience tells us that it is easier to identify one particular shade of red when there is only one other as compared to ten other shades of red to choose from. Regarding the second point, consider the structure of English words. Some letters, such as 'e' and 's', are more common than others. Suppose instead that all letters were equi-probable. In this case, reading would be more difficult without the advantage of our knowledge concerning the structure of the language.

In applying the concept of information measurement to music, notice first that most music compositions typically contain only a few discrete tones (or chroma) in an octave – only seven in the major scale, twelve in the chromatic scale – compared to the infinite continuum of available frequencies. Secondly, for any typical piece of music, tones are not equi-probable. Some tones occur more frequently or for longer than others. Therefore, theoretically, musical sets of sounds have relatively less uncertainty than if there were (a) more notes in the scale and (b) equal-probability of presentation of the notes. In short, music is redundant and listeners can take advantage of this redundancy.

Delayed recognition paradigm

The delayed recognition paradigm is useful for identifying the details that people can retain after hearing a piece of music. Employing this paradigm to study memory for musical surface features such as pitch and duration, Krumhansl (1991) presented to a group of music students the first part of an unfamiliar modern classical piece by the French composer Olivier Messiaen (1908–92).

Messiaen used a unique and generally unfamiliar 12-tone principle for composition. Within each of 3 simultaneous lines of music, all 12 notes of the musical alphabet (i.e. C C# D ... B) appeared. Each of the 12 notes always was presented at the exact same highness or lowness (pitch height), duration, and intensity. Thus, a particular duration was linked with a particular loudness and pitch height.

In the experimental procedure, the listeners heard the first half of the piece and then heard six test segments of six types. One type came directly from the presented music. Another was from the part of the music that had not been presented (still based on the same compositional principle). The third type preserved the overall up and down pattern in the melody but altered pitches by just one semitone (e.g. C moved down to B or up to C#). The remaining three types entailed other transformations of the original material.

The listeners were required to rate their confidence that the excerpt came from the piece by Messiaen (regardless of whether it came from the part of the piece they had heard, or the later part). If the segment was judged as part of the piece, then the rating would approach the high end of the scale; otherwise, the rating would approach the low end of the scale. The results revealed high ratings for segments that had actually been presented (the first test type) and also for segments from the unheard second half of the piece (the second test type). High ratings were also ascribed to those segments that had been only slightly changed but preserved the pattern of up and down of the melody of the piece (the third test type). The other three transformations were regarded as not in the piece. The results revealed that listeners can acquire an *abstract representation* of a new style so as to determine whether novel segments fit that style. The abstract representation is limited in its ability to preserve some detail (e.g. exact interval size as opposed to general directional information, i.e. contour). Thus, the experiment helps to define what the listener represents in his or her mind while listening to and remembering music, that is, what information about musical surface is and is not transmitted. Such information could explain, for example, what motifs are available to members of a jazz improvisation group as discussed by Sawyer (this volume). The abstract nature of this representation, the range as to what acceptably counts for the piece, can be regarded as a 'field of liberty', a term coined by J. E. Cohen (1962, p. 138) in reference to a musical score.

The delayed recognition paradigm has addressed other kinds of questions about musical communication as well: memory for familiar versus unfamiliar popular music styles to be discussed later (e.g. Cohen 2000), memory for film music (e.g. Boltz 2004; Cohen 1995) and memory for music versus lyrics in songs with words (e.g. Serafine *et al.* 1984).

Pattern goodness and information theory

Simplicity

The limitations on music communication discussed so far concerned memory. Another important aspect of musical experience is its appreciation or enjoyment. Here again, the brain sets a limit on which characteristics of music can be considered pleasing and which cannot. As already mentioned, the founders of experimental psychology had considered aesthetic issues. Fechner had written a text on experimental aesthetics, and Wundt had defined a function relating pleasingness to an optimum intensity level. The Gestalt psychologists believed that certain structures or characteristics of a pattern led to perceived good form or prägnanz. The task of quantifying these effects challenged the cognitive era.

Taking a communication-theory perspective, Garner (1962) addressed the challenge of quantifying pattern goodness. Consistent with communication theory, he believed that people saw or heard an event not simply as the event itself, but in terms of all the events that might have happened but did not in fact occur. In some cases an event would be one of a few possibilities, but in others, one of many possibilities. Take his example of the symbol ꓱ. It can be perceived as a member of a set of four three-pronged forks, the number 3 in the set of 10 numbers, or as a member of the set of 26 backwards letters (i.e. a backwards E). The set size differs in each case as either 4 (patterns), 9 (numbers), and 26 (letters) respectively. Garner reasoned that the smaller the inferred subset, the better (more beautiful) the perceived form of the item that was presented. Good form was then both in the object and in the eyes (brain) of the beholder.

Garner's (1970) article entitled 'Good patterns have few alternatives' reviews studies of pattern goodness. Using two-element tone sequences, Garner found that high goodness ratings of sequences were associated with small subsets (e.g. xxxxoooo is a better form than xxoxxxoo where x and o represent different tones). The relation between musical structural complexity, goodness ratings, and memory was later shown by Cohen (1976) and further demonstrated by Cuddy *et al.* (1981).

By quantifying the concept of inferred subset, Garner thus quantified the Gestalt concept of good form. He supported his hypothesis that pattern goodness is inversely related to the size of the inferred set. This is consistent with the communication theory notion that messages are quantified probabilistically, and rightly so, as it was this on which Garner's hypothesis was based. But the focus on an imagined subset is also reminiscent of Helmholtz' notion of unconscious inference. Garner had after all showed that the simplest patterns or messages from small subsets were regarded as more pleasing. The notion of simplicity is relevant to certain aspects of the pleasingness of music (e.g. the consonance of musical intervals, and the appreciation of rhythmic over arrhythmic patterns). But does the concept of simplicity or small subset limit musical appreciation too greatly? Surely it is not only simplicity that is enjoyable.

Optimum complexity

Consider the following experiment by Heyduk (1975). He composed samples of music varying in two dimensions of musical complexity, namely rhythm and harmonic accompaniment. For the simple rhythm, the tones fell on the beat. For the complex rhythm, some tones fell off the beat. Likewise, the simple harmony used fewer different harmonies than did the complex harmony. If simplicity is the only feature affecting pleasure, then pleasingness should decrease with increasing complexity. Instead, listeners assigned their highest rating to passages with intermediate complexity. Moreover, on subsequent hearings, pleasingness increased for the more complex patterns and decreased for the less complex patterns. Some factor other than simplicity must operate to affect the judgements of pleasingness, and this may be optimum complexity, associated with the Wundt curve.

Berlyne's group in Toronto also observed that the judgement of pleasingness followed Wundt's inverted U-shape in a variety of studies. High pleasingness was associated with a moderate degree of stimulus complexity as measured in accordance with information theory. North and Hargreaves (1997) have also discussed this with specific reference to music. The theory and data challenge the Gestalt notion of pattern goodness and simplicity. Platt (1961, p. 230) helps to settle the controversy by stating that individuals need both organization and change, '...what is beautiful is pattern that contains uncertainty and surprise and yet resolves them into the regularity of a larger pattern'.

More recently, Narmour's (1990) implication–realization theory implies the need to specify not only what happens in the music notation but also 'what might have been.' In theory, a quantification of the relative fulfilment of expectations could be compared with measures of aesthetic experience. The need to consider the real-world listening environment in predicting what music will be appreciated has also been emphasized by North and Hargreaves (1997).

Parsing

Another aspect of music communication is the segmentation into groups and phrases as the music unfolds in time. Lerdahl and Jackendoff (1983) applied notions of the Gestalt laws of similarity and proximity to this problem. Their rules represent limitations on the way music information is communicated.

Composers have intuitively exploited grouping principles. Baroque composers, for example, established two different streams of music by interleaving high and low pitched tones in a single sequence (Bregman 1993). What is notated is not what will necessarily be heard: A single melodic line consisting of large interval leaps played by a single instrument may be heard as two lines when played rapidly.

In a study of melodic parsing (Frankland and Cohen 2004), listeners heard a melody and were asked to press a key whenever they felt a breakpoint occurred (end or beginning of a unit). The data of over 100 listeners, for melodies each of which was presented three times for responses by the listener, provided a basis for testing several of the Lerdahl and Jackendoff grouping rules (see also Frankland 1998). Support for the significance of two rules based on proximity in time was obtained (i.e. Attack-Point and Rest). Deliège (1987), Clarke and Krumhansl (1990), and Peretz (1989) have also empirically explored the validity of various aspects of Lerdahl and Jackendoff's theory. Temperley (2001), also working within the Lerdahl and Jackendoff framework, developed computational models for determining perceived breakpoints in melodies. His impressive computational results remain to be tested against data of what listeners actually hear (Cohen 2004).

Liberties, limitations, and music literacy

Music literacy and language literacy

Literacy typically refers to the knowledge required for effective verbal communication – to listening, understanding, speaking, reading, and writing. Literacy is one of the primary factors influencing quality of life, and its aggregate effects contribute globally to the division between first and third world countries. Given the significance of literacy, much scholarship has been directed to factors influencing its acquisition. Sometimes the concept of literacy extends to music because there are parallels to verbal language in terms of listening, understanding, performing, reading notation, and composing. Language literacy arises through everyday exposure to spoken language and to adult models of reading and writing, but reading and writing are routinely attained through formal training. In the music domain, however, adult models of reading and writing music are uncommon (Barrett, this volume), and reading and writing music are not considered as a necessary part of education (cf. Hodges 1992, p. 469).

Notation

Music staff notation appears to precisely designate musical sounds, however, it represents a range of acoustic possibilities or, again, a 'field of liberty' (*cf.* J. E. Cohen 1962). Music notation, conventional or invented, reveals much of what is communicated by music to the listener but it also conceals what is communicated (Barrett this volume). Bamberger (this volume) describes her experiments with bells differing only in pitch for which children's invented notations have provided insight into the structures that music communicates at an early age to both novices and more musically experienced children.

Invented notations, freed from conventions, permit representation of patterns impossible to perform on fixed-pitch traditional instruments but that can be created by electronic means or the voice. Sounds such as quarter-tones, for example, 'fall between the cracks' of traditional notation. New notation systems are needed to represent these possibilities, yet other notation systems are needed to represent other structural characteristics, such as repeated themes or phrases that traditional notation ignores but that even children identify (Bamberger, this volume). Challenges of notation may eventually be met by cognitive psychology, in identifying more completely what sounds and patterns are to be heard when listening – be they groupings, segmentation, timbres, pitches, intensities, durations, or repetitions of these or other structures. Such a notation however might be so complex as to be more like a theory than a usable tool for reading music (e.g. Narmour 1990). From the practical as opposed to theoretical standpoint, the challenge is to develop an efficient but informative code that does not exceed the reader's channel capacity. Mrs. Touchett's remark on the cost of clarity is somehow applicable: 'I never know what I mean in my telegrams. ... Clearness is too expensive.' [*Portrait of a Lady* by Henry James (1881/1979, Chapter 5, p. 42)]

Exposure to music during early and adolescent development

Helmholtz' unconscious inference, Garner's application of communication theory, and Meyer's and Narmour's emphasis on the role of expectancy support the view that for any performance of music, what is heard depends on one's past exposure to music. None of these theorists, however, considers that the timing in the lifespan of this exposure may be critical. Using a linguistic comparison, sounds that function similarly in one language (allophones) may be differentiated as phonemes in another language. Failure to provide exposure to these linguistic distinctions during an early critical period (as early as the first year in life), impairs the ability to make these distinctions later (Werker and Tees 1999). Exposure to language during an early critical period facilitates both first and second language learning (Johnson and Newport 1989; Mayberry *et al.* 2002). Similarly, exposure to music during an early critical period may have lasting influence on hearing music. Gordon (1979) proposed that the child's musical ability was fixed by the age of 8 or 9 years (see also Hargreaves 1986). A program of research on the liberating and limiting role of exposure to music has been carried out for over a decade in my own laboratory at the University of Prince Edward Island.

This research program employs the same basic experimental paradigm with listeners from different age cohorts. The musical material entails short excerpts of popular music from the last 10 decades (e.g. Bing Crosby, Elvis Presley, Beatles, Madonna). Music from different decades of course has cohort-specific significance. In the first part of the experiment, listeners first rate randomly selected excerpts from each decade for familiarity or preference. The ratings reveal cohort-specific response patterns. For example, older adults, in contrast to younger adults, find recently popular excerpts less familiar and less preferred than excerpts popular several decades earlier. A second part of the study entails a surprise recognition test of some of the previously presented excerpts. Although all excerpts have been heard only minutes earlier, older and younger adults produce vastly different recognition patterns depending on the decade of popularity of the excerpt. The differences are generally consistent with the rule that music originally experienced prior to or during early adulthood tends to be recognized best regardless of age (Clyburn and Cohen 1996, see also Rubin et al. 1998). In a study that compared young children, pre-adolescents, and young adults, effects of style increased with increasing age (Bailey and Cohen 2002), suggesting an openness to acquire knowledge about any music in the earliest years.

Contemporary technological developments of the music industry and the Internet have increased public accessibility to music of every style and decade. In addition, there are increasingly more new styles, such as hip hop, techno, and rap, to name only a few (Gjerdingen 2003). Thus, the present generation is less easily characterized by its music than were past generations. Western-European music nevertheless contrasts with music of other cultures employing different musical scales, instruments, and rhythms. Therefore, to continue the inquiry into critical periods for music, responses to native music and music from unfamiliar cultures have been compared in our recent work (McFadden and Cohen 2003). This approach partially parallels developmental psycholinguistic studies that compare discrimination and memory for native and non-native language (e.g. Trehub 1976; Werker and Tees 1999).

Recent brain imaging research has surprisingly revealed continuing brain development during adolescence (Giedd et al. 1999). Clinical data also suggest that during adolescence, certain kinds of exposure have lifelong influence, and a developmental plasticity has been proposed as an account

(Steinberg *et al.* in press). Consistent with this view is our cross-sectional research which shows that music styles learned during adolescence influenced music preferences and memory well into senior years (Cohen *et al.* 2002). As Russell (1997, p. 146) states: '...musical tastes formed in youth tend to persist into and across the adult years, especially in the case of popular music' referring also to the work of Holbrook and Schindler (1989) and Stipp (1990). Along with brain plasticity during adolescence, sociobiological significance could also explain adolescent strong interests in popular music (Cohen *et al.* 2003), as also documented by Tarrant *et al.* (2002) and Zillman and Gan (1997).

The notion of critical periods for music acquisition can be accommodated by a Plasticity Framework for Music Grammar Acquisition (Cohen 2000, pp. 446–7) as shown in Fig. 4.4. Here, exposure to music during a critical period readies the brain for particular musical structures. This setting of parameters has a lifelong influence. Music that satisfies the parametric description can 'Go' ahead (be encoded); music that violates the description meets a 'Stop' sign. Thus, the interaction of predispositions and musical exposure both liberate and limit the potential for music communication throughout life. A corollary is that greater adult literacy of musical styles will follow from greater exposure early in life.

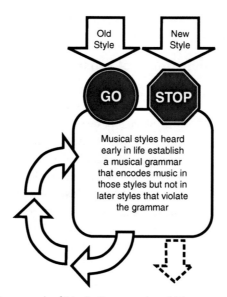

Fig. 4.4 Plasticity Framework of Music Grammar Acquisition as proposed by Cohen (2000).

Constraints on music communication from a cognitive perspective

Music tells us about mind

As the research on absolute pitch showed, by establishing a reference tone, memory for all tones in the set of tones improved. Moving the example from the laboratory to the everyday music listening situation, establishment of a reference tone facilitates memory for all tones in the piece. It enables the listener to remember what has just been presented so that it can be related to the rest of the music as it unfolds. Tonality could then well be a prominent feature of music because it is adaptive to the memory constraints of mind. The redundant structures in music may be there because the composer or performer (e.g. improvisor) can grasp them, and because they implicitly or explicitly know that the audience should also be able to grasp them. Lewis Thomas (1979), former president of the Memorial Sloan-Kettering Cancer Center in New York City and regular contributor to his own column *Notes of a Biology Watcher* in the prestigious *New England Journal of Medicine*, shared his insight that music reflects the mind – music tells us how the mind works. 'Music is the effort we make to explain to ourselves how our brains work. We listen to Bach transfixed because this is listening to a human mind'. (Thomas 1979, p. 154). Thus, the analysis of music itself will help to reveal secrets of human communication in general: what can and cannot be transmitted from composer, performer, or machine to the listener and back again.

Toward a cognitive model of musical communication

In summary, the early science of psychology provided strong roots for current research on musical communication, endorsing music as an obvious area for inquiry. Fechner established the goal of determining the functional relation between objective and subjective reality, quantifying this relation and defining its limits. Whereas his psychophysical methods provided solid data, in contrast, Wundt's introspective analysis of imagery and perception failed to do so, but his methods complement other forms of data collection, and his ideas on preference founded a quantitative approach to experimental aesthetics. The second phase of experimental psychology, behaviourism, supplanted introspection with an emphasis on objectively observable responses, much to the detriment of interest in music. While ignoring music, research methodology and data analysis developed and could be adapted to music issues when the time was once again right to address mind. Gestalt psychology advanced as a separate branch of psychology, establishing principles of good form and similarity that impacted the next period, cognitive psychology, that once again admitted mind into experimental psychology. Half-way through the twentieth century, political and technological developments led to a mathematical theory of communication and to information theory, which indirectly supported a renewed interest in mind and supplied metaphors for mental processes. Thus, began the third and present phase of experimental psychology, the cognitive zeitgeist, during which music has increasingly regained its place. The many research paradigms that followed started to define processes underlying music memory, emotional and aesthetic response, parsing, and the implications of notation. In many cases, these results can be looked on as elucidating the liberties and limitations placed by the mind on music communication. More studies on capacities and limits are needed (see e.g. Parncutt and Cohen 1995, on defining the limits of scale-step size for identification of sequential patterns of tones).

The chapter has touched on the heritage of concepts provided during the first century of experimental psychology: from Fechner, Helmholtz, and Wundt; the technical rigour of behaviourism and its concept of stimulus and response; the perspective of communication theory, the research paradigms of absolute judgement, delayed recognition, pattern classification, and parsing, and developmental studies of musical literacy. Together these furnish a rich foundation for understanding the liberties and limitations of musical communication as a result of the mind as source and receiver of music. History also reveals the constraints imposed on theorizing. There is no better reminder than the 40 years of behaviourism during which most psychology departments regarded the mental phenomena of music as tangential at best. Only slowly has this changed. The twenty-first century seems freer of ideological constraint and offers seemingly unbounded technology. Although history cautions us against complacency, the foundation seems well established for a cognitive theory of music communication that accommodates and defines the liberties and limitations arising from music structure and style, socio-cultural development, performance practices, and individual differences.

Acknowledgement

Research support from the Natural Sciences and Engineering Research Council and the Social Sciences and Humanities Research Council is appreciated as is the assistance of Elizabeth McFadden and Robert Drew. The historical context owes much to my mentors in psychology at Queen's University: Professors Lola Cuddy, Douglas Mewhort, David Murray as well as Albert Bregman at McGill University. Appreciation for feedback on the article is expressed to the editors of this volume.

References

Ash, M.G. (1995) *Gestalt Psychology in German culture 1890–1967.* Cambridge: Cambridge University Press.

Bailey, B.A. and Cohen, A.J. (2002) Acquisition of musical vernacular in children and young adults. *Canadian Acoustics,* **30,** 7–8.

Berlyne, D.E. (1960) *Conflict, arousal, and curiosity.* Toronto: McGraw.

Berlyne, D.E. (1971) *Aesthetics and Psychobiology.* New York: Appleton-Century-Crofts.

Blackwell, H.R. and Schlosberg, H. (1943) Octave generalization, pitch discrimination, and loudness thresholds in the white rat. *Journal of Experimental Psychology,* **33,** 407–19.

Boltz, M. (2004) The cognitive processing of film and musical soundtracks. *Memory and Cognition,* **32,** 1194–205.

Bregman, A. (1993) *Auditory scene analysis.* Cambridge, MA: MIT Press.

Clarke, E.F. and Krumhansl, C.L. (1990) Perceiving musical time, *Music Perception,* **7,** 213–51.

Clyburn, L. and Cohen, A.J. (1996) Memory for popular music in elderly and young adult listeners. *Canadian Acoustics,* **24,** p. 31.

Cohen, J.E. (1962) Information theory and music. *Behavioural Science,* **7,** 137–63.

Cohen, A.J. (1976) Perception of tone sequences from the Western-European Chromatic Scale: Tonality, transposition and the pitch set. (Thesis summary). *Journal of the Acoustical Society of America,* **60,** p. 1421

Cohen, A.J. (1991) Tonality and perception: Musical scales primed by excerpts from the *Well-Tempered Clavier* of J. S. Bach. *Psychological Research,* **53,** 305–14.

Cohen, A.J. (1994) Musical training and pitch schemata: Tonal influences in microtonal contexts. In *Proceedings of the 3rd International Conference for Music Perception and Cognition,* (ed. I. Deliège), pp. 79–82. Liege, Belgium.

Cohen, A.J. (1995) One-trial memory integration of music and film: A direct test.' Paper presented at the Annual Meeting of the Canadian Acoustical Association, Quebec City.

Cohen, A.J. (2000) Development of tonality induction: Plasticity, exposure, and training. *Music Perception,* **17,** 437–59.

Cohen, A.J. (2004) Review of D. Temperley's. *The cognition of basic musical structures.* Cambridge, MA: MIT Press. *Psychology of Music,* 111–26.

Cohen, A.J., Bailey, B.A., and Nilsson, T. (2002) Importance of music in older adults. In *Psychogeromusicology* (ed. A.J. Cohen). Special issue on the psychologies of music and aging. *Psychomusicology,* **18,** 89–102.

Cohen, A.J., Bailey, B.E., MacDonald, L.M., and McFadden, E.D. (2003) Popular music as a probe for adolescent brain development. Adolescent Brain Development [New York Academy of Sciences Conference Poster]. New York.

Cuddy, L.L. (1968) Practice effects in the absolute judgment of pitch. *Journal of the Acoustical Society of America,* **43,** 1069–76.

Cuddy, L.L. (1971) Absolute judgement of musically-related pure tones. *Canadian Journal of Psychology,* **25,** 42–55.

Cuddy, L.L., Cohen, A.J., and Mewhort, D.J.K. (1981) Perception of structure in short melodic sequences. *Journal of Experimental Psychology: Human Perception and Performance,* **7,** 869–83.

Cuddy, L.L., Pinn, J., and Simons, E. (1973) Anchor effects with biased probability of occurrence in absolute judgment of pitch. *Journal of Experimental Psychology*, **100**, 218–20.

Deliège, I. (1987) Grouping conditions in listening to music: An approach to Lerdahl and Jackendoff's grouping preference rules. *Music Perception*, **4**, 325–60.

Deutsch, D. (1969) Music recognition. *Psychological Review*, **76**, 300–07.

Eerola, T.U., Järvinen, T., Louhivuori, J. (2001) Statistical features and perceived similarity of folk melodies. *Music Perception*, **18**, 275–96.

Ehrenfels, C. von (1890) 'Über "Gestaltqualitäten"', Vierteljahrsschrift für wissenschaftliche Philosophie, **14**, 242–92, Eng. trans. In *Foundations of Gestalt Theory*, (ed. Barry Smith), Munich and Vienna: Philosophia, 1988, 82–117.

Ehrenfels, C. von (1937) On Gestalt-Qualities. (M. Focht, trans). *American Journal of Psychology*, **44**, 521–4.

Fechner, G. T. (1860/1966) *Elements of Psychophysics*. (trans H.E. Adler; eds D.H. Howes and E.G. Boring). New York: Holt, Rinehart and Winston.

Fechner, G.T. (1876) *Vorschule der Aesthetik*. Leipzig: Breitkopf and Härtel.

Frankland, B.W. (1998) *Empirical tests of Lerdahl and Jackendoff's (1983) Low-Level Group Preference Rules for the Parsing of Melody*. (Doctoral dissertation, Dalhousie University, Halifax, N.S.).

Frankland, B.W., and Cohen, A.J., (2004) Parsing of melody: Quantification and testing of the local grouping rules of Lerdahl and Jackendoff's *A Generative Theory of Tonal Music*. *Music Perception*, **21**, 499–543.

Garner, W. (1962) *Uncertainty and structure as psychological concepts*. New York: Wiley.

Garner, W. (1970) Good patterns have few alternatives. *American Scientist*, **58**, 3–42.

Garner, W. (1974) *The processing of information and structure*. Potomac, Maryland: Erlbaum.

Giedd, J.N., Blumenthal, J., Jeffries, N.O., Castellanos, F.X., Liu, H., Zijdenbos, A. *et al.* (1999) Brain development during childhood and adolescence: A longitudinal MRI study. *Nature Neuroscience*, **2**, 861–3.

Gjerdingen, R. (2003) What to listen for in rock: A stylistic analysis by Ken Stephenson. (Book review). *Music Perception*, 2003, **20**, 491–7.

Gordon, E.E. (1979) *Primary measures of music audiation*. Chicago, IL: G.I.A.

Haber, R.N. and Herschenson, M. (1980, 2nd edn). *The psychology of visual perception*. New York: Holt.

Hargreaves, D.J. (1986) *The developmental psychology of music*. Cambridge: Cambridge University Press.

Harnish, R.M. (2002) *Minds, brains, computers: An historical introduction to the foundations of cognitive science*. Malden, MA: Blackwell.

Helmholtz, H. von (1896/1962) *Treatise on physiological optics*. J. P. C. Southall (ed. and trans). New York: Dover.

Helmholtz, H. von (1887/1954) *On the sensations of tone as a physiological basis for the theory of music*. N.Y.: Dover. (Originally published, 1863; English translation of the 4th edition 1877 with additional notes by A. J. Ellis, 1885).

Heyduk, R.G. (1975) Rated preference for musical composition as it relates to complexity and exposure frequency. *Perception and Psychophysics*, **17**, 84–91.

Hodges, D. (1992) The acquisition of music reading skills. In *Handbook of research on music teaching and learning*, (ed. R. Colwell), pp. 466–71. N.Y.: Schirmer.

Holbrook, M.B. and Schindler, R.M. (1989) Some exploratory findings on the development of musical tastes. *Journal of Consumer Research*, **16**, 119–24.

Humphrey, G. (1927) The effect of sequences of indifferent stimuli on a reaction of the conditioned response. *Journal of Abnormal and Social Psychology*, **22**, 194–212.

James, H. (1881/1979/1996) *The portrait of a lady*. Toronto: Penguin Signet.

Johnson, J.S. and Newport, E.L. (1989) Critical period effects in second language learning: the influence of maturational state on the acquisition of English as a second language. *Cognitive Psychology*, **21**, 60–99.

Krumhansl, C.L. (1990) *Cognitive foundations of musical pitch*. New York: Oxford University Press.

Krumhansl, C.L. (1991) Memory for musical surface. *Memory and Cognition*, **19**, 401–11.

Lerdahl, F. and Jackendoff, R. (1983) *A generative theory of tonal music*. Cambridge, MA: MIT Press.

Lipps, T. (1905/1995) *Psychologische Studien*. Trans. W.E. Thomson as Consonance and Dissonance in Music. San Marino, CA: Everett Books.

Mach, E. (1886/1897) *Contributions to the analysis of the sensations*. Trans. C.M. Williams. Chicago, IL: Open Court Publishing.

Mayberry, R.I., Lock, E., and Kazmi, H. (2002) Linguistic ability and early language exposure. *Nature*, **17**, 38.

McFadden, E.D. and Cohen, A.J. (2003) Recognizing familiar and foreign words and music by children and adults: An examination of the critical period hypothesis. *Canadian Acoustics*, **31**, 7–8.

Meyer, L. (1956) *Emotion and meaning in music*. Chicago, IL: University of Chicago Press.

Miller, G.A. (1956) The magical number seven plus or minus two: Some limits on our capacity for processing information. *Psychological Review*, **63**, 81–97.

Moles, A. (1958/1968) *Information theory and esthetic perception*. Joel. E. Cohen (trans). Urbana, IL: University of Illinois Press.

Narmour, E. (1990) *The analysis and cognition of basic melodic structures: the implication-realization model*. Chicago, IL: University of Chicago Press.

Narmour, E. (1991) The top-down and bottom-up systems of musical implication: Building on Meyer's theory of emotional syntax. *Music Perception*, **9**, 1–26,

North, A.C. and Hargreaves, D.J. (1997) Experimental aesthetics and everyday music listening. In *The Social Psychology of Music*, (eds D.J. Hargreaves and A.C. North), pp. 84–103. Oxford: Oxford University Press.

Oram, N. and Cuddy, L.L. (1995) Responsiveness of Western adults to pitch-distributional information in melodic sequences. *Psychological Research/Psychologische Forschung*, **57**, 103–18.

Parncutt, R. and Cohen, A.J. (1995) Recognition of serial patterns in microtonal melodies. *Perception and Psychophysics*, **57**, 835–46.

Pavlov, I. (1928) *Lectures on conditioned reflexes: I*. Oxford: International. Republished, 1963.

Peretz, I. (1989) Determinants of clustering in music: An appraisal of task factors. *International Journal of Psychology*, **24**, 157–78.

Platt, J.R. (1961) Beauty: Pattern and change. In *Functions of varied experience*, (eds D. Fiske and S. Maddi), pp. 402–29. Homewood: Dorsey Press.

Pollack, I. (1952) The information of elementary auditory displays. I. *Journal of the Acoustical Society of America*, **24**, 745–49.

Pollack, I. (1953) The information of elementary auditory displays. II. *Journal of the Acoustical Society of America*, **25**, 765–9.

Razran, G. (1949) Attitudinal determinants of conditioning and of generalization of conditioning. *Journal of Experimental Psychology*, **39**, 820–9.

Rubin, D.C., Rahhal, T.A., and Poon, L.W. Things learned in early adulthood are remembered best. *Memory and Cognition*, **26**, 1998, 3–19.

Russell, P. (1997) Musical tastes and society. In *The Social Psychology of Music*, (eds D.J. Hargreaves and A.C. North), pp. 141–58. Oxford: Oxford University Press.

Schellenberg, E.G. (1996) Expectancy in melody: Tests of the implication-realization model. *Cognition*, **58**, 75–125.

Schmuckler, M. (1997) Expectancy effects in memory for melodies. *Canadian Journal of Experimental Psychology*, **51**, 292–306.

Seashore, C.E. (1938/1967) *Psychology of Music*. New York: McGraw-Hill, reprinted by Dover.

Serafine, M.L., Crowder, R.G., and Repp, B.H. (1984) Integration of melody and text in memory for songs. *Cognition*, **16**, 285–303.

Shannon, C.E. and Weaver, W. (1949) *The mathematical theory of communication*. Urbana, IL: University of Illinois Press.

Sloboda, J.A. (1985) *The musical mind: The cognitive psychology of music*. New York: Oxford University Press.

Steinberg, L., Dahl, R., Keating, D., Kupfer, D.J., Masten, A.S., and Pine, D. (in press). The study of developmental psychopathology in adolescence: integrating affective neuroscience with the study of context. In *Handbook of Developmental Psychopathology*, (ed. D. Cicchetti). New York: Wiley.

Sternberg, R.J. and Ben-Zeev, T. (2001) *Complex cognition: The psychology of human thought*. New York: Oxford University Press.

Stipp, H. (1990) Musical demographics. The strong impact of age on music preferences affects all kinds of businesses. *American Demographics*, August, 48–49 (cited by Russell, 1997).

Stumpf, C. (1883/1890) *Tonpsychologie* (Psychology of tone). *Vol 1*, 1883 /Vol 2, 1890 Leipzig: Hirzel.

Tarrant, M., North, A., and Hargreaves, D.J. (2002) Youth identity and music. In *Musical Identities*, (eds R.A.R. Macdonald, D.J. Hargreaves, and D. Miell), pp 151–62. Oxford: Oxford University Press.

Temperley, D. (2001) *The cognition of basic musical structures*. Cambridge, MA: MIT Press.

Thomas, L. (1979) On thinking about thinking. *The Medusa and the snail: More notes of a biology watcher* (pp. 151–4). New York: Viking.

Thompson, W.F., Cuddy, L.L., and Plaus, C. (1997) Expectancies generated by melodic intervals: Evaluation of principles of melodic implication in a melodyproduction task. *Perception and Psychophysics*, **59**, 1069–76.

Trehub, S.E. (1976). The discrimination of foreign speech contrasts by infants and adults. *Child Development*, **47**, 466–72.

Watson, J. (1913) Psychology as the behaviourist views it. *PsychologicalReview*, **20**, 158–77.

Watson, J.B. (1916) The place of conditional reflex in psychology. *Psychological Review*, **23**, 89–116.

Werker, J. and Tees, R. (1999) Developmental changes across childhood inperception of non-native speech sounds. *Canadian Journal of Psychology,* **37**, 278–86.

Wundt, W.M. (1874) *Grundzüge der Physiologischen Psychologie.* [Principles of Physiological Psychology] Leipzig: Engelmann.

Zillman, D. and Gan, S-l. (1997) Musical taste in adolescence. In *The Social Psychology of Music,* (eds D.J. Hargreaves and A.C. North), pp. 161–87. Oxford: Oxford University Press.

Chapter 5

From mimesis to catharsis: expression, perception, and induction of emotion in music

Patrik N. Juslin

Musical communication is often considered to be a transmission process through which meaning of some kind is conveyed from one person to another. Opinions vary drastically on the nature of the meaning, and on exactly 'who' or 'what' is doing the conveying. However, as pointed out by Meyer (1956) and Serafine (1980), the meaning–transmission idea is also evoked by formalists, who implicitly assume that there is some meaning to be received or 'decoded' by a listener. The question is: What does music communicate? Although this book provides a number of different answers to this question, probably the most common notion about what music communicates is emotion. Music is often referred to as 'the language of emotions' (e.g. Cooke 1959). This idea is not entirely accurate (there is not a semantics in music), but it does capture one important feature, namely that music is often seen as an effective means of expressing and inducing emotions:

> 'Nearly everyone enjoys listening to music. Why? Undoubtedly, because music moves the emotions. But this answer replaces one puzzle with two: how does music communicate emotions, and why do we enjoy having our emotions stirred in this way? No one knows...'
>
> (Johnson-Laird 1992, p. 13)

Johnson-Laird's final sentence is perhaps overly pessimistic. As we shall see later in this chapter, researchers are making *some* progress, at least, in explaining how music communicates emotions to listeners (see also Juslin and Sloboda 2001).

This chapter aims to provide a review of important theoretical concepts as well as empirical findings regarding musical emotions that may serve as a background to some of the following chapters of this volume, several of which touch upon emotional aspects of musical communication. Because it is sometimes hard to clearly distinguish instances of communication from instances of non-communication in regard to musical emotions – and because researchers often disagree about how emotional communication should be defined – I will deliberately cast a wide net on research on musical emotions that can help us understand musical communication. This will pave the way for a serious consideration of whether music really can be conceived of as a channel of emotional communication. The so-called 'transmission model' of music has been criticized by some authors (Swanwick 1985). This chapter might be construed as an attempt to convince a skeptic that there *is* a sense in which music communicates emotions to listeners – which is *not* to say that this is the sole or main value of music (Budd 1989).

The structure of this chapter is as follows: First, I critically examine the notion of music as a means of communication of emotion, and present some relevant evidence concerning this issue. Then, I provide a working definition of emotions and some conceptual distinctions for the study of musical emotion. Following that, I review mechanisms through which music may express and induce emotions, respectively. Finally, I consider various objections to music-as-communication and provide an agenda for future research. The discussion is generally limited to Western music, especially classical and popular music from the eighteenth century to present day.

Music as communication of emotion

Working definition of communication

Johnson-Laird (1992) offers a useful working definition of communication. First, he notes that communication is a matter of *causal influence*; that is, a communicator influences his or her recipient, one way or another (e.g. a musician influences the auditory impressions of a listener). However, Johnson-Laird notes that the concept of communication also calls for something more: a communicator has a *message* to transmit. Specifically, the communicator constructs an internal representation of some aspect of the world, such as an emotional state, and then – *intentionally* – carries out some symbolic behaviour that conveys the content of that representation. The recipient must first perceive this symbolic behaviour, and then recover from it an internal representation of the content it signifies. Like all symbolic behaviours, the communicative behaviour is arbitrary in at least one sense: different symbolic conventions could, in principle, have been used to convey the same contents. Yet, in any concrete instance of communication, the symbolic behaviour used may reflect natural principles, human conventions, or a combination of the two. The important thing is that there is a shared 'code' among senders and receivers (Shannon and Weaver 1949).

Communication in music

Application of the aforementioned definition of communication to music requires that we clarify the relationship between expression and communication. Figure 1 illustrates the 'chain' of musical communication as it is commonly conceived by music researchers, and may help us to compare various definitions of expression and communication. Moving from left to right, Fig. 5.1 shows (1) the composer's intention (e.g. the notation); (2) the performer's intention; (3) the acoustic features of the music; (4) the listener's perception of these features (involving both the detection of the features and the recognition of relevant patterns in them); and (5) the (possible) induction of mental states as an effect of this perception. Each of these aspects is, of course, embedded in a particular context, but the context is rarely modelled explicitly.

It is important to note that different definitions of expression and communication focus on different aspects. Particularly, they differ with regard to how many of these aspects are required in order for a particular instance to qualify as a case of 'expression' or 'communication'. It may seem natural to include *all* of the aspects in any definition of expression or communication, but this is seldom done explicitly, or in actual practice. More often, only sub-sets of the aspects are taken into account. The most extreme example is provided by researchers of expression in music performance, who often define 'expression' simply in terms of the large and small variations in timing, dynamics, timbre, and pitch that form the *microstructure* of a performance (e.g. Palmer 1997).

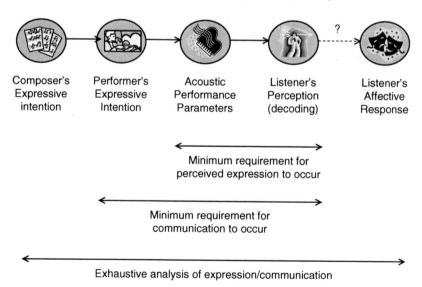

Composer's Expressive intention
Performer's Expressive Intention
Acoustic Performance Parameters
Listener's Perception (decoding)
Listener's Affective Response

Minimum requirement for perceived expression to occur

Minimum requirement for communication to occur

Exhaustive analysis of expression/communication

Fig. 5.1 Different aspects of the chain of musical communication of emotion.

This view implies that acoustic features alone are sufficient to define musical expression. This notion is problematic, however. Although musical expression originates in performers' and composers' behaviours, it is more appropriate to define expression from the listener's perspective: 'Expression's domain is the mind of the listener' (Kendall and Carterette 1990, p. 131).

In this chapter, *expression* refers to a set of perceptual qualities (e.g. structural, emotional, motional) that reflect psycho–physical relationships between 'objective' properties of the music, and 'subjective' – or, rather, objective but partly person-dependent – impressions of the listener. Expression does not reside solely in the acoustic properties of the music (different listeners *may* perceive the expression differently), nor does it reside solely in the mind of the listener (different listeners *usually* agree about the general nature of the expression in a piece of music). Expression depends on both of these factors, in ways that, although complex, can be modelled in a systematic fashion (see Juslin 2000). Our perception of expressive music reminds us, somehow, of the ways humans express their states of mind in real life; why would we otherwise use the term expression in the first place? We have a tendency to perceive *expressive form* even in inanimate objects. For instance, a tree may be sad-looking (e.g. Davies 1994). Sometimes, the perception of expressive music also evokes an *emotion* in the listener (he or she is 'moved'), though such a response is not *required* for a listener to hear the music as expressive (Davies 1994). Musical expression is often measured in terms of *listener agreement*: music is expressive of a certain quality to the extent that there is some level of agreement among listeners about the expression (presumably because there is something in the actual music that gives rise to similar listener impressions). Though studies of expression may well benefit from analyses of composers' or performers' intentions, perception of expression – as defined here – does not require that there is an expressive intention on the part of the composer or performer (Juslin 2003).

The concept of *musical communication* (of emotion for instance), in contrast, goes further: Communication, I propose, requires that there is both a composer's (or performer's) *intention* to express a specific concept and *recognition* of the same concept by a listener. The accuracy of the communication may be indexed in terms of the extent to which the composer (or performer) and the listener agree about the expression of the music: is the expression perceived as intended? That a definition of communication should include the composer's intention, the performer's intention, the acoustic features of the music, and the listener's perception is, perhaps, not controversial. The critical question is whether communication requires that the music, in addition, *induces* emotions in the listener (cf. Fig. 5.1). A review of the literature reveals that different authors have used the concept of emotional communication differently.

Some authors view communication in terms of perception (e.g. Juslin 1997a; Thompson and Robitaille 1992); that is, emotions are expressed by musicians and perceived by listeners – induction is 'optional'. Other authors limit the concept to instances where the emotion expressed is also *induced* in the listener. Both uses of the term could be legitimate, depending on the circumstances. Therefore, in this chapter, I shall review empirical findings regarding both perception and induction of emotions.

Does music communicate emotions?

Although some readers might find it obvious that music communicates emotions, this notion has been questioned by certain authors (Hanslick 1854/1986). On what basis can we really claim that music involves emotional communication? A natural point of departure is to consult listeners and musicians. Studies of popular music have revealed that listeners emphasize the role of music-as-communication: 'Popular musicians are loved, and even worshipped, not only for their abilities to write songs and perform them publicly, but for their ability to "speak" to their audiences. Even an artist whose only contact with the audience is through the sales of millions of compact discs and tapes communicates "personally" with each listener' (Lull 1992, p. 3). Such an impression is confirmed by recent findings from a questionnaire study featuring 141 listeners, aged 17–74, who responded to various questions about musical expression, communication, and emotion (Juslin and Laukka 2004). The majority of listeners (>67 per cent) reported (a) that they experience that music (or musicians) communicates with them, and (b) that music communicates emotions (as indicated by their own free responses to an open-ended question). All of the listeners believed that music can express emotions (as compared to, for instance, 51 per cent for 'personality characteristics') and 76 per cent of the listeners claimed that music expresses emotions 'often'.

Similarly, a questionnaire study featuring 135 expert musicians from three countries (England, Italy, Sweden) revealed that the majority of the musicians defined expression mainly in terms of 'communicating emotions' and 'playing with feeling' – as indicated by their own free responses (Lindström *et al.* 2003). When directly asked about whether music expresses emotions, 99 per cent of the musicians confirmed that this is the case. Moreover, 83 per cent of the musicians claimed that they try to express specific emotions in their musical performances 'always' or 'often'. These results are confirmed and extended in recent research by Minassian *et al.* (2003). They conducted a questionnaire study featuring 53 expert performers of classical music, and explored which factors were statistically associated with an optimal performance. Performances judged as optimal tended to be those where the performer (a) had a clear intention to communicate (usually an emotional message), (b) was emotionally engaged with the music, and (c) believed the message had been 'received' by the audience. Finally, an interview study by Burland and Davidson (2004) showed that performers in pursuit of a professional performing career were more inclined to think of music as a vehicle for communication than were performers in pursuit of a non-music career.

Numerous biographies and interviews with performers (both classical and popular) confirm that they often conceive of musical expression in terms of emotions and communication (Boyd and George-Warren 1992; Carreras 1991; Denski 1992; Menuhin 1996; King 1996; Persson 2001; Schumacher 1995). Apart from the fact that listeners and musicians appear to conceive of music in terms of emotional communication, there is also evidence that music really *can* communicate emotions to listeners. The following sections will be devoted to reviewing this evidence.

Key distinctions in musical emotion

The study of musical emotion has generally suffered from conceptual confusion. To enhance the cumulativeness of research efforts, and to promote fruitful debate, it may be heuristic to adopt a number of conceptual distinctions. These distinctions may help researchers to specify in a much more precise fashion *what* they are investigating and *how*. First, we need a working definition of emotion. There are many different ways to define emotions, but most emotion researchers would probably agree that emotions can be seen as relatively brief and intense reactions to goal-relevant changes in the environment that consist of many *sub-components* (Oatley and Jenkins 1996, Ch. 4):

- ◆ cognitive appraisal (e.g. you appraise the situation as 'dangerous')
- ◆ subjective feeling (e.g. you feel afraid)
- ◆ physiological arousal (e.g. your heart starts pounding)
- ◆ emotional expression (e.g. you scream and call out for help)
- ◆ action tendency (e.g. you are strongly inclined to run away)
- ◆ emotion regulation (e.g. you try to calm yourself)

Different researchers of musical emotion focus on different components, as these enter into the musical communication process. For instance, some focus on the emotional expression of the performance; others focus on the cognitive appraisal of the music that induces an emotion, or on how the induced emotion influences physiological measures; still others focus on how music may be used to regulate emotions. It is important to note that what counts for one emotion component, theoretically and empirically speaking, does not necessarily hold for another component.

Researchers disagree as to whether emotions are best conceptualized as *categories* (Ekman 1999), *dimensions* (Russell 1980), or *prototypes* (Shaver *et al.* 1987). Different theories of emotion have been adopted in studies of music, and it is fair to say that there is currently no theoretical paradigm that dominates studies of emotion in music. Most researchers have not explicitly adopted one or the other of these approaches, but their implicit orientation can still be inferred from the way in which they have operationalized listener responses. For example, the researcher who asks the participants to respond by choosing an emotion from a list of emotion labels is implicitly assuming that there are discrete emotion categories.

There are also different *sources* of emotion in music (Sloboda and Juslin 2001); that is, there are different 'psychological mechanisms' that may give rise to emotional responses through their interactions with music (see pp. 102–4 for some examples). Note that what counts for one particular source of emotion may not count for another source, and different theories may be required to explain each source. Furthermore, different sources of emotion may involve and be affected by a number of *causal variables*. Indeed, a serious problem is the manifold determinants of musical emotions. Gutheil (1952, Appendix A) listed, in a systematic fashion, all the variables that might potentially influence musical emotions, and this list may be unprecedented to this day. Given this complexity – later more concisely formulated as *an interaction between the music, the person, and the situation* (e.g. Jørgensen 1988; see also Gabrielsson 2001) – it is important that researchers are careful in how they select causal variables to include in their study.

Finally, it is important to make a distinction between *perception* and *induction* of emotions. We may simply perceive emotions in the music, or we may actually feel emotions in response to the music. This distinction, known since ancient Greece, is often but not always made in modern research. It is crucial to make this distinction for three reasons. First, the underlying mechanisms may be very different depending on the process involved. Second, measuring induced emotion is more difficult than measuring perceived emotion, and the methods must be adapted accordingly. Third, the types of emotions typically expressed and perceived in music could be rather different from the set of emotions typically induced by music.

Mechanisms of musical communication of emotion

Human communication commonly begins and ends with conscious messages. However, the intervening mental processes are almost completely unconscious (Johnson-Laird 1992). Indeed, the fact that many of the processes that underlie musical communication of emotion are implicit helps to 'mystify' the nature of musical expression to musicians (e.g. Denski 1992). However, a large number of studies have studied the mechanisms by which music communicates emotions to listeners. In the following overview, I adopt the previously noted distinction between perception and induction of emotion. This division must not be taken to imply that the two processes never occur together. On the contrary, they *do* co-occur, although perhaps not always in the simple one-to-one relationship (e.g. 'perception of sadness induces sadness') one may be tempted to believe.

Expression and perception of emotion

Can music express specific emotions? Emotion perception is relatively easy to measure and is a 'cognitive' process in the sense that it may well proceed without any emotional involvement on the part of the listener. In principle, a listener might perceive *any* emotion in a piece of music, and in a sense, it may be inappropriate to claim that the listener is 'wrong'. However, researchers are usually interested in cases where emotions in music are perceived *similarly* by many listeners (or perceived in the way *intended* by a composer or a performer), perhaps because such common impressions relate strongly to the nature of the music. Can music express various emotions in this way? This issue has been examined in terms of (a) *listener agreement* (where the music is said to express a particular emotion 'reliably' when there is a certain level of agreement among listeners about what the music expresses) and (b) *accuracy* (which refers to listeners' 'correct' recognition of emotional expression according to some 'independent criterion' such as the composer's or the performer's intention). The latter index corresponds better to the established meaning of the word communication, although most previous research has relied on measures of agreement, because it is usually difficult to obtain reliable indices of composers' expressive intentions. It can be argued that listener agreement is a necessary but not sufficient condition for communication to occur, in that a performer can hardly be described as successful in communicating a particular emotion to a group of listeners if the listeners totally disagree about the emotion expressed. On the other hand, even if there *is* listener agreement, listeners' judgements may not correspond with the performer's expressive intention, in which case the communicative process is still unsuccessful.

The results from over a hundred studies have suggested that listeners are generally consistent in their judgements of emotional expression in music. That is, listeners' judgements are systematic and reliable, and can thus be predicted with reasonable accuracy. However, there is usually high agreement among listeners about the *broad* emotional category expressed by the music, but less agreement concerning the nuances *within* this category (Campbell 1942; Downey 1897; Juslin 1997*c*). Hence, the precision with which music can convey different emotions is clearly limited. Listeners' agreement about the perceived expression varies depending on many factors (e.g. the piece of music, the musical style, the response format, the procedure), yet perception of emotions in music is robust in that listener judgements are only marginally affected by musical training, age, and gender of the listener (e.g. Gabrielsson and Juslin 2003). That musical training is not required to express (Yamasaki 2002) or recognize (Juslin 1997*a*) emotions in music suggests that general mechanisms of perception of emotion are involved – a hypothesis that is supported by the finding that abilities to decode emotions in music are correlated with measures of *emotional intelligence* (Resnicow *et al.* 2004).

Most studies have focused on discrete emotions. Attempts to reduce perceived emotions to a smaller number of dimensions have typically yielded dimensions corresponding to those obtained in other domains of emotion, such as *activation*, *valence*, and *potency* (Kleinen 1968; Nielzén and Cesarec 1981; Wedin 1972), but also some dimensions that probably are more typical for music (e.g. *solemnity*), and that might reflect a distinction between 'serious' and 'popular' music in the music excerpts used. Much of music's expressiveness lies in the *changes* in musical features over time, and a dimensional approach may be particularly suitable for describing gradual movements of the musical expression in the 'affective space'. Thus, there has recently been some progress in tracing listeners' perception of emotions in music over time, using 'continuous response formats' (Schubert 1999; Sloboda and Lehmann 2001). One interesting development is the use of synthetic facial expressions to display changes in perceived valence and activation (Schubert 2004).

However, while generally attractive, two-dimensional models of perception of emotion have certain problems associated with them. One such problem is that positive and negative affect may be two, partly independent dimensions (Cacioppo and Gardner 1999). If this is true, certain states cannot be properly represented by a two-dimensional space with a single 'valence' dimension. In addition, two dimensions may not adequately differentiate some emotions such as anger and fear that occupy a similar position in the affective space, but that really sound and feel very differently with respect to music. Therefore, findings obtained with continuous response formats need to be corroborated using other response formats (for an example, see Schubert 1999).

Knowledge gained from experimental studies of emotional expression is complemented by information gained from more 'impressionistic' studies of expression, for example, in sociology (Harris and Sandresky 1985; Middleton 1990), musicology (Cook and Dibben 2001), philosophy (Davies 1994), and psychoanalysis (Noy 1993). Freed from the constraints of operationalization (i.e. the translation of theoretical concepts into concretely defined measures) researchers are able to address more subtle and complex aspects of musical expression, although obviously with more uncertainty regarding the underlying causal relationships.

That listeners tend to agree about the emotional expression in music is one thing, but to what extent can music composers and performers actually *communicate* specific emotions to listeners? Few studies have explicitly investigated the extent to which composers can communicate specific emotions to listeners. However, a rare exception is the study by Thompson and Robitaille (1992). They asked five highly experienced musicians to compose short melodies that should convey six emotions: joy, sorrow, excitement, dullness, anger, and peace. They were required to rely on such information (pitch, temporal and loudness information) that is contained in musical scores. Deadpan performances of the resulting compositions by a computer sequencer were played to fourteen listeners moderately trained in music. They successfully recognized the intended emotions in the pieces. Thus, it would seem that music composers can really convey *some* emotions reliably.

Several studies have investigated the extent to which *performers* can communicate emotions to listeners. These studies have provided fairly precise estimates of the communication accuracy. In the most extensive review of emotional expression in music performance to date (see Juslin and Laukka 2003) including 41 studies, a meta-analysis of the communication accuracy showed that professional performers are able to communicate five emotions (happiness, anger, sadness, fear, tenderness) to listeners with an accuracy approximately as high as in facial and vocal expression of emotions. The overall decoding accuracy was equivalent to a raw accuracy score of $p_c = .70$ in a forced-choice task with five response alternatives (i.e. the mean number of emotions included in studies thus far). In accordance with what has been found in studies that use listener agreement as the dependent variable (as mentioned earlier), the evidence from performance research indicates that the communication process operates in terms of broad emotion categories, whereas finer distinctions within these categories are difficult to communicate reliably without additional context provided by, for instance, lyrics, program notes, or visual impressions.

What are the reasons for music's inability to communicate more specific emotions reliably? There are, in fact, several reasons: first of all, music's ability to communicate emotions is heavily dependent on its similarity to other forms of non-verbal communication and the kinds of emotions that are possible to communicate through *those* channels (cf. Clynes 1977; Davies 1994; Juslin 1997a); for instance, the patterns of communication accuracy for various basic emotions in music seem to closely mirror those of emotional speech (Juslin and Laukka 2003). Secondly, the musical features involved in communication of emotions are only *probabilistically* related to the emotions and are partly *redundant* (e.g. Juslin 2001), which limits the complexity of the information that can be conveyed (Shannon and Weaver 1949). Finally, because precision of communication is not the only criterion by which we value music, communicative reliability is frequently compromised for the sake of other virtues of music, such as beauty of form. Thus, for instance, emotion may be only one of many components of expression in music performance (Juslin 2003; Juslin *et al.* 2002).

How does music express different emotions? There are numerous features of music that have been reported to be suggestive of discrete emotions. Table 5.1 shows an updated summary of these features for the most commonly studied emotions. As can be seen in Table 5.1, the features include tempo, mode, harmony, tonality, pitch, micro-intonation, contour, interval, rhythm, sound level, timbre, timing, articulation, accents on specific notes, tone attacks and decays, and vibrato. Note that there are *different configurations of musical features for different emotions* as predicted by a categorical approach to emotion. Note also that the same feature can be used in a similar manner in more than just one emotional expression (e.g. fast tempo is used in both anger and happiness). Hence, each feature is neither necessary nor sufficient, but the larger the number of features used, the more reliable the communication (e.g. Juslin 2001). The relationships between features and emotions are only *probabilistic* (i.e. uncertain) and are therefore best thought of as correlational, as captured by the *Lens Model* (Juslin 1995). Most of the investigated features are rather simple, whereas more complex features (e.g. harmonic progression, melody, musical form) remain to be thoroughly investigated in future research. In addition to the overall features described in Table 5.1, there are several kinds of *musical ornaments* (e.g. the trill, the appoggiatura) that may be used to express emotions, as discussed in many treatises on interpretation (e.g. Bach 1778/1985) and as also demonstrated in recent research (Timmers and Ashley 2004).

What are the *origins* of these relationships between musical features and different emotions? There is no simple answer to this question, but the relationships most likely have several origins. Performance features such as tempo, loudness, and timbre, many of which music has in common with the non-verbal aspects of speech (Juslin and Laukka 2001), may largely reflect a speech code. We recently made a systematic comparison of 104 studies of emotional speech and 41 studies of emotion in music performance (Juslin and Laukka 2003). Results showed among other things that performers use primarily the same emotion-specific patterns of acoustic parameters that are used in emotional speech (as originally argued by Spencer 1857). This is one example of cross-modal similarities in expressive form between different non-verbal communication channels, which has been suggested by several authors (e.g. Clynes 1977; human movement is

Table 5.1 Summary of musical features correlated with discrete emotions in musical expression

Emotion	Musical features
Happiness	fast tempo, small tempo variability, major mode, simple and consonant harmony, medium-high sound level, small sound level variability, high pitch, much pitch variability, wide pitch range, ascending pitch, perfect 4th and 5th intervals, rising micro intonation, raised singer's formant, staccato articulation, large articulation variability, smooth and fluent rhythm, bright timbre, fast tone attacks, small timing variability, sharp contrasts between 'long' and 'short' notes, medium-fast vibrato rate, medium vibrato extent, micro-structural regularity
Sadness	slow tempo, minor mode, dissonance, low sound level, moderate sound level variability, low pitch, narrow pitch range, descending pitch, 'flat' (or falling) intonation, small intervals (e.g. minor 2nd), lowered singer's formant, legato articulation, small articulation variability, dull timbre, slow tone attacks, large timing variability (e.g. rubato), soft contrasts between 'long' and 'short' notes, pauses, slow vibrato, small vibrato extent, ritardando, micro-structural irregularity
Anger	fast tempo, small tempo variability, minor mode, atonality, dissonance, high sound level, small loudness variability, high pitch, small pitch variability, ascending pitch, major 7th and augmented 4th intervals, raised singer's formant, staccato articulation, moderate articulation variability, complex rhythm, sudden rhythmic changes (e.g. syncopations), sharp timbre, spectral noise, fast tone attacks/decays, small timing variability, accents on tonally unstable notes, sharp contrasts between 'long' and 'short' notes, accelerando, medium-fast vibrato rate, large vibrato extent, micro-structural irregularity
Fear	fast tempo, large tempo variability, minor mode, dissonance, low sound level, large sound level variability, rapid changes in sound level, high pitch, ascending pitch, wide pitch range, large pitch contrasts, staccato articulation, large articulation variability, jerky rhythms, soft timbre, very large timing variability, pauses, soft tone attacks, fast vibrato rate, small vibrato extent, micro-structural irregularity
Tenderness	slow tempo, major mode, consonance, medium-low sound level, small sound level variability, low pitch, fairly narrow pitch range, lowered singer's formant, legato articulation, small articulation variability, slow tone attacks, soft timbre, moderate timing variability, soft contrasts between long and short notes, accents on tonally stable notes, medium fast vibrato, small vibrato extent, micro-structural regularity

Note. Shown are the most common findings in the literature. For further details, see Gabrielsson and Juslin (2003), Juslin and Laukka (2003), and Juslin and Lindström (2003).

another candidate for explaining musical expressiveness, e.g. Davies 1994). Speech prosody may also help to explain some of the emotional connotations associated with melodic contours (e.g. Fónagy and Magdics 1963; Papoušek 1996), which seem to play an important role in the early interactions of infants and caregivers. Various other aspects of composed musical structure are not as easily explained. However, features of a piece of music that are usually indicated in the notation of the piece (e.g. harmony, tonality, melodic progression) are likely to reflect to a larger extent characteristics of music as a human art form that follows its own intrinsic rules and that varies from one culture to another. Some of the effects of composer-features (e.g. consonance/dissonance) may originate in psycho-physical relations between acoustic properties and basic perceptual mechanisms (Cooke 1959), but most probably reflect cultural conventions developed over the long course of music's history, and are in that sense more or less 'arbitrary'. At this stage of the historical development, these alternative but not mutually exclusive explanations are not easily teased apart.

Do we have sufficient knowledge about emotional expression in music to be able to actually model the communication process mathematically? Indeed, there have been successful attempts at *quantifying* various aspects of the emotional communication process, using a modified version of Brunswik's *Lens Model* (Juslin 1995, 2000). This model can help us understand many crucial issues concerning expression of emotion in music. One important goal in this domain is to better understand how composed and performed cues *interact* in expression of emotion (Juslin 1998, p. 50). The problem, of course, is the enormous complexity: there are so many musical features and their potential interactions to consider (see Table 5.1). Hevner's (1935, 1936) pioneering work was important, though she lacked a number of modern research tools, such as computer synthesis and certain multivariate techniques, that may be needed to make real progress. How can we approach the complex interplay between musical features in a practically feasible way?

We have recently proposed an *Expanded Lens Model* (Juslin and Lindström 2003; Fig. 5.2). The Lens Model was originally applied only to performance features (Juslin 2000). However, in the expanded version, both composer cues and performance cues are included to make it possible to explore their relative contributions. In addition, important interactions between performer and composition cues are included as predictors in the model. The goal is also to be able to model the emotion judgements of individual listeners. As in our previous research (Juslin 1997b, 2000), we are using a statistical approach based on multiple regression analysis. Contrary to popular belief, it is actually possible to investigate the relative contributions of interactions between predictors within the framework of multiple regression analysis. Recent studies

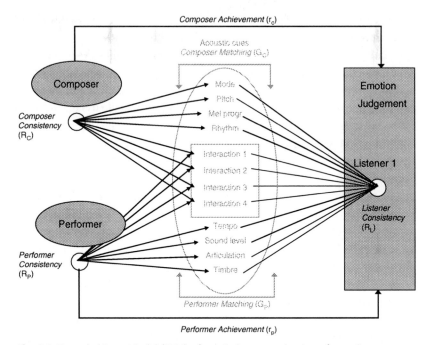

Fig. 5.2 Extended Lens Model (ELM) of musical communication of emotions. (Adapted from Juslin and Lindström 2003)

based on this framework, using both analysis and synthesis (e.g. Juslin and Lindström 2003), indicated that a large amount of the variance in listeners' emotion ratings could be explained by a linear combination of the main effects alone (typically around 75–85 per cent). Furthermore, results indicated that interactions between composed and performed features made small (but not negligible) contributions to the predictive power. Thus, an important lesson from this investigation was that, although there *are* interactions among musical features, we should not overstate their importance; they may be fewer and smaller than previously believed. (Further evidence that jugements of affective qualities of music reflect mainly an additive combination of musical features were reported by Makris and Mullet 2003.)

Much work remains to be done in order to fully understand musical expression, but it can be concluded that people can express and perceive different emotions in music (cf. Fig. 5.1).

Induction of emotion

Does music induce emotions in listeners? It might appear obvious from everyday experience that music induces emotions in listeners. Anecdotal evidence on the emotional powers of music is certainly abundant; yet we know better than to accept such reports at face value. Is there scientific evidence supporting the idea that music can induce emotions? Emotions are inferred on the basis of three kinds of evidence: (a) *self-report*, (b) *expressive behaviour*, and (c) *physiological reaction*. Empirical evidence of emotional reactions to music comes from several strands of research which are summarized in Table 5.2.

Table 5.2 Examples of evidence of emotional reactions to music from various strands of research.

Type of research	Finding
Experiments	Music produces differentiated effects on self-report, physiology, and behaviour (Davis and Thaut 1989; Kallinen 2004; Krumhansl 1997; Nyklíček *et al.* 1997; Panksepp, 1995; Pigniatello *et al.* 1989; Pike 1972; Vaitl *et al.* 1993; Waterman, 1996; Västfjäll, 2002).
Qualitative interviews	Listeners employ music to regulate, enhance, and change qualities and levels of emotion. They show considerable awareness about the music they need to hear in different situations to induce particular emotions (DeNora 2001; Gomart and Hennion 1999).
Brain imaging and EEG	Listeners' responses to music involve subcortical and cortical regions of the brain that are known from previous research to be involved in emotional reactions (Altenmüller *et al.* 2002; Blood and Zatorre 2001; Peretz 2001; Schmidt and Trainor 2001).
Field studies	Music influences consumer behaviour, helping, and interpersonal attraction and conflict (Fried and Berkowitz 1979; Honeycutt and Eidenmüller 2001; May and Hamilton 1980; North and Hargreaves 1997*a*; North *et al.* 2004).
Questionnaires	Music serves various emotional functions in everyday life: to change moods; to release emotions; as a source of comfort; to match current mood; as a source of enjoyment; to relieve stress, etc. (Behne 1997; Juslin and Laukka 2004; Panzarella 1980; Roe 1985; Sloboda 1991; Sloboda and O'Neill 2001; Zillman and Gan 1997; Wells 1990).
Music therapy	Music facilitates the expression, identification, and experience of emotions; improves the control of one's own emotional behaviour; helps to 'trigger' emotionally-laden memories of past events; and helps to diagnose patients' psychiatric conditions (Thaut 1990).
Ethnographic research	Emotional response to music is a 'universal' phenomenon, typically involving feelings of happiness and arousal, although the particular forms of engaging with music may differ from one culture to another (Becker 2001; Blacking 1973).

While each source of evidence is uncertain, the *combined* evidence is quite compelling. It should be noted, however, that few studies so far have investigated induction of emotion as part of a musical communication process (Fig. 5.1).

Which emotions does music typically evoke? If we accept the fact that music can induce real emotions in listeners, one might then ask whether the emotions induced by music include the full range of human emotions. In principle, depending on the particular situation, the person listening, and the music, it would indeed seem possible that music could arouse just about *any* emotion that can be felt in other realms of human life. A more interesting question, perhaps, is which emotions music *usually* induces in listeners. As we will see, the set of emotions typically *induced* by music may be a somewhat different set of emotions than that typically *expressed* by music – for natural reasons. The emotions that are most easy to express and perceive in music are the basic emotions (e.g. happiness, sadness, anger, fear, love/tenderness) that have distinct expressive characteristics in *other* non-verbal communication channels; notably, the non-verbal aspects of speech and human body movement (see Atkinson *et al.* 2004; Juslin and Laukka 2003). Emotions *induced* by music, on the other hand, are more determined by the nature of the appraisal of the musical event and the specific reasons for engaging with the music in a particular situation. Perhaps the most frequently cited reason for listening to music is *enjoyment*. Thus, we would expect joy to be one of the most frequently felt emotions in relation to music, which – as we shall see – may indeed be the case.

There is little research on the 'epidemiological' aspects of musical emotions (i.e. how often people experience different emotions to music under different circumstances). However, there is some preliminary evidence from questionnaire studies. Table 5.3 shows the emotions reported to be felt most frequently in response to music in a recent study of 141 music listeners (aged 17–74) by Juslin and Laukka (2004). These findings are interesting for several reasons. First, it is quite clear that positive emotions (e.g. happy, relaxed, moved) dominate among the most commonly evoked emotions. This is what we should expect. After all, people can usually (although far from always) exercise choice over what music to listen to. Given this choice, people will tend to prefer to listen to music that they like and that makes them 'feel good'. Hence, it should come as no surprise that positive emotions are most common in musical experiences (see also Becker 2001; Gabrielsson 2001; Sloboda and O'Neill 2001), whereas this may *not* be the case in 'everyday life' (e.g. Oatley and Duncan 1994). Secondly, the results in Table 5.3 clearly indicate that music *does* induce 'basic emotions' in listeners (contrary to some claims in the literature; Scherer 2003), although perhaps more often happiness and sadness than anger and fear (fortunately!).

Table 5.3 Preliminary evidence on the relative frequency of felt emotions in response to music, as estimated by listeners (based on Juslin and Laukka 2004). Note: Emotions are listed from the most commonly experienced to the least commonly experienced ($N = 141$).

1. Happy*	23. Empathic
2. Relaxed*	24. Proud
3. Calm*	25. Spiritual
4. Moved	26. Curious
5. Nostalgic	27. Relieved
6. Pleasurable*	28. Bored
7. Loving*	29. Indifferent
8. Sad*	30. Frustrated*
9. Longing*	31. Tense*
10. Tender	32. Disappointed*
11. Amused	33. Surprised*
12. Hopeful	34. Honoured*
13. Enchanted	35. Regretful
14. Expectant*	36. Contemptuous
15. Solemn*	37. Confused*
16. Interested	38. Anxious*
17. Admiring	39. Afraid*
18. Angry*	40. Jealous
19. Ecstatic*	41. Disgusted
20. Lonely	42. Guilty
21. Content*	43. Shameful*
22. Desiring	44. Humiliated

* These emotions were mentioned in free descriptions of strong experiences of music (SEM), as reported by Gabrielsson (2001, Table 19.2).

Evidence on what emotions music induces also comes from Gabrielsson's studies of strong experiences of music (SEM), which involved hundreds of extensive, retrospective verbal reports from listeners on their most profound musical experiences. Gabrielsson (2001) notes that 'in the reports, we find numerous examples of so-called "basic" emotions' (p. 446). He also notes, with respect to the question of whether there are emotions that music does *not* induce, that 'too hasty exclusions should be avoided' (p. 446). However, his results also suggest that positive emotions dominate in SEM. Those emotions in Table 5.3 that were mentioned in Gabrielsson's SEM reports are indicated with asterisks (based on Gabrielsson 2001, Table 19.2). Thus, it appears that some emotions are more commonly induced by music than others. Perhaps researchers should actually accommodate to this fact in regard to how they measure emotion? Indeed, some researchers have argued that we should develop specific rating scales for induced musical emotions. For examples of such scales, see Asmus (1985), Bartel (1992), and Juslin and Laukka (2004).

How, exactly, do musical events induce emotions in listeners? This problem is still puzzling to researchers. One problem appears to be that the conditions of emotion-elicitation in music are different from those in real life. In the paradigmatic case, an emotion is aroused when an event is appraised as having the capacity to influence the goals of the perceiver somehow (Oatley 1992). Because music has no direct capacity to further or block goals, a challenge for music researchers is to provide an alternative, but plausible, account of how music can arouse emotions (Sloboda and Juslin 2001). A number of different theoretical mechanisms have been proposed to explain how music may arouse emotions, including (but not limited to) the following ones:

- *Musical Expectancy.* Meyer's (1956) groundbreaking book on how musical expectations are created, maintained, confirmed, or disrupted offers one fruitful solution to the problem of the 'formal object' of musical emotions ('What is musical emotion about?'): Emotions to music are induced when our schematic expectations are interrupted. Research by Kraehenbuehl and Coons (1959) suggests that many listeners prefer places in musical patterns where their expectations are confirmed rather than places where they are interrupted. This can help to explain the wide-spread rejection of so-called 'contemporary music', which has a tendency to disrupt rather than confirm almost any melodic expectancy of the average listener. Meyer (1956) himself acknowledged that mere arousal through interruption of expectancies has little value. To have any aesthetic meaning, the arousal or tension must be followed by a satisfying *resolution* of the tension. While influential and respected, Meyer's theory has not actually stimulated much research, presumably because of the problems in testing the theory. A specific piece of music may produce many different musical expectations at different levels of the music (and these expectations may be different for different listeners), wherefore it is hard to understand or predict exactly what the listener is reacting to. For recent models of expectancy, see Eerola (2003), Hellmuth Margulis (2003), and Rozin (2000).

- *Mood Contagion.* There is evidence that people may easily 'catch' the emotions of others when seeing their facial expressions or hearing their vocal expressions, perhaps through primitive 'motor mimicry' (e.g. Hatfield *et al.* 1994;

Neumann and Strack 2000). Because music often features expressive acoustical patterns that are similar to those in emotional speech, it has been hypothesized that we get aroused by the voice-like aspects of music through a process in which a neural module reacts quickly and automatically to certain stimulus features, which leads us to 'mimic' the perceived emotion internally (Juslin and Laukka 2003, pp. 802–3).

- *Arousal Potential.* We do not only react to the emotion-specific patterns of acoustic cues in pieces of music (as noted earlier), we also react to the inherent 'arousal potential' of more general stimulus characteristics, such as its complexity, ambiguity, and familiarity. Part of our emotional responses could reflect our attempt to 'make sense' of the information in the music. According to Berlyne's (1971) influential theory listeners will tend to prefer music that gives them an optimum level of arousal: If the arousal potential of the music is too high, listeners will reject the music; if the arousal potential is too low, listeners will also reject the music. Hence, Berlyne hypothesized that listeners' preferences are related to arousal (or some aspect of it, e.g. perceived complexity) in the form of an inverted U-shaped curve. Berlyne's theory has received empirical support (e.g. North and Hargreaves 1997*c*), and has been especially influential in accounts of music *liking* and *preference*. It is less clear how his theory could account for the induction of discrete emotions by music (but for some interesting ideas, see North and Hargreaves 1997*b*). One particular feature of the musical stimulus that can explain many emotional responses is its perceived *beauty* (see, e.g. Gabrielsson 2001, p. 447). Unfortunately, there is no thorough theory of musical beauty that can guide work in this area.

- *Associations.* Emotions to music often reflect personal and idiosyncratic associations based on arbitrary and contingent relationships between the music experienced and various non-musical factors related to emotion (what Davies 1978, refers to as the 'Darling, they're playing our tune' phenomenon). Associative responses to music involve 'primitive' learning mechanisms (such as conditioning) that are not available to conscious introspection, but the responses typically evoke emotionally laden memories of specific places, events, or individuals (Gabrielsson 2001). In fact, research indicates that listeners often use music as 'a reminder of valued past events' (Sloboda and O'Neill 2001), and that specific pieces of music may be strongly associated with particular time periods of an individual's life (e.g. Schulkind *et al.* 1999). Hence, nostalgia may be one of the more commonly felt emotions in regard to music (Juslin and Laukka 2004).

- *Mental Imagery.* Music can be highly effective in stimulating mental imagery. The images may not necessarily be about the music (or the musicians), but could be about anything. Still, the music may be important in *shaping* the images. Guided imagery in music (GIM) is an established method in music therapy (Bonny and Savary 1973), where 'the traveller' is invited to 'share' his or her images as they are experienced in real time during a programmed music sequence. Emotions experienced are presumably the result of an interaction between the structure of the music and the structure of the images. Also in non-clinical settings, mental imagery may be an effective means to enhance emotional responses to music, both for listeners (Band *et al.* 2001–02) and musicians (Persson 2001).

Unfortunately most theories of musically induced emotion have not actually been thoroughly tested yet. However, one thing appears certain: there is no *single* theoretical mechanism that can account for *all* instances of musically induced emotion. Hence, Juslin (2004) recently proposed a multi-component model of musical emotions, featuring a hierarchy of psychological mechanisms at different levels of processing – each with its own evolutionary history and characteristics. This model leads to a number of predictions that could guide future research. A novel research project, *Appraisal in Music and Emotion (AMUSE)*, is currently testing the model using a combination of field and laboratory studies.

In sum, evidence indicates that music does not only express emotions that are recognized by listeners, it does also occasionally induce emotions in listeners (cf. Fig. 5.1).

Discussion

Objections to music-as-communication

It can be concluded from the previous review that there really is a sense in which music can be regarded as a means of musical communication. Performers and listeners actually *do* think of music as communication of emotion (perhaps particularly in popular music), and composers and performers actually *can* communicate discrete emotions to listeners, although there are definitive limitations on what music can communicate reliably. Thus, the communicative aspect of music is something that cannot be denied. Even so, the transmission model of music has been described as 'old-fashioned' (Serafine 1980) and 'naive' (Swanwick 1985), as a 'Romantic notion' of music (Budd 1989). Why has the transmission model of music so often been dismissed? Goehr (1992) notes that:

'As soon as we talk about music as communication, we imply a topography and arising from it a politics … The politics is played out between the sometimes complementary and sometimes conflicting concerns of [composers, performers, and listeners]

... Should the entire process be regarded as the recreation of the composer's original intention? ... Or then again is music really a performing art? ... Or again, should not everything be evaluated from the point of view of the recipient? After all it is he who pays!' (p. 125)

Indeed, the question of music's value seems to be a key issue (cf. Budd 1989). Music may communicate emotions. However, from this we must not conclude that the value of music resides only, or even primarily, in its emotional-communicative functions. Music is not merely a tool for communication of emotion, since 'Art can exist without the need to communicate anything at all' (Goehr 1992, p. 131). This is a fascinating aspect of some human communications: the symbols *themselves* rather than their interpretation may come to be the important part of the message (e.g. Johnson-Laird 1992). It is reasonable to assume that music developed from a means of emotion sharing and communication to 'an art form in its own right' (Juslin and Laukka 2003). Objections to music-as-communication often centre around the problem of how to do music justice as an art form, which is a legitimate concern. But the solution is not to deny music-as-communication, but rather to investigate the topic better (see the following section).

Another objection to music-as-communication involves its possible consequences for music teaching. Serafine (1980) argues that the transmission model of music has had a negative impact on music education by leading to an over-emphasis on passive-receptive skills (partly reflecting a research focus on perceptual processes) at the expense of more active skills, such as composition. Although it could be true that music education has over-emphasized skills related to perception, it should be noted that the transmission model actually implies an *equal* focus on 'active' processes (composition, performance) and 'passive' processes (listening) (see, e.g. Fig. 5.2). Thus, it may be premature to blame the transmission model for the current state of affairs in music education, which more likely reflects the fact that it is easier to study perception than it is to study skills like composition and performance (Sloboda 1994). In my estimation, the transmission model could have a positive influence on music education. Goehr (1992) observes that 'most performers and listeners still do consider music in terms of its affects', but that 'academic attention is principally focused upon problems of structure' (p. 128). The transmission model could help to counter this imbalance by focusing more on the *meaning* communicated by music – its contents. Such a focus would be more compatible with how musicians conceive of music (Persson 2001). Musicians as well as listeners relate to music in highly *personal* ways, and there is a strong *social* dimension in how we respond to music. It seems only reasonable that music education should accommodate to this fact in order to better reflect the essence of human music making. It is thus reassuring to note that the transmission model has recently contributed to computer applications in music education that focus on emotion and expression (Juslin *et al.* 2004).

Agenda for future research

If we accept the basic validity and utility of the transmission model, there are still a number of limitations of earlier research based on this model that offer incentives for further research. For example, a definitive conclusion that can be drawn on the basis of the present review is that most previous research on expression, perception, and induction of emotions has neglected *the social context* of musical emotion, including everything from the situation in which the musical activity takes place to the wider socio-cultural context (North and Hargreaves 1997c). This neglect may be particularly unfortunate for research on *induction* of emotions by music, because it has obscured several issues that could prove to be critical to an understanding of music and emotion, including, for instance, listeners' motivations for listening to music; epidemiological aspects of music and emotion; individual differences; and listeners' uses of music in various everyday contexts (Juslin and Laukka 2004). Neglecting the context of music listening might lead to a view that emphasizes sublime, aesthetic emotions to 'works of art'. While such a view may be popular with musicians, no doubt, it has limited validity in terms of fully accounting for how most *listeners* actually relate to music. The consequence might be theories of musical emotion that overly emphasize musical structures and sources of emotion related to structure (expectancy, iconic sources) at the expense of the rich personal associations listeners have to music, and that may involve a wider variety of human emotions. Thus, I argue that a move to extend research on music and emotion to everyday life contexts represents one of the most promising avenues towards a better understanding of how humans experience emotions in connection with music. This could involve diary studies (Bolger *et al.* 2003; e.g. Sloboda and O'Neill 2001), field observations (Miller and Strongman 2002), questionnaire studies (Juslin and Laukka 2004), qualitative interviews (DeNora 2001), and cleverly designed experiments (Szpunar *et al.* 2004).

One aspect of the context left out in previous studies is *the relationship between music and lyrics*. The work reviewed here concerns mainly instrumental music, and the conclusions about the limitations on what music can communicate reliably from the composer or the performer to the listener applies only to instrumental music. However, the great majority of everyday listening to music in different cultures arguably involves music linked with words (Clarke 1952), and the combination of words and music offers a very precise means of communication of emotions, in which the two 'channels' – verbal and non-verbal – complement each other (e.g. the suggestive 'mood' of the music renders emotional 'depth' to the precise cognitive contents of the lyrics). A number of studies have investigated the emotional characteristics and effects of lyrics (Anderson *et al.* 2003; Hansen and Hansen 1991; Whissell 1996) but there is little research on the *interaction* between lyrics and music (see Stratton and Zalanowski 1994, for one example). Further study of the combined effects of music and lyrics is thus urgently needed.

What are the implications of these future directions for the transmission model? First of all, it must be noted that very few studies so far have actually modelled the *complete* communicative process (Fig. 5.1). The expanded lens model (see Fig. 5.2) includes most aspects but still leaves out induction of emotion. However, a rare study by Lundqvist *et al.* (2000) investigated how a musician's composition and performance of two pieces of music intended to communicate happiness and sadness, respectively, affected listeners' perception and induction of emotions through the use of self-reports and continuous measures of physiological reactions and facial expressions. The results suggested that music intended to express happiness was perceived as happy and induced happiness, and that music intended to express sadness was perceived as sad and induced sadness. This study may serve as a model for future research, though even this study left out several aspects of the context, as well as lyrics. Clearly, the transmission model needs to be augmented by adding variables related to the social context to the analysis. In my view, there is nothing in the transmission model that precludes a consideration of social aspects. If anything, the transmission model serves to underscore that music making is at heart a social process. Thus, for instance, the expanded lens model could be used to model individual differences in emotional communication (e.g. due to different cultural backgrounds), also including predictors of specific social situations in the statistical analysis.

Ultimately, the value of the transmission model depends on the goals of the research: do we want to investigate musical *communication* of emotion (as defined on pp. 86–9) or emotional responses to music in general? All studies of communication must rely on *some* communication model (which cannot be altogether different from the transmission model). However, emotional responses to music are not always about communication, but could involve other processes and phenomena for which the transmission model does not really apply. In addition, the transmission model does not suffice to *explain* induction of emotions. What is needed is to develop a detailed model of the *cognitive appraisal process* that underlies emotional reactions to music (e.g. Juslin 2004). Given the extremely large number of different potential sources of musical emotion, such an endeavour is a formidable undertaking.

A cognitive appraisal model could, of course, be a part of a transmission model, but it could also stand alone. The point is that, as long as we realize that the transmission model is only part of the story, applicable to only some music phenomena (cases of *genuine* communication), the model is a highly valuable tool to describe how humans express, perceive, and induce emotions in music. Hence, continued use of the transmission model is likely to increase, rather than decrease, our appreciation and admiration for music as a human art form.

Acknowledgments

The writing of this chapter was supported by the Swedish Research Council and the Bank of Sweden Tercentenary Foundation. The author is grateful to the editors for helpful comments on a preliminary version of this chapter.

References

Altenmüller, E., Schürmann, K., Lim, V.K., and Parlitz, D. (2002) Hits to the left, flops to the right: different emotions during listening to music are reflected in cortical lateralisation patterns. *Neuropsychologia,* **40**, 2242–56.

Anderson, C.A., Carnagey, N.L., and Eubanks, J. (2003) Exposure to violent media: The effects of songs with violent lyrics on aggressive thoughts and feelings. *Journal of Personality and Social Psychology,* **84**, 960–71.

Asmus, E.P. (1985) The development of a multidimensional instrument for the measurement of affective responses to music. *Psychology of Music,* **13**, 19–30.

Atkinson, A.P., Dittrich, W.H., Gemmell, A.J., and Young, A.W. (2004) Emotion perception from dynamic and static body expressions in point-light and full-light displays. *Perception,* **33**, 717–46.

Bach, C.P.E. (1778/1985) *Essay on the true art of playing keyboard instruments* (Trans. and ed. by W.J. Mitchell). London: Eulenburg Books.

Band, J.P., Quilter, S.M., and Miller, G.M. (2001–02) The influence of selected music and instructions on mental imagery: Implications for practitioners of Guided Imagery and Music. *Journal of the Association for Music and Imagery,* **8**, 13–33.

Bartel, L.R. (1992) The development of the cognitive–affective response test – music. *Psychomusicology,* **11**, 15–26.

Becker, J. (2001) Anthropological perspectives on music and emotion. In *Music and emotion: Theory and research,* (eds P.N. Juslin and J.A. Sloboda), pp. 135–60. New York: Oxford University Press.

Behne, K.E. (1997) The development of 'musikerleben' in adolescence: How and why young people listen to music. In *Perception and cognition of music,* (eds I. Deliége and J.A. Sloboda), pp. 143–59. Hove, UK: Psychology Press.

Berlyne, D.E. (1971) *Aesthetics and psychobiology.* New York: Appleton Century Crofts.

Blacking, J. (1973) *How musical is man?* Seattle, WA: University of Washington Press.

Blood, A.J. and Zatorre, R.J. (2001) Intensely pleasurable responses to music correlate with activity in brain regions implicated in reward and emotion. *Proceedings of National Academy of Sciences,* **98**, 11818–23.

Bolger, N., Davis, A., and Rafaeli, E. (2003) Diary methods: Capturing life as it is lived. *Annual Review of Psychology,* **54**, 579–616.

Bonny, H.L. and Savery, L.M. (1973) *Music and your mind.* New York: Station Hill.

Boyd, J. and George-Warren, H. (1992) *Musicians in tune. Seventy-five contemporary musicians discuss the creative process.* New York: Fireside.

Budd, M. (1989) Music and the communication of emotion. *Journal of Aesthetics and Art Criticism,* **47**, 129–38.

Burland, K. and Davidson, J.W. (2004) Tracing a musical life transition. In *The music practitioner,* (ed. J.W. Davidson), pp. 225–49. Aldershot, UK: Ashgate.

Cacioppo, J.T. and Gardner, W.L. (1999) Emotion. *Annual Review of Psychology,* **50**, 191–214.

Campbell, I.G. (1942) Basal emotional patterns expressible in music. *American Journal of Psychology,* **55**, 1–17.

Carreras, J. (1991) *Singing from the soul: An autobiography.* Seattle, WA: YCP Publications.

Clarke, H.L. (1952) The basis of musical communication. *The Journal of Aesthetics and Art Criticism,* **10**, 242–6.

Clynes, M. (1977) *Sentics: The touch of emotions.* New York: Doubleday.

Cook, N. and Dibben, N. (2001) Musicological approaches to emotion. In *Music and Emotion: Theory and Research,* (eds P.N. Juslin and J.A. Sloboda), pp. 45–70. New York: Oxford University Press.

Cooke, D. (1959) *The language of music.* Oxford: Oxford University Press.

Davies, J.B. (1978) *The psychology of music.* London: Hutchinson.

Davies, S. (1994) *Musical meaning and expression.* Ithaca, NY: Cornell University Press.

Davis, W.B. and Thaut, M.H. (1989) The influence of preferred relaxing music on measures of state anxiety, relaxation, and physiological measures. *Journal of Music Therapy,* **26**, 168–87.

DeNora, T. (2001) Aesthetic agency and musical practice: New directions on the sociology of music and emotion. In *Music and emotion: Theory and research,* (eds P.N. Juslin and J.A. Sloboda), pp. 161–80. New York: Oxford University Press.

Denski, S.W. (1992) Music, musicians, and communication: The personal voice in a common language. In *Popular music and communication,* (ed. J. Lull), (2nd edn), pp. 33–48. London: Sage Publications.

Downey, J.E. (1897) A musical experiment. *American Journal of Psychology,* **9**, 63–9.

Eerola, T. (2003) *The dynamics of musical expectancy: Cross-cultural and statistical approaches to melodic expectations (Jyväskylä Studies in Humanities 9). Doctoral dissertation,* University of Jyväskylä, Jyväskylä, Finland.

Ekman, P. (1999) Basic emotions. In *Handbook of cognition and emotion,* (eds T. Dalgleish and M. Power), pp. 45–60. Sussex, UK: John Wiley and Sons.

Fónagy, I. and Magdics, K. (1963) Emotional patterns in intonation and music. *Zeitschrift für Phonetik, Sprachwissenschaft und Kommunikationsforschung,* **16**, 293–326.

Fried, R. and Berkowitz, L. (1979) Music that charms ... and can influence helpfulness. *Journal of Applied Social Psychology,* **9**, 199–208.

Gabrielsson, A. (2001) Emotions in strong experiences with music. In *Music and emotion: Theory and research,* (eds P.N. Juslin and J.A. Sloboda), pp. 431–49. New York: Oxford University Press.

Gabrielsson, A. and Juslin, P.N. (2003) Emotional expression in music. In *Handbook of affective sciences,* (eds R.J. Davidson, K.R. Scherer, and H.H. Goldsmith), pp. 503–34. New York: Oxford University Press.

Goehr, A. (1992) Music as communication. In *Ways of communicating,* (ed. D.H. Mellor), pp. 125–52. Cambridge: Cambridge University Press.

Gomart, E. and Hennion, A. (1999) A sociology of attachment: music amateurs, drug users. In *Actor network theory and after,* (eds J. Law and J. Hazzart), pp. 220–47. Oxford: Blackwell.

Gutheil, E.A. (1952) Introduction. In *Music and your emotions: A practical guide to music selections associated with desired emotional responses,* (eds A. Carpurso *et al.*), pp. 9–13. New York: Liveright.

Hansen, C.H. and Hansen, R.D. (1991) Schematic information processing of heavy metal lyrics. *Communication Research,* **18**, 373–411.

Hanslick, E. (1986) *On the musically beautiful.* (Trans. G. Payzant). Indianapolis, IN: Hackett. (Original work published 1854.)

Harris, C.T. and Sandresky, C. (1985) Love and death in classical music: Methodological problems in analyzing human meaning in music. *Symbolic Interaction,* **8**, 291–310.

Hatfield, E., Cacioppo, J.T., and Rapson, R.L. (1994) *Emotional contagion.* New York: Cambridge University Press.

Hellmuth Margulis, E. (2003) *Melodic expectation: A discussion and model.* Unpublished doctoral dissertation, Columbia University, New York.

Hevner, K. (1935) Expression in music: A discussion of experimental studies and theories. *Psychological Review,* **42**, 186–204.

Hevner, K. (1936) Experimental studies of the elements of expression in music. *American Journal of Psychology,* **48**, 246–68.

Honeycutt, J.M. and Eidenmuller, M.E. (2001) Communication and attribution: an exploration of the effects of music and mood on intimate couples' verbal and nonverbal conflict resolution behaviours. In *Attribution, communication behaviour, and close relationships: Advances in personal relations,* (eds V. Manusov and J.H. Harvey), pp. 21–37. New York: Cambridge University Press.

Johnson-Laird, P.N. (1992) Introduction: What is communication? In *Ways of communicating,* (ed. D.H. Mellor), pp. 1–13. Cambridge: Cambridge University Press.

Juslin, P.N. (1995) Emotional communication in music viewed through a Brunswikian lens. In *Music and expression: Proceedings of the Conference of DGM and ESCOM, Bremen, 1995,* (ed. G. Kleinen), pp. 21–5. Bremen, Germany: University of Bremen.

Juslin, P.N. (1997*a*). Emotional communication in music performance: A functionalist perspective and some data. *Music Perception,* **14**, 383–418.

Juslin, P.N. (1997 *b*). Perceived emotional expression in synthesized performances of a short melody: Capturing the listener's judgment policy. *Musicae Scientiae,* **1**, 225–56.

Juslin, P.N. (1997*c*) Can results from studies of perceived expression in musical performances be generalized across response formats? *Psychomusicology,* **16**, 77–101.

Juslin, P.N. (1998) *A functionalist perspective on emotional communication in music performance.* Comprehensive Summaries of Uppsala Dissertations from the Faculty of Social Sciences 78. Uppsala, Sweden: Uppsala University Library.

Juslin, P.N. (2000) Cue utilization in communication of emotion in music performance: Relating performance to perception. *Journal of Experimental Psychology: Human Perception and Performance,* **26**, 1797–813.

Juslin, P.N. (2001) Communicating emotion in music performance: A review and a theoretical framework. In *Music and emotion: Theory and research*, (eds P.N. Juslin and J.A. Sloboda), pp. 309–37. New York: Oxford University Press.

Juslin, P.N. (2003) Five facets of musical expression: A psychologist's perspective on music performance. *Psychology of Music*, 31, 273–302.

Juslin, P.N. (2004) *Musik och känslor–Ett evolutionärt perspektiv (Music and emotion– An evolutionary perspective)*. Paper presented at EuroScience Open Forum, the first pan-European General Science Meeting, Stockholm, Sweden, August 25–8, 2004.

Juslin, P.N., Friberg, A., and Bresin, R. (2002) Toward a computational model of expression in music performance: The GERM model. *Musicae Scientiae, Special Issue 2001–02*, 63–122.

Juslin, P.N., Friberg, A., Schoonderwaldt, E., and Karlsson, J. (2004) Feedback-learning of musical expressivity. In *Musical excellence: Strategies and techniques for enhancing performance*, (ed. A. Williamon), pp. 247–70. New York: Oxford University Press.

Juslin, P.N. and Laukka, P. (2001) Impact of intended emotion intensity on cue utilization and decoding accuracy in vocal expression of emotion. *Emotion*, 1, 381–412.

Juslin, P.N. and Laukka, P. (2003) Communication of emotions in vocal expression and music performance: Different channels, same code? *Psychological Bulletin*, 129, 770–814.

Juslin, P.N. and Laukka, P. (2004) Expression, perception, and induction of musical emotion: a review and a questionnaire study of everyday listening. *Journal of New Music Research*, 33(3), 216–37.

Juslin, P.N. and Lindström, E. (2003) *Musical expression of emotions: Modeling composed and performed features*. Manuscript submitted for publication.

Juslin, P.N. and Sloboda, J.A. (eds) (2001) *Music and emotion: Theory and research*. New York: Oxford University Press.

Jørgensen, H. (1988) *Musikkopplevelsens psykologi [The psychology of music experience]*. Oslo: Norsk Musikforlag.

Kallinen, K. (2004) Emotion-related psychophysiological responses to listening to music with eyes-open versus eyes-closed: Electrodermal, electrocardiac, and electromyographic measures. In *Proceedings of the 8th International Conference on Music Perception and Cognition*, (eds S.D. Lipscomb, R. Ashley, P.O. Gjerdingen, and P. Webster), pp. 299–301. Evanston, IL: ICMPC.

Kendall, R.A. and Carterette, E.C. (1990) The communication of musical expression. *Music Perception*, 8, 129–64.

King, B.B. (1996) *Blues all around me*. London: Hodder and Stoughton.

Kleinen, G. (1968) *Experimentelle Studien zum musikalischen Ausdruck [Experimental studies of musical expression]*. Hamburg, Germany: Universität Hamburg.

Kraehenbuehl, D. and Coons, E. (1959) Information as a measure of the experience of music. *Journal of Aesthetics*, 17, 510–22.

Krumhansl, C.L. (1997) An exploratory study of musical emotions and psychophysiology. *Canadian Journal of Experimental Psychology*, 51, 336–52.

Lindström, E., Juslin, P.N., Bresin, R., and Williamon, A. (2003) 'Expressivity comes from within your soul': A questionnaire study of music students' perspectives on expressivity. *Research Studies in Music Education*, 20, 23–47.

Lull, J. (1992) Popular music and communication: an introduction. In *Popular music and communication*, (ed. J. Lull), 2nd edn, pp. 1–32. London: Sage Publications.

Lundqvist, L.-O., Carlsson, F., and Hilmersson, P. (2000) Facial electromyography, autonomic activity, and emotional experience to happy and sad music. *International Journal of Psychology*, **35**, 225. (Abstract)

Makris, I. and Mullet, E. (2003) Judging the pleasantness of contour-rhythm-pitch-timbre musical combinations. *American Journal of Psychology*, **116**, 581–611.

May, J.L. and Hamilton, P.A. (1980) Effects of musically evoked affect on women's inter-personal attraction toward and perceptual judgements of physical attractiveness of men. *Motivation and Emotion*, **4**, 217–28.

Menuhin, Y. (1996) *Unfinished journey*. London: Methuen.

Meyer, L.B. (1956) *Emotion and meaning in music*. Chicago, IL: Chicago University Press.

Middleton, R. (1990) *Studying popular music*. Milton Keynes: Open University Press.

Miller, M.M. and Strongman, K.T. (2002) The emotional effects of music on religious experience: a study of the Pentecostal-Charismatic style of music and worship. *Psychology of Music*, **30**, 8–27.

Minassian, C., Gayford, C., and Sloboda, J.A. (2003) *Optimal experience in musical performance: a survey of young musicians*. Paper presented at the Meeting of the Society for Education, Music, and Psychology Research, London, March 2003.

Neumann, R. and Strack, F. (2000) Mood contagion: The automatic transfer of mood between persons. *Journal of Personality and Social Psychology*, **79**, 211–23.

Nielzén, S. and Cesarec, Z. (1981) On the perception of emotional meaning in music. *Psychology of Music*, **9**, 17–31.

North, A.C. and Hargreaves, D.J. (1997*a*) Music and consumer behaviour. In *The social psychology of music*, (eds D.J. Hargreaves and A.C. North), pp. 268–89. Oxford: Oxford University Press.

North, A.C. and Hargreaves, D.J. (1997*b*) Liking, arousal potential, and the emotions expressed by music. *Scandinavian Journal of Psychology*, **38**, 45–53.

North, A.C. and Hargreaves, D.J. (1997*c*) Experimental aesthetics and everyday music listening. In *The social psychology of music*, (eds D.J. Hargreaves and A.C. North), pp. 84–103. Oxford: Oxford University Press.

North, A.C., Tarrant, M., and Hargreaves, D.J. (2004) The effects of music on helping behaviour: A field study. *Environment and Behaviour*, **36**, 266–75.

Noy, P. (1993) How music conveys emotion. In *Psychoanalytic explorations in music*, (eds S. Feder, R.L. Karmel, and G.H. Pollock), 2nd edition, pp. 125–49. Madison, CT: International Universities Press.

Nyklíček, I., Thayer, J.F., and Van Doornen, L.J.P. (1997) Cardiorespiratory differentiation of musically-induced emotions. *Journal of Psychophysiology*, **11**, 304–21.

Oatley, K. (1992) *Best laid schemes: The psychology of emotions*. Cambridge, MA: Harvard University Press.

Oatley, K. and Duncan, E. (1994) The experience of emotions in everyday life. *Cognition and Emotion*, **8**, 369–81.

Oatley, K. and Jenkins, J.M. (1996) *Understanding emotions*. Oxford: Blackwell.

Palmer, C. (1997) Music performance. *Annual Review of Psychology*, **48**, 115–38.

Panksepp, J. (1995) The emotional sources of 'chills' induced by music. *Music Perception*, **13**, 171–208.

Panzarella, R. (1980) The phenomenology of aesthetic peak experiences. *Journal of Humanistic Psychology,* **20**, 69–85.

Papoušek, M. (1996) Intuitive parenting: A hidden source of musical stimulation in infancy. In *Musical beginnings. Origins and development of musical competence,* (eds I. Deliége and J.A. Sloboda), pp. 89–112. Oxford: Oxford University Press.

Peretz, I. (2001) Listen to the brain: A biological perspective on musical emotions. In *Music and emotion: Theory and research,* (eds P.N. Juslin and J.A. Sloboda), pp. 105–34. New York: Oxford University Press.

Persson, R.S. (2001) The subjective world of the performer. In *Music and emotion: Theory and research,* (eds P.N. Juslin and J.A. Sloboda), pp. 275–89. New York: Oxford University Press.

Pignatiello, M.F., Camp, C.J., Elder, S.T., and Rasar, L.A (1989) A psychophysiological comparison of the Velten and musical mood induction techniques. *Journal of Music Therapy,* **26**, 140–54.

Pike, A. (1972) A phenomenological analysis of emotional experience in music. *Journal of Research in Music Education,* **20**, 262–67.

Resnicow, J.E., Salovey, P., and Repp, B.H. (2004) Is recognition of emotion in music performance an aspect of emotional intelligence? *Music Perception,* **22**, 145–58.

Roe, K. (1985) Swedish youth and music: Listening patterns and motivations. *Communication Research,* **12**, 353–62.

Rozin, A. (2000) The intensity of musical affect: a model of experience and memory. *Dissertation Abstracts International Section A: Humanities and Social Sciences,* **61**(6-A), 2097.

Russell, J.A. (1980) A circumplex model of affect. *Journal of Personality and Social Psychology,* **39**, 1161–78.

Scherer, K.R. (2003) Why music does not produce basic emotions: a plea for a new approach to measuring emotional effects of music. In *Proceedings of the Stockholm Music Acoustics Conference 2003,* (ed. R. Bresin), pp. 25–8. Stockholm, Sweden: Royal Institute of Technology.

Schmidt, L.A. and Trainor, L.J. (2001) Frontal brain electrical activity (EEG) distinguishes valence and intensity of musical emotions. *Cognition and Emotion,* **15**, 487–500.

Schubert, E. (1999) Measuring emotion continuously: Validity and reliability of the two-dimensional emotion space. *Australian Journal of Psychology,* **51**, 154–65.

Schubert, E. (2004) EmotionFace: Prototype facial expression display of emotion in music. In *Proceedings of the 10th Meeting of the International Conference on Auditory Display* (CD rom), (eds S. Barrass and P. Vickers), Sydney, Australia: International Community for Auditory Display.

Schulkind, M.D., Hennis, L.K., and Rubin, D.C. (1999) Music, emotion, and autobiographical memory: They are playing our song. *Memory and Cognition,* **27**, 948–55.

Schumacher, M. (1995) *Crossroads. The life and music of Eric Clapton.* New York: Hyperion.

Serafine, M.L. (1980) Against music as communication: Implications for music education. *Journal of Aesthetic Education,* **14**, 85–96.

Shannon, C.E. and Weaver, W. (1949) *The mathematical theory of communication.* Urbana, IL: University of Illinois.

Shaver, P., Schwartz, J., Kirson, D., and O'Connor, C. (1987) Emotion knowledge: Further explorations of a prototype approach. *Journal of Personality and Social Psychology,* **52,** 1061–86.

Sloboda, J.A. (1991) Music structure and emotional response: Some empirical findings. *Psychology of Music,* **19,** 110–20.

Sloboda, J.A. (1994) Music performance: Expression and the development of excellence. In *Musical perceptions,* (eds R. Aiello and J.A. Sloboda), pp. 152–69. New York: Oxford University Press.

Sloboda, J.A. and Juslin, P.N. (2001) Psychological perspectives on music and emotion. In *Music and emotion: Theory and research,* (eds P.N. Juslin and J.A. Sloboda), pp. 71–104. New York: Oxford University Press.

Sloboda, J.A. and Lehmann, A.C. (2001) Tracking performance correlates of changes in perceived intensity of emotion during different interpretations of a Chopin piano prelude. *Music Perception,* **19,** 87–120.

Sloboda, J.A. and O'Neill, S.A. (2001) Emotions in everyday listening to music. In *Music and emotion: Theory and research,* (eds P.N. Juslin and J.A. Sloboda), pp. 415–30. New York: Oxford University Press.

Spencer, H. (1857) The origin and function of music. *Fraser's Magazine,* **56,** 396–408.

Stratton, V.N. and Zalanowski, A.H. (1994) Affective impact of music vs. lyrics. *Empirical Studies of the Arts,* **12,** 173–84.

Swanwick, K. (1985) *A basis for music education.* Windsor: NFER-Nelson.

Szpunar, K.K., Schellenberg, E.G., and Pliner, P. (2004) Liking and memory for musical stimuli as a function of exposure. *Journal of Experimental Psychology: Learning, Memory, and Cognition,* **30,** 370–81.

Thaut, M.H. (1990) Neuropsychological processes in music perception and their relevance in music therapy. In *Music therapy in the treatment of adults with mental disorders,* (ed. R.F. Unkeler), pp. 3–31. New York: Schirmer books.

Thompson, W.F. and Robitaille, B. (1992) Can composers express emotions through music? *Empirical Studies of the Arts,* **10,** 79–89.

Timmers, R. and Ashley, R. (2004) Communicating emotions through ornamentation. In *Proceedings of the 8th International Conference on Music Perception and Cognition,* (eds S.D. Lipscomb, R. Ashley, P.O. Gjerdingen, and P. Webster), pp. 194–97. Evanston, IL: ICMPC.

Vaitl, D., Vehrs, W., and Sternagel, S. (1993) Promts - Leitmotif - Emotion: Play it again, Richard Wagner. In *The structure of emotion: Psychophysiological, cognitive, and clinical aspects,* (eds N. Birnbaumer and A. Öhman), pp. 169–89. Seattle, WA: Hogrefe and Huber.

Västfjäll, D. (2002) A review of the musical mood induction procedure. *Musicae Scientiae, Special Issue 2001-02,* 173–211.

Waterman, M. (1996) Emotional responses to music: Implicit and explicit effects in listeners and performers. *Psychology of Music,* **24,** 53–67.

Wedin, L. (1972) Multi-dimensional study of perceptual-emotional qualities in music. *Scandinavian Journal of Psychology,* **13,** 241–57.

Wells, A. (1990) Popular music: Emotional use and management. *Journal of Popular Culture,* **24,** 105–17.

Whissel, C. (1996) Traditional and emotional stylometric analyses of the songs of Beatles Paul McCartney and John Lennon. *Computers and the Humanities,* **30**, 257–65.

Yamasaki, T. (2002) Emotional communication in improvised performance by musically untrained players. In *Proceedings of the 17th International Congress of the International Association of Empirical Aesthetics* , (ed. T. Kato), pp. 521–4. Osaka, Japan: IAEA.

Zillman, D. and Gan, S-L. (1997) Musical taste in adolescence. In *The social psychology of music,* (eds D.J. Hargreaves and A.C. North, pp. 161–87. Oxford: Oxford University Press.

Chapter 6

Representation, cognition, and communication: invented notation in children's musical communication

Margaret S. Barrett

Introduction

In a text that seeks to explore the topic of 'musical communication' it seems sensible to devote some thought to the role and function of music notation in musical communication. In this chapter I shall examine the communicative role of invented notation in children's musical experience. The study of children's invented notation has sparked considerable interest in recent years. Researchers have explored the signs and symbols children employ when inventing notations, speculated on 'what' is communicated in children's invented notations, and suggested developmental trajectories in musical cognition from the study of children's invented notations. In this chapter I shall: provide an overview of research in the realm of children's thinking as users of invented notation; examine the communicative role of invented notations as *initiation* into the use of conventional symbolic systems and/or *externalization* of musical thinking; and explore the potential relationship of invented notation to other forms of sign-making activity (drawing, writing, using mathematical symbols). To provide a context for these discussions I shall examine briefly some of the roles of notation in musical communication in the broader context of western music.

Music notation

The existence of a wealth of musical traditions that do not rely on representing music in visual form is ample evidence that music notation is neither universal nor necessary to the construction, communication, and conservation of musical meaning. However, the importance of music notation in western musical traditions is underlined in educational practices such as those developed by Glover, Curwen, Dalcroze, and Kodaly in which notation is a key element in pedagogical practice. The widespread tendency to begin instruction in instrumental music simultaneously with instruction in using music notation further illustrates the focus on music notation in music teaching and learning.

Music notation is a form of intra-and inter-musician communication that rests in particular traditions of generating and transmitting musical meaning. It serves several purposes, including the conservation of music, the communication of music, and the conception of music (Cook 1998, p. 52). Music notation serves as a memory aid, and makes possible the learning of musical works independent of the originator (Small 1987, p. 231). Consequently, the use of music notation can dramatically reduce the time needed to learn new works as musicians work within literate rather than oral traditions. However, whilst music notation has provided an effective means of conserving and communicating musical meaning across cultural, geographical, and temporal borders, the notational 'artefact' often conceals as much as it reveals. As Eisner reminds us 'No single form of representation can reveal all that can be experienced; hence, representation, like perception, is selective' (1994, p. 93).

For those able to crack the code, a music notation can function as a complex and detailed set of instructions for the realization of musical meaning in sound (for example an orchestral score), or as an outline 'sketch' that suggests a range of possible musical meanings (for example a jazz chart). In a more pessimistic view, music notation '...makes it possible to play without first understanding... one simply follows the coded instructions; understanding, it is assumed, will follow with repeated playings over' (Small 1987, p. 231). Consequently, a music notation, removed from its ecological context and the aural traditions from which it arose, is subject to a range of interpretations, evidence of the potential for concealment rather than revelation that rests in the notational artefact.

The limitations of western music notation are highlighted further through examination of aspects of its history, one in which notation in part '... developed...within the physical and cognitive constraints of performance and sight-reading. It deliberately fails to describe music in too much detail, since that would make it too difficult to read' (Friberg and Battel 2002, p. 201). This link between sight-reading in performance and the development of western music notation is elaborated further in an examination of the pre-nineteenth century practice of playing scores by sight in concert, where'...the musical idioms were familiar, most music was not performed more than a few times, (and) composers were afraid of plagiarism by orchestral musicians...' (Lehmann and McArthur 2002, p. 136). In these contexts competent sight-readers were musical problem solvers as, in dealing with the external demands of the sight-reading experience they had to 'guess, simplify, or improvise', processes that meant that '...the reader is actively reconstructing the musical material rather than simply taking it off the page and duplicating it on the instrument' (Lehmann and McArthur 2002, p. 141). These authors point to the co-existence of literate and non-literate practices in the pre-nineteenth century western classical musician's repertoire, a theme expounded upon by Small in earlier writing (1998). Small laments the total dependence on music notation in contemporary Western concert music, a circumstance he suggests that has resulted in a pejorative view of non-literate traditions in the concert hall, and an atrophying of self-directed performance (1998, pp. 110–12). Whilst music notation assists in the processes of conserving and communicating musical meaning, it is apparent that there are many dimensions of musical meaning that cannot be captured in the notational artefact.

Just as music notation serves as a means to conserve and communicate aspects of our musical intention and ideas, its very structures also shape our musical thinking, the ways in which we conceive and construct music. Any notational system simultaneously acts as a means of making aspects of our thinking public, and of shaping that thinking. Music notation enshrines particular features and these are the ones that become our concern creating a 'salient frame of reference for perception' (Eisner 1994, p. 41). This feature of notation is made apparent each time I transcribe a child's composition. Transcriptions of children's composition are adult notations and representations[1] of the child's work and inevitably reflect the transcriber's musical education and notational knowledge. The vehicle through which I make my understanding of a child's music public to others, inevitably shapes the ways in which her musical work is interpreted subsequently. Other examples of the ways in which notation systems shape our thinking are evidenced in the work of Davidson *et al.* (1988), and that of Jeanne Bamberger (1991, 1994, 1999). In a study of the ways in which musically trained and untrained adults and children notate a known song, *Happy Birthday,* Davidson and his colleagues found that musically untrained participants developed 'surprisingly rich' notations informed by their performance knowledge, whereas musically trained participants drew on their knowledge of music conventions to make 'surprisingly inaccurate' notations. The latter notated what they expected to hear derived from their knowledge of these conventions, rather than what was heard. Bamberger explores this issue from a different perspective as she differentiates between children as musical map-makers and musical path-takers (see Bamberger 1999, and this volume).

---

[1] Here I make the distinction put forward by Karmiloff-Smith (1992, 139) between a 'notation', something external to the mind, and a 'representation', something internal to the mind.

The examples provided here suggest that the processes and products of music notation constrain our thinking: paradoxically, they can also 'liberate' our thinking. Eisner observes that 'The selection of a form of representation not only functions as vehicle for conveying what has been conceptualised, it also helps articulate conceptual forms' (Eisner 1994, p. 41). Put another way, notation can be both a 'referential-communicative tool' and a 'formal problem-solving space' (Karmiloff-Smith 1992). This latter function is powerfully illustrated in Australian composer Andrew Ford's description of the last minutes of Gustav Mahler's orchestral song cycle *Das Lied von der Erde* and his subsequent contemplation of the score. He writes:

> The sonic allure of the music is ravishing. Even in the context of the piece itself, this coda has a special sound: the music has been playing for an hour, and yet it is only now, in these final two minutes, that we hear the mandolin. But these splashes of colour are more than merely decorative; they also bring a sense of weightlessness to the music. They are off the beat, out of time, and gradually they eliminate all sense of bar lines. Bit by bit, tempo is vanquished, until the music is left floating. This song – *The Farewell* – has no real end. The singer doesn't want to say goodbye. The music could go on forever – eternally. The celesta and the mandolin and the harps play less frequently, less predictably, their once florid figures reduced, bit by bit, to the odd note here and there (Ford, 2003, p. 6).

He goes on to describe his curiosity as to how this 'delicate balance' was achieved, a curiosity that was assuaged in an examination of the score.

> As I expected, the music could have been composed only with the help of notation... it is clear that Mahler has written the music down in such a way as to make sure the four players don't collide...With notation, Mahler has done more than avoid musical collisions, he makes the instrumental patterns intersect and interlock...It's a paradox... music which sounds improvised, unstructured, gently disintegrating before our very ears, is the result of the kind of careful planning that is possible only when something is worked out on paper (Ford 2003, p. 6).

Beethoven's sketchbooks provide us with another example of notation as a 'formal problem-solving space'. In these sketchbooks the record of his 'thinking out on paper' suggests that '...notation is much more profoundly implicated in the act of composition than many accounts of the compositional process might lead you to believe' (Cook 1998, p. 65). With the development of increasingly complex rhythmic, harmonic, and melodic structures through the nineteenth century and onwards, the subsequent 'break-down' of tonality, and the proliferation of musical genres and styles, notation took on an increasingly important role in the conception and construction of musical meaning.

To summarize, music notation provides a means to conserve, communicate, and conceive musical meaning, making the 'reconstruction' (any 'transmission' of cultural knowledge is inevitably a reconstruction) of musical meaning possible across borders of time, geography, and culture. Notation has made possible the independent learning of large amounts of musical repertoire, a repertoire that rests in an aural-literate tradition rather than an aural-oral tradition. Importantly, music notation is tied to particular musical traditions and its function is shaped by the cultural practices and symbolic demands of that tradition. For example, a jazz musician does not 'use' a score in the same way that a classical musician does. For the former, a faithful rendition of the 'notes' as they appear in the score is not a pre-requisite for 'accurate' and 'authentic' performance in the same way that it is for a classical musician. Given the above, music notation is a symbol system that refers in 'second-order' fashion to a 'basic symbol system' (Gardner 1982, p. 309), that of music. As such, music notation is a *partial representation* of musical meaning, and limited in the extent to which it can capture the full communicative intentions of the notator.

Music notation in education

Despite these limitations music notation as a form of communication has become an integral component of many systems of music education and for some, learning music and learning to read notation are synonymous. Factors such as the introduction of high-speed printing machines, the growth in publication of method and technique books (McPherson and Gabrielsson 2002, p. 100), the increase in numbers of amateur musicians in the nineteenth century (Small 1998), and the move from improvisation to reproduction in performance (Gellrich and Parncutt 1998; Small 1998) placed an emphasis on music as an aural-literate practice, with a subsequent emphasis on notation in teaching and learning practices. In relation to the contested issue of when and how to introduce notation into the musical education of the beginning instrumentalist, McPherson and Gabrielsson draw on historical, psychological, and pedagogical literature to argue that '…emphasizing notational skills too early can lead to a decreased sensitivity to the unified patterns that children spontaneously observe when listening to music' (2002, p. 113). They argue for an integrated approach to the learning of notation where '…performing music by ear serves as preparation for literacy development in the beginning stages of musical involvement, and where performing with or without notation is encouraged during all subsequent levels of development' (2002, p. 113). Bamberger reinforces this view when she suggests that rushing children by '…giving them labels based on organizing features that others have evolved over a long history) may be to deny them the experience of first becoming effective pathmakers' (1999, p. 73).

The emphasis here is on the introduction and use of conventional music notation in music education, and the ways in which this 'tool' 'enables' rather than 'disables' musical thinking and practice. In a complementary movement, music educators and researchers have been concerned with the role of invented notations in children's musical thinking and practice.

Children's invented notations: initiation or externalization?

> ...all cognition, whatever its nature, relies upon representation, how we lay down our knowledge in a way to represent our experience of the world...representation is a process of construction, as it were, rather than of mere reflection of the world (Bruner 1996, p. 95).

Bruner's emphasis on the process of representation as one of construction of knowledge rather than *mere reflection* of knowledge, echoes the view that a notation not only conserves and communicates musical meaning, it also plays a role in the conception and construction of musical meaning. The notion that musical meaning may be accessed through the examination of a notation has led a number of researchers to investigate children's invented notations as a means to understanding more of children's construction of musical meaning. Just as the function of conventional music notation may be viewed in a range of ways, so too may children's invented notations. Whilst researchers' focus has been on invented notations as an 'externalization' of children's musical thinking, for educators children's invented notations may be viewed as 'initiation' into the aural-literate tradition of music, and a precursor to the acquisition of skills in using conventional music notation.

Initiation

In viewing children's invented notations as initiation into the aural-literate traditions of music, educators (Barrett 1990; Upitis 1990*a*, 1992) have drawn on the study of children's acquisition of the conventions of written language as described by exponents of the 'whole-language' movement. Under the tenets of this movement, children's first attempts at writing occur after extensive immersion in a language-rich environment in which all the language modes, those of reading, writing, speaking, and listening, are used. As beginning language-users, prior to any formal instruction or schooling, children are encouraged, indeed 'expected' to engage in language use. This occurs through interaction with and emulation of others, and participation in the socio-cultural practices of the group, rather than through specific instruction in which the target skill is atomized and re-presented to the child. Children are encouraged to take responsibility, to initiate, and to practise language 'tasks' and are given many opportunities to use their developing skills and understandings.

Children are allowed to approximate, to make 'mistakes' as they acquire language skills, and are further encouraged through 'feedback' and interaction with more knowledgeable others (Cambourne 1988; Goodman 1987). In building on these practices in language classrooms, children's invented writing is a necessary precursor to the acquisition of conventional written language, and is valued as a means of connecting the child's early attempts at written communication with the other modes of language use (speaking, listening, reading), and the literate practices of the wider community.

It is salutary to compare the language learning environment just described to the music learning environment encountered by many young children prior to formal instruction in the school classroom or the private music studio. Although children may be immersed in music from birth as communicative participants (Malloch 1999) and audience listeners, few children have the opportunity to observe those who are significant in their lives (parents, siblings, peers) engaging in *all* modes of music behaviour, for example composing, improvising, listening, and performing. Crucially, few children are able to view significant others 'using' music notation in relation to these modes. How many children are able to experience the musical equivalent of being read a favourite story, by following the notation as a favourite musical work is played or sung? Children readily engage in the exploration of music through sound play and invented song (Davidson 1994; Davidson *et al.* 1981; Davies 1986, 1992, 1994; Dowling 1984, 1999; Moog 1976) yet, for how many children is that play extended through interaction with more knowledgeable others and encouragement of early attempts to record these events? Children are influenced strongly by the expectations of significant others. What expectations of engagement and participation in music are conveyed to young children? Are children's initial musical statements met with the same thrill and excitement as their first words? Are children encouraged to take control over their musical learning, to 'approximate' or make mistakes without fear of judgement of failure? Often the responses to these questions are negative.

When we examine the contexts in which many children's knowledge, skills, and understanding in written language are promoted, and those in which their knowledge, skills, and understanding in music notation are promoted, the contrast is more pronounced. This is particularly evident for those children whose first experience of notation occurs in conjunction with the commencement of instrumental tuition. It is too often the case that the sound of the instrument is secondary to the de-coding of the notation.

Children's early attempts at written language in the school setting are characterized by random, personalized symbols in which some written language conventions (conventional letters, left-to-right and top-to bottom directionality) may be discerned. Children's ability to de-code such writings is variable, often with little resemblance evident between the initial intention and the subsequent 're-telling' of the writing. Yet such symbolic activity is encouraged, as children engage in 'writing behaviour' and begin to perceive of themselves as members of a 'community of writers'. As a component of this approach, teachers provide children with the conventional models for recording their language attempts. These practices provide children with a powerful and contextually embedded demonstration of conventional models of language, and, in conjunction with other practices such as LCWRC (look, cover, write, review, check), build children's skills in written language.

If we view children's invented notations as a precursor to the acquisition of conventional notation, as invented writing is a precursor to the acquisition of written language, there are a number of implied teaching practices. For example, overt connections need to be made between children's invented notation output, the music practices that gave rise to the notation, and the conventional models for notating musical work. Children need assistance in recognizing the relationships between notational modes and other modes of musical engagement (for example, performing from notations, following scores, notating compositions). Whilst some are loathe to intervene in children's production of invented notations, viewing these products as a component of children's creative work, it is important to observe that notations are a record of a musical event, not an art-work. Through discussion, demonstration of alternative ways of recording their musical intentions, and performance from invented and conventional notations, children are provided with contextually embedded demonstrations of the uses of notation. Such strategies in conjunction with experiences in de-coding the notations of others, both invented and conventional, provide an effective link between the development of invented notation and the acquisition of conventional music notation.

When we view children's invented notations as 'externalization' of their musical thinking rather than 'initiation' into an aural-literate tradition, the practice of intervention and modelling is less appropriate. As externalization, we are more concerned with accessing the characteristic ways in which young children represent their musical thinking, and what this tells us of the nature of this thinking.

Externalization

In an 'externalization' view of invented notation, the processes and products of children's activity when using invented notations are viewed as 'representations' (see footnote 1) that communicate aspects of their musical thinking and understanding. Such 'representations' provide a 'window' (Davidson and Scripp 1988, 1992) onto children's musical cognition, albeit a 'window' that is at times opaque, and/or provides a 'view' that is subject to bias and distortion (Barrett 2000). This focus on using invented notations as a strategy for exploring musical thinking may be attributed to two viewpoints: one, the common (mis)perception that young children are unable to explain verbally the nature and content of their musical thinking; and two, the acknowledgement that words are an inadequate means to describe musical phenomena and a consequent desire to find other means to access musical thinking. In this latter view, invented notations may be viewed as 'cultural psychological' tools (Vygotsky 1978) that function as a 'secondary system' of representation for the 'primary system' of music (Gardner 1982, p. 309). Through their participation in musical experiences in which invented notation is used, children are developing a 'database' of representational strategies. Examination of these strategies holds potential to inform us about the ways in which children abstract and generate principles about music and construct their musical worlds. Research in the field of invented notation indicates that children draw on a number of practices of 'secondary representation' including writing, drawing, and notating number in order to record their musical thinking. This suggests that there are possible links between the various representational systems in which children work. However, one of the distinguishing features of invented notation in contrast to some of these systems is the focus on generating an idiosyncratic system of representation rather than acquiring a conventional system of representation (writing and number). In the following section I shall explore the ways in which the study of invented notation has provided insights into the nature of children's musical thinking, prior to considering the possibilities research findings in children's use of other representational systems offer us in furthering our understanding of musical thinking and communication.

Invented notation and children's musical thinking

Researchers have employed a range of strategies to elicit invented notations including asking children to notate:

- researcher-generated rhythmic and/or melodic fragments (Adachi and Bradshaw 1995; Bamberger 1982, 1991, 1994; Cohen 1985; Davidson and Colley 1987; Domer and Gromko 1996; Gromko 1994, 1998; Smith *et al.* 1994);
- known and unknown canonic song and/or invented song (Bamberger 1999; Barrett 1999, 2000; Davidson and Scripp 1988, 1989, 1992; Davidson *et al.* 1988);

- original compositions (Barrett 1997, 2001; Borstad 1989; Christensen 1992; Upitis 1987, 1987*a*,*b*, 1990, 1990*a*, 1992); and,
- responses to hearings of adult music (Hair 1993).

In other studies researchers have asked children to follow adult-generated invented notations (graphic listening maps) whilst listening to music (Gromko and Poorman 1998*a*, 1998*b*) or to engage in 'kinaesthetic analogues' (Cohen 1997) prior to following such notations whilst listening to music (Fung and Gromko 2001; Gromko and Russell 2002). Generally invented notation research has focused on young children, (aged four to eight), although studies have examined the notations of children aged two (Gromko 1998) through to those of musically trained and musically naive adolescents and adults (Smith *et al.* 1994).

Categories and typologies of invented notations

From these studies various categories or typologies of children's invented notations have emerged, some of which suggest a developmental progression, whilst others are less predictive of developmental issues. I distinguish here between those studies where the focus has been on notating the work of *others* and those where the focus has been on notating children's original musical works (see earlier listing). In Bamberger's (1982) study of children's drawings of researcher-generated rhythm patterns, three categories of invented notation emerged, those of pre-figural, figural, and metric. In this early study, figural notations, (notations that focus on the motivic groupings or 'figures') were the dominant method of notation employed by young children and musically naïve adults whilst metric notations (notations that arise from an underlying 'unit') emerged in the work of those children and adults who had access to musical training. Pre-figural notations, including 'primitives', 'rhythmic scribbles' and 'played drawings' (Bamberger, 1982, pp. 195–6) may be linked to Goodnow's (1977) 'action equivalents' of rhythmic sequences, where the emphasis is on representing the physical action of performing the rhythm (drawing hands or 'playing out' on paper), rather than the rhythmic content. Importantly, Bamberger (1994, p. 136) suggests that the strategy drawn upon (figural and/or metric) is reflective of the listener/performer's focus of attention, rather than a strict indication of a developmental stage, a theme she has pursued further in later work (see Bamberger 1999 and this volume).

Davidson and Scripp's (1988, 1989, 1992) progressive typology emerged from work in which children were asked to notate known song. This typology sees the child move progressively from 'enactive' scribbles, to pictorial images, rebus or strings of icons that represent aspects of the song text, to invented symbols or symbols adopted and adapted from other symbol systems that encode the dimensions of rhythm and/or pitch. In a descriptive model of artistic development that draws on these and related studies in a range of arts forms, Hargreaves suggests that children move progressively through four age-related phases in the domain of musical 'representation', those of: Scribbling: 'action equivalents' (0–2 years); Figural: single dimension (2–5 years); Figural-metric: more than one dimension (5–8 years); and Formal-metric (8–15 years) (1996, pp. 155–65). Here the emphasis is on a progressive movement from idiosyncratic recordings of a dimension of music to the acquisition of the conventions of western music notation, and the model may be viewed as a means to linking the views of invented notation as 'externalization' and 'initiation'.

Researchers who have focused on children's invented notation of their compositions and invented songs have also identified a number of commonalities in the ways in which children notate. When inventing notations for their own works children draw on a broad range of symbols borrowed from other domains including letters, words, numbers, directional signs, icons, pictographs (Upitis 1990*b*), and, in much the way that young children incorporate conventional letters into their invented writing, conventional music symbols. Categories or typologies of young children's (aged four to five years) invented notation of their work as composers and song-makers (Barrett 1997, 1999, 2000, 2001, 2003, 2004) that have emerged include: exploration, (random drawings or scribbles with little discernible relationship to the sound event – Fig. 6.1); notation of instrument (sketches of the instrument – Figs. 6.2 and 6.3); notation of instrument with modification (sketches of the instrument that include

Fig. 6.1 John: Drum (Reproduced with permission from *Invented notations: A view of young children's thinking*, published in number 8 (July 1997) of *Research Studies in Music Education*).

Fig. 6.2 Shaun: Agogo Bells (Reproduced with permission from *Invented notations: A view of young children's musical thinking*, published in number 8 (July 1997) of *Research Studies in Music Education*).

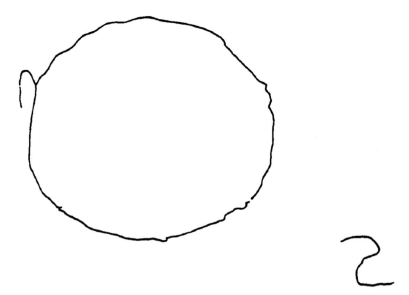

Fig. 6.3 Sabrina: Tambourine (Reproduced with permission from *Invented notations: A view of young children's musical thinking*, published in number 8 (July 1997) of *Research Studies in Music Education*).

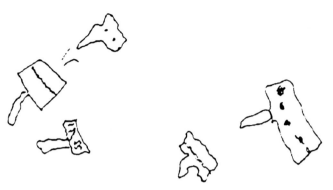

Fig. 6.4 Caitlin (dynamic change is indicated through varying size of the sketch) (Reproduced with permission from *Invented notations: A view of young children's musical thinking*, published in number 8 (July 1997) of *Research Studies in Music Education*).

modifications of size and/or shading to indicate a musical parameter such as dynamics or pitch – Figs 6.4 and 6.5); notation of gesture/enactive (imitation on paper of the actions used to produce the sound – Fig. 6.6); abstract/symbolic notation (use of lines, circles, dots, triangular shapes to represent discrete sounds, with a one-to-one correspondence between sound and symbol – Fig. 6.7); adopted symbols (for example attempts to write the lyrics – Fig. 6.8); pictographs (drawings of the lyric content of songs – Fig. 6.9); and conventional notation.

In studies that have sought to investigate the factors that influence the choice of strategy young children (aged four to five years) employ when notating

Fig. 6.5 Belinda: Agogo Bells (changes in pitch are indicated through varying size of the sketch (Reproduced with permission from *Invented notations: A view of young children's musical thinking*, published in number 8 (July 1997) of *Research Studies in Music Education*).

Fig. 6.6 Laura: Maracas (Reproduced with permission from *Invented notations: A view of young children's musical thinking*, published in number 8 (July 1997) of *Research Studies in Music Education*).

musical experience, a number of findings have emerged. As children notate their musical works over time, they appear to move back and forth between notational strategies rather than moving progressively through hierarchically distinct stages where prior strategies are abandoned in favour of newly acquired strategies. In short, they appear to be developing a database of strategies (Barrett 1997) on which they draw in subsequent work. It is worth noting that these early strategies appear to endure and emerge in children's work in later years. For example, a grade four child's (aged nine years six months) recording of a xylophone melody consists of a drawing of the 'grid' of the xylophone with the melody recorded by writing successive numbering (one to fifty-two) of the pitches. This 'notation of instrument with modifications' suggests that the notator's main concern was pitch as there is no indication of the rhythmic structure of the work.

The notational strategies children employ are influenced by the nature of the musical task, and those features children perceive to be dominant in the

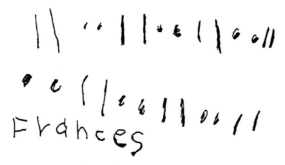

Fig. 6.7 Frances: Agogo Bells (Reproduced with permission from *Invented notations: A view of young children's musical thinking*, published in number 8 (July 1997) of *Research Studies in Music Education*).

Fig. 6.8 Jacob – Humpty Dumpty.

musical task (Barrett 1999). In this study kindergarten children were asked to notate canonic and original song, and instrumental compositions. Whilst all were content to notate instrumental works, the majority of children refused to notate song material. The reasons proffered included not knowing how to read yet, or not knowing 'my letters' yet. These children perceived the task as a language task. This perception was borne out in the work of those children who *did* notate song material, as they either attempted to write the lyrics of the

Fig. 6.9 Rowan – Humpty Dumpty.

song (see Fig. 6.8) or drew pictures of the lyric content of the song (see Fig. 6.9). In further studies, when notating song material (original and canonical), children tended to employ a strategy focused on representing lyric content, regardless of the musical complexity, diversity of genre, or emotional content of the song (Barrett 2000). Recent studies of children's song acquisition suggest that children commence schooling with a strong predisposition towards learning song text with a less well-developed ability to match pitch (Welch *et al.* 1998). Earlier, it has been noted that the 'linguistic topology' of songs tends to dominate children's early song-singing, characterized by a focus on textual features (Davidson *et al.* 1981) over musical features. Welch *et al.* suggest that children arrive at school '…"biased" towards words when they are attached to melodies (as in a song)' (1998, p. 70), and recommend that children's capacity to match pitch contour is perhaps best fostered without the 'contaminating influence of words' (1998, p. 71). These studies indicate that whilst we may be able to identify common notational strategies in children's musical work, such as the drawing of lyric content (see Davidson and Scripp's 1988, 1989, 1992), the factors that influence the choice of notation strategy, and what these notations indicate about children's musical thinking and *development*, are subject to debate.

Across these studies there is general agreement that children's early notations include 'action equivalents' or 'enactive' categories in which the focus of the notation is the 'playing out on paper' of a dimension of the musical work such as rhythm or dynamics. Similarly, pictorial notations are identified as a category across these studies. Bamberger refers to pictorial notation of the instruments as a sub-category of 'rhythmic scribbles', whilst Davidson and Scripp refer to a pictorial category that focuses on notation of aspects of the lyrics of song material. This differentiation is reflected in those studies that have focused on children's invented notations of their original songs and instrumental works (Barrett 1997, 1999, 2000), with the added dimension of some children striving to record more than one aspect of the musical work through modification of the pictorial notation (multiple sketches that vary in size). In the majority of studies, children adopt and adapt symbols from a range of other symbol systems. Finally, the employment of abstract symbols are common across the studies as children record musical dimensions, such as rhythm.

Those studies that have employed adult-generated invented notations (graphic listening maps) in conjunction with music listening tasks as a means to investigate children's musical thinking provide another perspective on the phenomenon of children's musical thinking when mediated by notation. The findings from these studies are varied. Whilst it is suggested that unstructured (Fung and Gromko 2001) and structured (Gromko and Poorman 1998b) kinaesthetic responses to music enhance children's perceptions of note groupings and rhythm patterns and perceptions of musical form respectively, these findings were not supported in more recent work. For example, in a study of second and third grade children's aural perception when reading graphic listening maps under unstructured and structured listening conditions, the researchers found that one listening under the condition of unstructured or structured kinaesthetic response was not sufficient to explain the variance in speed and accuracy of reading. Instead, those children with more advanced powers of aural discrimination (as measured by Gordon's (1986) IMMA (Intermediate Measure of Musical Ability) were '...predisposed to more accurate reading of graphic listening maps and (that) aural perception ability may have been the result of previous musical experience' (Gromko and Russell 2002, p. 340), specifically, keyboard instruction. The authors conclude that the link between aural perception ability and more accurate reading of the maps supports the '...idea that symbols must follow experience with sound...' (2002, p. 340).

Some functions of invented notation for children

Whilst some would suggest that young children are unable to explain verbally the nature of their music thinking, those studies that have explored children's accompanying verbal accounts have proven illuminating (Bamberger 1991; Barrett 1999, 2001, 2003, in press 2005; Christensen 1992; Davidson and Scripp 1992). Young children's immediate verbal accounts of their notations and music activity suggest that they are building a repertoire of strategies with meaningful intention (Barrett 2001), that the use of a strategy is the result of deliberate and considered choice.

The development of an invented notation involves the processes of selecting, recording, reporting, or representing, resulting in a 'cultural psychological' tool for encoding, storing, and retrieving meaning, as a prompt for memory. Consequently, children's invented notations may be viewed as evidence of *mediated* memory. Memory is a key component of children's cognition, and examination of *mediated* memory as evidenced in children's sign-using activity in music has the potential to provide us with further insight into the nature and extent of their musical thinking. In a study of young children's invented notations and mediated memory, abstract/symbolic notational strategies appeared more effective 'cultural psychological' tools when retrieving meaning over time, than pictorial notational strategies (Barrett 2003). This suggests that young children (aged five) understand the musical elements with which they are working and, importantly, are able to reflect on experience, to engage in an 'internalized dialogue' that can lead to higher order thinking. In these instances, the communicative function of the invented notation is both that of a memory aid, and a 'space' for the child's musical thinking.

From the preceding review of research a common finding is the adoption and adaptation of symbols from a range of symbol systems. Whilst such actions could be viewed as evidence of a common semiotic function, a recent study (Barrett in press, 2005) indicates that young children are conscious of the differing constraints that operate within and across symbol systems, and observe these constraints when employing symbols from other systems in their invented notations. In this study the invented notations, musical events, and accompanying dialogue of a young girl (4 years 6 months at study commencement) were collected over a one-year period. Her notations included rhythmic solfege, letter names, and iconic (pictorial) notations, with the same type of musical event (song) being notated using a range of different strategies (letters, drawings, rhythmic solfege). From the analysis of her explanations of these notations it is evident that she is neither confusing symbol systems nor making arbitrary selections from the representational repertoire she has built. Rather, she is imposing different constraints on her use of each symbolic choice, constraints that reflect her symbolic and musical intentions. This suggests that children's invented notations can also function as a 'problem-solving space' for them. In the following section I shall examine further the potential relationship between children's invented notations and other systems of symbolic representation.

Representation, cognition and notation: Looking beyond music

Karmiloff-Smith points to the '…pervasiveness of the human tendency to create notations of various kinds – to draw, to engrave, to paint, to sculpt, to make maps, and to invent systems for written language, for number notation, for music notation, and so forth' (1992, p. 139) as indicative of the human propensity to 'externalize' mental representations. In exploring this issue, she differentiates between a *representation*, 'something internal to the mind' and cognitive, and a *notation*, an external depiction of such representations (1992, p. 139). For Karmiloff-Smith, *human notations* are essentially intentional and communicative, and differentiated from the marks made by chimpanzees, for example, by the intention to communicate either to self (as memory) or to others. Importantly, the distinction between a *notation* as 'external depiction' and a *representation* as an indication of something 'internal to the mind' emphasizes that a notation is not a precise or 'exact' 'reflection' of an internal mental process, it is partial.

In an attempt to integrate nativism and constructivism Karmiloff-Smith argues for a domain-specific approach to representation and notation whereby each symbol system is seen to follow its own developmental path (Karmiloff-Smith 1992, pp. 141–3). However, this path is not hard-wired, rather

'Nature specifies initial biases or predispositions that channel attention to relevant environmental inputs, which in turn affect subsequent brain development' (Karmiloff-Smith 1992, p. 5). In a later work this modular view is described as one whereby 'domain-relevant mechanisms...*become* domain-specific over developmental time, through interaction with (these) differential inputs' (Thomas and Karmiloff-Smith 1999, p. 245). In short, modularity is progressive, an 'outcome' rather than the 'starting state' of development (Thomas and Karmiloff-Smith 1999, p. 245).

In studies of preliterate and pre-drawing toddlers' attempts to draw and write, findings suggest that these children approach the tasks of drawing and writing differently despite the apparent similarity in the end-products (Karmiloff-Smith 1992, p. 144). Consequently, 'It is essential to distinguish between product and process, because toddlers' notational products may at times appear domain-general to the observer whereas their notational intentions and hand movements bear witness to a clear differentiation that they have established between the two systems' (Karmiloff-Smith 1992, p. 144).

Karmiloff-Smith asserts that young children (four years) '...do *not* confuse writing, number notation, and drawing; they impose different constraints on each system' (1992, p. 145, emphasis in the original), a finding borne out by work in the domain of music (Barrett 1999, in press 2005). For example, children are able to distinguish between those notations that require (in their view) written language (recording of lyrics) rather than other forms of notation (drawings of lyric content or other forms of symbolization that recorded musical features), with many refusing to notate when they perceive the task to require writing, rather than other forms of symbolizing (Barrett 1999). Importantly, accessing children's *intentions* when notating indicates that children's symbolic choices are closely related to their musical and notational intentions, and that they impose different constraints on the use of symbols from differing systems (Barrett in press, 2005). In this, the notational functions of 'conservation' and 'communication' are emphasized, but what of those of 'conception', of 'construction'?

In a view of invented notations as 'cultural psychological tools' their role can be one of modifying and enriching cognitive activity (John-Steiner and Meehan 2000, p. 32), rather than simply 'reflecting' cognitive activity. This is evident when children's use of invented notations shapes their musical thinking (Barrett in press, 2005). Research in the fields of mathematics (Hatano *et al.* 1977) and astronomy (Schoultz *et al.* 2000) has demonstrated that the use of cultural psychological tools (such as notations and artefacts) transforms the nature of children's thinking and problem-solving. As Gauvain reminds us symbol systems not only enhance human thinking through representing, manipulating, and communicating ideas, they transform it (Gauvain 2001, p. 128). Significantly, this transformation can be in the form of both an affordance and a constraint. Valsiner defines signs as '...*subjectively constructed, interpersonally consolidated, and stored in both intra- and interpsychological domains.* By their main role – 'standing in' for some aspect of experience – signs acquire flexibility through their abstract generalizing role... Signs create *relative stability* within the field of experience – 'capturing' some (generalized) features of the irreversible flow of experience of a personal kind' (Valsiner 2001, p. 87). Semiotic mediation (using signs) described in this way holds both affordances and constraints as signs paradoxically both extend and inhibit our thinking through their dual emphasis on abstract generalization and context specification (Valsiner 2001).

Hatano and Wertsch (2001) maintain that '...(a) interaction with other people and artifacts plays an important part in learning and the development of mind, and (b) what occurs in the microenvironment in which individual learning is observed is affected by larger contexts, both at community and global levels...' (2001, p. 78). They go on to elaborate the role of practices in this process, commenting that

> ...practices may provide a database from which people abstract general principles and construct models of the world, and as a result those abilities that are valued in a culture tend to be enhanced over the long run. In short 'participation in practice' is the key concept linking social and cultural setting with individual cognitive development (Hatano and Wertsch 2001, p. 79).

The cognitive consequences of participation in a practice tend to be domain-specific (2001, p. 79) although 'some domain-general development can also be explained on the basis of experience with different practices...what is acquired in one domain may be used in others through analogies, abstraction, and the like' (Hatano and Wertsch 2001, pp. 79–80).

A number of implications for music learning and the furthering of our understandings of the nature of children's musical thinking and communication arise from these observations about symbol systems in general. First, humans externalize their thinking through the use of symbols and notations. However, such 'externalization' is not a 'direct' reflection of an internal process. It is partial in its capacity to 'represent' cognition. Nevertheless, invented notations do provide us with a partial view on a phenomenon, children's musical thinking, that is difficult to access in other ways. Second, notations not only 'reflect' aspects of cognitive activity, they assist cognitive activity, for example, as an aid to memory. Importantly, notations can also shape cognitive activity as they afford and/or constrain particular ways of thinking and acting. Third, young children differentiate between symbol systems and impose different constraints on their use of these systems.

Concluding remarks

Invented notation functions as an intra- and inter-musician means of communication. It provides opportunities for implicit and explicit representation and presentation of aspects of musical thinking. Whilst invented notation is an idiosyncratic system, there are some commonalities in the forms (types of symbols) children employ, and the functions of invented notation for them.

In common with conventional notation, invented notation provides a means of conserving, communicating, conceiving, and constructing musical meaning. Each of these uses examines children's invented notations from an adult perspective, focusing on the ways in which these notations inform us about children's developing knowledge of music. From this perspective, children's invented notations are seen as a transitory component of their musical learning. I suggest that children's invented notations also be viewed as part of a developing repertoire of ways of symbolizing their worlds, as an alternative and continuously useful means of representation and notation that reflects the diversity and richness of the ways in which children conceive and construct their musical worlds. Children acquire a repertoire of strategies for recording aspects of their environment: these include drawing, graphing, mapping, each of which functions in different ways. The acquisition of a repertoire of strategies for recording their *sound* environment provides children with equally useful and alternative strategies for conceptualizing their musical worlds.

So far, children's own musical discourse has been the focus. To limit children to that discourse alone may debar them from participating in other musical discourses. The acquisition of a range of notational systems, constitutes an important component of the child's developing repertoire. However, whilst all notation systems facilitate the conservation and communication of musical meaning within particular musical practices, they also shape musical thinking. The study of musical notation provides us with a means to ends, not an end in itself. Perhaps the most important challenge for teachers is not so much how and when to teach notation. Rather, it is how to establish with the child recognition of a 'need' to notate in ways that are less idiosyncratic and more accessible to others, of the need to participate in that form of musical discourse that is conserved, communicated, and conceived through conventional music notation. This entails acknowledgement and valuing of children's expanding repertoires of notational practice, rather than the substitution of one approach for another.

For some, the principle pedagogical imperative of schools is the mastery of a culture's major notational systems, those of written language and numerical systems. In critiquing the practices of schooling, Gardner examines two models of learning and acquiring expertise, those of the student in the institutional setting, and the apprentice. He comments:

> Much of school is deliberately decontextualised: one learns about things at a remove. And so the students spend time creating and decoding symbols and notations, which themselves denote concrete entities. In contrast, apprentices work directly with the objects of their craft and with the individuals – the master – who embody the requisite skills. The world of the apprentice may contain symbols, but these are likely to be introduced incidentally in the course of working with physical materials, rather than as substitutes for actual contact with concrete materials (1997, p. 29).

In using music notation in educational settings, our emphasis should be to develop children's capacity to participate in forms of musical discourse, where acquisition of music notation skills is a component of an apprenticeship in the sound worlds of music, not a substitute for participation in these worlds.

References

Adachi, M. and Bradshaw, D.H. (1995) Children's symbolic representations of rhythm patterns across tasks. Paper presented at the Biennial Meeting of the Society for Research in Child Development, Indianapolis, IN.

Bamberger, J. (1982) Revisiting children's descriptions of simple rhythms: A function for reflection-in-action. In *U-shaped behavioural growth,* (ed. S. Strauss), pp. 191–226. New York: Academic Press.

Bamberger, J. (1991) *The mind behind the musical ear.* Cambridge, MA: Harvard University Press.

Bamberger, J. (1994) Coming to hear in a new way. In *Musical perceptions,* (ed. R. Aiello), pp. 131–51. Oxford: Oxford University Press.

Bamberger, J. (1999) Learning from the children we teach. *Bulletin of the Council for Research in Music Education,* **142,** 48–74.

Barrett, M.S. (1990) Graphic notation in music education. In *Music education facing the future,* (ed. J.P.K. Dobbs). Christchurch: The Printery, University of Canterbury.

Barrett, M.S. (1997) Invented notations: A view of young children's musical thinking. *Research Studies in Music Education,* **8,** 2–14.

Barrett, M.S. (1999) Modal dissonance: An analysis of children's invented notations of known songs, original songs, and instrumental compositions. *Bulletin of the Council for Research in Music Education,* **141,** 14–20.

Barrett, M.S. (2000) Windows, mirrors and reflections: A case study of adult constructions of children's musical thinking. *Bulletin of the Council for Research in Music Education,* **145,** 1–19.

Barrett, M.S. (2001) Constructing a view of children's meaning-making as notators: A case-study of a five year old's descriptions and explanations of invented notations. *Research Studies in Music Education,* **16,** 33–45.

Barrett, M.S. (2003) Invented notations and mediated memory: A case-study of two children's use of invented notations. *Bulletin of the Council for Research in Music Education,* **153/154,** 55–62.

Barrett, M.S. (2005) Thinking about the representation of music: A case-study of invented notation. *Bulletin of the Council for Research in Music Education,* in press.

Borstad, J. (1989) But I've been pouring sounds all day. Paper presented at the annual meeting of the Canadian Society for the Study of Education, Quebec City, Quebec.

Bruner, J. (1996) Frames for thinking: Ways of making meaning. In *Modes of thought: Exploration in culture and cognition,* (eds D. R. Olson and N. Torrance), pp. 93–105. Cambridge: Cambridge University Press.

Cambourne, B. (1988) *The whole story: Natural learning and the acquisition of literacy in the classroom.* Auckland: Ashton Scholastic.

Christensen, C. (1992) *Music composition, invented notation and reflection: Tools for music learning and assessment.* Unpublished Doctoral dissertation, Rutgers, State University of New Jersey, New Jersey.

Cohen, S.R. (1985) The development of constraints on symbol-meaning structure in notation: Evidence from production, interpretation, and forced-choice judgments. *Child Development,* **56**(1), 177–95.

Cohen, V. (1997) Explorations of kinaesthetic analogues for musical schemes. *Bulletin of the Council for Research in Music Education,* **131,** 1–13.

Cook, N. (1998) *Music: A very short introduction.* Oxford: Oxford University Press.

Davidson, L. (1994) Song singing by young and old: A developmental approach to music. In *Musical perceptions,* (ed. R. Aiello), pp. 99–130. Oxford: Oxford University Press.

Davidson, L. and Colley, B. (1987) Children's rhythmic development from age 5 to 7: Performance, notation, and reading of rhythm patterns. In *Music and child development,* (eds J.C. Peery, I.W. Peery, and T.W. Draper). pp. 107–36. New York: Springer-Verlag.

Davidson, L. McKernon, P., and Gardner, H. (1981) The acquisition of song: A developmental approach. Documentary Report of the Ann Arbor Symposium. Reston, VA: MENC.

Davidson, L. and Scripp, L. (1988) Young children's musical representations: Windows on cognition. In *Generative processes in music: The psychology of performance, improvisation, and composition,* (ed. J.A. Sloboda), pp. 195–230. Oxford: Clarendon Press.

Davidson, L. and Scripp, L. (1989) Education and development in music from a cognitive perspective. In *children and the arts,* (ed. D.J. Hargreaves), pp. 59–86. Milton Keynes: Open University Press.

Davidson, L. and Scripp, L. (1992) Surveying the coordinates of cognitive skills in music. In *Handbook of research on music teaching and learning,* (ed. R. Colwell), pp. 392–431. New York: Schirmer Books.

Davidson, L., Scripp, L., and Welsh, P. (1988) "Happy birthday": Evidence for conflicts of perceptual knowledge and conceptual understanding. *Journal of Aesthetic Education,* **22**(1), 65–74.

Davies, C. (1986) Say it till a song comes: reflections on songs invented by children 3–13. *British Journal of Music Education,* **3**(3), 279–93.

Davies, C. (1992) 'Listen to my song': A study of songs invented by children aged 5–7 years. *British Journal of Music Education,* **9**(1), 19–48.

Davies, C. (1994) The listening teacher: An approach to the collection and study of invented songs of children aged 5–7. *Musical connections: Tradition and change.* pp. 120–27. Auckland, NZ: ISME.

Domer, J. and Gromko, J.E. (1996) Qualitative changes in preschoolers' invented notations following music instruction. *Contributions to Music Education,* **23**, 62–78.

Dowling, W.J. (1984) Development of musical schemata in children's spontaneous singing. In *Cognitive processes in the perception of art,* (eds W.R. Crozier and A.J. Chapman), pp. 145–63. Amsterdam: North-Holland.

Dowling, W.J. (1999) The development of music perception and cognition. In *The psychology of music,* (ed. D. Deutsch), pp. 603–25. San Diego, CA: Academic Press.

Eisner, E. (1994) *Cognition and curriculum reconsidered.* Teachers College Press: New York.

Ford, A. (2003) The power of pure contraption. *The Australian Financial Review,* October 3, 2003, 6–7.

Friberg, A. and Battel, G.U. (2002) Structural communication. In *The science and psychology of music performance: Creative strategies for teaching and learning,* (eds R. Parncutt and G.E. McPherson), pp. 199–218. New York: Oxford University Press.

Fung, V. and Gromko, J. (2001) Effects of active versus passive listening on the quality of children's invented notations and preferences for two Korean pieces. *Psychology of Music,* **29**(2), 128–38.

Gardner, H. (1982) *Frames of mind: the theory of multiple intelligences.* New York: Basic Books.

Gardner, H. (1997) *Extraordinary minds: Portraits of exceptional individuals and an examination of our extraordinariness.* London: Weidenfield & Nicholson.

Gauvain, M. (2001) Cultural tools, social interaction and the development of thinking. *Human Development,* **44**, 126–43.

Gellrich, M. and Parncutt, R. (1998) Piano technique and fingering in the eighteenth and nineteenth centuries: Bringing a forgotten method back to life. *British Journal of Music Education,* **15**(1), 5–24.

Goodman, N. (1987) *What's whole in Whole Language.* Portsmouth, NH: Heinemann.

Goodnow, J. (1977) *Children's drawing.* London: Fontana Open Books.

Gordon, E. (1986) *Intermediate measures of music audiation.* Chicago, IL: G.I.A. Publications, Inc.

Gromko, J. (1994) Children's invented notations as measures of musical understanding. *Psychology of Music,* **22**(2), 136–147.

Gromko, J. (1998) The development of musical language in preschool: From exploration to early symbolization. Poster presentation for the Seminar "Respecting the child in early childhood music education" XXII ISME Early Childhood Seminar, Capetown, South Africa, 12–17 July 1998.

Gromko, J. and Poorman, A.S. (1998a) Developmental trends and relationships in children's aural perception and symbol use. *Journal of Research in Music Education,* **46**(1), 16–23.

Gromko, J. and Poorman, A.S. (1998b) Does perceptual-motor performance enhance perception of patterned art music? *Musicae Scientiae: The Journal of the European Society for Cognitive Sciences of Muisc,* **2**(2), 157–70.

Gromko, J. and Russell, C. (2002) Relationships among young children's aural perception, listening condition, and accurate reading of graphic listening maps. *Journal of Research in Music Education,* **50**(4), 333–42.

Hair, H.I. (1993/1994) Children's descriptions and representations of music. *Bulletin of the Council for Research in Music Education*, **119**, 41–8.

Hargreaves, D.J. (1996) The development of artistic and musical competence. In *Musical beginnings: Origins and development of musical competence*, (eds I. Deliege and J. Sloboda), pp. 145–170. Oxford: Oxford University Press.

Hatano, G. and Wertsch, J.V. (2001) Sociocultural approaches to cognitive development: The constitution of culture in mind. *Human Development*, **44**, 77–83.

Hatano, G., Miyake, Y., and Binks, M. (1977) Performance of expert abacus operators, *Cognition*, **9**, 47–55.

John-Steiner, V.P. and Meehan, T.M. (2000) Creativity and collaboration in knowledge construction. In *Vygotskian perspectives on literacy research: Constructing meaning through collaborative inquiry*, (ed. C.D. Lee and P. Smagorinsky), pp. 31–48. Cambridge: Cambridge University Press.

Karmiloff-Smith, A. (1992) *Beyond modularity: A developmental perspective on cognitive science*. Cambridge, MA: MIT Press.

Karmiloff-Smith, A. (1999) Taking development seriously. *Human development*, **42**(6), 325–7.

Lehmann, A.C. and McArthur, V. (2002) Sight-reading. In *The science and psychology of music performance: Creative strategies for teaching and learning*, (eds R. Parncutt and G.E. McPherson), pp. 135–50. New York: Oxford University Press.

Malloch, S. (1999) Mother and infants and communicative musicality. Musicae Scientiae: Rhythms, Musical Narrative, and the Origins of Human Communication, Special Issue 1999–2000, 29–57.

McPherson, G.E. and Gabrielsson, A. (2002) From sound to sign. In *The science and psychology of music performance: Creative strategies for teaching and learning*, (eds R. Parncutt and G.E. McPherson), pp. 99–116. New York: Oxford University Press.

Moog, H. (1976) *The musical experience of the pre-school child*. (translation C. Clarke). London: Schott.

Shoultz, J., Saljo, R., and Wyndham, J. (2001) Heavenly talk: Discourse, artifacts, and children's understanding of elementary astronomy. *Human Development*, **44**, 101–16.

Small, C. (1987) *Music of the common tongue: Survival and celebration in Afro-American music*. London: John Calder.

Small, C. (1998) *Musicking: the meanings of performing and listening*. Hanover, NH: Wesleyan University Press.

Smith, K.C., Cuddy, L.L., and Upitis, R. (1994) Figural and metric understanding of rhythm. *Psychology of Music*, **22**(2), 117–35.

Thomas, M. and Karmiloff-Smith, A. (1999) Quo vadis modularity in the 1990's? *Learning and individual differences*, **10**(3), 245–50.

Upitis, R. (1987) Toward a model for rhythm development. In *Music and child development*, (eds J.C. Peery, I.W. Peery, and T.W. Draper), pp. 54–79. New York: Springer-Verlag.

Upitis, R. (1987a) Children's understanding of rhythm: The relationship between development and music training. *Psychomusicology*, **7**(1), 41–60.

Upitis, R. (1987b) A child's development of music notation through composition: A case study. Paper presented at the Annual Meeting of the American Educational Research Association, Washington, DC.

Upitis, R. (1990) Children's invented Notations of familiar and unfamiliar melodies. *Psychomusicology*, **9**(1), 89–106.

Upitis, R. (1990*a*) *This too is music.* Portsmouth, NJ: Heinemann Educational Books.

Upitis, R. (1990*b*) The craft of composition: Helping children create music with computer tools. *Psychomusicology,* **8**(2), 151–62.

Upitis, R. (1992) *Can I play you my song? The compositions and invented notations of children.* Portsmouth, NJ: Heinemann Educational Books.

Valsiner, J. (2001) Process structure of semiotic mediation in human development. *Human Development,* **44**, 84–97.

Vygotsky, L.S. (1978) *Mind in society.* Cambridge, MA: MIT Press.

Welch, G.F., Sergeant, D.C., and White, P.J. (1998) The role of linguistic dominance in the acquisition of song. *Research Studies in Music Education,* **10**, 67–74.

Chapter 7

How the conventions of music notation shape musical perception and performance

Jeanne Bamberger

> Of all affairs, communication is the most wonderful. That things should be able to pass from the plane of external pushing and pulling to that of revealing themselves to man, and thereby to themselves; and that the fruit of communication should be participation, sharing, is a wonder by the side of which transubstantiation pales. (Dewey 1927, p. 166.)

Introduction

Despite Dewey's eloquent and compassionate advocacy for the powers of communication, there is a subtle tension underneath these comments.

For example, Dewey goes on:

> Events when once they are named lead an independent and double life: their meanings may be infinitely combined and re-arranged in imagination... Meanings, having been deflected from the rapid and roaring stream of events into a calm and traversable canal, rejoin the main stream, and color, temper and compose its course (ibid).

The tension reveals itself when we ask: how are we able to transform

> '...the rapid and roaring stream of events... [so as to] turn events into objects, things with a meaning [that] may be referred to when they do not exist, and thus be operative among things distant in space and time, through vicarious presence in a new medium' (ibid).

And there is a further tension already foreshadowed by Dewey's claims: When events are 'turned into objects' the representations of those events are necessarily partial and they are so in two senses: they are *incomplete*, and they favour, or are *partial to* certain aspects of the phenomena while ignoring others. Moreover, in being selective, communications, whether invented by children, associated with social convention, or with a community of professional users, the privileged selection will guide the objects, events, and relations, sometimes even usurp, the selective attention of its communicants. In short, notations reflect a tacit ontological commitment.

To pursue the significance of the evolving symbiosis among musical notations, ontologies, theory, and practice, one should ideally follow the long and fascinating history of music notation, itself. While this is not the place for that discussion, the symbiosis becomes relevant when we notice that the historical evolution of modern notation in some eerie way is mirrored in the natural evolution over time of children's invented notations (Bamberger 1995, 2000; Barrett, Ch. 6 this volume; and Treitler 1982).

The two evolutions pursue a parallel course in that transformations over time can be characterized as a gradual emergence (invention) of systematic frameworks within which the noticeably invisible relations of pitch and time that are necessarily experienced as continuously going on, come to be represented as spatial, static, and invariant properties. Critical to this emergence is the extraction or 'lifting out' of pitch/time from the unique contexts and unique functions within the performed and perceived configurations of which they are members so as to represent them as invariant properties.

With respect to the representation of temporal relations, there was a long and circuitous process that eventually led to the emergence of the idea that the beat could serve as an invarient 'unit'. While initially a few ligatured rhythm patterns (modes) had served as the fundamental units of reference, the idea of the beat as an invariant 'unit' made it possible for discrete durations at the musical surface to be consistently measured and represented (Tanay 1999).

In turn, pitch notations evolved from representation of familiar musical patterns or 'gestures' associated with text and represented by graphical *neumes*. These were gradually replaced by the construction of an outside *fixed reference structure* that ordered pitch-properties according to what we metaphorically term 'low-high'. Represented eventually by modern staff notation, pitch and pitch-distance could be consistently measured and invariantly noted (Treitler 1982; Tanay 1999).

In accounts of children's cognitive development across domains of study, 'progress' is described in much the same terms. That is, 'getting better' is seen to be the transformations that occur over time from an initial responsiveness to present, unfolding contexts and the unique function of events and relations in that present, to the mental construction of outside fixed reference systems in terms of which properties can be invariantly named, placed, classified, and their relations consistently measured (e.g. Werner 1948; Piaget 1968; Vygotsky 1962).

With respect to the conventions of modern music notation, it is clear what is gained with the construction of fixed reference systems. Such systems make possible the use of symbols that consistently refer to pitch and time as stable, measurable, properties disengaged from the changes acquired through context and function. This, in turn, provides, an unambiguous conduit from composer to performer *within the constraints of the partial features represented*. But we need to ask, what is lost in these disambiguating evolutions? How can we tell, and how do we learn to respond to the utility of invariance while still being responsive to unique context and function?

To explore these questions, I will concentrate on three case studies, each of which brings into focus the tensions implicit in these questions as well as in those implicit in Dewey's comments quoted earlier. In particular, each study suggests that an early emphasis on teaching notation and the property invariances it names, may disguise and even discourage children's powerful and appropriate intuitive responsiveness to the changing meaning of notationally same pitch/time events when they become embedded in new tonal and/or rhythmic contexts.

In Part II, I look at the work of a nine-year-old musically untutored boy whom I call Brad. I compare Brad's work in Part III with that of two exceptionally gifted young violinists, Conan and Beth, who are 9 and 8 years old, respectively. Working on a task much like Brad's, surprising similarities emerge despite the children's strikingly different backgrounds. Specifically, all three children show a rather remarkable ability to shift their focus of attention among possible features and relations of the melodies.

Finally, in Part IV, I compare aspects of the children's work with actual conversations among members of the Guarneri String Quartet. These conversations touch upon the tensions between notational conventions and artistic performance that are already emergent among the children. I will discuss the ontological commitments implicit in these findings and the educational implications they entrain.

Brad: the materials, the task, and the working environment

The musical materials with which Brad, as well as Conan and Beth worked, are bells borrowed from the Montessori materials. Each individual metal bell, *all of which look the same*, is attached to a wooden stem with bell and stem, in turn, standing on a small wooden base making it easy to move them about.

Brad was given five Montessori bells and a small mallet or stick with which to play them. The task, as it was presented to Brad (and to some 50 other children between the ages of 8 and 12), is as follows:

'Build the tune, "Hot Cross Buns" with your bells. When you are finished, make some instructions so someone else can play the tune on your bells as you have set them up'.

Because the bells all look alike, the only way to tell them apart is to play them and listen. The bells differ in this regard from any other musical materials of which I am aware – for instance, size and/or spatial orientation of conventional instruments usually correspond to ordered pitch relations, as well. The visual anonymity of the bells plays a significant role in the children's need to invent means for differentiating and naming the bells in part to communicate with others in making 'instructions'.

The children's inventions also serve as clues to how they are organizing pitch and time. As Israel Rosenfield has said:

We perceive the world without labels, and we can label it only when we have decided how it's features should be organized (Rosenfield 1988 p. 187)

Taken seriously, these implicit organizing principles serve as foils in revealing assumptions in our notational conventions that might otherwise remain hidden from view.

Brad's work was influenced by the culture of the novel environment where it was carried out – an alternative public school classroom called The Laboratory for Making Things. For example, children were accustomed to informal conversations in which they explained to others how they were making sense of their working materials, including inventing graphic instructions/notations that could help someone else build what they had built. Particularly important in this small culture was the idea of 'chunking' or grouping their working materials. This initially grew out of the children's need to 'chunk' or parse a melody into workable 'blocks' which then became the 'units of work' in composing melodies.

The practice of 'chunking' was also related to marking off elements that were to be named. This cultural practice became most evident when we heard one child asking of another as they looked together at a musical, lego, or other work-in-progress, 'So what is a THING, here?' Indeed, the question became a very concrete way of posing a fundamental ontological question: What have you got here? What are the objects, the 'things' that your house or machine or melody is made up of and what do you call them? The question quite spontaneously focused a child's attention on, for instance, functions, repeating objects, patterns, boundaries, and groupings as they emerged.

Brad's evolving instructions

Undifferentiated objects

Brad began his work by anticipating the task of making instructions and with it the need to communicate with others. Without playing the bells, he cut out five paper squares, wrote numbers on them from 1 to 5, and placed a numbered square in front of each bell. Ordering the numbers *right-to-left* from 1 to 5, he ingeniously invented a way to name the undifferentiated objects, the 5 bells, on the table before him (Fig. 7.1).

Brad's number-labels cannot, of course, refer to the hidden pitch properties of the objects they name since, remaining silent, these properties have not yet been revealed. The numbers are simply 'paste-on' labels useful as long as the labels stay attached to the bells. His use of numbers is reminiscent of lessons in how to play the piano where keys are colour coded and instructions for playing a tune instruct the player which key-colour, like Brad's bell-numbers, to play when.

Building the tune

Playing the bells now, listening, and searching for each bell *as it was needed in the tune*, Brad built up a cumulating bell-path. Being careful to keep the labels attached to the bells as he moves them into place, Brad transformed his initial silent line-up into a bell-path where the position of each added bell matched its order of occurrence *in the unfolding of the tune*. Moving *on* his built bell-path, now, Brad made an *action path* through his unique, one-purpose instrument to play the whole tune (Fig. 7.2).

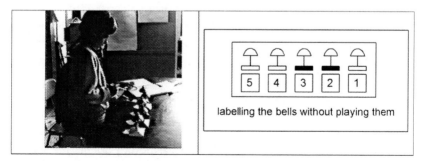

labelling the bells without playing them

Fig. 7.1

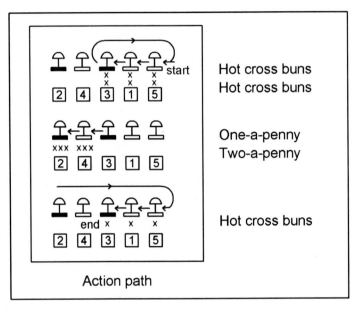

Hot cross buns
Hot cross buns

One-a-penny
Two-a-penny

Hot cross buns

Action path

Fig. 7.2

Notation 1: action and structural grouping

Brad makes his first instructions by so-to-speak 'peeling off' each number-name from a bell and placing it on paper *in the order in which he plays them*: his sequence of actions becomes a sequence of numbers in paper space.

Putting pencil to paper, Brad abandons the prevailing right-to-left direction of his *actions*, and spontaneously invokes the left-to-right directional convention associated with writing. Most significant is Brad's *spatial grouping* of numbers. The boundaries of these numeric groups coincide with *changes in direction* in Brad's action path and these together with repetition 'bundle' events to generate the *figural or motivic grouping boundaries* of the tune. The middle figure which Brad notates as **4 4 4 2 2 2**, is bounded by the move to new bells, the repeated events played on single bells, and by the subsequent return to the beginning figure. (Like many other children, Brad plays only 3 repetitions on each bell rather than four as in the original tune.) (Fig. 7.3)

Brad's spatial grouping boundaries bear a certain similarity to the historically early *neumes* in that they graphically represent contextually bounded figures. While the *neumes* were associated with the parsing of text, Brad's figures are more associated with the parsing of his actions. And like the early *neumes*, Brad's notation is primarily as a performance aid, communicating to the performer how to express the internal structural relations of just this tune (Treitler 1982).

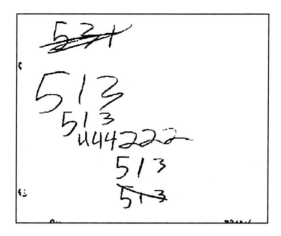

Fig. 7.3

I will call Brad's one-purpose bell path from which his notation derives, a *reference entity*. A *reference entity* is a uniquely built structure that 'holds still' in physical space a maker's situational knowledge of some present phenomena. Unlike staff notation which derives from a pre-fixed *reference structure*, a notation that derives from a reference entity cannot be generalized so as to apply to any instrument, to make comparisons across melodies, or, indeed, to map onto relevant structures in other domains. However, Brad's reference entity reflects motivic grouping and the function of events within these figures – aspects that are not shown in bare (un-annotated) staff notation at all (Fig. 7.4).

Fig. 7.4

Notation 2: just three bells

Brad's next instructions were triggered by an accidental discovery made by Celia who discovered that she could play the first part of *Hot Cross Buns* '...in two different ways so it sounds just the same' (Fig. 7.5).

The discovery remained simply a mystery for Celia. But in the spirit of collaborative learning in the Lab, I showed Celia's new way to Brad and asked, 'How do you explain this? See if it will work on your bells?'

Brad played the first figure of the tune in his usual way and used Celia's new action-path to play the repeat. Pausing for just a moment, he went on to play

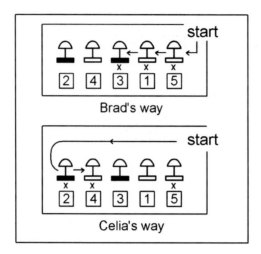

Fig. 7.5

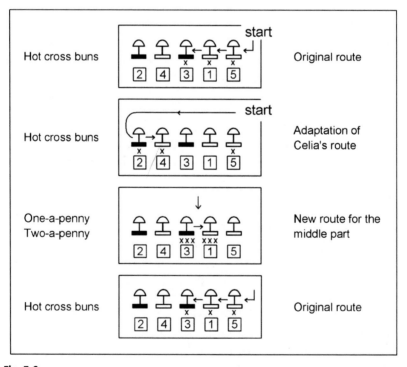

Fig. 7.6

the middle part of the tune using the two bells labelled **3 and 1**, that he had previously used *only to play the first part of the tune* (Fig. 7.6).

Finishing the tune by playing the return to the first part in his usual way, Brad paused, looked up with an expression of puzzlement and surprise, and said,

Oh, this is weird! I can play it with just three bells!

And he pushed aside the bell-pair labelled **4-2**.

It might seem obvious to those who are more musically experienced that Brad had simply recognized that the bell-pairs 4-2 and 3-1 played the same pitches. But Brad's own explanation makes clear that this is not the case. When asked by Mary Briggs, 'How'd you discover it? All of a sudden you said, "Wait a minute, I can do it with three", Brad explained:

...I was realizing that if I could play it one way – like **5 1 3** (pause).

Then I realized that two of these (pointing to the pair [**1 3**]) could be used in a different way instead of these two (points to the pair [**4 2**] (Fig. 7.7)).

Perhaps what is 'weird' for Brad is his discovery that bell-constituents can 'change who they are'. That is, the bell pairs, 2-4 and 1-3 can function effectively as members of the first motivic group or the middle motivic group. They are, in this sense, *functionally equivalent pairs*. Brad articulates that principle in his expression '...could be used in a different way instead of....' And since the two

Fig. 7.7

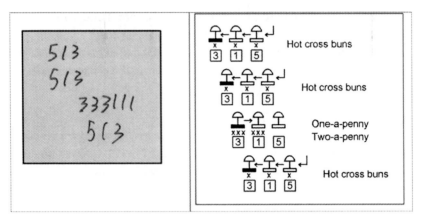

Fig. 7.8

pairs are functionally equivalent, either one or the other plus the single 5-bell is enough, and that makes just 3 bells in all.

Brad's accounting illuminates the importance of distinguishing between our conventional criterion for classifying events as 'the same', namely, 'same pitch property', and a classification of events as the same on the criterion, *functionally* equivalent. Brad's work also suggests that constructing a class of objects/events that can functionally substitute for one another may be a necessary intermediary step towards later recognizing de-contextualized same-pitch properties – for instance, the class of all Cs and all Ds.

Having proposed his 3-bell theory Brad successfully plays the whole tune using just the three remaining bells. His second notation gives instructions for how to do that (Fig. 7.8).

Questioned about why he has grouped together numbers [3 3 3 1 1 1], Brad again speaks of 'the same' in a functional way:

> Because they're kinda together ... cause it's kinda the same ... it's the same as these three. (He points to the previous numbers [5 1 3]).

The events numbered [3 3 3 1 1 1] are 'the same as' those numbered [5 1 3] in just one critical respect: the events 'go together' to form gestures or structural

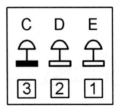

Fig. 7.9

entities. To use the children's expression, events that form a group, constitute the functional 'things' of this small universe.

Notation 3: a pattern

Saying, 'I see a pattern; I mean, you really could number them **1 2 3**', Brad uses his numbered paper squares to re-label the bells accordingly (Fig. 7.9).

Brad has replaced his *ad hoc* number-names (**5-1-3**) with ordinal numbers that refer to the sequence in which the bells enter the song as tune-events but still going right-to-left. Again giving new meaning to the bells and the sequence of events, Brad's verbal instructions along with his gestures

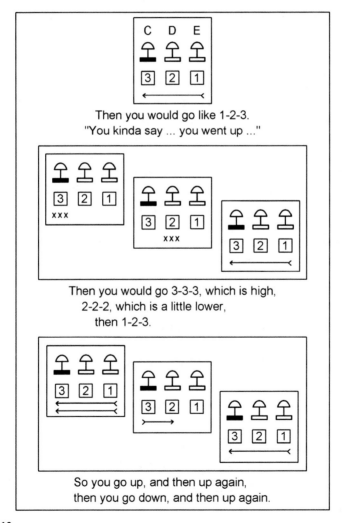

Fig. 7.10

become another embodied notation (Fig. 7.10). He says, 'I mean, let's say this was 1':

Borrowing from numeric directionality, Brad's numbers are metaphorically 'going up' but the beginning of the melody is equally metaphorically 'going down'. Dead metaphors can come alive under conditions of uncertainty and confusion (Lakoff, and Johnson 1987; Spitzer 2003; Schön 1963, 1979). Brad's use of directional metaphor, here, is illuminated by the work of Johnson and Larson (2003). They define 'conceptual metaphor' of musical time in terms of a 'Landscape/Motion opposition':

> Given that we typically conceptualize time either as "motion through space" ('The Moving Time Metaphor') or as a "landscape" through which we ourselves move ('The Time's Landscape Metaphor'), we can imagine music as either "moving" past us or as a structure which we navigate. (quoted in Spitzer 2003, p. 104)

Notation 4: pitch as an emergent phenomenon

The transformations in action as Brad constructed and re-constructed his notations gave evidence of emerging new entities and relations. But none of Brad's notations has referred to pitch or pitch relations, as such. Watching Brad's work, I asked myself what on-the-spot intervention might help him include as a factor in his ontology and his notations the existence of pitch and its invariance?

Pointing to the two 'discarded' bells, I asked Brad: "How come you don't need to use these bells? Do you know why it works"? Shaking his head, Brad said rather soberly, "No. I don't". This response tentatively confirmed my hunch that Brad was unaware of the duplicate pitches in his initial 5-bell collection (Fig. 7.11).

Going further, I pointed to one of the 'extra' bells (the D-bell) and said, 'Play this bell. Can you find one that sounds the same?'

Brad quickly found a match for the designated bell, I asked him, 'Do they sound the same?' Looking visibly surprised, he answered, 'Yeah, they do'. And without even playing the remaining 'extra' bell, Brad pushed it towards the matching C-bell saying, 'And these probably do too' (Fig. 7.12).

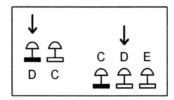

Fig. 7.11

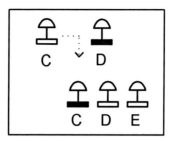

Fig. 7.12

Finally, pushing the two extra bells away again, he said, 'So you really only need—that's cool'. Coupled with their mates, the 'extra' bells had again changed their identity – no longer objects that were functionally equivalent, they were pitch equivalents (Fig. 7.13).

Brad had invented another new embodied notation and perhaps helped to account for the 'weirdness' of his 3-bell theory, as well.

Revisiting

Brad's work has provided evidence for a child's untutored intuitive sense of figures, their boundaries, and their structural functions within the unique contexts of an unfolding melody. In the course of my intervention, Brad caught a glimpse of categorical pitch class. But to understand the meanings implicit in the symbols of notation, he would still need to construct a fixed reference structure *external* to any particular tune in terms of which to place any pitch event, consistently name it, and measure its distance from others. In contrast, the constructions and notations that Brad made on his own rest entirely on relations and actions *internal* to the unique tune, itself. As instructions they could help to communicate to a performer how to shape phrasing and articulations at boundaries and implicitly the changing functions of pitch events – aspects that are only vaguely communicated by conventional music notation.

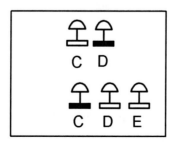

Fig. 7.13

As practicing musicians we value and depend on the consistency of fixed reference structures and the notations derived from them. But if responsiveness to function and context is central to the intuitive perception and communication of the musical novice and, as we will learn from the Guarneri, also deeply important to expert performance, we are left with the critical question raised earlier: How can we nurture rather than discourage musical responsiveness such as we see in Brad's work while still benefiting from the security of modern notational conventions?

In the next section this question will become more vivid through the disequilibrium of transition exhibited by the gifted violinists: On one hand, we see them expressing the intuitions of the musically novice child and, on the other, the ontological commitments associated with adult musicians who have fully internalized notational conventions.

The young violinists

I worked with Conan and Beth in the context of the Young Performers Program, a special program for musically gifted children in a community music school in Cambridge, MA. Conan and Beth, 9 and 8 years old, respectively, had each recently played impressive performances of violin concertos with the school orchestra. Conan and Beth could, of course, read music, fluently.

I enlisted five children as participants in the bell tasks including Conan and Beth, towards the end of a six-month period during which I had attended the children's private violin lessons, chamber music rehearsals, coaching sessions, and sat in on theory classes, orchestra rehearsals, and public performances.

Most memorable in these observations was the persistence with which I saw teachers encouraging children to shift their focus of attention and to experiment with playing a passage in different ways. This, in turn, contributed to the young performers' development of a network of what I have called 'organizing schemata' – i.e. multiple ways of actively understanding, thinking about, and/or performing a passage, a motive, or even a single note (Bamberger 1986). I borrow the notion of organizing schema from Bartlett's seminal book, 'Remembering':

> "Schema" refers to an active organization of past reactions, or of past experiences, which must always be supposed to be operating in any well-adapted organic response. (Bartlett 1932, p. 201).

The network of organizing schemata were important because they spawned the use of differing sensory modalities, different media, and different kinds of language or symbols, providing possibilities for different ways of communicating, conceptualizing and solving problems. The resulting hearings, re-hearings, playings and re-playings also allowed teacher and student tacitly to test their understanding of one another. For the children the schemata became a fluid, well-functioning system of reciprocities – an actively intertwined web.

It is, then, of particular interest that in the bell tasks these multiple foci of attention tended to come apart – to emerge separately, come into confrontation with one another, and even, at times, come into conflict. However, consistent with their experience in shifting focus and musical problem solving, the children were able to invent novel strategies to resolve conflicts among features and relations newly liberated from the previously well-functioning meld.

The task

The task given to the children was similar to Brad's except a bit more elaborate. The children were asked to make a somewhat longer tune, *Twinkle Twinkle Little Star*, and they were given a mixed array of 11 Montessori bells (rather than only 5) – all the pitches of the C-major scale, along with three matching E, G, and C bells. Further, they were asked to make instructions only *after* they had finished building the tune.

I focus on a few critical moments in the work of the two violinists which provide evidence that, despite their remarkably precocious violin performances, the children were still in musical and conceptual transition. Reminiscent of Brad's work, the disequilibrium of transition was most clearly expressed in the children's use of conflicting spatial metaphors. But unlike Brad, the children's conflicts took the form of images associated with conventional notation, on one hand, and on the other, with direction of pitch motion associated with actions on instruments. Indeed, the critical moments initially occurred when the tune goes down in pitch associated with going left on the keyboard, and simultaneously goes 'forward' in time, associated in notation with going right. While this potential conflict is ordinarily overridden in everyday practice before it even comes into one's awareness, it was clearly revealed in this unusual environment where pitches are embodied by bells that are free to be moved about, that have no identifying labels on them, and that are likely to change their identity in response to visual/spatial image and to context as the tune unfolds.

Given these aspects of potential conflict, it is not surprising that in the process of building the tune, critical moments most frequently occurred at structural boundaries. The diagram of *Twinkle Twinkle Little Star* (Fig. 7.14) will facilitate reference to these structural moments.

The pitch structure of *Twinkle* is prototypical of what Meyer calls a 'gap fill' melody: an initial leap up from tonic to dominant in Phrase a.1, the 'gap', followed by a descending stepwise progression from the dominant back down

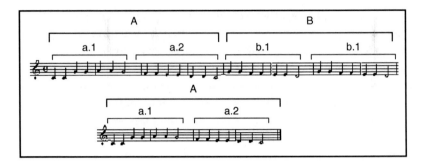

Fig. 7.14

to the tonic in phrase a.2, the 'gap fill' (Meyer 1973, p. 145). This structure turned out to be an active component in the work of both children.

Getting started

Since the children were certainly familiar with the major scale as a reference structure, and since the bells included all the pitches of the C Major scale, it was expected that they would begin by first building the scale. In fact none of the children did so. However, it is significant that older participants in the program did begin the task by building the C-Major scale – further evidence to suggest that the younger children were indeed, in transition. One 12-year old cellist said on seeing the mixed array of bells on the table, 'It makes me nervous to see them all mixed up like that; can I put them in order'?

The younger children all began the task just as Brad and other musically novice children did: finding the first bell (C), they added the next two bells to their cumulating bell path (G and A) in the order in which they occurred in the tune – an order-of-occurrence schema (Fig. 7.15).

But with the next event in Phrase a.1 the young violinists clearly deviated from their novice peers. The typical novice continues by adding another G-bell to the right of the previous A-bell (Bamberger 1995), but all of the violinists moved back *left* to play the same G-bell again (Fig. 7.16).

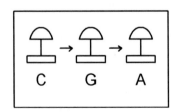

Fig. 7.15

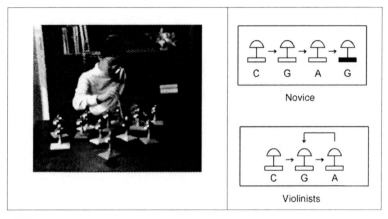

Fig. 7.16

For all the children the switch-back to the G-bell was a familiar action path. But this move held implications for generating conflict among schemata, leading the children into their first critical moments.

Critical moments

Conan: a double-classification strategy

Conan began like all the other children, turning back to end Phrase a.1 by striking the G-bell again. But with his next move, Conan slipped into momentary conflict. In search of the F-bell with which Phrase a.2 begins, Conan struck the C-bell sitting immediately to the left of G, exactly where the F-bell should have been if invoking the schema, pitches to the left are lower. For a fleeting moment the C-bell, which was already there as first-in-tune, and the F-bell that could have been there as lower-then, were fused in one identity. But quickly recouping, Conan backed off, swung his mallet *between* the C and G bells and said out loud to himself, 'Yah, it has to go there' (Fig. 7.17).

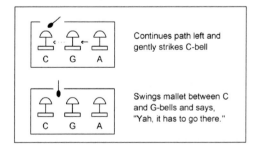

Fig. 7.17

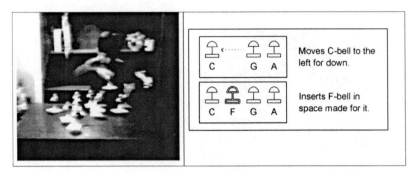

Moves C-bell to the left for down.

Inserts F-bell in space made for it.

Fig. 7.18

The 'it' is, of course, the needed F-bell and his comment makes clear that Conan has now shifted his strategy to invoke the new scale schema. With his next move Conan plays out a resolution to his conflict by inventing a *double classification strategy*. Finding an actual F-bell among the still unidentified bells on the table, he moves the C-bell to the left (for 'down'), and inserts the F-bell in the space made for it (Fig 7.18).

Playing out his double-classification strategy, Conan finds and adds bells in order of occurrence in the tune, but at the same time positions each new bell to the left of the previous one as next lower in the scale (Fig. 7.19).

With the completion of section A, Conan has also built most of the C-Major scale. This is, of course, a fortuitous function of the 'gap-fill' structure of the melody: the history of Conan's construction mirrors the history of the tune. Conan quickly completed the B and returning A sections of the tune using his bell path as the familiar fixed reference scale.

Beth: Phrases a.2 and b.1

Beth also turned back to strike the G-bell again. But like novice tune builders, she continued with the order-of-occurrence strategy adding new bells to the right of the A-bell into Phrase a.2. However, at the end of the phrase Beth broke

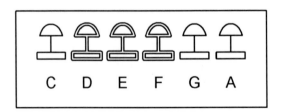

Fig. 7.19

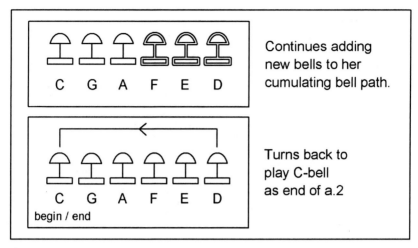

Continues adding new bells to her cumulating bell path.

Turns back to play C-bell as end of a.2

begin / end

Fig. 7.20

the prevailing order-of-occurrence schema, going back to the far left to strike the C-bell again (Fig. 7.20).

This shift in organizing schema, moving to the far left to use the C-bell again, throws her into acute confusion. With the anonymous bells lined up on the table, the C-bell at the far left which had just functioned as the *ending* event in Phrase a.2, changes its identity to become the *lowest* pitch of the bells as if organized in the C scale. As evidence, we see Beth reach from the 'low' C-bell 'up' to the far right where, on the scale-organized view the G-bell with which Phrase b.1 begins, should be. But with the just previous order of occurrence strategy, the D-bell was still there as the penultimate member of Phrase a.2 (Fig. 7.21).

To escape from the confusing situation, Beth went to the unused bells still on the table, found an *entirely new G-bell*, and added it on at the far right of the bell line-up. Still seeing the line-up of bells as the instantiation of the scale,

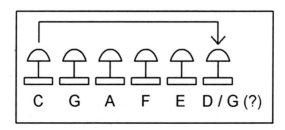

Fig. 7.21

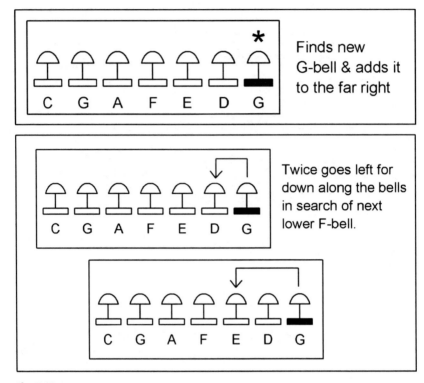

Fig. 7.22

she placed the new G-bell to the far right, just where it 'belonged' as 'high' and as the top of the descending b.1 phrase. Going on, Beth twice went left, 'down', from her new G-bell in search of the descending pitches (Fig. 7.22).

Painfully bewildered now, Beth paused, then all in one go quickly rearranged the bells to make the C-scale, left-to-right, low-to-high with the low C-bell still at the far left. The previous order-of-occurrence line-up of bells was transformed to conform with the structure she had been silently attributing to them. Except that the extra G-bell still remained at the far right, *maintaining its identity as the beginning* of the B section (Fig. 7.23).

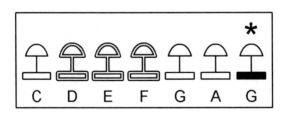

Fig. 7.23

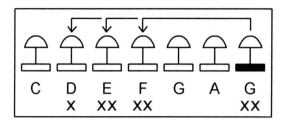

Fig. 7.24

Trying the B section again, Beth ignored the G-bell in the scale-ordered series, kept the identity of the extra G-bell as the beginning of Phrase b.1 using it to play the descending G-F-E-D-bells to complete the b.1 phrase (Fig. 7.24).

Repeating Phrase b.1 in the same way, Beth played the return of A, this time using the G-bell positioned within the scale-ordered series (Fig. 7.25). Constructed representations and situational identities do not disappear easily.

With the task completed, I asked Beth, 'What did you do back there? All of a sudden you re-arranged all the bells?' She answered quietly, 'I built a scale'. And when I asked her why, she said simply, 'So I could find the notes.' But the question of identity was not quite resolved. When I asked, 'Do you have any bells that play the same pitch?' after a moment's thought she answered simply, 'No'.

Paradoxically, while both children initially started building the tune by constructing its unique *internal* relations, they left behind a static, *outside* fixed reference structure, the scale, as if confirming its efficacy. Indeed, without having followed the evolution, the 'becoming,' of this structure, someone entering the room would most likely have assumed that Conan and Beth had started out by building the scale.

But there is a critical point here: the children's emerging multiple schemata are possible only because in the unfolding of a melody, even a single musical event potentially embodies multiple aspects and can assume multiple identities simultaneously. Aspects (pitch register, function, order of occurrence, etc.) are carried over across schemata as the player sees/hears a feature or an event now as a constituent of one schema, now of another; now with one identity, now

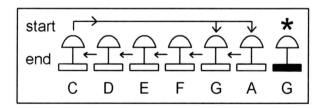

Fig. 7.25

with another. With respect to communication, we are faced again with the same questions: Is there a logical incommensurability between a representation that consistently communicates invariant properties, and a representation that can communicate changing identities in response to contextual function?

Making instructions

I expected that when asked to make instructions, the children would simply use conventional staff notation, but not one of the young violinists did so. Moreover, none of the children included rhythm in their instructions. However, not surprisingly, both Beth and Conan used their scale-ordered bells as a reference structure, numbering the bells sequentially and then using the number-names to make their instructions (Fig. 7.26).

Like his construction strategy, Conan's notation also implicitly involves double classification between two well-formed structures: numbers refer to the *fixed* position of pitches along the reference structure, while the *sequence* of numbers refers to the unique order of occurrence of tune events. It is through the intersection of the two that '...we can imagine music as either 'moving' past us or as a structure upon which we navigate' (Johnson and Larson, *op cit*).

Revisiting the tune-builders

A comparison among all three children points up their differences but also what they share, namely, a rather remarkable capacity to engage conflict, and to find ingenious resolutions through shifting attention among their organizing schemata. For Brad this meant, in part, borrowing organizers from other domains (language, math) together with his ingenuity in discovering or

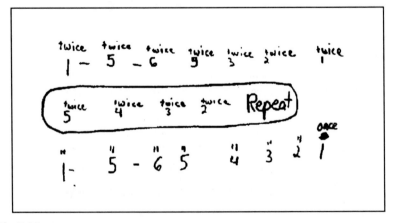

Fig. 7.26

inventing a series of new 'possibles' – figural grouping, his 3-bell theory, the ordinal number notation with its implied directionality.

For Conan and Beth, it was a matter of side-slipping, sometimes out of control, among a wider network of musical organizers. This active network of multiple organizing schemata which functioned smoothly and reciprocally in performance on their violins, only became visible as the network came apart in the novel environment of the bell task.

Looking back, one is tempted to ask if the ability of all three children to invent or to invoke a network of organizers, to confront conflict, and to see an event or an object differently as they situate it in different organizing schemata, has something to do with what makes them special? Indeed, I will propose, now, that we see the broad network of organizers emerging again in new guise as an important factor contributing to the artistry of mature performers.

The Guarneri quartet

We are fortunate to have intimate documentation of the actual work that contributes to such artistry through conversations with the Guarneri String Quartet (Blum 1986). The documentation includes accounts of conversations among players and also conversations between players and the score. Ben Shahn speaks of the conversations between the painter and his painting in much the way performers speak of their conversations with the score:

> But idea itself must always bow to the needs and demands of the material in which it is to be cast ... So one must say that painting is both creative and responsive. It is an intimately communicative affair between the painter and his painting, a conversation back and forth, the painting telling the painter even as it receives its shape and form (Shahn 1957/1972, p. 49).

I have chosen just two passages that I believe show how the children's evolving network of intuitive organizing schemata may develop into means that contribute to artistic performance of complex, large compositions.

In this first example, Soyer, the cellist of the quartet, comments on a very brief passage from the coda of the first movement of the Beethoven Quartet Op. 59 #2. In this passage a notated G-natural and G-sharp each change their functional identities. But now, unlike the functional identity changes that are out of control and cause confusion for the children, these occur with Soyer's full awareness of rapidly changing harmonic environments. Indeed, identity change emerges in part to account for the paradoxical constancy with which same pitch is notated – what you see is not necessarily what you hear or play.

> Soyer: ....The passage begins in the key of G-sharp minor; the G natural in bar 216 is clearly a simplified way of writing F double-sharp, which, as the leading note, has an

Fig. 7.27

upwards attraction towards the tonic G sharp. For this reason I'd avoid using the open
G-string and would play the passage on the C string (Fig. 7.27).

When G natural comes again [bar 224], its harmonic function is altered; it's now
the fifth degree of C major and thus not sharpened. The subsequent G sharp [bar 225]
is no longer the tonic but acts as the leading note in A minor and should be sharpened. This is the explanation from the harmonic standpoint, but your hearing once
sensitized to such things, will often be able to put you there quite of itself without
your needing to think it out (Blum, p. 33).

Soyer is here reflecting on his own decision-making as it happens in real time
performance. To this he brings a totally conscious awareness of the interactive
communication between the givens of the score, the instrument and his actions
on it, and the musical meaning of the passage. Soyer makes a close analysis
and description of why and how the notated pitches 'change who they are', but
the way in which description becomes intuitive performance leaves some big

Fig. 7.28

questions: how does a 'hearing' evolve and how does one become 'sensitized' to 'such things' so that in conversation with the score, the 'same' becomes both the same and different? How does a performer benefit from the invariance of pitch class notation and still use it as a means of communicating functional musical meaning? When, then, is again? These are some of the deep questions of a musical education.

Michael Tree, the violist, elaborates on Soyer's comments, now with respect not only to conversation with the score but also communication among the four players in coming to agreement:

> Tree: When four string players have passages in unison, the question is always who is to adjust to whom – especially when expressive intonation is involved. Take the second movement of Beethoven's Op. 132 (Fig. 7.28):
>
> Close semitones are called for here, but if someone exaggerates, it can throw things out of kilter. There has to be discretion. As Dave (Soyer) says, the problem is in coming to an agreement as to how much the note strives upwards or downwards (Blum, p. 33).

And so once again the metaphor of directionality enters. While directionality involved actual movements in space for the children, it was also associated with tacit metaphoric directionality – up and down in pitch space, numeric space, or symbolic time-space. But for these performers, it is as if the note, itself is given volition and animus – an 'upwards attraction', 'the note strives upwards or downwards'. In this way artists, in conversation with the score, the instrument, and the unfolding process of the composition, animate a static list of invariant symbols so as to communicate functional variance in response to contextual change.

Conclusions

Through the three case studies, Brad, Conan, and Beth, along with the Guarnari Quartet, we catch a glimpse of before, during, and after in the influence of conventional notation on perception and performance. Each phase is reflected in the participants' actions and representations in the course of communicating with themselves and others. The communications, in turn, reflect the musical objects that hold their attention – those which in practice, they take to exist.

Brad shows us the changing face of 'before': his ontology, while evolving, includes primarily motivic grouping of events as they unfold in time and the classification of some events as functionally equivalent, neither aspect of which exists in conventional notation.

The gifted young violinists show us the influence of notation most vividly through the conflicts of transition between, on one hand, assumed pitch-objects and their ordering as represented in conventional notation and as these map onto the geography of instruments, and on the other, an ontology shared with Brad that is still actively working in the background – motivic groups as bounded objects and the shifting function of pitch-events within these groupings.

The Guarneri show us the fully internalized and, of course, effective use of conventional notation, but also the necessity to go beyond its limits. Most interesting, 'going beyond' involves probing for, engaging, integrating, and projecting through performance, responsiveness to context and function that we saw in nascent form in Brad's work. But it would be too easy to draw from this a simple correspondence between the naive child and the mature, sophisticated artist performer. Indeed, Soyer and Tree in their conversations with the score and with each other are resolving the contentious conflicts in organizing schemata we saw among the gifted children by projecting the multiple aspects and the changing meanings of even a single note as their performance unfolds in time.

> ...what can it mean in a truly temporal sense to say that the same is repeated? (Hasty 1997, p. 8).

Returning to my opening forays concerning musical communications, notations, ontologies, and the ever present danger of notational imperialism, a big question emerges that harks back to the tensions voiced by Dewey and reflected in the children's inner and outer communications with the bells?

How can we give children the security and the communicability of pitch invariance as represented by a shared notation, while still helping them go beyond its limits to develop their musical responsiveness to temporally changing identities?

Remarkably, Aristoxenus in c. 350 B.C.E. was already aware of this tension. He says:

> ...the signs fail to distinguish the functional differences, and consequently indicate the magnitudes of the intervals, and nothing more... Mere knowledge of magnitudes does not enlighten one as to the functions of the tetrachords, or of the notes, of the differences of the genera..., or the distinction between modulating and non-modulating systems, or the styles of melodic composition, or indeed anything else of the kind. (Aristoxenus (c. 350 B.C.E., p. 31)).

I propose that we embrace these tensions by embedding them in an environment where children are encouraged to confront and puzzle over the potential for multiple organizing schemata. This would include recognizing and valuing both the mobility associated with pitch and rhythm in changing contexts, as well as the invariance associated with the traditional classifications of musical objects. For without the latter we could not marvel at how identities shift for there would be no resilient identities at all. With such puzzlements, conventional notation would also come to be seen as an invention, the gradually emergent organizing schema that it is – one among a repertoire of possibles.

In this way the tension among these possibles becomes creative but only if we have the courage to join the landscape of well-trodden, well-learned static communication paths that we move *on*, and the sensory action paths along which we sometimes become lost as we both make and follow them through space and time in the ever present present.

References

Aristoxenus (c. 350 B.C.E.) *The Harmonic elements*. In *Source readings in music history: Antiquity and the middle ages*. (ed. O. Strunk, 1950), pp. 27–31. New York: W.W. Norton & Co.

Bamberger, J. (1986) Cognitive issues in the development of musically gifted children. In *Conceptions of giftedness* (eds R.J. Sternberg and J.E. Davidson), pp. 388–413. Cambridge: Cambridge University Press.

Bamberger, J. (1991; 1995) *The mind behind the musical ear*. Cambridge, MA: Harvard University Press.

Bamberger, J. (1996) Turning music theory on its ear. *International journal of computers for mathematical learning*. Volume 1 No. 1, pp. 33–55.

Bamberger, J. (2000) *Developing musical intuitions: A project-based approach to music fundamentals*. New York: Oxford University Press.

Bartlett, F.C. (1932) *Remembering: An experimental and social study*. Cambridge: Cambridge University Press.

Blum, D. (1986) *The art of quartet playing: The Guarneri quartet in conversation with David Blum*. New York: Alfred A. Knopf.

Dewey, J. (1927; 1958) *Experience and nature*. New York: Dover Publications.

Hasty, C. (1997) *Meter as rhythm*. New York: Oxford University Press.

Lakoff, G. and Johnson, M. (1987) *Metaphors We Live By*. Chicago, IL: University of Chicago Press.

Meyer, L.B. (1973) *Explaining Music*. Berkeley, CA: University of California Press.

Piaget, J. (1968; 1976) *The Psychology of Intelligence*. Patterson, NJ: Littlefield, Adams, & Co.

Rosenfield, I. (1988) *The invention of memory: A new view of the brain*. New York: Basic Books.

Shahn, B. (1957; 1972) *The shape of content*. Cambridge, MA: Harvard University Press.

Schön, D.A. (1963) *Displacement of Concepts*. New York: Humanities Press.

Schön, D.A. (1979) Generative Metaphor. In *Metaphor and thought* (ed. A. Ortony), pp. 254–84. Cambridge: Cambridge University Press.

Spitzer, M. (2003) "The metaphor of musical space." *Musicae Scientiae*, Vol. 7(1), 101–18.

Tanay, D. (1999) *Noting music, marking culture: The intellectual context of rhythmic notation, 1250–400*. American Institute of Musicology, Hanssler-Verlag, Holzgerlingen.

Treitler, L. (1982) The early history of music writing in the west. *Journal of the American Musicological Society*, Vol XXXV, Summer, Number 2, 239–79.

Vygotsky, L. (1962) *Thought and Language*. Cambridge, MA: MIT Press.

H. Werner, (1948/1973) *Comparative Psychology of Mental Development*. New York: International Universities Press, Inc.

Wittgenstein, L. (1960) *The blue and brown books*. New York: Harper and Row.

Chapter 8

Rhythm, human temporality, and brain function

Michael H. Thaut

Music and communication

Throughout human history, music has been considered as a form of communication. However, the nature of what and how music communicates has been the subject of long-standing and fascinating inquiries in philosophy, religion, the arts, and the sciences. Music has been frequently described as a language-like form of human expression although musical sounds do not carry designative meaning like speech sounds. Communication, defined in broadest terms as the process involving any exchange of meaningful information between two or more participants (Gillam *et al.* 2000), requires signs and symbols to exchange information between the originator and the recipient. Signs are frequently defined as anything that 'stands for' something, usually with rather specific references, whereas symbols, as subforms of signs, evoke less specified meaning and are much more subjective. They must have significance for the originator producing them (*cf.* Kreitler and Kreitler 1972; Berlyne 1971). In submitting music to communication analysis, the comparison to speech and language is intriguing and has been invoked many times (*cf.* Aiello 1994). Both speech and music have structural acoustical similarities in regard to prosodic features: pitch, duration, timbre, intensity, and inflection patterns built from those elements. Music can also be studied in analogy to phonological analyses of single speech sounds. A case could also be made for possible morphological analogies in regard to the analysis of smallest sound units that convey meaning. One of the most important overlaps in comparative analysis between music and speech occur within syntax and pragmatics. Music and speech both are built on syntactical systems which organize sound patterns into rule-based structures. Parallels between music and speech from a syntactical point of view have been made, for example, by comparing Noam Chomsky's linguistic model of deep and surface structure in language with musical structure analyses, such as Heinrich Schenker's 'Ursatz' (Schenker 1935;

Bernstein 1976; Sloboda 1985). Although the common existence of syntactical systems in music and speech is undisputed, the exact function and meaning within both communication systems, however, is not necessarily viewed as common (*cf.* Deutsch 1979).

Furthermore, the pragmatic elements of communication – meaning shaped and conveyed by social and cultural context , learning and enculturation, as well as communicative intent of the participants in the communication process – are also found to play important roles in music and speech (Merriam 1964; Kraut 1992). Speech and music both take on meaning within the cultural background, the social context, and the intents and expectations of the situation in which the communication takes place.

However, most likely the most important difference between speech and music lies in the lack of semantic or referential meaning in music. Musical sounds and sound patterns communicate themselves in abstract fashion. They do not intrinsically denote or refer to extramusical events, objects, concepts, or cognitions. Musical meaning is embodied and its nondiscursive symbols cannot be translated directly into referential denotations. One must note, of course, that attempts at infusing direct referential systems into music have been attempted throughout history, for instance, in the 'Doctrine of Affections' in the Baroque period or, through associative prescriptions, in the program music of the nineteenth century which was composed around a nonmusical plot of action (e.g. Berlioz' *Symphonie Fantastique*). A further and very clear distinction between music and speech is found in the differences in the neurological basis of processing speech and music. Whereas expressive and receptive speech functions can be localized in a relatively constrained and lateralized neural network, the neuroanatomical basis of music is widely distributed neurologically and quite dependent on subfunctions of music processing.

Dowling and Harwood (1986) have proposed a system of terms that summarizes comprehensively the different ways in which music is thought to communicate meaning (Peirce 1935; Langer 1942; Meyer 1956; Berlyne 1971): indexically, by learned association with extramusical material; iconically, by likeness or resemblance to extramusical events, experiences, etc; symbolically, by communicating the role and value of its symbols (i.e. musical events) within the structure of musical patterns. Arguably, the symbolic, embedded, form of communication has been often called the core function of musical communication because this is what the listener or performer actually hears, and without meaningful and salient perception of musical structure little associative learning value or iconic representation would be possible (Meyer 1956).

Considering the nonreferential embodied meaning as a core function in musical communication, an understanding of the major organizing syntactical elements in music, those that create meaningful sound patterns, is of utmost importance. Musical 'grammar' is obviously very complex, has undergone significant historical developments, and manifests itself in large diversity across different cultures. A specific musicological review and analysis is not the topic of interest for this chapter. For this reason, a somewhat reductionistic conceptualization must suffice. One of the most important characteristics of music – also when compared to other art forms – is its strictly temporal character. Music unfolds only in time, and the physical basis of music is based on the time patterns of vibrations. Within this temporal basis two additional dimensions emerge: sequentiality and simultaneity. Music's particular nature permits to express both at once. Language is sequential but monophonic. Visual art has analogies of time expressed, for example, in the fascinating writings and paintings of Kupka, Klee, Delauney, or the Cubist movement (Shaw-Miller 2002) but it is essentially spatial. Music's whole physical and cognitive – perceptual nature, however, rests solely within this two – dimensional temporality. Translated into musical terms, we may speak of rhythm and polyphony as the two core dimensions of music. Rhythm and polyphony organize sounds sequentially and simultaneously into meaningful patterns and structures that create 'the language' of music. However, distinct from speech, music is not a referential, associative language – it is initially a perceptual language whose intrinsic pattern structure conveys meaning to the human brain. The significance and meaning of the musical symbols within that pattern structure depend on their place and role in the pattern, relative to the other symbols in a syntactical network which is organized sequentially and simultaneously in time (Meyer 1956; Berlyne 1971). Thus, in taking the liberty to slightly modify a famous quote by Igor Stravinsky, we may state that one of the most important aspects of musical meaning is that music communicates time. In music, the human brain creates and experiences a unique, highly complex time-ordered and integrated process of perception and action.

One of our major research interests for several years has been in the neurological basis of such processes, especially of rhythm as one of the main elements of temporal organization in music. The capability for the perception and volitional production of rhythms is unique to the human brain and is dependent on the capacity for stable, precise, rapid, and complex time organization in the brain. Recent research efforts are beginning indeed to elucidate the neural substrates for rhythmicity in the human brain that are not fully known or understood yet. However, the study of rhythm may yield not just insights into musical time but into temporality of information processing in the human brain in general, using music and rhythm as a fruitful model to study general brain function (Avanzini *et al.* 2003; Parsons 2001). Furthermore, as will be discussed at a later part of this chapter, these investigations have also led to a fundamental need to rethink the role of music in therapy and medicine. This evolving role includes the capacity of music to serve as a powerful sensory stimulus, capable of engaging the brain in retraining neural and behavioural functions that can then be applied to nonmusical contexts (Thaut *et al.* 1999).

In summary, rhythm in music is the core element that binds simultaneity and sequentiality of sound patterns into structural organizational forms underlying what we consider musical 'language' (Snyder 2000; Parncutt 1994). In this function, rhythm assumes a critical syntactical role in communicating symbolic as well as associative meaning in music. In the following sections we will examine what we know about the neural basis of musical rhythm formation in the human brain. The findings will contribute a significant step in understanding how one of the core elements in musical communication is processed in the brain. Reciprocally, the findings will also give us insights in how music shapes the brain that engages in music through listening, performance, composition, or improvisation. Within the context of a comprehensive book about the very broad, diverse, and fascinating aspects of 'musical communication' this chapter will try to extend an understanding of communication in music to an examination of some of its neurological bases and functions. Informing a behavioural approach by data from brain sciences and vice versa provides a potent framework in which a synergistic understanding of brain and behaviour can evolve.

We will examine the evidence, including data from our own research, in three sections. First, behavioural data from psychophysical studies will be presented in terms of how these behavioural data give insight into assumed brain function on a theoretical level. Second, we will review studies using brain imaging and brain wave recordings to shed some light on what we know so far about neurophysiological processes mediating rhythm perception and rhythm production. Third, biomedical implications of music's influence on brain and behaviour function will be reviewed in light of a changing paradigm for music in therapy and medicine. Traditionally, music in therapy has been based mostly on social science models in which the cultural role of music was interpreted as an effective facilitator for therapeutic concepts of 'well being' (Gaston 1968). Neuroscience research in music has created new insights into the therapeutic benefits of music, shifting the models of music in therapy from social science and interpretative models to models that are based on how music perception and music production engage the brain in ways that can be meaningfully translated and generalized to nonmusical therapeutic learning and training.

Although the following sections contain some neurological detail, summarizing statements should help an understanding with less comprehensive knowledge in technical aspects of the brain sciences required.

Rhythmic synchronization: evidence from psychophysics and behavioural data

One of the questions in regard to the scientific investigation of musical behaviour deals with formulating study designs that have a valid relationship to the actual complexity of music's nature. In relation to rhythm from a musicological point of view, converging evidence (Parncutt 1994) shows pulse salient models as underlying rhythm processing. Conceptually, these are models that require synchronization of acoustical events, at various hierarchical levels of rhythmic organization, into perceptually identifiable pulse patterns that function as isochronous (patterns of pulses that are equidistant in duration) temporal templates of a given duration. If the concept of periodic perceptual grouping, based on mapping sound events unto pulse-driven internal template structures, represents one of the most appropriate bases for a structural understanding of musical rhythm, then active rhythmic synchronization tasks belong to the most meaningful experimental models to be used to study rhythm processing. The study of the neural substrates of rhythm would closely reflect the process of intrinsic temporal pattern formation within synchronized pulse structures, which is the core effort in the perception and production of rhythm. Study designs using the production or recognition of sound patterns without an implicitly-felt pulse structure, or tasks which rely predominantly on discrimination efforts, would be less central for rhythm processing because they rely largely on shared processes with other forms of non-rhythmic time processing.

Furthermore, most researchers studying rhythm have given preference to experimental designs involving simple tasks, such as finger tapping in synchrony to metronome-like pulse beat sequences. Time-span reduction theory supports the validity of these designs as one fruitful approach to the study of rhythm, since all rhythms can eventually be reduced to isochronic prototypes (Jackendoff and Lehrdahl 1982; Vos and Helsper 1992).

We have conducted several experiments to investigate the neural mechanisms by which motor response may be synchronized to an auditory rhythm. Several important findings have helped to build an understanding of how rhythm formation is controlled in the brain. First, as has been shown previously (Michon 1967; Hary and Moore 1987), steady and stable couplings between the rhythmic cue and the rhythmic motor response are achieved almost instantaneously, within one to two repetitions of the rhythmic stimulus interval. In a study employing random changes in the tempo of metronome sequences, we found an interesting nonlinear change in the response mechanisms employed to keep the rhythmic motor response (finger tap) synchronized to the beat. In small changes – below the level of conscious perception – the duration or period errors (time difference between metronome *interval* and the tap *interval*) are corrected first, and then synchronization errors (time difference between tap and onset of sound) are adjusted gradually. During larger step changes – consciously perceived step changes of at least 5 per cent of the period duration – synchronization error and period error are corrected conjointly by temporary overcorrection of the response period (Thaut *et al.* 1998*a*). Thus a nonlinear neural control system can be proposed in the human brain that employs multiple synchronization strategies, the choice of which depends on the dynamical state of the synchronization system relative to the magnitude and the perceptual threshold of the tempo change.

These data show that auditory rhythm communicates stable and precise interval-based temporal templates to the brain, to which the motor system has 'privileged' access even below levels of conscious awareness (Large *et al.* 2002). Evidence of such direct frequency entrainment in rhythmic synchronization provides support for the notion that rhythm in music can have a profound influence on the organization of movement in time and space. We are defining entrainment, using the traditional definition from physics, whereby the frequency of one moving system becomes locked to the frequency of another 'driver' system.

The data of the experiment described here were replicated in a recent study by using a syncopated synchronization design in which the beat and the motor response were 180 degrees out of phase (Thaut and Kenyon 2003). Randomly presented step changes of 2 per cent of the stimulus interval were immediately compensated for by the motor response adapting to the new stimulus period, even though the size of the tempo modulation was not consciously perceptible. A recursive mathematical model showed a predominant weighting factor of 5:1 in favour of correction of the period error over the synchronization error, when adapting the motor response to the new tempo. The model shows further support for strong frequency or period-based entrainment mechanisms between motor and auditory system, similar to oscillators that become coupled in frequency to one another.

Further evidence of subliminal coupling mechanisms between auditory rhythm and motor response was demonstrated in a study where we employed a metronome pattern with continuous modulation rates – similar to a cosine wave – with amplitudes of 1, 3, 5, and 7 per cent of a base interval of 500 ms (Thaut *et al.* 1998*b*). Response curves of the timing of the rhythmic movement followed precisely the temporal dynamics of the modulating rhythm, with continuous correction always one beat behind. This consistent lag time provided evidence for the interesting insight that the brain never recognized the periodicity pattern of the modulated rhythm but continued to operate in an anticipatory mode in which previous time information was used to predict the next interval duration in a continuous anticipation – correction process.

In all studies of rhythmic synchronization, one of the more difficult and complex aspects of data analysis is that the timing of the rhythmic motor response on a level of milliseconds is not consistent from beat to beat but exhibits considerable temporal fluctuations in relationship to the beat interval. Yet, the *averaged* response is very tightly synchronized to the rhythmic stimulus. Statistical models have tried to explain parts of these fluctuations as indicators of some ongoing correction process based on short-range correlations (Pressing 1999; Vorberg and Wing 1996). However, in a recent study we used a method from mathematical physics developed by Salvino and Cawley (1994) to investigate whether the time series fluctuations were deterministically chaotic or truly random (Roberts *et al.* 2000). A direct test for determinism using this powerful method failed to demonstrate the presence of determinism. Fractal analysis showed the absence of long-range correlations for the periods of the motor response but presence of long-range correlations for synchronization errors. Taken together, the synchronization mechanisms appear to be characteristic of a self-correcting system with stochastic noise attributes – i.e. containing random fluctuations – (Mitra *et al.* 1997; Kelso 1995), but with bounded phase errors which indicate 'thermostat-like' set point limits of perceived simultaneity between motor rhythm and auditory rhythm (Hassan and Thaut 1999). These set point limits are most likely driven by perceptual constraints of the human brain, whereas the rhythmic entrainment mechanisms are most likely based on the strong resonant physiological attractor functions of the neural activation patterns in the auditory system which project into motor structures. Thus, precise timing of rhythm is achieved in a system state of the human brain that resembles directed Brownian motion – which is random rather than chaotic – but which also contains correlations. As one can imagine, the exact nature and function of neural noise in brain information processing continues to present a challenging and difficult yet fruitful field of inquiry but these data provide some very interesting insight into some of the very complex brain mechanisms underlying time perception and the temporal control of behaviour such as found in music.

Neurophyisological and neuroanatomical evidence

In order to understand the dynamics of how neuronal activation patterns unfold in time during information processing involving rhythmic synchronization, we again used the step change experiment described above in conjunction with brain wave measures using magnetic encephalography (MEG)

(Tecchio *et al.* 2000). We performed a series of MEG measurements to investigate whether the brain wave response of the auditory cortex exhibited markers that were correlated with interval changes randomly interspersed in sequences of metronome beats. In line with our previous experiments, we again compared brain cortical responses during rhythmic tempo changes above and below levels of conscious perception. The step changes were either 2 or 20 per cent of a base interval of 500 ms. Results revealed for the first time that the strength of a specific component brain wave (M 100, a specific brain wave potential that emerges 100 ms after the stimulus) of the measured magnetic field of the brain scales proportionally to changes in rhythmic interval duration, regardless if the tempo modulation was perceived consciously or not. Previous dependency of the M100 magnitude on temporal stimulus characteristics has been shown (cf. Imada *et al.* 1997; Lu *et al.* 1992) but not with time measures as brief and in millisecond ranges as in our experiment. We used a technique called dipole analysis to locate the source of this particular brain wave. The analysis showed that the M100 brain wave was generated stably in localization and latency within the supratemporal Heschl's gyrus (primary auditory cortex), where the primary analysis of all aspects of perceived sounds occurs in the cortex of the brain. The change in magnitude of the brain wave in relation to the duration of the beat interval indicates that the cerebral time coding was caused by the synchronized firing of more activated neurons (within an ensemble or circuit of neurons) working together in a fixed time pattern, similar to an orchestra performing together. It is clear that such mechanisms in brain activity are part of the brain's way to code and process time in rhythm and music. It is of course a natural assumption that subcortical cell ensembles may also contribute to or generate the cortical activity patterns. Indirect evidence for such an assumption – as well as support that they activate subcortical neuronal loops necessary for the rhythmic motor performance, e.g. via the reticulospinal pathway in the brain stem and spinal cord – comes from work by, e.g. Rossignol and Melvill Jones (1976) and Paltsev and Elner (1967).

From the data presented here we can conclude several interesting facets on how auditory rhythm is processed in the brain. The data demonstrate convincingly that the rapid and precise adaptations of rhythmic movements to subliminal tempo changes during our behavioural experiments have a precise neurological basis in the brain. The data show that these small time fluctuations in the ranges of a few milliseconds are indeed registered and coded in the brain by changes in the strength of the brain wave currents measured over the primary auditory cortex. Since changes in brain wave power are a function of more neurons firing together in synchrony, the use of the analogy of neurons working like a rhythm band when detecting timing changes is tempting. Longer durations of intervals require higher levels of synchronization of neuronal oscillations, i.e. more neurons are firing at more precise synchronization patterns. Furthermore, these perceived time patterns must then be projected into motor structures to generate the precise changes in temporal motor control. The exact location of these transfer points in the brain is still unclear and the subject of much debate. However, the foregoing studies provide some suggestive and intriguing neurological evidence for a notion that music communicates temporal order in auditory perception through its time ordered sound structures, and it is an obvious conclusion that the brain takes great delight in perceiving and producing these time-ordered sound shapes within the simultaneity and sequentiality of music's syntax of rhythm and polyphony.

In a series of recent brain imaging experiments we have begun to explore how the neuroanatomical networks of the brain are activated during rhythmic motor synchronization (Thaut 2003). Several different experimental tasks were used, such as isochronous finger tapping, tapping to random rhythms, or tapping to rhythms whose tempo fluctuations followed the pattern of a cosine wave similar to experiments described earlier (Stephan *et al.* 2002*a*). Using Positron Emission Tomography (PET) – measuring oxygenation changes in the brain as an indicator of activity levels of brain structures – we were able to identify the basic neural network underlying rhythmic synchronization. We found that the basic network consists of a relatively simple array of auditory and sensorimotor areas, including primary sensorimotor areas, sensory association areas, opercular premotor areas, basal ganglia, and thalamus. Additional significant increases in regional cerebral blood flow were seen in right prefrontal cortex. Within the cerebellum, right cerebellar vermis and right anterior hemispheres were activated. This network is not substantially different – with the exception of some prefrontal and cerebellar areas – from rhythmic finger tapping without tones, suggesting that the neural network underlying rhythmic motor synchronization is essentially a composite of auditory and motor areas with no specific brain structure dedicated to time transduction and entrainment mechanisms. If this suggestion is correct it would imply that rhythmic time information coded in the auditory system is directly projected into motor tissue entraining rhythmic motor responses similar to a resonance function in a musical instrument, for instance, between vibrating strings.

Rhythmic finger tapping to tempo changes was associated with additional parieto-thalamic and premotor activity, right prefrontal, anterior cingulate, and intraparietal areas, as a well as posterior cerebellar areas. Prefrontal activation which is typically associated with higher perceptual and cognitive control functions of the brain, showed an expanding regional network depending on the magnitude of the modulation.

Our research in mapping brain activation in regard to rhythm processing also gave insights into the function of the cerebellum. In general, the cerebellum is thought of as being involved in many critical optimizing aspects of sensory perception and cognition functions, as well as motor control. Two major conclusions may be derived from our research in music and the cerebellum. First, the cerebellum is not a unifunctional structure rather than different parts of the cerebellum subserve different functions related to the control movement, sensory information acquisition, as well as higher perceptual processes which can all be mapped onto rhythmic synchronization tasks. Second, the observations suggest that the cerebellum contributes to at least three distinct cortico-cerebellar brain networks related to different aspects of temporal control during rhythmic synchronization (Stephan *et al.* 2002*b*).

The basic neural network for isochronous rhythmic synchronization was also described in a study my colleagues Jerome Sanes, Martina DeMartin, and I (2001) conducted recently to compare isochronous with polyrhythmic synchronization. The subjects were asked to tap musical hemiola patterns, i.e. 2 beats versus a 3 Hz rhythm and vice versa, at two different movement frequencies. Hemiolas belong to the most complex rhythmic patterns performed in music. The hemiola synchronization showed more activation strength compared to the isochronous condition, yielding more activation in cortical motor area as well as the cerebellum. Interestingly, activation in basal ganglia structures was reduced during hemiola performance compared to isochronous tapping. The data from this study add another dimension to the possible functions of the cerebellum and its involvement in musical processing. Higher complexity in the rhythmic task clearly was associated with higher activation patterns in the cerebellum. As such, the cerebellum may play an important role in learning, sensory acquisition, and optimization of complex motor and perceptual functions. These roles are supported in general by current theories about cerebellar function (Schmahmann 1997) and the involvement of the cerebellum in experiments studying musical tasks.

Finally, my colleague Larry Parsons and I (2001) investigated whether distinct neural activation patterns mediate different components of rhythm. We used discrimination tasks of paired comparisons of brief rhythm motives. We separately studied perception of differences in tempo, duration, pattern, and meter. We also tested nonmusicans and musicians. Results showed impressively that distinct and partially overlapping neural networks subserve each component rhythm. The complex nature of rhythm thus was also reflected neurologically in distinct networks of neurons in the brain active during different rhythmic tasks. The data of the study clearly support the notion that it is crucial for neurobiological investigations in musical rhythm to be specific in conceptual definitions of rhythm. These definitions must be consistent with theoretical concepts of rhythm in musicology to do justice to the complexity of rhythmic processes and to avoid misunderstandings or misinterpretations between musicians and neuroscientists. Furthermore, the data provide very interesting evidence for the partial neurological independence of different components of rhythm processing in the human brain. Thus, the neurological evidence would support the capability of the human brain to independently develop a large degree of syntactical diversity in rhythmic structures as existent in the music of different cultures, e.g. by comparing meter-based rhythms of western music with Indian Raga music utilizing set rhythmic modes. The neurological data seem also to put question marks to theories of rhythm that consider the structural time elements (pulse, meter, pattern, tempo, etc.) of rhythm as contingently embedded into each other in hierarchical form. Since very different neurological networks, that seem to be fairly independent of each other in circuit architecture, subserve different components of rhythm, hierarchical rhythmic structures, such as in western musical 'language systems', may be more based on structural developments in then music specific to certain musical cultures than based on a culturally independent intrinsic function of 'musical biology'.

Neurologic music therapy

The study of the neurobiological basis of music, discussed here, is also inherently linked to music's influence on brain function. In other words, the brain that engages in music is changed by engaging in music. This reciprocal relationship in music and brain function – discovered over the past 10 years within the larger context of a very fascinating line of research demonstrating the experience-dependent plasticity of the brain – is one of the most powerful motors of change in the historical paradigm of music therapy. In the modern history of music therapy – encompassing roughly the past 60 years – social science concepts of music's influence and role in human life and society have dominated music therapy. The therapeutic value of music was believed to stem from music's cultural role in facilitating social learning and emotional 'well being'. More recently, under the influence of new data in brain research in music, new findings suggest that music can stimulate complex cognitive, affective, and sensorimotor processes in the brain, which can then be generalized and transferred to nonmusical therapeutic purposes. Studies have shown impressively over the past 10 years that rhythmic entrainment of motor function can actively facilitate the recovery of movement in patients with stroke (*cf.* Thaut *et al.* 1993, 1997, 2002; Hummelsheim 1999; Whitall *et al.* 2000; Mauritz 2002), Parkinson's Disease (*cf.* Miller *et al.* 1996; Thaut *et al.* 1996; McIntosh *et al.* 1997; Howe *et al.* 2003, Freedland *et al.* 2002; Pacchetti *et al.* 2000; Fernandez del Olmo and Cudeiro 2003), cerebral palsy (Thaut *et al.* 1998) , or traumatic brain injury (Hurt *et al.* 1998). There is strong physiological evidence that rhythmic sounds act as sensory timers, entraining brain mechanisms that control the timing, sequencing, and coordination of movement. Recovery of speech functions can also be facilitated with music (*cf.* Pilon *et al.* 1998; Thaut *et al.* 2001; Boucher *et al.* 2001; Bonakdarpour *et al.* 2003; Glover *et al.* 1996; Belin *et al.* 1996). Music's strong timing mechanisms are thought to entrain oscillatory circuits in the speech centers of the brain (Warren *et al.* 2003). Recognizing the importance of temporal organization in cognitive functions, new frontiers in biomedical music research study the effect of music and rhythm on critical aspects of timing in learning, attention, executive function, and memory (Hommel *et al.* 1990; Baur *et al.* 2000; Chan *et al.* 1998; Foster and Valentine 2001; Haslam and Cook 2002; Ho *et al.* 2003; Kilgour *et al.* 2000; Rainey and Larsen 2002; Son *et al.* 2002; Overy 2003). The current scientific model searches for therapeutic mechanisms of music by studying if and how music stimulates and engages parallel or shared nonmusical brain function in cognition, motor control, and emotion (Thaut 2000). For example, rhythmicity is a universal function in the control of movement, and thus can be effectively accessed and regulated with music in patients with neurological movement disorders. Temporal organization and appropriate arousal – universally important functions in perception, attention, memory, and executive function – can be modulated by music in patients with, for example, dementia or traumatic brain injury.

Building analogies between neuroscience, acoustics, the elements of music, and aesthetics, we may surmise that music, written in the time code of rhythm which creates meaningful sound patterns in time, simulates or resembles the oscillatory 'rhythmic' synchronization codes of neural information processing in the brain, thus becoming a powerful stimulus to communicate sensory and cognitive-perceptual information to the brain (Merzenich *et al.* 1993). To put it simply: music may be a 'language' the brain can read with ease because its temporal-based grammar is fundamental to how the brain processes information. For example, sounds – as neurophysiological studies have shown – can arouse and excite the spinal motor neurons mediated by auditory – motor connections at the brainstem and spinal cord level (Rossignol and Melvill Jones 1976). This priming effect sets the motor system in the brain in a state of readiness, facilitating the execution of movements. However, rhythmic sounds also entrain the timing of the muscle activity, thereby providing a physiological template for cueing the timing of movements. Patients with neurological movement disorders can benefit from this effect of music and rhythm to retrain their motor functions. Thus, music provides a stimulus that substitutes for compromised internal functions, accesses compensatory networks in the brain, and may help build new pathways shaping the plasticity of the brain. The rhythmic patterns of music can help patients with Parkinson's disease overcome extreme slowness and episodes of 'freezing' of movement because the music acts as a sensory sequencer that provides critical neural 'movement' command signals that are not generated reliably in time by brain areas affected by the disease (Hausdorff *et al.* 2003; Thaut *et al.* 2001).

For illustration of the influence of music on a very different brain function, we may simply think of the ABC song in which a child learns to sing a song with the letters of the alphabet as the song lyrics. The organizing element of chunking, a critical element in memory coding, is always present in all music as a necessary component to build musical forms through melodic, harmonic, and rhythmic phrasing (Wolfe and Hom 1993). Therefore, music can function as an excellent memory template for nonmusical declarative or procedural learning (Wallace 1994; Gfeller 1983; Claussen and Thaut 1997). Studies with memory disorders, such as Alzheimer's Disease, frequently show retention of musical information in patients that is preserved longer and out of proportion with their concurrent state of memory loss (Cowles *et al.* 2003). Such data suggest that neuronal memory traces built through music are deeply ingrained and more resilient to neurodegenerative influences (Foster and Valentine 2001; Haslam and Cook 2002). The organizational basis of music as a temporally 'overstructured' language of sound patterns may play a critical role in such effective memory formation (Deutsch 1982). Recent research has shown that neuronal oscillations, which build rhythmically synchronized firing patterns in network ensembles of neurons, form the neurobiological basis of perception and learning. The precise synchronization of neuronal activation patterns is a crucial element in building the tightly-coupled networks that physiologically underlie the process of effective learning (Klimesch *et al.* 1998). Thus, music's temporality, expressed in its rhythmic nature, may optimize the formation of such rhythmic neuronal networks because music, as the learning stimulus that drives the physiological activations in the brain, is already tightly organized within temporal structures. (Peterson and Thaut 2002, 2003).

Conclusion

The preceding discussion may indeed widen our understanding of how and what music can communicate. Through neurologic processes, music communicates information to the brain that has profound effects on learning, development, recovery of function, and aesthetic engagement. Research into the neurobiology of music has made great and unprecedented progress in the last decade due to a fruitful merger of lines of investigation from neuroscience, psychophysics, and musicology, supported by other disciplines such as mathematics, physics, and engineering (Zatorre and Peretz 2001; Avanzini *et al.* 2003). Music, especially rhythm, can serve as a model of temporality in the human brain (Harrington and Haaland 1999; Rao *et al.* 2001). In support of similar views by other researchers, we may propose that music is indeed related to core functions of the biology of the human nervous system and therefore serves adaptive evolutionary purposes beyond that of the functional interpretation of art. Music must be viewed as a biological fact, not just as a cultural phenomenon. In both arenas, the cultural and the biological, music is a powerful communicator.

Furthermore, in musical aesthetics, a great deal of emphasis in understanding musical semantics, i.e. the meaning in music, is given to the temporal nature of music as a pivotal element in conveying its rule based 'language' structure (Berlyne 1971). Thus, we may propose that a scientific study of music always needs to study the various elements of music within a temporally ordered context of musical patterns.

Several key findings in rhythmic synchronization research have emerged that contribute to an understanding of the neurobiological basis of music and temporal information processing in the brain. Musical rhythm rapidly creates stable and precise internal templates for temporal organization of motor responses. The motor system is very sensitive to arousal by the auditory system. Neural impulses of auditory rhythm project directly into motor structures. Motor responses become entrained to the timing of rhythmic patterns. The entrainment process can be modelled well via resonant network functions and coupled oscillator models. The motor system has access to temporal information in the auditory system below levels of conscious perception. Rhythmic synchronization appears to emerge in a fuzzy biological system characterized by stochastic time fluctuations which are embedded in self-correcting nonlinear coupling functions. The dynamics of such process cannot be captured by simple statistical models of local stationary corrections using, e.g. variance analysis.

The neurobiology of rhythm shows a widely distributed cortical and subcortical network subserving motor, sensory, and cognitive aspects of rhythm processing (Platel *et al.* 1997; Penhune *et al.* 1998; Schlaug 2001). Consistent engagement of distinct neural circuits in the cerebellum across musical-rhythmic tasks suggests a central role of the cerebellum in the temporal organization of cognitive and perceptual processes in music (Schmahmann 1997). However, cerebellar pathology does not affect the capacity of auditory rhythms to entrain rhythmic motor responses (Molinari *et al.* 2001) suggesting that sensory rhythms can compensate for brain mechanisms related to timing that are dysfunctional due to disease or injury.

The basic neural network underlying isochronous pulse synchronization consists mainly of composite motor and auditory areas with no clearly designated functionally separate brain area for 'synchronization'. It appears that the temporal information processing in rhythm follows multiple parallel and possibly hierarchically ordered neural computation processes. Such processes may be coded on a cellular level in the emerging timing patterns of synaptic network coupling. In the case of music perception or production, these processes may originate in the auditory system and subsequently entrain other brain areas via resonant physiological network functions. Thus, the neuronal activation patterns that precisely code the perception of rhythm in the auditory system spread into adjacent motor areas and activate the firing patterns of motor tissue. One may think of it – using a 'nonscientific' image – as a process similar to the vibrating strings of a violin which resonate the wood molecules of the violin's body setting them into the same vibrating motion as the strings themselves. Neuroimaging maps of rhythm (and other musical functions) suggest that on the 'macro level' of regional brain activations, the connectivity between widely distributed brain areas in precisely timed relationships may be one of the most essential system components in musical processing.

Finally, many clinical studies have shown striking evidence that auditory rhythm and music can be effectively harnessed for specific therapeutic purposes in the rehabilitation of patients with different neuropathologies (Thaut *et al.* 1999). Such findings underscore further the complex ways in which music engages and communicates to the human brain and in which the brain that engages in music can be – even in states of brain injury – changed by engaging in music (Pascual Leone *et al.* 1995; Thaut and Peterson 2002).

In conclusion, we have reviewed new aspects of the neurological basis for key elements of musical communication. Rhythm and time are among the most eminent concepts in understanding the nature of music as an organized and rule-based 'sensory language'. As we have seen, the brain is neurologically superbly sensitive to processing the time elements of music in a rapid, precise, and meaningful manner. Thus, in closing we may return to Stravinsky's famous quote by restating that indeed one of the core functions of music may be to communicate time. And so, the structured flow of time, made audible in music's temporal architecture of sound, rhythm, and polyphony, may be what excites, moves, and gives order to our feelings, thoughts, and sense of movement.

References

Aiello, R. (ed.) (1994) Music and language: Parallels and contrasts. In *Musical Perceptions*, pp. 40–63. New York: Oxford University Press.

Avanzini, G., Faienza, C., Minciacchi, D., Lopez, L., and Majno, M. (eds) (2003) The neurosciences and music. New York: *Annals of the New York Academy of Sciences*, 999.

Baur, B., Uttner, I., Ilmberger, J., Fesl, G., and Mai, N. (2000) Music memory provides access to verbal knowledge in a patient with global amnesia. *Neurocase*, 6, 415–21.

Belin, P., Van Eeckhout, P., Zilbovicius, M., Remy, P., Francois, C., Guillaume, S., *et al.* (1996) Recovery from nonfluent aphasia aster melodic intonation therapy. *Neurology*, 47, 1504–11.

Berlyne, D.E. (1971) *Aesthetics and Psychobiology*. New York: Appleton, Century & Croft.

Bonakdarpour, B., Eftekharzadeh, A., and Ashayeri, H. (2003) Melodic intoniation therapy Persian aphasic patients. *Aphasiology*, 17, 75–95.

Boucher, V., Garcia, J.L., Fleurant, J., and Paradis, J. (2001) Variable efficacy of rhythm and tone in melody-based interventions: Implications of the assumption of a right-hemisphere facilitation in non-fluent aphasia. *Aphasiology*, 15, 131–49.

Bernstein, L. (1976) *The unanswered question: Six talks at Harvard*. Cambridge, MA: Harvard University Press.

Chan, A.S., Ho, Y.C., and Cheung, M.C. (1998) Music training improves verbal memory. *Nature*, 396, 128.

Claussen, D.W. and Thaut, M.H. (1997) Music as a mnemonic device for children with learning disabilities. *Canadian Journal of Music Therapy*, 5, 55–66.

Cowles, A., Beatty, W.W., Nixon, S.J., Lutz, L.J., Paulk, J., Paulk, K., *et al.* (2003) Musical skill in dementia: A violinist presumed to have Alzheimer's disease learns to play a new song. *Neurocase*, 9, 493–503.

Deutsch, D. (1979) Language and music as communication: A discussion. *Music Educators Journal*, 65, 68–71.

Deutsch, D. (1982) Organizational processes in music. In *Music, Mind and Brain*, (ed. M. Clynes), pp. 119–31. New York: Plenum Press.

Dowling, W.J. and Harwood, D.L. (1986) *Music cognition*. New York: Academic Press.

Fernandez Del Olmo, M. and Cudeiro, J. (2003) The timing in Parkinson's disease: Effects of a rehabilitation programme based on rhythmic sound cues. *Proceedings of the Society for Neuroscience*, 734, 2.

Foster, N.A. and Valentine, E.R. (2001) The effect of auditory stimulation on autobiographical recall in dementia. *Experimental Aging Research*, 27, 215–28.

Freedland, R.L., Festa, C., Sealy, M., McBean, A.,Elghazaly, P., Capan, A., *et al.* (2002) The effects of pulsed auditory stimulation on various gait measurements in persons with Parkinson's disease. *Neurorehabilitation*, 17, 81–7.

Gaston, E.T. (1968) *Music in therapy*. New York: McMillan.

Gfeller, K.E. (1983) Musical mnemonics as an aid to retention with normal and learning-disabled students. *Journal of Music Therapy*, 20, 179–89.

Gillam, R.B., Marquardt, T.P., and Martin, F.N. (2000) Communication sciences and disorders: From science to clinical practice. San Diego, CA: Singular Publishing Group.

Glover, H., Kalinowski, J., Rastatter, M., and Stuart, A. (1996) Effect of instruction to sing on stuttering frequency at normal and fast rates. *Perceptual and Motor Skills*, **83**, 511–22.

Harrington, D.L. and Haaland, K.Y. (1999) Neural underpinnings of temporal processing: A review of focal lesion, pharmacological, and functional imaging research. *Reviews in Neuroscience*, **10**, 91–116.

Hary, D. and Moore, P. (1987) Synchronizing human movement with an external clock source. *Biological Cybernetics*, **56**, 305–11.

Hasan, M.A. and Thaut, M.H. (1999) Autoregressive moving average modeling for finger tapping with an external stimulus. *Perceptual and Motor Skills*, **88**, 1331–46.

Haslam, C. and Cook, M. (2002) Striking a chord with amnesic patients: Evidence that song facilitates memory. *Neurocase*, **8**, 453–65.

Hausdorf, J.M., Schaasma, J.D., Balash, Y., Bartels, A.L., Gurevich, T., and Giladi, N. (2003) Impaired regulation of stride variability in Parkinson's disease subjects with freezing of gait. *Experimental Brain Research*, **149**, 187–94.

Ho, Y.C., Cheung, M.C., and Chan, A.S. (2003) Music training improves verbal but not visual memory: Cross-sectional and longitudinal explorations in children. *Neuropsychology*, **17**, 439–50.

Hommel, M., Peres, B., Pollak, P., and Memin, B. (1990) Effects of passive tactile and auditory stimuli on left visual neglect. *Archives of Neurology*, **47**, 573–6.

Howe, T.E., Lovgreen, B., Cody, F.W., Ashton, V.J., and Oldham, J.A. (2003) Auditory cues can modify the gait of persons with early-stage Parkinson's disease: A method for enhancing Parkinsonian walking performance. *Clinical Rehabilitation*, **17**, 363–7.

Hummelsheim, H. (1999) Rationales for improving motor function. Current Opinion in *Neurology*, **12**, 697–701.

Hurt, C.P., Rice, R.R., McIntosh, G.C., and Thaut, M.H. (1998) Rhythmic auditory stimulation in gait training for patients with traumatic brain injury. *Journal of Music Therapy*, **35**, 228–41.

Imada, T. M., Watanabe, T., Mashiko, M., Kawakatsu., and Kotani, M. (1997) The silent period between sounds has a stronger effect than the interstimulus interval on auditory evoked magnetic fields. *Electroencephalography and Clinical Neurophysiology*, **102**, 37–45.

Jackendoff, R. and Lehrdahl, F. (1982) Grammatical parallels between music and language. In *Music, Mind, and Brain*, (ed. M. Clynes), pp. 83–118. New York: Plenum Press.

Kelso, J.A.S. (1995) Dynamic Patterns: The Self-Organization of Human Brain and Behavior. Cambridge MA: MIT Press.

Kilgour, A.R., Jakobson, L.S., and Cuddy, L.L. (2000) Music training and rate of presentation as mediators of text and song recall. *Memory and Cognition*, **28**, 700–10.

Klimesch, W., Doppelmayr, M., Russeger, H., Pachinger, T., and Schwaiger, J. (1998) Induced alpha band power changes in the human EEG and attention. *Neuroscience Letters*, **244**, 73–6.

Kraut, R. (1992) On the possibility of a determinate semantics for music. In *Cognitive Bases of Musical Communication*, (eds M. Riess Jones and S. Holleran), pp. 11–22. Washington DC: American Psychological Association.

Kreitler, H. and Kreitler, S. (1972) *Psychology of the arts*. Durham, NC: Duke University Press.

Langer, S. (1942) Philosophy in a new key. New York: Mentor Books.

Large, E.W., Fink, P., and Kelso, J.A.S. (2002) Tracking simple and complex sequences. *Psychological Research*, **66**, 3–17.

Lu, Z.L., Williamson, S.J., and Kaufman, L. (1992) Human auditory primary and association cortex have different lifetimes for activation traces. *Brain Research*, **572**, 236–41.

Mauritz, K.H. (2002) Gait training in hemiplegia. *European Journal of Neurology*, **9** Suppl.1, 23–9, discussion 53–61.

McIntosh, G.C., Brown, S.H., Rice, R.R., and Thaut, M.H. (1997) Rhythmic auditory-motor facilitation of gait patterns in patients with Parkinson's disease. *Journal of Neurology, Neurosurgery and Psychiatry*, **62**, 122–6.

Merriam, A.P. (1964) *The anthropology of music*. Evanston, IL: Northwestern University Press.

Merzenich, M.M., Schreiner, C., Jenkins, W., and Wang, X. (1993) Neural mechanisms underlying temporal integration, segmentation, and input sequence representation: Some implications for the origin of learning disabilities. *Annals of N.Y. Academy of Science*, **682**, 1–22.

Meyer, L.B. (1956) *Emotion and meaning in music*. Chicago, IL: University of Chicago Press.

Michon, J.A. (1967) *Timing in temporal tracking*. Assen, NL: Van Gorcum.

Miller, R.A., Thaut, M.H., and Aunon, J. (1996) Event-related brain wave potentials in an auditory-motor synchronization task. In *Music Medicine*, (eds R. Pratt and R. Spintge), Volume 2, 76–84. St.Louis, MO: MMB Music.

Mitra, S., Riley, M.A., and Turvey, M.T. (1997) Chaos in human rhythmic movement. *Journal of Motor Behavior*, **29**, 195–8.

Molinari, M., Thaut, M.H., Gioia, C., Fillipini, V., Cerasa, A., and Leggio, M.G. (2001) Motor entrainment to auditory rhythm is not affected by cerebellar pathology. *Proceedings of the Society for Neuroscience*, **950**, 2.

Overy, K. (2003) Dyslexia and music: from timing deficits to musical interventions. *Annals of the New York Academy of Sciences*, **999**, 497–505.

Pacchetti, C., Mancini, F., Aglieri, R., Fundaro, C., Martignoni, E., and Nappi, G. (2000) Active music therapy in Parkinson's disease: An integrative method for motor and emotional rehabilitation. *Psychosomatic Medicine*, **62**, 386–93.

Paltsev, Y.I. and Elner, A.M. (1967) Change in the functional state of the segmental apparatus of the spinal cord under the influence of sound stimuli and its role in voluntary movement. *Biophysics*, **12**, 1219–26.

Parncutt, R. (1994) A perceptual model of pulse salient and letrical accent in musical rhythm. *Music Perception*, **11**, 409–64.

Parsons, L.M. (2001) Exploring the functional neuroanatomy of music performance, perception, and comprehension. *Annals of the New York Academy of Sciences*, **930**, 211–31.

Parsons, L.M. and Thaut, M.H. (2001) Functional neuroanatomy of the perception of musical rhythm in musicians and nonmusicians. *Neuroimage*, **13**, 925 (abs).

Pascual-Leone, A., Nguyet, D., Cohen, L.G., *et al.* (1995) Modulation of muscle responses evoked by transcranial magnetic stimulation during the acquisition of new fine motor skills. *Journal of Neurophysiology*, **74**, 1037–45.

Peirce, C.S. (1931–1935) *Collected Papers*, (eds C. Hartshorne and P. Weiss), (Vols 1–6). Cambridge, MA: Harvard University Press.

Penhune, V.B., Zatorre, R.J., and Evans, A. (1998) Cerebellar contributions to motor timing: A PET strudy of auditory and visual rhythm reproduction. *Journal of Cognitive Neuroscience*, **10**, 752–65.

Peterson, D.A. and Thaut, M.H. (2002) Delay modulates spectral correlates in the human EEG of nonverbal auditory working memory. *Neuroscience Letters*, **328**, 17–20.

Peterson, D.A. and Thaut, M.H. (2003) Plasticity of alpha and theta synchronization during verbal learning with a music template. Proceedings of the Society for Neuroscience, **194**, 21.

Pilon, M.A., McIntosh, K.W., and Thaut, M.H. (1998) Auditory versus visual speech timing cues as external rate control to enhance verbal intelligibility in mixed spastic-dysarthric speakers: A pilot study. *Brain Injury*, **12**, 793–803.

Platel, H., Price, K., Baron, J.C., *et al.* (1997) The structural components of music perception. *Brain*, **120**, 299–43.

Pressing, J. (1999) The referential dynamics of cognition and action. *Psychological Review*, **106**, 714–47.

Rainey, D.W. and Larsen, J.D. (2002) The effect of familiar melodies on initial learning and long-term memory for unconnected text. *Music Perception*, **20**, 173–86.

Rao, S.M., Mayer, A.R., and Harrington, D.L. (2001) The evolution of brain activation during temporal processing. *Nature Neuroscience*, **4**, 317–23.

Roberts, S., Eykholt, R., and Thaut, M.H. (2000) Analysis of correlations and search for evidence of deterministic chaos in rhythmic motor control by the human brain. *Physical Review E*, **62**, 2597–607.

Rossignol, S. and Melvill Jones, G. (1976) Audiospinal influences in man studied by the H-reflex and its possible role in rhythmic movement synchronized to sound. *Electroencephalography Clinical Neurophysiology*, **41**, 83–92.

Salvino, L.W. and Cawley, R. (1994) Smoothness implies determinism: A method to detect it in time series. *Physical Review Letters*, **73**, 1091–4.

Sanes, J.N., Demartin, M., Weckel, J., and Thaut, M.H. (2001) Brain activation patterns for producing symmetrically and asymmetrically synchronized movement rhythms. *Neuroimage*, **13**, 1249 (abs).

Schenker, H. (1935) *Der freie Satz*. Vienna: Universal Edition.

Schlaug, G. (2001) The brain of musicians: A model for functional and structural adaptation. *Annals of the New York Academy of Sciences*, **930**, 281–99.

Schmahmann, J.D. (ed.) (1997) *The Cerebellum and Cognition*. New York: Academic Press.

Shaw-Miller, S. (2002) Visible deeds of music. New Haven, CT: Yale University Press.

Sloboda, J.A. (1985) *The musical mind: The cognitive psychology of music*. Oxford: Oxford University Press.

Snyder, V. (2000) *Music and memory*. Cambridge, MA: MIT Press.

Son, G.R., Therrien, B., and Whall, A. (2002) Implicit memory and familiarity among elders with dementia. *Journal of Nursing Scholarship*, **34**, 263–7.

Stephan, K.M., Thaut, M.H., Wunderlich, G., *et al.* (2002a) Conscious and subconscious sensorimotor synchronization: Prefrontal cortex and the influence of awareness. *Neuroimage*, **15**, 345–52.

Stephan, K.M., Thaut, M.H., Wunderlich, G., *et al.* (2002b) Cortico-cerebellar circuits and temporal adjustments of motor behavior. *Proceedings of the Society for Neuroscience*, **462**, 8.

Tecchio, F., Salustri, C., Thaut, M.H., Pasqualetti, P., and Rossini, P.M. (2000) Conscious and preconscious adaptation to rhythmic auditory stimuli: A magnetoencephalographic study of human brain responses. *Experimental Brain Research*, **135**, 222–30.

Thaut, M.H. (2000) *A scientific model of music in therapy and medicine.* San Antonio TX: IMR-University of Texas San Antonio Press.

Thaut, M.H. (2003) Neural basis of rhythmic timing networks in the human brain. *Annals of the New York Academy of Sciences,* **999**, 364–73.

Thaut, M.H., Hurt, C.P., Dragan, D., and McIntosh, G.C. (1998) Rhythmic entrainment of gait patterns in children with cerebral palsy. *Developmental Medicine and Child Neurology,* **40**, 15.

Thaut, M.H. and Kenyon, G.P. (2003) Fast motor adaptations to subliminal frequency shifts in auditory rhythm during syncopated sensorimotor synchronization. *Human Movement Science,* **22**, 321–38.

Thaut, M.H., Kenyon, G.P., Hurt, C.P., McIntosh, G.C., and Hoemberg, V. (2002) Kinematic optimization of spatiotemporal patterns in paretic arm training with stroke patients. *Neuropsychologia,* **40**, 1073–81.

Thaut, M.H., Kenyon, G.P., Schauer, M.L., and McIntosh, G.C. (1999) The connection between rhythmicity and brain function: Implications for therapy of movement disorders. *IEEE Engineering in Medicine and Biology,* **18**,101–8.

Thaut, M.H., McIntosh, G.C., McIntosh, K.W., and Hoemberg, V. (2001) Auditory rhythmicity enhances movement and speech motor control in patients with Parkinson's disease. *Functional Neurology,* **16**, 163–72.

Thaut, M.H., McIntosh, G.C., and Rice, R.R. (1997) Rhythmic facilitation of gait training in hemiparetic stroke rehabilitation. *Journal of Neurological Sciences,* **151**, 207–12.

Thaut, M.H., McIntosh, G.C., Rice, R.R., Miller, R.A., Rathbun, J., and Brault, J.M. (1996) Rhythmic auditory training in gait training with Parkinson's disease patients. *Movement Disorders,* **11**, 193–200.

Thaut, M.H., Miller R.A., and Schauer, L.M. (1998*a*) Multiple synchronization strategies in rhythmic sensorimotor tasks: Phase vs period correction. *Biological Cybernetics,* **79**, 241–50.

Thaut, M.H., Rice, R.R., McIntosh, G.C., and Prassas, S.G. (1993) The effect of auditory rhythmic cueing on stride and EMG patterns in hemiparetic gait of stroke patients. *Physical Therapy,* **73**, 107.

Thaut, M.H. and Peterson, D.A. (2002) Plasticity of neural representations in auditory memory for rhythmic tempo: Trial dependent EEG spectra. *Proceedings of the Society for Neuroscience,* **373**, 8.

Thaut, M.H. and Schauer, L.M. (1997) Weakly coupled oscillators in rhythmic motor synchronization. *Proceedings of the Society for Neuroscience,* **298**, 20.

Thaut, M.H., Tian, B., and Azimi, M. (1998*b*) Rhythmic finger tapping to cosine wave modulated metronome sequences: Evidence of subliminal entrainment. *Human Movement Science,* **17**, 839–63.

Vorberg, D. and Wing, A.M. (1996) Modeling variability and dependence in timing. In *Handbook of Perception and Action,* (eds H. Hewyer and S.W. Keele), pp. 181–262. New York: Academy Press.

Vos, P.G. and Helsper, E.L. (1992) Tracking simple rhythms: On-beat versus off beat performance. In *Proceedings of the NATO Advanced Research Worshop on Time, Action, and Cognition,* (eds F. Macar and V. Pouthas), pp. 287–99. Amsterdam: Kluwar Academic Publishers.

Wallace, W.T. (1994) Memory for music: Effect of melody on recall of text. *Journal of Experimental Psychology- Learning, Memory and Cognition*, **20**, 1471–85.

Warren, J.D., Warren, J.E., Fox, N.C., and Warrington, E.K. (2003) Nothing to say, something to sing: Primary progressive dynamic aphasia. *Neurocase*, **9**, 140–53.

Whitall, J., McCombe, W.S., Silver, K.H., and Macko, R.F. (2000) Repetitive bilateral arm training with rhythmic auditory cueing improves motor function in chronic hemiparetic stroke. *Stroke*, **31**, 2390–5.

Wolfe, D.E. and Hom, C. (1993) Use of melodies as structural prompts for learning and retention of sequential verbal information by preschool students. *Journal of Music Therapy*, **30**, 100–18.

Zatorre, R.J. and Perez, I. (eds) (2001) The biological foundations of music. *Annals of the New York Academy of Sciences*, **930**. New York: NYAS.

Chapter 9

Musical companionship, musical community. Music therapy and the process and value of musical communication

Gary Ansdell and Mercédès Pavlicevic

All music calls to an ear that is not the musician's own…(Buber 1947/2002, p. 30)

To be means *to communicate*… To be means to be for another, and through the other, for oneself. A person has no internal sovereign territory, he is wholly and always on the boundary; looking inside himself, he looks *into the eyes of another* or *with the eyes of another*. (Bakhtin 1984, p. 287)

Introduction

Disorders of communication and their 'musical solutions'

Benjamin Britten wrote the Foreword to a small book called *Therapy in Music for Handicapped Children* by pioneer music therapists Paul Nordoff and Clive Robbins (1971). At a time when music seemed to be losing its power to communicate, wrote Britten, here was a use of music 'where the concentration is entirely on this, on communication pure and simple' (p. 9).

In our culture, where it is seemingly always 'good to talk', disorders or failures of communication stand out – whether the cause is autism, brain injury, psychosis, dementia, or depression. Amongst the approaches treating such 'pathologies of communication' music therapy is increasingly acknowledged as being especially successful. Music therapists are trained to understand the processes of musical communication, and to use music as a medium and a tool for initiating or enhancing interpersonal or social communication through developing musical companionship and musical community. Nordoff and

Robbins also stated that music, and what it can do for people's ability to communicate with each other, brings a 'moral reality into the world' (1971, p. 144). Most music therapists likewise see their work as not just a technology of communication, but as part of a value system which links music to the wellbeing of people and society. Music therapy perhaps shows us why we have music.

Although this latest incarnation of Music therapy arrived only in the mid twentieth century (Bunt 1994) it stands within a perennial tradition, almost unbroken since Antiquity, of linking music and healing (Horden 2000) – summed up by Novalis' famous dictum that 'every illness is a musical problem, its healing a musical solution'. There are, however, two notable differences between this perennial tradition of music-healing and contemporary music therapy. Firstly, in traditional practices music was usually only played *to* the patient, with musical communication being an indirect effect. In contrast, most contemporary music therapy has concentrated on eliciting clients' participation in direct communicative musicing[1], with therapist and client often improvising together (Nordoff and Robbins 1977; Ansdell 1995; Bunt and Pavlicevic 2001; Pavlicevic 1997). A second difference that can be noted is a distinct move away from a discourse of healing (or curing) to one where, for music therapists today, communication itself is the more modest therapeutic aim. It seems that, as music therapy develops further as a global health profession, it increasingly presents itself as a psychosocial intervention, rather than a curative medical one.

Contemporary music therapy is nevertheless a varied practice, discipline, and discourse. It has allied itself over the last forty years to a variety of prevailing treatment theories such as behaviourism, psychoanalysis, humanistic psychology, and social therapy (Ruud 1980; Bunt 1994). Each of these epistemologies has led to different constructions of the music-therapeutic enterprise, and to different accounts of how and why it works. Recent metatheoretical work on music therapy (Ruud 1998; Stige 2002; Ansdell 2003) is showing how closely its theory mirrors the ever-shifting cultural stories told about how music, individual, society, and health interrelate. Music therapy will perhaps always tell a different story about itself in different times and places.

'Music as communication' is, however, perhaps the key theme used by contemporary music therapists to describe and legitimate their work – linking

---

[1] We will use the form 'musicing' (Elliott 1995) in this chapter to suggest 'musicianship-in-action', music as lived experience, as well as music as a social and cultural phenomenon. Christopher Small (1998) also proposes a similar and useful notion of *'musicking'* which relates to our argument in this chapter.

it with much contemporary interdisciplinary work on the relationships between health and social interaction. In this chapter we outline this perspective and show how it can be empirically supported by interdisciplinary theory that shows how human communication is fundamentally musical – and how disorders of communication can be amenable to 'musical repair'. This is illustrated by examples from music therapy work in an adult psychiatric setting – an area that graphically presents the challenges to communication chronic illness can bring, and how music can often help.

We also highlight some current areas of debate, both in the discipline of music therapy today, and in the culture of contemporary healthcare. Is music therapy's concept of musical communication as 'intimate relating' too limited? This question has led to recent appeals (Ansdell 2002; Stige 2003; Pavlicevic and Ansdell 2004) to consider music therapy beyond the traditional therapy dyad and group, and in relation to broader contexts of community and culture. A second question concerns whether a tendency bred by 'evidence-based medicine' to establish a 'science of music therapy' (and with this a 'technology of musical communication') does damage to music therapy as a 'healing art' practiced by gifted musicians. Consequently, music therapists emphasize how the idea of 'music as communication' within music therapy can embody and foster a humanistic value system of musical dialogue as companionship and community – as ways of being musically with people in need.

We hope to show how music therapy, as an exemplar of musical communication in difficult circumstances, can generate thinking on the processes, uses, and values of music and musicing in contemporary society in general.

Musical companionship

> *Communicative musicality*… is the dynamic sympathetic state of a human person that allows co-ordinated companionship to arise. (Trevarthen 2002, p. 22)

The case of 'Jay'

Jay[2] is a young woman, detained under the Mental Health Act in a locked psychiatric provision. She was presumed to be electively mute, and was unresponsive to any attempts to communicate with her. A psychiatrist described her as

---

[2] The case description is taken from the clinical work of one of us (as is the group example which follows in the second half of the article). These cases have been partly fictionalized to preserve confidentiality. Certain events in the description are indexed with a number in square brackets and referenced within the theoretical discussion that follows.

being on 'psychic retreat'. The music therapist was asked to see Jay, to report to the team on how he experienced her, and to attempt to encourage her to communicate non-verbally. Below are extracts from the therapist's notes.

This is a complex case on many levels – and here we present only the first stage of Jay's work in music therapy. Much could be commented on from a clinical angle – on why Jay was refusing to communicate verbally and interpersonally, on the intra-personal and inter-personal dynamics of her pathology. We will, however, limit our comments more directly to the process of communication that music seems to offer her in this situation, and on how and why this seemed therapeutically helpful.

> I visit Jay in her room on the ward by request of the psychiatrist, who finds her 'uncommunicative, on psychic retreat'. Jay has not spoken for weeks, withdrawing from all social contact, reducing her life to silence and stillness. Nobody knows why – it is difficult to understand a silent story. There is currently no diagnosis (the hypothesis – 'dissociative fugue state') [1]. She barely registers my presence, makes no verbal response to my questions or comments, but sits very still, searching my eyes as if trying to find something. I 'listen' to how she is – to the 'music' of her stillness [2].
>
> I try using a musical channel to communicate with Jay. I give her a small hand-drum and a drumstick, and, using a similar instrument myself, play a few soft beats and wait – my communication neither question nor demand, but perhaps an invitation – related directly to the qualities of her current state [3]. There's a silence, then she responds with a similar musical gesture consisting of a slightly rhythmically disordered sequence of beats [4].
>
> We repeat this sequence a few times more (confirming that her response is intentional). The second time I register more of the quality and character of it, and tune-in in my reply to match this, modulating my gestures to hers [5]. After which she retreats again into silence and stillness [6].
>
> Three days later something similar happens, but this time our halting dialogue takes on greater shape and flow, becoming a modest musical game as we trade musical patterns between us [7]. Here's a beginning of mutuality – a 'musical between'. Finally I offer the cliché rhythm **da da-da daa daa...** and Jay completes it... **DA, DA!** – then she smiles (I'm told for the first time in weeks). The ice has been broken, contact established [8]. Jay has also re-entered the cultural world as we share a musical joke.
>
> A week later Jay comes down to the music therapy room where there is a piano, and a variety of percussion instruments. She speaks a few words reluctantly, but I feel little sense of personal connection with her – she is still distant, her presence elsewhere, her body inexpressive [9]. At first she's unwilling to play, then says 'I'll play piano' and clearly can, improvising washes of sound in A and D minor broken chords in a New Age-like style. She fills musical space with a breadth and volume of sound, but it's a monologue [10]. Her music communicates *to* me (about her), but not *with* me.
>
> I try to join her music, playing a second piano, matching the character and quality of her playing, unsure she even registers my playing with her [11]. But she stops and says 'I can't play at the same time, sorry'. I ask whether playing together is uncomfortable and she says 'I don't know how to' [12]. We are playing in parallel, not together.

The fifth session begins with more of her 'cut-off' playing – a self-referential musical reverie, a wash of sound as she plays a metallophone. The only audible connection between our respective musics is of my trying to 'catch' her music, which leads to a forced sense of communication – we inhabit the same musical space but are not meeting [13].

Then suddenly there is a shift. On the piano I change my music – to a syncopated South American idiom (which takes shape as a tango). It's a musical offering to Jay. She changes instrument too, to the crisper sound of a wooden xylophone, and her playing finds more intention, she orientates to the idiom (her body moves to it), to the rhythm (she begins to syncopate her music), and to the melodic direction (her music goes somewhere). In just 30 seconds we have established musical dialogue [14].

It feels as if something about the music itself has called to our musical relatedness, has made this increasingly congruous in these minutes. Our mutual listening, timing and expressive matching of each other seems to have happened in the service of making this music work - this music which has spontaneously attracted us both, which has led to our 'joint action' on its behalf. I test this congruity between us in the music, playing with a little *rubato*, and Jay follows, then she leads me a little. We mutually accommodate to these micro-variations of musical timing (which also stylistically define the tango). Not only musical relatedness, but Jay's musical creativity has been called by this music's character – she offers new melodic shapes and rhythmic variations. It is satisfying [15].

At first these qualities of fluency, expressiveness, and communication within music are in marked contrast to her 'outside' behaviour – though this too begins to change. Perhaps this 'We', created fleetingly in the music, allowed the re-experiencing and rehearsing of a level of relatedness needed to reestablish interpersonal communication in everyday life – music therapy functioning as a trial run for Jay's return to everyday communication.

Towards the end of the period described Jay and the music therapist were walking to the session. She says to him: 'Nobody understands me here, nobody listens…'. He asks 'Does that include me'? 'No, you listen' she says. Then later in the session 'We're good at making something out of nothing, aren't we'? and smiles. There's a moment of natural, authentic communication here between them. Jay is back from psychic retreat. This ends the first phase of their work together. The re-establishment of authentic human communication seems to be an index of her return to a degree of mental health.

We will now explore this case from a variety of theoretical perspectives in the sections that follow, attempting to balance our discussion between the processes and values of musical communication in music therapy.

Changing communicative channel

Jay's withdrawal from communication – her 'psychic retreat' – can be described medically as a 'negative symptom' of mental illness. Whilst drugs can often treat florid 'positive symptoms' of psychotic states, it is often the chronic withdrawal from social communication that is so disabling for patients and carers. The way people described Jay at this time – that they couldn't 'reach her', couldn't 'make contact' – suggests also that the problem was not just that Jay wouldn't talk, but that others couldn't talk *with her*. Attempts at this time to communicate with Jay were verbal, and happening within perceived professional relationships that were, even with the best of intentions, innately hierarchical, and based on challenging questions. Though my colleagues probably used more tact, their basic question to Jay was: *Why aren't you talking to us?* [1].

When, instead of being questioned, Jay is musically invited, the channel of communication changes, and a bridge to communication is found [3]. These kinds of events in music therapy have been seen by some recent thinkers on music as exemplary of how music works to help gain access to human and cultural others. The musicologist Nicholas Cook writes:

> If music can communicate across barriers of gender difference, it can do so over other barriers as well. One example is music therapy, where music communicates across the cultural barrier of mental illness. (Cook 1998, p. 120)

But this brings us to the difficult territory of what *kind* of communicative channel music is, and how far it resembles a language. Some might suggest that what happened with Jay could be explained by considering music as an alternative 'language of emotion'. But is it possible to say more than this rather general cliché? What specifically about musical communication makes the barrier easier to cross?

Certainly the therapist offers a communicative channel that is an invitation to participation, rather than a demand for explanation. He offers to do something *with* Jay as he listens to the 'music' of her silent presence, then makes the first musical sounds and waits for a response [2–3]. The potential of music, its allure, has a motivational effect on Jay, who finds herself responding. To put it simply, the therapist offered to *play* with her – to play music. Music is not just a *means* used to the end of communicating something, but a *medium* in which a different quality of communication, one perhaps closer to more basic forms of non-verbal communication, is invited and taken up (Ansdell 1995; Garred 2002).

This process does not, however, fit well into traditional models of communication – summed up in Laswell's classic formula, dating from 1948: *Who says what in which channel to whom and with what effects?* (cited in Brooker 1999). This is both too linear and too mechanical for our example. It also shows up the basic problem of thinking about music as a language – does '*Who says what?*' have any meaning in musicing?

Thankfully, the 'language analogy' is increasingly seen as a misleading one, music at best having only resemblances with verbal language (Scruton 1997). Kofi Agawu (1999) sums up: 'music [is not a] system of communication in the ordinary sense, although it can be used to communicate' (p. 146). Arguably the whole music/language analogy is built on a misunderstood view of language as just transmitting information, in a linear and mechanical sequence of *sender* (encoder) → *message* → *receiver* (decoder), with its over-transparent differentiation between form and content (Martin 1995).

Interestingly, instead of the now rather outdated 'telegraph model' of communication (of messages 'sent' and 'received'), an 'orchestral model' has recently been suggested. Here coactivity, harmonization and co-regulation *in context* define the process of communication as meaning created or shared (Tonsberg and Hauge 2003). So music is perhaps better understood as a complex *social* phenomenon, where the meaning of any musical utterance lies within the context of its social use.

Both musicology and music psychology have grappled with the complexities of these issues. Re-examining how music communicates has been central to the 'new musicology', with its emphasis on the social and contextual factors of music's meanings (Williams 2001; Cook and Everist 1999). The more 'ecological' and cultural paradigm within the latest psychology of music (Clarke 2003) and the 'new' sociology of music (DeNora 2000, 2001) have added further perspectives. We suggest music therapy also contributes to this interdisciplinary investigation into a specifically musical phenomenology of communication – which can perhaps in turn explain why music is often therapeutically effective.

'Musical companionship' through communicative musicality

Research is beginning to show how musical communication is built upon physiological foundations and innate biological mechanisms. A study by a music therapist and music therapy researcher (Neugebauer and Aldridge 1998) set up an experiment to track the physiological process of two players in a simulated music therapy session (comprising a dialogical improvisation, but using a well subject instead of a patient). By tracking the music against the heart-beat responses of the two players they saw how physiological events parallelled significant moments in the musical dialogue. Here is evidence that playing music together involves mutual physiological response ('two hearts beating as one' in the authors' words), and that musical dialogue emerges as a co-produced simultaneous effect – communication emerging as a mutual coordination of intention and action within concrete events in real time.

Research from developmental psychology gives us another important perspective on this phenomenon. What began in the 1970s and 1980s as studies of the seemingly musical nature of mother–infant communication (Pavlicevic 1997) has led to key insights into human communication in general, with implications for the therapeutic situations we examine in this article, where communication has been 'damaged' and needs 'repairing'. This research on the 'protomusicality' of infants has led to an empirically grounded theory of non-verbal intersubjective communication, which is seen to have a neurobiological substrate[3]. The mutual communication between mother and infant comprises a musically determined and jointly created 'dance' of co-operation which allows the emergence of the infant's sense of self within a social world.

This theory, which sees all human communication as foundationally musical, has recently been appropriately named *communicative musicality* by Trevarthen and Malloch (Trevarthen and Malloch 2000; Trevarthen 2002, 2003), and defined as '…the dynamic sympathetic state of a human person that allows co-ordinated companionship to arise' (Trevarthen 2002, p. 21). They further suggest that because our communications are made musically, so too they can perhaps be 'repaired' musically:

> Music, as it changes, evokes motive universals in the human experience of moving, the unfolding of purposeful projects and their dramatic cycles of emotional expecta-tion and consummation. It has the capacity to give emotional companionship, and to heal, because it supports intrinsic, neurobiologically founded needs for qualities of human communication that are organized within musicality, 'in time' with the mind. (Trevarthen 2002, p. 25)

Cross-cultural studies in early mother–infant interaction show that commu-nicative musicality is innate: it is present from birth, grounded in neurological functioning, and helps secure the infant's survival. From an evolutionary and biological perspective, musicality can be understood as a sequence of behav-iours (vocal, gestural, and kinesic) that signal our existence, our agency, and our capacity for co-acting with others (Dissanayake 2000). Unlike language, which is in constant process of being overlaid with more or less fixed terms and meanings assigned by cultures and social groups, musicality is a funda-mental prototype that 'holds together' the mutually constructed speaking, moving, and 'being with' of persons in a social world (Malloch 1999). In other words, music-as-communication is understood as an abstract but embodied tool: a constantly shifting combination of pulse, rhythmicity, contours, timbres, and intensity, which underpins our speaking, vocalizing, facial

---

[3] Trevarthen (1999) postulates a mechanism he terms the IMP ('a fundamental intrinsic motive pulse generated in the human brain' p. 25).

expressions, gestural acts and movement. Communicative musicality is founded on[4]:

◆ *Pulse* – the timing of movements (and the coherence of such timing)

◆ *Dynamic Quality* – the force, direction, texture, 'intensity shape', modulation and 'harmonic coherence' of movements

◆ *Narrative* – the shaping of movements over longer stretches of time, their groupings and coherence

These parameters of communicative musicality are clearly analogous to the phenomenology of musicing itself ('pulse', 'quality/intensity', and 'narrative' being homologies of rhythm, melody/dynamics/timbre, and form). These elements of 'proto-musicality' communicate the intention and emotional energy of a subject, and allow another subject to create a responsive and sympathetic co-action of pulse, dynamic quality, and narrative (which may, of course, be perceived directly as rhythmic, melodic, and formal parameters). As Trevarthen writes, the peculiarly human form of relatedness we have with each other '…begins as a music-like composition, an improvised song or dance of companionship with someone we trust…'(2002, p. 35).

There are interesting parallels between this theory and the earlier discoveries of music therapists such as Nordoff and Robbins who, working with children with impaired communication, discovered unexpected and spontaneous intensities of musical response and communicativeness – leading them (as early as the 1960s) to infer a 'core musicality' in children, which was both motivational and communicational (Nordoff and Robbins 1977, p. 1). Consequently, music therapists have developed two main skills for their work of 'repairing' damaged 'communicative musicality'. The first involves 'reading' human behaviour 'as' music, and the second is to 'translate' such a hearing into responsive musical improvisation, using musically communicative mechanisms such as sequencing, repetition, overlapping, alternating, extending, turn-taking, leading, and following. You can therefore hear the co-improvisation between a music therapist and client both as music in the conventional sense, but also as psycho–neuro–biological communication at the same time (Bunt and Pavlicevic 2001; Pavlicevic 1997, 2000).

The case example of Jay can be understood in these terms of 'communicative musicality' and 'musical companionship'. The therapist begins by musically 'reading' the non-verbal communications Jay is making: her posture, tense quietness, and hesitancy [2–3]. These qualities are then 'transposed' into the

---

4 We make here a conflation of the categories of Trevarthen's IMP and Malloch's work (both in Trevarthen 2002, 2003).

tempo, texture, and shape of his first beats on the hand-drum [5]. They reflect the qualities of Jay's current state, as the therapist 'hears' this 'musically'. But they also convey to Jay that he has a sense of her in that moment – which she hears through his careful listening [4]. Their increasing non-verbal attunement is made concrete as both play and listen to each other's musical utterances. As they get into the initial turn-taking exchange of simple rhythmic motives they also begin to co-construct a musical *narrative*, to plot their communication [4–5, 7–8].

Attunement is not all, however. Just as a mother is seen not just to mirror, but also to extend her infant's proto-conversation by playful and carefully judged *mis*-attunements, so the therapist's playing with Jay does not just passively *reflect* her gestures, but also offers the possibility that greater musical conversation is possible. This basic pattern of musical communication has been shown to underlie highly sophisticated patterns of musical relatedness in performance traditions such as jazz and rock, and termed 'participatory discrepancies' by Charles Keil (Keil and Feld 1994). He writes that 'music, to be personally involved and socially valuable, must be "out of time" and "out of tune"'(p. 4). The 'groove' of music is its attuned flow, but the aliveness of the musical communication between the musicians depends on how they *play around* the set-up expectations. In just this way, Jay's attention to the therapist as someone worth playing with needed this tension of difference, this space to 'play around'.

All of this in just a few simple rhythms – just as a mother's intimate communication with an infant is established in a few vocalizations. The vital component in each case is the 'musicality' of shared utterance, which becomes organized, as Trevarthen suggests, as shared 'time in the mind'. That is, there comes a *synchronization* of the music between two people – *musical companionship*.

'Health performances' and cultural communications

Unlike the verbal dialogue between a psychotherapist and patient, a music therapist usually plays *with* his patient (as in the case of Jay). In music it is natural to play together, and consequently the musical companionship we have explored so far naturally reaches beyond such intimacy, into a social and cultural space. With Jay, at [7, 14] musical culture enters the interaction, with the beginning of a mutual musical performance (of an admittedly unusual type).

This natural performance dimension in music therapy has led David Aldridge (1996, 2001) to suggest that personal identity, health, and music are all performed phenomena, and that what we witness in music therapy are 'health performances' through musical performances.

> My contention is that we are improvised performed beings; that is, we realize ourselves in the world, mentally, physically, and socially as performers *in* time and *of* time. (Aldridge 2001, p. 2)

Illness (especially chronic illness – whether physical or psychological) can be seen then as a 'failing performance' of health. In illness we fall too far out of time and out of tune with ourselves and others. An intervention such as music therapy is then a way of promoting and retaining, as well as actively working on, the 'performance of the self'. The 'performance' of communicative musicality demands both self-coherence of gesture, and the interactional synchrony of joint timing in dialogue. For Aldridge, as for Trevarthen, the essence of dialogue, in sickness or in health, is *time*. Communication pathologies are pathologies of time, and what music offers is an alternative form of structuring time:

> '...when the relationship fails, then the mutuality of time is lost... We literally fall out with each other, fall out of time and thereby understanding. This is the process of becoming isolated. To repair performance, then we have to offer a structure in time. (Aldridge 2001, p. 10)

We could see Jay as re-initiating the 'performance of herself' and a performance of her *health* through her music therapy sessions, using her communicative musicality to initiate participation in the 'joint action' of musicing with the therapist. Key to the success of the 'performance' in this session is the ability of the therapist and Jay to find, and play with, shared time.

An equally key aspect is how therapist and client also share *culture* within their musicing. The cultural dimension of musical communication in music therapy is being increasingly emphasized (Stige 2002) as a natural corrective to exclusively biological or psychological explanations. Culture and its musical codes decisively enter into the therapist's interaction with Jay with the cliché rhythm at [8]. Here they share cultural as well as musical knowledge, and this helps cement their musical and personal contact. Later, the New Age-like style Jay plays on the piano [10] is the first music in which she communicates something of her relationship to musical culture 'outside' herself. Still later, the real meeting point of their playing is in the tango-style improvisation, where both share the active and emotional affordances of the idiom [14–15].

The cultural theorist Bakhtin made the observation that language is never our own: there can be no such things as a private expression, a 'free association'. Rather, he stated that 'the word in language is half someone else's' (cited in Shotter 1999, p. 80). In our communications we are partaking in socially conventional 'speech genres', and even in a monologue there are still two talking. Perhaps, then, this is also true of musical communication – the tone is half somebody else's, and music as culture is a third player in any musical dialogue.

Arguably there is no musical communication which is not at the same time a cultural communication.

This has been a major theme in much of the so-called 'new musicology' and its creative rapprochement with the empirical tradition of the sociology of music (Williams 2001). In particular Tia DeNora's work (2000, 2001) has been influential in showing how people in their everyday life assemble and use the cultural materials which music affords for 'being, doing, feeling' – or, as she puts it, 'the musical composition of subjectivity' (2001, p. 176). One of her examples of this is a music therapy case.

Any further research and thinking on the nature of musical communication will need to address these question of just how, in DeNora's phrase, 'cultural material "gets into" social psychological life' – and how it helps there. Music therapy may be a fruitful area of study here, showing as it does the fine interface between the biological, psychological, and cultural factors in musical communication.

The values of musical communication: the 'dialogical principle'

As a discipline, music therapy attempts to balance empirical perspectives on musical communication with the philosophical, spiritual, and musical discourses on the values of musical dialogue as a way of 'being in the world with others'. Here music therapy moves from a medical model of treatment to a humanistic one of relationship and care; from the 'mechanisms' of communication to the values of dialogue. This is consistent with the feedback we get from our clients, who report experiencing within musical dialogue moments of 'pure communication' – whose qualities of authenticity, intersubjectivity, and presence are healing for them (Ansdell 1995; Hartley 1999; Lee 1996).

So we might say (after Bakhtin) that it takes two to music. A musical utterance always already addresses someone, and is in dialogue with someone – even where one partner is silent. What we will call the 'dialogical principle' (derived from a tradition of 'philosophers of dialogue'[5]) suggests that being in dialogue is a fundamental human reality – even when this is distorted or thwarted by situation or illness. Bakhtin's phrase '*To be* means *to communicate*', could stand as a summary of many twentieth century critical challenges to Descartes' monological and solipsistic vision of a self which *is* because it thinks, and does

---

[5] A role-call of such 'philosophers of dialogue' would include: Hegel, Novalis, Jacobi, Freud, Dilthey, Husserl, Jaspers, Heidegger, Merleu-Ponty, Levinas, Buber, Gadamer, Wittgenstein, Adorno, Bakhtin, Bohm, Kristeva – taking us from German idealism to contemporary social constructionism.

so privately (Shotter 1999). Reacting against this stance, several generations of thinkers have instead re-defined Man as the *dialogical* creature – we *are* because we communicate, help create each other, live as communal creatures.

To take here just one example of how a philosophy of dialogue may give a music therapist a way of conceptualizing musical dialogues in music therapy within a framework of a humanistic value system, we will discuss Ansdell's use of the Jewish theologian and philosopher Martin Buber's concept of the 'life of dialogue'. Buber's belief in the value of dialogue can be summed up in his phrase 'All real living is meeting'. He advocated a form of face-to-face authentic human encounter that is (at best) immediate, intersubjective, mutual and authentic (Friedman 2003). For Buber there *is* no 'single *I*' – we only exist in relationship 'companying with the other'. We address the world (each other, as well as works of art, nature, and God), with two 'basic words', which in turn indicate a 'basic stance' of relatedness: either *I–It* – creating a world of subject–object, where we manipulate things and people whilst living in our own world, or, alternatively, *I–You*[6] an inter-subjective world where we enter into direct relatedness with people and things, where they influence us, where we share a world *between* us, where there is immediacy, presence, mutuality, responsibility (Buber 1947/2002). The 'life of dialogue' is an *interhuman* realm, which both defines our values as communicative human beings, as well as being a potential vehicle for revelation. 'The basic movement of the life of dialogue' writes Buber, 'is the turning towards the other' (p. 25). Music helps us here, for as Buber wrote: 'All music calls to an ear that is not the musician's own' (p. 30).

Ansdell (1995) developed a schema of musical relatedness for use in music therapy, drawing directly from Buber's dialogical perspective. Looked at this way we could see the shifts in relatedness between Jay and the therapist as follows:

It is difficult within doctor–patient roles for a diagnostic session [1] not to assume an I–It relationship, characterized by knowledge sought (and resisted in this case). Each retains their own stance. In contrast, at [3] the therapist's musical invitation, which we could characterize as $[I \triangleright You]$ quickly moves to an incipiently reciprocal and symmetrical communication $[I \triangleright You \leftrightarrow (You?) \triangleleft I]$ at [4]. When Jay completes the musical cliché rhythm [7–8] there is definite shared communication in the 'musical between' $[I \triangleright You \leftrightarrow You \triangleleft I]$. The relatedness retreats at [9–12] into the musical monologue of her piano playing $[I \triangleright You \leftrightarrow I]$ before finally changing again into the creative dialogue of [14–15], where what Buber would call a *meeting*, and Ansdell a 'musical meeting' as [*We*] takes place.

---

[6] Buber's 'Thou' is translated as 'You' here – following arguments by Buber scholars on the correct translation of the original *Ich und Du*.

We want to emphasize here the connection between the micro-phenomenology of the shifts in musical relatedness represented in this schema (which also mirrors that of Trevarthen's 'communicative musicality') with the ethical dimensions of human communication emphasized by Buber. We see Jay taking steps back to relatedness through dialogue grounded in the concrete musical reality which she and the therapist commonly shape.

In this first section we have outlined how 'musical companionship' is a biologically grounded, but culturally directed form of human socialization articulated through the processes of communicative musicality. Music therapy, in which music is both the medium and the tool, can allow the creative 'performance of health' even from within illness. It may also be possible to talk of the 'repair' of communicative musicality. Musical companionship, however, also naturally reaches outwards to widening contexts of musical community: to being-with-others in music.

Musical community

Community is where community happens. (Buber 1947/2002, p. 37)

The case of 'The Group'

An open group meets weekly on the ward in a psychiatric unit. The room is organized with a variety of percussion instruments set out for people to select, and also an upright piano mostly played by the therapist. It's difficult to predict who will turn up, how many 'regulars' or new members, or what the mix of the group will be like in terms of ability, illness, character. The session has a loose structure, which is improvised (as is most of the music) according to the needs and mood of the group. There are some group 'rituals' such as members introducing themselves to each other at the beginning of the group and singing goodbye to each other at the end. The therapist sometimes intervenes to provide more or less structure – but in theory anything is possible.

> Most of the group has arrived. Tom is loud and forceful; Jack is speedy, inappropriately jovial; Jane is timid; Shanti is puzzled; Kevin is withdrawn; Leila is upset... [1]. The 'group' is hypothetical – just a collection of individuals.
>
> The sense of these people being in their own worlds carries over into the music they improvise. Barely listening to each other, the music sounds fragmented, disjointed and monotonous – a collage of monologues [2]. We are in the same space and time physically, but not musically.
>
> The lack of communication within the group feels unsatisfactory – there is little acknowledgement of each other, physically or musically. Instead each person stays in his or her own world and we travel nowhere together [3].
>
> Then Simon comes into the room, ecstatically giggling, picks up a cymbal and plays loudly in a way unrelated to the music already happening [4]. This at least sets off a

reaction: Tom plays louder, Jane withdraws more, Leila looks even more anxious... But still the group struggles to find a way of acting together [5].

My job as a music therapist is to intervene in these situations, and to do so musically where possible [6]. My aim is firstly to get people listening to each other as they play. I start by musically contacting each of them in turn, playing the piano so as to match how they are playing on their instrument at the time, joining them in *their* world of musical time and space, initiating musical companionship [7].

At the same time I'm still keeping my ears on what is happening in the group as a whole. By bringing each person into musical communication with me I can then bring their awareness to others' playing and to the group as a whole, as they hear their playing being echoed by someone else's [8]. When contact happens I can work musically to moderate Tom's loud playing, to slow down Jack's, to enhance Kevin's, to encourage Leila [9].

After a while we stop playing as a group, and I get each person to improvise a dialogue with another, responding exactly as the other plays [10]. Then we go a stage further, passing around improvised fragments of melody with our voices.

In a final phase of the group I initiate from the piano an improvised lilting jazzy music to which each person sings an improvised turn and passes it on to the next person. Then the group spontaneously sings the theme together, there's a sudden crescendo in the singing and a spontaneous call-and-response form takes shape between me and the group as a whole. The group had been connected link by link, and is now a group [11].

People rush for small instruments which they play as they sing – we keep the lilting jazz going – maracas and tambourines complement voices. The group's music balances and coheres, people are really listening to each others' music, and to the music of the whole. The group really plays together for the first time today [12].

The music segues into a mutual singing of goodbye. The members sing to each other, and sing their appreciation of each other. The quality of communication we've now achieved is at the heart of this 'feeling well' together, being well together [13].

The outcome is positive by the end of the session. Community here was forged against the odds. Not 'community-building' as a utopian goal, but community 'happening' as a need and an achievement.

Our theoretical comments on this example are in many ways a continuation of those on musical companionship – but asking this time what different forms of musical communication can be seen within 'The Group'. In the same way as the case of 'Jay' illustrated some interesting facets of interpersonal communication through the particular medium of musical communication, so we suggest also that group musical communication can present some of the complexities of social communication and social action – and of the possibilities of creating musical community.

Social dialogue and coupled neurodynamics

The social and the empirical sciences again provide interesting perspectives on the kind of musical communications taking place in such a music therapy group.

There are also important overlaps between them: whilst both Bahktin and Buber see community as elaborated dialogue, the contemporary cognitive neuroscientist William Benzon (2001) states 'Cartesian individuals do not make music'. Musicing illustrates how we are social creatures.

The pioneer sociologist Alfred Schutz considered musical communication paradigmatic of human social communication. He cites the famous ensemble pieces in Mozart's operas, where the way music works gives us both the individual perspectives of each character *and* how they are 'bound together in [the] intersubjective situation of a community, in a *We*' (Schutz in Martin 1995, p. 200). Schutz suggests this to be different from normal linguistic communication. When people music together, they synchronize their experience (either with the composer, or the players), not in 'clock time' but in the 'inner' subjective time of individual and shared consciousness. Music is then 'a meaningful arrangement of tones in inner time', and musical communication involves what he calls a 'mutual tuning-in relationship', where 'the subjectivities of two or more people are brought into alignment through being synchronised' (cited in Martin 1995, p. 200), creating an 'intersubjective lifeworld':

> This sharing of the other's flux of experiences in inner time, this living through a vivid present in common, constitutes... the mutual tuning-in relationship, the experience of the 'We', which is at the foundation of all possible communication. (Schutz in Martin 1995, p. 200)

The cognitive neuropsychologist William Benzon's (2001) work on music's role in social experience has many parallels with Schutz' ideas. Benzon re-frames Schutz' phenomenological speculations in cognitive neuroscience terms, focusing on the intersubjective 'tuning-in relationships' of players. Benzon's view is that musical communication at these points is no less than a coupling between brains through shared activity. As such 'the neurobiology of music and the neurobiology of social attachment appear to be intimately intertwined' (p. 113). This also clearly links with Trevarthen and Malloch's 'communicative musicality'.

Benzon suggests that the forms of precise coordination that happen in musicing groups are mediated by drawing on several neural structures at once: both sub-cortical motor and affective neural systems along with higher cortical conceptual systems. Drawing on Condon's famous research on interactional synchrony, Benzon suggests how the brain is motivated to attune to the sounds of a musicing group, and then to reorganize the nervous system to form a 'collective neural state space' – a single system which comprises the whole group: 'The individuals are physically separate, but temporally integrated. It is one music, one dance' (p. 164).

Both Schutz and Benzon are of course presenting scenarios of 'ideal communicative musicing' here – where timing, intersubjectivity, and social communication are achieved. Music therapy, as we have seen previously, is often a needed intervention where such performance is failing, where pathology is preventing 'ideal communicative musicing' happening. The case example of 'The Group' shows a situation developing from problem to solution in this regard.

The Group begins with seven individuals, their illnesses militating against an easy 'tuning-in' with each other. Their playing is at first [1–5] unsynchronized, unaligned – both in terms of *pulse*, but also in the *dynamic quality* and *narrative* aspects of communicative musicality – the energy, shape, and 'story' of their playing. They are in their own world – together in physical time and space, but not in the shared 'inner time' that Schutz describes. Whilst out-of-time-together, intersubjective feeling is low, and the overall experience feels unsatisfactory. As Benzon comments, the opposite of musical pleasure is where overall 'neural flow is poorly timed and incoherent' (p. 86). The Group has, as Aldridge (2001) suggests, 'fallen out with each other'. Through the interventions and 'communication exercises' [6–10] the therapist manages to change this situation – by coming into interactional synchrony with each person, by encouraging the group's listening, literally musically coupling each player to the whole like links in a chain. Finally at [11–12] there comes what Schutz would call a 'We', which has the sense of 'vivid presence' and a flow of shared experience – or what Benzon calls a 'collective neural state space'. What both of these complementary descriptions share is the centrality of *time* and *timing* being at the heart of musical community – quite simply *being-in-time-together*.

Culture and communitas

What of the music at [11–12]? At this arrival point of musical community the group is not just playing and singing at the same time together, it is also somehow in the same 'place' together. By this I mean a shared experience of the music's idiom – with its connotations of laid-back jazziness, its characteristic body movements, its modes and textures of playing and singing. The group falls collectively into the 'groove' of this music – which is a cultural 'place' to be together. Music therapists such as Ken Aigen (2002) are beginning to write about how social experiences in music are mediated through shared cultural experiences. You can only establish a groove within communicative playing, and this in turn is its reward – the experience of common feeling. You can also only establish groove within a musical *culture*, because it depends on recognizing and being able to participate in the particular 'feel' of the music. This, we would suggest, is what is happening at [11–12] – the groove of the jazz idiom is participated in and enjoyed because it moves the body and the mind in certain culturally pleasurable ways.

How a cultural artefact such as an idiom can 'get into' social life in this way, and how it specifically organizes it once there, has been an increasingly important theme in the sociology of music – in particular Tia DeNora's (2000, 2001) work. Equally, the more psychobiologically grounded theories of Trevarthen and Benzon would not disagree with this emphasis on the cultural underscoring of successful musicing. Benzon is at pains to emphasize that, as culture moulds musicing, so too the forms of sociality music affords in turn moulds the nervous system. Not only do we have to be-in-time-together for successful musical communication to happen, but also *be-in-place-together* – where 'place' is somewhere shared and good to be in.

A way of describing this experienced place might be the concept of *communitas,* which the anthropologist Victor Turner characterized as a way of being-together which contrasts with usual structured social experiences. Several music therapists (Ruud 1998; Aigen 2002) have used this concept to model those experiences in music therapy where the ritual quality of joint improvisation in a particular context allows an experience of *communitas*, with its sense of mutual presence, dialogue, levelling of social roles and flow of musical communication.

The experience of 'The Group' could be seen in this way: as a gradual negotiation and achievement of *communitas*. The members of the group were, by circumstance of their mental illness, in a marginal state both in society and in terms of their difficulty in being-with-others. The musicing gradually helps shift modes of communication, feeling, action, and awareness, leading to a different quality of experiencing-together. It might be remarked that the interventions needed from the therapist indicate role differentiation and structuring. But this stage was only a temporary and preparatory one, for the experience of *communitas* was achieved by the end of the group session – shared by clients and therapist alike.

Conclusion

Playing together in time

A dominant theme of this chapter has been time. Trevarthen writes of human communication as musically grounded, 'in time with the mind'; Schutz of the 'inner time' of tuning-in relationships; Benzon of coupled nervous systems which are 'physically separated but temporally integrated' and that 'music, more than any other human activity is an exercise in timing'; Aldridge that 'at the heart of this understanding [of dialogue] is time'; Aigen that 'groove' is 'a place of timing'. There is, it would seem, substantial agreement that time and timing are key (perhaps *the* key) to the processes of successful musical communication.

What, then, of the work of music therapists, who attempt to facilitate (and sometimes to 'repair') musical communication? The two clinical cases we have examined (and indeed much of the work by music therapists) concerns work with people living with *chronic* illness – where time is experienced as a negative factor. David Aldridge (1996, 2000, 2001) has written of the relevance of the two forms of time, as defined by the Greeks – *chronos* and *kairos* – in relation to illness and music therapy. He links this to his metaphor that, whilst scientific medicine would have us as 'mechanical beings' (acting within and treated within mechanical time as *chronos*), what is perhaps needed in music therapy is an understanding of the person as a 'symphonic being', where time is *kairos*:

> If *chronos* is time as measured, *kairos* is time considered as the right or opportune moment. It contains elements of appropriateness and purpose. (Aldridge 2001, p. 4)

Musical time is *kairos* – allowing both moments of timelessness as well as the kind of 'being-together-in-time' we have discussed throughout this chapter. Communicative musicality, musical companionship, and musical community all operate within the opportunity, appropriateness, and purposefulness of musical time as *kairos*. It is these qualities of musical communication that allows music therapy to address the problems of communication that people with chronic illness can have. Musical communication both gives a more optimistic view of the nature of our innate biological and cultural capacity of being-together, and also a way of helping people and communities to 'repair' their 'communicative musicality' so they can experience better ways of being together. Such 'musical companionship' and 'musical community' bring us close to the original function of a *therapeutes* – one who helps by accompanying.

References

Agawu, K. (1999) The challenge of semiotics. In *Rethinking Music*, (eds N. Cook and M. Everist). Oxford: Oxford University Press.

Aigen, K. (2002) *Playin' in the Band: A Qualitative Study of Popular Music Styles as Clinical Improvisation*. New York: Nordoff-Robbins Center for Music Therapy, New York University.

Aldridge, D. (1996) *Music Therapy Research & Practice in Medicine*. London: Jessica Kingsley.

Aldridge, D. (2000) *Spirituality, Healing & Medicine: Return to the Silence*. London: Jessica Kingsley.

Aldridge, D. (2001) Music therapy and neurological rehabilitation: Recognition and the performed body in an ecological niche. *Music Therapy Today* [online]. www.musictherapyworld.info

Ansdell, G. (1995) *Music for Life*. London: Jessica Kingsley.

Ansdell, G. (2002) Community Music Therapy and the winds of change [online]. *Voices: A World Forum for Music Therapy.* http://www.voices.no/discussions/discm4_03.html

Ansdell, G. (2003) The stories we tell: some metatheoretical reflections on music therapy. *Nordic Journal of Music Therapy,* 12(2),152–9.

Bakhtin, M. (1984) *Problems of Dostoevsky's Poetics.* Mineapolis, MN: University of Minnesota Press.

Benzon, W. (2001) *Beethoven's Anvil: Music in Mind & Culture.* New York: Basic Books.

Brooker, P. (1999) *A Concise Glossary of Cultural Theory.* London: Arnold.

Buber, M. (1947/2002) *Between Man and Man.* London: Routledge.

Bunt, L. (1994) *Music Therapy: An Art Beyond Words.* London: Routledge.

Bunt, L. and Pavlicevic, M. (2001) Music and emotion: perspectives from music therapy In *Music and Emotion,* (eds P. Juslin and J. Sloboda). Oxford: Oxford University Press.

Cook, N. (1998) *Music: A Very Short Introduction.* Oxford: Oxford University Press.

Cook, N. and Everist, M. (1999) *Rethinking Music.* Oxford: Oxford University Press.

Clarke, E. (2003) Music and psychology. In *The Cultural Study of Music: A Critical Introduction,* (eds M. Clayton, T. Herbert, and R. Middleton). London: Routledge.

DeNora, T. (2000) *Music in Everyday Life.* Cambridge: Cambridge University Press.

DeNora, T. (2001) Aesthetic agency and musical practice: new directions in the sociology of music and emotion. In *Music and Emotion,* (eds P. Juslin and J. Sloboda). Oxford: Oxford University Press.

Dissanayake, E. (2000) Antecedents of the temporal arts in early mother-infant interaction. In *The Origins of Music,* (eds E. Wallin, N. Merker, and S. Brown). Cambridge, MA: MIT Press.

Elliott, D. (1995) *Music Matters.* New York: Oxford University Press.

Friedman (2003) Martin Buber and dialogical psychotherapy. In *Understanding Experience: Psychotherapy and Postmodernism,* (ed. R. Frie). London: Routledge.

Garred, R. (2002) The ontology of music in music therapy – A dialogical view. In *Contemporary Voices of Music Therapy: Communication, Culture, and Community,* (eds C. Kenny and B. Stige), Oslo: Unipub forlag.

Hartley, N. (1999) A music therapist's personal reflections on working with those who are living with HIV/AIDS. In *Music Therapy in Palliative Care: New Voices,* (ed. D. Aldridge). London: Jessica Kingsley.

Horden, P. (2000) *Music as Medicine: The History of Music Therapy since Antiquity.* Aldershot: Ashgate.

Keil, C. and Feld, S. (1994) *Music Grooves.* Chicago, IL: University of Chicago Press.

Lee, C. (1996) *Music at the Edge.* London: Routledge.

Malloch, S. (1999) Mothers and infants and communicative musicality. *Musicae Scientiae* Special Issue 1999–2000, 29–53.

Martin, P. (1995) *Sounds and Society: Themes in the Sociology of Music.* Manchester: Manchester University Press.

Neugebauer, L. and Aldridge, D. (1998) Communication, heart rate and the musical dialogue. *British Journal of Music Therapy,* 12(2), 46–53.

Nordoff, P. and Robbins, C. (1971) *Therapy in Music for Handicapped Children.* London: Gollancz.

Nordoff, P. and Robbins, C. (1977) *Creative Music Therapy.* New York: John Day.

Pavlicevic, M. (1997) *Music Therapy in Context.* London: Jessica Kingsley.

Pavlicevic, M. (2000) Improvisation in music therapy: human communication in sound. *Journal of Music Therapy,* 37(4), 269–85.

Pavlicevic, M. and Ansdell, G. (eds) (2004). *Community Music Therapy.* London: Jessica Kingsley Publishers.

Ruud, E. (1980) *Music Therapy and its Relationship to Current Treatment Theories.* St. Louis, MO: Magna-Music Baton.

Ruud, E. (1998) *Music Therapy: Improvisation, Communication & Culture.* Gilsum, NH: Barcelona Publishers.

Scruton, R. (1997) *The Aesthetics of Music.* Oxford: Oxford University Press.

Shotter, J. (1999) Life inside dialogically structured mentalities: Bakhtin's and Voloshinov's account of our mental activities as out in the world between us. In J. Rowan and M. Cooper (eds), *The Plural Self.* London: Sage Publications.

Small, C. (1998) *Musicking: The Meanings of Performing & Listening.* Hanover, NH: Wesleyan University Press.

Stige, B. (2002) *Culture-Centered Music Therapy.* Gilsum, NH: Barcelona Publishers.

Stige, B. (2003) Elaborations towards a notion of Community Music Therapy. Oslo: Unipub.

Tonsberg, G. and Hauge, T. (2003) The musical nature of human interaction [online]. *Voices: A World Forum for Music Therapy.* Retrieved June 2, 2003 from http://www.voices.no/mainissues/mi40003000116.html

Trevarthen, C. (1999) Musicality and the intrinsic motive pulse: evidence from human psychobiology and infant communication. *Musicae Scientiae* Special Issue 1999–2000, 155–215.

Trevarthen, C. (2002) Origins of musical identity: evidence from infancy for musical social awareness. In *Musical Identities,* (eds R.A.R. Macdonald, D.J. Hargreaves, and D. Miell). Oxford: Oxford University Press.

Trevarthen, C. (2003) Neuroscience and intrinsic psychodynamics: current knowledge and potential for therapy. In *Revolutionary Connections: Psychotherapy & Neuroscience,* (eds J. Corrigall and H. Wilkinson). London: Karnac Books.

Trevarthen, C. and Malloch, S. (2000) The dance of wellbeing: defining the musical therapeutic effect. *Nordic Journal of Music Therapy,* 9(2), 3–17.

Williams, A. (2001) *Constructing Musicology.* Aldershot: Ashgate.

Chapter 10

Bodily communication in musical performance

Jane W. Davidson

Outline

This chapter deals with three central aspects of musical communication which focus on how the human body is used to produce a musical performance, namely how biomechanical constraints operate; how expressive intentions and social codes influence the production; and how that production is then interpreted by co-performers and audiences. The theoretical basis of the work presented has emerged from the study of the physical and mental skills involved in playing, ranging from basic biomechanics through to general social psychology and the effects of different social contexts on individual behaviour. Overall, the chapter demonstrates the need to adopt an integrated perspective in order to understand the role of the bodily communication in musical performance. That is, the distinct research domains have provided specialist evidence, giving partial explanations of the body's function, but in order to gain a comprehensive understanding, it is necessary to develop a theoretical and practical approach to bodily communication which integrates the range of evidence from biomechanics through to social psychology. Existing studies are used to present theoretical explanations and these are then explored in practical investigations. Two case studies from my own research provide the empirical data: one of a jazz singer and accompanist, Rosie Brown and Mark Slater; and the other of the pop band, The Corrs. The scant research in this area limits the discussion in this chapter to Western styles of music perform-ance, though non-western performance is considered in Martin Clayton's chapter (this volume). It is hoped that the reader will be able to extract the general principles under current discussion and apply them to other musical forms and contexts, just as they may do the same for Clayton's work.

The chapter is divided into sub-sections. In the first sub-section, the physical and mental processes involved in generating a performance are considered. A range of empirical work is drawn upon to reveal that performance movements have specific physical characteristics necessary for the biomechanical accomplishment of the task, and in addition, expressive effects. However, it is also made apparent that both types of characteristics coexist and occur in an integrated movement stream. This means that measuring the movements in order to see how and where the different characteristics occur offers only very partial data. To understand the movement components, the onlooker's perception of the performance, alongside an analysis of the musical content, needs to be taken into account in establishing whether or not the movements are being used for expressive effect. In fact, it is demonstrated that the onlooker (audience and/or co-performers) not only identifies these movements, but is also involved in a social communication with the performer. Therefore, it seems that the generation and subsequent meaning of the movement behaviours of the performer are more or less consciously created for the onlooker (audience/ co-performer), for social and musical ends. The onlooker's reception of the movement behaviours will depend on stylistic knowledge and familiarity.

At this point, the second sub-section of the chapter reveals how research into onlooker perception can help to investigate which types of movement lead to communication of a performer's intentions. The movement types and associated meanings are explored by drawing parallels between the movement accompanying speech. Also, the roles of specific social influences such as individual training and the musical culture and style are explored, as well as their relative impacts on the development of a performer's movement behaviour.

Having already established the communicative function of performance from the onlooker's perspective, the third sub-section of the chapter considers other aspects of the social nature of the performer's task. Case studies of musicians are then used to illustrate the types of codes that are most useful for social communication on stage.

The chapter concludes by suggesting that bodily communication is a crucial aspect of musical performance, and that performers can benefit from understanding how they produce their music, not only for musical understanding, but also for audience and co-performer engagement.

Musical performance production

Playing a piece of music depends on developing a range of complex and interactive skills. They require cognitive, perceptual, and action processes (Davidson and Scripp 1990), and so depend on mental representations; that is, the internal representation in memory that the performer produces while trying to encode or manipulate a relevant stimulus for a specific performance event. The ability to generate and use mental representations efficiently is the hallmark of expert performers. Consider the following contrasting examples: a beginning piano student's mental representation of a piece of music might typically consist of a sequence of difficult and laborious fingering combinations, while a more advanced player might also represent the chordal progression with some expressive information, some aural image of the sounds, and maybe a visual representation of how the score looks.

Lehmann and Ericsson (1997) have developed a model of musical performance skills which assumes that musicians require at least three different types of mental representations to play, corresponding to (i) a goal representation, (ii) a production representation, and (iii) a representation of the current performance. Woody (1999) has renamed these as goal imaging, motor production, and self-monitoring. We might explain the bodily engagement of the performer, therefore, as being the consequence of performance goals (technical and expressive aims) and the self-monitoring that goes on during the course of the performance. All of these processes are codependent, combining intellectual/conceptual understanding and motor skill.

Of course, knowledge and experience shapes the performer's goals and level of achievement: a child is far less fluent and expressive than an expert soloist, for example. A key feature of music practice is to ensure that the playing activity and the piece being learned become so well established in thought and motor activity that the player is more mentally 'free' to deal with the 'in the moment' aspects of problem-solving during a performance, such as coping with a sticking piano key while trying to play with the same degree of technical fluency and expressive content as achieved in rehearsal. Having the skill to play automatically, and also the potential to focus consciously on detail if necessary is a desired state of mastery, and it is a state that differs from the novice's possibilities (see Lehmann and Davidson 2002, for a more detailed discussion).

In association with the development of mental representations, our anatomies and the instruments we play also have a critical role in shaping the musical outcome. For instance, someone of light weight and small physique will have to develop his or her way of playing to achieve a fortissimo in a Beethoven sonata which will be slightly different from a much heavier, larger person, even if the technicalities of playing are based on the same principles. As for the instruments themselves, the English ethnomusicologist John Baily has shown how the music of the Dutar, a stringed instrument from Herat, in Afghanistan, evolved from music associated with a neighbouring instrument, and in the process acquired characteristics that were specifically related to the ergonomics of the Dutar itself (see Baily 1985). We may apply the principles of ergonomics to the differences in the repertoire as well as the physical approach required when playing, for example, the same piece of music on a harpsichord versus the piano, or the viola versus the violin.

Economy of bodily movement in the production of a musical performance

The earliest studies on how motor control is achieved show that humans will rehearse actions until they achieve an incompressible minimum; that is, the minimum action time involved in doing a specific task, which produces an economy of movement, such as in rowing, or box packing (see Bernstein 1967). In music, Shaffer (1982), working only with timing data, demonstrated that piano key presses do indeed have their own 'incompressible minimum', with a specific combination of key presses having a unique timing profile. But, there are other manipulations which are dependent on representations of musical expression, rather than simple biomechanics: timing extensions at phrase boundaries, for example. Thus, in Shaffer's view, it seems that the two kinds of movement information are involved in the physical action of music performance: those for the requirement of playing the notes, and those to achieve musical effects. When a skilled performer plays a well-learned piece, these actions become co-specified, especially if the piece is extremely well learned and performed with a high degree of automaticity (see Shaffer 1984, for more details).

Research on musical performance production until the early 1990s generally tended to focus on the musical effects produced in sound, rather than investigating how they are achieved through the body. This was clearly a very limited approach to understanding performance production. It was in this context that I began to research the body in performance, and attempted to bring understanding to a completely un-explored area. I began with case study investigations of a pianist to map how he assembled and produced a musical performance through his body. I needed to establish how a body 'negotiated' a piece of music (see Davidson, in press, to follow up some of the current discussion in more detail). In order to trace the bodily actions, I used video cameras and an x- and y- axis video position analyser to follow markers on his face, shoulder, and hands to track the principal movements of his body. These measurements revealed that the hand(s) engaged in rotations of the wrist over the keys, and meandering lifts of one hand, during musical passages where the other hand was active in note playing. The head made a swaying, circular type of motion. Even if these movements were approaching an incompressible biomechanical optimum, in line with Shaffer's ideas, they would include expressive information.

In order to attempt to differentiate between what may constitute technically necessary movement from movement for expressive effects, I asked the pianist to play pieces varying the expressive intention: playing without expression, exaggerating all the expressive features of the music, and playing a 'normal' or desired expressive intention. In statistical analyses of the resulting movement tracks, it was discovered that in terms of quantity and scale of the movements, there were no differences in how the hands were used, presumably because of the technical constraints of the more or less constant note playing. But, with the head/upper torso, there were significant differences, especially between the inexpressive interpretation and the other two performances. The most striking difference was in the degree of the movement. Also, there was a near continuous swaying movement across all three performances, though the movement was very small in the inexpressive performance, and increased in amplitude across the two other performances.

In a further study of the same pianist (see Clarke and Davidson 1998), it was discovered that the swaying was critical in shaping the expression of the performance, perhaps as well as reflecting some of it too. This finding coincides with Todd's (1999) proposal that we enjoy the vestibular activity involved in moving with music, and it could be that in generating the performance, the swaying helps in the production of the expressive timing effects, providing a regulatory device (the constant sway) around the musical timing which ebbs and flows as the *rubato* effects operate.

Moreover, following from the work of Cutting and his associates Kozlowski and Proffitt (Cutting and Kozlowski 1977; Kozlowski and Cutting 1977; Cutting, *et al.* 1978; Cutting and Proffitt 1981), the swaying might provide an account for a physical centre within the body through which the musically expressive information is produced. In physics, the term for such a point is the *centre of moment*. According to Cutting's theoretical proposal, it could be that the pianist's waist region functions as the central physical core for the musical expression, for that is the point from which the swaying action emanates: rotating the body from the waist, through to the hip area and upwards to the shoulders and head. My own schematic representation of the possible 'expressive' *centre of moment* for a pianist is shown in Fig. 10.1.

Cutting and collaborators established their theoretical propositions on experimental work investigating the physical expression of gender in walking style. They found that the gender information was available from a single marker placed on each walker's leg, the centre being implied, though not visible, and providing the information about gender. In a replication of the single marker study, but working with the pianist playing in the inexpressive, normal, and exaggerated manners, I discovered that all the information about musical intention was indeed contained in any single marker, though the head was the best overall indicator (see Davidson 2002a). It is important to be aware that

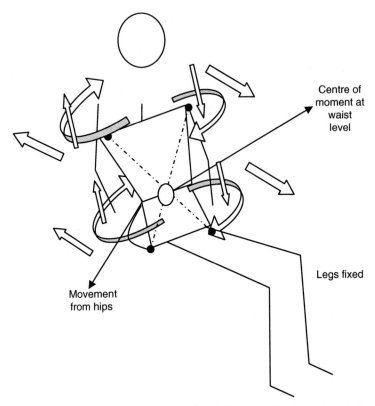

Fig. 10.1 The 'centre of moment' principle applied to a pianist. Note the rotational possibilities of the torso around the waist. As a hierarchical structure, the rotations observed at torso levels would be reflected in head/neck and arm/hand movements.

the *centre of moment* theory for movement expression argues that there is a movement hierarchy, with different body parts expressing the same information but at a more local level. Thus, forearms and wrists might trace similar types of movement patterns to the overall body sway.

Of course, the reader might wonder how I can propose such a theory based on one single case. In fact, during the period of work with the pianist, I recorded other data from other pianists which appeared to be very similar, but at that time, there was not sufficient computer technology available to me to analyse more than one person. More recently, Vines and Wanderley (2003) have discovered similar sorts of movement traces in clarinet players; and Windsor, Ng, and I have found similar evidence by studying three other pianists (Windsor, *et al.* 2003), as have Williamon and I (Williamon and Davidson 2001). Most recently, similar data are emerging in a new research collaboration (Davidson *et al.* in preparation), which examines flute and clarinet players.

The centre of moment theory accounts mainly for the generation of bio-mechanical action related to technical and some expressive aspects of performance. As a theoretical account, it does not deal specifically with the many socially learned and developed movement techniques that we know performers use for specific co-performer and audience affect. Indeed, in the work undertaken in 1998 (see Clarke and Davidson), it was shown that the pianist used a consistently identifiable repertoire of discreet movements which included actions like wiggling his back, or lifting his hand in a swirling gesture that seemed unnecessary for technical purposes, but which – at some level – appeared to be connected to an intention to express something about the music and the performance itself. These smaller movements were integrated into the overall swaying. In terms of how different representational processes interact, it is possible to assume that the discreet movements may be more socially focused, but that they become integrated into the overall representation (goal) and final movement (production/self-monitoring processes) of a performance.

Audience reactions to body movements used in music production

In order to explore the performance movement, and to decide whether or not the discreet movements may be for social communication effects, it seems necessary to understand which aspects of performance movement provide useful cues for the audience. Minimum visual information (the simple use of points of light reflecting the action of body joints) showed that expressive differences in interpretations of the same piece could be detected (Davidson 1993, 1995). Moreover, a follow-up study revealed that only two seconds of information was necessary for such a judgement to be made (Davidson 1994). However, repeated observations and recordings showed that the pianist I studied would use the same gestures at the same points in the music, but the specific gestures themselves were different. For example, for performances of a Beethoven Bagatelle, comparing two interpretations, it was discovered that although the movements occurred at more or less the same points in the musical structure, the types of movement used were different across the two interpretations, though the performer's expressive intentions were identical.

Audience observations suggested that the pianist was doing things like reflecting the force of a technical activity such as playing fortissimo by, for instance, nodding in agreement with the force of the movement required. Or, generating a musical effect such as sustaining a note by wiggling his torso in a metaphorical attempt to express vibrato – rather like he were playing an instrument like a violin and so creating vibrato effects with his own body. In order to make a reasoned explanation of these more local movements and their variations across similarly intentioned performances, we find some answers in the literature on the physical gestures that accompany speech.

Although speech is a different channel of communication to music, Juslin and Laukka (2003) have argued that there is a cross-modal nature to expressive intention and effects. It is also important to recall that up to 90 per cent of everyday human behaviour involves gestures used to 'convey some information from one person to another', and most typically these gestures accompany speech (Vaananen and Bohm 1993).

The communicative power of gesture in speech is illustrated when a hesitation or a word fails to be verbalized in a conversation – a hand or other body part gesture will often occur first (McNeill 1992). People even gesture when they know that their movements cannot be seen (e.g. gestures accompanying a telephone conversation). Thus, gestures help to formulate thoughts into utterances (McNeill 1992; Kendon 1980). That is, they are critical parts of the representational system of verbal communication. Therefore, these principles ought to apply to the representation of music and its communication.

Physical gestures and function: parallels between speech and music

At the most general level, hand gestures begin and cease as speech starts and finishes. At the most specific local level, individual gestures and words are synchronized so that the most energetic part of the gesture occurs just before or with the most prominent syllable of the accompanying speech segment. These gestures aid speech production, and also serve as cues for the communication of intention. When speech is ambiguous, for example, gestures help observers/listeners to understand. Furthermore, although speech errors occur, gestural errors virtually never occur. For example, if someone says 'left' but means 'right', the hand gesture will be with the right hand (McNeill 1992). This might also be the case in music. For example, a head gesture might trace the air in a very smooth legato line – an intention of the performer's – yet the played notes may not be so smooth or expressive.

We know that physical gestures are not pre-requisites to understanding either speech or music, such as in a phone conversation or music played on a CD recording. But, since we make fewer gestures when there is no face-to-face contact in both speech and music, it would seem that whilst some gestures are specifically oriented towards generating the music, a proportion would seem to be used for audience communication effects.

An intriguing example of the differences between musical and audience concerns is demonstrated in the case of Canadian pianist, Glenn Gould. One of the greatest modern interpreters of the keyboard, Gould is most well known for his 'clean' articulation of Bach's keyboard music on piano. Early in his career, Gould performed in all the top classical concert venues including Carnegie Hall. Later in his career, he decided to give up public performance, focusing solely on recording studio performances. Delalande (1990) has made a study of Gould's performances taken from rare film footage of both periods. What is striking is that in the recording of the studio playing, Gould's movements are highly repetitive and often quite disturbing to watch. By contrast, those of the public recitals have smooth, flowing movements. Thus, there is some evidence that in the studio case, Gould's concerns were entirely focused on the music, whereas in the public context, he was taking into account the audience's presence.

In an effort to comprehend the local physical gestures used in music, it seems useful to ask what gestures are commonly used in speech. Might these be similar to those used in music? For speech, Cassell (1998) explores commonly used speech-accompanying gestures. She refers to these including conscious *propositional gestures*, such as 'it was *this* big'! (hands being used to demonstrate the size). The gesture is a key part of the speech, the '*this*', being a significant part of the meaning.

There are other unconscious gestures such as *iconic* ones in which some feature of the action or event is described. For example, 'make sure you close it tightly', with the hands tracing the precision of the potential action. There are *metaphoric* gestures such as – 'she went on and on' being illustrated in a rolling process hand movement. The *conduit metaphor* is particularly common is speech. For example, talking about this chapter, I might say 'in the next section I shall'… and I might contain the words 'next section' in a box-shaped hand gesture. *Deictic* gestures locate in the physical space in front of the narrator aspects of the discourse, e.g. pointing left and then right when saying 'she was looking at him across the table'. Also, *beat* gestures, those small baton like gestures that do not change in form over the content of the speech, appear to have a pragmatic function, commenting on the speaker's own linguistic contribution. For example, consider speech repairs and reported speech, such as 'she talked first, I mean second'. Here, the hands flap up and down, displaying the error.

If the parallel between speech and music is drawn, the specific gestures made by the pianist I studied could indeed mirror the speech pattern. The musical sound produced may have been '*that* big!'. For example, he plays one solo right hand passage in the Beethoven Bagatelle whilst tracing it in the air with the left hand. Here, at least, a significant function of the gesture would involve acting out the expressive idea in space. But, how might we explain the differences gestures over successive performances? Gestures do not rely on a one-to-one mapping of form to meaning. For example, in one circumstance, a finger pointing down might mean 'look at the kitten on the floor', whilst at another point, the same gesture might mean 'pick up that paper'. So, it could be that the movement repertoire itself is limited, but what it has the potential to express is endlessly variable, depending on the context in which it is used.

Of course, if we are principally considering gestures for audience effect, we might ask if these gestures are really useful for the optimal performance of the musical ideas biomechanically and expressively. Using a series of different pianists, Jeremy Dawson and I (Davidson and Dawson 1995) asked pianists to learn a specially composed piece which did not require any large scale movement, yet when completely free to move, the pianists made quite extravagant movements in their performances, including both sways and identifiable gestures. Some were asked to learn the piece in a physically restraining harness to prevent them from moving around, though they were free to reach the keyboard and play all the notes required. In this condition, the performances were never as musically expressive or indeed as visually 'pleasing' as the freely learned pieces. This indicates that freedom of movement is obviously important in the generation of musical expression.

There may be 'optimal' forms of movement production, both for performer and onlooker. Jazz pianist Keith Jarrett, for example, despite his phenomenal expertise, is a source of great controversy with regard to the function of bodily posture and gesture. He makes many extreme gestures and adopts strange postures at the keyboard, often shouting and grunting as he plays. He has stated that he would not be able, nor would he want to produce his performances differently. Indeed, as an improviser, he says that the way he produces the music through his body is for him a 'shadow of an attempt' to represent in sound what he hears in his mind (see Elsdon 2003). For Jarrett, this is the only way to play. However, he has been highly criticized for the fact that his piano performances include him producing extraordinary physical movements and bizarre vocalizations, which, some believe, detract from the musical content. This is a fascinating case, because for Jarrett, the very particular gestures and sounds he makes are a part of his representation of the music, and so arguably are essential to the musical improvisation. Those on-lookers and listeners who object seem to want him to perform by complying with what other performers do on stage.

Thus, the skills involved in music production do seem to vary, and whether an audience is present or not might indeed affect the way in which the music is conceived and then produced, and sociocultural influences seem to have a crucial role in the 'presentation' and 'reception' of the musical performance. Associated with this is the entire social context from which the performer has emerged, with style and training having a significant influence.

Style and training

The link between instrument, bodily production, musical material, and expression has been discussed by pedagogues across musical cultures. In the Western style, in 1834, for example, the violinist and professor at the Paris Conservatoire, Balliot wrote a treatise on violin playing which suggested that performers could employ different types of body movements to perform music at different musical speeds. He remarked that the adagio speed requires 'more ample movements' than the allegro where notes are 'tossed off', whereas in presto there is 'great physical abandon' (see Stowell 1985). Of course many teachers do work on the basis that expressive musical effects seem to require specific physical postures and gestures. I know an expert violin teacher; for example, who gets all her students to play with their knees bent in a very particular manner. All her students are identifiable from this posture. Additionally, I recall that in my own vocal training, many technical aspects of voice production involved copying my teacher's physical actions.

Along with those postures and gestures associated with optimal technical and expressive performance, some techniques of body alignment have been developed in order to prevent repetitive strain injury, and unnecessary physical tensions in playing. The story of the actor F.M. Alexander and the complete physical tension which gripped his body, causing a paralysis, is a case in point. The Alexander Technique operates on the principle that the body needs to be in a subtle state of physical balance, and that an optimal achievement of control and expression comes though minimizing movements (rather like Bernstein's discussion of the physical 'incompressible minimum' for action). But, as we have discussed in the previous section, the movements of the player have many functions, whether in terms of helping to generate the musical ideas through the body, or to reflect what has already occurred. Therefore, I would suggest that any sensible trainer or musician would want to optimize the way in which the body produces and controls the many different aspects of the performance. In my own vocal and movement training, I decided to break away from Alexander Technique for at a certain point I experienced some conflict between what I wanted to do with my body and what I was able to do by channelling the performance through the movement technique. However, different people work in different ways, and personal style needs to be acknowledged and respected.

Of course, sociocultural practice has a key role here too; for example, Gellrich (1991) has considered some of the physical gestures used by musicians within their cultural contexts. Take, for instance, the tradition in jazz saxophone playing when the bell of the saxophone is raised high into the air, and the players close their eyes, seeming to show effort at playing very loudly and emphatically. As one saxophonist said to me: 'we do it in order to give the impression that we are playing even louder!'. Allied to this point, it is not surprising to note that highly creative and rule-breaking expressive effects are sometimes achieved through daring physical demands being placed upon the body in note production. An example comes from the jazz piano performances of Keith Jarrett. According to Elsdon (2003), Jarrett's mental energies in his lengthy improvisations are often concerned with rigorously applying physical constraints on himself. One example is where he holds his thumb and index finger in a minor third position and then attacks the piano keys with this held position: rather than anticipating tonal effects, Jarrett reacts to the newly created sound effects of the held finger position. Thus, by doggedly applying physical constraints on his fingering patterns, Jarrett forces himself to create new kinds of note clusters, and is able to explore new tonal effects.

Having considered the need for mental representations and how the link between physical control, expression, and socially mediated movement/musical gestures seems to function, I investigate bodily communication in performance adopting an integrated analysis approach to explore the specific social actions involved in performance.

The performer's tasks

Frith (1996) points out that performers have multiple social tasks to execute in a performance situation: they present their musical material; they interact with their co-performers to coordinate the performance task; and they have to communicate with and sometimes interact with the audience. For a singer, there are arguably more layers to the performance task, for not only is there the music, but there is the narrative of the lyric. The singer's role is also to 'become' the character in the song. In order to achieve a certain character, and working with Runeson and Frykholm's (1983) principle that actions specify their causes, we know that physical behaviour must be taken into account in this characterisation process. Frith (1996) also observes that performance involves gestures that are both false (put on for the occasion) and true (i.e. appropriate and authentic to the emotions being described or expressed). Indeed, it could be said that singers constantly create a tension between the story within the song and the real one: – the singer on the stage. Thus, it seems that pop stars work simultaneously with both their star personality and presentation of self which portrays the content of the song.

In a study of Annie Lennox (Davidson 2001) and several leading specialist Baroque style countertenors (Davidson 2002*b*), I also found that singers adopted these roles, and that they were clearly revealed in very different types of non-verbal communication. For instance, Annie Lennox literally shows off to her audience using provocative sexual body postures. The countertenor Michael Chance creates a sense of poise and 'performance occasion' by making a large and slow sweeping forward arm movements over the course of the whole introduction to a Bach solo cantata. Of course, it is necessary to point out that there is a difference according to whether the singing takes place in a community choir, or in a pop venue, or on an opera stage. There are different demands on the performers. In the larger group contexts, the behaviours might be more cooperative, or more focused towards a leader, such as a conductor. With the soloist, there are co-performers and audience, but the soloist emphasizes him or herself at the core of this social interaction.

Bearing in mind the role of gestures used in speech and the parallels with musical material explored here, an attempt to understand which specific social postures and gestures work to enhance co-performer and audience understanding and enjoyment of any musical performance is perhaps best attained by exploring what singers do in interaction with instrumentalists. In order to explore this further, I turn to examples of a jazz singer working with a pianist and of a pop band for further discussion.

Rosie Brown and Mark Slater

Rosie Brown is a successful professional solo jazz singer in her mid-30s, well established on the North of England circuit. Mark Slater is a fine composer and pianist with a growing reputation as an accompanist in both jazz and classical styles. I wish to discuss a performance they gave of *Summertime* which was recorded on video as part of a larger study to analyse performance style (see Davidson and Coulam, in press, for more details).

For both performers, *Summertime* is a jazz standard, something they have been performing for years, in styles ranging from slow ballad to up beat or swing, in this version a swing interpretation is offered.

The first thing to note is that Rosie and Mark had never worked together prior to this session. They were instructed, as part of the large-scale study, to rehearse and then perform the song, but immediately, Rosie looked at Mark and said, 'I'll show you what to do'. Clicking her fingers, she set the tempo and then with a series of head nods and arm gestures, she controlled when and how he should play a solo, stop playing, or change a section.

Undoubtedly, these are established non-verbal communicative codes in jazz playing that may be found in almost any rehearsal or performance, nonetheless it is important to indicate that it was these non-verbal codes that made it possible for the two performers to 'get into a groove'. Also, there was never a separate rehearsal prior to the performance. When they had finished playing, Rosie simply said, 'That's it, it's fine!' When asked about this she commented further:

> 'Well, I liked the way we "communicated", I mean Mark was really looking out for me. We didn't need to practice, we both could read the signs. Of course, I was reading him too. It was cool. I think we both felt it was good.'

Mark noted:

> 'Fantastic! It was all very clear. That's good music-making!'

Allied to these comments, striking features of the performance were as follows: there was lots of eye contact; Mark swayed and Rosie made many dance-like movements as they seemed to 'give and take' within the music, for instance, Rosie swirled around to the pulse of the music, leaning towards Mark and the video 'audience'. Rosie had a general tendency to lean towards Mark, whilst Mark looked very directly at her for more that 70 per cent of the time he was playing. Although Mark used mainly head nods for instructional purposes (for example, 'let's go to the verse now'), he did other things like trace the melody line with the upper torso movement, and sometimes lift his hands in rather extravagant gestures, appearing to follow the 'flow' of the music (as the pianist mentioned earlier had done in solo repertoire). Mark made no direct movement towards the video 'audience', but Rosie directed many movements toward the audience, with lots of dance steps, and some movements including head shakes and eyes closing on quiet slow music, clearly reflecting on the narrative content of the song.

Frith (1996) suggests that dance movement functions for the body to say something, with music performers using dance to draw attention to themselves as a means of 'display'. It certainly seemed that Rosie was displaying herself in the dance movements, this was a very extravert 'public' display. It is important to note that Rosie combined movements for musical coordination (*regulators*), and illustration of the song's narrative with gestures such as literally 'spreading' her arms as she sang the words 'spread your wings' with what have been labelled by Ekman and Freisen (1969) as *illustrators* – extravagant and publicly focused movements. But, in addition, Rosie used the kinds of gesture used in speech which reveal unconscious processes of self-stimulation, and may help to control the individual in some way (referred to as *adaptors*). For example, rubbing the ear lobe in a gentle manner, or flicking the finger tips in a particularly soft but repetitive manner. Mark did not make these types of movement, and when the types and frequency of all gestures made by Rosie were calculated, it became apparent that adaptors were as frequent as the illustrative gestures. Furthermore, when Rosie's data were compared with other singers in the main study (see Davidson and Coulam, in press) she was the singer who proportionally made the most adaptor behaviours, and was perceived by Mark and subsequent video raters to be by far the most interactive and communicative of the performers studied.

Adaptors for Rosie included a 'floppy arm', and touching her face with her hand when singing. It could be, therefore, that adaptor movements are important factors in determining performance quality: that is, Rosie is an individual who shows inner, 'intimate' states as well as projected 'public' states. Rosie 'shows confidence' in her movements, especially those related directly to the regulation of the performance with Mark (finger clicking) and the illustration of the lyrics of the song, but we also have glimpses of Rosie's own vulnerabilities as a person in her soft, floppy arm swings and face touching.

In order to explore these types of movement in more detail, Kaori Kurosawa and I (Kurosawa and Davidson 2005) have made a detailed case study of the Irish pop band, The Corrs. This band is interesting for several reasons:

- all four members are siblings
- the three female members take turns singing solo
- all female members play instruments too, when they are not singing solo

Thus, we can make potential comparisons within the group, relating kinds of movements made when singing and playing to see how the gestures are used and perceived by audience members.

The Corrs

The line up of the band is as follows:
Andrea (vocals and tin whistle)
Sharon (violin and vocals)
Caroline (drums and vocals)
Jim (guitars and keyboard)
The data I shall discuss come from a video taped live performance at Lansdowne Road (Warner: 8536-53120-3, 2000). Two songs were analysed: *What can I do*, where Andrea sings lead vocals, and *No frontiers,* in which Sharon and Caroline take the vocals. In each song, the movement behaviours were categorized by both authors (Kurosawa and myself; see Kurosawa and Davidson 2005, for further details) and verified by an expert independent viewer. Given that Jim never takes a vocal solo, we limited our analyses to the sisters. We observed their actions as solo singers from the beginning to end of the songs,

labelling movements according to the following categories: hand/arm gestures (emblematic, illustrative, display, regulator, adaptor), posture (that is a fixed pose), direction of eye gaze, touch and facial expression. Tables 10.1–10.3 show the types and frequencies of the non-verbal behaviours used by each sister.

We had hoped that the female Corrs – as sisters – may have used very similar kinds of movement gestures, but in fact they were quite idiosyncratic, more

Table 10.1 The types and frequency of kinetic nonverbal behaviour in the performance of : *What can I do* by Andrea Corr in 2000

	Type	NB	%
1	Illustrator	16	29.1
2	Display	10	18.2
3	FE	8	14.6
4	Regulator	7	12.7
5	Emblem	6	10.9
6	Posture	5	9.1
7	Adaptor	2	3.6
8	Gaze	1	1.8
9	Touch	0	0
	Total	**55**	**100**

Type = Types of nonverbal behaviour, NB = the number of behaviour, FE = facial expression

Table 10.2 The types and frequency of kinetic nonverbal behaviour in the performance of: *No Frontiers* by Sharon Corr in 2000

	Type	NB	%
1	FE	5	20.8
2	Regulator	5	20.8
3	Illustrator	4	16.7
4	Gaze	3	12.5
5	Adaptor	3	12.5
6	Posture	2	8.3
7	Touch	1	4.2
8	Emblem	1	4.2
9	Display	0	0
	Total	**24**	**100**

Type = Types of nonverbal behaviour, NB = the number of behaviour, FE = facial expression

Table 10.3 The types and frequency of kinetic nonverbal behaviour in the performance of: **No Frontiers** by Caroline Corr in 2000

	Type	NB	%
1	Gaze	8	38.1
2	FE	4	19.0
3	Posture	3	14.3
4	Emblem	2	9.5
5	Regulator	2	9.5
6	Touch	1	4.8
7	Adaptor	1	4.8
8	Illustrator	0	0
9	Display	0	0
	Total	**21**	**100**

Type = Types of nonverbal behaviour, NB = the number of behaviour, FE = facial expression

obviously being influenced by the types of musical instruments and the musical roles they play within the band.

Examining the movement styles used by the three sisters, it is apparent that Andrea uses the most illustrators and display behaviours. Indeed, she is the one who 'engages' most obviously with her audience. She dances and jumps with them responding, apparently supporting her actions. Sharon also used illustrative gestures, which focused on communicating a story to the audience. She did not try to elicit a specific audience response, other than through her focus of gaze, but she seemed to ask for their attention to listen to the song and understand its musical and poetic content. Generally speaking, Caroline was much less 'powerful' in her role as a solo singer. She seemed to be reticent rather than communicative, and most of her movements are regulatory. Some of these differences were evidently to do with the content of the material being sung: movements within the style, tempo, and lyrical framework of the song. Andrea's song is of loss and heart-break, and is very dramatic with a strong pulse. Caroline and Sharon have a song with more constrained emotion in terms of the song's lyrical and harmonic content. By contrast to Andrea's large and flamboyant movements on stage, the other two sit side-by-side, making much smaller and fewer movements, restricted by the sitting position and musical and lyrical content. But, even singing the same song, Caroline and Sharon use their bodies differently, with Caroline using more emblems, gaze and general facial expression, and Sharon using regulators and illustrators.

We have attempted to contextualize some of the data above by exploring the biographies of the siblings, and we note that Caroline is reported to be the most shy, as well as being the youngest sibling. Also, it is important to note that she plays the drums, instruments which fully engage the limbs and which operate within the tight constraint of 'keeping the musical pulse', so she may have developed a general performance style which relies entirely on coordinating and regulating rather than exploring expressive content. By contrast, the violin, played by Sharon, has far more movement possibilities, the arms, hands, and fingers arguably being used through their mechanical action through the bow and on the strings to create the musical expression. Finally, Andrea is the most clearly defined as a lead vocalist, and her data reflect more strongly than those of Rosie and other lead vocalists I have studied (see Davidson 2001, 2002, for example).

The data from The Corrs verifies that instrumentalists also use non-verbal gestures of the type that might be categorized under the socially defined labels of illustrator, regulator, display, and thus have similar underlying intentions: illustrating a key point in the music, coordinating timing, even showing off to the audience. But, the more soloistic an individual's performance role, the more he or she will make illustrative and emblematic gestures. Perhaps most importantly, the adaptor is used as a sign of intimacy, which perhaps counterbalances the large public display gestures. The singer is perhaps dealing more with 'acted out' (illustrative/emblematic ideas) movements combined with self-concerns (as seen in adaptors), than the accompanying instrumentalist whose primary concern is for coregulation.

Conclusion

From the discussion so far, it is evident that the body plays an integral role in musical performance. The performer has three representations of the work: the ideal or goal, the actual skills involved in the production, and the performance as it unfurls. We have discovered that in the performance the expression of the musical sounds and the social intentions of the performer in context are integrated in the bodily production. It has been argued that within the body there is a physical centre for the expression of musical intention, with the performer's musical expression being severely impaired if the body is constrained in the musical production. However, it is also recognized that whilst note-playing technique and musical expression become integrated in the generation and execution of the work, some individuals can create unnecessary and even damaging physical approaches to their playing. It is recognized that some specific body management techniques such as the Alexander technique, for instance, have been developed to assist performers in the elimination of negative tension.

By contrast, since movements specify their causes (Runeson and Frykholm 1983), some idiosyncratic movements, though perhaps 'tense', might be useful for the creation and generation of musical expression – a case that Keith Jarrett has argued in his own playing.

In addition to the idea of a bodily centre for expression, it has been demonstrated that performers make a series of gestures which serve to clarify and coordinate certain ideas for communication to coperformers and the audience, and which are embedded within a cultural framework. These movements might be learned from a teacher (like the violin players using certain performance movements such as knee bending). Some of these movements seem to reveal expression of the musical structure itself (for instance, an emphatic nod at a cadence point, to signal the 'ending' created in the musical sound). Additionally, movements express the communication with coperformers and/or audience (showing the coperformer to 'enter now', or thanking the audience for listening so attentively).

In instrumental music, much more research is necessary to define the nature of these gestures more clearly. But, in vocal performance, research progress has been possible owing to the clear link between singing and speech, and the strong historical precedents of researching non-verbal communication in spoken language. Considering the work done on singing performance, it seems that the singer produces his or her performance by relying on non-verbal codes of the same type as those used in speech for coordination purposes, and the expression of narrative ideas about the song.

The vocal research outlined in this chapter has shown that performers' bodies also express information about inner personal states. The research on performance perception has shown that audiences are able to identify a range of performer characteristics, and indeed that the audience is presented with different levels of information about the performer: the performer in the music, the performer showing off in the public context of the performance, the performer revealing thought processes through the personal movement style, and the use of the adaptor. From the preliminary investigations of Rosie and The Corrs, it seems that within the Western tradition at least, a range of adaptive intimate behaviours with display and illustrative behaviours seem necessary as core elements. It is also apparent that there are some performer behaviours which are more or less acceptable or understandable to audiences. While some performers remain inflexible about their performance presentation style (for example, Keith Jarrett), others appear to be profoundly influenced by whether or not a live audience is present and who that audience is (for instance, the apparent change in Glenn Gould's piano performances between live audiences and the recording studio).

This chapter has revealed that the body is a critical element in understanding and producing musical performance: it is part of the generation and perception of the performance. Of course, performers do not have to be seen in order to be understood, but the significance of visual cues cannot be underestimated.

Although there has also been some consideration of the fact that music generated in and through the performer's body is then 'read' by the audience member, little has been said about the spectator's own participation in a performance. We know from work presented elsewhere in this volume (see Clayton, this volume) that there are physical consequences for the perceiver: for example, toes tap and heads nod, along with the music. A number of authors (for example, Jackendoff 1988, and Lidov 1987) have proposed that movement, and especially the sense of motion or desire to move is a key part of creating and responding to music. Our own representations of our bodies to ourselves are critical in our response to any information that has an actual bodily origin (for example, vestibular activation, as Todd has implied), or that may be associated with such bodily origins (for example, sights and sounds that convey a sense of bodily movement). So, the body and its capacity to move are essential aspects for generation of music, and audience participation in response and towards a performance. The audience may well experience the performance partly through a physical identification or empathy with the performer's movements, and partly in terms of generating a performance (accompanying hand claps, head shakes etc.) themselves. This idea is consistent with the theoretical direction of the chapter, suggesting that audiences are drawing upon experiences and knowledge similar to those of the performers (this issue is discussed in a much greater detail by Davidson and Correia 2002). Additionally, it is important to note that performers often use visual cues from their audiences to develop their own performance expressions: for example, Annie Lennox waited until her audience responded to her coaxing hand gestures before moving onto the next section of her song. Audience members can thus potentially be physically involved in shaping the performance, though this clearly varies according to the performance tradition, with pop performance being oriented far more towards movement and participation than classical performance.

Given the results presented and discussed in this chapter, it seems that performers can and should study what is effective in the body movements involved in the generation of their music, and also to engage their audiences and coperformers. For instance, a choral conductor needs to know which kinds of non-verbal signals are best; a solo pop singer might like to know which elements of physical presentation make Mick Jagger a more appealing performer to certain audiences than say Bruce Springsteen, even though both performers are highly successful and perform within the same musical genre.

Understanding body movement is a key area for performers to explore and reflect upon, as it is central to the conception, production, and performance of music and how it is perceived.

References

Baily, J. (1985) Music structure and human movement. In *Musical Structure and Cognition,* (eds P. Howell, I. Cross, and R. West). London: Academic Press.

Bernstein, N. (1967) *Coordination and Regulation of Movement.* London: Pergamon.

Cassell, J. (1998) A framework for gesture generation and interpretation. In *Computer Vision in Human-Machine Interaction,* (ed. R. Cipolla), pp. 248–65. Cambridge: Cambridge University Press.

Clarke, E.F. and Davidson, J.W. (1998) The body in music as mediator between knowledge and action. In *Composition, Performance, Reception: Studies in the Creative Process in Music,* (ed. W. Thomas), pp. 74–92. Oxford: Oxford University Press.

Cutting, J.E. and Kozlowski, L.T. (1977) Recognising friends by their walk: Gait perception without familiarity cues. *Bulletin of the Psychonomic Society, 9,* 353–6.

Cutting, J.E. and Proffitt, D.R. (1981) Gait perception as an example of how we may perceive events. In *Intersensory Perception and Sensory Integration,* (eds R.D. Walk and H.L. Pick). New York: Plenum.

Cutting, J.E., Proffitt, D.R., and Kozlowski, L.T. (1978) A biomechanical invariant for gait gait perception. *Journal of Experimental Psychology: Human Perception and Performance, 4,* 357–72.

Davidson, J.W. (in press) Qualitative insights into the use of expressive body movement in piano performance, *Psychology of Music.*

Davidson, J.W. (1993) Visual perception of performance manner in the movements of solo musicians. *Psychology of Music, 21,* 103–13.

Davidson, J.W. (1994) What type of information is conveyed in the body movements of solo musician performers? *Journal of Human Movement Studies, 6,* 279–301.

Davidson, J.W. (1995) What does the visual information contained in music performances offer the observer? Some preliminary thoughts. In *The Music Machine: Psychophysiology and Psychopathology of the Sense of Music,* (ed. R. Steinberg), pp. 105–13. New York: Springer Verlag.

Davidson, J.W. (2001) The role of the body in the production and perception of solo vocal performance: A case study of Annie Lennox. *Musicaie Scientiae, 5*(2), 235–56.

Davidson, J.W. (2002) *The performer's identity.* In *Musical Identities,* (eds R.A.R. MacDonald, D.J. Hargreaves, and D. Miell), pp. 97–116. Oxford: Oxford University Press.

Davidson, J.W. (2002a) Understanding the expressive movements of a solo pianist. *Musikpsychologie, 16,* 9–31.

Davidson, J.W. (2002b) An exploration of the solo singer's skills. *Conference Proceedings of the International Conference on Music Perception and Cognition.* University of New South Wales, Australia, July.

Davidson, J.W. and Correia, J.S. (2002) Body movement in performance. In *The Science and Psychology of Music Performance: Creative Strategies for Teaching and Learning,* (eds R. Parncutt and G.E. McPherson), pp. 237–50. Oxford: Oxford University Press.

Davidson, J.W. and Coulam, A. (in press) Summertime, again and again. In *Musical Creativity: Current research in theory and practice*, (eds G. Wiggins and I. Deliege). Oxford: Oxford University Press.

Davidson, J.W. and Dawson, J.C. (1995) The development of expression in body movement during learning in piano performance. *Conference Proceedings of Music Perception and Cognition Conference*, University of California, Berkeley, June, p. 31.

Davidson, J.W., Malloch, S., and Whittaker, D. (in preparation) Moving musicians: investigating musical coordination of solo and duo flute and clarinet players through tracks and maths.

Davidson, L. and Scripp, L. (1990) Education and development in music from a cogntive perspective. In *Children and the Arts*, (ed. D.J. Hargreaves), pp. 59–86. Philadelphia, PA: Open University Press.

Delalande, F. (1990) Human movement and the interpretation of music. Paper presented at the Second International Colloquium on the Psychology of Music, Ravello, Italy.

Elsdon, P. (2003) Keith Jarrett and the muse. Conference proceedings, international Conference on Music and Gesture, p. 35, University of East Anglia, August.

Ekman, P. and Friesen, W.V. (1969) The repertory of nonverbal behaviour: Categories, origins, usage, and coding, *Semiotica*, 1, 49–98.

Frith, S. (1996) *Performance Rites*. Oxford: Oxford University Press.

Gellrich, M. (1991) Concentration and tension. *British Journal of Music Education*, 8, 167–79.

Jackendoff, R. (1988) *Consciousness and the Computational Mind*. Cambridge: Cambridge University Press.

Juslin, P and Laukka, P. (2003) Communication of emotions in vocal expression and music performance: Different channels, same code? *Psychological Bulletin*, 129, 770–814.

Kendon, A. (1980) Gesticulation and speech: two aspects of the process. In *The Relation Between the Verbal and Nonverbal Communication*, (eds M.R. Key), Mouton.

Kozlowski, L.T. and Cutting, J.E. (1977) Recognising the sex of a walker from a dynamic point-light display. *Perception and Psychophysics*, 21, 575–80.

Kurosawa, K. and Davidson, J.W. (2005) Nonverbal interaction in popular performance: A case study of The Corrs. *Musicae Scientiae*, IX, 111–37.

Lehmann, A.C. and Davidson, J.W. (2002) Taking an acquired skills perspective on music performance. In *Second Handbook on Music Teaching and Learning*, (eds R. Colwell and C. Richardson), pp. 542–60, Oxford: Oxford University Press.

Lehmann, A.C. and Ericsson, K.A. (1997) Expert pianists' mental representations: Evidence from successful adaptation to unexpected performance demands. In *Proceedings of the Third Triennial ESCOM Conference*, (ed. A. Gabrielsson), (pp. 165–9). Uppsala, Sweden: Uppsala University.

Lidov, D. (1987) Mind and body in music, *Semiotica*, 66, 69–97.

McNeill, D. (1992) *Hand and mind: What gestures reveal about thought*. Chicago, IL: Chicago University Press.

Pierce, A. (1994) Developing Schenkerian hearing and performing Integral, 8, 51–123.

Runeson, S. and Frykholm, G. (1983) Kinematic Specification of Dynamics as an informational basis for person-and-action perception: Expectations, gender, recognition, and deceptive intention. *Journal of Experimental Psychology: General*, 112, 585–615.

Schacher, C. (1994) The prelude in e minor op. 28, no. 4: autograph sources and interpre-tation. In *Chopin Studies 2*, (eds J. Rink and J. Sansom). Cambridge: Cambridge University Press.

Shaffer, L.H. (1982) Rhythm and timing in skill. *Psychological Review*, **89**, 109–23.

Shaffer, L.H. (1984) Timing in solo and duet piano performances. *Quarterly Journal of Experimental Psychology*, **36A**, 577–95.

Stowell, R. (1985) *Violin technique and performance practice in the late eighteenth and early nineteenth centuries*, Cambridge: Cambridge University Press.

Todd, N.P. Mc Angus. (1999) Motion and Music: A neurobiological perspective. *Music Perception*, **17**(1), 115–26.

Vaananen, K. and Bohn, K.(1993) Gesture-driven interaction as a human factor in virtual environments – an approach with neural networks. In *Virtual Reality Systems*, (eds R.A. Earnshaw, M.A. Gigante, and H. Jones). London: Academic Press.

Vines, B. and Wanderley, M. (2003) Seeing music: What does the visual component of a clarinet performance convey? Conference proceedings, International Conference on Music and Gesture, University of East Anglia, August.

Williamon, R.A. and Davidson, J.W. (2002) Exploring co-performer communication. *Musicae Scientiae*, **6**(1), 1–17.

Windsor, W.L., Davidson, J.W., and Ng, K. (2003) Investigating musicians' natural upper body movements, Conference proceedings, international Conference on Music and Gesture, University of East Anglia, August.

Woody, R.H. (1999) Getting into their heads. *American Music Teacher*, **49**(3), 24–36.

Chapter 11

Singing as communication

Graham F. Welch

Introduction: the significance of voice in the ontogeny of communication

Vocal sound is one of the defining features of humanity. Its commonality, plurality, and development distinguish the species. Within the wide range of sounds that humans make with their voices, there are two constellations that commonly have the greatest socio-cultural significance. These are categorized as speech and singing, but there is potential (and actual) significant overlap between the two, because both sets of behaviours are generated from the same anatomical and physiological structures and initiated/interpreted by dedicated neuropsychobiological networks whose development and function are shaped by cultural experience.

Our predisposition to perceive particular vocal sounds as singing or speech is dependent on the dominant acoustic features. Perception begins when the sensory system is stimulated by acoustic information that is filtered according to principles of perceptual organization which group the sounds together according to key features, such as pitch range, temporal proximity, similarity of timbre, and harmonic relationships. Perception is contextualized by the listener's age, family, community membership, enculturation, and the development of the vocalizer. The first few months of life, for example, are often characterized by vocal play ('euphonic cooing', Papoušek [H], 1996) in which the growing infant's vocalizations could be interpreted as musical *glissandi* as well as the precursors of prosody in speech. Such categorical perceptions of vocal sound as being either 'musical' or 'speech(like)', however, are a product of the layers of enculturation that inform our socially constructed interpretations.

To the developing infant, any such distinction is relatively meaningless, because speech and singing have a common ontogeny. As far as sound *production* is concerned, infant vocal behaviours are constrained by the limited structures and behavioural possibilities of the developing vocal system (*cf.* Kent and Vorperian 1995). The first vocalizations are related to the communication of an affective state, initially discomfort and distress (crying), followed by sounds of comfort and eustress. The predisposition to generate vocal sounds that have quasi-melodic features first emerges around the age of two to four months (Stark *et al.* 1993), with increasing evidence of control during the three months that follow (Vihman 1996). These pre-linguistic infant vocalizations are characterized by a voluntary modulation and management of pitch that emulates the predominant prosodic characteristics of the mother tongue (Flax *et al.* 1991), whilst also exploring rhythmic syllabic sequences with superimposed melodies and short musical patterns (Papoušek [M] 1996).

With regard to sound *reception*, hearing is normally functioning before birth in the final trimester of pregnancy (Lecanuet 1996) and the newborn enters the world capable of perceiving tiny differences in voiced sound (Eimas *et al.* 1971). Infants are 'universalists' (Trehub 2003) in the sense that they are perceptually equipped to make sense of the musics and languages of any culture. This predisposition will lead developmentally to the discrimination of vowel categories and consonantal contrasts in the native language by the end of the first year (*cf* Kuhl *et al.* 1992, Vihman 1996). During these initial twelve months of life, it is the prosodic (pitch and rhythm) features of 'infant-directed' speech (also known as 'motherese' or 'parentese') that dominate early communication from parent/caregiver to child (Papoušek [H], *op cit*). The prosodic envelopes that define spoken phrases are thought to be essential perceptual building blocks in the infant's developing comprehension of language (Jusczyk *et al.* 1992).

The mother's infant-focused utterances are also typified by having a regulation of pulse, vocal quality, and narrative form, theorized collectively as a 'communicative musicality' (Malloch 1999) that engages with an 'intrinsic motive pulse', an innate ability to sense rhythmic time and temporal variation in the human voice (Trevarthen 1999). The expressive prosodic contours, pitch glides, and prevalence of basic harmonic intervals (3rds, 4ths, 5ths, octaves) of 'infant-directed speech' (Fernald 1992; Papoušek [H], *op cit*) occur alongside the mother's 'infant-directed singing' (Trehub 2001), a special limited repertoire of lullaby and play song which is characterized by structural simplicity, repetitiveness, higher than usual pitches (somewhat nearer the infant's own vocal pitch levels), slower tempi and a more emotive voice quality.

> 'In general, the maternal repertoire of songs for infants is limited to a handful of play songs or lullabies that are performed in an expressive and highly ritualised manner. From the neonatal period, infants prefer acoustic renditions of a song in a maternal style (performances from mothers of other infants) to non-maternal renditions of the same song by the same singer. Moreover, they are entranced by performances in which they can both see and hear the singer, as reflected in extended periods of focused attention and reduced body movement in the infant'. (Trehub 2003, p. 671)

Early vocalization is intimately linked to perception (Vihman, *op cit*) in which the primacy of developing pitch control in infant utterances occurs alongside adult-generated sounds that are dominated perceptually by melodic contour. As such, although the 'precursors of spontaneous singing may be indiscriminable from precursors of early speech' (Papoušek [M], *op cit*: p. 104), the weight of available evidence on the origins of language and music in the child suggests a common dominance of 'the tune before the words' (Vihman, *op cit*: p. 212), related both to the developing child's own 'tunes' as well as the 'tunes' of others.

The text that follows focuses initially on the nature of the physical realities involved in singing as a form of communication. These psycho-acoustic features of the singing voice and their development underpin the nature of intra- and inter-personal communication in singing.

Singing as a physical activity: structure and communicative function

Probably because of the ubiquity and bipotentiality of the human voice for speech and singing (both in reception as well as production), the outputs of the vocal instrument are central components in many of the world's diverse performing arts. Examples include hugely popular Bollywood genre of *filmi* music from the Indian subcontinent, virtually all the musics of Africa, in which singing is often the core group activity, other indigenous musics, such as the traditional 'throat musics' of Southern Siberia, Mongolia, and Tibet in which two musical lines are sung simultaneously by a single voice, as well as the musical narrative forms of Japan, such as *Nohgaku* and *Shinnai*, which challenge a bipolar Western conceptualization of vocal behaviour as either singing or speech.

Underpinning this worldwide use of the voice for musical performance and communication is a common anatomy and physiology (Fig. 11.1, Welch and MacCurtain, private archive) that are shaped by biological maturation, experience, cultural imperative, and tradition. Vocal *pitch* is essentially a product of patterns of vocal fold vibration, vocal *loudness* relates to changes in air pressure from the lungs, vocal *colouring* is generated by the interface between vocal fold vibration and the configuration of the elements of the vocal tract (see Welch and Sundberg 2002 for an overview).

Young children have smaller vocal folds than adults and so have higher pitched voices. Perhaps surprisingly, although boys tend to have slightly larger vocal folds than girls, they both use a similar vocal pitch for speech (Titze 1994), although girls attain a wider vocal range earlier in singing (Welch 1979b). Up to the age of twelve when adult-like breathing patterns emerge, children can achieve similar vocal loudness levels to that of adults by using relatively more breath (Stathopoulos 2000).

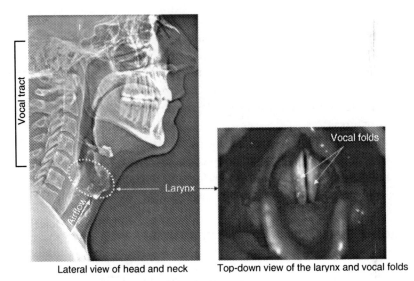

Lateral view of head and neck   Top-down view of the larynx and vocal folds

Fig. 11.1 Anatomical structure of the singing voice.

The onset of adolescence brings growth in the average size of both male and female vocal tracts, but there is a disproportionate increase in the length and circumference of the male tract and size of the larynx, resulting in the adult male having a customary vocal pitch range that is between a fifth to an octave lower than that of the adult female (see also the *gender* section below on 'inter-personal communication').

Crying is the first vocal act and it forms the substrate for all subsequent vocalization, including singing, '…prosodic elements such as variation in intensity and pitch, rhythmic patterning, and phrasing are all present in cry long before they enter into vocal play' (Vihman, *op cit*: p. 104). Greater variety of vocalization is only possible when the facial skeleton has grown downwards and forward, thus increasing the size of the oral cavity, and the proprioceptive sense receptors in the vocal tract (such as tongue tip and pharynx) are more mature (Kent and Vorperian 1995). The perceptual ambiguity of infant vocalization (as pre-speech and pre-singing) is a product of the functioning of its basic vocal anatomy as well as our adult categorical perception.

A theory of intra- and inter-personal communication in singing
Neuropsychobiological perspectives

Technological advances in brain imaging over the past decade have provided valuable insights into the neural basis for a variety of cognitive and affective functions, including those related to music. Hemispheric asymmetries are often evidenced, as are relative biases towards particular neural locations, depending on the type of musical behaviour under consideration. Recent findings suggest, however, that musical perception can also involve cross-hemispheric processing (Schuppert *et al.* 2000), such that initial right-hemispheric recognition of melodic contour and metre are followed by an identification of pitch interval and rhythmic patterning via left-hemisphere systems, at least in musically experienced adults.

Musical behaviours in adulthood appear to depend on specific brain circuitry that is relatively discrete from the processing of other classes of sounds (Zatorre and Krumhansl 2002), such as speech and song lyrics. A modular model of functional neural architecture has been proposed to explain neuro-psychobiological musical processing (Peretz and Coltheart 2003), based on case studies of musical impairments in brain-damaged patients. Separate systems within the brain are responsible for the analyses of language, temporal organization, and pitch organization. These systems relate incoming information to existing knowledge banks (a phonological lexicon and a musical lexicon) as well as previous experience of emotional expression.

Adapting the Peretz and Coltheart model to *singing* (see Fig. 11.2), there is evidence to suggest that song lyrics are processed separately and in parallel with song melody. In performance, these are enacted by simultaneous cooperation between areas within the left and right cerebral hemispheres, respectively (Besson *et al.* 1998), with likely common cortical processing of the syntactical features of music and language (Patel 2003). Other neurological studies that compare song imagery (thinking through a song in memory) with actual song perception offer support for this adapted model. An integration of lyrics and melody in song representation is achieved through the combined action of two discrete systems for auditory-tonal and auditory-verbal working memory, based on bilateral activation of the temporal and frontal cortex and of the supplementary motor area (Marin and Perry 1999). There is also evidence that song imagery alone can activate auditory cortical regions (Marin and Perry, *op cit*).

The original Peretz and Coltheart model proposes that any acoustic stimulus is subjected to an initial acoustic analysis. This is then 'forwarded' to a range of discrete 'modules' that are specifically designed to extract different features, namely *pitch* content (pitch contour and the tonal functions of successive intervals) and *temporal* content (metric organization = temporal regularity, and rhythmic structure = relative durational values). Both pitch and temporal outputs are further 'forwarded' to a personal 'musical lexicon' that contains a continuously updated representation of all the specific musical phrases experienced by the individual over a lifetime. The output from this

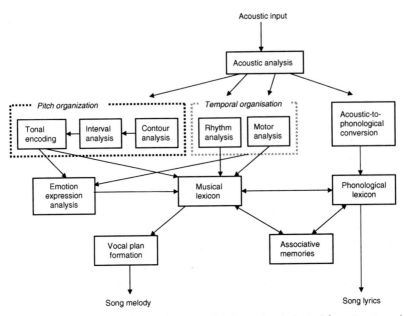

Fig. 11.2 A modular model of music processing in singing (adapted from Peretz and Coltheart 2003). Each box represents a processing component and arrows represent pathways of information flow or communication between processing components.

musical lexicon depends on the task requirements. In relation to singing, if the goal is a song, then the melody from the musical lexicon will be paired with its associated lyrics that are theorized as being stored in the 'phonological lexicon'.

This is not to say, however, that the resultant *sung* output would necessarily be an ideal musical 'match' to an original stimulus model. A significant proportion of young children often experience difficulty (and for a small minority this can be a long-term difficulty) in performing accurately both the lyrics and melody of songs from their culture (*cf.* Welch 1979a, 2000; Davidson 1994). Analysis of longitudinal empirical data on young children's singing development (*cf.* Welch *et al.* 1996, 1997, 1998) indicates that most young children are usually very accurate in remembering and communicating the lyrics of particular songs that they have been taught (or heard informally), but can often be less accurate in reproducing the same songs' constituent pitches. A similar bias is reported in adult singers' biased ability to make fewer errors in memorizing the words of new songs compared to the musical elements (Ginsborg 2002). In relation to the model, children's singing research data indicates that the average English-speaking five-year-old's 'phonological lexicon' is often more developmentally advanced than their 'musical lexicon'.

The original Peretz and Coltheart neuropsychobiological model also accords with an earlier developmental model of children's singing that drew together a large number of independent studies (Welch 1986, 1998). This developmental model and its associated literature suggest that an important phase in the child's journey towards accurate vocal pitch matching is the ability to match a song's melodic contour (Welch 1986; Hargreaves 1996). The child data support the model's notion of a pitch 'contour' module that has a basic primacy over other perceptual pitch organization. Young children who were rated as 'out-of-tune' when singing particular focus songs were much more pitch accurate vocally when asked to match pitch glides (*glissandi*) that had been deconstructed from the melodic contours of the same songs for the purposes of assessment of singing development. Furthermore, a recent pedagogical study of the conscious development and manipulation of vocal pitch contour in six-year-olds (including the use of computer-assisted learning and visual feedback) produced significant improvements in vocal pitch matching and in an extended vocal pitch range (Western 2002).

The symbiotic interweaving of singing and emotion

The Peretz and Coltheart model proposes that in parallel, but independently, outputs from the pitch and temporal perceptual modules are fed into an 'emotion expression analysis' module, facilitating an emotional response to the musical sounds. With regard to the emotional evaluation of vocal sounds, various distinct cortical and sub-cortical structures, primarily (but not solely) in the right hemisphere, have been identified as significant (Peretz 2001). As part of our basic communication, six primary emotions – fear, anger, joy, sadness, surprise, and disgust – are all commonly expressed vocally (Titze 1994) and are differentiated by strong vocal acoustic variation (Scherer 1995). Voice is an essential aspect of our human identity: of who we are, how we feel, how we communicate, and how other people experience us.

The ability to generate concurrent emotional 'tags' to vocal outputs (singing and speech) is likely to relate to the earliest fetal experiences of its acoustic environment, particularly the sound of the mother's voice heard in the womb during the final trimester of pregnancy. Although speech is partially muffled and the upper frequencies of the sound spectrum are reduced, the pitch inflection of the mother's voice – its prosodic contour – is clearly audible (see Thurman and Grambsch 2000 for a review). The final trimester is also marked by the fetus developing key functional elements of its nervous, endocrine, and immune systems for the processing of affective states (Dawson 1994). As a consequence, a mother's vocalization with its own concurrent emotional correlate

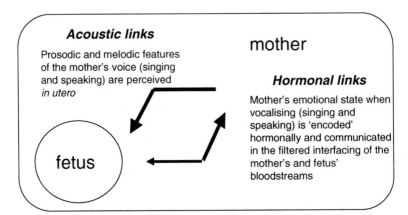

Fig. 11.3 The shaping of an integrated fetal emotional response to sound through concurrent experience of the mother's prosody, sung melody, and affective state.

(*pace* Peretz and Coltheart, *op cit*) is likely to produce a related neuro-endocrine reaction in her developing child (*cf.* Thurman and Grambsch, *op cit* Keverne *et al.* 1997). The filtered interfacing of the maternal and fetal blood-streams allows the fetus to experience the mother's endocrine-related emotional state concurrently with her vocal pitch contours (see Fig. 11.3). Feelings of maternal pleasure, joy, anxiety, or distress will be reflected in her vocal contours and her underlying emotional state. Given that singing (to herself, listening to the radio, in the car, with others) is usually regarded as a 'pleasurable' activity, this will be reflected in a 'positive body state' (Damasio 1994) that is related to her endocrine system's secretion of particular neuropeptides, such as β-endorphin, into her bloodstream (Thurman 2000). Her musical pleasure (expressed vocally and hormonally) will be communicated to her fetus.

At birth, neonates are particularly sensitive to the sound of their own mother's voice, which derives from their fetal experiences of their mother's singing and reading aloud (DeCasper and Fifer 1980). The perceptual salience of maternal pitch contour is also shown in the reported ability of infants aged three to four months to imitate an exaggerated prosodic pitch contour presented by their mothers (Masataka 1992), as well as an ability to imitate basic vowels at the same age after only fifteen minutes laboratory exposure (Kuhl and Meltzoff 1996). Similarly, six-month-old infants demonstrate increased amounts of sustained attention when viewing video-recordings of their mothers' singing as compared with viewing recordings of them speaking (Trehub 2001).

Singing as emotional capital

Thus the child enters the world with an emotional 'bias' towards certain sounds, linked to their earliest acoustic and affective experiences of maternal vocal pitch contour. Arguably, this biasing will shape the way that developing infants respond to other sounds, supplemented and expanded by concurrent auditory and affective experience of their own voices, beginning with the acoustic contours of their first cries. As suggested earlier, the available data suggests that there is a priming of the neuropsychobiological system from pre-birth through early infancy in which vocal melodies are associated with various emotional correlates. These associations provide a basis for musical communication across the lifespan, both in the production and reception of voice-based melodies and also for other intra-personal and inter-personal musical communications that draw on similar acoustic features.

This integration of early musical experience with its affective correlates can be construed as basic *emotional capital*, a resource which is employed as the developing humans interact with, relate to, deal with, and make sense of their immediate and expanding sonic environments. Auditory experiences can be interrelated with six basic emotions that are evidenced in the first nine months of life. Initial tripolar emotional states that relate to distress (evidenced by crying and irritability), pleasure (indicated by satiation), and being attentive to the immediate environment lead to the emergence of interest (and surprise), joy, sadness, and disgust by the age of three months, followed by emotional displays of anger and fear by the age of eight months (Lewis 1997). As mentioned, each of these basic emotions has a characteristic vocal acoustic signature and an acoustic profile that is associated with a strong characteristic emotional state. Sounds that have similar acoustic profiles are likely to generate related or identical emotions. Musical performance relies on expressive acoustic cues, such as changes in tempo, sound level, timing, intonation, artic-ulation, timbre, vibrato, tone attacks, tone decays, and pauses to communicate emotion, such as tenderness, happiness, sadness, fear, and anger (Juslin 2001). Analyses of recorded performances indicate that virtually every performance variable is affected in ways specific to each emotion (Gabrielsson 2003). In performance, the patterns of continuous changes in such variables consti-tute an 'expressive contour' and have been likened to the prosodic contour of speech (Juslin, *op cit*). Thus there appears to be a close correspondence between the acoustic characteristics of voiced emotion in everyday life and the expres-sive cues used to convey emotion in musical performance (Lavy 2001). For example, a mother suffering from post-natal depression will have a different vocal quality (quieter, lower pitched, longer pauses) than her non-depressed peers (Robb 1999). As children get older, they become more expert at recog-nizing and expressing intended emotion in singing as well as speaking (Gabrielsson and Örnkloo 2002). Arguably, this correspondence has its roots in mother–fetus/mother–infant vocalization and human neuropsychobio-logical development from the third trimester of pregnancy.

The acoustic features of the maternal voice and her immediate sonic environment are socially and culturally located, such that the initial generic plasticity demonstrated by the neonate for the discrimination of differences in any group of sounds (Eimas *et al.* 1971) is soon shaped towards a biased detection of the particular distinguishing features of salient local sounds. This, in turn, affects related behaviours. So by the age of one year, for example, infants from different cultures are sufficiently cued into the maternal language to babble differently: French infants babble with French speech units, Russian infants with Russian, and Japanese with Japanese (Meltzoff 2002). It is hypothesized, therefore, that any auditory contour event that is perceived as 'alien' to the dominant sound culture (as previously experienced) is likely to be noticed and 'tagged' emotionally on a positive/negative continuum, depending on its acoustic profile. These ongoing concurrent experiences act as one of the bases for the generation of musical 'preference' within the developing musical lexicon. Examples of early musical 'preference' in relation to singing are:

- two-day-old neonates who listen longer to audio recordings of women singing in a maternal ('infant-directed singing') style than to their usual singing style (Masataka 1999);
- infant preferences for higher rather than lower pitched singing (Trainor and Zacharias 1998), which is one of the characteristics of 'infant-directed singing';
- two- to six-month-old infants that listen longer to sequences of consonant musical intervals than to sequences of dissonant intervals (Trehub 2003);
- endocrine (cortisol) changes in six-month-old infants after listening to their mothers singing (Trehub 2001).

These 'preferences' for particular vocal pitch contours, vocal timbres, and interval consonance, linked to underlying endocrine and emotional states, may also be seen as early examples of how musical experience (including singing) is multiply processed within the overall functions of the nervous, endocrine and immune systems – the integrated human 'bodymind' (Thurman and Welch 2000).

Singing as intra-personal communication

Sounds can be self-generated as a basis for *intra-personal* musical communication, such as the earliest melodic vocal sounds that emerge around eight weeks (Papoušek [H] 1996), the vocal play that begins around four to six months (Papoušek [M] 1996) and subsequently in pre-schooler's spontaneous 'pot-pourri' songs (Moog 1976) and 'outline songs' (Hargreaves 1996) that draw on aspects of the dominant song culture. The sounds can also be part of *inter-personal* communication, such as the interactive and imitative vocal play of infant and parent (Papoušek [M] 1996; Tafuri and Villa 2002), or adult-initiated song improvisations and compositions (Barrett 2002). As the human develops social awareness and communicative vocal skills, there is shift from communication that is biased towards the *intra-personal* to the possibilities of *inter-personal* communication in singing, but the former will always be present.

The developing singer communicates intra-personally in a variety of ways related to the nature of the feedback system. Feedback can be auditory, visual, tactile, kinaesthetic, or vestibular (Welch 1985; Gabrielsson 2003) and it is used in the construction of individual musical identity, both in the sense of 'identity in music' – as a musician – as well as in the sense of 'music in identity' – as a feature of an individual's overall personal identity (Hargreaves *et al.* 2002). At one level, there is an internal psychological feedback system that is essentially outside conscious awareness and which relates to a moment-by-moment self-monitoring of the singing behaviour (*cf.* 'vocal plan formation' – Peretz and Coltheart 2003). In the first months of infancy, this system is being developed in the vocal behaviours that are the precursors of spontaneous singing and early speech, prior to their use in the emergence of a 'coalescence between spontaneous and cultural songs' (Hargreaves 1996, p. 156) from the age of two onwards.

A schema theory of singing development (Welch 1985) proposed that any initiation of a specific singing behaviour (termed 'voice programme' in the original model), such as copying an external song model, would generate expectations of proprioceptive and exteroceptive feedback that are compared to the actual feedback received from the sense receptors and auditory environment (as both bone and air conducted sound) respectively. This internal motor behaviour feedback system also provides the basis for self-reflective psychological judgements as to the 'appropriateness' of any given example of singing behaviour, such as its correspondence to an external song model or to an internal mental representation of a target melody's key, tonal relationships, loudness, and/or timbre. In the absence of evaluative feedback from an external source (termed 'knowledge of results'), the singer has to make their own judgement of the 'appropriateness' of their sung response compared to their internal model. This comparison is likely to depend on the relative developments within and between their 'musical lexicon' and 'phonological lexicon' (*cf.* Peretz and Coltheart, *op cit*), in the sense that accurate reproduction of songs from the dominant culture requires the combination of a range of musical and linguistic skills (Davidson 1994; Welch *et al.* 1996, 1997, 1998). In some cases, there will be a realization of a mismatch between the intended and actual singing behaviour and a subsequent correction can take place.

Awareness, however, is not a necessary guarantee of vocal accuracy or singing development. 'Out-of-tune' singing can persist, for example, because singers do not know how to change their behaviour, even though they may realize that something is 'incorrect' or 'inappropriate'. It can also persist because there is no awareness that their singing behaviour needs to change.

At a conscious, reflective level, the singer's intra-personal communication is a form of self-monitoring that is essential for the development of skilled performance behaviour of diverse pieces in a wide variety of acoustic contexts. Adjustments, both mental and in physical coordination, may need to be made as the performer moves from the individuality of the singing studio to the more public rehearsal environment, as well as in relation to the demands of the actual performance, when stress levels may be higher due to the efferent stimulation of the adrenal gland (Rossi 1993; Sapolsky 2003). In addition, there are other context effects. Performance behaviours are subject to social and cultural imperatives, as shown in classical singing styles by a shift in emphasis from vocal agility in the eighteenth century to vocal resonance in the late nineteenth century (Mason 2000). Practice, particularly deliberate practice, may be regarded as an essential feature of intra-personal communication and the development of performance expertise. Lehmann (1997) suggests that there are three necessary mental representations involved, namely concerning the desired performance goal, the current performance, and the production of the music.

At the other end of the performance skill continuum are those who are less developed as singers. Some may have experienced extreme disapproval about their singing, usually from a significant person in their life (such as parent, teacher, peer) (Welch 2001). Their internal representations of themselves as (non)singers and, by association, as (non)musicians are constructed by their negative experience of singing, usually in childhood. This self-image is normally sustained by singing avoidance behaviours, at least in public (Knight 1999), although there is evidence that even those who regard themselves as singing disabled can be improved in an appropriately nurturing environment (Richards and Durrant 2003). Such labelling can also be environmentally and culturally sensitive, as demonstrated by the woman who had been born in Barbados and moved to the USA when she was four years of age. When questioned as to why she was convinced that she was a 'non-singer', she replied: 'Now that I think about it, when I go home to Barbados I am a 'singer'. I'm just not a 'singer' in this country' (Pascale 2002, p. 165). She had two different internal representations of a 'singer': a USA 'singer' was someone who could lead songs, sing solos, and perform easily, whereas a Barbadian 'singer' was someone who could sing fast, 'upbeat' songs and who generally participated with others in singing.

However, even less skilled singers may sing alone and to themselves, either as an accompaniment to another activity (such as showering, housework, driving, deskwork, gardening) or just for its own sake. This is further indication of pleasurable intra-personal musical communication, first evidenced in infancy, and of the interrelated nature of singing, emotion, and self. When provided with an appropriately nurturing environment, developing singers are likely to increase their range of vocal behaviours, improve their self-image, and generally feel better. For example, fourteen weeks of individual, twice-weekly singing and speaking lessons that were aimed at generating a wider range of vocal dynamics and colour, alongside greater ease in vocal production, also produced a significant reduction in stress levels (related to both physical health and cognitive stress), an increased sense of personal well-being, more self-confidence, and a more positive self-image (Wiens *et al.* 2002). 'Voice training became a metaphor of self-discovery' (Wiens *et al. op cit*: 231).

Singing as interpersonal, social, and cultural communication

Cross (2001) argues that the essence of music may be found in its grounding in social interaction and personal significance, as well as being rooted in sound, movement, and heterogeneity of meaning. In singing, Salgardo (2003) goes further by suggesting that the communication of emotion is at the heart of sung performance through the combined use of acoustical (vocal) and visual (facial) expressive cues. He undertook a series of empirical experiments to demonstrate how the singer's movements and gestures (vocally and facially) facilitate the communication of their interpretation of the intended meaning of the composer's notation, including its emotional character. Furthermore, such vocal and facial expressions in performance are similar to those used to convey emotional meaning in everyday life. Salgardo (*op cit*) concludes that the emotions portrayed by a singer, although performed, are not 'faked', but are built on the recollections of real emotions. A performance that is regarded as 'authentic' or of high quality will have a close correspondence between such vocal and visual gestures and the nature of the original features of the musical structure; it is a form of corroboration.

In addition to the communication of a basic emotional state, the act of singing conveys information about *group membership*, such as age, gender, culture, and social group. Several studies have demonstrated that listeners are able to identify and label certain features of both the singer (as a 'child') and the singing (as 'child-like'). Often there is an accurate correspondence between the listener assessment and the acoustic item, but this is not always the case because of the variables involved, both in relation to the listener and to the singer. As outlined above (see 'singing as a physical activity'), the vocal performer's manipulation of the pattern of vocal fold vibration and the configuration of the vocal tract are basic to the act and art of singing. The acoustic output is dependent on the physiological patterning and this, in turn, is closely related to the singer's age, gender, experience, skill levels, social and cultural background, and the particular musical genre.

With regard to *age*, a study of three hundred and twenty untrained child singers aged three to twelve years found a highly regular and linear relationship in listener judgements between the estimated age and the true chronological age (Sergeant *et al.* unpublished ms). Where listeners made erroneous judgements, they tended to underestimate the age of those singers aged seven years and older, irrespective of gender, suggesting perhaps that there was a categorical perception of child-like vocal quality that influenced judgements towards some notional mean age. The ability to recognize that a singer is a child is closely related to the nature of the acoustic output. Although development occurs across childhood, the child's vocal apparatus is significantly different in size and structure from that of the adult (Kent and Vorperian 1995; Stathopoulos 2000) to produce a relatively distinctive sung vocal timbre.

At the other end of the age continuum, older voices also have a characteristic acoustic signature, both in singing and in speech, that relate to changes in the underlying voice mechanism. However, there can be a significant difference between the chronological and biological ages of a singing voice (Welch and Thurman 2000). It is possible for a person to 'sound' several decades younger (or older), depending on their lifelong voice use and vocal health (Hazlett and Ball 1996). 'Older-sounding' voices may have relatively weaker vocal musculature and reduced functioning of the respiratory system, leading to qualitative changes in vocal output, such as a more 'breathy' sound, reduced loudness, greater variation in pitching, and perhaps vocal tremor on sustained pitches.

In between these age extremes there are other 'ages' of singing, each related to the underlying anatomical and physiological realities of the voice mechanism. These physical realities have acoustic correlates, suggesting that there are at least seven 'ages': early childhood (1–3 years), later childhood (3–10 years), puberty (8–14 years), adolescence (12–16 years), early adulthood (15–30/40 years), older adulthood (40–60+ years), and senescence (60–80+) years. However, there is considerable overlap between these 'ages', not least because of individual and sex differences in biological (maturational) and chronological vocal ages.

With regard to *gender*, there is evidence of differences between the sexes in vocal fold patterning across the lifespan from mid-childhood onwards. Females tend to have slightly incomplete vocal fold closure, resulting in a 'breathier' production that is acoustically distinctive spectrally, with more 'noise' in their vocal products above 4000 Hz. Males, on the other hand, tend to have stronger vocal fold closure and a steeper spectral drop-off acoustically. Gender appears to be communicated by the amount of perceived 'breathiness' and the formant patterning within an overall spectral shape. The aforementioned study of untrained children's singing (Sergeant *et al.*, *op cit*) found that listeners made greater sex identification errors for boys aged below 7 years. There was a highly significant linear trend in which correct sex identification was closely correlated with boys' ascending age: pre-pubescent boys became perceptibly more 'masculine' in their singing as they got older. No such trend was evident with the girl singers, but there were relatively few identification errors for all age groups.

The effects of education and training on the communication of gender in singing provide similar evidence of both distinctiveness and similarity between the sexes. A range of studies (*cf.* Welch and Howard 2002) have demonstrated that there is a slight tendency for trained male choristers to be more correctly identified than trained female choristers, but this perception accuracy is sensitive to individual performance, the particular group of singers, their age and experience, the choice of repertoire, and the individual listener. Nevertheless, both acoustic analyses and perceptual outcomes suggest that trained girl singers are capable of singing with a perceptibly 'male-like' voice quality. The same singers are also capable of singing in a more characteristically 'feminine' manner. There is also evidence of gender confusability in 'collective' (choral) as well as solo singing.

The effects of *experience, training,* and *skill levels* are evidenced in studies of trained singers, child, adolescent, and adult. Singers who have undertaken classical music training tend to produce a more even timbre across their vocal range. The relatively lower larynx position creates a particular perceptual colour to the trained singer's voice, although this is also culturally sensitive (such as may be evidenced in the differences between German and Italian opera performance styles). There is an intriguing interaction between *gender* and *training* at the highest sung pitches. For males, the trained *falsetto* register is distinctive, as in the countertenor voice, being a form of vocal production that uses a particular configuration of the male vocal structure to produce a female sung pitch range. This style of singing is exploited in both classical and popular musics across the world and can communicate a sense of *sexual* ambiguity or androgyny (*cf.* Koizumi 2001). In contrast, the highest sung female register (employing a similar voice coordination as the male – termed the 'flute' or 'whistle' register) presents challenges in the communication of text in singing because all vowels share approximately the same formant frequencies so that vowel intelligibility becomes problematic (*cf.* Welch and Sundberg 2002).

There is an extensive literature on different musical genres and singing and there are certain key features about singing as communication with regard to *social* and *cultural* groups, which can be summarized as follows:

- Singing can be a form of group identification and social bonding. Examples are found in the use of specially composed company songs to reinforce a senior management's definition of company culture (Corbett 2003) and in many diverse choral settings, such as bringing disadvantaged individuals together to create a 'Homeless Males Choir' (Bailey and Davidson 2002), as well as in the traditional choral communities of Iceland and Newfoundland.

- Singing can also be a transformational activity culturally, in which members or groups evolve new musical styles or sub-genres or modify established performance practices. Examples of such communities of practice are found in the fusion music of South Asian youth groups (Farrell *et al.* 2001) and also in the recent influx of female singers into the traditionally all-male cathedral choir that offers the potential of a wider 'vocal timbre palette' in the performance of the established repertoire (Welch 2003). Here the messages are about musical innovation, modernity, challenge, and/or social justice, the latter being demonstrated by the emergence of rap (Toop 2000).

- Regular singing activities can communicate a sense of pattern, order, and systematic contrast to the working day and week, such as in use of songs in the special school classroom to frame periods of activity and in the seasonally related rehearsals and performances of the amateur choir/choral society.

- Singing can also be used as an agent in the communication of cultural change, such as in the recent identification of certain 'Singing Schools' by the Ministry of Education in New Zealand (Boyack 2003) as part of their promotion of a new arts curriculum.

In each of these cases, the act of singing, whether as an individual or as part of a collective, can facilitate both musical and non-musical communication, a sense of belonging or of being on the 'outside'.

Conclusions

It is impossible to imagine singing without some form of communication that is multi-faceted and concurrent, with different messages being produced and perceived at the same time. The singer communicates intrapersonally by the moment-by-moment acoustic stream providing diverse forms of feedback concerning musical features, vocal quality, vocal 'accuracy' and 'authenticity', emotional state, and personal identity. To the external listener (parent, peer, audience), there is also interpersonal communication that is musical, referential (through the text), emotional, and non-musical, such as in the delineation of membership of a particular social and/or cultural group. To sing is to communicate – singing as communication.

References

Bailey, B.A. and Davidson, J. (2002) Emotional, social and cognitive enrichment through participation in group singing: Interviews with members of a choir for homeless men. In *The Phenomenon of Singing III*, (eds A. Rose and K. Adams), pp. 24–32. St. John's, NF: Memorial University Press.

Barrett, M. (2002) Freedoms and Constraints: Constructing Musical Worlds through the Dialogue of Composition. In *Why and How to Teach Music Composition: A New Horizon for Music Education*, (ed. M. Hickey), pp. 3–27. Reston, VA: MENC.

Besson, M., Faïta, F., Peretz, I., Bonnel A.-M., and Requin J. (1998) Singing in the brain: independence of lyrics and tunes. *Psychological Science*, 9, 494–8.

Boyack, J. (2003) *Hearing the Voices of Singing Schools*. Paper presented at The Phenomenon of Singing IV, St. John's, Newfoundland, June 26–9, 2003.

Corbett, M. (2003) I Sing the Body (In) Corporate: Identity, Displacement and the Radical Priority of Reception. *Paper presented to the Critical Management Conference, Lancaster University, July 2003*.

Cross, I. (2001) Music, Cognition, Culture and Evolution. In *The Biological Foundations of Music*, (eds R.J. Zatorre and I. Peretz), Vol. 930, pp. 28–42. New York: Annals of the New York Academy of Sciences.

Damasio, A.R. (1994) *Descartes' Error: Emotion, Reason, and the Human Brain*. New York: Avon Books.

Davidson, L. (1994) Songsinging by Young and Old: A Developmental Approach to Music. In *Musical Perceptions*, (eds R. Aiello with J. Sloboda), pp. 99–130. New York: Oxford University Press.

Dawson, G. (1994) Development of emotional expression and emotional regulation in infancy: contributions of the frontal lobe. In *Human Behavior and the Developing Brain*, (eds G. Dawson and K.W. Fischer), pp. 346–79. New York: Guilford.

DeCasper, A.J. and Fifer, W. (1980) Of human bonding: newborns prefer their mother's voices. *Science*, 208, 1174–6.

Eimas, P.D., Siqueland, E.R., Jusczyk, P.W., and Vigorito, J. (1971) Speech perception in infants. *Science*, 171, 303–6.

Farrell, G., Welch, G.F., and Bhowmick, J. (2001) South Asian Music and Music Education in Britain. *Bulletin of the Council for Research in Music Education*, 147, 51–60.

Fernald, A. (1992) Meaningful melodies in mothers' speech to infants. In *Nonverbal vocal communication: comparative and developmental approaches*, (eds H. Papoušek, U. Jurgens and M. Papoušek), pp. 262–82. Cambridge: Cambridge University Press.

Flax, J., Lahey, M., Harris, K., and Boothoyd, A. (1991) Relations between prosodic variables and communicative functions. *Journal of Child Language*, 18, 3–19.

Gabrielsson, A. (2003) Music performance research at the millennium. *Psychology of Music*, 31(3), 221–72.

Gabrielsson, A. and Örnkloo, H. (2002) Children's Perception and Performance of Emotion in Singing and Speech. Paper presented at the ISME Early Chilhood Conference, Copenhagen, Denmark, 5–9 August, 2002.

Ginsborg, J. (2002) Classical Singers Learning and Memorising a New Song: An Observational Study. *Psychology of Music,* **30**(1), 58–101.

Hargreaves, D.J. (1996) The development of artistic and musical competence. In *Musical Beginnings,* (eds I. Deliege and J. Sloboda), pp. 145–70. Oxford: Oxford University Press.

Hargreaves, D.J., Miell, D., and MacDonald, R.A.R. (2002) What are musical identities and why are they important? In *Musical Identities,* (eds R.A.R. MacDonald, D.J. Hargreaves, and D. Miell), pp. 1–20. Oxford: Oxford University Press.

Hazlett, D. and Ball, M.J. (1996) An acoustic analysis of the effects of aging on the trained singer's voice. *Logopedics Phoniatrics Vocology,* **21**(2), 101–7.

Jusczyk, P.W., Kemler Nelson, D.G., Hirsh-Pasek, K., Kennedy, L., Woodward, A., and Piwoz, J. (1992) Perception of acoustic correlates of major phrasal units by young infants. *Cognitive Psychology,* **24**, 252–93.

Juslin, P.N. (2001) Communicating emotion in music performance: a review and a theoretical framework. In *Music and Emotion,* (eds P.N. Juslin and J.A. Sloboda), pp. 309–37. Oxford: Oxford University Press.

Kent, R.D. and Vorperian, H.K. (1995) Development of the Craniofacial-Oral-Laryngeal Anatomy: A Review. *Journal of Medical Speech-Language Pathology,* **3**(3), 145–90.

Keverne, E.B., Nevison, C.M., and Martel, F.L. (1997) Early learning and the social bond. In *The Integrative Neurobiology of Affiliation* (eds C.S. Carter, I.I. Lederhendler, and B. Kirkpatrick), Vol. **807**, pp. 329–39. New York: Annals of the New York Academy of Sciences.

Knight, S. (1999) Exploring a cultural myth: what adult non-singers may reveal about the nature of singing. In *The Phenomenon of Singing II,* (eds B.A. Roberts and A. Rose), pp. 144–54. St. John's, NF: Memorial University Press.

Koizumi, K. (2001) Male Singers in Japanese Visual Rock Bands: Falsetto as an Alternative to Shout in Rock. In *Proceedings,* (eds Y. Minami and M. Shinzahoh), pp. 148–51. Third Asia-Pacific Symposium on Music Education Research and International Symposium on 'Uragoe' and Gender. Nagoya, Japan, 23–26 August, 2001.

Kuhl, P.K., Williams, K.A., Lacerda, F., Stevens, K.N., and Lindblom, B. (1992) Linguistic experience alters phonetic perception in infants by 6 months of age, *Science,* **255**, 606–8.

Kuhl, P.K. and Meltzoff, A.N. (1996) Infant vocalizations in response to speech: vocal imitation and developmental change. *Journal of the Acoustical Society of America,* **100**, 2425–38.

Lavy, M. (2001) Emotion and the Experience of Listening to Music: a framework for empirical research. Unpublished PhD Thesis, University of Cambridge.

Lecanuet, J.P. (1996) Prenatal auditory experience. In *Musical Beginnings,* (eds I. Deliege and J. Sloboda), pp. 3–34. Oxford: Oxford University Press.

Lehmann, A.C. (1997) The acquisition of expertise in music: Efficiency of deliberate practice as a moderating variable in accounting for sub-expert performance. In *Perception and Cognition of Music,* (eds I. Deliege and J. Sloboda), pp. 161–187. Hove: Psychology Press.

Lewis, M. (1997) The Self in Self-Conscious Emotions. *The Self Across Psychology.* Vol. 818, pp. 118–42. New York: Annals of the New York Academy of Sciences.

Malloch, S.N. (1999) Mothers and infants and communicative musicality. *Musicae Scientiae, Special Issue,* pp. 29–57.

Marin, O.S.M. and Perry, D.W. (1999) Neurological Aspects of Music Perception and Performance. In *The Psychology of Music* (2nd edition), (ed. D. Deutsch), pp. 653–724. London: Academic Press

Masataka, N. (1992) Pitch characteristics of Japanese maternal speech to infants. *Journal of Child Language,* **19,** 213–23.

Masataka, N. (1999) Preference for infant-directed singing in 2-day old hearing infants of deaf parents. *Developmental Psychology,* **35,** 1001–5.

Mason, D. (2000) The teaching (and learning) of singing. In *The Cambridge Companion to Singing,* (ed. J. Potter), pp. 204–20. Cambridge: Cambridge University Press.

Meltzoff, A.N. (2002) Elements of a developmental theory of imitation. In *The Imitative Mind,* (eds A.N. Meltzoff and W. Prinz), pp. 19–41. Cambridge: Cambridge University Press.

Moog, H. (1976) The musical experience of the pre-school child. (trans. C. Clarke). London: Schott.

Papoušek, H. (1996) Musicality in infancy research: biological and cultural origins of early musicality. In *Musical Beginnings,* (eds I. Deliege and J. Sloboda), pp. 37–55. Oxford: Oxford University Press.

Papoušek, M. (1996) Intuitive parenting: a hidden source of musical stimulation in infancy. In *Musical Beginnings,* (eds I. Deliege and J. Sloboda), pp. 88–112. Oxford: Oxford University Press.

Pascale, L. (2002) "I'm Really NOT a Singer": Examining the Meaning of the Word Singer and Non-Singer and the Relationship Their Meaning Holds in Providing a Musical Education in Schools. In *The Phenomenon of Singing III,* (eds A. Rose and K. Adams), pp. 164–70. St. John's, NF: Memorial University Press.

Patel, A.D. (2003) Language, music, syntax and the brain. *Nature Neuroscience,* **6**(7), 674–681.

Peretz, I. (2001) Listen to the brain: A biological perspective on musical emotions. In *Music and Emotion,* (eds P.N. Juslin and J.A. Sloboda), pp. 105–34. Oxford: Oxford University Press.

Peretz, I. and Coltheart, M. (2003) Modularity and music processing. *Nature Neuroscience,* **6**(7), 688–91.

Richards, H. and Durrant, C. (2003) To Sing or Not to Sing: A study on the development of 'non-singers' in choral activity. *Research Studies in Music Education,* **20,** 78–89.

Robb, L. (1999) Emotional musicality in mother-infant vocal affect, and an acoustic study of postnatal depression. *Musicae Scientiae Special Issue,* 123–54.

Rossi, E.L. (1993) *The Psychobiology of Mind-Body Healing.* (Revised edition). New York: W.W. Norton.

Salgardo, A. (2003) *A psycho-philosophical investigation of the perception of emotional meaning in the performance of solo singing (19th century lied repertoire).* Unpublished PhD Thesis, University of Sheffield.

Sapolsky, R. (2003) Taming Stress. *Scientific American,* **289**(3), 67–75.

Scherer, K.R. (1995) Expression of emotion in voice and music. *Journal of Voice*, **9**(3), 235–48.

Schuppert, M., Münte, T.F., Weiringa, B.M., and Altenmüller, E. (2000) Receptive amusia: evidence for cross-hemispheric neural networks underlying musical processing strategies. *Brain*, **123**, 546–59.

Sergeant, D.C., White, P., and Welch, G.F. *Listeners' identification of gender differences in children's singing.* Unpublished ms.

Stark, R.E., Bernstein, L.E., and Demorest, M.E. (1993) Vocal communication in the first 18 months of life. *Journal of Speech and Hearing Research*, **36**, 548–58.

Stathopoulos, E.T. (2000) A review of the development of the child voice: an anatomical and functional perspective. In *Child Voice*, (ed. P.J. White), pp. 1–12. Stockholm: Royal Institute of Technology Voice Research Centre.

Tafuri, J. and Villa, D. (2002) Musical elements in the vocalisations of infants aged 2 to 8 months. *British Journal of Music Education*, **19**(1), 73–88.

Thurman, L. (2000) The human endocrine system. In *Body, Mind and Voice: Foundations of Voice Education*, (eds L. Thurman and G. Welch), pp. 61–7, Iowa: National Center for Voice and Speech.

Thurman, L. and Grambsch, E. (2000) Foundations of human self-expression during prenate, infant and early childhood development. In *Bodymind and Voice: Foundations of Voice Education*, (eds L. Thurman and G. Welch), pp. 660–95. Iowa: National Center for Voice and Speech.

Thurman, L. and Welch, G.F. (eds) (2000) *Bodymind and Voice: Foundations of Voice Education*. Iowa: National Center for Voice and Speech.

Titze, I. (1994) *Principles of voice production*. Englewood Cliffs, NJ: Prentice-Hall.

Toop, D. (2000) The evolving language of rap. In *The Cambridge Companion to Singing*, (ed. J. Potter), pp. 42–52. Cambridge: Cambridge University Press.

Trainor, L.J. and Zacharias, C.A. (1998) Infants prefer higher pitched singing. *Infant Behaviour and Development*, **21**, 799–806.

Trehub, S.E. (2001) Musical Predispositions in Infancy. In *The Biological Foundations of Music*, (eds R.J. Zatorre and I. Peretz), Vol. 930, pp. 1–16. New York: Annals of the New York Academy of Sciences.

Trehub, S.E. (2003) The developmental origins of musicality. *Nature Neuroscience*, **6**(7), 669–73.

Trevarthen, C. (1999) Musicality and the intrinsic motive pulse: evidence from human psychobiology and infant communication. *Musicae Scientiae, Special Issue*, 155–215.

Vihman, M.M. (1996) *Phonological Development*. Oxford: Blackwell.

Welch, G.F. (1979a) Poor pitch singing: A review of the literature. *Psychology of Music*, **7**(1), 50–58.

Welch, G.F. (1979b) Vocal range and poor pitch singing. *Psychology of Music*, **7**(2), 13–31.

Welch, G.F. (1985) *A schema theory of how children learn to sing in tune*. Psychology of Music, **13**(1), 3–18.

Welch, G.F. (1986) A developmental view of children's singing. *British Journal of Music Education*, **3**(3), 295–303.

Welch, G.F. (1998) Early childhood musical development. *Research Studies in Music Education,* **11**, 27–41.

Welch, G.F. (2000) Singing development in early childhood: the effects of culture and education on the realisation of potential. In *Child Voice,* (ed. P.J. White), pp. 27–44. Stockholm: Royal Institute of Technology Voice Research Centre.

Welch, G.F. (2001) *The misunderstanding of music.* London: Institute of Education.

Welch, G.F. (2003) *The nature and development of the female cathedral chorister.* Arts and Humanities Research Board Report B/SG/AN8886/APN14717.

Welch, G.F. and Howard, D. (2002) Gendered Voice in the Cathedral Choir. *Psychology of Music,* **30**(1), 102–20.

Welch, G.F. and Sundberg, J. (2002) Solo Voice. In *The Science and Psychology of Music Performance,* (eds R. Parncutt and G.McPherson), pp. 253–68. Oxford: Oxford University Press.

Welch, G.F. and Thurman, L. (2000) Vitality, health and vocal self-expression in older adults. In *Bodymind and Voice: Foundations of Voice Education,* (eds L. Thurman and G. Welch), pp. 745–53. Iowa: National Center for Voice and Speech.

Welch, G.F., Sergeant, D.C., and White, P. (1996) The singing competences of five-year-old developing singers. *Bulletin of the Council for Research in Music Education,* **127**, 155–62.

Welch, G.F., Sergeant, D.C., and White, P. (1997) Age, sex and vocal task as factors in singing "in-tune" during the first years of schooling. *Bulletin of the Council for Research in Music Education,* **133**, 153–60.

Welch, G.F., Sergeant, D.C., and White, P. (1998) The role of linguistic dominance in the acquisition of song. *Research Studies in Music Education,* **10**, 67–74.

Western, B. (2002) *Fundamental Frequency and Pitch-Matching Accuracy Characteristics of First Grade General Music Students.* Unpublished PhD Thesis, University of Iowa.

Wiens, H., Janzen, H.L., and Murray, J.B. (2002) Heal the Voice-Heal the Person: A Pilot Study on the Effects of Voice Training. In *The Phenomenon of Singing III,* (eds A. Rose and K. Adams), pp. 228–34. St. John's, NF: Memorial University Press.

Zatorre, R.J. and Krumhansl, C.L. (2002) Mental Models and Musical Minds. *Science,* **298**, 2138–9.

Chapter 12

Musical communication and children's communities of musical practice

Margaret S. Barrett

Introduction

In their endeavours to investigate children's experience and understanding of music, researchers have moved beyond the boundaries of the experimental laboratory and the music classroom to study children's engagement with music in a range of settings (for example, Addo 1997; Campbell 1998; Harwood 1998a,b; Marsh 1999; Russell 2002). This 'change of location' in the research environment reflects the influence of socio-cultural theory in the study of children's development, and the view that development may be conceptualized as a process of socialization into existing systems of meaning and cultural practice. In socio-cultural theory children are viewed as active social agents who internalize cultural meanings through interaction with knowledgeable others in their *zone of proximal development* (Vygotsky 1986). This process of internalization occurs through two types of engagement in the ZPD: engagement in problem-solving with more competent members of the society; and/or engagement in play (Gaskins and Göncü 1988).

Recognition of the role of children's play in the learning process has necessitated an understanding of the role of musical play in children's musical development (see Young, this volume). This has led researchers to examine children's participation in 'communities of musical practice' (Barrett 2003; Barrett and Gromko 2002; Harwood 1998a,b; Marsh 1995a,b, 1997; Riddell 1990; Russell 2002), communities in which children are active agents in the determination of the location, the participants, and the nature and range of the activities involved. In this chapter I shall explore the notion of a community of practice (Wenger 1998; Wenger *et al.* 2002) in relation to children's music-making. This shall be illustrated by recent research in the realm of children's communities of musical practice that investigates the communicative processes that hold between the persons and practices in these communities and the nature of musical engagement in these settings.

Recognition of children's musical culture as a location of meaning making and communication holds potential for the further development of our understanding of the meaning and value of music in the lives of children and the ways in which this may be promoted in both school and community settings. In examining children's communities of musical practice, this chapter shall explore further dimensions of the questions '*where* does music communicate?' and '*why* does music communicate?'

Musical communication: a perspective from socio-cultural theory

The emergence of socio-cultural theory has been attributed to both George Herbert Mead (1934/1956) and Lev Vygotsky (1978) who simultaneously developed theories that sought to provide an account of human thought and development that acknowledged the role of social interaction and setting. Whilst researchers and theorists in subsequent decades have drawn on the fields of psychology, sociology, and anthropology in further attempts to understand the nature of human functioning and development in culture (Rogoff 2003; Shore 1996), Cole (1996) traces the development of this 'cultural psychology' from the work of the eighteenth century Neopolitan scholar, Giambattisto Vico (1725/1948). Vico argued against the application of natural science models of inquiry to the investigation of human thought and action. As Cole summarizes Vico's argument, '…human nature must necessarily be understood through an historical analysis of language, myth, and ritual' (1996, p. 23). This view has been taken up by 'cultural psychologists' including Cole, for whom any study of human development must acknowledge the role of social and cultural practices and settings.

In the field of contemporary psychology it is Vygotsky's version of socio-cultural theory, built upon by Soviet (Luria 1961; Leontev 1981) and American (for example, Bruner 1996; Cole 1996; Wertsch 1988) colleagues that has become most influential. In his 'genetic' approach, Vygotsky queried the notion of an 'eternal' child whose development may be explained through reference to universal laws that hold across time and culture. Rather, he proposed the notion of an 'historical' child, whose development may be understood through examining the nature of the child's participation in the socio-cultural practices of her life-world, including those of family, school, community, and the wider culture in which these operate (Vygotsky 1987). As Wells describes it '…to the biological inheritance carried in the genes is added the cultural inheritance carried in the meanings of artefacts and practices in the individual's environment' (2000, p. 55). However, in a socio-cultural view, culture is no mere 'add-on', or causal factor; rather, it is formed by and formative of human thought and action, and inseparable from human development.

Rogoff outlines the orienting premise of a socio-cultural perspective on any sphere of human activity as one that acknowledges that '...*people develop as participants in cultural communities. Their development can be understood only in light of the cultural practices and circumstances of their communities – which also change*' (Rogoff 2003, pp. 3–4). In this view, all human thought and activity is social and cultural in nature, and is advanced by and through communicative processes. This emphasis on communication does not confine us to a logocentric view of the world, where all processes are mediated through language as word, thought, and/or speech. Rather, a socio-cultural perspective acknowledges the arts, particularly music, as cultural practices that provide a powerful means of communicating human thought and feeling, without recourse to language as supplementary to our understanding.

The study of communication has emerged from a range of disciplines including anthropology, cultural studies, information theory, linguistics, media studies, and political science (Mattelart and Mattelart 1998; Schirato and Yell 2000). Such diverse approaches have resulted in a range of definitions of communication. Key to a socio-cultural approach to the study of communication however, is recognition of communication as a 'contextualized practice', concerned with '...producing meanings, a practice which always takes place under specific social, cultural and political conditions' (Schirato and Yell 2000, p. x). This emphasis on the context of the communicative act as well as the content may be traced from the early work of the 'Palo Alto School' (founded by anthropologist Gregory Bateson in the early 1940s) who proposed the idea of communication as '...an ongoing social process involving a number of behavioural modes: speech, gestures, facial expressions and the physical space between individuals' (Mattelart and Mattelart 1998, p. 52). This early emphasis on communication as an interactive situated social process has been extended in the work of later theorists. Bourdieu for example, moves beyond the immediate context of the communicative act or practice to link communicative processes to larger cultural structures and institutions. Bourdieu introduces the notions of 'cultural capital' (Bourdieu 1986), an entity that gives the holder status, prestige, power, and 'habitus' (Bourdieu 1991) the adoption of dispositions, rules, and values from the 'cultural field', to explain the ways in which meanings are produced and negotiated. Drawing on the work of Bourdieu, Schirato and Yell (2000) suggest that communication practices are 'contextualized practices', shaped by cultural contexts. For these authors, effective communication draws on 'cultural literacy', defined as '…a familiarity with the rules and conventions of a culture; and a feel for negotiating those rules and conventions' (2000, p. 17). This focus on communication as the production and negotiation of meaning through 'contextualized practices' that are informed by an understanding of the rules of a specific culture and the ability to negotiate these (for example, an understanding that 'crowd surfing' as performed at a rock concert communicates a very different meaning when attempted in a symphony concert), further emphasizes that communicative practices are not solely speech and/or writing events.

Paradoxically, it is through language that musical meaning is contested in attempts that argue alternatively that its communicative function is to extrapolate to meanings beyond music, or that such a function is impossible. These debates are focused on issues of 'what' music communicates and are located in the philosophy of music. Associated questions such as 'how music communicates' and 'where' and 'why' music communicates lead to a focus on the sociocultural settings of music and return us to an acknowledgement of communicative practices that are not dependent upon language-based thought. Non-verbal communicative practices such as modelling, and non-verbal cues including gaze, gesture, posture, and timing (Rogoff 2003, p. 314) are essential to on-going participation in, and development of human thought and action. As Rogoff notes, 'The opportunities to observe and pitch in allow children to learn through keen attention to ongoing activities, rather than relying on lessons out of the context of using the knowledge and skills taught…'(2003, p. 9). Drawing on a musical example of such opportunities, she points to the Suzuki approach to music education as a powerful example of communication through modelling (2003, p. 318). In the pedagogic practices of this approach, the development of keen observation skills on the part of the learner, both visual and aural, and the capacity to extract the key components of modelled action and sound in the context of the learning environment, are essential (Rogoff *et al.* 2003).

Working within socio-cultural theory Engestrom puts forward a view of context as an 'activity system' (1993) that '…integrates the subject, the object, and the instruments (material tools as well as signs and symbols) into a unified whole. An activity system incorporates both the object-oriented productive aspect and the person-oriented communicative aspect of the human conduct. Production and communication are inseparable' (Engestrom 1993, p. 67). Activity theory focuses on examining the relationships that hold between the individual and her environment, relationships that involve 'situated cognition' (Greeno 1998; Lave and Wenger 1991). Situated cognition refers to a form of meaning-making that is contextually bound as specific capacities are afforded and constrained by the situations in which they occur. Such situational affordances and constraints may be located in the cultural tools, the objects, processes and practices of specific activities, and are dependent on the communicative processes that hold within specific settings. In a related concept, that of 'distributed cognition' (Salomon 1993) the notion of 'in-the-head' or individual cognition is further challenged by arguing that intellectual activity is 'distributed' amongst persons, activities, artefacts, and settings. Resnick suggests that

> ... the social invisibly pervades even situations that appear to consist of individuals engaged in private cognitive activity. Social construals of the situation (e.g., what are the rules of the game? Who is in charge? What are the stakes?) influence the nature and course of thinking. And the tools of thought (ranging from external memory devices and measuring instruments to tables of arithmetic conversions and dictionaries, thesauruses, and maps) embody a culture's intellectual history. Tools have theories built into them and users accept these theories – albeit often unknowingly – when they use these tools (1994, pp. 476–7).

In such a view all music practices, from solitary listening to participation in a group improvisation are fundamentally 'social' and inherently 'communicative'.

Play and musical play

In recent work Dissanayake (2001) argues that aesthetic imagination arises from early mother–infant interactions, playful social interactions that draw on an inherent capacity for 'pretense'. She draws on a broad range of research to demonstrate that infants are not passive recipients of the communicative intentions of their mothers or caretakers. Rather, through their responses they influence the pace, intensity, and nature of such interactions. In her account Dissanayake argues that human minds are 'inescapably and unconditionally social' (2001, p. 97) and suggests that the arts function '...as ways of creating and sharing emotional communion with other humans, thereby transmitting group knowledge and instilling a sense of "coping" that could relieve individual anxiety, and foster one-heartedness and social solidarity' (2001, p. 98). In locating the foundations of aesthetic imagination in these earliest of human interactions, Dissanayake highlights the role of play in learning, and, by inference musical communication. This latter is taken up in recent research that points to the vital role of interactive vocalization or 'communicative musicality' (Malloch 1999) between infant and care-giver in the health and well-being of the developing infant. This research suggests that music is deeply rooted in human nature and plays a powerful role in building memories and establishing the foundations of the infant's social identity

(Trevarthen 2002, p. 22). It is evident that the onset of socio-cultural and musical agency as meaning-makers occurs early in the infant's life and is fostered through communicative play.

One explanation of how this occurs in the child's on-going development is provided by Vygotsky's concept of the *Zone of Proximal Development (ZPD)*. Described as '...the distance between the actual developmental level as determined by independent problem-solving and the level of potential development as determined through problem solving under adult guidance or in collaboration with more capable peers' (1978, p. 86), the ZPD emphasizes the social nature of learning and development, and recognizes the role of play in children's learning and development (Gaskins and Göncü 1988; Göncü and Becker 1992). A related concept, that of scaffolding (Wood *et al.* 1976, p. 98), refers to six key strategies employed by adult guides when working with children to solve problems. These strategies, recruitment, reducing degrees of freedom, direction maintenance, marking of features, frustration control, and demonstration, are features of adult-mediated learning environments. As will be noted later in this chapter, research that examines child-mediated learning environments in children's communities of musical practice, demonstrates that there are some notable differences in children's 'scaffolding' strategies.

A number of researchers have developed the notion of the ZPD further to encompass social situations beyond that of the adult–child dyad (Lave and Wenger 1991; Rogoff *et al.* 1993) and its emphasis on direct person-to-person interaction (Guberman 1996). Lave and Wenger (1991) suggest that the ZPD be explained not only in terms of person-to-person interaction, but also in cultural and societal terms. The former is described as '...the distance between cultural knowledge provided by the sociohistorical context, usually made accessible through instruction, and the everyday experience of the individual' (Lave and Wenger 1991, p. 48). Drawing on Engestrom's work they describe the ZPD in societal terms as '...the distance between everyday actions of individuals and the historically new form of societal activity' (Engestrom 1987, in Lave and Wenger 1991, p. 49). In this expanded view, the individual may work in the ZPD through interaction with the cultural tools of the domain, as well as guided interaction with a more expert other. This latter is of particular interest to music education researchers when considering the co-learning and auto-didactic practices that occur in communities of musical practice beyond those of the school. For example, a child who adopts and adapts the musical conventions of popular music learnt through electronic media in constructing her own songs (see Barrett 2003) is working within a cultural view of the ZPD. Here her new musical knowledge is 'scaffolded' through engagement with cultural tools as a participant in a 'virtual' community of musical practice.

Communities of practice

The notion of a community of *musical* practice draws on the work of Lave and Wenger (1991) and Wenger (1998, Wenger *et al.* 2002). The theoretical foundations of a community of practice are built on four premises: 1. 'We are social beings...; 2. Knowledge is a matter of competence in valued enterprises...; 3. Knowing is a matter of participation ... of active engagement in the world; 4. Meaning – our ability to experience the world and our engagement with it as meaningful – is ultimately what learning is to produce' (Wenger 1998, p. 4). Through these premises, Wenger links *learning* to participation in social practices, a transformative process that impacts the construction of identities. He maintains that '...learning – whatever the form it takes – changes who we are by changing our ability to participate, to belong, to negotiate meaning. And this ability is configured socially with respect to practices, communities, and economies of meaning where it shapes our identities' (1998, p. 226).

For Wenger a social practice is '...a process by which we can experience the world and our engagement with it as meaningful' (1998, p. 51). In such a view participants in practices are continuously negotiating meaning, a process that is not always mediated by direct interaction with others. The emphasis on a social perspective does not necessarily entail learning in groups or collective participation in practices. Learning in a community of practice can at times be undertaken individually. In music for example, an individual may work with the cultural tools of a practice such as songs, recordings, or notations rather than with another in developing musical meaning and understanding. This is evident in accounts of the ways in which some popular musicians learn repertoire from 'purposive' listening to recordings and copying recordings 'by ear' (see Green 2002; Campbell 1995). Of course, such cultural tools are in themselves 'social products' and emphasize that '...our engagement with the world is social, even when it does not clearly involve interactions with others' (Wenger 1998, p. 57).

Communities of practice are characterized by three dimensions, those of mutual engagement, joint enterprise and shared repertoire (Wenger 1998, p. 70). Through these dimensions, communities of practice become 'shared histories' of learning, with a shared 'localized' discourse, a *'locally negotiated regime of competence'* (Wenger 1998, p. 137) and the privileging of certain meanings and practices (Wenger 1998, p. 199). Newcomers are admitted to a community of practice through 'legitimate peripheral participation' (Lave and Wenger 1991), a process by which neophytes to the community are exposed to the practice and the dimensions of mutual engagement, joint enterprise, and the repertoire in use (Wenger 1998, p. 100). Children are legitimate peripheral participants in many of the mature cultural practices of their community (Rogoff 2003, p. 318) including the musical practices of that community. Conversely, children also construct their own communities of musical practice, a notion I shall explore further here.

In later work Wenger and colleagues define a community of practice as '...group(s) of people who share a concern, a set of problems, or a passion about a topic, and who deepen their knowledge and expertise in this area by interacting on an ongoing basis' (Wenger *et al.* 2002, p. 4). Crucially, communities of practice are seen as effective structures for knowledge management and communication, a concept that includes the creation of new knowledge and practices, the systematic evaluation of current and past knowledge and practices, and the communication of such knowledge and practices. As such, communities of practice 'fit' a socio-cultural view of development, recognizing the social nature of learning whether that be realized in human interaction, in person-to-person encounters or in human interaction mediated through the cultural tools of a domain.

It is important to note that whilst 'communities of practice' involve shared social practices and goals for the individuals within that community, this does not necessarily imply that these communities are characterized by a sense of 'harmony' or concord between all participants. Rather than romanticizing communities of practice we should be aware of negative features such as the potential to '...hoard knowledge, limit innovation, and hold others hostage to their expertise' (Wenger *et al.* 2002, p. 139). At their worst, communities of practice may lead to a '...toxic coziness that closes people to exploration and external input' (Wenger *et al.* 2002, p. 144). Tensions between individuals may lead to the formation of subgroups that precipitate a re-negotiation of the activity, tasks, and goals by which the community is defined, a process by which members of communities of practice '...have agency and thus take up, resist, transform, and reconstruct the social and cultural practices afforded them...' (Gee and Green 1998, p. 148).

Whilst communities of practice may take a variety of forms, they are characterized by three fundamental elements '...a *domain* of knowledge, which defines a set of issues; a *community* of people who care about this domain; and the shared *practice* that they are developing to be effective in this domain' (Wenger *et al.* 2002, p. 27). Communities of practice are distinguished from other types of community by their purpose (knowledge management and the development of individual capacities), personnel (self-selected through expertise or interest), boundaries (fluid), cohesive factor (identification with group and/or expertise), and longevity (determined by the interest in the topic) (Wenger *et al.* 2002, p. 42).

These distinguishing features have considerable overlap with the learning environments of popular musicians described by Lucy Green in her recent book *How popular musicians learn* (2002). In this book Green's focus is the teaching and learning practices that occur in informal music settings. Whilst she refers to Lave and Wenger's notions of apprenticeship or 'situated learning', and 'legitimate peripheral practice' Green suggests that:

> ... informal Western popular music learning practices tend to be marked by certain differences from both traditional and apprenticeship music learning contexts, particularly in the following two senses. First, most young popular musicians in the West are not surrounded by an adult community of practising popular musicians, and therefore 'legitimate peripheral participation' of the sort studied by Lave and Wenger is largely unavailable to them. Hence they tend to engage in a significant amount of goal-directed solitary learning. Second, in so far as a community of practice is available to young popular musicians, it tends to be a community of *peers* rather than of 'master-musicians' or adults with greater skills (2002, p. 16).

Whilst these disparities between Lave and Wenger's original conceptualizations of 'legitimate peripheral participation' and 'apprenticeship learning', and Green's descriptions of the learning experiences of young popular musicians in the West are compelling, I suggest an expanded view. When participation in a social practice is viewed through the lens of mediated practice with cultural tools, such 'goal-directed solitary learning' as 'purposive listening' (Green 2002, pp. 60–8) can be viewed as a form of 'legitimate peripheral participation' and 'apprenticeship learning' as the young musician strives to learn to play an '...exact copy or cover of a song' (Green 2002, p. 24). In such instances, interaction with the practices of a 'master-musician' is mediated through the cultural tool of the recording, and at times, the commentary of other 'apprentices'. This former aspect is illustrated through one of Green's participant's descriptions of learning from slowed-down recordings:

> And there were several benefits to that. One, great ear training, great training in listening; two, some of these things were really quite technically advanced, those people were world class players, so it improved my technique no end; and thirdly, it gave me an understanding, you know, it gave me an insight into the way other musicians were thinking, the way they were conceiving, the way they'd approach a problem (Bernie, quoted in Green 2002, p. 73).

When such mediated interaction with a cultural tool is acknowledged as 'legitimate peripheral participation' it is evident that we participate in a number of intersecting communities of musical practice. These include localized communities that feature direct human interaction, and 'globalized' virtual communities where interaction is mediated through electronic media such as MTV and sound recordings.

Children's communities of musical practice

Thompson and Bresler remind us that 'Not only do the great majority of young children spend their days in education or care settings outside the home or in the company of paid caregivers; they spend their days increasingly in the company of other children, in a culture of their peers, absorbing rhythms and routines far different from those their parents may recall' (2002, p. 5). In addition to the musical practices they may encounter in such 'peer' communities, children are also active participants in the musical practices of the 'local' communities they encounter through family, church, and community, and, the musical practices of 'global' virtual communities they encounter through various media presentations. Through these various types of participation children become 'meme engineers' (Barrett 2003), engaged in the production and communication of musical culture. This is evident in the ways in which children appropriate and adapt components of adult music-making and the popular media in their invented songs (Barrett 2000, 2003), their musical compositions (Stauffer 2002), and their musical play (Marsh 1999, 2001). A number of studies that have investigated the transmission of children's musical chants and games in informal contexts such as playgrounds also highlight children's agency as 'pedagogues' who employ a range of teaching and learning strategies (Addo 1997). In the following section I shall provide an overview of research that has explored the nature of adult and child-mediated communities of musical practice.

Joan Russell's (2002) ethnographic study of communal singing practices in the Fiji Islands provides an example of children's participation in a cross-generational community of musical practice, where the management and communication of 'traditional' musical knowledge is a priority. Drawing on Wenger's theory of social learning she illustrates the ways in which the intersecting communities of musical practice that children encounter in church, school, family, and peer groups provide powerful musical learning opportunities. Russell suggests that 'Church communities of practices are sites where young people learn sacred repertoire, musical idioms, and singing behaviours and attitudes from the practices of significant and respected adult community members' (2002, p. 35). She also emphasizes the importance of group over individual musical practice, a value she suggests that '...is a necessary condition for the maintenance of constellations of communities of practice' (2002, p. 36). In addition, Russell identifies 'adult authority', 'shared repertoire', 'sites of learning' and 'belief in ability' as key aspects of children's musical development as singers in Fiji and emphasizes the role of 'informal' learning in community contexts. However, Russell does note that the emphasis on the replication of traditional practices that is characteristic of Fijian musical practices appears to 'limit innovation' through constraining children's capacities to respond to improvisational challenges, a constraint that is less evident in those communities of musical practices where children hold authority.

Children's playground cultures where the transmission and learning of chants and musical games is practised are examples of communities of musical practice where children hold authority. Kathryn Marsh's (1995a, 1995b, 1997, 1999) ongoing studies of the transmission of children's singing games highlights the ways in which children communicate in and through 'musical action'. In her original study, Marsh investigated children's variation and transmission processes when engaged in musical play (singing and clapping games), in an inner-city school playground. Children adapted components of an established repertoire of familiar games and songs using a 'battery of innovative techniques', including: reorganization of formulae; elaboration through addition of new material or expansion of known material; condensation through omission or contraction of formulae; and, recasting of material (1995b, p. 4). Importantly, the transmission and learning practices employed involved group processes of collaborative interaction that relied on close observation, kinaesthetic modelling, the shadowing of musical sound and action, and 'reiterated complete renditions of the games' (Marsh 1999, p. 7). This latter element, where the practice to be learnt was always presented as a complete 'model-in-action' with few concessions to the learner (for example, breaking down into component parts, or slowing down the tempo of musical action) beyond that of beginning again when break-down occured, highlights the differences between teaching and learning practices in classroom settings and those employed in children's communities of musical practice (see also Harwood 1998a, 1998b).

A notable exception to this presentation of a complete model-in-action is described in Addo's (1997) study of the transmission and learning practices of Ghanaian schoolgirls. In this study, student participants taught adult observers and participants through a segmentation method, yet retained a version of the holistic method described above for their own purposes. The use of the segmentation method in this instance is similar to the scaffolding strategy of 'Reducing degrees of freedom' (Wood et al. 1976, p. 98). This involves simplifying the task by reducing its size and breaking it down into smaller parts. Wood and colleagues describe the adult tutor's role as one where it was '…she who controlled the focus of attention … who, by slow and often dramatized presentation, demonstrated the task to be possible … the one with a monopoly on foresight. She kept the segments of the task on which the child worked to a size and complexity appropriate to the child's powers' (Wood et al. 1976, p. 75).

It is interesting to note that in Addo's study it is only in child-to-adult inter-actions that these scaffolding strategies were employed. In child-to-child interactions no such concessions were made.

In a study of the transmission of singing games amongst year five (approximately ten years of age) children, Riddell identifies close observation, gaze, posture and timing, and gestural and musical cues as key elements in the co-construction and communication of variations in traditional hand-clapping games. She writes:

> Two children who are hand-clapping are involved in a more intense situation than is created by learning a song from the music teacher at school. They are touching one another, they are watching each other intently for cues and for responses which are difficult to describe in terms of musical concepts. They are creating something which is fresh, something that contains surprises; the players can't predict the outcome because it depends upon another person. It is never boring. It can't be done casually; full concentration is always required. Often its seriousness is punctuated by silliness and laughter (Riddell 1990, p. 391).

Harwood's (1998*a*, 1998*b*) study of the improvisation practices of adolescent African-American girls when participating in singing games provides an example of legitimate peripheral participation in a community of musical practice. Harwood suggests that the process of improvising 'in the game' is the domain of a few 'acknowledged masters' and 'game leaders' who have 'special dispensation' to vary the musical tradition, that is the 'locally negotiated regime of competence' (Wenger *et al.* 2002). Of particular interest is what occurs on the periphery of the main activity or in the transitions between different games. Here, participants with different levels of skills learn by keen observation of the 'complete model' in action, and 'peripheral practice' of aspects of that model. As legitimate peripheral participants, they employ diverse strategies to acquire the 'shared repertoire' of the community, including singing along sotto voce, shadowing actions of the 'acknowledged masters' in performance, and rehearsing in spaces between performances. Through these processes, participants are admitted to a community of musical practice, and contribute to the continuing evolution of that community through observation of established rules and the accommodation of individual variations within these. Key to this process is a shared repertoire that makes allowances for a range of levels of competence and the musical and social support provided by fellow players (Harwood 1998*a*, p. 123).

Acknowledgement of varying levels of competence within a community of practice does not necessarily imply that expertise and agency are confined to more experienced or long-term members of the community, and communicated in a unidirectional (expert to novice) manner. Rather, neophyte and long-term members of the community can contribute to the on-going development of the community through the process of 'brokering' (Wenger 1998) whereby practices from one community of practice are introduced and integrated into another. Communication and learning can become multidirectional (participant to participant) rather than unidirectional (expert to novice). These aspects were highlighted in a study that sought to probe the nature of children's musical thinking as learners in a community of musical practice focused on the performance of three new works composed specifically for that community (Barrett and Gromko 2002). Child participants in this study (aged nine to twelve years) drew on the expertise of others (peers, composers, and ensemble director), their previous experiences, and their observations of the learning processes of their peers in ways that at times subverted the teaching practices of the classroom. As with other studies of children's learning practices in communities of musical practice, close observation and kinaesthetic modelling were key aspects. In addition, children 'brokered' their learning in adopting and adapting practices from other learning contexts such as private music lessons. This was particularly evident in children's descriptions of memorization strategies which included '...singing "in their heads", writing out their parts, "playing" the parts away from an instrument, and playing the parts on other instruments to those used in the ensemble' (Barrett and Gromko 2002). Importantly, these strategies helped children in taking up, resisting, transforming and reconstructing 'the social and cultural practices afforded them' (Gee and Green 1998, p. 148) in their learning processes.

Perhaps one of the most extensive descriptions of children's participation in varying communities of musical practice is that provided by Patricia Shehan-Campbell (1998). She remarks that it is difficult to conceive of a singular children's culture (1998, p. 184) and refers to the "super", "sub", "inter" (Slobin 1993), and "idio" cultures in which children operate. This also pertains to children's communities of musical practice, which are equally diverse and idiosyncratic, with intersections between the "super-cultures" of the global music media, and the "sub", "inter" and "idio" musical cultures children encounter. Key to a conception of children's communities of musical practice is the recognition of children as active social and musical agents, and a desire to understand children's cultural practices.

Campbell demonstrates in her study the diverse ways that children engage in all modes of musical engagement in their communities of musical practice, including those of the 'appreciation', generation, and transmission of music. For example, her conversation with four-year-old Michael is revealing of the ways in which joint listening experiences can become rich inter-personal communicative experiences. Michael's descriptions of listening sessions with his father, where each plays his favourite music (*The Lion King* and

Willie Nelson respectively), with his mother (*Mozart's Fantasy*), and the whole family ("Peter, Paul, and Mommy") illustrates powerfully the role of music listening in both his musical development, and his relationships with his family (Campbell 1998, pp. 75–7). Campbell argues that children 'use' music for a variety of purposes in their various musical cultures (2002, p. 61). Distinct functions that she identifies are: Emotional expression; Aesthetic enjoyment; Entertainment; Communication; Physical response; Enforcement of conformity to social norms; Validation of religious ritual; Continuity and stability of culture; and Integration of society (2002, pp. 61–4). Whilst communication is separated out in this listing, I suggest that all of these purposes are fundamentally social and communicative in nature. These functions are also evident in other studies of children's communities of musical practice.

The modes of communication that researchers have observed in children's communities of musical practice tend to be non-verbal as children depend on participation in 'music-in-action' to communicate their intentions. The modes most commonly described are: close attention to musical models presented in both person-to-person, and cultural tool-to-person interactions; keen observation of musical action in both real and virtual settings; kinaesthetic modelling; the shadowing of musical sound and action in both real and virtual settings; gestural and musical cues; gaze, posture, and timing; and the demonstration of 'complete' musical models in action. Significantly, these communicative modes are at times at odds with those employed in the formal music learning environment of the classroom. Additionally, in children's communities of musical practice children take on diverse roles. This is reflected in Wenger's assertion that 'Unlike in a classroom, where everyone is learning the same thing, participants in a community of practice contribute in a variety of interdependent ways that become material for building an identity' (1998, p. 271). What are the implications of such differences for the advancement of musical communication and learning?

Implications for music education

Schools need to develop '…instruction that builds on children's interests in a collaborative way…(where)…learning activities are planned by children as well as adults, and where parents and teachers not only foster children's learning but also learn from their own involvement with children' (Rogoff *et al.* 2001, p. 3). Whilst an understanding of the nature and functioning of children's communities of musical practice may assist in working towards this aim, there is an inherent paradox in cultivating informal structures for implementation in formal institutional settings such as schools.

Communities of practice are characterized by the dimensions of mutual engagement, joint enterprise, and shared repertoire. Their distinguishing elements relate to purpose, personnel, boundaries, cohesive factors, and longevity. One of the challenges for music education lies in generating the positive dimensions of a community of practice in an environment where the distinguishing elements of a community of practice would appear to be oppositional to the prevailing norms and practices of the institutional setting. For example, the purposes of teachers and students may be diverse, rather than mutual, leading to potential conflicts in terms of mutual engagement and joint enterprise. Personnel in teaching and learning interactions in institutional settings are selected often through factors other than expertise and interest, resulting in class groupings where not only is there a broad range of expertise, there is also a broad range of interest. Music teaching and learning environments in school settings are characterized by boundaries that are set (school time-tables) rather than fluid, where the cohesive factor is often unrelated to the practice (all year sevens), and longevity is determined by external constraints (an eight week compulsory music module), not by interest in the topic (Wenger *et al.* 2002, p. 42).

A second challenge for music education lies in drawing on the positive features of children's communities of musical practice as they exist beyond formal schooling in ways that strengthen and provide a legitimate role for such practices, and simultaneously contribute to the development of music learning in formal settings. Whilst these two challenges may appear daunting, they are not insurmountable.

In establishing principles for the cultivation of communities of practice the following are identified:

1. Design for evolution
2. Open a dialogue between inside and outside perspectives
3. Invite different levels of participation
4. Develop both public and private community spaces
5. Focus on value
6. Combine familiarity and excitement
7. Create a rhythm for the community (Wenger *et al.* 2002, p. 51).

In applying these principles to music education, the following points may be helpful to music educators:

1. be prepared for change in individual theories and practices of music education over the course of a teaching career. Acknowledgement of the evolutionary nature of social and cultural practices involves music educators

in on-going professional learning not only in issues related to pedagogy, and curriculum and assessment, but also in contemporary developments in music practice;

2. be open to the range of perspectives on musical thought and action brought to the classroom by all participants. Music is practiced in a broad range of social and cultural settings, each generating distinctive forms of 'cultural literacy'. In developing a community of practice in the music classroom knowledge of these 'literacies' is needed to promote dialogue and discussion, and the interrogation of a range of perspectives;

3. design learning experiences in collaboration with student participants that foster different levels of participation and invite a range of ways of participating. Acknowledgement of the diverse music practices with which students engage beyond the school setting, and the roles they take in these practices (for example, composer, critic, DJ, performer) provides a range of possibilities for broadening the nature of participation in the classroom music learning environment;

4. consider the ways in which the physical constraints of the music classroom shape the musical practices undertaken. Whilst the physical structure of a music classroom is shaped by the institution in which it is located, minor structural changes such as the identification of designated spaces for specific music practices may assist in creating public and private spaces for individual, small group and large group engagement;

5. provide an environment where musical values are identified and interrogated. A view of music as a contextualized cultural practice, where meaning is produced and negotiated, entails recognition of differing musical values, and the promotion of forms of discourse that encourage the interrogation of these differing values;

6. acknowledge and value the public and private ways in which we engage with music experience. In a view of education as preparation for life, acknowledgement and accommodation of the diverse ways in which individuals experience music is helpful in promoting a 'life-long' view of music engagement and music education.

Concluding remarks

Whilst the study of children's communities of musical practice is still comparatively new, a number of key issues have emerged from these investigations. It is evident that children's communities of musical practice are diverse in their nature. Children exercise considerable autonomy and agency in these communities, and draw on a range of communicative practices in producing and negotiating meaning. Children build and hold considerable cultural capital in these communities and demonstrate a 'cultural literacy', 'a feel' for negotiating the rules and conventions in a range of musics. Research is needed to explore potential applications of the structures and practices of children's communities of musical practice to music education as it is practised in more formal settings. Crucially, research is needed to understand the ways in which children's communities of musical practice intersect with those of adults, and the ways in which these assist children to take part in the large and small 'conversations' of our musical worlds.

References

Addo, A.O. (1997) Children's idiomatic expressions of cultural knowledge. *International Journal of Music Education*, **30**, 15–25.

Barrett, M.S. (2000) Windows, mirrors and reflections: A case study of adult constructions of children's musical thinking. *Bulletin of the Council for Research in Music Education*, **145**, 43–61.

Barrett, M.S. (2003) Meme engineers: Children as producers of musical culture. *International Journal of Early Years Education*, **11**(3), 195–212.

Barrett, M. S. and Gromko, J.E. (2002) Working together in 'communities of musical practice': A case-study of the learning processes of children engaged in a performance ensemble. *Paper presented to the ISME 2002 conference Bergen, Norway (published on CDROM)*.

Bourdieu, P. (1986) The forms of capital. In *Handbook of Theory and Research for the Sociology of Education*, (ed. J. Richardson). Westport, CT: Greenwood Press.

Bourdieu, P. (1991) *Outline of a theory of practice*. Cambridge: Cambridge University Press.

Bruner, J. (1996) *The culture of education*. Cambridge, MA: Harvard University Press.

Campbell, P.S. (1995) Of garage bands and song-getting: The musical development of young rock musicians. *Research Studies in Music Education*, **4**, 12–22.

Campbell, P.S. (1998) *Songs in their heads*. New York: Oxford University Press.

Campbell, P.S. (2002) The musical cultures of children. In *The arts in children's lives: Context, culture and curriculum*, (eds L. Bresler and C.M. Thompson), pp. 57–69. Dordrecht: Kluwer Academic Publishers.

Cole, M. (1996) *Cultural Psychology: A once and future discipline*. Cambridge, MA: Harvard University Press.

Dissanayake, E. (2001) Becoming *homo aestheticus*: sources of aesthetic imagination in mother-infant interactions. *SubStance*, **94/95**, 85–103.

Engestron, Y. (1993) Developmental studies of work as a testbench of activity theory: The case of primary care medical practice. In *Understanding practice: Perspectives on activity and context*, (eds S. Chaiklin and J. Lave), pp. 64–103. Cambridge: Cambridge University Press.

Gaskins, S. and Göncü, A. (1988) Children's play as representation and imagination: The case of Piaget and Vygotsky. *The Quarterley Newsletter of the Laboratory of Comparative Human Cognition*. **10**, 104–7.

Gee, J.P. and Green, J.L. (1998) Discourse analysis, learning, and social practice: A methodo-logical study. In *Review of research in education, No 23*, (eds P. D. Pearson and A. Iran-Nejad), pp. 119–70. Washington, DC.: American Educational Research Association.

Göncü, A. and Becker, J. (1992) Some contributions of a Vygotskian approach to early education. *International journal of cognitive education and mediated learning*, 2(2), 147–53.

Greeno, J. (1998) The situativity of knowing, learning, and research. *American Psychologist*, 53(1), 5–26.

Guberman, S.R. (1996) The development of everyday mathematics in Brazilian children with limited formal education. *Child Development*, 67, 1609–23.

Harwood, E. (1998a) Go on girl! Improvisation in African-American girls' singing games. In *In the course of performance: Studies in the world of musical improvisation*, (eds B. Nettl and M. Russell), pp. 113–26. Chicago, IL: University of Chicago Press.

Harwood, E. (1998b) Music learning in context: A playground tale. *Research Studies in Music Education*, 11, 52–60.

Lave, J. and Wenger, E. (1991) *Situated learning: Legitimate peripheral participation*. Cambridge: Cambridge University Press.

Leontev, A.N. (1981) The problem of activity in psychology. In *The concept of activity in Soviet psychology*, (ed. J.D. Wertsch), pp. 37–71. Armonk, NY: Sharpe publishers.

Luria, A.R. (1961) *The role of speech in the regulation of normal and abnormal behavior*. New York: Liveright.

Malloch, S. (1999) Mothers and infants and communicative musicality. *Musicae Scientiae, Special Issue*, 29–57.

Marsh, K. (1995a) Creative processes in children's musical play: the playground and the classroom. In *Honing the craft: Improving the quality of music education, Proceedings of the Australian Society for Music Education 10th National Conference*, (eds H. Lee and M. Barrett), pp. 184–91. Hobart: Artemis Press.

Marsh, K. (1995b) Children's singing games: Composition in the playground? *Research Studies in Music Education*, 4, 2–11.

Marsh, K. (1997) Lessons from the playground: Teaching and learning singing games in a multicultural society. Paper presented at the Australian Society for Music Education X1 National Conference, Brisbane.

Marsh, K. (1999) Mediated orality: The role of popular music in the changing tradition of children's musical play. *Research Studies in Music Education*, 13, 2–12.

Marsh, K. (2001) It's not all black or white: The influence of the media, the classroom and immigrant groups on children's playground singing games. In *Play today in the primary school playground: Life, learning and creativity*, (eds J.C. Bishop and M. Curtis), pp. 80–97. Buckingham: Open University Press.

Mattelart, A. and Mattelart, M. (1998) *Theories of Communication: A short introduction*. London: Sage Publications.

Mead, G.H. (1934/1956) *The social psychology of George Herbert Mead*. Chicago, IL: University of Chicago Press.

Resnick, L.B. (1994) Situated rationalism: Biological and social preparation for learning. In *Mapping the mind: Domain specificity in cognition and culture*, (eds L.A. Hirschfeld and S.A. Gelman), pp. 474–494. Cambridge: Cambridge University Press.

Riddell, C. (1990) *Traditional singing games of elementary school children in Los Angeles.* PhD dissertation, University of California.

Rogoff, B. (2003) *The cultural nature of human development.* New York: Oxford University Press.

Rogoff, B., Mistry, J., Göncü, A., and Mosier, C. (1993) Guided participation in cultural activity by toddlers and caregivers. *Monographs of the Society for Research in Human Development* **58** (7, serial no 236).

Rogoff, B., Paradies, R., Mejia Aeauz, R., Correa-Chavez, M., and Angellilo, C. (2003) Firsthand learning through intent participation. *Annual review of psychology,* **54**.

Rogoff, B., Turkanis, C.G., and Bartlett, L. (eds) (2001) *Learning together: Children and adults in a school community.* New York: Oxford University Press.

Russell, J. (2002) Sites of learning: Communities of musical practice in the Fiji Islands. In *Samspel–Together for our musical future! Focus area report,* (ed. M. Espeland), pp. 31–9. Stord: ISME.

Salomon, G. (1993) *Distributed cognitions: Psychological and educational considerations.* (ed.) New York: Cambridge University Press.

Schirato, T. and Yell, S. (2000) *Communication and cultural literacy.* St Leonards, NSW: Allen & Unwin.

Shore, B. (1996) *Culture in mind: Cognition, culture and the problem of meaning.* Oxford: Oxford University Press.

Slobin, M. (1993) *Subcultural sounds: Micromusics of the West.* Hanover, NH: University Press of New England for Wesleyan University Press.

Stauffer, S. (2002) Connections between the musical and life experiences of young composers and their compositions. *Journal of Research in Music Education,* **50**(4), 301–22.

Thompson, C.M. and Bresler, L. (2002) Prelude. In *The arts in children's lives: Context, culture and curriculum,* (eds L. Bresler and C.M. Thompson), pp. 5–8. Dordrecht: Kluwer Academic Publishers.

Trevarthen, C. (2002) Origins of musical identity: Evidence from infancy for musical social awareness. In *Musical identities,* (eds R.A.R. MacDonald, D.J. Hargreaves, and D. Miell), pp. 21–38. Oxford: Oxford University Press.

Vico, G. (1725/1948) *The new science,* (Trans. T.G. Gergin and M.H. Fish). Ithaca: Cornell University Press.

Vygotsky, L.S. (1978) *Mind in society: The development of higher psychological processes,* (eds M. Cole, V. John-Steiner, S. Scribner, and E. Souberman). Cambridge, MA: Harvard University Press.

Vygotsky, L.S. (1986) *Thought and language.* Translation newly revised by Alex Kozulin. Cambridge, MA: MIT Press.

Vygotsky, L. (1987) Thinking and speech. In *The collected works of L. S. Vygotsky (Volume 1): Problems of general psychology,* (eds R.W. Reiber and A.S. Carton), pp. 39–285. New York: Plenum.

Wells, G. (2000) Dialogic inquiry in education: Building on the legacy of Vygotsky. In *Vygotskian perspectives on literacy research: constructing meaning through collaborative inquiry,* (eds C.D. Lee and P. Smagorinsky), pp. 51–85. Cambridge: Cambridge University Press.

Wenger, E. (1998) *Communities of practice: Learning, meaning and identity.* New York: Cambridge University Press.

Wenger, E., McDermott, R., and Snyder, W.M. (2002) *Cultivating communities of practice.* Boston, MA: Harvard Business School Press.

Wertsch, J.V. (1998) *Vygotsky and the social formation of mind.* Cambridge, MA: Harvard University Press.

Wood, P., Bruner, J., and Ross, G. (1976) The role of tutoring in problem-solving. *Journal of Child Psychology and Psychiatry,* **17**, 89–100.

Chapter 13

Musical communication between adults and young children

Susan Young

Through musical interaction, two people create forms that are greater than the sum of their parts, and make for themselves experiences of empathy that would be unlikely to occur in ordinary social intercourse. (Blacking 1987, p. 26)

Introduction

Young children produce many types of playful behaviour which can be described as 'musical'. These include spontaneous vocalizations, rhythmic movements, play with sound-making objects and moving and vocalizing in response to live or recorded music (Young 2002, 2003a). These musical behaviours integrate and blend with many other kinds of play, so that it is difficult to isolate them or, at least, to identify them as musical activity as conventionally conceived. A concern to identify developmental pathways of isolated musical competencies has dominated early childhood music education research until relatively recently. However, important theoretical shifts are emphasizing the ways in which music, thought, and social activity are related. Consequently, interest has turned to understanding how children's self-initiated musical behaviours are shaped by their situations and settings and embedded in play with the people and things around them.

These theoretical shifts for music educators have received their impetus from various sources. Educational theorists, strongly influenced by Vygotsky (1978) and the many who are developing his sociocultural approach (see: Valsiner and van der Veer 2000), are focussing interest on the adult as mediator between child and forms of knowledge encapsulated in culturally defined practices.

Taking a lead from the work of Blacking (1976, 1987), ethnomusicologists emphasize the shift from music as the outcome of individual thinking to music-as-action constituted within and gaining its meaningfulness through interactions with what Blacking termed 'extra-musical' processes. Within such conceptions of music, interest turns to the active processes of making music, and the interactions between players and their environment which are generative of music. These revisions of theoretical thinking challenge traditional conceptions of what constitutes music. As conceptual boundaries loosen, become flexible and expand, interesting dilemmas arise. Where, for example, are the lines now drawn between what is defined as musical or extra-musical? When thinking about the playful activity of young children, what counts as intrinsically musical, as hybridized with other forms of play, or as something quite separate? Developing our understanding of young children's musical activity must go hand-in-hand with reflecting carefully on assumptions about music and musical process (Young 1999).

This chapter looks closely at musical interaction between adults and three- to five-year-old children who are attending preschool education. It takes as its focus a play episode between Chris Foster, a community musician, and Jake, who is just four years old. The chapter is organized into five main parts. In the first, I will discuss musical communication in early childhood and set out my definition. I then go on to describe two studies which are particularly relevant as they reveal forms of musical dialogue between adults and children in preschool settings. In part three, Chris and Jake's exchange will be described and analysed so that the communicative processes can be drawn out and explored. I take, therefore, a level of analysis which is grounded and specific. But at the same time the analysis and interpretations offer a version of musical communication which might usefully transfer to, or provide comparisons with, other musical situations. In the final part, I will consider the role of the adult and how he can be seen to be mediating between his own stock of musical knowledge and experience and the child's emerging musical competencies in a way which fosters creative transformation and does not stifle it. This leads into a discussion of pedagogical strategies. The chapter concludes by setting this discussion of what turns out to be quite complex, interlocking music play into a bigger picture of varying levels of engagement observed among young children – from completely disengaged to highly merged, synchronous play. I posit the view that creative productivity in music rests on the ability to hold in tension the individual and the social and thus that enabling children to negotiate musically between their own musical ideas and those of many musical traditions is a central aim of music education.

Musical communication in early childhood

The term 'communication' is broad and diffuse, incorporating many shades of meaning. It is important, therefore, to make a clear statement of the definition I will adopt here to illuminate the processes of young children's musical activity. In doing so I am drawing on theories of infant–adult communication as developed by a number of researchers including Fogel (e.g. 1993*a*), Kaye (e.g. 1982), Stern (e.g. 1985) and Trevarthen (e.g. 1979), the dialogical approaches of Bakhtin, a literary scholar whose writing has enriched contemporary thinking theoretically (e.g. Lodge 1990; Wertsch 1991) and writings on cultural psychology (e.g. Cole 1996). First, it is my view that musical communication cannot be separated out as if it were a thing unto itself, but is a manifestation of communication broadly and generally conceived as a human need for affiliation, to belong, and to connect with others. The next few paragraphs consider theoretical models of communicative processes, thereby contextualizing musical communication and elucidating processes common to communication in whatever mode it may manifest.

Psychology has taken a lead in the recent considerable expansion of interest in the competencies of infants in their first year. Much of this work has drawn attention to the fundamental importance of non-verbal communicative characteristics such as timing, rhythm, pitch inflexion, and dynamic contouring within infant–adult exchanges. That these are, in fundamental ways, also essentially 'musical' characteristics has led to interesting lines of thinking about the biological origins of what Trevarthen has termed 'communicative musicality' (Trevarthen 2000). In contrast, research driven by educational concerns has considered children when they enter formal schooling, around four years old in the UK and older still in the US and Europe. As yet, within music, there is little which connects these two domains and age phases of research activity. This lack of research contrasts, interestingly, with the field of language development, in which accumulated studies track language acquisition from infancy through to early childhood, often by studying children in home settings (e.g. Halliday 1975; Wells 1985). The key idea, therefore, which orientates this chapter, is that there is a continuity linking the communicative processes between caregiver and infants and the music-play behaviours that may take place between adults and young children in early childhood settings. In a nutshell, I propose that the reciprocal nature of early caregiver–child interplay leaves internalized templates of interactive processes which can become a generative source of musical ideas among young children with other adults – though only in circumstances which are conducive. To develop this proposition, I need to explain what these 'internalized templates of interactive processes' might be and in doing so, I will continue to define communication.

Among the just born and very young infants, Trevarthen (1995) has proposed that non-verbal communicative processes are mobilized initially by a basic motivation to relate to others and to make contact (also Rochat 2004, p. 277). This function of communication immediately moves away from the idea of communication as implicitly denoting the transfer of information from one to another. In infant–caregiver interaction, once this connection is initiated, the communicative processes evolve in order to establish and sustain interaction and to guide it in ways which best serve the infant's needs. The adult caring for the infant is, in turn, predisposed to be the responsive and reciprocating partner. In early infancy, much communicative behaviour is concerned with the regulation of emotional and physical states (Reddy et al. 1997) and is closely connected to the smooth management of care routines.

As the infant matures, these interactive processes serve the infant's growing needs for stimulation, for interest, and curiosity. The exchanges become increasingly meaningful by carrying inferences derived from the exchanging patterns of non-verbal play. These inferences, in turn, feed back into the interaction in the creation of small, shared games of repetitive actions (Bruner 1983). If communication is going well, the interactions will be increasingly elaborated in order to continue and consolidate them. Conversely, if communication is faltering, the process may regress to simpler, less elaborated forms so as to repair and re-establish connection, otherwise it may break off altogether.

This view of communication rests on the assumption that information does not pre-exist in individual minds nor – to think specifically of music – in the music itself, only to be revealed through analysis, but is continuously recreated in action. It importantly changes the view of communication from a process which implicitly carries information to an active process which brings people together and then sustains, enhances, and strengthens that connection. Theoretical understandings of infant–adult interaction draw attention to its adaptive importance for young children in relating to their surroundings and the adults around them, for those adults can be harnessed to provide them with what they need to thrive, not only physically but also emotionally and cognitively.

This interpretation of communication is not, as often conceived, a directional process shunting back and forth between two individuals in turn, but operates continuously as an active, dynamic system in which both or all participants are simultaneously fully engaged. Fogel (1993b) refers to 'continuous process communication systems' to capture this characteristic. Furthermore, the communicative processes are not static, but are evolving and transforming within the ongoing exchange. This creates inferences about what has just preceded and what will follow. A good example is the familiar and universal game of peep-bo. Each new move in the game, hiding for a moment longer, hiding in a different way, showing a more exaggerated surprise, and so on, depends on what has just gone before and, crucially, on how the baby or toddler is reacting. Each consequent contribution by one partner begins to take on meaning in the light of its predecessor. In an accumulative, cyclical process, the retrospective inference increasingly sets up anticipation for what is to come. So, in a kind of feedback loop, the engendering of meaning between participants increases the communicative potential of the exchange. As a consequence, the initial motivation to connect with another is satisfied. The outcome of effective communication is a sympathetic contact which is mutually rewarding to both partners.

Bruner (1983) has proposed that these games of early childhood, extended and elaborated versions of the early interaction in infancy, provide a raft for the development of language. He proposes that language used as meaningful depends on children's ability for intersubjectivity – the ability to infer the meaning of others through the reading of non-verbal cues and actions with objects. This is the world of non-verbal, gestural meaning proposed by Donald (1981) as the evolutionary precedent to verbal language. And Donald's mimetic communication has close links to the multi-modal forms of communication described by those concerned with infant communication, particularly Stern's 'vitality affects', which he explains as basic impulses of emotionally charged energy (Stern 1985). It is logical to propose that this game-playing of toddlerhood, relying as it does on multi-modal, time-phrased interactions could lead smoothly into early music-making. To explore this possibility will be the purpose of the description of musical exchange which follows later in the chapter. Having set out a version of communication, we need now to ask how it can operate in young children's music-making. There are valuable sources of information to begin to answer this question in two prior studies of children's improvising to which I now turn.

Musical dialogues

The Pillsbury Foundation Nursery studies were carried out over 60 years ago but remain an important longitudinal, observational source of information about young children's spontaneous musical behaviours (Moorhead and Pond, 1941/1978). The nursery was set up for the purpose of studying the 'innate musicality' of young children aged between 18 months and eight years. It was generously equipped with adult instruments, including percussion drawn from a range of musical traditions, some wind, and stringed instruments. The children were free to initiate play with these instruments and, over time, developed their musical activities in varied and idiosyncratic ways.

Donald Pond, a composer and performing musician, was musical director from 1937–1940. While not claiming to be undertaking systematic, experimental research, Pond made copious notes from his observations (Pond 1981). Significantly, he did not hold back from joining in with and playing with the children if they invited his participation, often taking part in what he termed 'rhythmic dialogues' (Pond 1981, p. 8). He maintained that, as a composer, he possessed listening sensibilities and an open-mindedness to the value and potential of the children's musical play that enabled him to be more alert and perceptive to their ways of making music.

Veronica Cohen's study (1980) took its lead from the Pillsbury study. A period of observation of children's free play in a kindergarten music corner narrowed to focussed case studies of two selected children. The main theoretical outcome of Cohen's study was a conception of children's music-making as 'kinaesthetic gesturing'. Micro-analyses of short episodes revealed how the children communicated their musical intention through gestures of bodily movement adapted to the technical demands of producing sound with instruments. Although Cohen was not explicitly concerned with the interpersonal dimension – her primary purpose was to explain how these gestures operate as deep structuring devices – it is significant that both children selected for further study were making their music for and/or with others. The first selected child was experiencing difficulty in making friendships with other children and so played alone. He frequently invited others to listen to his playing on a set of bongo drums, interpreted by the researcher as him looking for a means to 'reach out to others'. The second child and the researcher improvised at the piano, each taking a turn at producing short phrased melodies.

Significantly, both Pond and Cohen refer to improvised 'dialogues' between adult and individual children. Their willingness to participate in playing with the children contrasts with several studies of young children's improvising and composing in which researchers have been careful to remain detached from the children's activity (e.g. Kratus 1994; Webster and Hickey 2000). Their detachment derives from concern that participation could bias the objective investigation of what are conceived to be individualistic processes of improvising. In most research into young children's musical activity, Western musical forms and processes, based on assumptions of individual activity, have been taken as unquestioned norms (Young 1999).

Chris and Jake playing together

The research which provides the main example and the background to this chapter has taken place in early childhood settings typical of the English education and child-care systems. These systems have a long tradition of providing environments believed to be conducive for young children's self-selected and self-guided play. In keeping with this tradition, musical instruments designed to be appropriate for early years educational purposes were set out for free choice play. When children opted to play, the adult would typically wait and watch to determine whether joining in would be welcomed or not. Young children usually cued the adult, either by making eye contact, by gesturing with the instruments (often by pausing with them in readiness) or by verbally inviting the adult to play. Although a majority of children welcomed the adult as play partner, particularly when the adult was familiar to them, there were exceptions. No children were coaxed or coerced into playing with the adult.

The instruments available were for the most part educational percussion. These are designed to be technically undemanding, to be held and played by small hands, and inexpensive to purchase. All of these features have corresponding effects on the musical potential in terms of quality of tone and resonance and variety of pitch and timbre. Frustrated by these musical limitations and interested in exploring the challenges of instrumental design for very young children, Chris had made instruments and imported sound-producing objects to create an outdoor play environment. Within a conception of music as action, the generative potential of musical instruments determines the kinds of musicians – and correspondingly musical communicators – we can be when playing, and how the music sounds. In turn this draws attention to the representations and expectations of young children as musicians which are carried in the provision of instruments and situations for playing them. This line of thought is a diversion from the main theme of this chapter, but it is worth holding in mind when the communicative play potential of Chris's 'climbing frame pitch pipes' becomes evident in the description later.

The play episode we are considering here consisted of quite a long musical dialogue between Chris and Jake played on wooden pipes. The setting was a local education authority nursery school which serves a predominantly white working class and Anglo-Asian community in a suburb of Birmingham, central England. I selected this episode because it lends itself more easily than many to being described in words; each pipe plays only one pitch and the musical exchanges were relatively clear-cut. A member of the project team, standing at some distance and using a zoom lens so that his recording was non-intrusive, recorded the whole play session, including this episode, on video camera[1].

---

[1] The project, entitled 'How to Catch and Moonbeam and Pin it Down' is run by BASS (Birmingham Advisory and Support Service, Birmingham City Council Education Service) and focusses on the role of professional artists working in a range of early years settings.

This recording also enabled a process of reviewing, documenting and reflecting on the play episode. Details of the context, the children and their play were captured in hand-written field-notes.

To describe this musical exchange I have converted some rhythms into short units of conventional musical notation and adopted terms such as motif, imitation, variation, and turn-taking. These symbols and terminology are useful to convey the musical interactions with one form of precision. My aim, however, is not to provide a conventional 'music theory' transcription and analysis of the music as sound onto which I then map communicative processes, but instead to explain composite music-communicative processes as one and the same. These are structural terms, but used in the sense of a series of small interactive events sequentially organized within a longer play episode.

In the outdoor play area Chris had created set-ups designed to stimulate music play, including an arrangement of several hand-made wooden single-note pipes, all differently tuned, hanging on short strings from a climbing frame. The children could climb on the frame and discover these pipes. Chris stood within the frame surrounded by children who came and went as they pleased. By clambering on the frame, they could choose to position themselves close by, at his level, as Jake did. Turning to face Chris, Jake blew a short call (Fig. 13.1) on a single-pitched pipe. Chris, although occupied with several children, heard this and echoed it on a differently pitched pipe. Jake reciprocated. A turn-taking sequence of these simple calls continued in exact imitation of one another for eight or so turns. Now the turn-taking was established, Jake changed the rhythm slightly (see Fig. 13.2). Again, Chris imitated the change and a few matched turns continued. Next Chris introduced a variation by changing pipes so that he could play a matching rhythm on a new pitch. After a pause, Jake had pulled up another suspended, differently pitched pipe for himself. Each now had the possibility of two pitches. With this increased potential, the

Fig. 13.1 First short call

Fig. 13.2 Varied rhythmically

musical motifs became more varied. And now that the turn-taking had become well established, both partners introduced new ideas and variations, but always adhering to the established turn-taking structure maintained by the interlocking timing of short 'one bar' calls. The game reached a climax with a new idea, a kind of joke. Chris stuffed both pipes in his mouth to produce a loud, double-pitch hooting. Jake tried to copy, failed, laughed, dropped both pipes and ran off.

Before I look more closely at this play session, the willingness of Jake to play, to remain for several minutes by choice, suggests at the very least that he found the activity intrinsically rewarding. The motivation to engage with others and generate increasing interest and pleasure is what sustains participation. Such forms of activity are rewarding because they are intended to generate a state of togetherness, of sharing, which is, of its own sake, pleasurable and satisfying.

Processes of musical communication

Imitation

For Chris to imitate Jake's initial pipe call may seem a simple act, yet imitation signals willingness to join in, to participate, and crucially that the initiative lies with Jake. The direct echo is an open invitation for further imitations. Jake, probably drawing on prior experiences of the unfolding pattern of similar interactive exchanges with others, immediately anticipates that the game will continue with more turn-taking. Exact imitation by both partners is therefore a primary communicative strategy which establishes turn-taking as they feel their way in the early stages of the episode (Nadel *et al.* 1999).

The process is subtle, however, for the echoes must be well-timed. If they are too late or too early, they will fail to link rhythmically with the previous idea, thus diminishing the echo's communicative potential. It is not just the repetition of ideas which establishes turn-taking but, importantly, the exact timing of exchanges, so that they co-ordinate to create a 'continuous communication process system' (Fogel 1993*b*) – one stream of music created by the two players. The length of pauses at the change-over point is crucial in the successful establishment of the system. In a simple experimental manipulation, when playing with some three- and four-year-olds, I either over-shortened or over-lengthened these swap-over pauses. Although the variations were only slight, they nevertheless upset the rhythm of interchange (Young 2000). Faced with a poorly coordinating adult partner, one child continued to play but increasingly disconnected from the adult partner to play independently, while the other verbally expressed her frustration and struggled to regain control over the turn-taking. Similar emotional responses of dismay or frustration have also been observed in infants when the timing of interaction is perturbed in some way (Trevarthen 1979).

Comparative inter-cultural studies from ethnomusicology (Sager 2003) and anthropology (e.g. Shore 1996) are beginning to suggest that members of a common cultural group will connect most successfully when tempi, rhythm, timing, and intensity contours have a 'rightness' about them according to their cultural norms. Similarly, particular musical traditions and styles have preferred rhythmic and dynamic relationships. This is a similar notion to the interactional synchrony of which Sawyer talks (this volume). But while Sawyer emphasizes the rhythmic basis of synchrony, rhythm is but one component of generously conceived non-verbal, dynamic forms encompassing qualities of intensity, shape, and movement which are communicatively potent: the parameters of communicative musicality described by Ansdell and Pavlicevic (this volume). It may be that Jake and Chris share common characteristics of communicative musicality as a result of similarities in their cultural backgrounds. I also suggest that successful partnering of young children by adults is likely to depend on the adult being susceptible to the dynamic style of individual children and acquiring a repertoire of music-communicative styles to draw upon (Young and Gillen 2000).

From certain viewpoints, the young child's capacity and apparent need for repetition through imitation might seem unproductive and even regressive. The usual yardsticks for evaluating children's music are typically drawn from Western art music, a tradition in which certain emphases on repetition, variation, and novelty are prized. These criteria have been automatically adopted in many studies of young children's musical competence, which has often led to poor assessments. In keeping with the analytical conventions of Western art music, musical motifs have been detached from the activity of making and analysed without reference to their use within a context. If the repetition of musical motives serves as a communicative device for starting and continuing to play together, it is more appropriate to see them as productive and competent. As Glover (1999) has argued, in looking for an interpretation of children's music, it is essential to ask what was intended and whether the musical activity succeeds in relation to that intention. The case for valuing imitative strategies is strengthened by the existence of musics in which repetition and continuity are structural devices essential to the musical aesthetic, for example, in some musical traditions from sub-Saharan Africa. It is no coincidence that those musics which value these features tend to be semi-improvised aural forms in which the communal dimension is a priority. Nzewi (2003) referred to the 'cruciality of interpersonal relationships in African music'. Participation is facilitated by predictability. Where the possibilities are reduced, musical consensus is more likely to emerge.

Elaboration

Once the turn-taking was established, Jake disturbed it with a variation which served to provide new impetus. The variation from the original was slight, however. At this point, the interpersonal understanding, relying on inferred patterns and regularities, was still becoming established and might have been upset by too wide a deviation. Yet, at the same time, the gradual introduction of some measure of unpredictability became increasingly important in heightening interest and thus sustaining the exchange. Once communication is established through a mutually understood structure, a precariousness between continuity and the introduction of novelty can begin to evolve. As Dissanayake (2000) points out, this precariousness is fundamental to socially constructed, time-based performance arts and ritualistic events. Through copious examples, she explains how it is as central to the dyadic game playing of infancy and toddlerhood as it is to the stylized forms belonging to culturally defined practices. The creation of new ideas within social interaction, both as a means to connect with others and to share expressively significant ideas, is a form of creativity arising from participatory processes which has been overlooked by traditional views of creativity as the product of the individual mind.

As Chris and Jake's imitative turn-taking develops into more elaborated turns, the thematic relationship between 'before' and 'after' turns becomes more established. Both forward and retrospective relationships begin to impinge on the immediate turns. Sawyer has referred to the 'localized rules' which guide the evolution of turns in socially constructed improvisation (Sawyer 1999). The unfolding interaction takes on the form of a game which is rule-guided, and develops creatively around shared ideas, but is not rule-bound. Thus the game begins to provide a format for collaborative activity, recognized by both partners, which provides a framework at a structural level beyond the immediate exchange of turns. The game sets up both forward and retrospective relationships which arch over and beyond the immediate moment to provide a kind of 'meta-format', positioning each individual playing action within an inferred plan. Now established, creative elaboration can proliferate within the emerging frame, as demonstrated by Chris and Jake's playing. Their increasingly inventive motifs were extended by the possibilities for variation by the pitches of the two pipes they each held. Their game reached a peak of involvement when Chris played the two-pipe hoot. Perhaps because Chris sensed the play episode had run its course and might begin to wane, he disturbed the flow of turns, creating a potential climax, a point of closure with the two-tone hooting. Jake accepted the ending. Thus the adult acted as boundary-setter; an idea I will come back to later.

Organization

This detailed analysis of one episode of shared musical play reveals how the music arises as a transformation of participatory play into the medium of sound. The responsive play between Jake and Chris channelled and organized their socio-musical ideas. The communicative, interactional forms with which the child is already familiar provide templates for musical action. Coordinating and sustaining the game of playing together gives the music-making coherence, and a sense of intention and forward progression (Young 2003–4).

At this level, Jake's lack of musical skills, experience, and knowledge of musical styles means that the music is a transformation of interaction at a relatively direct and immediate level. The musical coherence and its evolving significance to both players are heavily dependent on the immediate 'here and now'. Young children's music would be unlikely, yet, to display structural transformations of social processes exactly corresponding to those found in more refined and stylized adult cultural forms. However, the processes of children's music-making are similar to Keil's conception of 'music in process', in which 'good spontaneity and flow are at the premium' (Keil 1966, p. 347). Drawing his ideas from broad musical interests including rock and contemporary jazz, Keil likens 'music in process' both to the nature of children's play and to a river, in which each moment pushes forward the next, emerging contingently from the prior flow. He contrasts this linear unfolding of 'music in process' with music as architecture, in which the whole musical event is hierarchically structured in advance.

The music is not an exact moulding of the social processes, however. Many other factors, including bodily movements to produce the sound required by the instruments, introduce constraints and possibilities which impinge on how the music is played out. The resulting sound is therefore generated from many sources which interact with one another. However, the fundamental impetus is Jake's motivation to make playful contact with others, his confidence to do so, and his abilities to coordinate with Chris socially. This communicative play provides the medium through which to articulate musical ideas and the making of music together, in turn, heightens the experience of connecting one with another. The communication is experienced as successful and the music as it sounds is enhanced by the emotional potency which arises from successful communication.

But it is interesting to consider how the instrument itself and how it is played also partly determine the kinds of communicative processes that are available to players. For example, educational percussion instruments played with mallets or sticks require a wider range of whole-body movements to produce sound (Young 2003b) than the wooden pipes that Chris and Jake used and so can potentially carry more expressive meanings through bodily gesture

(Davidson, this volume). Singers are even more liberated, having comparatively fewer technical restrictions on bodily movement to produce their sound. They are free to use expressive physical gestures and facial expression (Welch, this volume). Blown instruments, in contrast, severely restrict upper body movement and facial expression. Within these limitations, however, Jake articulated the blown sounds on the pipes with a rhythmic clarity which probably could not have been achieved with mallet-struck or shaken percussion. This rhythmic clarity enabled the interplay of the rhythmic variations which became the main theme of their playing together. Other generative sources of musical play may have been so pared down that the turn-taking of short rhythmic patterns (limited by breathing capacity too), liberated by the pipes, emerged as a fruitful source of musical ideas. Pipe calls are, after all, literally used to signal between people.

The adult as play partner and pedagogue

A view of children's music as emerging from playful interactions with an adult partner draws attention to the nature of the adult role. Although all musical relationships will be characterized by inequalities and differences which are likely to require compensatory adaptations on the part of participants if communication is to flow, the partnership between adult and young child is strikingly asymmetrical. In Western cultures, however, playful interactions between adults and children in which the boundaries of status and power are minimized through the adaptive behaviour of the adult are acceptable, and indeed form an important pedagogical principle in the early years of education. In other cultures such adaptation may not be the norm, or may be acceptable in certain situations but not within others. Adults are clearly more skilled than children and can harness this skill to alter their actions to fit better with children's abilities – in this way enabling them to become creative participants. Adults, however, determine the outer boundaries within which the children can act. Recall that Chris wound up the play episode when he intuitively sensed that 'enough was enough', and was monitoring and managing the children's play within certain margins in other subtle ways.

In a small study, practitioners who were well known to children joined in with their playing in ways which were experimentally altered across different features (Young 2000, 2003a). Some allowed the children to self-initiate play with the instruments but then intervened with direct verbal instructions, whilst others modelled ways to play 'correctly', and yet others intervened minimally, showing little interest and leaving prematurely. In all three versions; directing, correcting or low-interest, interceptions either closed down the children's play, caused it to falter and fold eventually, or were simply ignored. There are parallels to be found in infant–caregiver interaction, where research has revealed that when children are active in determining the nature, content, pacing, and direction of interaction and the caregiver, in turn, is sensitive and responsive to the infant's communicative strategies, exchanges flow successfully (Stern 1985). It is, therefore, not readiness to interact *per se*, but how the adult interacts which is the key factor in fostering creative, participatory play.

Although in many respects the children's position is weaker than the adults', and their repertoire of adaptive behaviours is limited, they are not passive if given clear boundaries within which to act. They are full of initiative in applying already mastered forms of interaction. Young children have stored a good deal of experience enabling them to initiate various forms of interaction with adults. As we have seen in Jake and Chris's play episode, they can possess a range of strategies which they draw upon to guide and direct the interactions in ways which meet their own needs. Having said this, of course children bring sets of expectations based on varying prior experiences of interacting with adults, and not all children will do so with Jake's confidence and competence.

A view of participatory music play emerges from this analysis in which the child's processes of music-making are facilitated within widely set boundaries by the adult, but towards which the children nonetheless actively contribute. The children's need to retain control in communicative exchanges – or at least to feel that they do so through the adaptive behaviour of the adult – becomes crucial. We can be more receptive to the contributions of others, and become fully creative participants, from a position of feeling in control – and this applies at all ages. It was noticeable, for example, that the playful contributions of Jake reached a peak of inventiveness in mid-episode. Adults present themselves to the child as responsive, controllable, contingent, and predictable within a carefully judged margin of deviation; just enough to enable the music-making, to generate interest and fun, but not enough to hi-jack it. Straightforward though this may sound, it demands in practice a set of skills specifically honed for this kind of work in early childhood music – and indeed in adult–child interaction more generally.

For a community musician like Chris, working in a range of musical situations, different types of music and musical roles require him to draw from a repertoire of musical communicative styles and patterns. For work in early childhood settings, this includes a pedagogical musical role which requires 'child-appropriate musical communication'. What, communicatively, is essential to one interactive mode, say, highly attuned imitative responses with young children – may not be assumed in another. The making of interpersonal musical relationships between adults and children to bring about learning and how these relationships might be conceived within educational institutions are interesting areas to explore. Current training of music educators focusses more on content and curriculum structure than on developing a repertoire of musical interactive styles to foster learning.

It only remains to consider how learning can be defined within this kind of interactive improvisation and to consider its usefulness as a pedagogical strategy. In straightforward terms it fulfils a basic educational principle, namely to use familiar means to achieve new ends, grafting music-making onto what children already know well how to do. But learning involves induction into the cultural practices of communities to which the child belongs. Up to this point the emphasis has been on the significance of the musical exchange only within itself and not beyond.

Adults inevitably hear children's contributions through a filter of experience and common usage. In responding contingently they will automatically subtly rework and 'repair' children's contributions to normalize them within prevailing cultural versions of music with which they are familiar. For example, the rhythms may be slightly reorganized, the melodic patterning remembered with slight alterations to fit tonal systems, and so on. This process can be usefully likened to that of children learning to speak, in which the adult repeats the child's utterance, or replies to it, with a repaired version so as to assist the process of language learning. The child, in turn, hears her own musical ideas mirrored back but slightly reworked. Moreover, as the exchanges reach a level of elaboration and transformation, when the child's autonomy is on a firm footing, the adult has the opportunity to introduce new musical ideas more explicitly. Chris's two pitched melodies, minimal though they were, conformed to certain stylistic musical expectations. By this strategy, the adult's responses become a source of information for the child: a learning resource. Thus, Chris has the potential to mediate between Jake's idiosyncratic playing and cultural versions of music.

However, it is important to stress that the process is one of creative exchange of ideas in improvisational dialogue. This moves away from the conception of the adult as providing guided participation (Rogoff 1990) in which the structure of the activity and its direction is relatively fixed. Some pedagogical practices in early childhood music education advocate improvised activity as a means for children to develop musical skills and understanding (e.g. Frazee 1987). But these activities are highly 'rule-bound' so as to guide the children towards given goals. The model of improvised dialogues I propose here is open-ended. If we hold that music is, by its very nature, in a continual process of transformation, there can indeed be no fixed cultural practices to which the child is introduced. There are methods, approaches, processes, and ideas which will be valuable resources for creative action and transformation, but no orthodoxies to be taught dogmatically.

Conclusion: levels of engagement

While this chapter has focused on communicative processes within paired musical play between adults and young children, and has emphasized the reciprocity of musical ideas, one caveat is required, otherwise this emphasis may be misleading. It is useful to view this kind of interactive play within a wider spectrum of social engagement. At one extreme, from a range of studies in early years settings, it is noticeable that some forms of musical activity flourish when children play quite alone (Young 2000; Glover 2000). For example, some forms of spontaneous singing (Young 2003b), common hybrid play forms such as blending role play, number patterning into play with the instruments, or finding pleasing sequences of sounds, all seem to require bouts of concentrated solitary play. Arguably, the children may still be playing 'as if' communicating with others imaginatively, even though apparently alone.

At the other extreme, children commonly enjoyed synchronizing their instrumental play with others, typically maintaining an exactly matched steady beat together for a continuous period of time. This kind of highly coordinated action represents a simpler level of interaction which makes fewer demands on communicative skills. Perhaps for this reason it often occurred between some of the youngest children playing together, or among those who found social interaction with others more difficult to achieve. Stern (1985) has suggested that synchronous experiences may be the ones that 'come closest to the notions of merging or of dissolution of self/other boundaries, at least on perceptual grounds' (p. 107). Forms of playing together characterized by exact coincidence and merging can be an outcome of successful musical communication and can create a point of arrival, an affirming consolidation likened to the moments in jazz improvisation or post-cadenza in a classical concerto where all the players reunite to play out the theme. But continuous, exact synchronization is by its very nature unchanging and unproductive, without variation and elaboration.

To conclude, I suggest that attempting to find and maintain a balance between merged synchronicity and non-collaborative individual play, and their musical counterparts, involves a tension between different forces which are managed through the interplay of communicative processes. This allows for the meeting of musical minds and their creative adaptations of one with another. Young children have competencies for engaging with others which they can exploit in first music-making experiences when responsive adults, provision of equipment, and the practical arrangements of educational settings allow. I see this interplay between individuality and social connection as the driving force and creative potency of musical activity. It follows that a key aim of education is to enable children to become proficient musical communicators so that they can negotiate musically with other 'players' in all manner of musical styles and practices.

References

Blacking, J. (1976) *How Musical is Man?* (2nd edition). London: Faber and Faber.

Blacking, J. (1987) *A Commonsense View of All Music.* Cambridge: Cambridge University Press.

Bruner, J.S. (1983) *Child's Talk: Learning to Use Language.* Oxford: Oxford University Press.

Cohen, V. (1980) *The Emergence of Musical Gestures in Kindergarten Children,* unpublished Doctoral dissertation, University of Illinois, Urbana.

Cole, M. (1996) *Cultural Psychology: A Once and Future Discipline.* Cambridge, MA: The Belknap Press of Harvard University Press.

Dissanayake, E. (2000) *Art and Intimacy.* Seattle, WA: University of Washington Press.

Donald, M. (1991) *Origins of the Modern Mind.* Cambridge, MA: Harvard University Press.

Fogel, A. (1993*a*) *Developing Through Relationships: Origins of Communication, Self and Culture.* New York: Harvester, Wheatsheaf.

Fogel, A. (1993*b*) Two Principles of Communication: Co-regulation and Framing. In *New Perspectives in Early Communicative Development,* (eds J. Nadel and L. Camaioni). London: Routledge.

Frazee, J. (1987) *Discovering Orff: A Curriculum for Teachers.* New York: Schott.

Glover, J. (1999) '"Don't ask for the Meaning: Ask for the Use": Issues in Researching and Contextualising Children's Composition', paper presented at the conference: *Research in Music Education.* Exeter University, April, 1999.

Glover, J. (2000) *Children Composing 4–14.* London: Routledge Falmer.

Halliday, M.A.K. (1975) *Learning to Mean – Explorations in the Development of Language.* London: Edward Arnold.

Kaye, K. (1982) *Mental and Social Life of Babies.* Chicago. IL: Harvester.

Keil, C. (1966) 'Motion and Feeling Through Music', *The Journal of Aesthetics and Art Criticism,* **24**, 337–49.

Kratus, J. (1994) 'The Ways Children Compose'. In *Musical Connections: Tradition and Change,* (ed. H. Lees). Proceedings of the 21st World Conference of the International Society for Music Education, held in Tampa, Florida. Auckland, New Zealand: Uniprint, The University of Auckland, 128–41.

Lodge, D. (1990) *After Bakhtin: Essays on Fiction and Criticism.* London: Routledge.

Moorhead, G.E. and Pond, D. (1941, reprinted 1978) 'Music of Young Children: 11. General Observations', *Music of Young Children: Pillsbury Foundation Studies.* Santa Barbara: Pillsbury Foundation for Advancement of Music Education.

Nadel, J., Guérini, C., Pezé, A., and Rivet, C. (1999) 'The Evolving Nature of Imitation as a Format for Communication'. In *Imitation in Infancy,* (eds J. Nadel and G. Butterworth). Cambridge: Cambridge University Press.

Nzewi, M. (2003) 'The Juncture of Music, Space and Humanning: reflections on African musical arts scholarship', Keynote Address: *A Symposium celebrating the work and legacy of John Blacking,* Callaway Centre, School of Music, the University of Western Australia, Perth, 12–14 July.

Pond, D. (1981) 'A Composer's Study of Young Children's Innate Musicality', *Bulletin: Council for Research in Music Education,* **68**, 1–12.

Reddy, V., Hay, D., Murray, L., and Trevarthen, C. (1997) 'Communication in Infancy: Mutual Regulation of Affect and Attention'. In *Infant Development: Recent Advances,* (eds G. Bremner, A. Slater, and G. Butterworth). Hove, East Sussex: Psychology Press.

Rochat, P. (2004) 'Emerging Co-Awareness'. In *Theories of Infant Development*, (eds G.Bremner and A. Slater). Oxford: Blackwell Publishing.

Rogoff, B. (1990) *Apprenticeship in Thinking: Cognitive Development in a Social Context.* Oxford: Oxford University Press.

Sager, R. (2003) 'Blacking's theory of musical transcendence: the other, self and socio-cultural identity reconsidered', paper presented at *A Symposium celebrating the work and legacy of John Blacking*, Callaway Centre, School of Music, the University of Western Australia, Perth, 12–14 July.

Sawyer, K. (1999) 'Improvised Conversations: Music, Collaboration and Development', Keynote presentation for the conference '*Research in musical improvisation: Issues and methodologies*', University of Reading, March 13, 1999.

Shore, B. (1996) *Culture in Mind: Cognition, Culture and the Problem of Meaning.* Oxford: Oxford University Press.

Stern, D. (1985) *The Interpersonal World of the Infant.* New York: Basic Books.

Trevarthen, C. (1979) 'Communication and Co-operation in Early Infancy: a Description of Primary Intersubjectivity'. In *Before Speech: The Beginning of Interpersonal Communication*, (ed. M. Bullowa). Cambridge: Cambridge University Press.

Trevarthen, C. (1995) 'The Child's Need to Learn a Culture', *Children and Society*, 9(1), 5–19.

Trevarthen, C. (2000) 'Musicality and the Intrinsic Motive Pulse: Evidence from Human Psychobiology and Infant Communication', *Musicae Scientiae*, Special Issue 1999–2000, 155–215.

Valsiner, J. and van der Veer, R. (2000) *The Social Mind: Construction of the Idea.* Cambridge: Cambridge University Press.

Vygostsky, L.S. (1978) *Mind in Society: The Development of Higher Mental Processes.* Cambridge, MA: Harvard University Press.

Webster, P. and Hickey, M. (2000) 'The Development and Refinement of a Computerized Version of the Measure of Creative Thinking in Music', report presented at the MENC National Convention Special Research Interest Group: Creativity, Washington, DC, March 10, 2000.

Wells, G. (1985) *Language Development in the Pre-School Years.* Cambridge: Cambridge University Press.

Wertsch, J. (1991) *Voices of the Mind: A Sociocultural Approach to Mediated Action.* Cambridge, MA: Harvard University Press.

Young, S. (1999) 'Just Making a Noise? Reconceptualising the Music-making of Three- and Four-year-olds in a Nursery Context', *Early Childhood Connections: Journal of Music and Movement-based Learning*, 5(1), 14–22.

Young, S. (2000) *Young Children's Spontaneous Music-making in Nursery Settings*, Unpublished PhD thesis, University of Surrey.

Young, S. (2002) 'Young Children's Spontaneous Vocalisations in Free-play: Observations of two- to three-year-olds in a day-care setting', *Bulletin of the Council for Research in Music Education*, 152, (Spring) 43–53.

Young, S. (2003a) *Music with the Under Fours.* London: Routledge Falmer.

Young, S. (2003b) 'Time-space structuring in spontaneous play on educational percussion instruments among three- and four-year-olds', *British Journal of Music Education*, 20(1), 45–59.

Young, S. (2003–4) 'The Interpersonal Dimension: a potential source of musical creativity for young children?' in *Musicae Scientiae: Musical Creativity: 10th Anniversary Conference Issue – Award Papers*. 175–91.

Young, S. and Gillen, J. (2000) 'Sharing the Initiative with 3-4 year old Children in Two Areas of Educational Research (Instrumental Music-making and Telephone Discourse): Exploring Challenges and Rewards', paper presented at the British Educational Research Association Annual Conference, held in Cardiff, Wales, September 7–9, 2000.

Chapter 14

Pedagogical communication in the music classroom

Charles Byrne

Introduction

This chapter is concerned with the ways in which music teachers communicate with pupils in secondary school music classrooms while engaged in music making, teaching, and learning. I suggest that good teaching is essentially about good communication, which involves the teacher in thinking about how to prepare, plan, implement, and communicate lesson ideas and content in such a way that learning takes place. Talking about music and communicating musically are two different activities in the music classroom. The music classroom is an environment in which music making can be the dominant activity but in which talking about music can inadvertently take over. Remembering to ask a single question before playing a short musical extract can allow pupils to focus their listening, while asking a question during the listening period can easily become a distraction from the intended purpose of listening to the music in the first place. There is evidence (Byrne and Sheridan 1998; Byrne *et al.* 2001) that teachers are sometimes uncomfortable with certain aspects of the musical domain, including talking with children about their compositions and improvisations.

For children, communicating thoughts, ideas, and emotions through musical composing activities is an important part of both their general and musical development (Scottish Office Education Department 1992; Odam 1995; Paynter 2000). Active learning in music engages learners in experiencing musical concepts and features, during which they learn how to play and recognize these features and begin to explore how to consolidate and enrich their understanding through short composing tasks which make use of them. Musical composition as part of the curriculum offers the learner opportunities to communicate in new ways and to express ideas, moods, and emotions through music that may have remained unexplored in the performing and listening less practical areas of teaching. This 'comprehensive musicianship' approach, in which one area of musical activity informs and supports the other, places creative music making at the centre of the musical development of young people (Choksy *et al.* 1986) and was central in the successful development of Standard Grade (ages 13–15) music in Scotland (Scottish Examination Board 1988). Since performing and listening are also involved during composing activities, it may be helpful to explore communication issues through learning and teaching in creative music making. Swanwick (1999) suggests that 'composing offers the greatest scope for choosing not only *how* but *what* to play or sing and in which temporal order' (p. 55). In addition, during composing, decisions are made by the participants, as opposed to being made for them by teachers and others, which provides a compelling argument for viewing composing as 'an educational necessity, not some optional activity when time permits' (ibid.). Placing composing activities at the centre of the learning experience for young musicians promotes higher standards of general musicianship since performing, listening, and composing skills complement and inform one another, and support the development of each (Sheridan and Byrne 2002). As a result, the communication skills used by the teacher in the classroom around compositional tasks, both musical and verbal, are powerful aids to the development of musical skills in the learner. The ways in which teachers design, set up, and communicate the aims of musical tasks in order to promote creative thinking are also seen as being important (Byrne *et al.* 2001). However, performance and listening skills are clearly important in the music classroom, and ways in which communication impacts on integrated learning and teaching in all three areas of activity will be explored.

This chapter begins by examining some theoretical ideas associated with communication as part of the learning process, and communication within the learning environment, and makes links between these ideas, the music classroom, and the different ways in which teachers and learners communicate in the classroom to bring about learning and understanding. Next, I will suggest some ways in which verbal and musical communication might be used to engage pupils in open-ended creative tasks using a number of different communication strategies such as direct teaching and scaffolding. I will examine the ways in which such tasks can offer opportunities for teachers and pupils to interact with one another, posing and answering questions using both verbal and musical communication. The ways in which teachers think and talk about music will have a direct bearing on the ways in which they communicate with learners, and so both thinking about music and talking about music will be considered. Finally, the ways in which verbal, non-verbal, and musical communication can be utilized in the classroom will be examined with reference to a proposed model of interaction in teaching and learning in the music classroom which draws together some of the theoretical ideas discussed, and provides a template for teachers to assist in the planning and implementation of teaching activities with individuals and small groups. The types of communication deployed by the teacher and learner are necessarily different; the teacher adopts a pro-active role in guiding the learning process, and learns to interpret the cues and clues which the learner gives to the teacher as to what further teaching is needed. Teachers use verbal and musical communication to present, outline, and develop musical ideas and features, to check for pupil understanding and to help fill in gaps in knowledge. Learners, on the other hand, will communicate their own level of understanding of musical ideas and features and will prompt teachers to provide either further explanation or musical examples. The new model will clearly show the different stages of the learning process and highlight the potential for improved teacher and learner communication about music.

Communication and the learning process

In music, good classroom practice requires clear objectives for both short term and long term attainment by pupils, who are likely to have a wide range of abilities and needs. Teachers need to communicate clearly and effectively with learners using verbal, non-verbal, and musical communication as well as setting clearly defined targets within tasks and classroom materials. The discrepancy between what learners can achieve with and without assistance is known as the zone of proximal development, wherein children can be shown a method for solving a problem that they will be able to apply to another, more advanced problem later on. Vygotsky (1978) describes the zone of proximal development as

> The distance between the actual developmental level as determined by independent problem solving and the level of potential development as determined through problem solving under adult guidance or in collaboration with more capable peers (p. 86).

This gap between what a child can achieve on his or her own and what can be achieved with adult guidance is conceived of as an area in which the child learns and in which observations can be made of the cognitive change that takes place (Newman *et al.* 1989). The teacher could fulfil a number of tutoring roles such as 'establishing and maintaining an orientation towards task-relevant goals, highlighting critical features of the task that the child might overlook, demonstrating how to achieve goals and helping to control frustration' (Wood and Wood 1996, p. 5). This role of keeping the child on task and helping to minimize frustration requires an understanding by the teacher of the learner's present level of development.

> Sensitive instruction at the novice's cutting edge of understanding, in Vygotsky's zone of "proximal development", encourages participation at a comfortable yet challenging level and provides a bridge for generalizing skills and approaches from familiar to novel situations (Rogoff 1984, p. 7).

Defining the learner's 'cutting edge of understanding' is crucial in affording the learner opportunities to continually improve skills and knowledge. This process of continual improvement or 'growing edge' (Bereiter and Scardamalia 1993), is developed through working on the five to ten percent of the aspects of one's craft or occupation which are found to be genuinely challenging. Just as an expert in any field is able to 'develop quick and relatively effortless ways to make additions to their repertoires of facts, techniques, cases or whatever' (Bereiter and Scardamalia 1993, p. 153), so the novice is able to build upon what he or she has previously learned and applied. Sensitive instruction must not only involve awareness of the stage of development of each pupil, but must also rely on the ability of the teacher to communicate his or her conceptions of what the child should achieve. Later, I will look in more detail at the ways in which teachers describe and discuss specific tasks with children but I would first like to introduce the key phases of what DeCorte (1990) refers to as a 'powerful learning environment'.

This four stage model explains what happens during the different phases of the learning process and describes aspects of teacher/pupil communication which are commonly used. The oral tradition in music, in which knowledge of musical repertoire and technique has been communicated from one generation to the next by word of mouth, has many direct parallels with the powerful learning environment and has clearly been an influential means of maintaining many musical traditions over the centuries (Goldsworthy 1997; Stock 2002, 2003). Both the oral tradition, which has served many cultures in continuing musical traditions, and the apprenticeship model, which was prevalent before the introduction of printed music (Gellrich and Sundin 1993/4) provide important teaching strategies which inform the way teachers communicate in the classroom and the private teaching studio today. Discussion of the powerful learning environment is not common in the music education literature (Byrne and Sheridan 2000), although music educators will recognize the different phases. Each involves a specific action on the part of the teacher or capable peer during which verbal, non-verbal, and musical communication may be used. Communication lies at the heart of this model and is intrinsic to both the teaching and the learning process.

Communication and the learning environment

DeCorte's (1990) idea of the classroom as a powerful learning environment represents one practical application of Vygotsky's theories, and builds upon the work of others in this field (Bliss *et al.* 1996; Wood *et al.* 1976). Just as good teaching requires a balance between talking and listening, DeCorte has proposed a working model for a powerful learning environment which is characterized by 'a good balance between discovery learning and personal exploration on the one hand, and systematic instruction and guidance on the other, always taking into account the individual differences in abilities, needs, and motivation between students' (DeCorte 1990, p. 12). Teachers take into account the differing needs and abilities of individual children as well as facilitating and maintaining motivation. The powerful learning environment provides a strong supporting framework for the teacher, within which '…students need to observe an expert performing the task (modelling), to be given hints and feedback on their own performance (coaching), to be given direct support (scaffolding) in the early stages of task execution, and to gradually move from other-regulation to self-regulation (fading)' (McGuinness and Nisbet 1991, p. 180).

The following descriptions of each phase of the powerful learning environment, with appropriate illustrations within a music learning context, provides the teacher with opportunities to make judgements as to when to move between teaching and allowing the learner to regulate his or her own learning through 'discovery learning and personal exploration' (DeCorte 1990, p. 12). The teacher can create situations in the classroom during which learners are involved and during which musical ideas and features, as well as musical skills, are communicated highly effectively within an enjoyable, active environment.

Modelling

A good musical example can explain a complex musical concept without the need for words. This involves pupils observing and hearing the task being performed by an expert.

Modelling using musical and verbal communication: Canon and syncopation

In this example the musical model provided by the teacher is 'Canon in the snow (Frosty Fugue)' by Maurice Chernick (Stannard 2003). The following phrase is used as a canon - two different groups speak the same words but start at different times:

> 'Gosh it's flippin' cold it's really cold it's freezin', it's really freezin'. I can't feel my toes or fingertips. Get a bag o' chips that'll warm you up, John' (p. 3).

The teacher models one way of saying each phrase with short phrases being repeated by the class after each hearing. The whole piece can be learned in this rote learning mode. It can then be performed as a canon in two, three, four, or more parts and there is plenty of opportunity for fun and rap style performance. Both musical and verbal communications are deployed here by the teacher through musical performance of the material, and spoken encouragement and advice on how to perform or modify the class's performance. While learning how to perform this canon, the class will have also explored the rhythmic use of words to create interesting musical textures, with each part maintaining an independent rhythmic line while other parts are heard at the same time.

As a creative exercise to follow on from the performance, the teacher might suggest that the word 'syncopation' could be explored in a similar way. The teacher would begin by asking the class to chant the word rhythmically (with the second and third syllables forming a syncopated rhythm) and, when mastered, would add a second part as a canon to the first part being chanted by the class.

At this stage in the learning process, the class as a whole has provided the 'expert performance' of Frosty Fugue, which serves as a model for the next creative music making activity. There are many possible responses to this model but essentially, the meaning of the word 'syncopation' and how syncopation can be used musically is effectively communicated to pupils. It could be argued that the learning which takes place as a result of such participation is deeper and more likely to be remembered than by memorizing a written definition. Therefore, the method of communication which the teacher has selected is crucial in bringing about understanding of what is a fairly complex musical concept. In this case, musical communication, by both teacher and class, has allowed the teacher to exemplify the concept through the use of the word 'syncopation' in a musical way. This is an example of using musical performance as a powerful communication tool.

Modelling using verbal and non-verbal communication: Chord structure

In this case, the teacher prepares to introduce a class to the construction of the major triads, I, IV, and V.

Nine children stand in a line holding large cards on each of which is a letter name. These are, C, D, E, F, G, A, B, C', and D'. The teacher asks that cards C, E and G be held up at the same time and asks all of the class to remember that this is now to be called chord I. Similarly, cards F, A, and C' are to be known as chord IV and G, B, and D' as chord V. The children who hold the cards C, F, and G are to be known as the 'root' of their respective chords and the other two members as the 'third' and 'fifth' respectively. The teacher points to each 'root' card in turn to check that the card holders understand what is required and all three cards for each chord should be held up. At this point, the holder of the G card will have noticed, or had it pointed out by an observant classmate, that G now seems to belong to two chords; it is both the fifth of chord I and the root of chord V. The teacher would explain to the class that it is perfectly alright for a note to belong to more than one chord, but it can only be the root in one chord during this particular activity. The teacher now points to each root card in turn and says the letter names of all three notes of the chord while pointing to each. The class could be encouraged to say the letter names along with the teacher.

Non-verbal and verbal communications have been used here to illustrate the construction of major triads in root position and the degrees of the scale upon which the chords are built. Verbal communication has been used by the teacher to explain the functions of each member of the chord, and non-verbal (pointing to and holding up cards) communication has reinforced the teaching points and allowed the teacher to check that the class have understood the different notes that make up each chord. Verbal communication has also been used by the class as they say each chord's letter name out loud. This provides the class teacher with another means of checking that all pupils understand the principle and can clearly see each card as it is held up. Non-verbal communication also helps to verify that each card holder has understood the function of their note in the chords.

Modelling using musical and non-verbal communication: Chord structure

This involves a further refinement to the lesson mentioned earlier during which the teacher repeats many of the same steps but limits the communication to musical and non-verbal. The teacher should demonstrate how to sing each letter name for the chords, encouraging the class to sing along and perhaps allocating some children to 'hold' each note. Alternatively, members of the class could play single notes on keyboards or percussion instruments as specific cards are held up, thus creating vocal and instrumental harmony for each triad.

Clearly, a mixture of all styles of communication is required, but it should be possible to move to a teaching style in which musical communication predominates.

Moving the class on to an understanding of chord inversions and an explanation as to why the lower D card has not been used will require a short explanation, but the demonstration and reinforcement of the concept can make use of non-verbal and musical communication. Several musical games could be developed from this activity.

This modelling process is the first phase of the powerful learning environment, the second phase of which takes the learner from what they can just achieve, with some assistance, to being able to achieve it without assistance.

Scaffolding

The metaphor of 'scaffolding' within the context of teacher and pupil interaction was introduced by Wood et al. (1976) in order to explore the nature of adult support for the novice while carrying out tasks that could not be achieved without assistance.

The best sort of teacher is one who helps you do what you couldn't do by yourself, but doesn't do it for you (Child aged eight, in Fisher 1995, p. 107).

Scaffolding requires the teacher to simplify the child's role in the learning process while holding the task constant (Greenfield 1984) and to offer 'questions and prompts, suggestions of where to look for inspiration, and advice. It does not involve simplifying the task' (Byrne *et al.* 2001, p. 71). Clearly, the learning objective may be broken down into manageable steps by the teacher in such a way that the children's responses can be fairly simple while leading to the acquisition of a more complex skill.

Just as modelling can be achieved by musical, verbal, and non-verbal communication or a combination of all three, scaffolding can be effected by a mixture of communication styles. It is important that teachers create structures around which learners can build their existing knowledge and skills. The more experienced adult or capable peer offers support during the learning of new skills or knowledge. Pattern and echo is a specific technique designed to develop a specific musical skill, listening, in order to develop improvisational ability (Byrne 1996). The child listens to a two bar, two note phrase. The learner plays back, as accurately as possible, the phrase that has just been played. This highly interactive process allows the teacher to decide when to move on to the next pattern or whether to play the same pattern again in order to elicit a more accurate echo. Such 'contingent instruction' (Wood *et al.* 1976) can take account of pupils' different paces of learning. As the learner begins to hear the pattern clearly and is able to correct any errors quickly, so the pacing of the sequence of patterns becomes more fluent. If the learner does not accurately play back the given phrase, then the teacher can indicate, through repetition of the pattern, that the response needs to be modified. This might be described as non-verbal communication using musical cues, since it is the repetition of the pattern which provides the cue to the learner to try again and is contingent upon the learner's response. This may or may not be accompanied by a raised eyebrow or a shake of the head from the teacher, but it is also a non-verbal response. 'Here is the pattern again because the response was not completely accurate' is what the teacher is not saying out loud, but is clearly implying by his or her actions. This non-verbal, musical scaffolding takes place within a live music-making environment.

In terms of learning to play a musical instrument, scaffolding which makes use of the learner's knowledge of a chord shape on the guitar, for example, can bring about new learning when this shape is applied to a different position on the fret board. The tutor asks the learner to move the left hand up by one fret and to listen to the effect that is produced. A simple E chord shape, treated in this way, produces a new Spanish sounding chord. This chord and its various transformations become part of the learner's actual level of development and forms part of their cutting or growing edge. The learner's knowledge of this new chord, and how it was created, can now be applied to other chords and different positions on the fretboard, which in turn will become part of their developing musical vocabulary. Of course, this type of scaffold could also be conveyed in a purely non-verbal manner through demonstration and listening.

A purely technical, paper-based illustration of this chord and how it relates to the E chord would be possible, and may suit the learner who likes to have things written down and filed neatly away for future reference. What such a paper-based explanation would miss are two important factors in new musical learning. Firstly, the feeling of the new chord shape under the fingers can only be experienced by actually sliding the fingers of the left hand from the first to the second fret. Secondly, part of the excitement of learning to play a musical instrument is being able to experience the magical sound of the new chord as some new notes are introduced while some of the same open strings are still there from the first chord.

Coaching and fading

As the child's learning and development progress in a given domain, the scaffold gradually diminishes, the roles of the learner and teacher become increasingly equal, and the point is finally reached where the child or learner is able to do alone what formerly could be done only in collaboration with the teacher (Greenfield 1984, p. 117).

At this point, the learner has moved through a zone of proximal development to a new developmental level. In order to ensure that additional tutoring is contingent upon the children's responses, the teacher now reduces the amount of scaffolding that is given. This *fading* phase of the powerful learning environment can also be accompanied by the *coaching* phase, during which encouragement and advice continue to be offered but in which more responsibility for learning has clearly been transferred to the child.

During the coaching phase, the teacher needs to be available to offer advice and encouragement by talking to the learner and answering any questions they may have. Hints and guidance can also be offered through the use of musical communication, dependent upon the level of help which the learner requires. Importantly, the learner should now be able to define questions, both verbal and musical, while moving towards fuller understanding and self-regulated learning. During the fading phase, the learner may continue to ask questions but should be communicating their understanding musically through performing, and the teacher will adopt more of a listening role.

Thinking about music

The value of learning how to learn has been identified as being important by a number of authors (Candy 1991; Brookfield 1985; Mezirow 1985) and Kreber (1998) has indicated that there is a strong relationship between learners' success in self-directed learning and their critical thinking. Byrne and Sheridan (1998) established the Strathclyde Consortium for Action Research in Learning Approaches and Teaching Techniques in Inventing (SCARLATTI) Project in order to identify good practice in teaching composing, improvising and arranging in Scottish secondary schools.

In an interim report on the SCARLATTI project, we wrote:

> Open learning activities (are) characterized as those having no single predetermined possible outcome but provide pupils with frameworks within which they can engage and develop their own critical thinking skills in a musical context. In our view, exploration in sound, experimentation with pitch and rhythm, musical play and opportunities to work in groups are key ingredients of open learning activities (Byrne and Sheridan 2001, p. 178).

Open-ended creative music making activities might include using music cells to develop ideas, creating ostinato figures which can be combined in an infinite variety of ways, or using a set of pentatonic notes to improvise along with a MIDI backing track. Adding a melody to a given or well-known chord scheme can be done effectively using musical communication alone. A prepared backing track can be used to play along with, experiment with new notes and patterns, in order to create a unique musical response from each pupil. This requires the teacher to prepare the musical communication in advance of the lesson, being available to respond to individual questions and to allow the pupils to respond musically.

Children could also use a Japanese Haiku or a short poem to create a new melody, allocating specific notes from a pentatonic set to certain syllables. This could be achieved through non-musical means, by allocating letter names to syllables, or musically through musical exploration of the vocal or instrumental sounds that might fit best with certain words and phrases. Such open-ended tasks allow individuals to respond to given stimuli at their own pace and to begin to communicate musically through the activity.

These types of activity will provide opportunities for teachers and pupils to ask questions, for pupils to acquire new knowledge and to move through the phases of the zone of proximal development. Again, a balance between guidance and exploration is important and this balance will be explored in a model of interaction for teaching and learning in the classroom that I will discuss later on in this chapter.

Talking about music

The music curriculum in Scotland tends to over-emphasize the acquisition of facts about music (propositional knowledge) at the expense of providing opportunities for learners to engage in activities such as learning about music through playing, or improving improvising and listening skills while performing. Clearly, there will be times when teachers and learners need to talk about music by asking and answering questions, as not all situations can be dealt with by responses involving purely musical communication. Experienced teachers develop the skills of knowing when to ask questions and when to allow the learner to ask questions, ensuring that a positive and helpful response is given. As the mediator in the active learning process, the teacher recognizes not only that children should know how to answer questions, but also that they should know 'how to ask them and how to formulate the right question' (Williams and Sternberg 1993, p. 320). Of course, having encouraged children to ask and formulate questions, these should be answered in as stimulating a manner as possible in order to 'enhance the child's intellectual development' (ibid. p. 321). A music teacher's ability to talk about children's composing and improvising strategies will, of course, be based upon a number of factors but it is worth considering some general points about posing and answering the learner's questions.

A conceptual model of interaction for teaching and learning in the classroom is proposed in the next section which draws upon the ideas of Williams and Sternberg (1993), in particular their account of the ways in which teachers respond to learners' questions. It also draws on the four stages of DeCorte's (1990) powerful learning environment, and suggests ways in which teachers can distinguish between the different types of learning that are needed in the music class. It has been suggested that good learning occurs when there is a balance between learning by discovery and by guidance and instruction (DeCorte 1990). The management of this balance is important when dealing with questions and issues which the learner may have. Williams and Sternberg (1993) propose seven levels of response to children's questions which range from the total rejection of the question, to an admission of ignorance, encouragement to seek a response from another authority, such as a dictionary, consideration of other explanations, ways of evaluating these other explanations and practical follow up of the evaluations. This seven level model of parent–child or teacher–child interaction is highly relevant for music teachers as it provides specific strategies for helping the learner move through the zone of proximal development from assisted to unassisted completion of tasks (Sternberg 1994). Level 4 involves encouraging the learner to seek a response through authority. There are two possible strategies the teacher can deploy when a child encounters a problem. The following case illustrates the possible strategies the teacher can deploy when the learner encounters a musical problem.

A young bass guitarist is struggling with the ringing sound of the open D and G strings which are played consecutively within a bass part and asks the tutor for help. The tutor knows how to correct the problem but starts by asking how the D string might be stopped from ringing at the same time as the G is sounding. Both are open strings, and the student suggests that he could stop the D with the flat of his hand just before plucking the G string with his thumb. He tries this with some success although more practice would help. The tutor then suggests a different right hand technique, showing the student how to use the right hand fingers in a walking style on the strings. At the end of this short period of interaction, the young bass player has made significant improvement by taking an active role in finding a solution to a musical problem.

In this case, responsibility is with the learner, who is beginning to learn that he can take control of this aspect of his learning. He has avoided being a *passive learner* (with the teacher providing all of the solution) and is becoming an active learner. 'Active learning is better than passive learning; through active learning, children develop their own information-seeking skills, rather than becoming dependent on others' (Williams and Sternberg 1993, p. 322). The teacher's role may become less active; guiding the learner towards discovering some possible solutions rather than showing or suggesting some possible solutions. Depending on the learner's level of knowledge of chords and their origins, the teacher can link the chords to what is already known. Scaffolding clearly requires a 'light touch' approach as the teacher and learner move to the 'fading' and 'coaching' stages. The teacher becomes less active and the learner more active and self-regulatory.

As learners move from learning that is regulated by the teacher (modelling) to self regulation (fading), they pass through the current zone of proximal development and arrive at their next own 'growing edge' of skill or understanding. The model suggests four separate stages through which both teacher and learner will move during periods of interaction in the classroom. Teachers may use the model to help identify the different stages and develop their own teaching skills as they recognize the stage the learner is in, to respond with some type of support which is dependent on the needs of the learner, and to plan the next stages of the learning for that individual.

The new model proposed here sets out the different phases of the powerful learning environment and explains the types of learning and their characteristics that can be expected in each. The model is laid out as a series of steps, but is essentially fluid in that it provides a framework which, with practice, teachers and students will be able to use to monitor learning and teaching while moving from working with assistance to working without assistance. At any given moment, learners will find themselves at one particular stage, but they will move to an earlier or later phase as required. The model will also help teachers to know what they want to communicate to learners, when to do this and what type of communication to use, verbal, non-verbal, or musical.

Alongside the powerful learning environment framework, I have developed the idea suggested by Williams and Sternberg (1993) that the learner can move from passive to active learning and I describe the types of activity which may indicate each. I have extrapolated from this the types of teaching that may be required, and suggest that the teacher's role in each phase of the powerful learning environment moves from active to passive teaching. During active teaching in the modelling phase, for example, the teacher sets tasks and demonstrates for the learner. This could involve written communication, verbal communication, musical communication through printed materials, and musical communication through performing and singing. Active teaching in the coaching phase might require the teacher to use verbal communication to give positive encouragement and advice to the learner, who is now engaged in active learning, as well as using musical communication to provide further guidance and to help the learner refine their responses to given tasks. During the fading phase, the learner is still engaged in active learning while the teaching becomes passive. At this point the teacher offers less guidance and support although is prepared to do so if necessary. The teacher will listen and observe during this phase and may join in any practical work with the learner.

The model is designed to offer teachers insights into the different phases of the learning process, the types of teaching and learning that may go on during each, and indicate the possible different modes of communication that may be effectively deployed.

Communication between teacher and learner – a new model

Communication of targets, ideas, suggestions, and advice is important in allowing teachers to transfer their own, more advanced knowledge to the learner, and each phase of the powerful learning environment assists in this process. Furthermore, the idea that the quality of the teacher's responses to the learner's questions moves the learner from being passive to active also implies a shift in emphasis from active to passive teaching. This shift has been built into the model (Table 14.1), but readers should note that there is no implication that either teacher or learner adopts a passive role. On the contrary, 'passive learning'

Table 14.1 A conceptual model of interaction for teaching and learning in the classroom

Teacher	Phase of powerful learning environment	Learner
active teaching sets tasks demonstrates Performs Provides exemplars	MODELLING teacher regulated learning	*passive learning* listens, observes, practical involvement
active teaching supports the learner asks questions defines goals provides further exemplars offers contingent instruction provides supporting material	SCAFFOLDING mediated learning	*active learning* answers teacher's questions attempts task
active teaching encouragement hints and guidance helps answer questions helps test hypothesis	COACHING mediated learning	*active learning* defines own questions answers own questions refines response to task develops hypothesis seeks help from others (peers, teachers)
passive teaching ready to offer guidance and support listens, observes, practical involvement	FADING self-regulated learning	*active learning* evaluates hypothesis tests possible solutions

means learning that is regulated by the teacher but which involves learner participation. In effect, the learner is learning through carrying out tasks that have been assigned by the teacher prior to moving to a more active role through the scaffolding phase. Although actively participating in the lesson, the learner is not actively learning at this stage. During 'active learning', learners have more regulation of their own learning and become more involved, answering questions and attempting different tasks.

The model presented in Table 14.1 defines the different stages of practical music making, creating music, and learning about music through listening. Underpinning the model is the learning through music approach outlined earlier in the chapter. Using the model, teachers can learn to plan for teaching that involves modelling and scaffolding, recognizing opportunities for supporting learning, providing further exemplars when needed, and to manage the learning environment in a positive and stimulating way.

When new material or musical concepts are being introduced, the model suggests how the teacher can allow each learner's pace of learning to influence the appropriate phase of the powerful learning environment to work within. In mixed ability classes, for example, instruction and guidance will be contingent upon students' different levels of understanding and response to the material being introduced. As the student attempts more active learning tasks, the teacher provides further questions and offers support. Crucially, the types of support which the teacher offers at this point should help to remind the learner of the task and avoid frustration. As students begin to be able to define and answer their own questions, so the teacher moves to an encouraging and helping role before moving to the passive teaching phase, during which it is suggested that the students are beginning to evaluate their own hypotheses and test possible solutions. At this stage in the learning process, the roles of learner and teacher begin to change as the learner asks questions, both verbally and musically, and the teacher provides answers.

Keeping this model in mind while working with children engaged in creative music making tasks may well help the teacher to ask the right questions and to encourage the learner to formulate questions. The working model in the music classroom (Table 14.2) articulates with the types of open-ended activities mentioned earlier such as creating groups of ostinato figures which fit together, or composing pentatonic melodies with a backing track. Pattern and echo work in improvising can also make use of this model and the teacher and learner can use verbal and musical communication while engaged in the process. Common sense and awareness of the four stages of the model will guide the teacher as to the exact balance between verbal, non-verbal communication, and purely musical communication. Continuous pattern and echo work requires very little verbal communication whereas advising on small listening and composing projects will require verbal responses from both teacher and learner along with musical examples. Question and answer technique can be used sensitively in order to define goals and to offer encouragement and advice.

While this model may help teachers to consider different types of communication and to develop ways of selecting appropriate modes of communication, the exact type of communication deployed will always depend on the specific needs of individual pupils, groups, and classes.

When the overall goal of a series of lessons is the development of creative work in music, such as composing, the working musical model (Table 14.2) illustrates how some of the musical examples can benefit from the application of the model. During the passive learning phase, the learner listens, observes, and perhaps plays a song arrangement. Parts of other related tunes could also be explored and examined for shape, pattern etc. so that the term 'sequence' is

Table 14.2 A model of interaction for teaching and learning in the music classroom

Teacher	Phase of powerful learning environment	Learner
active teaching sets tasks – compose 8 bar song using sequence, repetition and inversion demonstrates Performs existing song Provides exemplars – suggest other exemplars	MODELLING teacher regulated learning	*passive learning* listens, observes, Participates in performance
active teaching supports the learner – suggests strategies, ideas asks questions defines goals – reminds learner of sequence, plays excerpt provides further exemplars offers contingent instruction provides supporting material – offers chord scheme plays backing track	SCAFFOLDING mediated learning	*active learning* attempts task tries out initial ideas performs melody of song with teacher answers teacher's questions
active teaching encouragement hints and guidance helps answer questions helps test hypothesis	COACHING mediated learning	*active learning* defines own questions – possible combinations of phrases answers own questions – limits number of combinations refines response to task develops hypothesis – template for 8 bar scheme seeks help from others (peers, teachers) – plays ideas with others Adds chords
passive teaching ready to offer guidance and support listens, observes, practical involvement	FADING self-regulated learning	*active learning* evaluates hypothesis – listens critically to structure, effect of 8 bars tests possible solutions – suggests and plays other ideas, new ideas

fully understood before moving on to create a new one. The teacher continues supporting the learning by asking questions and offering additional support in the form of suggested patterns or starting notes. Advice might be offered in the form of short musical examples or spoken comments. As students begin to suggest their own possible combinations of phrases the teacher can offer help and encouragement as both move toward the end of the mediated learning phase of the process and begin to test and help test new ideas. Finally, students listen critically to the structure of their response and perhaps play and evaluate some new ideas. A passive teaching role is adopted as students become responsible for their own learning. Peer learning and support is also allowed for in the model, particularly in the scaffolding and coaching stages as opportunities occur quite naturally during informal lunchtime and after school sessions when youngsters gather together to make music and learn from one another.

This model will help the teacher to deploy effective communication with the learner and remind the teacher to allow the learner to communicate verbally, musically and with any other means at their disposal in order to indicate the amount of teaching – passive or active – required at any given stage. Such two-way communication throughout the learning process should ensure that effective communication produces effective learning.

Conclusion

Learning in the music classroom is a complex business, and we have seen that both the learner and the teacher play various roles in the learning process. Movement through the zone of proximal development is crucial if the learner is to be kept on task, interested and motivated. The four stages of the powerful learning environment show that teachers and students continually change the way they interact with one another. Awareness of the model of interaction for teaching and learning in the classroom highlights for the teacher the different types of communication needed. Opportunities for scaffolding which may, in the past, have been missed, may now form a key part of teaching in the music classroom. The model may help teachers plan a series of lessons for whole classes or small groups and individuals since the stimulus, exemplar and support materials for possible scaffolding, and further targets and activities for pupils can all be prepared in advance.

The model may help teachers plan a series of lessons for whole classes, small groups, and individuals as the starting point, or exemplar material (modelling), support material for possible scaffolding and further targets and activities for pupils can all be prepared in advance.

Musical communication in the music classroom is multifaceted, and the importance of music teachers' awareness of the role they play in creating, setting, directing, mediating, and regulating the learning environment for young learners in music has been highlighted. While music teachers would expect to have a clear idea of what they wish to achieve in the classroom, it is also reasonable to expect learners to know what is required of them and the proposed teaching and learning model provides various signposts for classes, groups, and individuals.

We have seen that there is much value in questioning in the classroom, that children learn well when they ask questions, and that teachers teach well when they ask the right questions. Helping children learn to formulate their own questions and to develop and test their own hypotheses ensures that ownership of the learning process does not rest solely with the teacher. Teachers are sensitive to the needs and abilities of individuals and are aware of the level of development or 'growing edge' of children. Teachers who wish to develop the potential for peer learning in the classroom might study the proposed model and use it to reflect upon their current practice. Teacher educators might also consider the model outlined here and the theories discussed since, as gatekeepers of music education, they are well placed to introduce student teachers to models of teaching and learning which may be suited to their skills and abilities.

References

Bereiter, C. and Scardamalia, M. (1993) *Surpassing ourselves: an inquiry into the nature and implications of expertise.* Chicago, IL: Open Court.

Bliss, J., Askew, M., and MacRae, S. (1996) Effective Teaching and Learning: scaffolding revisited, *Oxford Review of Education,* 22(1), 37–61.

Brookfield, S. (1985) 'Self-directed learning: a critical review of research'. In *Self-directed Learning: from theory to practice,* (ed. S. Brookfield), pp. 5–16. *New Directions for Continuing Education no.25.* San Francisco, CA: Jossey-Bass.

Byrne, C. (1996) The use of pattern and echo in developing the creative abilities of secondary school pupils, *British Journal of Music Education,* 13(2), 143–54.

Byrne, C., Halliday, J., Sheridan, M., Soden, R., and Hunter, S. (2001) Thinking Music Matters: Key Skills and Composition. *Music Education Research,* 3(1), 63–75.

Byrne, C. and Sheridan, M. (1998) Music: a source of deep imaginative satisfaction? *British Journal of Music Education,* 15(3), 295–301.

Byrne, C. and Sheridan, M. (2000) The Long and Winding Road: The Story of Rock Music in Scottish Schools. *International Journal of Music Education,* 36, 46–57.

Byrne, C. and Sheridan, M. (2001) The SCARLATTI Papers: development of an action research project in music. *British Journal of Music Education,* 18(2), 171–183.

Candy, P.C. (1991) *Self-direction for Lifelong Learning.* San Francisco, CA: Jossey-Bass.

Choksy, L., Abramson, R.M., Gillespie, A.E., and Woods, D. (1986) *Teaching Music in the Twentieth Century.* Englewood Cliffs, NJ: Prentice-Hall.

DeCorte, E. (1990) Towards powerful learning environments for the acquisition of problem solving skills. *European Journal of Psychology of Education* , 5, 5–19.

Fisher, R. (1995) *Teaching Children to Learn.* Cheltenham: Stanley Thornes.

Gellrich, M. and Sundin, B. (1993/94) Instrumental Practice in the 18th and 19th Centuries. *Bulletin of the Council for Research in Music Education.* IV, 137–45.

Goldsworthy, D. (1997) Teaching gamelan in Australia: some perspectives on cross-cultural music education. *International Journal of Music Education*, **30**, 3–14.

Greenfield, P.M. (1984) A Theory of the Teacher in the Learning Activities of Everyday Life. In *Everyday Cognition: Its Development in Social Context*, (eds B. Rogoff and J. Lave), pp. 117–38. Cambridge, MA: Harvard University Press.

Kreber, C. (1998) The relationships between self-directed learning, critical thinking, and psychological type, and some implications for teaching in higher education. *Studies in Higher Education*, **23**, 1, 71–86.

McGuinness, C. and Nisbet, J. (1991) Teaching Thinking in Europe. *British Journal of Educational Psychology*, **61**, 174–86.

Mezirow, J. (1985) 'A critical theory of self-directed learning'. In *Self-directed Learning: from theory to practice*, (ed. S. Brookfield), pp. 5–16. *New Directions for Continuing Education no.25*. San Francisco, CA: Jossey-Bass.

Newman, D., Griffin, P., and Cole, M. (1989) *The Construction Zone – Working for Cognitive Change in School*. Cambridge, Cambridge University Press.

Odam, G. (1995) *The Sounding Symbol*. Cheltenham: Stanley Thornes.

Paynter, J. (2000) Making progress in composing. *British Journal of Music Education*, **17**(1), 5–31.

Rogoff, B. (1984) Introduction: Thinking and Learning in Social Context. In *Everyday Cognition: Its Development in Social Context*, (eds B. Rogoff and J. Lave), pp. 1–8. Cambridge, MA: Harvard University Press.

Scottish office Education Department (1992) *Expressive Arts: 5–14, National Guidelines*. Edinburgh: HMSO.

Scottish Examination Board. (1988) *Scottish Certificate of Education: Standard Grade Arrangements in Music*. Dalkeith, Scottish Examination Board.

Sheridan, M. and Byrne, C. (2002) Music Education. In *Scottish Education*, (eds T.D.G. Bryce and W.M. Humes), (second edition) 575–9. Edinburgh: Edinburgh University Press.

Stannard, K. (2003) *Junior Voiceworks*. Oxford: Oxford University Press.

Sternberg, R.J. (1994) Answering Questions and Questioning Answers: Guiding Children to Intellectual Excellence. *Phi Delta Kappan* **76**(2), 136–8.

Stock, J. (2002) Concepts of world music and their integration within western secondary education. In *Aspects of Teaching Secondary Music: Perspectives on practice*, (ed. G. Spruce), pp. 182–96. London: Routledge Falmer.

Stock, J. (2003) Music education: perspectives from current ethnomusicology. *British Journal of Music Education*, **20**(2), 121–45.

Swanwick, K. (1999) *Teaching Music Musically*. London: Routledge.

Vygotsky, L.S. (1978) *Mind in Society: The Development of Higher Psychological Processes*. Cambridge, MA: Harvard University Press.

Williams, W.M. and Sternberg, R.J. (1993) Seven Lessons for Helping Children Make the Most of Their Abilities. *Educational Psychology*, **13**(3&4), 317–31.

Wood, D.J., Bruner, J.S., and Ross, G. (1976) The role of tutoring in problem solving. *Journal of Child Psychology and Psychiatry*, 17, 89–100.

Wood, D. and Wood, H. (1996) Vygotsky, Tutoring and Learning, *Oxford Review of Education*, Vol. **22**(1), 5–16.

Chapter 15

Talking about music: a vehicle for identity development

Raymond MacDonald, Dorothy Miell, and Graeme Wilson

Introduction

This chapter considers a rather different aspect of musical communication from others in this volume. Rather than examining how music itself communicates, we will be considering the ways in which *talk about* music can be seen as integral to musical communication, since such talk is seen to serve a number of important personal, social, and musical functions for people. Even amongst groups of musicians who work and perform together, many find that talking about music – as distinct from playing music – constitutes a considerable volume of their interaction time together as musicians; during a tour, for example, bands are likely to spend more time in conversation about music than actually playing together.

The social constructionist model of communication adopted here is one in which talk is seen as a tool of social action – people are seen as being able to achieve certain personal and social ends through their talk (Edwards and Potter 1992; Potter and Wetherell 1987), rather than using it purely as a means of transmitting information. When individuals describe their tastes and interests in music, for example, this model suggests that they are not only conveying to other people certain information about their particular preferences for a musician, band, or piece of music, but also that they are doing some important personal 'business' by positioning themselves (e.g. as 'knowledgeable fans') in relation to others (Wetherell and Maybin 1996). This model of communication suggests that the meaning of any particular talk will vary according to the context in which it is said, and the perspectives of the people involved (Antaki 1998). For example, someone listening in on musicians talking about a particular performance could take a very different meaning from what they say than might those who were involved with the performance themselves – the same words would convey very different information to the different audiences.

This model of communication also challenges the traditional distinction between talk about a world 'out there', and talk about our own internal world of thoughts and motivations, suggesting instead that the way people build arguments and express themselves about a range of issues (such as, in the instances we are interested in here, their views on various musical genres, and on their involvement in musical activities) characterizes them in a particular way and attempts to avoid less desirable characterisations (Billig 1997). As a result, communication is not seen as simply a vehicle that transparently conveys thoughts and views between people, but as a system that is *actively used* to construct both the world and the self within dialogue (Edwards and Potter 1992). If a large proportion of musicians' interaction is through talk, this model of communication has important implications for any research on their musical interaction. According to this model, a musician's awareness or understanding of another's musicality, or of their musical goals in common, will inevitably be shaped by the identity work taking place in their conversations (Munro 2005).

We will be considering examples of such communication from two British data sets: one from interviews with young people who are involved with music making in their own free time outside school (e.g. with rock bands and choirs) and another from focus groups and interviews with professional jazz musicians. Whilst these two groups have a number of rather different experiences in music, we will see that many of the same processes can be seen in extracts of the discourse from both data sets – for example through their talk they can be observed to claim membership of communities that they value and/or aspire to, and to work to avoid identification with less desirable groups.

In talking about music, people are both signalling their membership of and also contributing to a 'community of reasoners' – a community of likeminded others:

'...to think or to reason well in a situation is, by definition, to take on the forms as well as the substance of a community of reasoners and thus to join that community. Much of discourse, and thus [much] of cognition serves to situate an individual with respect to others, to establish a social role or identity' (Resnick, Pontecorvo, and Saljo 1997, p. 9 in Light and Littleton 1999, p. 99). This view of talk as a means through which people establish their identities (and, through talk about music, to establish their musical identities) allows us to gain an interesting insight into the functions of this form of musical communication. When people mark themselves out in their talk as, for example, an 'aficionado', 'amateur', or 'professional' these are in fact artificial categories and only exist in talk in order to perform the function of identity positioning relative to others. Involvement in the production of music might be conceived of as ranging from singing along with a radio on one's own, through karaoke or jamming at parties, to public performances with amateur orchestras and/or professional playing. Marking out categories of musical involvement in this way is an interpretative act, however; membership of any category is not an individual attribute, though it is often treated as such. Part of the process of musical identity production is to control the reception of talk by stipulating one's relationship to it (hence the common phrase 'I'm not really a musician, but ...'). Thus we saw the woman cited in Graham Welch's chapter earlier in this volume state that "when I go home to Barbados I am a 'singer' – I'm just not a 'singer' in this country".

There may also appear to be a distinction between 'listeners' and 'players', yet this is not a simple dichotomy either. Fans of music become knowledgeable enough about, for example, riffs, lyrics, or hook lines to be able to 'quote' them to each other, using recognition ('you know that one too!') or the resulting process of explanation (e.g. 'you must know that, it's on "Pretzel Logic"...'). This can cement or build a common identity. Their talk about music is characterized by considerable assumed knowledge. In the above example, mentioning the name of the album 'Pretzel Logic', by the US group Steely Dan, suggests that the listener can access a body of implicit knowledge. Fans in this instance are likely to prize the recognition of common tastes and practices in their communication partners' contributions. Talk about music, then, functions both to categorize the spectrum of involvement in music and position oneself and others on it; and to engage with, and signal membership of, the 'community of reasoners' associated with that position (Fischlin and Heble 2004). As such, talk about music can be seen as an important element in the production of music and musical identities (MacDonald and Miell 2002; Monson 1996). Musicians who play professionally (perhaps particularly in some genres such as jazz and rock) will also spend time discussing their listening, when they talk about favourite albums, musicians or musical practices. Thus, although we are suggesting there may be a distinction between 'listeners' and 'players', these two categories are by no means mutually exclusive.

In the following sections we give examples of these processes from two groups we have recently studied – young people talking about their extra-mural musical activities, and professional jazz musicians. These two groups were chosen for discussion here as they provide insights into different aspects of engagement with music. The young people were all involved in music at school, but also took part in a range of other voluntary musical activities such as being members of rock bands, musical theatre, and choirs in their spare time. They also spent a considerable amount of time listening to music and talking about it with their friends and family. They were aged between 13 and 16, were contacted through notices in youth clubs and music centres, and were interviewed individually about their musical tastes and interests, their views about school music lessons, and their involvement in musical activities outside school. The second data set came from a series of focus groups and interviews with professional jazz musicians. One focus group comprized five male participants: one drummer, one trumpeter, a guitarist, and two bass players, ranging in age from early 20s to mid-60s. The second focus group comprised six participants, again all male: two trumpeters, two saxophonists, a drummer and a bass player, all in their mid-20s except for one musician of 37. A further series of semi-structured individual interviews was conducted with 10 (6 male and 4 female) professional UK jazz musicians. In both studies, the conversations were tape recorded and transcribed. Following repeated inspection of the transcripts, researchers coded the data under individually developed categories representing emergent themes. Extracts from the talk included below are examples of these themes. Using thematic analysis techniques (Denzin and Lincoln 1998), these categorizations were then compared and refined into a single system and checked back for consistency against the data. The analysis examined ways in which the participants' talk about their involvement in musical activities (including listening) constructed and maintained particular musical identities, and in particular how they used their talk about music to claim and mark their relationship to various communities such as knowledgeable others.

Signalling membership of musical communities

Young people's accounts

The young people who were interviewed used their talk about their tastes in music and their accounts of their involvement in musical activities to locate themselves and others, especially their peers, within various musical communities. This is not surprising, since as Cook (1998) noted, 'In today's world, deciding what music to listen to is a significant part of deciding and announcing to people not just who you 'want to be' … but who you *are*. 'Music' is a very small word to encompass something that takes as many forms as there are cultural or sub-cultural identities' (p. 5, cited in MacDonald and Miell 2002). In this way, by claiming membership of various sub-cultures, music can be seen to act as a resource used by the young people in their ongoing construction and presentation of self. This activity is an almost all-consuming preoccupation throughout the teenage years, when young people are exploring, trying out, and rejecting a range of different possible identities. In a series of studies by North and Hargreaves and colleagues (North *et al.* 2000; Tarrant *et al.* 2000), adolescents were asked to comment on the extent to which possible reasons for listening to music applied to them. These researchers found that in both UK and US populations, the factor that explained most of the variance in responses was one labelled 'impression management', which included agreement with statements such as 'I listen to music in order to create a particular self-image', 'I listen to be trendy/cool', and 'I listen in order to please others (e.g. peers)'. These young people are achieving a great deal through their engagement with music, notably in managing their self-presentation and sense of identity in relation to their peer group.

If we turn to look at what the young people said in their interviews, we can see that signalling membership of particular groups involved not only listening to particular music but also, at least for some groups, wearing identifiable clothing and accessories (e.g. Andy, in the extract below, talks about the 'chains and studs' worn by those who like heavy metal music). There were interesting differences, however, in the ways in which they interpreted their own behaviour and that of others, especially of others who they saw as less musically knowledgeable than themselves. When explaining how these others signal their membership of groups by listening to particular genres of music and, linked to this, wearing a recognizable style of dress associated with that genre, all those we interviewed signalled their disapproval of this form of 'slavish' following of what they saw as fashion-based peripheral features of the music rather than knowledge and appreciation of music itself:

Extract 1[1]:

Andy:	I mean, people who get into music for an example and they get into it because it's a cool thing to do, like people are branded in a huge hideous sort of (·) they, you know, they don't have any idea about the band they're into or what they're trying to put across with their music, it's just purely (x) and it's all
Researcher:	So it's like an identity thing?
Andy:	Yeah it's like (·)
Researcher:	People keep telling me this, it's all kind of like groups of people who dress a certain way and act a certain way, and listen to certain types of music
Andy:	Yeah, if you're heavy metal it's huge chains and studs, I'm mean if you're a proper (x) that's cool but if you're just someone who's tagging along, you know, sheep in the flock as you do, it's fake.

It was certainly more important for the young people we interviewed to stake claims for authentic, individual, often idiosyncratic musical tastes than

---

[1] See appendix for transcription key

to be seen as 'following the crowd' in the way that they saw less knowledgeable others doing. As we see below, they preferred to display their individuality by claiming tastes that they did not associate with 'the masses'. The notion of individuality is evident in Katia's claim that she is 'less likely to be swayed by something that everyone else likes' and her search for new bands or sounds that she can make her 'own':

Extract 2:

Katia:	Yeah, I often sort of, find myself quite em encouraged to find out new bands, or sort of new sounds or something and say 'what's that?' and then I listen to it. So (·)
Researcher:	Yeah
Katia:	I mean if you've got quite a diverse taste in music you can't, it can't be given to you in any way
Researcher:	mmm
Katia:	So you have to look for it yourself but even so, sort of, you're proud when you've found something (·) something else you can sort of make your own

As John explains below, he listened to Nirvana initially in order to claim a 'rebellious' and 'cool' identity, but later stopped when 'everyone else' started to listen to it as well – he wanted to avoid the imputation of just being 'one of a crowd' of fans:

Extract 3:

| John: | there's loads of people into Nirvana and stuff – and that's probably why I don't listen to it any more. I started to listen to it when I was 12, and it was quite rebellious and cool to listen to it then … and then like everyone else started listening to it so I just felt like 'everyone else is listening to it – I'm going to stop listening to it' [...] and then I got into this kind of weird stuff and [...] other people kind of (·) respect it and stuff but I mean (·) I don't know – I just think it's too challenging for people who just want to kind of sit there |

His change of taste towards what he calls 'weird stuff' (he later explains that it is a genre called industrial music that he is referring to here) communicates to others that he is distinctive and unusual. By explaining how 'challenging' and 'weird' it is, he also claims an identity as a knowledgeable music listener – he can appreciate the type of music that those 'who just want to kind of sit there' with music on purely as a background wouldn't understand. John wasn't alone in making these sorts of claims in his talk about what he sees as his sophisticated music tastes. Below, Ossie explains how he has developed a taste for 'very underground hip hop', which necessitated deliberate efforts on his part to cultivate an appreciation of 'quite obscure, hard to listen to things' by 'very clever musicians' – things that 'a lot of people' wouldn't like.

Extract 4:

Ossie: I was sort of growing into hip hop, very underground hip hop, which, so, quite obscure, hard to listen to things, like people like James Ravell and people like that who are actually very clever musicians to be able to make the tunes that they do, and drum and bass – I know a lot of people don't like it but I think it's good

Inherent in these accounts is the importance of appreciating complexity, often through effortful engagement with music that involves shunning what Andy earlier said the 'sheep in the flock' listened to. This was particularly the case with those who were actively involved in music making through membership of bands. However, the young people we interviewed *were* sometimes keen to associate with the tastes of others – but only when those others were friends or members of a group that they aspired to belong to, and were happy to be publicly identified with:

Extract 5:

Craig: most musicians tend to like the same sort of thing, for example everyone at the Academy who I know likes Jamiroquai, but a lot of people who don't play instruments don't – it's probably because of some of the musical aspects of their music – it's got quite a lot of depth to it – a lot of the chords might sound a little weird to people […] a lot of their music is really complicated'.

Once again we see positive reference being made to music that is 'weird' – that is, appreciating music that most (implication, less musical) people would not understand because it is too complex. In such ways, young people talking about their musical tastes can be seen to be communicating about music in a multi-faceted way that suggests that a number of complex psychological processes are at work. They are doing more than straightforwardly conveying information about their preferred bands – they are actively claiming certain desirable identities ('musical', 'unique', 'passionate about music', 'sophisticated') and resisting problematic ones ('sheep in the flock', 'not serious listener', 'most people'). As Dan explains later, such distinctions may not be evident in observed behaviour – he and his sister listen to music about as much as each other, but he believes that there is a difference in their appreciation and understanding. He is carefully presenting himself as different from her – by talking about the apparent similarities in their observed behaviour whilst making a point about his greater musical understanding or appreciation by drawing attention to the subtle differences between them – he is saying that he is more discriminating than her.

Extract 6:

> Dan: My sister listens to a lot of music but (·) probably just as much as me (·) but I can tell that there's something (·) not quite [...] she's just sort of willing to let anything play in the background

It is clear that in their talk about music they can display their musical dedication and commitment, which contrasts so much with those others who they believe, like Dan's sister, just 'let anything play'. John and Dave both talk about how important and personal music is for them and how this contrasts with less committed others:

Extract 7:

> Dave: They aren't sort of strongly into music as much as I am I don't think (·) I mean they like music but they're not really (·) they are not exactly passionate about it

Extract 8:

> John: Music is my life

The young people talked about the need for similar levels of passion and commitment from other members of their bands if they were going to work together successfully. There were many disparaging comments about band members who failed to attend practices, or who didn't take their share of the work of arranging gigs or rehearsals. Along with this commitment, however, the young people also explained the need for both trust between band members (in order to allow the sort of risk taking that led to creative music making) and a level of technical proficiency that enabled all members to contribute successfully. As Rachel explains, band members need to be at least 'mediumly good':

Extract 9:

> Rachel: the first three times [at 'young band' workshops] it was excellent, it was just really good cos it was just a major jamming session [...] and we [her band] sort of got together through fun, like having a laugh. It wasn't like, 'oh we've got to do music', it was more, 'oh let's go and have fun', which sounds really weird, but it was just like that at the time.
>
> Interviewer: Well, that's what works.
>
> Rachel: Yeah, cos that got the trust between us, but gradually now more people come, that's sort of gone (·) The people that have come now are really shy and they don't want to say much about their opinion, about anything really, and that sort of, they really want to be there to sing, but you can't say (·) you expect them to be mediumly good singers.
>
> Interviewer: But they are not?
>
> Rachel: There's like two of them that just aren't (·) they are not really good at anything really, which sounds really bad, but it's true.

And in the extract below from John's interview he sees a different role for his two fellow band members – his friend Mike is there because he is a friend who John trusts to say what sounds good, but Mike is clearly not as proficient an instrumentalist, songwriter, or improviser as the drummer Jim or indeed as John himself:

Extract 10:

> John: […] we just have our little Sunday jams and I'll have been writing during the week and I'll kind of go along […] and I'll have written Mike's, the other guitarist's part and I'll give it to him. And then me and Jim, I mean Jim is our drummer I mean he's pretty mental, I mean he's really good, I mean he's a grade A drummer, so I mean I don't really need to tell him what to do (·) me and Mike maybe say what sounds good and stuff (·) the thing is like our guitarist [Mike] isn't that good. And em there might be reasons why like he's in the band cause like he's a really good friend of mine, he's a really good friend of Jim's, so we kind of (·) it's not like he's a charity or anything, we want him to be in the band, but I don't think he's that good at writing stuff

In the following extracts from jazz musicians we will see similar careful balancing between the benefits of working with known others and with those who are seen as highly competent.

Talk about music between young people, then, can be seen to be used in order to protect, claim, or resist various musical identities. These identities are used not only to differentiate the self from some ostensibly similar individuals but also to position the self as like certain desirable others. If, as was argued in the introduction to this chapter, involvement in music represents a continuum, we might expect to find similar functions of talk about music when we look at the ways in which professional musicians operate within their community of reasoning.

Accounts of professional jazz musicians

In this section, we will consider how individual UK jazz musicians treat the social context of their music in relation to their musical practice. We shall then show how their discussions of music and musical practice are characterized by implicit knowledge and the establishment of musical common ground. Finally, we shall examine how a community of reasoners is thus constituted in discourse in the pursuit of identity production.

In their talk in the individual interviews, the jazz musicians we spoke to affirmed the idea of a musical community linked to the music they played, much as the young people identified communities based around their own listening and playing practices. While these two data sets come from very different populations, we suggest that the extracts presented here share a number of important common features. In both the young people's interviews and the following extracts from jazz musicians' conversations, we see how individuals use talk about music to construct and negotiate identities that are inextricably linked to their musical tastes and preferences. Moreover, for both these populations, their musical identities are crucially intertwined with a social and cultural milieu that is constantly evolving (MacDonald and Miell 2000). It is thus useful to present two apparently diverse data sets together; and taking a qualitative discursive approach also allows us to investigate the functions of communicating about music in these populations in significant detail.

Extract 11:

> Most of the people I hang around with or meet occasionally are, if not players, people who like the music. That's my circle because that's where I move. And then I have others who really don't like my playing but they're my friends, they like me and they think it's okay that I do it but they don't want to listen to it. But if I play a love song for them when I'm in a good mood that makes them happy for a while. (10)

The working practice of professional jazz musicians whose principal income is from performance involves few regular line-ups. Most of those operating on a freelance basis play regularly, with little or no rehearsal, in groups put together according to who is available on that date (Wilson and MacDonald, 2005). It is not unusual for musicians to meet each other for the first time as they are about to perform together. Successful performance in this milieu, in which a group activity depends on the collaboration of interchangeable individuals, is accounted for by musicians as being dependent on objective qualities of musicianship. This ethos of professional status as a jazz musician being meritocratic has been noted elsewhere (MacDonald and Wilson, 2005). Such an account is furthermore treated as communal reasoning; the idea that being a 'busy' musician equates with being a 'good' musician is implicitly assumed to be axiomatic, as the following extract demonstrates:

Extract 12:

> So I think it works both ways as to people enjoying it and also, you know (·) But I suppose the way to measure that is "are you working?" because if people didn't like it, you wouldn't be working. (1)

In extract 12, the speaker's use of the second person – '**you** wouldn't be working'- implies that this rating applies not just to him, but to *any* jazz musician. Meritocracy is therefore treated as a commonplace among the jazz community. However, he also aligns himself as someone who shares this commonplace view –'I suppose'. In effect, recounting this piece of reasoning in this way works both to define the point of view of a professional community and to position the speaker himself as a member of such a community. This account of prowess as a jazz musician is strongly individualistic.

However, the musical identities revealed in these interviews also tended to be based on the idea of belonging to a community of musicians with common practices (rather than membership of a particular band, more characteristic of rock or pop musicians, for example):

Extract 13:

> [...] there are people who improvise a lot on violin but most of them are in the kind of Celtic music tradition. That's kind of very different sound and you've got people on the Grappelli (·) the Grappelli thing and play all the sort of different licks and (·) Hang around with people with all the same model guitar you know. So it's kind of really boxed in and kind of I think I've got a different sound to that. Because I try and do sort of straight-ahead, jazzy-type stuff. (3)

The community may be treated as subdivided by particular factions. In the same way that Ossie (extract 4) differentiates hip hop and drum and bass enthusiasts, the speaker in extract 13 makes distinctions between groupings of 'Celtic', 'Grappelli', or 'jazzy-type' improvizers.

Although it may be a professional requirement for jazz musicians to be able to play with strangers, those we spoke to often prized working with people they saw as part of their own enclave within the jazz community. This could have varied implications for professional life:

Extract 14:

> But often the people in your inner group are people that you also socialise with and you do identify the groups. So there's a lot of grouping. Lots of small sub-divisions within the jazz scene and very often the people you work with are the people you hang with. Definitely. There's a lot of that. You know. And I guess it's because creating together is about creating that trust. You have to really (·) you trust people and (·) I mean having said that, yeah, I suppose that also some (·) you know (·) some people don't book people that, they're really close. They book people because they're just really good but they might not have that connection with. (8)

In the aforementioned extract, the speaker initially suggests that a jazz musician will 'work with the people you hang with' since 'creating together is about creating that trust'. Yet in the young people's accounts (see extracts 9 and 10), it was seen that there was a balance to be struck between wanting to play with those who were known and trusted yet needing band members who were good enough to play with the others and enhance the music. Similarly, the speaker in Extract 14 subsequently qualifies her endorsement of playing with those you know ('having said that') by proposing that sometimes musicians book each other 'because they're really good', whether they have a 'connection' with each other or not. Such wavering demonstrates that musicians playing in the jazz milieu may express differing rationales for why they play together, depending on the identity they wish to construct in that context – as a 'member of a fraternity' (or sorority), or a 'freelancer' of competitive quality.

Reasoning as a jazz musician (seen in the speaker's use of 'you' and 'they' rather than 'I') the same speaker below also talks about these alternative rationales for playing together – 'identity/history in common', *vs* 'objective quality as a musician'. This interplay of reasoning when positioning self and others was described by the interviewee as integral to playing together.

Extract 15:

> Q. What's it like the first time you improvise a song or if you play with a musician you've not played with before on a jazz gig?
>
> A. Oh it's exciting. It's always exciting meeting new people and that's the best thing about the jazz scene is. You think you know everybody, but then you know, somebody comes along and it's like "oh wow, you've learnt to play" and it's just (·) it's just great to always meet new people. You always meet new people. So when you first play with somebody (·) well, I guess (·) there's part of you that is (·) that just wants to enjoy their playing but there's also part of you that's saying "okay, could I play with this" (·) you know, "is this somebody whose number I want to take and do they want to take my number?" There's all those sort of things so it's about where you put them in relation to you musically. Are they from a similar planet, kind of thing. You know. So yeah, because you're always looking for people, you know, that's like in life isn't it? You know. You're drawn to people who think like you and have similar values. (8)

The speaker here describes simultaneous processes of evaluating and appreciating another musician's playing; while enjoying another's playing, one would also 'put them in relation to you musically'. This tension may be experienced internally, or individually, as Sawyer (1992) suggests; but might also be expected to have implications for the interpersonal processes of collaborative music-making. These processes are crucial to the broad theme of musical communication in a number of ways. Critiquing and appreciating a co-performer's playing in situ will influence the nature of an individual's own musical contribution, and thus fundamentally influence the nature of the musical communication processes. Thus, it is possible to experience uncertainty in connection with which of the two possible options – playing with those you know, or playing with those who are 'best' – is appropriate. Moreover, in the earlier two extracts, the speaker vacillates between the two, and in Extract 15 describes experiencing this uncertainty while playing. Neither emerges as the definitive basis for playing together; hence they are 'alternative rationales'.

Extract 16:

> I've been in situations with drummers where they have a certain preconception about how you play, like they might have heard me play on a lot of very straight-ahead things so they think [names himself] is a very straight-ahead British mainstream pianist so they play like that (1)

In Extract 16, a particular identity ('straight-ahead British mainstream pianist') is treated as a possible version of self, one that evokes a particular musical response from others ('they play like that'). However, the speaker positions himself separately from this identity, describing it as a 'preconception'; he implies that being a straight ahead mainstream player is only *one* way that he might be seen. In such instances of talk, musicians indicate not only that musical activity can be shaped by perceptions of identity amongst those taking part, but that those identities do not represent an essential self.

In all the material discussed so far, identity as a jazz musician tends to be supported by claims of what 'you' (i.e. jazz musicians) would do in this identity, and the treatment of such claims as commonplaces (e.g. 'you're **always** looking for new people', extract 15 above, emphasis added) In the following extract, the speaker outlines the reasoning underlining diverse claims of identity in relation to jazz, employing some deft attribution in relation to supposed other groups of musicians:

Extract 17:

> Also you find a lot of non-jazz musicians are quite intimidated by some jazz musicians because they feel (·) the amount of times I've had people say to me, various guitarists or keyboard players or whatever, "oh yeah, well, you know...". There's a few things. There's the argument "well I could have gone into jazz but there's no money in it", or there's "I never learnt all my Charlie Parker solos so I can't play jazz". Sometimes you get the feeling that people are at ease with it, and constructively in admiration but they're not insecure in their own thing. Then you get some people that are insecure about their own thing and they make some excuse why they don't want to play jazz rather than saying "it's just not something I do", which is fair enough. Certainly I'm not going to bother about it (1)

A series of generalized accounts are attributed by this speaker to musicians who do not play jazz, in order to explain why they do not. In doing so, an opposite list is implied as a commonplace definition of *being* a jazz musician – no money, have learnt all Charlie Parker solos, secure in playing jazz as their own thing. He also casts these qualities as positive strengths of musical identity within a jazz context, positioning some generalized others in a curious formulation as being 'constructively in admiration' of jazz players, or even 'intimidated' by them. Yet by suggesting that he is paraphrasing what has often been said to *him* in the past by non-jazz players ('the amount of times I've had people say to me') the speaker aligns himself with the jazz musician qualities that these generalized others have distinguished themselves from; he positions himself as someone whom non-jazz musicians address as a jazz musician.

The picture emerging from the individual interviews with UK jazz musicians is of a broad sub-cultural community defined by a music – jazz. Among the musicians themselves, 'factions' or sub-communities are formed according to shared tastes or practices. A tension emerges between a stated preference for playing with others of one's sub-community, and the ethos that employment should be meritocratic. Improvising with unfamiliar musicians thus involves simultaneous processes of appreciation and evaluation. However, these may not be directly voiced by the musicians to each other. Attributions of identity can affect how musicians play together, and involve the use of reasoning that is treated as commonplace among jazz musicians. This may be facilitated by a tendency to assume implicit knowledge (MacDonald and Wilson, in press). The nature of the musical environment in which jazz musicians work (e.g. a strong emphasis on improvisation) creates assumptions amongst jazz musicians that their colleagues will understand certain key features of the music (e.g. play melody first and then improvize). These issues emerge in their talk with the assumption that they will be understood without an explicit statement of these features; i.e. they rely on shared implicit knowledge.

Examples from focus group interviews of talk between jazz musicians about their music show more clearly how the negotiation of that community may occur within musicians' own discourse to each other, and illustrate its reasoning in action:

Extract 18:

5	[...] People'll get up and play solos right outa context, it'll never <u>work</u>. It'll never <u>really</u> work properly unless the, whole fuckin' team's thegether.
4	Mm. Mmhm.
5	Music=
1	=An' they're all playin' the same tune ((couple of laughs))
5	All playin the same tune?
1	Well. Ye know. Ye cannae dae a solo over, a set of chords if the band's playin' a different set a chords ((general loud laughter))
2	((over laughter)) Right enough, I can tell ya -

In this exchange, the musicians reach a consensus on when improvisation is successful; their ability to do so is marked in their joint laughter, which illustrates their access to a common set of assumptions and knowledge. Everybody present has to show that they are able to find the idea of a band playing different sets of chords funny. There is, then, an assumption of implicit knowledge; to someone who did not claim identity as a jazz musician, it may not be clear why in a group improvisation everybody should stick to the same set of chords. Not doing so might even appear as a creative or individualistic strategy. By not explaining why this might be a recipe for musical disaster, speaker 5 positions all those present as individuals whose experience lets them appreciate that 'ye cannae dae that'. The general laughter and speaker 2's affirmation ('right enough') both serve to signal that they can share 5's understanding.

As well as presenting a particular understanding of how improvisation works, then, 5's statement carries out identity work in that it sets up a particular understanding of what it is to be a jazz musician, and positions that identity as applicable to all those present.

Implicit knowledge is also deployed where famous names are invoked. The conversation below taps into a recurrent argument among brass players over the relative merits of Miles Davis in relation to other famous jazz trumpeters:

Extract 19:

> Drummer: I mean we've sat and had Miles Davis on in our house an' you've said 'oh I can't listen to that because, because of his tone and everything'. Whereas for me I don't hear that it's just a voice //
>
> Tpter1:   Yeah but the thing is that that //
>
> Tpter 2:   Is it hard for you to listen to because you're a trumpeter?//
>
> Tpter 1:   Yeah oh yeah if I wasn't a trumpeter I would think it's fantastic like ehm I could listen to someone play the drums who wasn't quite on it and not notice //I dunno// like fluctuations in time if he was doin stuff that wasn't quite on it but you would instantly recognize that// but// but it might still appeal to you//

The drummer cites another participant stating dislike for Miles Davis 'because of his tone and everything'; without explaining any further, the drummer then states that he himself doesn't 'hear that'. While the conversation is dialogic at that point, it is being delivered in the context of a focus group interview. There is, therefore, an implicit assumption that those present will be able to receive the reference to wider criticisms of Davis as a brass player ('his tone and everything') as sufficient justification for a stated dislike of a trumpeter of considerable iconic status. Another participant, however, probes for further explanation. His question offers an account of this dislike that positions participant 1 according to a specific instrumental identity ('you're a trumpeter') and expands (perhaps for the purpose of the interview) on why 'it's just a voice' for the drummer. It also invokes a repertoire of common reasoning, according to which Davis' unconventional brass technique often leads experienced professionals to criticize what can be construed as 'flaws' in his playing (Cole 1974; Kernfeld 1995). Participant 1's reply signals strongly ('yeah oh yeah') that he is familiar with this line of argument and views it as an appropriate explanation here; he goes on to recast it in relation to drumming technique. This exchange above, then, shows musicians' implicit treatment of knowledge and reasoning as available to those with common identity as jazz musicians.

The final extract shows a sustained attempt to find a suitable way of explaining and accounting for the closure of an orchestra that manages to maintain and support a positive identity for jazz musicians that can be shared by those present.

Extract 20:

5	There <u>did</u>. There used to be the Radio, big band up here.
6	//((sighs)) Yeh.
5	//was a full time funded thing and the ((6 – yeh)) guys who were in it were piss artists and they wrecked it for everybody and the, the BBC shut it down. (·)
4	I don't think (·) the wh- the BBC shut it down for more than the reason everyone was drunk.
5	I don't think so. I think that was a big part of it.
3	Well they shut it down – they sh- shut it down –
4	There wasn't money for it, was there?
3	Well they shut it down because, em, what happened was they, they axed the, BBC Symphony Orchestra. And then all the musicians – from the, Symphony and the Radio Orchestra went and picketed outside the, BBC. But then – so the BBC saw this and says right we – we'll reinstate the symphony orchestra. But we'll get rid of the, radio orches-tra. And then when that happened, none of the symphony orchestra came out to picket with – the, the radio orchestra to help them –
5	Cause they got what they needed.
3	Cause they got – they then had what they needed and – That's actually what happened. 'S mental. ((…))
3	But they <u>were</u> pissed all the time as well. ((loud laughter, M2 & others))
5	I don't think that – I really don't think that//was the only cause of it, I really don't //think that at all cause I think that was like part of it.
6	//Maybe that's why they didn't turn up to the -
3	//Oh of course, yeh. Oh, yeh. Oh yeh. Oh totally is though totally. (·) Oh yeh.

The negotiation here proceeds through a series of identities for the jazz musicians in the former radio orchestra that are proposed to account for its demise. At first, they are portrayed as 'piss artists', blaming the closure on the failings of those jazz musicians in the old days. This runs the risk of casting an unfavourable light on the identity of the participants as current jazz musicians, however. Instead, it is suggested that the orchestra was unviable, blaming economic circumstances. But this would imply that being a jazz musician in a large, ongoing ensemble is unsustainable; again, not favourable to the professional identity of those present. Finally, blame is apportioned to the fickle nature of musicians in another ensemble, casting the jazz musicians in a nobler role as victims of a lack of solidarity. To authorize this version of events as the most authentic, the speaker presents a fuller narrative as the basis of his claim.

Conclusion

The material discussed in this chapter has highlighted a number of ways in which *talking about* music can be viewed as an important aspect of musical communication. For example, jazz musicians articulate conflicting priorities of social groupings and individual qualities to authorize their musical identities. To resolve this tension in their discourse, these musicians often resort to the same strategies as the young people whose accounts were presented earlier in this chapter. They shape a particular identity as positive and claim it for themselves, while positioning others as non-jazz musicians assigning them more negative identities. Yet the data here show that these identities are negotiated within the context of conversation. By negotiating what can be treated as commonplace, they arrive at a workable definition of identity as a jazz musician that enables them to treat each other as both social compatriots and a gathering of players of equivalent status. These identity needs for both subcultural membership and musical insight or authority are parallel to those of the Nirvana or Jamiroquai fans discussed earlier; whatever their level or stage of musical involvement, all use talk about music to shape and claim musical identities. Moreover, the discourse presented in this chapter not only functions to fulfil identity needs for the participants but it also helps to shape the participants' experiences of music itself. For example, laying claim to particular musical identities involves describing musical preferences and showing allegiances to particular cultural subgroups. Music listening for all individuals will then take place with reference to these particular subgroups, and the musical communication process is crucially influenced by the construction of musical identity highlighted in our selected extracts. Talking about music is a vitally important aspect of the overall process of musical communication and can illuminate, in many different ways, the power and richness of that process.

References

Antaki, C. (1998) Identity ascriptions and their time and place: 'Fagin' and 'The Terminally Dim'. In *Identities in talk*, (eds C. Antaki and S. Widddicombe), pp. 71–86. London: Sage Publications.

Billig, M. (1997) Rhetorical and discursive analysis: How families talk about the royal family. In *Doing qualitative analysis in psychology*, (ed. N. Hayes), pp. 39–54. Hove: Psychology Press.

Cole, B. (1974) *Miles Davies: A musical biography.* New York: Morrow Quill Paperbacks.

Cook, N. (1998) *Music: A very short introduction.* Oxford: Oxford University Press.

Denzin, N.K. and Lincoln, Y.S. (1998) *Collecting and interpreting qualitative materials.* London: Sage Publications.

Edwards, D. and Potter, J. (1992) *Discursive psychology.* London: Sage Publications.

Fischlin, D. and Heble, A. (2004) *The other side of nowhere: Jazz, improvisation and communities in dialogue.* Middletown, CT: Wesleyan University Press.

Kernfeld, B. (1995) *What to listen for in jazz.* New Haven, CT: Yale University Press.

Hargreaves, D.J. and North, A.C. (1997) *The social psychology of music.* London: Oxford University.

Light, P. and Littleton, K.S. (1999) *Social processes in children's learning*. Cambridge: Cambridge University Press.

MacDonald, R.A.R. and Miell, D. (2000) Creativity and music education: The impact of social variables. *International Journal of Music Education* **36**, 58–68.

MacDonald, R.A.R. and Miell, D. (2002) Music for individuals with special needs: A catalyst for developments in identity, communication and musical ability. In *Musical identities,* (eds R.A.R. MacDonald, D.J. Hargreaves, and D.E. Miell), pp. 163–179. Oxford: Oxford University Press.

MacDonald, R.A.R. and Wilson, G.B. (2005) The musical identities of professional jazz musicians: A focus group investigation. *Psychology of Music,* in press.

MacDonald, R.A.R. and Wilson, G.B. (in press) 'Constructions of jazz: How jazz musicians present their collaborative musical practice' *Musicae Scientiae*, in press, 2005.

Monson, I. (1996) *Saying something: Jazz improvisation and interaction*. Chicago, IL: University of Chicago Press.

Munro, G. (2005) I sing therefore I am: A discursive investigation of work, performance, and identity. Unpublished PhD thesis, University of Adelaide.

North, A.C., Hargreaves, D.J., and O'Neill, S. (2000) The importance of music to adolescents. *British Journal of Educational Psychology*, **70**, 255–72.

Potter, J. and Wetherell, M. (1987) *Discourse and social psychology*. London: Sage publications.

Wetherell, M. and Maybin, J. (1996) The distributed self: A social constructionist perspective. In *Understanding the self,* (ed. R. Stevens), pp. 219–81. London: Sage publications.

Sawyer, K. (1992) 'Improvisational creativity: An analysis of jazz performance'. *Creativity Research Journal*, **5**(3), 253–63.

Tarrant, M., North, A.C. and Hargreaves, D.J. (2000) 'English and American adolescents' reasons for listening to music'. *Psychology of Music*, **28**, 166–73.

Wilson, G.B. and MacDonald, R.A.R. (2005) 'The meaning of the blues: Musical identities in talk about jazz'. *Qualitative Research in Psychology,* in press.

Appendix - Transcription key

Participants were assigned an identifying letter (A, B, C ...) according to order of first contribution; moderators are indicated as M1 & M2. Spelling reflects participants' dialects.

(·)	pause
	pause of one second or longer
=	no pause between turns
//	overlap; next line starts here
...	omitted text from original transcript
(x)	unclear word or phrase – not transcribed

Emphasis in original speech indicated by underlining
LOUDER speech written in upper case
>Faster< speech enclosed thus.
Explanatory material is included within square brackets [ ]
Short interlocutory material is enclosed in doubled parentheses ((...)), with an attribution where possible.

Chapter 16

Hippies vs hip-hop heads: an exploration of music's ability to communicate an alternative political agenda from the perspective of two divergent musical genres

Janis McNair and John Powles

Introduction

The role and effectiveness of music in communicating and disseminating political ideas has resonance throughout the world. Historically, political songs, often inextricably linked with mass movements, have been used to provide a voice to the silenced, to sustain political campaigns, to express discontent, to generate support, to motivate, to provoke, to educate, and to mock. Political songs have reflected upon a multitude of concerns, both international and local, from worker's rights to civil rights, nationalism, peace movements, feminism, environmentalism and anti-globalization. Music and song can cause, facilitate, and reflect personal, social, cultural, and political change; music is a medium through which intentions and meanings can be shared and intellectual and emotional messages communicated. With specific reference to two very divergent musical genres – 1960s protest music and hip-hop – we will seek to examine the politicization of music and its impact on the audience. Both musical and lyrical qualities will be considered in their ability to inspire, inform, engage, and communicate with the listener. The two musical genres although disparate in time, musical form and sociological circumstances can be used together to demonstrate the capacity for music to communicate an alternative political agenda.

Our interest in the field of political song extends beyond these two genres; the aim of our work at the Centre for Political Song is to promote and foster an awareness of all forms of political song. Our collection contains material from almost all musical genres: popular music, punk, folk, hip hop, reggae, opera, world music and jazz. Woody Guthrie, Riot Grrrl, and Verdi exist side by side.

The Centre for Political Song was founded in January 2001 in Glasgow Caledonian University. Since its inception, the Centre has grown organically with a developing awareness that political song covers the whole political spectrum, ranging throughout time, and embracing all musical genres. Our emphasis throughout this chapter on the 1960s protest music and the hip hop is based partly on the authors' own affinities and experiences, and is used to support our conjecture that music, and more specifically politically edged lyrics, can function as agents of resistance and opposition. As the work of the Centre has developed, we have come to realize that music and song can be a political force even in the absence, partly or wholly, of overt political statement. For example the punk era in Britain in the 1980s – which spawned many classic political anthems such as *Anarchy in the UK*, *God Save the Queen* and *Ghost Town* – was a youth subculture identified by its distinct style, dress, language, and music. The music, although not wholly overtly political, was rendered political by its association with a movement, which emerged from the quagmire of Thatcher's Britain. Punk, as a musical genre, became a tool to communicate and motivate subversion, identity, and opposition.

Lyrical expression need not be the only means of communicating opposition – Elvis Presley's own brand of rock and roll in the late 1950s employed a musical statement and image to signify a spirit of anti-establishment rebellion. The explosion of dance culture in 1990s Britain signalled the emergence of a new youth movement founded on a spirit of euphoria and community spirit fuelled by the drug Ecstasy and repetitive beats. The essentially faceless nature of dance music, the absence of lyrical content, and the hedonism of the rave generation rendered the movement essentially apolitical. The 1994 Criminal Justice Act, which sought to criminalize the clubbing generation, injected the necessary oppositional fervour.

Music is used often to raise the profile of a political campaign: Billy Bragg and Paul Weller, and The Communards supported Labour's 1987 election campaign with the formation of Red Wedge. Stevie Wonder, Peter Tosh, The Specials, and Peter Gabriel contributed to the international campaign against Apartheid in South Africa with the hit songs *Apartheid (It's Wrong)*, *Fight Apartheid*, *Nelson Mandela*, *and Biko* respectively. The activities of Live Aid, Farm Aid, Rock Against Racism, The Concert for Bangladesh, and the recent Concert for New York (in honour of the New York Fire Fighters who worked at Ground Zero) are all relevant to the Centre's work.

The Centre for Political Song has therefore progressed from the simple collection and archiving of overt political statements and anthems. Our definition of a 'political song' assumes a very broad perspective – hence the collection of material held at the Centre is eclectic: international and local; well known and obscure; explicitly political or adopted and adapted for political purposes.

To help contextualize and emphasise the role of music and song in communicating political ideas, and in the evolution of politically defined subcultural movements, we will now examine our chosen subcultures in turn. However, an account of the efficacy of music, and more specifically politically charged lyrics, in communicating political ideas and aiding the development of oppositional identities must consider at the outset the impact of mainstream and commercial forces on the integrity of such music. The creation, recording, distribution, marketing, and performance of music and the appreciation and interpretation of such music must be considered in developing an understanding of the way in which music communicates with the listener. The potential to communicate a message to a wide audience has obvious constraints – the influence of the recording industry and its tendency towards the homogenization of cultural products in an attempt to exact maximum commercial gain. The pervasiveness of the profit motive often ensures alternative musical styles, which offer resistance to dominant ideologies, are often marginalized. However, a recognition of the market potential of political music, which addresses philosophical concerns, political issues, or social problems, often ensures the commercial appropriation of such radical strands of popular culture and assimilation into the mainstream; such trends are often characterized as 'selling out'.

The analysis of the hippie subculture will be structured around a Spenglerian-like cycle of birth, growth, maturity, decline and decadence, and death. It will chronicle the development of hippie sensibilities from the various 1950s manifestations of rebellion throughout the 1960s – characterized by key figures such as Bob Dylan, Phil Ochs, and Joan Baez, the 'love-ins' and 'happenings', the shaman-like performances of Jim Morrison and mind expanding drugs. With growing commercial pressures and the resulting corruption of the subcultural ideals, true hippiedom became embedded in a maze of alternative and underground movements. The 1960s protest music encapsulated a youth movement eager to disassociate itself from straight society, hell-bent on rebellion and seeking to channel existentialist yearnings.

The analysis of the hip-hop, or more specifically political or conscious rap lyrics, follows a traditional subcultural cycle from its origins in the Bronx, to prominence via lyrical protestations of Public Enemy, X-Clan, Poor Righteous Teachers, Paris and The Coup, and its eventual displacement by the more controversial and nihilist genre of gangsta rap. The hip-hop movement secured an oppositional niche in which to represent a growing underclass suffering the effects of racism, police brutality, and economic marginalization.

Peace, love, and politics

Introduction

The most prominent of the 1960s youth movements – the hippies – outstandingly demonstrates the role of music and song in the identification of, and communication within, social groupings.

The 1960s witnessed an intensive developing of musical forms, which stimulated, and in turn was stimulated by, the development of the hippie movement, one of the 1960s major subcultures. This period also illustrates how music can actively enable and cause change within a social group or subculture. In the USA at the start of the 1960s mainly traditional forms of folk music communicated intellectual and political (left) messages. The emerging genre of rock and roll, based on rhythm and blues and urban blues forms, was a vehicle for non-intellectual rebelliousness among young people, with James Dean as a typical hero figure. However, to many the use of folk musical forms seemed to impose a rigidity of both musical expression and political thinking

This section explores how the musical fusion of folk with rock and roll caused a liberation in thinking, and a realization that rock could be 'intellectual', thus allowing the emergence of new areas of political and sociological development. The section examines the work of Bob Dylan, who developed folk-rock to facilitate his increasingly poetically complex lyrical forms, and above all to communicate his increasingly subjective messages of personal exploration and subjective thinking. The infamous account of Pete Seeger and Alan Lomax trying to cut the electricity cable feeding Dylan and his group onstage at the Newport Folk Festival in 1965 may be apocryphal, but it wonderfully captures the split between the traditional folk left and the new creativeness of the liberated young.

The hippies were never a single coherent group or movement, but rather a kaleidoscope of merging and morphing foci with no clear or consistent philosophical base. It is entirely appropriate that it should be thus. Having emerged from the clearly defined civil rights movement, with folk as its musical messenger, the hippies sought a solution to existentialist yearnings rather than the practical living and promotion of a revealed manifesto. Music played a vital role in that quest.

Although the anarchic nature of hippiedom resists any attempt to impose rigid definitions or classifications, we believe that four reasonably clear phases can be distinguished – a nascent period from 1960 to 1964; an intense blossoming from 1964 to 1966; maturity from 1966 through 1968; and a phase of decay and eventual incorporation into mainstream popular culture from 1968 to 1970. As will be shown, Bob Dylan had a crucial influence on the birth and maturation of the movement.

Youth rebellion and hippie sensibilities

The 1960s was a period of growing affluence in the USA and Britain. The young had more disposable income than ever before; Abrams estimated that the 'discretionary spending' power of 'teenage consumers' in the UK and the USA doubled during the period 1938–1959 (Abrams 1959, p. 9). This new affluence enabled the young to translate the growing feelings of rebelliousness against parental and other authoritarian control agents (including school, government, and other elements of 'straight society') into action. Aware of their parents becoming increasingly 'family minded, home-centred, ... and acquisitive-celebrated,' the young recoiled against this materialism by intensifying their 'commitment to style, music, leisure and consumption' (Clarke *et al.* 1976, p. 21) within the context of various, and disparate, youth groupings. The ability to buy records, to travel to concerts, and to watch television, facilitated effective communications within, and out from, the groups.

The hippie movement (more than some other social units of the period, such as the Teddy Boys, Mods, and Rockers) drew membership from the increasingly prosperous middle and professional classes. The ability of many hippies to rebel – initially skipping college to hang out and listen to music in the coffee bars of Greenwich Village in New York, or Soho in London, and to adopt a romanticised version of the 'outsider' hobos and drifters of earlier times, was often based on support, however grudgingly accepted, from affluent parents. The hippies did not spring from impoverished urban ghettoes, or poor farming areas, but from suburbs and prosperous rural heartlands. The Beatles came from Liverpool, but were all ex-grammar school boys from suburban estates. Dylan, coming from a respectable shop-owning background, learned his craft not in cotton fields or on freight trains, but by dropping out of University to perform in coffee bars and folk clubs. Dinkytown in Minneapolis was typical, providing 'a funky, out-of-the-way roost for practising ... the "existential" lifestyle ... [where] the most striking aspect of Dinkytown society was the interplay of cultural bohemianism and political militancy' (Spitz 1989, pp. 75–7).

The hippie movement was an intellectually enabled movement, as evidenced in its songs and music. Many students became rebels and hippies by moving from formal courses at colleges and universities to exploring romanticism or existentialism, and onto 'digging' Beat poets like Ginsberg and Ferlinghetti, the writings of Kerouac with its advocacy of 'the road' as a way of life, and, later, the mind expanding testaments of Leary, Hesse and Huxley. The writers and musicians known as the Beat Generation were particularly important – 'by the mid-sixties, their *[the hippies]* ideas of love and peace, open sexuality, and the use of consciousness-expanding drugs, had reached hundreds of thousands of people world-wide. The hippie movement, in this respect, had its roots directly in the Beat Generation' (Miles 2002, p. 237).

The ability to bring a developed intellect to the creation and understanding of the music produced by the movement was crucial for the communication of hippy subcultural messages. From the use of didactic, explicit, language and song structures in the nascent phase, language became more subliminal, metaphoric, coded, and oblique during the blossoming and mature phases, before moving into simpler forms of delivery and eventual triteness as the movement collapsed. Music followed a similar path from straightforward folk and 'protest' formulaics, into the liberation of folk rock and acid rock, and eventually into stylistically simple stadium rock. With the degeneration of the musical forms, advocates of the true hippie ethos, such as Third Ear Band and Soft Machine, moved 'underground' into ever more experimental and complex music.

If the Beat Generation was the intellectual and philosophical cradle of the hippie subculture, then the folk revival, running through the 1950s and into the 1960s, was its musical precursor. With figures like Woody Guthrie and Pete Seeger as its heroes, and young practitioners like Bob Dylan, Phil Ochs, and Joan Baez, the songs and music inspired, informed, and communicated the messages of the civil rights movement and spread into wider movements of protest and revolt. City derelicts, the marginalized and the excluded were common subjects for songs, extending into more general political protests against government, the military, and the bureaucrats. Dylan, for example, established himself in New York in 1961 and 1962 by playing at coffee bars and folkclubs such as Folk City and Gaslight. Many songs on his second and third albums, *Freewheelin' Bob Dylan* (May 1963) and *Times They are a Changin'* (January 1964) typify the messages and modes of delivery common throughout the folk revival. Dylan's songs, more than those of any other performer or writer of the period, communicated protest, galvanizing action by performers and audiences alike at concerts and rallies; songs like *Masters of War, Blowin' in the Wind, Oxford Town,* and *The Ballad of Hollis Brown* are outstanding examples. Two main types are evident – the anthem and the narrative. Anthems raise morale and act as an identifier for participants at a march or rally; *Blowin' in the Wind* came to be the protest movement's most famous anthem:

> 'Yes, 'n' how many times must the cannon balls fly
> Before they're forever banned?
> …
> Yes, 'n' how many years can some people exist
> Before they're allowed to be free'

Narratives can educate and raise awareness by concentrating on a specific illustrative event. Dylan's *Lonesome Death of Hattie Carroll*, a polemic against injustice, tells the true story of William Zanzinger, a tobacco farmer 'with rich wealthy parents' who is charged with the murder of a maid, and whose sentence from 'the courtroom of honor' is 'a six-month sentence'.

Hippies break free – drugs and Dylan

By early 1964, the energy and drive of the protest movement was waning. The hippie spirit of rebellion against all constraints on creativity and wholeness was growing. Many of the most important exponents of the folk revival were, comparatively, not young (Pete Seeger was 44 in 1964). The musical forms of the folk revival now started to merge with other musical genres. Dylan provided the stimulus for this development; his song *The Times they are a Changin'* brilliantly articulates generalised rebellion rather than a specific 'protest' issue:

'Come mothers and fathers throughout the land
And don't criticize
What you can't understand
Your sons and your daughters
Are beyond your command
Your old road is rapidly agin'.

Another Side of Bob Dylan (August 1964) contained two songs far removed from mainstream protest, but with a clear message for alienated youth. *My Back Pages* starkly details the young/old antithesis whilst questioning the often simplistic statements of the protest movement:

'Yes my guard stood hard when abstract threats
Too noble to neglect
Deceived me into thinking
I had something to protect
Good and bad, I define these terms
Quite clear, no doubt, somehow.
Ah, but I was so much older then,
I'm younger than that now'

whilst *Chimes of Freedom* illustrates how lyrics became more complex and poetic, and drug-vision inspired, in their presentation:

'Far between sundown's finish an' midnight's broken toll
We ducked inside the doorway, thunder crashing
As majestic bells of bolts struck shadows in the sounds
Seeming to be the chimes of freedom flashing'

By the mid-sixties the use of drugs, especially psychedelics, in order to facilitate insight and song writing was intensifying. Timothy Leary had been advocating the use of psychedelics throughout the sixties, and coined the hippies' creed – 'Turn on, Tune in, Drop out'. Some of Leary's work was later collected and published as the hugely influential *Politics of Ecstasy* (Leary 1968). Dylan's *Mr Tambourine Man*, impregnated with drug imagery, and social and political detachment, from *Bringing it all Back Home* (March 1965), captures the hippie ideal:

'Yes to dance beneath the diamond sky with one hand waving free
Silhouetted by the sea, circled by the circus sands,
With all memory and fate driven deep beneath the waves,
Let me forget about today until tomorrow'

Dylan further developed and communicated the move away from the folk movement in the albums *Bringing it all Back Home* (March 1965) and *Highway 61 Revisited* (August 1965), in which *Subterranean Homesick Blues, Maggie's Farm, It's Alright Ma,* and *Ballad of a Thin Man* are exemplars of songs as agents of general and personal change. The political message had become subjective and introverted, and the authority of the protest movement was challenged explicitly: 'you don't need a weatherman/to know which way the wind blows' and 'don't follow leaders'.

As the movement progressed, so did its music, with bands like the Grateful Dead, The Doors, and Velvet Underground emerging as communication and identification agents; and with the hobo figure being replaced by the romantic archetypal seer, visionary, and shaman as icons – a typology personified by Jim Morrison, poet and singer with the Doors. Life was to be lived on the edge; exclusion from the values and lifestyles of mainstream society was self-selected rather than imposed. The association of the subculture with intellectualism and literary modes of expression became stronger. Group names celebrated a drug orientated, 'drop out', lifestyle: Steppenwolf (from Hesse's novel of alienation), The Doors (Huxley's *Doors of Perception*), and Soft Machine (Burrough's novel) used this technique.

Dylan was also a catalyst for change in the UK, including introducing the Beatles to marijuana in August 1964. The Beatles' role in the hippie movement has been underestimated, with their pop music associations and major commercial success diminishing their credibility for many hippie purists. *Revolver* (August 1966) was important, and *Sgt. Pepper's Lonely Heart's Club Band* (June 1967) quickly became a major text for the movement with songs like *Lucy in the Sky with Diamonds* (interpreted by many as advocating the use of LSD).

Through their much hyped and publicized meeting with the Maharishi Mahesh Yogi in August 1967 and their two trips to India, the Beatles strengthened the hippies' developing preoccupation with Eastern mysticism. Later *The Beatles* (November 1968), which became known as the *White Album*, would play a part in the subculture's death throes.

Dylan's performance of folk-rock songs using electric instruments at the Newport Folk Festival in July 1965 (much to the fury of Pete Seeger and Alan Lomax) was a defining moment for the movement. Cohen has written: 'Dylan's unveiling of what would quickly be called folk-rock at Newport was a continuation of his move to electric instrumental work paired with imaginative, introspective, sometimes nightmarish lyrics'; he goes on to make clear its importance in stating 'Dylan's performance would dominate all memories and future discussions, marking the festival as a watershed, both real and symbolic.' (Cohen 2002, p. 238). Dylan's UK electric concerts in late 1965 provided a stimulus for groups like the Beatles, the Rolling Stones, and the Animals to expand their songs and music, both intellectually and creatively.

Alternatives and the underground

By late 1966, the hippie subculture was at a zenith of wholeness and integrity. Dylan's *Blonde on Blonde* (May 1966), a double album of long tracks full of drug-induced abstractions, like *Visions of Johanna,* is, again, typical:

'While my conscience explodes …
The ghost of 'lectricity howls in the bones of her face'

The surrealism of lyrics and the rock-driven music was anathema to many on the traditional left, still immersed in folk music forms, and seeing surrealism (in any form of artistic expression) as an enemy of their social realism agendas.

Dylan was now a strung out, drug driven, Rimbaudian prophet – a true hero of the movement; then came his motorcycle accident, his move to Woodstock, and his virtual withdrawal from public life until 1969; Dylan would be unavailable in person as an icon for the movement for over two years, by which time he would again have moved on into new artistic explorations; unlike the hippie movement, Dylan would never stagnate.

From 1966 media and major commercial interests increasingly infiltrated the movement, beginning the commercialization which would eventually contribute to its collapse (for example the transfer of former cottage industry merchandizing to mass-production and marketing). The songs, often becoming massive popular hits, were identified by mainstream society with hippie 'Love-ins' and 'happenings'; Scott Mackenzie's *San Francisco (Be Sure to Wear Some Flowers in Your Hair)* illustrates this deterioration:

'For those who come
To San Francisco
Summertime
Will be a love-in there
In the streets of San Francisco
Gentle people
With flowers in their hair'

The political message of 'peace and love' became a trite buzz-phrase, rather than a statement of commitment. Meanwhile, the core movement shifted underground to become increasingly 'alternative'. The music and songs became more eccentric, experimental. Groups like The Edgar Broughton Band, Third Ear Band, and Soft Machine exemplify this trend. Edgar Broughton's *'Demons Out'* was a long audience-participation chant, an attempt both to exorcise bad karma, and, perhaps, to ward off the growing commercial threat. The Third Ear Band developed a typical hippie interest in things other-worldly, in this case an almost Pre-Raphaelite dwelling on mediaevalism and Celtic cultures; their first album *Alchemy* (1969) contained instrumental tracks such as *Stone Circle* and *Dragon Lines*. The Soft Machine took an equally distanced stance, through improvised fusions of modern jazz, folk, and eastern elements.

This musical diversity also helped new ways of thinking to develop and alternative political agendas to emerge. The 'politics' of liberating and realizing the self (which in turn, it was felt, would lead to the emergence of a new society) further distanced thinking away from the politics of the traditional left. The emergence of New Age thinking and DIY politics were facilitated by this musical melting pot, along with an emerging 'back to the land' commune-based movement.

Festival culture now also became increasingly commercialized. What had started as mainly free gatherings developed into commercial promotions. Even free events such as the Hyde Park Concerts increasingly promoted groups like the 'supergroup' Blind Faith – although it was still possible to catch sets by subcultural icons such as Ritchie Havens and Edgar Broughton at these events. Overtly political singers did continue to mingle with the movement; Country Joe and the Fish's *I-Feel-Like-I'm-Fixin-To-Die Rag* (1965) is a typical expression of the anti-Vietnam message, which continued the earlier protest phase throughout the decade:

'And it's one, two, three,
What are we fighting for?
Don't ask me, I don't give a damn,
Next stop is Vietnam;
And it's five, six, seven,
Open up the pearly gates,
Well there ain't no time to wonder why,
Whoopee! we're all gonna die'

Decadence and decay

In the two years preceding the end of the decade, commercialization and over-hype of the movement precipitated its decay, and a fin de siecle mode of decadence set in. The Woodstock Festival in the summer of 1969, heralded by many mainstream commentators as a statement of the hippie ideal (and later hailed as such by some of the performers there like Ritchie Havens and Joan Baez) proved to be the swansong of the subculture. The Woodstock festival was exploited by corporate interests on an unprecedented scale. Dylan, speaking about the hippie ethos, summarised the situation well – 'It just got suffocated. Like Woodstock – that wasn't anything. It was just a whole new market for tie-dyed t-shirts' (Dylan 1984). Violence became increasingly associated with the movement, and hastened its demise. The Rolling Stones at Altamont in 1969 sang *Sympathy for the Devil* whilst Hell's Angels minders stabbed a member of the audience to death and seriously assaulted several others. Meanwhile, cult leader Charles Manson claimed to be heavily influenced by the Beatles' *White Album*, believing that they were sending him coded messages through their lyrics which confirmed his predictions of Armageddon.

As Udo (Udo 2002) has pointed out, music and song developed angry, strident strands in songs like the Rolling Stones' *Street Fighting Man* (1968) and the MC5's debut album *Kick Out the Jams* (1969); the Doors' song *Five to One* (1968) is typical:

'The old get old
And the young get stronger
May take a week
And it may take longer
They got the guns
But we got the numbers
Gonna win, yeah'

The second Isle of Wight Festival, two months after Woodstock, retained some of the idealistic and amateur feel of the free festivals. The festival presented, in a highly eclectic way, a range of musical expressions which had influenced the development of the subculture, and which now mirrored its equally eclectic political thinking. From The Who's 'mock opera' Tommy, to the more or less traditional folk of Julie Felix and Tom Paxton; and from the rock of Family and Free, to the ethereal pseudo-mediaevalism of the Third Ear Band. The festival culminated with the re-emergence of a mellowed Bob Dylan.

However, the Isle of Wight Festival in 1970 was, despite outstanding performances by the Doors and Hendrix, an over-commercialized failure, with major disruption being caused by the violence of French anarchists. The hippie movement was all but dead.

The protest music of the 1960s translated the ideals of the hippie generation – peace, love, freedom, and self-realization – in both practical and surreal terms. The music which characterized the era articulated the concerns of a generation intent on changing the world or dropping out of society. The potential for music, and in particular lyrical expression, to engage, inspire, and reflect upon a range of philosophical concerns, political issues, or social problems and to galvanize an oppositional identity is undisputed. Was the hippie generation the archetypal model for the evolution of protest music? Did the ability to communicate an oppositional agenda through music end with Altamont?

Rap, rhyme, and resistance
Introduction

The contemporary rap artist has become something of a caricature: dripping in gold, adorned in fur, at the wheel of a Lexus with a scantily clad woman draped off his arm. Gangsta rap is renowned and reviled for its inherent sexism and materialism, for the glamourisation of violence and associations with criminality. Yet rap music can be understood as an oppositional realm and breeding ground for alternative politics.

'Rap music is a contemporary stage for the theater of the powerless' (Rose 1994, p. 101)

Hip-hop originated in New York's poverty-stricken South Bronx during the mid 1970s, where it supplied the soundtrack to New York's block parties. Hip-hop culture consisted of four main elements: graffiti art, break dancing, DJing, and MCing and formed a distinct youth culture with its own lifestyle, language, style of dress, music, and mind set. Although the terms 'rap' and 'hip-hop' are used interchangeably, rap artist KRS-One made the crucial distinction between rap as 'something one does or performs' and hip-hop as "something one lives or experiences".

Hip-hop should not be considered as a homogenous artistic category. Various classifications such as East Coast, West Coast, teen rap, party rap, gangsta rap, Southern rap, acid rap, dance-centred rap, dirty South, and political rap are used to differentiate the genre. Early or 'old skool' hip-hop was a form of party music and was dominated by the turntable acrobatics of DJs. As Jeff Chang commented in *Selling the Political Soul of Hip Hop*:

> 'The Bronx community-center dances and block parties where hip-hop began in the early 1970s were not demonstrations for justice, they were celebrations of survival. Hip-hop culture simply reflected what the people wanted and needed – escape' (Chang, Jeff 2003).

The sphere of 'political rap' or 'conscious' rap will be analysed in the context of hip-hop's ability to serve as the vehicle for the effective dissemination of political ideas. Political hip-hop was heralded by Public Enemy whose second album *It Takes a Nation of Millions to Hold Us Back* (1988) identified them as rap's leading political agitators.

Rap as social commentary

Hip-hop comprises both a musical genre and a cultural movement and can be understood in the context of a long history of African-American creative expression, which included field hollers, toasts, and sermons.

> 'Music has been a prime source of identity for African Americans and was a core element in the notion of a distinct black perspective and way of life' (Eyerman and Jamison 1998, p. 89)

As a form of cultural subversion and an opportunity for social critique, hip-hop culture generally and rap lyrics specifically represented an oppositional and counter-cultural response to the severe economic and social marginalization endemic to black inner city life. Rap lyrics addressed and attempted to negotiate extreme socio-economic circumstances; its counter-cultural discourse provided an opportunity to challenge existing patterns of exclusion and marginalization in urban life. Rap's social commentary offered a form of social critique and an opportunity to empower, to educate, and raise awareness.

The manifestation of hip-hop from the South Bronx is not coincidental: geopolitical factors specific to New York, such as depleted federal funding for arts, radical changes in housing policy, and social service cuts, provided the impetus for the development of rap music (Rose 1994, pp. 21–34). The concentration of a Black and Latino underclass in a specifically urban environment rife with poverty, crime, drug addiction, unemployment, and neighbourhood gangs provided the context for rap's emergence and germinated ample lyrical content.

'Rap music has become one of the principle vehicles by which young African Americans express their views of the world, attempting to create a sense of order out of the mayhem and disorder of contemporary urban life' (Ernest Allen Jr 1996, p. 159)

Rap's social commentary, or an 'electrified folk poetry of the streets' (Eyerman and Jamison 1998, p. 105), facilitated the identification of a shared experience of economic marginalization and social exclusion, an interpretation of these social conditions, and an opportunity to formulate resistance. *The Message* by Grandmaster Flash and his Furious Five, released in 1982 and widely regarded as hip hop's first political release, infused social commentary about ghetto life into a genre dominated by party raps and battle rhyming.

Afrika Bambaataa, one of the founding fathers of hip-hop, upheld the four elements of hip-hop as providing an alternative competitive arena to the violent and pervasive gang culture. Originally a gang leader and later influenced by Louis Farakhan's Nation of Islam, Bambaataa strived to mitigate youth gang violence through the redirection of creative efforts into the street culture of DJing, MCing, break dancing and graffiti art. The pursuit of social identity and respect could be alternately fulfilled through street competition.

'Rap music, more than any other contemporary form of black cultural expression, articulates the chasm between black urban lived experience and dominant, "legitimate" (eg. Neoliberal) ideologies regarding equal opportunity and racial inequality.' (Bennett 2001, pp. 88–103)

Political rap received mainstream attention through the commercially successful rap group Public Enemy. Dressed in military fatigues and led by activist Chuck D, known as the 'Messenger of Prophecy', Flavor Flav, Terminator X and Professor Griff condoned revolutionary activity and demanded social activism through their biting social criticism. Flavor Flav or 'The Joker' notoriously wore an imposingly large clock around his neck to denote 'Time Is Now', adopting the Black Nationalist style of the Nation Of Islam and the Black Panther Party.

As the ultimate 'prophets of rage', Public Enemy infused rap with social and political urgency and their lyrically abrasive rhymes informed on a range of social problems affecting the Black community. Also known as the 'lyrical Terrorist', 'The Hard Rhymer', and 'The Architect', Chuck D's authoritative baritone voice spewed forth militant lyrics, against a backdrop of raw beats, throbbing bass and dark, urban sounds, which offered the black community an appreciation of their heritage, and attempted to mobilize the community into action: 'I don't rhyme for the sake of riddlin' (Public Enemy, *Don't Believe the Hype* from *It Takes A Nation Of Millions To Hold Us Back*, 1988).

Famously claiming rap music was 'the black CNN', Public Enemy considered rap music as a social force to inform and mobilize the black community. The political rhetoric and explosive polemic concerned a range of issues spanning the inherent racism of the movie industry (*Burn Hollywood Burn, Fear of a Black Planet*, 1995), social exclusion (*Black Steel in the Hour of Chaos, It Takes a Nation of Millions to Hold Us Back*, 1988), the plight of drugs in African American communities (*Night of the Living Baseheads, ibid*), and revolutionary activity (*Party for Your Right to Fight, ibid*). The powerful fusion of politics and music could not be underestimated, as Public Enemy became the definitive rap group of all time.

From slavery to Rodney King: political rap lyrics

Hip-hop has become a conduit for African American culture and its primary sources of critique reflect the African-American experience, both past and present: slavery, racism, economic marginalization, social exclusion, and police harassment and brutality. Thus, rap music provides a collective challenge to existing social relations.

> 'Rap music uses the language of nation to rearticulate a history of racial oppression and struggle which can energise the movement toward black empowerment and independence' (Decker in Ross and Rose 1994, p. 100).

The subject of police harassment and brutality provides the impetus for many political rap lyrics: the police are seen to wield excessive power unchecked and to be pursuing an explicitly racist agenda. In *Illegal Business*, from the album *By All Means Necessary* (1988), Boogie Down Productions articulate a vision in which police powers are readily abused:

> 'The police department is like a crew. It does whatever they want to do'

Boogie Down Productions is the brainchild of KRS-ONE (an acronym for Knowledge Reigns Supreme Over Nearly Everyone) and, until his untimely death by a fatal shooting, DJ Scott La Rock. The philosophically enlightened rapper KRS-One, or 'The Teacher', criticizes the boundless authority of the police force and its lack of accountability in *Who Protects Us From You?*:

> 'You were put here to protect us
> But who protects us from you?
> Every time you say "That's illegal"
> Doesn't mean that that's true
> Your authority's never questioned
> No-one questions you'

The Oakland-based hardcore rap group The Coup express a similar critical stance against the police force and the perception of their role as conditional to the effective functioning of a capitalist economy; in *Drug Warz* MC Boots Riley states 'police are the fist of the imperial'. Furthermore, The Florida-based political rap duo Dead Prez regard the police and the institutions of capitalism as mutually compatible in *Propaganda*, 'now, buster, can you tell me who's greedier/ big corporations, the pigs, or the media?'. Dead Prez, who consist of Sticman and M-1, are so-called hip-hop freedom fighters denouncing the economic roots of injustice. Influenced by Malcolm X and the African People's Socialist Party, Dead Prez advocate the development of a revolutionary consciousness as a necessary precursor to the overthrow of the social system. As a result, political rap lyrics can be seen to contribute significantly to a revolutionary awakening via their potential to educate, empower, and formulate resistance.

Brooklyn-based rapper Talib Kweli, whose name literally means 'the seeker of truth', and who is well known for his collaborations with underground rap artist Mos Def, explored the issue of misuse of police power in *The Proud*. Kweli makes reference to the death of Amadou Diallo, an unarmed innocent man who died in a hail of police bullets in February 1999: 'It's in they job description to terminate the threat/So 41 shots to the body is what he can expect.' The incident sparked a heated debate over the crime-fighting policies of Mayor Rudolph Giuliani and the NYPD's excessive use of force.

Kweli points to the police's routine identification of the black urban male as a threat, thereby rendering acceptable the use of force at any cost. Tricia Rose in *Black Noise: Rap Music and Black Culture in Contemporary America* noted that, 'Rap music is fundamentally linked to larger social constructions of black culture as an internal threat to dominant American culture and social order' (Rose 1994, p. 144).

The thorny issue of police brutality was addressed by the original gangsta rappers NWA (Niggaz With Attitude) in their infamous song *Fuck tha Police* (*Straight Outta Compton*, 1988) which predicted 'a bloodbath of cops, dyin' in LA'. The song elevates Dr Dre to the status of judge presiding in the case of NWA versus the LAPD. Members of the group offer testimony to mistreatment and harassment at the hands of the LA police department.

> 'Fuckin with me cuz I'm a teenager
> With a little bit of gold and a pager
> Searchin my car, lookin for the product
> Thinkin every nigga is sellin narcotics'

This anti-police brutality anthem is regarded by some as a verbal prelude to the 1992 LA riots, which followed the acquittal of the police officers involved in the Rodney King beating. It caused further controversy when an FBI representative sent a letter to Priority Records stating that the song was an incitement to violence against the police.

The censorship of rap lyrics

Revenge fantasies within rap music have received intense press attention and precipitated demands for the censorship of rap lyrics. However, as Janet Harvey stated, 'revenge fantasies are an important (and peaceful) form of public resistance to mainstream stereotypes which barely mask the interests of hegemony' (Harvey 2000).

San Franciscan rapper Paris is perhaps best known for the release of the graphic revenge fantasy *Bush Killa*. Injecting a militant, politically charged message into hip-hop, *Bush Killa* (*Sleeping With the Enemy*, 1992) called for the assassination of President George Bush Snr; the album's inner-sleeve depicted an armed Paris assuming a sniper's position and the song concludes with Bush Senior's speech being halted by gunfire. The controversy surrounding the militaristic image, originally intended for the front cover, was partly responsible for Paris' defection from Tommy Boy Records and the album's release on his own label Scarface.

The debate regarding the censorship of rap lyrics in the USA was intensified by Tipper Gore and the Parents' Music Resource Center, who identified gangsta rap as a pollutant to the minds of the American youth. The controversy centred on the East Coast phenomenon of gangsta rap, or G-Funk, pioneered by NWA, which has been vilified for its sexually explicit lyrics, violent imagery, material emphasis, and glamourization of violence. However, is the portrayal of hip-hop by the mainstream media as male-dominated, money-oriented, nihilistic, violent, and exploitative of women an accurate representation of the genre? Or is this a form of demonization of a musical genre by a media dominated by a white middle class elite?

Indeed, the negative press attention devoted to gangsta rap has sought to discredit rap music as a whole and serves to detract from the potentially positive impact of political rap: as a display of cultural values, a vehicle for self-expression, and a political forum for the disenfranchised.

Moreover, the negative reporting of rap music can be understood as a reactionary strategy adopted by a largely mainstream conservative American press to undermine subversive or challenging transcripts. Cheryl L. Keyes (2002, p. 5) retorts that 'controversial forms that threaten mainstream sensibilities will always face intense scrutiny from powerful political forces'.

Rap lyrics and violence

Attempts to frustrate the positive potential of rap were reinforced by the focus on rap-related violence: the fatal shooting of DJ Scott La Rock (of Boogie Down Productions) and the high profile instances of violence at rap concerts. Nevertheless, this provided the impetus for the development of a hip-hop anti-violence movement. In the song *Stop the Violence* (*By All Means Necessary*, 1988) KRS-ONE appealed for an end to the internecine violence within the black community.

> 'When you're in a club, you come to chill out
> not watch someone's blood just spill out
> That's what these other people want to see
> another race fight endlessly'

KRS-ONE and author and columnist, Nelson George, established the *Stop the Violence* movement to counter the rising tide of violence associated with rap music, and to identify and address the real causes of black on black violence. The single *Self Destruction* was released and featured a collective of hip hop artists including KRS-ONE, Kool Moe Dee, MC Lyte, and Public Enemy endorsing the campaign.

Furthermore, the hip-hop community sought to question and undermine the erroneous link between rap lyrics and violence. The conflation of rap lyrics and violence was seen to simplify and distort the problem of gun crime. Atlanta rap group Goodie Mob (Good Die Mostly Over BullShit) received criticism for the track *Cell Therapy* (*Soul Food*, 1995): 'Who's that peeking at my window/Pow/Nobody now'. However, such criticism fails to acknowledge the context of gang violence and drug warfare endemic to the urban ghetto. The songs suggests the necessity to pursue self-preservation through violent means, and this necessity is often overlooked due to the isolationism of the inner city ghetto: 'Every now and then, I wonder if the gate was put up to keep crime out or to keep our ass in'.

Similarly, socially conscious rapper Talib Kweli was rebuked for *Gun Music* (*Quality*, 2000), denigrated as a pro-gun anthem rather than understood as a personal commentary on the effects of gang culture and violence on the community: 'Punk niggas feel inferior/Guns make us superior'. Indeed rather than glorifying black on black violence, such commentaries offer a realist and, sometimes, brutal portrayal of dire social circumstances.

Hip-hop versus capitalism

Prison expansion and the disproportionate number of young black men in prison is a further source of enquiry for rap artists. Raptivism Records and the Prison Moratorium Project released a hip hop compilation, *No More Prisons* (2001), to raise awareness and funds to fight prison construction across the USA. The compilation features *The Plan* by The Reepz, which explores the association between economic deprivation and criminal activities resulting in incarceration.

'Jump off the train and the first thing that I see
when I see the daylight, is a prison
I guess the government is tryin' to plant negative seeds
Could it be my destiny's in the prison.
I keep awareness, cause that's where they want us
they put us in the projects, so projects become us'

Goodie Mob similarly determine an explicit link between extreme poverty and the prison population in *Live at OMNI (One Millions Niggaz Inside, Soul Food,* 1995) by asserting 'Plenty niggas sittin in jail just to eat a decent meal' whilst Dead Prez, in *Enemy Lines (Lets Get Free,* 2000), regard the social conditions of the ghetto as restrictive as the prison complexes themselves: 'You don't need to be locked up, to be in prison/Look how we livin'

Dead Prez's revolutionary rhetoric identifies the forces of capitalism, imperialism, and white supremacy as manifest in a racist educational system, which seeks to marginalize the African-American perspective. In *They Schools (Lets Get Free,* 2000), the structures of education are seen to reinforce the social and economic stratification of society: 'The same people who control the school system control the prison system and the whole social system, ever since slavery'.

Talib Kweli, in *The Proud (Quality,* 2002) cites the intoxicating potential of education to raise consciousness within the black community, and as an impetus to the overthrow of the existing balance of power: 'Niggaz with knowledge is more dangerous than niggaz with guns, they make the guns easy to get and try to keep niggaz dumb'. Goodie Mob similarly attribute to preservation of existing social structures to a government conspiracy in the song *Fighting (Soul Food,* 1995): 'You'll find a lot of the reason we behind is because the system is designed to keep our third eyes blind'.

Hip-hop narratives endeavour to compensate for the failures inherent within the education system, which marginalizes or neutralizes a black historical perspective. Black Nationalist rappers such as Paris, Ice-T, X-Clan, Poor Righteous Teachers, and Brand Nubian attempt to redress this cultural balance, sampling speeches of Black Nationalist figures such Malcolm X, Martin Luther King and Huey Newton and offering historical accounts within their lyrics. In *They Schools (Lets Get Free,* 2000), Dead Prez highlight Malcolm X's conversion to the Nation of Islam whilst in prison and the subsequent relinquishing of his surname Little which he considered to be his slave name and in *Enemy Lines* (ibid), Dead Prez refer to the conviction for arson of Fred Hampton Jnr, local President of the National People's Democratic Uhuru Movement in Chicago and son of murdered Black Panther leader: 'They said he set a fire to a Arab store/But he ignited the minds of the young black and poor'. Chicago-bred rapper Common, in *A Song for Assata (Like Water for Chocolate,* 2000), recounts the story of Assata Shakur, a Black Panther activist who was pulled over by the New Jersey State Police on May 2 1973, shot twice and then charged with murder of a police officer. Assata spent six and a half years in prison under brutal circumstances before escaping and seeking exile in Cuba.

These examples demonstrate that political empowerment engendered by conscious rap is a requisite in the quest to develop a revolutionary consciousness. However, the inescapable allure of consumerist culture, as personified by gangsta rappers, seeks to detract from the politicization process as demonstrated in Dead Prez's *Hip Hop* (*Lets Get Free*, 2000): 'Would you rather have a Lexus or justice? A dream or some substance? A Beamer or necklace or freedom?'

Has the commercial success and pervasive quality of gangsta rap sounded the death knell for political or conscious rap? Can rap lyrics continue to inspire, engage and educate, communicate and politicize as the rap music market becomes saturated with nihilist, sexist and violent lyrics and imagery?

The terrorist attacks on New York and Washington on 11 September 2001, which left more than 3 000 people dead, sent shock waves around the world. The hip-hop community contributed with fervour to the post 9/11 and subsequent anti-war debate demonstrating the capacity of the hip-hop community to offer a platform for the unanswered questions which emerged from the fog of the transformed New York skyline. Talib Kweli, in *The Proud* (*Quality*, 2002), reflected on the irony that the masses are expected to demonstrate patriotic fervour in a time of national crisis:

'But it's hard for me to walk down the block/Seeing rats and roaches, crack vials and 40 ounce posters/People broken down from years of oppression/Become patriots when they way of life is threatened'.

Mr Lif, in *Home of the Brave* (*Emergency Rations*, 2002), rejects such flag-waving patriotism and attributes US foreign policy as a major contributory factor to the terrorist attacks:

'You can wave that piece of shit flag if you dare/But they killed us 'cause we've been killing them for years.'

Whilst revolutionary rapper Paris in *What Would You Do?* (*Sonic Jihad*, 2003) contributed scepticism to the debate:

'Now ask yourself who's the people with the most to gain (Bush)/'fore 911 motherfuckas couldn't stand his name (Bush)/Now even brothas wavin' flags like they lost they mind/Everybody got opinions but don't know the time'.

The hip-hop community clearly remains firmly engaged in dispensing polemic. The era of Public Enemy represented the pinnacle of political rap's influence both within the hip hop community and beyond. However, the hip-hop community continues to engage, inspire, and dissent.

Conclusion

The effectiveness of music, specifically politically edged lyrics, within the 1960s protest scene and the hip-hop movement to articulate, crystallize, and communicate an oppositional identity cannot be underestimated. The significance of these two strands of popular culture – reflecting a shared experience, interpreting a common cause, and mounting a collective challenge against authority (parental or governmental) through music – is indisputable. The hippies' use of music as a medium for their political agenda was less prescriptive and more opaque than their hip-hop counterparts, with the former influenced by Herman Hesse and Aldous Huxley whilst the latter drew their influences from Malcolm X, Huey Newton, and Martin Luther King.

Music is, of course, more memorable than a political speech and a music concert more alluring than a political rally. Despite cynical attempts to appropriate such radical strands of popular culture and market its products, lyrical expression, as a form of protest, continues to survive underground.

References

Abrams, M. (1959) *The teenage consumer* London: London Press Exchange

Allen, E., Jr, (1996) Making the strong survive: The contours and contradictions of message rap. In *Droppin' science: Critical essays on rap music and hip hop culture*, (ed. W.E. Perkins). Philadelphia, PA: Temple University Press.

Bennett, A. (2001) *Cultures of popular music*, Buckingham: Open University Press.

Chang, Jeff. (2003) *Selling the political soul of hip hop*, http://www.alternet.org/story.html? StoryID=14902

Clarke, J., Mall, S., Jefferson, T., and Roberts, B. (1976) 'Subcultures, cultures, and class: a theoretical overview'. in *Resistance through rituals: youth subcultures in post-war Britain*, (ed. S. Hall and T. Jefferson). London: Hutchenson Press.

Cohen, R.D. (2002) *Rainbow Quest: the folk music revival and American society, 1940–1970.* Amherst, MA: University of Massachusetts Press.

Decker, J.L. (1994) 'The state of rap: Time and place in hip hop nationalism'. In *Microphone fiends: Youth music and youth culture*, (ed. A. Ross and T. Rose). New York: Routledge.

Dylan, B. (1984) An interview with Mick Brown, London: The Sunday Times.

Eyerman, R. and Jamison, A. (1998) *Music and social movements: Mobilizing traditions in the twentieth century*, Cambridge: Cambridge University Press.

Harvey, J. (2000) *Hip-hop and cultural identity* Deepsouth v.6.n.1 http://www.otago.ac.nz/ deepsouth/index.html

Keyes, C.L. (2002) *Rap music and street consciousness*, Urbana, IL: University of Illinois Press.

Leary, T. (1968) *The politics of ecstasy*, London: Ronin Publishing.

Miles, B. (2002) *Allen Ginsberg: a biography,* London: Virgin Books.

Rose, T. (1994) *Black noise: Rap music and black culture in contemporary, America* Hanover, NH: University Press of New England.

Spitz, B. (1989) *Dylan: a biography,* New York: W. W. Norton and Company.

Udo, T. (2002) *Charles Manson: Music mayhem murder,* London: Sanctuary Publishing Limited.

Chapter 17

Communication in Indian raga performance

Martin Clayton

Introduction

Performances of raga music in the North Indian tradition are events rich in communicative potential and practice. Communication takes place in various directions (not only from performer to listener), and through multiple channels (not only auditory), and this variety and multidimensionality is part of what makes these events enjoyable and enriching events for those who participate in them.

The *sound* of raga music itself is open to multiple interpretations and engagements – its meaning arises as affordances for particular listeners (see Clayton 2001). Many of these affordances seem to relate to patterns of movement, especially movement of the human body – patterns that have obvious implications for temporality, space and agency (since movement implies something moving somewhere for a reason and at a particular pace). The engagement of listeners with the music depends on an understanding of the movements necessary to produce the sound, particularly the gestures and posture of a singer, as well as imagined analogues of movement (for instance if a melody rising in pitch is associated to an image of a bird rising in the air).

I will explore this theme mainly through a particular ethnographic example. By doing so I hope to make a case for the importance of ethnography in the study of musical communication. It is only through ethnography that we can build up a nuanced picture of the communication that takes place in performance, and of the meanings people ascribe to musical practices. One of the limitations of ethnographic music research however is that citable evidence is often limited to what participants are able and willing to express verbally. If what makes musical communication particularly powerful is that it conveys what we are unable (or unwilling) to express verbally, then any research method tied exclusively to verbal testimony is bound to be limited in its effectiveness (see Clayton 2003).

This chapter, therefore, considers how methods of studying nonverbal communication can be applied in this context, especially gestural analysis of individuals involved in musical interactions. The performance of raga music in the north Indian tradition is rich in gestural communication (see Clayton 2000, pp. 1–3). Performers and listeners communicate with each other not only through sound but also with a variety of head, eye, and hand movements; gestures produced by performers seem to amplify, or even explain the meaning of musical patterns; and these in turn evoke gestures of response from appreciative listeners.

This chapter is illustrated with a case study from my own research into North Indian raga performance. It sets preliminary observations of musical practice in the context of theory and investigative methods developed in other fields concerned with nonverbal communication, and reflects on what these methods might contribute to ethnographic studies of music as communication.

My understanding of 'communication' in raga performance is a synthesis of observations of behaviour (especially sound production and physical gesture), of introspection regarding my own experience of such events, and of conversations with both performers and other listeners. I have not imposed a strict definition of 'musical communication'. Rather, I take communication to include any kind of interactive behaviour where the behaviour of one individual has an impact on the behaviour or understanding of another individual; and 'musical' to mean that the behaviour involves the use of humanly organized sound.

Space does not allow me to place this study definitively in the context of previous research, but my approach is influenced by Feld's notion of 'interpretive moves' (1984/1994). Other ethnomusicological precedents include the work of Blacking (e.g. 1977, 1995:38ff), Kubik (e.g. 1979), and Baily (e.g. 1985), who write on the embodiment of musical process and meaning; and Qureshi, who has applied methods of video-based discourse analysis to South Asian Sufi music (1987, 1986/1995). Although not couched in terms of semiotic theory, it is consonant with certain approaches to the semiotics of music, especially those of Tagg (1999) and Middleton (1993); the latter overlaps with studies in musical aesthetics which highlight gesture and/or motion (Coker 1972; Scruton 1997). I borrow concepts from ecological perception theory such as the idea of 'affordance' (Gibson 1966, 1979/1986), which have previously been applied to musical motion and gesture by Clarke (2001) in particular. The importance of metaphorical transfer and image schemata is articulated most clearly by Lakoff and Johnson (1980) and Johnson (1987). Studies of meaning in Indian music are many, but empirical studies are few: those of Deva and Virmani (1968, Deva 1981) and Keil and Keil (1966), and by Balkwell and Thompson (1999) stand out.

This chapter continues with a general discussion of the dimensions of communication in raga performance, considering the issue from a broad ethnographic perspective. The following sections consider a particular ethnographic example, and how it might be explored further by using gestural analysis; finally a summary section draws the various theoretical and empirical strands together.

Dimensions of communication in raga performance

In any raga performance, we can identify several ways in which inter-personal communication takes place. I will concentrate for much of this chapter on the communication of character and mood through musical sound, since ethnographic evidence suggests that to be the primary focus of most participants' experience of this music. This is not, however, the only level, or the only direction (performer → listener) of communication taking place: here I discuss the wider context of social interaction too, and consider the different ways in which people can participate in communicative behaviour (*cf.* chapters by Ansdell and Pavlicevic, Cross, and Welch in this volume).

There are several possible ways in which to express this multidimensionality, and to begin to characterize the different communicative dimensions. One possible scheme is as follows:

i. The participants in a musical performance – principally, the performers and audience – make a statement of **identification** by their very presence and participation: *this is the kind of event I* (and by extension, *people like me) attend.* Extensions or inversions of this proposition are not difficult to read: I belong to the group of people who enjoy this kind of music; people like me listen to this kind of music; and so on. When such statements are not made explicitly but read into others' actions they can nonetheless be very effectively communicated.

ii. Within the performance event, different participants are assigned (or assume) different roles, and those roles may carry with them implications of greater or lesser power: an individual's mode of participation communicates his or her **status**. (Status in the musical context may not, of course, correlate with social or economic status in everyday life.) Musicians express, and sometimes contest, their status and musical knowledge relative to each other and to other musicians (who may be present or absent). In intimate settings in particular, this kind of exchange extends across the audience, with mutual respect, deference, self-assurance, or (rarely) antagonism expressed both verbally and nonverbally.

iii. **Interpersonal communication,** gestural and verbal, continues throughout the event. One function of this is to regulate the event itself and the continuity of the music (the latter mainly between performers, the former involving a wider group). This kind of communication is dependent, in principle, on a shared identification as participants in a musical event (i), and a shared understanding of the role and status of each participant (ii).

iv. **The presence of musical sound** itself communicates to all participants that they are situated within the time and space of the performance. It is important to remember, before discussing the meaning of sound element A (as opposed to element B or C), or the meaning of sound A for listener A (as opposed to listener B or C), that the *generic* qualities of the sound of raga music (e.g. the ubiquitous and quotidian drone) are themselves communicative, and also that they establish the conditions within which sound elements can be mutually distinguished.

v. The most difficult dimension to characterize, perhaps, is what is communicated through the specific sound patterns. One important aspect of this appears to be the communication of **character or mood** through sound (and accompanying gestures). This communication seems to depend on the empathic reception of particular body states and patterns of movement. The musical sound affords the communication of such states, without over-determining their reception. The extent to which this communication is predictable may depend on 'cultural' factors – such as shared language or a repertoire of gestural signs – although the evidence described below suggests that the ranges of affordances for Indian and European listeners overlap considerably. My findings suggest that this process also comes into play where the performer's gestures are not seen – for instance when listening to an audio recording. It seems probable that even here the reception of the music is strongly influenced by each listener's memory of either performing, or watching performances of similar music.

vi. Of interest to a subgroup of those present will be the domain of **intramusical communication**. Individual ragas can be regarded as elements of a global raga system. A raga performance may clarify that raga A has affinities with raga B, but on the other hand is clearly distinct from raga C (with which it may share a scale). Those listeners with insufficient knowledge to understand these dimensions are not, however, hampered in their appreciation of other communicative dimensions. (For an introduction to north Indian raga and basic bibliography, see Ruckert and Widdess 2000.)

The types of communication described in points i and (especially) ii above clearly depend on a degree of shared knowledge – dress, posture, gesture and so on are deployed in ways that would not be fully understood by cultural 'outsiders', who may consequently respond to the superficially 'exotic' features of the event. Point iii (interpersonal communication) depends on understanding which may be partly cultural, or even restricted to fellow musicians; (vi) (intramusical communication) is definitely for this group. What everyone has access to is (iv) – understanding that one is situated in relation to a musical performance, and (v), understanding that the performance conveys something about mood or character. Thus each participant has access to a different set of communicative possibilities.

In the next section I will focus on a particular musical event, as a way of keeping the theoretical and methodological arguments grounded in musical reality. The discussion concentrates on the use of sound to convey character and mood (my aforementioned point v.) – I will return briefly to the other points at the end of the chapter.

Raga, meaning, and communication: an ethnographic example

A raga performance

In April 2003 I visited Mumbai (formerly Bombay) with the intention of filming music performances, and a variety of follow-up interviews and experiments, in order to explore how people experience musical performance, and how the meaning of a performance is constructed discursively after the event. The first performance recorded for the project was by the khyal singer Veena Sahasrabuddhe, accompanied by Vishwanath Shirodkar (tabla) and Seema Shirodkar (harmonium), and two of Veena's students (tanpura). It was recorded in an auditorium on the campus of the Indian Institute of Technology, Bombay (IITB), where Veena teaches. Veena sang three items: Shree Raga, Raga Des, and a bhajan (devotional song). The performance began at about 6.30pm and was filmed by a locally hired crew using two DVCAM video cameras, in the presence of an audience of about 100 people.

After the performance we retired to the IITB guest house for dinner, and I talked about my research with Veena and some of her students. I suggested that I would like to interview some of them, as well as other listeners, and ask them what kind of mood or image was conveyed by the performance. Veena immediately asked me, 'Well, what do *you* think it conveys?' Posed the question myself, I could barely think beyond the fact that the performance had been superb, and that I had felt a strong sense of engagement with the music. I was aware that the music had had quite a specific effect on me, but I was a long way from being able to put it into words – so I could only reply, 'I'll tell you after the interview...'

Reviewing the video footage the next evening, I wondered what the performance was conveying to me. My first thought was again of engagement – *I feel like I could be singing this, as if I'm expressing something along with Veena.* But what was 'I' expressing – what was the music expressing with which I identified so strongly? I listened more, and a few key words presented themselves – it was 'strong' and 'powerful', but overall 'calm'. The subject of the performance (was it Veena, the raga, or who?) seemed to be saying, 'Here I am: I'm calm and at peace. But don't think that I'm weak, because underneath I have great strength and power'.

How I felt this, of course, is another question – was it all conveyed through the sound alone, or was it also signalled by the singer's physical gestures? Although Veena is not a particularly demonstrative singer – at times she seems introverted, and there is no hint of the kind of theatrical gestural display one would expect of some other khyal singers – nor is she static (unlike some Western singing traditions, no premium is placed on the restraint of physical gesture in performance). It struck me there was, for instance, something about the way she marked the Pa (5th scale degree) that might have contributed to my response: Veena slowly, precisely, raised her left hand and held it as if to say *this is exactly where the Pa sits – right here* (see Fig. 17.1(c)).

When I had a chance a couple of days later to ask Veena why she had chosen to sing Shree, she made a number of observations:

- She had intended to sing Shree for me – and the Open University – when we had filmed her in Pune in 1996, but had had to change the plan at the last moment (see Clayton 1999).

- She likes the mood of the raga, which is one of her favourites: she also knows that audiences appreciate the ways she sings Shree, and her accompanists often ask her to sing it.

- Shree is a Gwalior gharana raga, and she identifies herself as a Gwalior gharana singer. (Although the raga repertory is largely shared across the tradition as a whole, a gharana or stylistic school may have a more restricted repertory of ragas with which singers feel a particular affinity, and which they may develop in particular ways.)

- It's not a sampurna ('complete') raga – Shree depends heavily on just a few phrases, and it's very difficult not to repeat oneself while performing (making it difficult to sustain a performance).

- The distances between the notes also make it challenging for the singer (The scale, Sa Re̲ Ga Ṁa Pa Dha̲ Ni, equates to roughly A B*b* C♯ D♯ E F G♯ in this case. Six of the seven notes, then, fall within a semitone of either the tonic or fifth.)

Fig. 17.1 Examples of gestural communication from a performance by Veena
Sahasrabuddhe (VS). (a) At the end of an episode of improvisation, VS (left) marks
the cadence with a sharp downward movement, followed after the beat by a movement upwards and in towards her body. Madhuchhanda Sanyal is seated behind VS.
(b) As she begins her jor alap, VS introduces a periodic beating gesture to illustrate
the newly introduced pulse. Harmonium accompanist Seema Shirodkar taps the
index finger of her left hand in synchrony. Bageshree Vaze is seated to the left of
the picture. (c) As she holds the Pa (5th), VS raises her hand and holds the position.
(d) Listening to VS's alap, Vishwanath Shirodkar (left) shows his appreciation with
a sweeping head movement from right to left (from his perspective), then looks up
to the audience to share the moment.

(References to Shree Raga are scattered through an extensive literature: Sorrell
and Narayan include a complete performance of this raga by Pandit Ram
Narayan on the sarangi, with a transcription (1980).)

What was particularly interesting for me was her description of what she felt
Shree Raga was about. She had to approach this question obliquely – a few
moments earlier she had put the answer off to another day, but in the context
of discussing the character of another group of ragas, she made a comparison
with Rag Bhimpalasi:

> I was teaching Madhu [Rag] Bhimpalasi. I was just telling her, the gandhar komal,
> it has some request: 'Can you do this? *Please* do it, I will be obliged...' But in Shree,

no question, there is no request at all. There is not only not [a] request, not even [an] order – 'This is it – I can't change. If you like it, take it, if you don't like it, OK, forget about it...' I think Shree rag says that 'I have experienced all the worldly things, and I have come to the conclusion that this is my personality, this is my identity, and I have perfectly tested everything and I am very satisfied, whatever I am. I am fully satisfied with myself.' (Veena Sahasrabuddhe, interview, 12 April 2003. Gandhar komal is the flat third degree of the scale.)

When I commented that this was very close to what I had felt, citing my keywords – strong, calm, powerful – she replied,

Yes! Shree is a little bit – it's going inside, it's very serious... The day-to-day life, whatever's going on, Shree's not interested in that kind of a conversation. It is much more deep philosophy... meditative mood... calm, quiet, you said it yes... (Veena Sahasrabuddhe, interview, 12 April 2003)

I don't believe that in either case – singer or researcher – the 'standard' descriptions or associations of Shree Raga wholly drove our reflections, although the latter are consistent with some of them. Bor writes that 'Shri is usually personified as a calm, self-controlled hero, and portrayed as a royal and prosperous person.' (1999, p. 146), and Kaufmann cites the following from the Sangita-Darpana: 'Shree raga impressive and majestic like a king, with features like the god of love himself, has his ears adorned with tender leaves and is dressed in red' (1968, p. 281). Martinez concludes, on the basis of this and other evidence, that Shree is an ideal raga with which to describe a calm, self-controlled hero (1997, p. 320). (An interesting comparison could be drawn here with Davidson's reference to the idea of a singer 'becoming a character', discussed in this volume.)

But Shree's range of associations is rather diverse. One common association, for instance – which others have suggested to me but which did not come up at all in discussion with Veena – is with death and mourning. Shree is performed at, and associated with sunset, the rainy season, or the winter months (see Kaufmann 1968, p. 281). Kaufmann writes that 'Its character is mysterious, gentle, and often depicts the meditation of love and the nostalgic and prayerful mood of early evening'. Another reason to believe that neither my response nor Veena's description were simply a case of recycling 'standard' descriptions is that, contrary to my expectation, listeners who responded in terms similar to Veena's description included several with little exposure to raga music, who could not even recognize Shree Rag, let alone recall its usual associations.

I was struck by the extent to which I had perceived Veena's verbally expressed intention in her performance. This apparent evidence of effective communication left me with numerous questions: Did it work the same way for other listeners? How could this apparent communication be accounted for – how was the apparent 'strength' and 'certainty' conveyed by the music? *Whose* voice was strong and calm, who was the subject of the performance? In so far as I can answer these questions, I shall do so in the following sections.

Does the music communicate the same thing to all listeners?

I began to investigate this question by conducting short listening experiments in a variety of contexts. I worked with a few individuals at IITB, some of them Veena's students; I also tried the same experiment on a larger scale with a group at IITB – largely comprising Veena's 'music appreciation' class, to whom I had been invited to give a guest lecture (16 April 2003), and shortly afterwards with another group in a guest lecture at the University of Cambridge Music Faculty (30 April 2003). In both cases participants were highly selected, and could not be taken as representative samples of the Indian or UK populations. For these experiments I edited a section of Veena's alap, the unmeasured exposition of the raga, comprising roughly the first 7 minutes of this performance. In some cases I also used a second example, part of her performance of Rag Des, which is agreed to have a very different content: the results were indeed rather different, but they are not described in this chapter. I gave all participants an A4 sheet of paper, with an empty box drawn and the simple instruction:

> While I play the music extract, please note down any thoughts, feelings, images, or associations that come to your mind. Feel free to write or draw anything that comes into your head: there are no 'right answers'!

With the individual listeners, I left the room while they listened, then came back in at the end and asked them to summarize, orally, what they had noted down. In each case I also made video recordings, partly in the hope of recording listeners tapping or otherwise gesturing in response to the music. In fact, such responses were minimal, whether because they were listening alone or because of the artificial listening environment and the presence of the camera. One participant in the IITB group wrote, 'Felt like responding with my hand movement... Felt like responding by tapping my feet'.

Written, spoken, and in some cases drawn responses did however prove to be an extremely rich source of data: a single sound recording is capable of eliciting a vast range of responses. Listeners focus on different levels – some listen *analytically* and describe the sounds in terms of music theory; others are inspired to think of events in their own past, or other extra-musical *associations*; while yet others think of quite specific *moods*, *images* or *characters* (*cf.* Feld's 'interpretive moves', 1994: 92–3). I will quote here some of the comments offered in response to my queries.

Association…

Brings back pleasant memories of days when I had received a particular cassette as a gift, and I was just beginning to listen to Indian classical music. Anon, IITB

A live performance of Indian music, 1999 Stanford CA… Relaxation after yoga… Camden market. Anon, Cambridge

… shades into imagined context…

Sitting cross-legged on the floor… Musty smell of floor mats… Cramps in my legs. Anon, IITB

I was also feeling that I am sitting beside the Powai Lake just after the sunset. Madhuchhanda Sanyal, student of VS

… observations and fantasies involving space, time, and movement…

Lotus, morning, water in a canal next to a field waving in the breeze. Anon, IITB

It gives the feeling of Sun rising. Anon, IITB

A quiet evening; peace and repose descend. Anon, IITB

Voice is floating & flying like a bird in the air now – saw bird. Anon, IITB

Sailing slowly down a river in hot, humid weather at dusk. Sailing past various landscapes and images, all the time very slowly as if in a (nightmarish?) dream. Anon, Cambridge

…or involvement in the music…

Wonderful concert by Veenaji, Making you forget everything and get fully involved in it. Anon, IITB

… or on musical processes and theory…

Long rishabh makes us anticipate what's to come next, is it Puriya Dhanashree or which raga. Not clear yet, but elongated rishabh builds suspense…Re-Pa, when she hits pancham, it's clear it's Shree. Bageshree Vaze, student of VS. (Rishabh or Re is the second scale degree; pancham is Pa, the fifth.)

Voice entry completely changed harmony + feel of music… More notes added almost imperceptibly to what appeared to be B$^\flat$-A resolution at first. Anon, Cambridge

…on mood or emotion…

Sounds 'sad' > feeling of loneliness – being alone (of searching for something)… feeling of having lost something that is really close to you. Anon, IITB

After a harsh day, the soul is being relaxed, entering to a meditative mood, contemplating on the things that go by and getting ready for the new day to come. The soul experienced along the day happy things as well as less pleasant ones but she expresses strength and power to go beyond earthly things. Keren Porat, Israeli student of VS

Seems somehow to hold back, like having anxiety or other emotions that are not let out, but held in… A mindscape, not a landscape. Internal, not social. Anon, Cambridge

… and finally, on character

I imagine Lord Shiva, or a brave king or queen, one who cannot be challenged, is majestic in nature. Bageshree Vaze, student of VS

A lonely woman standing in the terrace in retrospection. Anon, IITB

Responses engaged in different discursive domains – often consecutively within a single sheet or even sentence. The most common responses, for listeners in both Mumbai and Cambridge, concern particular places (imagined either as contexts for listening, or scenes depicted by the music); images of movement (a bird, a boat, water flowing); and mood (calm and meditative, or sad and lonely). Listeners who imagined the music expressing character saw a figure either strong, calm and dignified (as Veena and I did), or contemplative and sad. Several of the Cambridge group described a feeling of 'oppression' which seems to have no equivalent in the Mumbai responses. Apart from the obvious differences in musical terminology among those who used it, the other distinction I notice is that the amount and range of imagery is richer for the Mumbai group - but where Cambridge listeners did write in imagistic terms the responses were not obviously distinguishable.

On the basis of verbal reports, then, what seems to have been communicated by Veena in this seven–minute clip of alap in Shree raga? She spoke in terms of the raga having a character or personality, and this character being self-confident, at peace with him or herself, introspective, and unconcerned with worldly troubles and trivia. Relatively few listeners responded explicitly in terms of a character in this way - for those who did the description was either consistent with Veena's, or couched in terms of sadness and loss. Others talked in terms of mood - again, variously calm and meditative, or expressing the sadness of one experiencing loss. The idea of sadness and loss might appear to contradict Veena's characterization (and intriguingly, take us closer to the theme of mourning referred to earlier). Seen in terms of embodied movement, however, it is easy to see how 'calm' could be interpreted as 'sad', since both would be associated with slow, introverted movements.

There may be a connection here with the findings of studies by Deva and Virmani and by Keil and Keil in the 1960s. These researchers used a set of four alap recordings and asked listeners – Indian and US respectively – to judge them using 7-point adjective rating scales. For the raga Puriya Dhanashree, which is closely related to Shree, they reported that 'There are clear indications that its affect is sweet and colourful and it is stable in its formation. Moreover, the moods of sobriety, weariness and darkness are also being communicated with the same piece... A noteworthy point... is that while Westerners "disliked" the music, Indians felt it rather "sweet" and deep.' (Deva and Virmani 1968, pp. 69–70; Deva 1981, p. 166). This would appear to be an interesting area of cultural difference in affect, which could be investigated further.

The other large group of responses concerned images of place, time, and movement. Time was characterised variously as suspended ('timeless'), as distinct from 'everyday time', or more concretely as either dawn or dusk. Places were those in which one could imagine relaxing and forgetting worldly troubles – in the sky, by the side of a lake or river, in the desert. Descriptions of movement were either circular, or spiral, or naturally flowing (a body of water, a lotus floating down a stream, a bird, a boat, plants blowing in the wind). The idea of the music taking one out of 'everyday' time is consistent with Veena's image of something 'inside' rather than social. Images of movement are plentiful in Veena's discourse as well as in these responses, as will be discussed in the next section, although the visual images to which they are attached (the bird, boat, water, or grass) did not figure in her description.

In summary then, although listeners' responses are varied and in many cases very personal, and although only a minority explicitly match Veena's description of the raga, I would suggest that the responses are overwhelmingly consistent with that description. There are relatively few exceptions – particularly the images of sadness (for some Mumbai listeners), or of oppression (in Cambridge). But in all the responses there is no mention of anger, jealousy, fear, doubt, disappointment, unrestrained joy, rapid, mechanical or graceless movement, dancing, or any kind of social meeting or relationship (except one brief reference to romantic feelings experienced as transitory). In short, there is plentiful evidence here of communication taking place through the medium of sound, with a degree of consistency between listeners in India and the UK.

How is the meaning communicated?

I suggest that the communication demonstrated earlier is at least partly mediated by images of movement (and the implications of that movement for space, time, and agency). First, let me return to Veena's description of her own expression in singing. She explained to me that she experiences her music as movement, and that this movement can be visualized.

> If I want to reach from rishabh to the upper rishabh, in the meanwhile all the swaras [notes] in the middle, re ma pa ni... I don't care [about them]. I know from rishabh to rishabh... I'm just going to... it's just like a curve, OK? I know I am perfectly going there, I have full confidence... I see rishabh there, waiting for me. And I will just go there. Because there has to be a fluency also, a flow, how you reach that. And from there, coming down, I make all kinds of designs, and the designs are in my mind...

Instead of swaras, I'm just thinking, imagining about the curves and the lines. (Veena Sahasrabuddhe, interview, 12 April 2003. Rishabh or Re is the second scale degree.)

When pressed specifically on the hand gestures she makes while singing, Veena suggested that 'Those gestures, I think [come] very *naturally*... because I am visualising it, even the flow and the continuation.' In summary, Veena reports experiencing the music as the expression of a character – a human being, or at least a consciousness with human-like characteristics. She also experiences the music as movement – directed movement through space, in curves and lines of various kinds. While singing, she also moves her body (especially her left hand, since she plays the tanpura with her right), in patterns which – we may hypothesize – relate closely to the imagined abstract movement, and/or to the movements her imagined character would make. Listeners, it appears, are able to pick up on those movement patterns – even in the absence of the visual clues afforded by her gestures – and seem to experience the music largely in terms of motion and its corollaries, space, time, and agency.

Thus, Veena might imagine the same phrase as either a calm, self-possessed character in a contemplative mood, or a graceful curve: the listener may perceive in the same phrase either the imagined character ('in a meditative mood'), or another image of motion ('Voice is floating & flying like a bird in the air'). There is no one-to-one mapping between sound and image, but rather a perception of motion, which maps onto images that are diverse but not arbitrary.

Who is the subject of the performance?

I found that the question *who is the subject of the performance?* is entwined, for Veena, with her identity in relation to both the music and the audience. She was clear that she sees the principal agent as being the raga itself, and that she places the character of the raga before her own personality when she performs.

> MC: [When] you sing Shree, is it always the same experience, or do you sometimes feel that the audience is giving more of a response, or that you're communicating more?
>
> VS: Earlier when I started performing on stage, I used to open my eyes and look for the audience: what are their responses? But these days [after 20 years on the stage] whatever I want to sing I will sing, and I am fully involved into that rag. And not only that. When I'm singing any rag, I'm forgetting my identity. I started thinking that I am Rag Shree, or I am Rag Kalyan, or I am Rag Desh...
>
> And suppose if audiences gave a good response that's fine, if it doesn't <LAUGHS> I don't get nervous... You must have noticed actually, when I am singing I am singing with my closed eyes sometimes. I am imagining or I am seeing some other things, maybe those notes. I'm not interested what the audience [is doing] (Veena Sahasrabuddhe, interview, 12 April 2003).

According to this account Veena is not so much projecting the mood or character of the raga. Rather, she is identifying with, and giving voice to an imagined, or virtual character. (This interpretation is consistent with a long tradition of Indian musical writing, where ragas are described as human or divine characters, and often pictorially represented in particular settings, performing particular actions: see the descriptions of Shree quoted earlier.) Ideally the character does not change, and nor does the mood; the full performance (of the alap at least) thus takes on the character of contemplation more than it suggests dramatic narrative. This creates the possibility that listeners may experience something similar – either observing, or themselves participating in, this virtual character. A listener may find that the music affords a quite different image, that is also nonetheless mediated by the same patterns of embodied movement.

The ethnographic evidence, then, points to the importance of embodiment and movement in the communication process. The performance does offer, of course, both auditory and visual information which may be analysed directly, and I hinted earlier that the performer's movements may be regarded as analogous to the movement specified by the music. In the next section I develop this theme further, discussing how gestural analysis can be applied in this context.

From ethnography to gestural analysis

Gestural analysis

I have suggested that a particular musical extract can communicate many things, and that what seems to link many of those things with the performer's intentions are real and imagined patterns of movement in space and time. I came to this understanding based on what musician and listeners told me, supported by the evidence of the singer's gestural communication. In this section, I will offer a preliminary discussion of the ways in which ethnographic work can be enriched by means of gestural analysis, such as has been developed in the context of speech communication. In the case of this extract, since there is no text, gestural analysis implies investigating Veena's movement in relation to the music's melodic and rhythmic processes, rather than in relation to the linguistic meaning of a text, but the challenge is otherwise similar to speech-based studies. I shall briefly describe some important studies of gestural communication, before locating my own categories in relation to those of other researchers.

An influential study by Ekman and Friesen offers descriptions of five categories of nonverbal behaviour – emblems, illustrators, affect displays, regulators and adaptors (1969: 62ff, *cf.* Davidson, this volume). By 1977, Ekman had simplified his scheme to four categories:

i. emblems (movements tied to specific verbal meanings)

ii. body manipulators (head scratching, nose picking etc)

iii. illustrators (gestures tied to the content or flow of speech), and

iv. emotional expressions

This work has been developed further by scholars including Kendon (1981, 1982) and McNeill. McNeill makes a distinction between gestures and non-gestures, the latter including 'self-touching (e.g., stroking the hair) and object-manipulations' (1992, p. 78), before offering five categories of gesture:

i. iconics, '[bearing] a close formal relationship to the semantic content of speech' (78)

ii. metaphorics, which 'present an image of an abstract concept' (80)

iii. deictics (pointing gestures)

iv. beats, that 'do not present a discernible meaning, and ... can be recognized positively in terms of their prototypical movement characteristics' (80) and

v. 'Butterworths' (gestures associated with 'speech failures', e.g. a hand grasping the air as the speaker searches for a word)

The last scheme to be discussed here is that described by Rimé and Schiaratura as a 'revised Efron system' (1991, p. 242ff, drawing on Efron's pioneering study of 1941). They distinguish gestures on the basis of the movement's referent. In outline, they identify:

i. Gestures referring to the ideational process: broken down into two sub-categories, speech-marking hand movements and ideographs (hand or finger movements 'sketching in space the logical track of the speaker's thinking' (244))

ii. Gestures referring to the object of speech (depictive type): broken down into iconic gestures 'that parallel the speech by presenting some figural representation of the object evoked simultaneously' (244) and pantomimic gestures (mimetic actions)

iii. Gestures referring to the object of the speech (evocative type): broken down into deictic gestures (pointing) and symbolic gestures (or emblems, see earlier)

In one of the very few empirical studies of gesture in vocal musical perform-ance to be published to date, Davidson (2001, see also this volume) adapts the framework suggested by Ekman and Friesen, applying their terms to a performance by Annie Lennox. In this case the scheme is adequate, because Davidson can interpret gestures in relation to lyrical content. I nonetheless find Rimé and Schiaratura's scheme more flexible when applied to gestures accompanying textless singing (as in the present example), and it may be use-ful in extending Davidson's approach to textless performance. Next, I will refer to my own set of five headings, which I came to inductively on the basis of

Table 17.1 Categorization of gestures used in *khyal* vocal performance (partly derived from Rimé and Schiaratura 1991, p. 248)

A. Gestures classified by Rimé and Schiaratura 1991	Applied to the present example
Gestures referring to the ideational process	
1. Nondepictive gestures: speech markers	I. Markers of pulse or tala structure; markers of cadence (mukhra). See Fig. 17.1, (a) and (b)
2. Depictive gestures: ideographs	II. Gestures which appear analogous to the melodic flow or "motion". See Fig. 17.1 (c)
Gestures referring to the object: depictive kinds	
1. Iconographic or iconic gestures	N/a (but can occur in other Indian vocal performances)
2. Pantomimic gestures	N/a (but can occur in other Indian vocal performances)
Gestures referring to the object: evocative kinds	
1. Deictic gestures or pointing	N/a (but could be an alternate interpretation of some ideographic gestures)
2. Symbolic gestures or emblems	III. Instructions to subordinate performers; appreciation. See Fig. 17.1(d)
B. Movements not included in speech-based studies, or classified as 'non-gesture'	
Physical movements necessary to produce sound	IV. Vocalization, striking strings, keys or drum heads
Manipulators of the body and the immediate physical environment	V. Tuning instruments, adjusting microphones, adjusting clothing

observation of this performance. Table 17.1 sets out how they are related to the 'revised Efron' system.

Gesture in khyal performance

In the present example (Veena Sahasrabuddhe's alap in Shree raga), the performers' movements can be divided into five categories, as described earlier. I introduce each group with my own shorthand term, and with the equivalent term used by Rimé and Schiaratura in parentheses, where applicable. The first three are illustrated with stills from the performance, marked with arrows to indicate the direction of movement (Fig. 17.1).

I. Markers (nondepictive gestures; analogous to speech markers)

These are markers of musical process or structure, and include marking focal moments such as cadences (mukhra, Fig. 17.1 (a)), or beating out a regular pulse or the tala structure (Fig 17.1(b)). This category could also be taken to include listeners' gestures of tapping or nodding in time with the music, counting tal or sympathetically marking the cadence; gestures which may also have an emblematic function ('I got it!', 'I'm in time'). (Counting the tala structure could be categorized as both nondepictive and emblematic, since the particular signs used have semantic functions.)

II. Illustrators (depictive gestures or ideographs)

In this case illustrators are tied to the content of the singing, rather than (as with Ekman, see earlier) to speech. Examples here include the gesture of raising and holding the hand, associated with the Pa (Fig. 17.1(c)).

III. Emblems (symbolic gestures)

These gestures have verbal equivalents: 'Well done', 'Now you take a solo', and so on. This type of gesture is often used by musicians to instruct subordinate musicians (e.g. telling tanpura players to play louder, or tabla players to play faster), to offer approval, or to invite the audience or fellow musicians to share appreciation of the music (Fig. 17.1(d)).

IV. Sound producers: movements necessary to produce the sound

In this example this category would include plucking tanpura strings, striking harmonium keys or tabla drum heads. These gestures can have a multiple function: for instance it may be necessary to adjust posture and head position in order to produce a vocal sound, but this may nonetheless be effected in a more or less 'dramatic' manner.

V. Manipulators: movements manipulating the physical environment

This category includes adjusting clothing or microphone placement, taking a drink, or retuning an instrument.

This scheme can be used to analyse the flow and exchange of gestural communication amongst musicians (and listeners) at a gross level, while also providing the context for finer-grained studies of short fragments of the performance. These gestural analyses, in turn, may be correlated with the audio data so that the relationship between sound and gesture can be studied in much greater detail. Even a preliminary analysis of this performance suggests that, for instance, the speed and density of gestures increase with the tempo of the music. It is also apparent that Veena shifts from continuous, flowing ideographic gestures in the slow, unpulsed section of alap to the 'jor alap' section, where she marks a clear pulse with her hand, seeming to superimpose gestures illustrating the movement of the melody over those marking the pulse. It is clear that analogous musical events or processes are illustrated with similar gestures (the gestures in Fig. 17.1(a–c) were selected from many similar moments), but detailed investigation of variation in both (is the time she holds the Pa proportional to the time her hand is held steady?) needs to be carried out.

Another area for future investigation is the degree to which gestures, as observed from the listener's perspective, actually communicate anything that is not also accessible through the sound. (Apart from the emblem category, of course, which is clearly not redundant.) It is clear that listeners perceive motion in the absence of visual clues (the responses quoted earlier are all drawn from occasions on which participants responded to audio recordings only; cf. Clarke 2001). It can also be demonstrated that a mute film of the performance conveys something to viewers: when I tried this experiment at the European Seminar in Ethnomusicology (Gablitz, Austria, 20 September 2003), mutterings audible from the podium changed from 'Where's the sound? Turn the volume up!' to 'Ah, look, you can see the music!'. If the singer's movements are analogous to musical processes, it should follow that they are redundant from the point of view of reception: however, it may be that experienced listeners are able to imagine the singer's likely gestures from the sound information. In any case, redundancy does not imply uselessness, and gestures may be used as clues in the interpretation of the sound, particularly by novice listeners.

Summary: communication, gesture and cultural competence

I started this chapter by describing the different dimensions of communication in raga performance, mentioning (i) identification, (ii) status, (iii) interpersonal communication, (iv) sound situating one within the performance space and time, (v) sounds communicating character or mood, and finally (vi) intramusical communication. I suggested that different individuals could participate in communication in different ways – some of these dimensions are open to all, some depend on a general cultural competence, others rely on detailed music-theoretical knowledge.

The bulk of the chapter has used a particular ethnographic and musical example to investigate the communication of character and mood. The singer Veena Sahasrabuddhe reports her own experience of the piece, Shree Raga, in terms of (1) assuming the identity of a virtual character, Shree Raga itself, who expresses a state of calm and dignified detachment; as well as (2) abstract patterns of motion, visualized in performance as trajectories ('curves and lines') toward locations ('I just go there'). Listeners engage with the sound in a variety of ways: a minority explicitly report the presence of a character, while most listeners (at least, most Indian listeners) report images of place, time and/or motion involving themselves, other people, animals or natural phenomena. Other modes of discourse, including music-theoretical and personal-associative ('reminds me of...') are reported more rarely.

I suggested that these reports confirm the idea that the music affords interpretation on the basis of embodied motion: seen in terms of patterns of bodily movement, even the apparently contradictory responses (sad, oppressive) seem consistent with the performer's intentions, and the performance seems to have been highly effective as a communicative act. In the last section, I suggested that this ethnographic evidence could be followed up using techniques of gestural analysis borrowed from the field of nonverbal communication, and made some initial proposals as to how this might be achieved.

Musical sound, with its associated gestures, is a specialized form of nonverbal behaviour used for communicative means: other musicians and listeners in turn use forms of nonverbal behaviour to express to each other and to the soloist that they understand and appreciate what she is doing, and can participate in the event appropriately. The demonstration that each participant can apply the appropriate codes of nonverbal communication is what facilitates the sense of identification described here; use of these codes also affirms that each understands their relative status and specialized roles, and allows individuals to effectively manage the event and the musical performance. The generic qualities of the sound establish a space and time within which participants can identify and interpret the specific musical sound elements, structures and processes presented: these are interpreted in various ways which seem to be largely dependent on patterns of embodied motion, while certain individuals can engage at another level by interpreting the performance in the light of intramusical associations. Thus, the ethnographic approach described here relates not only to musical communication in the narrow sense but to the whole multidimensional complex of communication in raga performance.

Acknowledgements

I cannot begin to express my gratitude to Veena Sahasrabuddhe, her husband Hari, their accompanists, students, and everyone else whose generous co-operation made this study possible. Thanks also to the staff of IITB, who did so much to make the research both successful and enjoyable, and to everyone involved in the filming and audio recording. Thanks to the editors, and to Laura Leante, Jennifer Lanipekun, and Bageshree Vaze for the helpful comments on drafts of the chapter, and to Laura Leante for help with Fig. 17.1. This project was supported by British Academy grant SG-35623.

References

Baily, J. (1985) Music structure and human movement. In *Musical structure and cognition*, (ed. P. Howell, I. Cross, and R. West), pp. 237–58. London: Academic Press.

Balkwell, L.L. and Thompson, W.F. (1999) A cross-cultural investigation of the perception of emotion in music: psychophysical and cultural cues. *Music Perception*, **17**(1), 43–64.

Blacking, J. (1977) Towards an anthropology of the body. In *The anthropology of the body*, (ed. J. Blacking). London: Academic Press.

Blacking, J. (1995) *Music, culture and experience. Selected papers of John Blacking*. Edited with an introduction by R. Byron. Chicago, IL: University of Chicago Press.

Bor, J. (1999) *The raga guide. A survey of 74 Hindustani ragas*. Nimbus Records and Rotterdam Conservatory of Music.

Clarke, E. (2001) Meaning and the specification of motion in music. *Musicae Scientiae*, **5**(2), 213–34.

Clayton, M. (1999) *Khyal: Classical singing of North India*. Milton Keynes, OU Worldwide (ETHNO VC01). [To download the accompanying booklet go to www.open.ac.uk/arts/music/mclayton.htm]

Clayton, M. (2000) *Time in Indian music: Rhythm, metre and form in North Indian rag performance*. Oxford: Oxford University Press.

Clayton, M. (2001) Introduction: towards a theory of musical meaning (in India and elsewhere), *British Journal of Ethnomusicology*, **10**(1), 1–17.

Clayton, M. (2003) Comparing music, comparing musicology. In *The cultural study of music; A critical introduction*, (ed. M. Clayton, T. Herbert, and R. Middleton), pp. 57–68. New York: Routledge.

Coker, W. (1972) *Music and meaning*. New York: Free Press.

Cox, A. (2001) The mimetic hypothesis and embodied musical meaning. *Musicae Scientiae*, **5**(2), 195–212.

Davidson, J. (2001) The role of the body in the production and perception of solo vocal performance: A case study of Annie Lennox. *Musicae Scientiae*, **5**(2), 235–56.

Deva, B.C. (1981) *The music of India: A scientific study*, pp. 141–222. New Delhi: Munshiram Manoharlal.

Deva, B.C. and Virmani, K.G. (1968) Meaning of music. An empirical study of psychological responses to Indian music. *Sangeet Natak* **10**, 54–93.

Efron, D. (1941/1972) *Gesture, race and culture*. The Hague: Mouton.

Ekman, P. (1977) Biological and cultural contributions to body and facial movement. In *The anthropology of the body*, (ed. J. Blacking), pp. 39–84. London: Academic Press.

Ekman, P. and Friesen, W.V. (1969) The repertoire of nonverbal behavior: Categories, origins, usage, and coding. *Semiotica*, **1**, 49–98.

Feld, S. (1984/1994) Communication, music, and speech about music. In *Music grooves*, (ed. C. Keil and S. Feld), pp. 77–95. Chicago, IL: University of Chicago Press.

Gibson, J.J. (1966) *The senses considered as perceptual systems*. Boston, MA: Houghton Mifflin.

Gibson, J.J. (1979/1986) *The ecological approach to visual perception*. Hillsdale, NJ: Lawrence Erlbaum Associates.

Johnson, M. (1987) *The body in the mind. The bodily basis of meaning, imagination and reason*. Chicago, IL: University of Chicago Press.

Kaufmann, W. (1968) *The ragas of north India.* New Delhi: IBH Publishing.

Keil, C. and Keil, A. (1966) Musical meaning: A preliminary report. *Ethnomusicology,* **10,** 153–73.

Kendon, A. (1981) Introduction: Current issues in the study of "nonverbal communication", In *Nonverbal communication, interaction and gesture (Selections from Semiotica),* (ed. A. Kendon), pp. 1–53. The Hague: Mouton.

Kendon, A. (1982) The organization of behavior in face-to-face interaction: observations on the development of a methodology, In *Handbook of methods in nonverbal behavior research,* (ed. K. R. Scherer and P. Ekman), pp. 440–505. Cambridge: Cambridge University Press.

Kubik, G. (1979) Pattern perception and recognition in African music. In *The performing arts,* (ed. J. Blacking and J. W. Kealiinohomohu), pp. 221–49. The Hague: Mouton.

Lakoff, G. and Johnson, M. (1980) *Metaphors we live by.* Chicago, IL: University of Chicago Press.

Martinez, J. L. (1997) *Semiosis in Hindustani music.* Acta Semiotica Fennica V. Imatra, International Semiotics Institute.

McNeill, D. (1992) *Hand and mind. What gestures reveal about thought.* Chicago, IL: University of Chicago Press.

Middleton, R. (1993) Popular music analysis and musicology: bridging the gap. *Popular music,* **12**(2), 177–90.

Qureshi, R.B. (1986/1995) *Sufi music of India and Pakistan.* Chicago, IL: University of Chicago Press.

Qureshi, R.B. (1987) Musical sound and contextual input: A performance model for musical analysis. *Ethnomusicology,* **31,** 56–86.

Rimé, B. and Schiaratura, L. (1991) Gesture and speech, In *Fundamentals of nonverbal behavior,* (ed. R. S. Feldman and B. Rimé), pp. 239–81. Cambridge: Cambridge University Press.

Ruckert, G. and Widdess, R. (2000) Hindustani Raga. *The Garland Encyclopedia of World Music Volume 5. South Asia: The Indian Subcontinent,* (ed. Alison Arnold), pp. 64–88. New York: Garland.

Scruton, R. (1997) *The aesthetics of music.* Oxford: Oxford University Press.

Sorrell, N. and Narayan, R. (1980) *Indian music in performance. A practical introduction.* Manchester: Manchester University Press.

Tagg, P. (1999) *Introductory notes to the semiotics of music.* http://www.tagg.org/texts.html, accessed 13 Oct 2003.

Chapter 18

The role of music communication in cinema

Scott D. Lipscomb and David E. Tolchinsky

Prelude

Past research leaves no doubt that music is an effective medium for communication. When one considers, however, the matter of *what it is that is being communicated* 'the plot begins to thicken,' to use a filmic metaphor. In the following pages, after presenting a general model of music communication, we will introduce models – both empirical and theoretical – of film music perception and the role of music in film, referencing some of the most significant research investigating the relationship between sound and image in the cinematic context. Finally, we shall enumerate the many ways in which the motion picture soundtrack can supplement, enhance, and expand upon the meaning of a film's narrative, providing specific cinematic examples. Throughout this chapter, the terms film, cinema, and motion picture will be used interchangeably. The authors acknowledge the distinction between the three terms and the variety of media types upon which each may exist. Because sound can be congruent with an image, in dramatic opposition to what is expected, or simply different from what is conventionally anticipated, 'the sound track can clarify image events, contradict them, or render them ambiguous' (Bordwell and Thompson 1985, p. 184). The relationship between the auditory and visual components in cinema is both active and dynamic, affording a multiplicity of possible relations that can evolve – sometimes dramatically – as the narrative unfolds. This chapter will take a cognitive approach to the study of musical communication in cinema. As a result, much attention will be paid and credence given to the results of experimental research investigating the perception of human beings in response to the motion picture experience.

Prior to the 1990s, as noted by Annabel Cohen (2001), the study of film music and its role in the cinematic context had been widely neglected by both musicologists and psychologists. There is now a significant amount of research confirming that the presence of film music affects the perceived emotional content of a visual scene (e.g. Boltz 2001; Bullerjahn and Güldenring 1994; Iwamiya 1994; Krumhansl and Schenck 1997; Lipscomb and Kendall 1994; Marshall and Cohen 1988; Tannenbaum 1956; Thayer and Levenson 1983), influences the specific aspects of a scene that are remembered (Boltz 2001; Boltz *et al.* 1991), and is capable of providing a sense of closure (Thompson *et al.* 1994). Music also has the potential to evoke emotion in a scene that would, in its absence, be perceived as neutral. A well-known excerpt demonstrating this fact can be found in Alfred Hitchcock's *Psycho* (1960; timing [represented as *hh:mm:ss*] was taken from the Collector's edition DVD, Universal 20251). In the 'rainstorm sequence' scene (25:35), Bernard Herrmann's musical score creates the jarring tension felt by the audience, a tension not present when the scene is viewed sans music (Smilow and Waletzky 1992; Waletzky 1995).

We will argue for a more inclusive definition of the term 'film music' than that proposed in previous publications. In our view, film music is one component of a spectrum of sound that includes the musical score, ambient sound, dialogue, sound effects, and silence. The functions of these constituent elements often overlap or interact with one another, as will be described and demonstrated in the following pages. Using one extended excerpt from *2001: A Space Odyssey* (1968), the present authors have suggested that, in the absence of a composed musical score, other elements (e.g. ambient sound) can function similarly to music, providing dynamically shifting and structurally meaningful sound to propel the narrative forward (Tolchinsky and Lipscomb, in preparation). Before proceeding, however, let us reflect briefly upon the music communication process in general.

A model of music communication

Many studies have investigated various aspects of musical communication as a form of expression (Bengtsson and Gabrielsson 1983; Clynes 1983, Gabrielsson 1988, Senju and Ohgushi 1987; Sundberg *et al.* 1983). A tripartite communication model was proposed by Campbell and Heller (1980), consisting of simply a composer, performer, and listener. Using this previous model as a foundation, Kendall and Carterette (1990) elegantly expanded upon this model of music communication, elaborating upon and clearly defining the constituent parts and elucidating the specific interrelationships that exist (Fig. 18.1). In an attempt to determine how, specifically, a performer conveys composer-intended information to a listener, they outline a process involving multiple states of coding, decoding, and recoding. Because music is a culturally defined perceptual artefact, existing in the mind of enculturated listeners (Hood 1982; Lomax 1962; Merriam 1964; Nettl 1983), successful communication must involve shared implicit and explicit knowledge structures. In the context

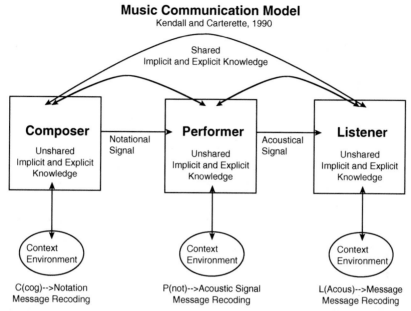

Fig. 18.1 Kendall and Carterette's (1990) model of music communication. (© *1990 by The Regents of the University of California.* Reprinted from *Music Perception*, Vol. 6, No. 2, Issue: *Winter 1990,* pp. *129–163,* with permission.)

of music communication, we would suggest that the degree to which a composer/director 'succeeds' in communicating a musical message is in direct proportion to the level of agreement between the emotional and/or expressive intent of the message and that perceived by the listener. Kendall and Carterette suggest that this process involves the 'grouping and parsing of elementary thought units' (p. 132), these 'thought units' (metasymbols) are mental representations involved in the process of creating, performing, and listening to musical sound. For additional information related to these topics, see the discussion of communication theory – specifically, information theory – by Cohen (this volume) and Juslin's chapter on the expression of emotion through music (also this volume).

Models of film music communication: empirical evidence

Several researchers have proposed models specific to the perception and cognition of music within the cinematic context. Initiating this systematic effort, Marshall and Cohen's (1988) bipartite 'congruence–associationist' model suggests that the meaning of a film is altered by the music as the result of two complex cognitive processes. Based upon subject responses, the researchers determined that musical sound directly effects subject ratings on the Potency (strong–weak) and Activity (active–passive) dimensions, while the Evaluative dimension (good–bad) relies on the degree of congruence between the audio and visual components on all three dimensions, as determined by a 'comparator' component. The second part of the model describes how musical meaning is ascribed to the film. Marshall and Cohen claim that attention is directed to the overlapping congruent meaning of the music and the film. Referential meanings associated with the music are ascribed to the overlapped (congruent) audio – visual components upon which attention is focused. As a result, 'the music alters meaning of a particular aspect of the film' (1988, p. 109).

Marshall and Cohen also acknowledge the important role played by temporal characteristics of the sound and image, stating that 'the assignment of accent to events will affect retention, processing, and interpretation' (1988, p. 108). Incorporation of this important component of the developing model was provided by Lipscomb and Kendall's (1994) Film Music Paradigm, in which two implicit processes are considered as the basis for whether attentional focus is shifted to the musical component or whether it is likely to remain at the subconscious – cognitively 'inaudible' – level (Fig. 18. 2). Analysing the results of two experiments in which excerpts from *Star Trek IV: The Voyage Home* (1986) were used as experimental stimuli, the authors suggested that these two implicit processes include an association judgement (similar to Marshall and Cohen's assessment of 'congruence') and an evaluation of the accent structure relationship between the auditory and visual components, i.e. the extent to which salient events in the musical score occur simultaneously with significant events in the visual scene.

Based on the results of a series of three experiments utilizing stimuli ranging from extremely simple, single-object animations to actual movie excerpts, Lipscomb (1995) determined that the role of the two implicit judgements appears to be dynamic such that, with simple stimuli (such as that used in Lipscomb 1995, Experiment 1 and Marshall and Cohen 1988), accent structure alignment plays a dominant role. As the stimuli become more complex – complex animations and actual movie excerpts – the primary determinant of meaning in the auditory domain appears to shift to the associational judgement, with the accent structure alignment aspect receding to a supporting role, i.e. focusing audience attention on certain aspects of the visual image (Boltz 2001). The changing relationship revealed in Lipscomb (1995) provides confirmation of an early warning stated by Lipscomb and Kendall (1994). The authors proposed that generalizing results of studies

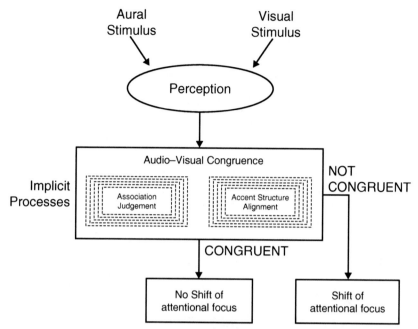

Fig. 18.2 A revised version of Lipscomb and Kendall's (1994) film music paradigm. (The original model was printed as Figure 7 in S. Lipscomb and R. Kendall: Perceptual judgement of the relationship between musical and visual components in film. *Psychomusicology, 13*(Spring/Fall), 1994, p. 91. Reprinted with permission of *Psychomusicology.*)

incorporating highly reduced stimuli (like Marshall and Cohen 1988) to the actual motion picture experience is problematic. The extreme simplicity of the visual imagery and the musical 'score' (which is itself highly repetitive) 'fail[s] to provide an accurate representation of the highly developed craftsmanship evident in a typical movie score' (p. 63). As shown by Lipscomb (1995), the level of stimulus complexity does appear to alter the manner in which the various audio–visual components and their interrelationships are processed in human cognition.

The most complex and fully developed model of film music perception proposed to date is Cohen's (2001) 'congruence–associationist framework for understanding film-music communication' (p. 259; see Fig. 18.3). This multi-stage model attempts to account for meaning derived from the spoken narrative, visual images, and musical sound. Level A represents *bottom-up processing* based on physical features derived from input to each perceptual modality. Level B represents the determination of cross-modal congruence, based on

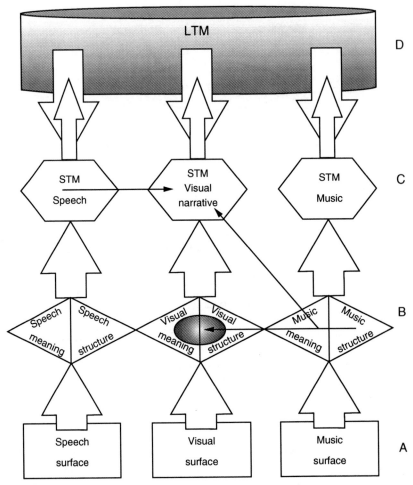

Fig. 18.3 Cohen's (2001) congruence–associationist framework for understanding film music communication. (The original model was printed as Figure 11.3 (p. 259) in *Music and Emotion* by P.N. Juslin and J.A. Sloboda (2001). Reprinted with permission of Oxford University Press.)

both semantic (associational) and syntactic (temporal) grouping features. Level D represents *top-down processing*, determined by an individual's past experience and the retention of that experience in long term memory. According to this model, the input from levels B (bottom-up) and D (top-down) meet in the observer's conscious mind (level C), where information is prepared for transfer to short term memory. In its details, clearly documented in Cohen (2001), this model is based on an assumption of visual primacy, citing several studies that have suggested a subservient role for the auditory component (Bolivar *et al.* 1994; Driver 1997; Thompson *et al.* 1994). Though a common assumption throughout the literature, the present authors would like to express reservation about this assumption and suggest that additional research is required before such a claim can be supported.

The role of music in cinema: theoretical models

Richard Wagner, creator of the idealized *Gesamtkunstwerk* (total art work) in the form of the nineteenth century music drama, claimed that 'as pure organ of the feeling, [music] speaks out the very thing which word speech in itself can not speak out ... that which, looked at from the standpoint of our human intellect, is *the unspeakable*' (Wagner 1849/1964, p. 217). According to Suzanne K. Langer, 'music has all the earmarks of a true symbolism, except one: the existence of an *assigned connotation*' and, though music is clearly a symbolic form, it remains an 'unconsummated symbol' (1942, p. 240). Royal Brown (1988) suggests that this 'unconsummatedness' accounts for the predominance of the orchestral film score. Excluding the highly effective marketing strategy of using commercially viable hit singles in an attempt to both increase box office receipts and bring in additional revenue in the form of soundtrack sales, he claims that there is an 'almost total lack' of the voice in the classical score. Brown argues that 'the very human presence felt through the performance of a vocalist tends to move the musical symbol one step closer toward consummation.... The fact that the audience *can* ask where a single human voice is coming from without questioning the presence of a large symphony orchestra on that same music track says a lot about the relationship between film and classical music' (p. 167). Therefore, in order for a film to make the greatest possible impact, there must be an interaction between the verbal dialogue (consummated symbol), the cinematic images (also a consummated symbol), and the musical score (unconsummated symbol).

To answer the question 'How does music in film narration create a *point of experience* for the spectator?,' Gorbman (1987) suggests three methods by which music can 'signify' in the context of a narrative film. *Purely musical signification* results from the highly coded syntactical relationships inherent in the association of one musical tone with another. Patterns of tension and release provide a sense of organization and meaning to the musical sound, apart from any extramusical association that might exist; Hanslick's (1891/1986) *absolute music. Cultural musical codes* are exemplified by music that has come to be associated with a certain mood or state of mind; Meyer's (1956) *referentialism*. These associations have been further canonized by the Hollywood film industry into certain conventional expectations – implicitly anticipated by enculturated audience members – determined by the narrative content of a given scene. Finally, *cinematic codes* influence musical meaning merely due to the placement of musical sound within the filmic context. Opening credit and end title music illustrate this type of signification, as well as recurring musical themes that come to represent characters or situations within the film.

As stated previously, there is a commonly held belief that film music is not to be heard (Burt 1994; Gorbman 1987). Instead, it is believed to fulfill its role in communicating the underlying psychological drama of the narrative at a subconscious level (Lipscomb 1989). There is, however, certain music that is intended to be heard by the audience as part of the cinematic diegesis, i.e. 'the *narratively implied spatiotemporal world of the actions and characters*' (Gorbman 1987, p. 21). This 'world' includes, of course, a sonic component. Therefore, all sounds – including music – that are understood to be heard by characters in the narrative are referred to as *diegetic*, while those that are not part of the diegesis (e.g. the orchestral score) are referred to as *nondiegetic*. This would suggest that diegetic music is more likely to be processed at the conscious level while nondiegetic music might remain at the subconscious level, though research is needed to determine whether this is true, in fact. It is worth noting also, that the source of diegetic sound can be either seen or unseen. Michel Chion (1990/1994) distinguishes these two types of diegetic forms using the terms 'onscreen' and 'offscreen,' respectively (pp. 76–8).

Two extant models related to the role and function of film music are worthy of consideration. Gorbman (1987) compiled a list of principles for composition, mixing, and editing in the 'classical' Hollywood film, emphasizing primarily the period between the late 1930s and 1940s and based on the scores of Max Steiner, composer of more than three hundred film scores (Thomas 1991), including *King Kong* (1933), *Casablanca* (1943), and *Gone With the Wind* (1947). The seven principles were considered by Gorbman as 'a discursive field rather than a monolithic system with inviolable rules' (p. 73). Table 18.1 contains six of the seven principles quoted directly from Gorbman's text. To confirm her intention that none of these principles was to be considered sacrosanct, the seventh principle states that 'a given film score may violate any of the principles mentioned earlier, provided the violation is at the service of the other principles' (Gorbman 1987, p. 73). Though the present authors would question the subordination of the musical component to image and dialogue, as stated in the 'inaudibility' principle, many aspects of this model will be incorporated into our own list of film music functions.

The second model is one proposed by Nicholas Cook (1998), conceived for the express purpose of analysing musical multimedia. Like the present authors,

Table 18.1 Gorbman's list of principles for composition, mixing, and editing in the 'classical' Hollywood film (1987, p. 259).

Principle	Description
Invisibility	The technical apparatus of nondiegetic music must not be visible.
"Inaudibility"	Music is not meant to be heard consciously. As such it should subordinate itself to dialogue, to visuals—i.e. to the primary vehicles of the narrative.
Signifier of emotion	Soundtrack music may set specific moods and emphasize particular emotions suggested in the narrative, but first and foremost, it is a signifier of emotion itself.
Narrative cueing	*referential/narrative*: music gives referential and narrative cues, e.g. indicating point of view, supplying formal demarcations, and establishing setting and characters.
	connotative: music 'interprets' and 'illustrates' narrative events.
Continuity	Music provides formal and rhythmic continuity—between shots, in transitions between scenes, by filling 'gaps'.
Unity	Via repetition and variation of musical material and instrumentation, music aids in the construction of formal and narrative unity.

Cook takes issue with the oft-stated 'fact' that music plays a subsidiary role to the image; what he refers to as 'the deceptive translucency of music' (p. 21). Not content to settle for Gorbman's classification of the music-image and music-narrative relationship as 'mutual implication' (Gorbman 1987, p. 15), Cook suggests considering the various roles played by these components in terms of denotation and connotation. He explains that 'words and pictures deal primarily with the specific, with the objective, while music deals primarily with responses – that is, with values, emotions, and attitudes. . . . the connotative qualities of the music complement the denotative qualities of the words and pictures' (p. 22). Cook sets forth three basic ways in which different media can relate one to another: *conformance, complementation,* and *contest.* Predicated upon the identification of similarities and differences between the component media, the model provides a two-step process for determining the existing relationship. The initial stage, identified as the 'similarity test,' involves the determination of whether component media are consistent with one another. To apply this test to a motion picture, one would ask 'Is the same information being presented via both the auditory and visual modalities?' To use Cook's terminology, we are asking whether the music and image are *consistent* or merely *coherent,* i.e. providing a variant meaning or differential elaboration.

Ultimately, if we can state that the relationship is invertible without changing the perceived meaning (i.e. it is equally valid to say that the music projects the meaning of the image or the image projects the meaning of the music), then the multimedia example has passed the similarity test and the relationship exhibited is one of *conformance*. In those instances where component media are determined to be coherent rather than consistent (i.e. failing the similarity test), one moves to the second step of the model: the 'difference test.' The answer to this query determines whether or not the inter-media relationship is one of contradiction in which the meanings of the component media are in opposition to one another, producing a collision or confrontation. If such contradiction exists, the relationship is one of *contest*. Otherwise, the relationship is one of *complementation* – neither consistency nor contradiction – in which the various media 'are generally aligned with one another and share the same narrative structure, but each medium elaborates the underlying structure in a different way' (Cook 1998, p. 102). Cook's model has proven quite useful, both as an analytical tool and as a means of providing a consistent and coherent vocabulary for the discussion of dynamic inter-media relationships.

What film music conveys

As confirmed by dozens of published theoretical treatises, the words of film music composers themselves, and the research cited previously, it is undeniable that a film score, in its typical role, serves to reinforce and/or augment the emotional content of a cinematic narrative. In the paragraphs below, we will propose an extended set of ways in which the soundtrack can serve to communicate meaning through sound (including music), taking into account the director's – and, therefore, the composer's – intentions, the narrative content of the film, and the overall strategy of the director in constructing the multi-faceted soundtrack. Throughout the remainder of this chapter we will use the term 'director' as a metonymy for the complex collaboration and decision-making process involving composer, sound designer, screenwriter, editor, and director, but which is ultimately shaped and controlled by the director, to whom the responsibility for the final decision typically falls. The following list of methods by which a cinematic soundtrack can communicate from director to audience represents the various ways a soundtrack can elicit emotional response and/or convey the dramatic intentions of the film narrative. Once delineated, we will further clarify the enumerated possibilities by analysing two well-known boxing movies, revealing specifically how choices made by directors, composers, and sound designers determine the meaning that the soundtrack – and, thus, the motion picture – will convey to the audience.

Music can convey the general mood of a film

Musical sound provides a cue for the listener concerning whether the narrative is supposed to be perceived as scary, romantic, funny, disturbing, familiar, comforting, other-worldly. In this capacity, the role of music is significantly enhanced by the *level of ambiguity* inherent in the visual scene. This character-istic was referred to as 'abstraction' by Lipscomb and Kendall (1994, p. 80) and was used by Boltz (2001) as a criterion for visual stimulus selection. Specifically, the more ambiguous the meaning of the visual image, the more influence is exerted by the musical score in the process of interpreting the scene.

Music can convey the *scope* of a film, effectively communicating whether the motion picture is an epic drama (*Star Wars* 1977; *Gone With the Wind* 1947) or a story that exists on a more personal scale (*Ghost World* 2001). Music can convey the *quality and size of a space*; what Gorbman refers to as 'depth in space' or 'physical volumes' (1987, p. 25). For example, in *Alien* (1979) and Olivier's *Hamlet* (1948) the music serves at times to make small and/or artificial spaces seem more grand and to enhance the sense of realism. In addition, music can establish a narrative's *placement in time*. Motion picture scores often serve to 'authenticate the era' or to provide a sense of *nostalgia* (Stuessy and Lipscomb 2003, pp. 410–11). Examples of the former would include *Amadeus* (1984) and *Immortal Beloved* (1995), while a sense of nostalgia is communicated through the music selected for films such as *American Graffiti* (1973) and *The Big Chill* (1983).

Music can convey a sense of *energy*. In narrative theory and screenwriting, it is understood that stories are often driven by the manipulation of perceived energy. For example, a loaded gun pointed directly at a character has a lot of potential energy, while a post-coital couple has a low level of energy. Music and sound can reinforce or alter the perceived level of energy at a given point in a film and/or the overall perceived energy level of the film. For example, the level of perceived energy is significantly increased by the presence of Herrmann's musical score and the repetitive sound of the windshield wipers in the previously mentioned 'rainstorm sequence' from *Psycho* (1960), and the tranquil image of a seascape is dramatically transformed from relaxing and peaceful to menacingly frightening with the appearance of John Williams' well-known musical motive in *Jaws* (1975). Alternatively, the level of perceived energy can be manipulated downward by the presence of music, as happens when Barber's 'Adagio for Strings' appears on the soundtrack during battle scenes in *Platoon* (1986).

Music is also capable of *conveying the overall perspective or message intended* by the director, as related to both characters and on-screen events. The same events can be portrayed differently – resulting in changed audience interpretation – by altering only the musical content (Bullerjahn and Güldenring 1994; Lipscomb and Kendall 1994; Marshall and Cohen 1988). Spaceships can be portrayed as elegant and beautiful (*2001: A Space Odyssey* 1968) or threatening machines of war (*Star Wars* 1977). Boxing can be portrayed as heroic (*Rocky* 1976), strategic (*When We Were Kings* 1997), or brutally tragic (*Raging Bull* 1980). Based on the use of different music and sound, the topic of war can be presented as brutal and chaotic (battle scenes in *Terminator 2: Judgment Day* 1991), tragic (the 'Letters' scene in *Saving Private Ryan* 1999), transcendent (the use of Samuel Barber's 'Adagio for Strings' in *Platoon* 1986), romantic and filled with adventure (*Casablanca* 1942; *African Queen* 1952), insane (*Apocalypse Now* 1979; *Barry Lyndon* 1975), heroic (*Schindler's List* 1993; *Glory* 1989), or even comic (*M*A*S*H* 1970). Borrowing from the field of linguistics, Gorbman applies the term '*commutation*' to describe the capability of music to influence the meaning of a film in this way (1987, p. 16). As an example of the dynamic manner in which cinematic meaning can be manipulated by sound, the musical score is often used to accompany montage sequences, conveying not only the passage of time but implying changes that have occurred – personal, interpersonal, or even global – during the intervening period (e.g. the well-known 'breakfast montage' from *Citizen Kane*; see Gorbman 1987, p. 26)

Music can convey the internal life, thoughts, and feelings of a character

One of the most effective ways in which a musical score can augment the narrative is to express the unspoken thoughts and unseen implications that underlie the drama; what Prendergast refers to as 'psychological refinements' (1992, p. 216). Music can convey *character*. Rather than just associating a character with a particular musical theme, a director can choose to define a character by sound, musical or non-musical. Without the sound, the character(s) would cease to exist or be less than fully realized (e.g. the mother character in *Psycho* or Hal in *2001: A Space Odyssey*).

The most consistently used technique to communicate musically through association is the *leitmotif*, used to great effect in Wagner's nineteenth century music dramas (including *Lohengrin* 1850; *Tristan und Isolde* 1857–59; *Der Ring des Nibelungen* 1857–74). A leitmotif is …

> a theme, or other coherent musical idea, clearly defined so as to retain its identity if modified on subsequent appearances, whose purpose is to represent or symbolize a person, object, place, idea, state of mind, supernatural force or any other ingredient in a dramatic work.' (Whittall 2003)

The history of film music is replete with examples of such recurring themes, one of the most familiar is the set of themes composed by John Williams for George Lucas' *Star Wars* series ... both the original trilogy (*Star Wars* 1977; *The Empire Strikes Back* 1980; and *The Return of the Jedi* 1983) and the two prequels released to date (*Episode I: The Phantom Menace* 1999; and *Episode II: Attack of the Clones* 2002). The appearance of any of the character themes serves an identical purpose to that of the leitmotif in the Wagnerian music dramas.

Music can convey narrative structure

In addition to communicating general mood or character representation and development, a well-crafted musical score can clarify – or even establish – a sense of order by presenting a clearly perceived formal structure. According to Prendergast (1992), 'music can provide the underpinning for the theatrical buildup of a scene and then round it off with a sense of finality' (p. 222). In films that incorporate extant compositions (*2001: A Space Odyssey* 1968; *32 Short Films About Glenn Gould* 1993), it is arguable that the visual scene is structured around the musical form, rather than vice versa. It is also possible that the shape of the music determines – or assists in determining – the shape of the narrative. The appearance, disappearance, and reappearance of musical sound can *provide or clarify the narrative structure* of the film. There are instances in which the narrative structure and the formal structure of the music coalesce to create the resulting sense of order. The narrative in both *The Thin Blue Line* (1988) and *Magnolia* (2000) can both be perceived in a manner similar to the movements of a large-scale musical composition. In this way, music can be used to *emphasize beginnings or endings*. Likewise, a sense of structural *unity* is provided by the recurrence of musical themes.

Music can convey messages about where in the frame the audience should *focus attention*. Research has shown that music that is assigned a 'negative' or 'positive' connotation 'significantly biased viewers' interpretation and subsequent remembering of a film in a mood-congruent fashion' (Boltz 2001, p. 427). Specifically, when music with an assigned connotation is combined with an ambiguous scene, memory of objects in the visual scene is influenced significantly by the music. In her discussion, Boltz states that

> overall results from the recognition memory task illustrate that *music does not simply convey different moods* that can bias the interpretive framework or visual imagery of an individual, even in the absence of an accompanying film. Instead, *music appears to exert a direct influence on the cognitive processing of a film* by guiding selective attending toward mood-consistent information and away from other information that is inconsistent with its affective valence. (p. 446; emphasis added)

In addition to mood congruent relations between audio and visual components, salient moments in the musical sound draw attention to salient events occurring concurrently within the visual image. This *'temporal coincidence'* (Gorbman 1987, p. 16) or 'accent structure alignment' (Lipscomb 2005; Lipscomb and Kendall 1994) is an important *focusing device* at the disposal of a film music composer and can range on a continuum from Mickey-mousing (Alan Silverstri's score for the opening scene of *Who Framed Roger Rabbit* 1983) to mid-range level synchronization (Bernard Herrmann's score for the 'shower scene' in *Psycho* 1960) to the use of 'stingers' to emphasize significant events (examples from Max Steiner's score for *Mildred Pierce* are cited in Gorbman 1987, p. 88).

Music can readily convey *pace*. By establishing patterns in the use of music, sound effects, and silences and then manipulating these established patterns, a film can be made to feel subjectively like it is speeding up or slowing down. For example, in the 'Dawn of Man' section at the beginning of *2001: A Space Odyssey*, each scene ends with a fade to silence. As the sequence continues, the silences between scenes are eliminated and the ambient shift between scenes becomes more extreme, creating the impression of a quickening pace. Alternatively, music can *facilitate the continuity* of or *provide background filler* for the narrative; smoothing cuts between shots, scene transitions, and filling 'gaps' to serve as modern day incidental music over scene changes (Gorbman 1987, p. 34). Within a cinematic context, the presence of film music serves to lower the audience member's 'threshold of belief' (Gorbman 1987, p. 6). The fact that nondiegetic music is heard in places where it would not appear as part of the diegesis, allows the audience to more readily become lost in the drama.

Mismatch conditions between the audio and visual components

All of the previous functions of music assume a certain level of coherence between the meaning of the visual image and the sound heard ... music, as well as other auditory components. There are numerous instances in the cinematic repertoire in which an intentional mismatch or disconnect occurs between the information sent to each sensory modality (*contest*). Music can convey *irony*. For example, a scene involving murder or graphic violence can be accompanied by upbeat music (e.g. 'Singin' in the Rain' accompanies a violent rape scene in *A Clockwork Orange* 1972; 'Somewhere Over the Rainbow' is heard during an intense shootout in *Face/Off* 1997). Such a mismatch can *invite intellectual processing* and active participation (Lipscomb and Kendall 1994). The audience member asks – consciously or unconsciously – what is the intended meaning? How do I resolve the conflict between the incompatible meanings I am receiving from the sound and image? If the music is familiar, the audience member may ask: How does this music I am used to hearing in one context relate to what am seeing now?

Another type of mismatch, results when we hear a *leitmotif* but do not see the associated character. The musical sound causes us to anticipate the arrival of the referenced character, to understand that a visible character is thinking about the referenced character, or realize that the referenced character is significant in relation to events occurring onscreen (Bordwell 1985, Chapter 3). It is also possible that the *absence of music* (or other sounds) may create a sense of mismatch. If based on the conventions of a genre or an established pattern set up within the specific film, there is an expectation for the presence of music in a specific scene, but no music is heard, the affected audience member asks: Why has the music been deleted? How does it change the perception of a character or the audience interpretation of the narrative? Emotionally, such realization tends to make the audience uneasy, desiring – perhaps unconsciously – some kind of cognitive resolution of the perceived dissonance. Silence in the cinema can be deafening ... silence beyond any that can occur in real world experience. With the high quality of sound reproduction systems in most theatres – and now in many homes – and the greatly improved signal-to-noise ratio inherent in digital recording and media formats, theatrical silence can be near complete. Such '*nondiegetic silence*' (Gorbman 1987, p. 18), involving either the entire soundtrack or excluding the sound associated with selected characters or objects, can be quite unsettling. An example of the former, *Y Tu Mamá También* (2001) incorporates complete silence prior to the narrator's dialogue, while the 'Omaha Beach' scene in *Saving Private Ryan* (1999) exemplifies an obvious incongruity between action and sound, with the intentionally muffled accompanying soundtrack effectively communicating both the physical trauma and mental anguish of Tom Hanks' character.

Analyses: film music as an integral part of cinematic sound

Now that we have enumerated the various ways in which musical sound can communicate within a cinematic context, analysis of excerpts from two classic films will provide an opportunity to illustrate and make tangible the abstract categories discussed earlier. The following paragraphs will describe musical functions in two of the three boxing films, incorporating bracketed italicized text to identify references to specific musical techniques enumerated in the preceding pages. Similarly detailed analyses of the science fiction dramas and westerns have been performed but, due to length restrictions for the present chapter, will be published elsewhere (Lipscomb and Tolchinsky in preparation). The following paragraphs will provide a comparative presentation concerning the role of music in *Raging Bull* and *Rocky*. Timings referenced for these excerpts are taken from the DVD releases: *Raging Bull* (MGM 906040), *When We Were Kings* (Polygram 4400458472), and *Rocky* (MGM 1001736).

Raging Bull (1980)

In *Raging Bull*, music serves two primary roles. First, the use of contemporaneous popular music is practically omnipresent throughout the film, authenticating the era during which the events portrayed actually occurred [*placement in time*]. Second, and more unique to this example, music is used to structure the film at a macro level [*provide narrative structure*] and communicate the intended meaning of the narrative [*convey the overall perspective or message intended*]. Only three times during the motion picture do we hear foregrounded nondiegetic instrumental music: with the opening credits, during a montage sequence in the middle of the film, and accompanying the end credits. In contrast to the music one might expect to accompany a movie about athletic competition, however, the instrumental music we hear is that of nineteenth century Italian operatic composer Pietro Mascagni, an example of Cook's (1998) 'contest' relationship. The orchestral selections are excerpted from *Cavalleria rusticana* (1890), *Guglielmo Ratcliff* (1895), and *Silvano* (1895), operatic tragedies from the late Romantic period. It is no coincidence that Giovanni Verga's play, upon which the first of these was based, is credited with 'inaugurating the *verismo* period in Italian theatre' (Girardi 2003) and Mascagni's compostion is cited as the first operatic example (Sansone 2003). The verismo style presented human circumstances and emotions realistically, as typical in everyday experience rather than in the idealized form represented in previous theatrical eras. *Raging Bull* fits the mold of a verismo tale perfectly … a boxer whose life story becomes – through his own actions – nothing short of a full-scale tragedy.

The use of 'Intermezzo' from *Cavalleria rusticana* underneath the opening credits and to accompany the image of Robert DeNiro as Jake La Motta warming up in the boxing ring sets the tone for the film [*convey the general mood*]. This scene provides an exemplary illustration of the use of *nondiegetic silence* in which Robert DeNiro, as Jake La Motta, shadowboxes in slow motion around a boxing ring, apparently in preparation for a match. There is no roar of the audience, no Foley sounds representing the boxer's footsteps or sweeping arm motions, only the tragic strains of the 'Intermezzo.' The music flawlessly foreshadows the events to come. The appearance of 'Barcorolle' from *Silvano* underneath the end credits confirms the tragedy. Only the middle appearance of 'Intermezzo' from *Guglielmo Ratcliff* requires explanation. This music supports a montage of home movies, representing the passage of a significant amount of time during which La Motta is married, his brother gets married, children are born and raised, and La Motta's boxing career continues on an upward trajectory, as represented by intercut still images. As with both other appearances of nondiegetic music, there is no dialogue or sound effects … the music of Mascagni is the sole component of the soundtrack. The isolated music at this point in the narrative effectively serves the important structural function of letting the audience know that this is the culmination of the 'happy' part of the film … and of La Motta's life [*emphasize beginnings and endings*]. The remainder will turn out to be La Motta tumbling downwards. The music underscores and reminds us of the tragedy that is about to occur [*reinforces the intended tone*]. It also acts as a respite from the violence and in-your-face sound effects that accompany the boxing sequences. The absence of sound effects, coupled with still images and grainy-looking 'home movies' throughout this montage sequence point to the film as separate from reality, reminding the audience – if only temporarily – that they are observing voyeuristically, not participating in, the unfolding drama.

Rocky (1976)

The use of music in *Rocky*, when compared with the soundtrack for *Raging Bull*, is much more typical of the functions associated with a mainstream classical Hollywood film score. Throughout the movie, it serves to enhance or augment the emotional content of the narrative, primarily through either conformance or complementation (Cook 1998) [*convey the general mood* and *convey the intended message*]. The opening title sequence presents a brief brass fanfare preparing us for the eventual victory – in life, if not in the boxing ring – that the protagonist will experience [*foreshadowing* and *character development*]. This music is heroic and reveals at the outset that Rocky will prevail, as the tragic music in La Motta's story foreshadows the boxer's ultimate failure. Though the boxing scenes themselves are bereft of musical scoring, examination of two non-boxing scenes will dramatically illustrate the use of music to underscore the actions of Rocky Balboa as he prepares for his shot at the title. The first (1:11:46), accompanies the 'Morning Run' scene in which Rocky begins his workout routine; the second is from the chapter entitled 'In Training' (1:30:32) and reveals the tremendous change that has occurred to the underdog as a result of his mental and physical conditioning. 'Morning Run' begins with a solo French horn playing open fourths and fifths, a legato performance in a slow, relatively free tempo. As his jog progresses, strings enter and a piano assumes the lead melodic role, gradually taking over completely as he climbs, practically stumbling, up the 99 steps of the Philadelphia Museum of Art. This is hardly the kind of music that generates a sense of urgency, proclaiming the presence of a contender. Instead, the audience is led to wonder if Rocky is up to the challenge [*convey character*]. After a series of scenes documenting his training, we see (and hear) a new challenger ... ready this time. This second jogging scene reveals, visually, a much more invigorated challenger with an energetic bounce in his step. The brass-dominated music, initiated by the same fanfare heard at the beginning of the film, supports this dramatic change in character. What appeared initially to be a pitiful attempt at working out has become second nature to the man ... now a worthy contender. The rock beat, the densely voiced brass fanfare, and stable harmonies portray the man musically as ready for any challenge. The lyrics for the song ('feeling strong now') become superfluous ... the instrumental music and imagery say it all.

Conclusions

Citing many empirical studies, this chapter has shown that recent research into the combination of sound and image is beginning to reveal to us unambiguous ways in which the auditory component of a motion picture adds depth and meaning to the cinematic experience. Several of these studies have gone so far as to propose specific models of film music perception (Cohen 2001; Lipscomb 1995; Lipscomb and Kendall 1994; Marshall and Cohen 1988). In addition, many scholars have developed unique theories regarding the various ways in which the coexistence of sound and image symbiotically produces affect in the audience member (Brown 1988; Cook 1998; Gorbman 1987; Wagner 1849/1964). Though few who have experienced a motion picture will deny the important role fulfilled by the musical soundtrack, this chapter attempted to identify many specific ways in which musical sound in this context can communicate information to the listener, enhancing the filmic experience. An analysis of two specific cinematic examples served to provide a practical application of this set of possibilities, identifying which specific techniques were utilized by the composer within the excerpts discussed. The dramatically different uses of music in these two films (*Raging Bull* and *Rocky*) demonstrate several of the many ways that music – as a primary component of the motion picture soundtrack – can serve and, at times, expand upon, the dramatic demands of the cinematic narrative.

Postlude

Though the title for this chapter includes the phrase '*music* communication,' the present authors maintain that 'music,' in a cinematic context, may move beyond the boundaries of what is typically recognized as such. Within a film, the soundtrack contains not only the musical score, but ambient sound, dialogue, sound effects, and silence, any of which may be either diegetic or nondiegetic. We would argue that the composite mix of these sounds becomes a complex communicative form that could be considered – in toto – 'music' (i.e. ordered sound), existing 'in harmony' with the visual image. As musical harmony can be consonant, dissonant, or anywhere on the continuum between these two extremes, so can the relationship between sound and image be consistent, contradictory, or anywhere on the continuum connecting these extremes (Cook 1998; Lipscomb and Kendall 1994). Expanding the definition of music is not an unprecedented step to take and, in fact, a similar leap has already been accomplished in the world of Western art music. For example, many works by John Cage (*4'33'* 1952; *Radio Music* 1956) and György Ligeti (*Poème symphonique* 1962) challenge willing listeners to reconsider the fundamental concept regarding what constitutes 'musical sound,' as the Dadaist movement of the early twentieth century did for visual art. The present authors' analysis of *2001: A Space Odyssey* (Tolchinsky and Lipscomb, in preparation) reveals that, when music is not present as part of the soundtrack, ambient sounds and (quasi-)dialogue can perform many of its typical functions. The roles of each component of the soundtrack became more blurred as the Hollywood film evolved toward the twenty-first century. Is it possible any longer to separately consider – in the context of the dramatic scenes of conflict in a given segment of the *Stars Wars* saga, for example – the function of John Williams' massive orchestral score, the sound effects, ambient sounds, etc.? The orchestral 'hits' merge with the sound effects and alternately share the spotlight with dialogue and other salient auditory events … all supporting and augmenting the emotional impact of the visual image. If the *Star Wars* example alluded to can be considered a representative example – and we believe it can – it may be time to consider expanding the definition of 'film music.' Rather than insisting upon its consideration as a separate and distinct entity, the present authors encourage analysis of the entire soundtrack, upon which musical sound, dialogue, sound effects, silence, and some sounds that fall in the cracks between traditional categories all exist for the purpose of enhancing the intended message of the motion picture. One might ask whether music does have a unique function that rightly justifies its being set apart from these other auditory components. Currently, there appears to be an implicit assumption on the part of film theorists and film music researchers, that the musical score is a separate entity. There is certainly a benefit, especially within the context of experimental investigations, in limiting the world of empirical inquiry. We suggest, however, that as the field continues to mature, the constituent elements that comprise the soundtrack should be studied as a whole. Cognitive models of music communication, carefully formulated on the basis of results from past experimental research, can undoubtedly serve as a valuable starting point for such future investigations, though the design for these studies was intentionally more reductionist to gain the necessary experimental control. Now that a significant amount of this empirical work has been completed, investigators can begin to incorporate stimuli that more closely resemble sounds and images experienced in authentic cinema and to consider the various components of the soundtrack either in isolation or in their symbiotic relationship to one another.

Within the framework of a finished motion picture, roles of the various individuals involved in the music-sound communication process – like the sonic components themselves – become multifaceted and difficult, if not impossible, to disentangle one from another. It may, in fact, be absolutely essential to revise the basic components of Kendall and Carterette's (1990) model of music communication to include additional creative partners in the process, when considering the role of music within a cinematic context. The role of the *composer*, typically, is dramatically influenced by the wishes and expressed input of the *director* (altered model component: *composer-director*). The sonic component generated by the *performers* involved in recording the score cannot be separated from the role of the *sound editor*, who is eventually responsible for the manner in which the sound and image are combined and the final audio-visual product (altered model component: *performer-sound editor*). Finally, the *listener* is transformed from a hearing-only individual into a *listener-viewer*.

Though the ideas expressed here may appear radical upon initial consideration, they provide yet another means of moving from the realm of reductionist methodology toward the real, ecologically valid world of the *Gesamtkunstwerk* – or *Gestalt* – that cinema has become.

References

Bengtsson, I. and Gabrielsson, A. (1983) Analysis and synthesis of musical rhythm. In *Studies of music performance*, (ed. J. Sundberg), pp. 27–60. Stockholm: Royal Swedish Academy of Music.

Bolivar, V.J., Cohen, A.J., and Fentress, J.C. (1994) Semantic and formal congruency in music and motion pictures: Effects on the interpretation of visual action. *Psychomusicology*, **13**, 28–59.

Boltz, M. (2001) Musical soundtracks as a schematic influence on the cognitive processing of filmed events. *Music Perception*, **18**(4), 427–54.

Boltz, M., Schulkind, M., and Kantra, S. (1991) Effects of background music on the remembering of filmed events. *Memory and Cognition*, **19**, 593–606.

Bordwell, D. (1985) *Narration in the fiction film*. Madison, WI: University of Wisconsin Press.

Bordwell, D. and Thompson, K. (1985) Fundamental aesthetics of sound in the cinema. In *Film sound: Theory and practice*, (eds E. Weis and J. Belton), pp. 181–99. New York: Columbia University Press.

Brown, R. (1988) Film and classical music. In *Film and the arts in symbiosis: A resource guide*, (ed. G.R. Edgerton), pp. 165–215. New York: Greenwood Press.

Bullerjahn, C. and Güldenring, M. (1994) An empirical investigation of effects of film music using qualitative content analysis. *Psychomusicology*, **13**, 99–118.

Burt, G. (1994) *The art of film music*. Boston, MA: Northeastern University Press.

Campbell, W. and Heller, J. (1980) An orientation for considering models of musical behavior. In *Handbook of music psychology*, (ed. D. Hodges), pp. 29–36. Lawrence, KS: National Association for Music Therapy.

Chion, M. (1994) *Audio-vision: Sound on screen* (C. Gorbman, Trans.). New York: Columbia University Press. (Original work published in 1990)

Clynes, M. (1983) Expressive microstructure in music, linked to living qualities. In *Studies of music performance*, (ed. J. Sundberg), pp. 76–181. Stockholm: Royal Swedish Academy of Music.

Cohen, A.J. (2001) Music as a source of emotion in film. New York: Oxford University Press.

Cook, N. (1998) *Analysing musical multimedia*. New York: Oxford University Press.

Driver, J. (1997) Enhancement of selective listening by illusory mislocation of speech sounds due to lip-reading. *Nature*, **381**, 66–8.

Gabrielsson, A. (1988) Timing in music performance and its relations to music experience. In *Generative processes in music*, (ed. J.A. Sloboda), pp. 27–51. Oxford: Clarendon Press.

Girardi, M. (2003) Pietro Mascagni. In *The new Grove dictionary of music online*, (ed. L. Macy). Grove's Dictionaries, New York. [Retrieved August 20, 2003 from http://www.grovemusic.com].

Gorbman, C. (1987) *Unheard melodies: Narrative film music*. Bloomington, IN: Indiana University Press.

Hanslick, E. (1986) *On the musically beautiful: A contribution towards the revision of the aesthetics of music*, (8th ed., G. Payzant, trans.). Indianapolis, IN: Hackett Publishing Co. (Original work published in 1891)

Hood, M. (1982) *The ethnomusicologist*. Kent, OH: Kent State University Press.

Iwamiya, S. (1994) Interactions between auditory and visual processing when listening to music in an audio-visual context: 1. Matching 2. Audio quality. *Psychomusicology*, **13**, 133–54.

Kendall, R.A. and Carterette, E.C. (1990) The communication of musical expression. *Music Perception* **8**(2), 129–63.

Krumhansl, C. and Schenck, D.L. (1997) Can dance reflect the structural and expressive qualities of music? A perceptual experiment on Balanchine's choreography of Mozart's Divertmento No. 15. *Musicae Scientiae*, **1**(1), 63–85.

Langer, S.K. (1942) *Philosophy in a new key: A study of the symbolism of reason, rite, and art*, (3rd ed.). Cambridge, MA: Harvard University Press.

Lipscomb, S.D. (1989) Film music: A sociological investigation of influences on audience awareness. Paper presented at the Meeting of the Society of Ethnomusicology, Southern California Chapter, Los Angeles.

Lipscomb, S.D. (1995) *Cognition of musical and visual accent structure alignment in film and animation*. Unpublished doctoral dissertation, University of California, Los Angeles.

Lipscomb, S.D. (2005) The perception of audio-visual composites: Accent structure alignment of simple stimuli. *Selected Reports in Ethnomusicology,* **12**, 37–67.

Lipscomb, S.D. and Kendall, R.A. (1994, Spring/Fall) Perceptual judgment of the relationship between musical and visual components in film. *Psychomusicology,* **13**, 60–98.

Lipscomb, S.D. and Tolchinsky, D.E. (in preparation) Boxing films: A detailed comparison. Pre-publication draft available from <http://faculty-web.at.northwestern.edu/music/lipscomb/docs/BoxingFilmsAnalysis.pdf>

Lomax, A. (1962) Song structure and social structure. *Ethnology* **1**, 425–51.

Marshall, S.K. and Cohen, A.J. (1988) Effects of musical soundtracks on attitudes toward animated geometric figures. *Music Perception,* **6**(1), 95–112.

Merriam, A.P. (1964) *The anthropology of music.* Evanston, IL: Northwestern University Press.

Meyer, L.B. (1956) *Emotion and meaning in music.* Chicago, IL: University of Chicago Press.

Nettl, B. (1983) *The study of ethnomusicology.* Urbana, IL: University of Illinois Press.

Prendergast, R.M. (1992) *Film music: A neglected art.* W.W. Norton and Co., New York.

Sansone, M. (2003) Verismo. In *The new Grove dictionary of music online,* (ed. L. Macy). Grove's Dictionaries, New York. [Retrieved August 16, 2003 from http://www.grovemusic.com]

Senju, M. and Ohgushi, K. (1987) How are the player's ideas conveyed to the audience? *Music Perception* **4**, 311–23.

Smilow, M. (Producer) and Waletzky, J. (Director) (1992) *Music for the movies: Bernard Herrmann* [Documentary]. New York: Sony Classical Film and Video.

Stuessy, J. and Lipscomb, S. (2003) *Rock and roll: Its history and stylistic development* (4th ed.). Upper Saddle River, NJ: Prentice-Hall.

Sundberg, J., Frydén, L., and Askenfelt, A. (1983) What tells you the player is musical? An analysis-by-synthesis study of music performance. In *Studies of music performance,* (ed. J. Sundberg), pp. 61–67. Stockholm: Royal Swedish Academy of Music.

Tannenbaum, P.H. (1956) Music background in the judgment of stage and television drama. *Audio-Visual Communication Review,* **4**(2), 92–101.

Thayer, J.F. and Levenson, R.W. (1983) Effects of music on psychophysiological responses to a stressful film. *Psychomusicology,* **3**(1), 44–52.

Thomas, T. (1991) *Film score: The art & craft of movie music.* Burbank, CA: Riverwood Press.

Thompson, W.F., Russo, F.A., and Sinclair, D. (1994) Effects of underscoring on the perception of closure in filmed events. *Psychomusicology,* **13**, 9–27.

Tolchinsky, D.E. and Lipscomb, S.D. (in prepation) *2001: A Space Odyssey* – 'Music' in the absence of a score. Pre-publication draft available from <http://faculty-web.at.north-western.edu/music/lipscomb/docs/2001Analysis.pdf>

Wagner, R. (1964) Orchestra's power of speech; analogy with gesture. In *Wagner on music and drama: A compendium of Richard Wagner's prose works,* (eds A. Goldman and E. Sprinchorn; H.A. Ellis, trans.). New York: Dutton. (Original work [*The Artwork of the Future*] published in 1849)

Waletzky, J. (1995) *Hollywood sound* [Documentary]. Great Britain: British Broadcasting Corporation.

Whittall, A. (2003) Leitmotif. In *The new Grove dictionary of music online,* (ed. L. Macy). Grove's Dictionaries, New York. [Retrieved August 16, 2003 from http://www.grovemusic.com]

Chapter 19

Musical communication in commercial contexts

Adrian C. North and David J. Hargreaves

The use of music in shops, bars and the like has long been the source of considerable light-hearted derision. As Lanza's (1994) fascinating *Elevator Music* describes, the playwright J. B. Priestly once bragged of having 'had it turned off in the best of places', and comedian Lily Tomlin once expressed fears that the guy who invented piped music might be inventing something else! However, it is a popular misconception that the power of background music is a recent discovery. For example, Greek mythology tells that Orpheus played his lyre to inspire Jason and the Argonauts' quest for the Golden Fleece, and that Hermes charmed the 100-eyed Argus with a reed flute lullaby. The third century Roman grammarian Censorinus wrote that 'music serves to make toil as bearable as may be, as when it is used by the steersman in a moving galley', and a flute orchestra purportedly accompanied the erection of the walls of Rome's Messina. During the Middle Ages, Christian soldiers of the early Crusades hired battlefield musicians to play the same Arabic military music that the Saracens had used to help defeat them in previous battles, and monks would provide Gregorian plainsong outside the monastery to uplift agricultural workers. In the present day, music in commercial practice is a hi-tech, multi-million dollar industry that employs the latest satellite and computer technology. Many chain stores now have their own nationwide 'radio' station that is broadcast from a central location to all branches. Indeed, in the financial year 2000–1, royalty payments alone on in-store music were worth £242M in just the United Kingdom. When this figure is multiplied by the number of countries where piped music can be heard then it becomes clear that this is a very large industry.

To complement the public derision to which piped music is subject, there is also a pressure group, 'Pipedown', dedicated to its removal. Founded in the 1990s, Pipedown has managed to attract a number of celebrity endorsers from the world of music, entertainment, and journalism, and now has branches world-wide. These write letters to organizations that use piped music, and members are issued with calling cards to be left with businesses: These say for example 'I left your establishment without buying anything simply because of the piped music', or, 'I have enjoyed my meal/drink here, but I will not return for one reason only: the piped music'. Indeed numerous anecdotes point to just how controversial piped music can be, some of which can be found in Fig. 19.1.

- London's well-known musical duo Chaz and Dave promised in their manifesto for the city's 2000 mayoral election that they would ban piped music in pubs. This was despite another of their manifesto promises that legislation concerning busking would be loosened!

- In May 2000, golfers in Stuart, Florida were in conflict with neighbouring pig farmer, Paul Thompson: The dispute centred over the country music Thompson played to his pigs which could also be heard from the 15th hole. Thompson plays the music since he claims it 'reduces stress, enhances tenderness of the meat, lets the animal grow faster and fatten quicker'

- In France, piped music is being introduced into some newly pedestrianized streets

- Military and law enforcement agencies have long used piped music to break the fighting spirit of opponents. For example, during the 1993 siege at Waco, Texas, Bruce Springsteen was played through loudspeakers to members of the Davidian religious cult

- The Glastonbury pop music festival which takes place in the south-west of England has long been well-known for it's primitive washing facilities and promotion of counter-culture attitudes: In recent years however it has featured piped music in it's toilets (which is where many would say it belongs!)

- An American man recently sued a bus company successfully over the piped music played on board. Apparently he saw no reason why he should have to listen to music he didn't order, and eventually had his argument upheld by the USA Supreme Court: His right to the freedom of assembly had been violated, contravening the first amendment to the USA's constitution.

Fig. 19.1 Some conflicting attitudes concerning piped music.

Campaigners' arguments seem to have two bases. The first is that piped music is a 'freedom of choice' issue. As Peter Donnelly, a director of the Canadian 'Right to Quiet Society' explains, 'Owners and staff justify forcing music on us by saying most people like it. But that argument ignores the right of individuals to make their own choices. Most people like coffee, but the greeter at Wal-Mart doesn't force you to drink a cup before letting you shop in the store.' The second argument is that piped music alienates customers and harms profits. Using arguments such as these, protesters against piped music won perhaps their biggest victory to date in 2000. British Conservative politician Robert Key received the backing of fellow MPs for his attempt to ban piped music in public places such as airports, doctors' surgeries, and bus stations. Only a lack of Parliamentary time meant that Key's proposals never became law.

Balanced against claims such as these are those of the companies that provide in-store music. Unsurprisingly, their opinion regarding the effectiveness of piped music is very different from that of protesters. Perhaps the most famous provider of piped music, the Muzak Corporation, features many testimonials from businesses on its web site (www.muzak.com). A manager from fast food chain McDonald's states that their piped music 'is an excellent vehicle to support ... McDonald's core equities, special offers and products ... [and is] designed to generate increased traffic within a site.' Another executive claimed that 'The audio (marketing) worked so well, (our) video tape sold out'. Another said 'We generate ... sales daily from the Muzak on-hold messages.' Most of the other in-store music companies make similar claims. Obviously it's easy to put these kind of statements to the test, and this is precisely what psychologists have been doing for several years. Specifically, researchers have been investigating what music communicates in commercial contexts, and how it might do this. Two conclusions concerning musical communication are clear from this literature. Whereas other chapters within this volume concern active music listening, exposure to piped music is an inevitably passive phenomenon. Second, this is because control of the music is in the hands of commercial operators rather than individual listeners.

Customer activity

Perhaps the most consistent set of findings concerning musical communication in commercial environments has come from research looking at how music can influence the speed with which customers behave. In short, there is quite a lot of evidence now showing that the faster in-store music is, so the quicker customers act. Perhaps the best demonstration of this came from a study by Milliman (1986). He watched 1392 groups of customers who visited a medium-sized restaurant over eight consecutive weekends. The restaurant was 'above-average priced' (p. 287), and attracted middle-aged upper-middle income patrons. One particular feature of the restaurant is that it was frequently crowded, with diners often being asked to wait for 60 minutes before being seated. Slow music was played on four Fridays and four Saturdays, and fast music was played on four Fridays and four Saturdays. Although spending on food was not influenced by the music, the latter did influence three other factors. First, customers who heard slow music took an average of 56 minutes to finish their meals: In contrast, customers who heard fast music took an average of only 45 minutes. Second, groups of customers who heard fast music spent on average $21.62 on drinks from the bar during their meal, whereas when they heard slow music, the average group of customers spent $30.47. To find out the 'bottom line' effect of this, the restaurant estimated the gross profit margin they made per customer group. When slow music was played this margin averaged out at $55.82 whilst the corresponding figure for fast music was $48.62. In short, the restaurant made more profit from customers when slow music was played than when fast music was played, and it seems likely that this is because 'slow music customers' ate more slowly and bought more drinks as a consequence. This finding suggests that fast music can be used to speed customers up, and slow music leads to customers being on the premises longer and (perhaps as a direct consequence of this) spending more money.

Several other studies have reached similar conclusions. For example, Milliman (1982) conducted very similar research in a supermarket, reporting that when fast music was played people shopped approximately 15% more quickly, but spent approximately 33% less money than when slow music was played. McElrea and Standing (1992) asked people to drink a can of soda, and found that they took 9.70 minutes when fast music was played in the background versus 13.52 minutes when slow music was played: Fast music caused fast drinking. Roballey et al. (1985) took a measure that is surely unique in the psychological literature, finding that fast music even leads to cafeteria customers taking more bites per minute than does slow music (with averages of 4.40 bites versus 3.83 bites respectively). It is also worth noting one study which suggests that the *volume* of in-store music has a similar effect as its tempo. Smith and Curnow (1966) found that customers spent approximately 5% more time in store when quiet rather than loud music was played.

How might such apparently consistent effects be explained? Although this has been the subject of very little research, one possible answer lies in Smith and Curnow's (1966) rather neglected study. They explained the effects of musical volume in terms of an 'arousal hypothesis'. This stated that loud music should increase the degree of autonomic nervous system arousal experienced by customers, causing them to shop more quickly. Such a process may also explain the effects of musical tempo indicated by more recent studies, since Berlyne (1971) and numerous other researchers have suggested that this factor may influence arousal in the autonomic nervous system. Such a conclusion is of course speculative since none of the studies considered here actually took physiological measures of arousal experienced by customers: Nevertheless the results are clearly consistent with this psychobiological explanation.

The business implications of such an effect are obvious and extensive. For instance, if music can increase or decrease the speed of customer behaviour then it may be wise to play different types of music in different parts of a store. Fast music could be used to relieve congestion in busy areas: Slow music could be played to encourage customers to linger in neglected areas. Similarly, slow music could be used when stores believe that the probability of making a purchase will increase with the amount of time spent considering the product(s) in question: Slow music could encourage a 'browsing effect' on sales. A more general implication of some of these studies is that there may be a trade-off between the speed of customer activity and the amount which customers spend: No manager wants a completely crowded store, but the slow music he/she plays to encourage spending may lead to an excessive number of customers in-store at any one time. The optimal resolution to this conflict depends on the goals that a given business is attempting to address with its music. For example, the manager of a town centre fast food restaurant should perhaps play fast music during weekend lunchtimes when the premises are over-crowded; but play slow music early on a weekday morning when the premises are quiet, as this may encourage customers to linger and perhaps spend more.

'Musical fit' and atmosphere

A second group of effects plays on the associations that people have with music. A limited number of studies have investigated how this might be turned to commercial advantage by using music to communicate certain thoughts and behaviours to customers as they move about commercial environments. For instance, in-store music might remind customers of certain products or make them consider those products in a particular way.

To test this, North *et al.* (1999*a*) conducted a study in the wines department of a supermarket. Their display had four shelves, with each shelf featuring one type of French wine and one type of German wine. The wines on each shelf were matched closely for their degree of sweetness and also their price: To all intents and purposes the only way in which they differed was in terms of their country of origin. On the top shelf of the display was a small tape deck. On alternate days over the course of two weeks this played either stereotypically French music (e.g. the French national anthem played on an accordion) or stereotypically German music (e.g. Bierkeller songs). When German music was played then German wine outsold French by two bottles to one. However, when French music was played then French wine outsold German by five bottles to one. Customers seemed to be predisposed to buying the wine that 'fitted' with the music playing from the display.

This parallels findings by Areni and Kim (1993), who investigated the effect of music on the amount of money that customers spend. They found that classical music and Top 40 songs had no effect on the number of bottles of wine sold in a wine cellar; but that classical music led to more expensive wine being bought, with customers spending on average $7.43 compared with $2.18 when top 40 music was played. The authors argued that spending more money on wine fits with the affluent, sophisticated image of classical music. If correct this argument has obvious and important implications, and a similar study by North and Hargreaves (1998) was carried out to investigate the effect in more detail. Over four days, pop music, classical music, easy listening music, or no music were played in a university cafeteria, and customers were asked to rate the premises according to several adjectival scales. When pop music was played the cafeteria was perceived as being 'fun' and 'upbeat'. When classical music was played the same cafeteria was perceived as 'sophisticated' and 'upmarket'. When easy listening was played, the cafeteria suddenly became rather 'downmarket' and 'cheap'. The absence of music led to a mixture of these different images. More interestingly, after rating the atmosphere of the cafeteria, diners were given a list of 14 items on sale (e.g. a slice of pizza, a pot of fruit yoghurt, a can of soft drink), and asked to state the *maximum* they would be prepared to pay for each item that day. The amounts for each of the 14 items were added up for each participant, showing that when no music was played, diners said they would spend on an average a total of £14.30 on the 14 items. The corresponding figure for when easy listening was played was £14.51. In contrast, the corresponding figures for when pop and classical music were played were £16.61 and £17.23 respectively. Overall the difference between the highest and lowest maximum prices was over 20%, and there was even some evidence that this was reflected in actual sales! As with the earlier Areni and Kim study, customers seemed to behave in a way that 'fitted' with the music, being willing to spend more when the cafeteria seemed 'sophisticated' or 'fun' than when it seemed 'downmarket' or had an unclear image. It's also worth noting that a recent replication study in an Australian restaurant (Wilson 2003) found similar results, even when diners' income, age, reason for dining out (e.g. with friends, attending a business convention), and level of familiarity with the restaurant were accounted for. Similarly, North *et al.* (2003) played classical music, pop music, and no music over 18 nights in a restaurant and found that classical music was associated with higher spending per head (£32.52) than was either pop music (£29.46) or no music (£29.73).

Although there is clear scope for more research on the notion of musical fit, the consistent pattern of findings obtained so far has obvious commercial implications. Businesses can boost sales of certain products by playing music that fits with them, or can boost overall spending by using music to make their premises feel more exclusive. Furthermore, the existing technology already allows businesses to go much further than this. For example, several companies install 'sound umbrellas' in shops. Made of clear perspex, these allow different types of music to be played in very specific areas of the store by different products. In other words, throughout a whole store, individual products can be paired with appropriate background music in order to communicate a particular ambience or message.

These practical implications raise four further issues that deserve attention. First it could be argued that using music to such ends is unethical since it could help to persuade customers to spend more money than they would otherwise. While we would not deny that such a potential exists (at least only because it has yet to be addressed by research), it is also worth considering whether the use of *music* to achieve such ends is any more unethical than other means used by businesses. For example, most people would not regard it as unethical for restaurant waiters to dress smartly in order to create an atmosphere thought to be conducive to spending.

Related to this is a second issue, namely whether it is possible to employ musical fit to persuade customers to purchase products they would not normally consider. Although this issue could only be resolved by further research, it is difficult to believe that piped music could influence major purchases. For example, it is extremely unlikely that a customer would choose to buy a Renault car rather than a Volkswagen simply because the showroom played French music. Although obviously speculative we would only expect musical fit to influence purchasing when customers are in a state of moderate involvement with the product in question. Involvement is a concept drawn upon heavily within the marketing literature to describe the extent to which the consumer views the focal object as a central part of their life, or as a meaningful and engaging object in their life which is important to them (O'Cass 2000). Involvement with a product also depends on the personal relevance of that product, and whether the product category in question is central to the consumer's self concept (Grewal *et al.* 2000). Following from this it would be surprising if music fit could influence purchase intentions under conditions of either very high or very low levels of involvement. Under conditions of high involvement, the purchase would be so important to the customer that they would carefully consider *all* the product information available, and not just be influenced by in-store music. Under conditions of low involvement the consumer may be paying so little attention to the entire purchasing process that any background music would simply be ignored.

This in turn leads to the third issue raised by the limited research that has already been carried out on musical fit, namely why such effects should occur. Although the existing research is far too under-developed to allow this question to be answered with confidence, one possible explanation is provided by a recent study by North *et al.* (2004a). This presented participants with specially produced radio adverts for five fictional products. Three versions of each advert were prepared featuring respectively music that did not fit the advertised product, music that did fit the advertised product, and no music. After hearing the advert and completing a short distracter task, participants were asked to recall as much as possible about the adverts. Recall was significantly higher when the participant had heard the 'musical fit' version of the advert. This provides some concrete cognitive evidence for the notion that musical fit perhaps operates by raising the salience of product attributes in the mind of the listener. The music perhaps operates as a mnemonic cue that facilitates recall and primes related behaviours.

The final issue raised by research such as this concerns how exactly 'musical fit' might be defined in a degree of detail that is commercially useful and scientifically testable. Indeed, the research described in this section of the chapter has indicated that the impact of music on store image can be a crucial factor that influences shoppers' behaviour and spending intentions, and this indicates that is it important to specify the main dimensions along which music influences the atmosphere of commercial environments. In an attempt to do this North *et al.* (2000) played classical music and easy listening music in a city centre bar, and also played classical music and pop music in a city centre bank. In both cases, customers were asked to rate the atmosphere of the premises along numerous adjectival scales and factor analyses of the two sets of ratings yielded three factors, namely 'aggressive', 'upbeat', and 'sophisticated'. Although a great deal more work is required to verify these factors, they may prove to be the means by which musical fit can be defined and by which music can be controlled carefully as a means of communicating a particular store atmosphere. (See also Turley and Milliman (2000) for a review of the effects of store atmosphere on shopping behaviour.)

Time perception and waiting time

One of the most prevalent (and most frequently complained about) uses of music in commercial environments concerns those occasions when it is played to customers while they are kept waiting in a physical or telephone queue. Several studies have shown that music can indeed influence customers' temporal judgements by for example reducing the number of people hanging up while being kept waiting 'on hold' (North *et al.* 1999*b*; Ramos 1993); in affecting participants' estimations of the duration of a 25 second period (Palmquist 1990); in reducing estimations of queuing time (Stratton 1992); and increasing the amount of unplanned time spent in-store (Yalch and Spangenberg 1990).

The explanation of effects such as these is by no means simple however, and this may explain why so many studies of the relationship between music and time perception have shied away from addressing theoretical issues. In a fascinating series of studies, James Kellaris has attempted to provide an explanation of the relationship between music and time perception based on the mainstream cognitive psychological literature concerning the latter. In particular, Kellaris has argued against the frequently cited claim that customers should be played music that they enjoy in order to make time seem to pass more quickly: Instead, Kellaris has claimed the opposite, namely that time does *not* fly when you're having fun, in showing that experimental exposure to disliked music seems to lead to participants making the shortest time estimates. This has been explained in terms of two cognitive psychological principles. First, the 'Pollyanna principle' (see e.g. Matlin 1989) states that pleasant information is processed and recalled more effectively. Second, time perception is positively related to the number of events that are processed within a given event period (Levin and Zackay 1989). In the context of disliked music, the Pollyanna principle dictates that less information should be encoded from this music as compared to liked music. Second, because fewer events are encoded when disliked music is heard, this means that less time is perceived to have passed than when liked music is heard. Although providing a neat theoretical explanation, it should be noted that the effect has only been demonstrated for females (Kellaris and Altsech 1992; Kellaris and Mantel 1994), and future research may indeed yield findings that are less counter-intuitive. Perhaps the major limitation of this approach however is that most businesses attract a diverse range of customers with a diverse range of musical preferences: Any attempt to influence time perception based on customers' musical preferences therefore seems unlikely to succeed, and we return to this point later.

Some of Kellaris' other research has investigated how time perception might be influenced by structural properties of the music in question. Such an approach is more likely to be commercially applicable given that perceptions of e.g. tempo vary far less from person to person than do musical preferences. For example, Kellaris and Altsech (1992; see also Kellaris *et al.* 1996) suggested that loud music caused females to give longer time estimates than did soft music because the former should have required more processing. As we have already seen, this increased processing load would indeed have been expected to increase the amount of time that participants perceived to have elapsed. Although this increases the extent to which any piece of music would be expected to have a universal effect on time perception, individual differences in musical preference may still prevent businesses from using music to mediate customers' time perception. Take the case for example of somebody who likes slow, quiet music. The structural properties of this music would be expected to lead to low estimates of elapsed time: There is little information to encode relative to other types of music. However, the fact that this music is liked might lead to the opposite effect on customers' time perception: As we have already seen, liked music may well lead to *increased* perceptions of elapsed time. In other words, the same piece of music has the potential to both increase and decrease estimations of time perception within any given individual. This must surely hamper attempts to employ such effects in commercial environments and future research. Indeed, the failure of Chebat *et al.* (1993), North and Hargreaves (1999), and North *et al.* (1998) to produce findings consistent with the theoretical framework described earlier suggests that a great deal more research is needed in order to isolate those aspects of music that are necessary and sufficient to have a predictable effect on listeners' perceptions of elapsed time.

The workplace

So far we have discussed the effect of piped music solely on customers, and neglected its impact on another group who cannot avoid it, namely those working in the premises in which it is played. Given that they comprise a captive sample of potential research participants it is perhaps surprising that so little research has considered the effects of piped music on staff in the workplace. Indeed, the existing literature has been published only intermittently since World War 2 in a wide variety of sources, and this diverse pattern of information makes it extremely difficult to reach any conclusions with confidence. Nevertheless, it is possible to argue that the literature does at least provide some indication of the likely findings that would accrue from any prolonged, systematic research programme.

Most of the existing research can be interpreted in terms of numerous psychologists' claims that there exists a generally 'inverted-U' shaped relationship between arousal of the nervous system and performance. Put simply, these models argue that humans usually perform at their best on a range of tasks when the nervous system is moderately aroused, and that performance tails off gradually at more extreme levels of arousal. In practical terms, this means that music should improve the performance of employees doing mundane jobs, since it can increase the low level of arousal (i.e. boredom) induced by the job itself. For example, Fox and Embrey (1972) reported how lively music could increase the number of faulty parts that production line workers were able to identify. Oldham *et al.* (1995) found that 'employees in relatively simple jobs responded most positively' (p. 547) when music was introduced to their office. Smith (1947) found that the introduction of music on a piecework production line was associated with a 7% increase in productivity on the day shift and a 17% increase on the night shift. Several other (now rather dated) studies show that employees under such circumstances report highly favourable attitudes towards piped music (Beckett 1943; Kerr 1942*a*; Newman *et al.* 1966; Smith 1947).

The same argument holds true also at the opposite end of the performance-arousal inverted-U. Several studies indicate that performance on an intellectually demanding task is hampered by background music that places further strain on the listener's cognitive capacity. Ransdell and Gilroy (2001) found that background music reduced the number of words per minute produced by undergraduates writing essays (although no indication is given concerning the effect of the music on the *quality* of the students' output). Similarly, Nittono (1997) reported that background music hampered performance on a short-term memory task.

However, this research has tended to be carried out in the laboratory using rather artificial tasks, there are also several caveats that should be remembered before concluding that piped music would always have a negative effect on those engaged in intellectually-demanding jobs. First, as Lesiuk (2000) demonstrated, piped music may reduce anxiety among those carrying out demanding jobs, and we might reasonably expect that this reduction in anxiety could have a positive impact on performance. Second, the extent to which piped music has a negative effect may depend very much on the personality of the employee, and particularly his/her level of extraversion (see e.g. Daoussis and McKelvie 1986). Extraverts of course have a sub-optimal baseline level of cortical arousal: Playing them music would increase this, and may subsequently improve performance. Third, music may mask other forms of workplace noise that could have a worse impact on employee performance (Young and Berry 1979). Fourth, some studies indicate that background music may have a short-term effect in increasing employees' creativity (Adaman and Blaney 1995; Kaltsounis 1973), such that performance on creative tasks may be aided by background music. Fifth, a small number of studies report findings contradictory to those outlined earlier and have indicated simply that music did not hamper the performance of people engaged in intellectually-demanding tasks (Freeburne and Fleischer 1952; Smith 1961; Zimmer and Brachulis-Raymond 1978). Sixth, there is (albeit rather dated) evidence that, although music may hamper employees carrying out intellectually demanding tasks, these people do at least enjoy it (Gatewood 1922; Smith 1961), and two further studies provide direct evidence concerning the positive effect of piped music on employee morale (Devereux 1969; Kerr 1942b). Seventh, a few studies indicate that background music can increase the incidence of pro-social behaviour which we might expect would lead to a more pleasant working environment (Fried and Berkowitz 1979; North and Hargreaves 1996; North *et al.* 2004b), and Blood and Ferriss (1993) provided direct evidence that background music can increase satisfaction with concurrent conversations. In short, it seems that there may well be scope for the provision of background music even for employees engaged in some intellectually demanding tasks.

One final line of evidence in support of this argument is provided by recent research suggesting that music may be able to improve the health of listeners. Although the field of music therapy has a long history, more recent research suggests that music may have a much more direct effect on the physical health of people exposed to it. Eight studies reported over the past few years have suggested that exposure to music can increase levels of secretory immunoglobulin-A and interleukin-1, both of which serve as indicators of the efficiency of the immune system (Bartlett *et al.* 1993; Brennan and Charnetski 2000; Charnetski *et al.* 1998; Goff *et al.* 1997; Hucklebridge *et al.* 2000; McCraty *et al.* 1996; Rider *et al.* 1990; Rider and Weldin 1990). The demonstration of these effects has not always been clear-cut and the mechanism by which music might be helpful can only be speculated upon, but research on the physiological aspects of musical communication nevertheless represents an exciting development.

Campaigners revisited

Let us conclude by returning to the campaigners against piped music with whom we began this chapter. As we noted, campaigners' protests are based on two claims. The first of these concerns 'freedom of choice', with people arguing that piped music should not be forced upon customers who do not like it. We agree. However, we would also point out that since customers are always free to leave commercial premises in which piped music is played, those businesses that offend too many customers will soon cease to exist. If the right to choose a music free environment really does excite consumers then the market will soon eradicate piped music.

However, we are more interested in the second claim made by protestors, namely that piped music hampers profits. We would certainly not deny that there is abundant scope for further investigation in this area, and the scarcity of research means that it is difficult to be completely confident concerning those effects outlined so far. Nevertheless, the existing evidence provides some initial positive indication that music can serve a positive commercial function. This raises the issue of what exactly is the 'right' kind of music that businesses should play in order to increase profits. The evidence suggests two factors that should be considered by businesses.

First, as we have already seen, music can have a variety of different effects. For example, variations in tempo can mediate the speed of shopping, and variations in style can convey different types of atmosphere to the customer. Before deciding on their music policy, businesses first need to decide what the goals of their music use are. Which of the effects described earlier is the business in question hoping to achieve?

Second, music is of course an extremely complex stimulus and, as we have argued elsewhere (North and Hargreaves 1997), a complete understanding of any individual response to music can only be obtained by considering three factors, namely the music itself, the listener, and the listening situation. With regard to the music itself, we have already seen numerous instances of how different properties of piped music can have different effects on customers. However, consideration of this alone would still not produce an effective music policy unless the listener and listening situation are also accounted for. With regard to the former for example, the music of Britney Spears may be popular in a shop aimed at young people but disastrous in a shop aimed instead at the elderly. Similarly, with regard to the listening situation, even a piece as universally popular as Beethoven's Fifth Symphony would be a poor choice for a chic city centre bar; and a musical style as unpopular as modern classical music would probably be regarded by most people as more tolerable in a modern art gallery.

More generally, this raises an interesting distinction between two different ways in which music might have commercial benefits. It is arguable that one of the reasons for antipathy towards piped music is simply that businesses might sometimes fail to play music that customers actually like. We have already seen in the section on time perception that any effects of music based on 'like-dislike' responses are necessarily dependent on the accuracy of an initial assessment of customers' musical preferences. *Any* intended effects of piped music based on customers' subjective preferences are necessarily subject to the risk of failure due to a failure to predict what music customers will and will not like. This in turn relates to the issue of the nature of 'musical communication' in commercial contexts. As Juslin and others have argued elsewhere in this volume, one common feature of many models of musical communication involves a chain in which the composers'/performers' communicative intentions are passed to the listener. In the field of piped music however, this process of direct communication between composer/performer and listener breaks down in at least four ways. First, on their way from the composer/performer to the listener, pieces of music are first selected in or out by businesses according to various commercial criteria. For example, high levels of swearing in the lyrical output of controversial pop musicians means that their music is unlikely to be played in any but the most specialized commercial premises. Other less offensive pieces of music may simply fail to match the desired image of a particular company. Second, the music that survives this selection process is then sometimes appropriated in such a way as to convey not just the message intended by the composer/performer but also that intended by the business. For example, as we have already seen, customers' knowledge of certain pieces and the associations that they have with them can be used to give a 'piggy back' to a commercial message that the company wishes to pass to customers. Thus, the stereotype of civilization and grandeur that is often attached to a Strauss waltz may be subverted by the business playing it in order to convey the message that 'Our company is upmarket'. Strauss certainly never intended to convey the impression that one supermarket has better baked beans than another, but any business could use the music to effectively imply the composer's endorsement. Similarly, piped music is experienced in a particular social context, and this context can itself distort or add further meaning to that intended by the composer/performer of the music in question. One obvious example of this is the particularly strong emotional reaction of the crowd to a national anthem played just prior to a sporting event. Third, in 'normal' music listening there is often some form of feedback loop whereby the listener helps to shape the composer's/performer's future output: For example, a rock concert audience's enthusiastic cheering of a particular song can help to shape the kind of songs the group will record for their next album. However, in the case of piped music, there is little room for such a feedback mechanism. A particular supermarket customer may not like piped music, but he/she is unlikely to leave the store without buying anything simply because going to a competing supermarket is usually too inconvenient. Indeed, with the exception of a small number of direct complaints to management from particularly aggrieved customers, communication via piped music rarely involves any listener feedback whatsoever. Finally, there remains the possibility with piped music that the target of that music (i.e. the customers) will simply fail to pay any attention to it, such that any attempt at musical communication is fruitless. This contrasts sharply with musical communication in a concert hall or other situations in which people deliberately choose to listen to music, and the composer/performer can be confident of the full attention of the audience: The message intended by the composer/performer may still be misinterpreted, but the audience is at least *trying* to understand.

In conclusion, the contention surrounding piped music tends to be characterised as whether it should be present or not. We would disagree and propose instead that it might be more accurate to consider the merits of various kinds of music or indeed of no music. Inappropriate and insensitive uses of music would offend many people and be detrimental to the businesses playing it. However, the evidence here also suggests that when it is carefully selected to correspond with the tastes of customers and the goals of the businesses playing it, then the communicative power of music can be used extremely effectively in marketing.

References

Adaman, J.E. and Blaney, P.H. (1995) The effects of musical mood induction on creativity. *Journal of Creative Behaviour*, **29**, 95–108.

Areni, C.S. and Kim, D. (1993) The influence of background music on shopping behaviour: classical versus top-forty music in a wine store. *Advances in Consumer Research*, **20**, 336–40.

Bartlett, D., Kaufman, D., and Smeltekop, R. (1993) The effects of music listening and perceived sensory experiences on the immune system as measured by interleukin-1 and cortisol. *Journal of Music Therapy*, **30**, 194–209.

Beckett, W. (1943) *Music in war plants*. Washington, D.C: War Production Board.

Berlyne, D.E. (1971) *Aesthetics and psychobiology*. New York: Appleton-Century-Crofts.

Blood, D.J. and Ferriss, S.J. (1993) Effects of background music on anxiety, satisfaction with communication, and productivity. *Psychological Reports*, **72**, 171–7.

Brennan, F.X. and Charnetski, C.J. (2000) Stress and immune system function in a newspaper's newsroom. *Psychological Reports*, **87**, 218–22.

Charnetski, C.J., Brennan, F.X., and Harrison, J.F. (1998) Effects of music and auditory stimuli on secretory immunoglobulin A. *Perceptual and Motor Skills*, **87**, 1163–70.

Chebat, J.-C., Gelinas-Chebat, C., and Filiatrault, P. (1993) Interactive effects of musical and visual cues on time perception: an application to waiting lines in banks. *Perceptual and Motor Skills*, **77**, 995–1020.

Daoussis, L. and McKelvie, S.J. (1986) Musical preferences and effects of music on a reading comprehension test for extraverts and introverts. *Perceptual and Motor Skills*, **62**, 283–9.

Devereux, G.A. (1969) Commercial background music: Its effect on workers' attitudes and output. *Personnel Practice Bulletin*, **25**, 24–30.

Fox, J.G. and Embrey, E.D. (1972) Music: An aid to productivity. *Applied Ergonomics*, **3**, 202–5.

Freeburne, C.M. and Fleischer, M.S. (1952) The effect of music distraction upon reading rate and comprehension. *Journal of Educational Psychology*, **43**, 101–9.

Fried, R. and Berkowitz, L. (1979) Music hath charms … and can influence helpfulness. *Journal of Applied Social Psychology*, **9**, 199–208.

Gatewood, E.L. (1922) An experiment in the use of music in an architectural drafting room. *Journal of Applied Psychology,* **5**, 350–8.

Goff, L.C., Pratt, R.R., and Madrigal, J.L. (1997) Music listening and S-IgA levels in patients undergoing a dental procedure. *International Journal of Arts Medicine,* **5**, 22–6.

Grewal, R., Mehta, R., and Kardes, F.R. (2000) The role of social-identity function of attitudes in consumer innovativeness and opinion leadership. *Journal of Economic Psychology,* **21**, 233–52.

Hucklebridge, F., Lambert, S., Clow, A., Warburton, D. M., Evans, P.D., and Sherwood, N. (2000) Modulation of secretory immunoglobulin A in saliva; response to manipulation of mood. *Biological Psychology,* **53**, 25–35.

Kaltsounis, B. (1973) Effect of sound on creative performance. *Psychological Reports,* **33**, 737–8.

Kellaris, J.J. and Altsech, M.B. (1992) The experience of time as a function of musical loudness and gender of listener. *Advances in Consumer Research,* **19**, 725–9.

Kellaris, J.J. and Mantel, S.P. (1994) The influence of mood and gender on consumers' time perceptions. *Advances in Consumer Research,* **21**, 514–8.

Kellaris, J.J., Mantel, S.P., and Altsech, M.B. (1996) Decibels, disposition, and duration: the impact of musical loudness and internal states on time perceptions. *Advances in Consumer Research,* **23**, 498–503.

Kerr, W.A. (1942a) Factor analysis of 229 electrical workers' beliefs in the effects of music. *Psychological Record,* **5**, 213–21.

Kerr, W.A. (1942b) Psychological effects of music as reported by 162 defense trainees. *Psychological Record,* **5**, 205–12.

Lanza, J. (1994) *Elevator music.* London: Quartet Books.

Lesiuk, T. (2000) The effect of music listening on a computer programming task. *Journal of Computer Information Systems,* **40**, 50–7.

Levin, I. and Zackay, D. (eds) (1989) *Time and human cognition.* Amsterdam: Elsevier Science.

Matlin, M.W. (1989) *Cognition.* Chicago, IL: Holt, Rinehart, and Winston.

McCraty, R., Atkinson, M., Rein, G., and Watkins, A.D. (1996) Music enhances the effect of positive emotional states on salivary IgA. *Stress Medicine,* **12**, 167–75.

McElrea, H. and Standing, L. (1992) Fast music causes fast drinking. *Perceptual and Motor Skills,* **75**, 362.

Milliman, R.E. (1982) Using background music to affect the behaviour of supermarket shoppers. *Journal of Marketing,* **46**, 86–91.

Milliman, R.E. (1986) The influence of background music on the behaviour of restaurant patrons. *Journal of Consumer Research,* **13**, 286–9.

Newman, R.I., Hunt, D.L., and Rhodes, F. (1966) Effects of music on employee attitude and productivity in a skateboard factory. *Journal of Applied Psychology,* **50**, 493–6.

Nittono, H. (1997) Background instrumental music and serial recall. *Perceptual and Motor Skills,* **84**, 1307–13.

North, A.C. and Hargreaves, D.J. (1997) Experimental aesthetics and everyday music listening. In *The social psychology of music,* (eds D.J. Hargreaves and A.C. North). Oxford: Oxford University Press.

North, A.C. and Hargreaves, D.J. (1998) The effect of music on atmosphere and purchase intentions in a cafeteria. *Journal of Applied Social Psychology,* **28**, 2254–73.

North, A.C. and Hargreaves, D.J. (1999) Can music move people? The effects of musical complexity and silence on waiting time. *Environment and Behaviour*, **31**, 136–49.

North, A.C., Hargreaves, D.J., and Heath, S. (1998) The effects of music on time perception in a gymnasium. *Psychology of Music*, **26**, 78–88.

North, A.C., Hargreaves, D.J., and McKendrick, J. (1999a) The effect of music on in-store wine selections. *Journal of Applied Psychology*, **84**, 271–6.

North, A.C., Hargreaves, D.J., and McKendrick, J. (1999b) Music and on-hold waiting time. *British Journal of Psychology*, **90**, 161–4.

North, A.C., Hargreaves, D.J., and McKendrick, J. (2000) The effects of music on atmosphere and purchase intentions in a bank and a bar. *Journal of Applied Social Psychology*, **30**, 1504–22.

North, A.C., Hargreaves, D.J., MacKenzie, L., and Law, R. (2004a) The effects of musical and voice 'fit' on responses to adverts. *Journal of Applied Social Psychology*, **34**, 1675–708.

North, A.C., Tarrant, M., and Hargreaves, D.J. (2004b) The effects of music on helping behaviour: a field study. *Environment and Behaviour*, **36**, 266–75.

North, A.C., Shilcock, A., and Hargreaves, D.J. (2003) The effect of musical style on restaurant customers' spending. *Environment and Behaviour*.

O'Cass, A. (2000) An assessment of consumers' product, purchase decision, advertising and consumption involvement in fashion clothing. *Journal of Economic Psychology*, **21**, 545–76.

Oldham, G.R., Cummings, A., Mischel, L.J., Schmidtke, J.M., and Zhou, J. (1995) Listen while you work? Quasi experimental relations between personal-stereo headset use and employee work responses. *Journal of Applied Psychology*, **80**, 547–64.

Palmquist, J.E. (1990) Apparent time passage and music preference by music and nonmusic majors. *Journal of Research in Music Education*, **38**, 206–14.

Ramos, L.V. (1993) The effects of on-hold telephone music on the number of premature disconnections to a statewide protective services abuse hot line. *Journal of Music Therapy*, **30**, 119–29.

Ransdell, S.E. and Gilroy, L. (2001) The effects of background music on word processed writing. *Computers in Human Behaviour*, **17**, 141–8.

Rider, M.S., Achterberg, J., Lawlis, G.F., Goven, A., Toledo, R., and Butler, J.R. (1990) Effect of immune system imagery on secretory IgA. *Biofeedback and Self-Regulation*, **15**, 317–33.

Rider, M.S. and Weldin, C. (1990) Imagery, improvization, and immunity. *Arts in Psychotherapy*, **17**, 211–6

Roballey, T.C., McGreevy, C., Rongo, R.R., Schwantes, M.L., Steger, P.J., Wininger, M.A., and Gardner, E.B. (1985) The effect of music on eating behaviour. *Bulletin of the Psychonomic Society*, **23**, 221–2.

Smith, H.C. (1947) Music in relation to employee attitudes, piece-work production, and industrial accidents. *Applied Psychology Monographs*, No. 14.

Smith, W.A.S. (1961) Effects of industrial music in a work situation requiring complex mental activity. *Psychological Reports*, **8**, 159–62.

Smith, P.C. and Curnow, R. (1966) 'Arousal hypothesis' and the effects of music on purchasing behaviour. *Journal of Applied Psychology*, **50**, 255–6.

Stratton, V. (1992) Influence of music and socializing on perceived stress while waiting. *Perceptual and Motor Skills*, **75**, 334.

Turley, L.W. and Milliman, R.E. (2000) Atmospheric effects on shopping behaviour: a review of the experimental evidence. *Journal of Business Research*, **49**, 193–211.

Wilson, S. (2003) The effect of music on perceived atmosphere and purchase intentions in a restaurant. *Psychology of Music*, **31**, 93–109.

Yalch, R. and Spangenberg, E. (1990) Effects of store music on shopping behaviour. *Journal of Consumer Marketing*, **7**, 55–63.

Young, H.H. and Berry, G.L. (1979) The impact of environment on the productivity attitudes of intellectually challenged office workers. *Human Factors*, **21**, 399–407.

Zimmer, J.W. and Brachulis-Raymond, J. (1978) Effects of distracting stimuli on complex information processing. *Perceptual and Motor Skills*, **46**, 791–4.

Index